Sufism in Central Asia

Handbook of Oriental Studies

Handbuch der Orientalistik

SECTION EIGHT

Uralic and Central Asian Studies

Edited by

Nicola Di Cosmo
Paolo Sartori

VOLUME 25

The titles published in this series are listed at *brill.com/ho8*

Sufism in Central Asia

New Perspectives on Sufi Traditions, 15th–21st Centuries

Edited by

Devin DeWeese
Jo-Ann Gross

BRILL

LEIDEN | BOSTON

Cover illustration: At the tomb, near Bukhara (Uzbekistan), of Bahāʾ al-Dīn Naqshband (d. 1389), eponym of the Naqshbandī Sufi *ṭarīqa* (2013, Jo-Ann Gross).

The preparation and publication of this volume were supported by a generous grant from the Poullada Fund.

Library of Congress Cataloging-in-Publication Data

Names: DeWeese, Devin A., 1956– editor. | Gross, Jo-Ann, 1949– editor.
Title: Sufism in Central Asia : new perspectives on Sufi traditions, 15th–21st centuries / edited by Devin DeWeese, Jo-Ann Gross.
Description: Leiden ; Boston : Brill, [2018] | Series: Handbook of Oriental Studies. Section 8, Uralic and Central Asian studies ; volume 25 | Includes bibliographical references and index.
Identifiers: LCCN 2018023815 (print) | LCCN 2018033920 (ebook) | ISBN 9789004373075 (E-book) | ISBN 9789004367876 (hardback: alk. paper)
Subjects: LCSH: Sufism—Asia, Central.
Classification: LCC BP188.8.A783 (ebook) | LCC BP188.8.A783 S84 2018 (print) | DDC 279.40958—dc23
LC record available at https://lccn.loc.gov/2018023815

Typeface for the Latin, Greek, and Cyrillic scripts: "Brill". See and download: brill.com/brill-typeface.

ISSN 0169-8524
ISBN 978-90-04-36787-6 (hardback)
ISBN 978-90-04-37307-5 (e-book)

Contents

Acknowledgments VII
List of Figures and Maps IX
Contributors XI
Note on Transcription and Style XIV
Maps XVII

Introduction 1
Devin DeWeese and Jo-Ann Gross

1 Re-Envisioning the History of Sufi Communities in Central Asia: Continuity and Adaptation in Sources and Social Frameworks, 16th–20th Centuries 21
Devin DeWeese

2 Naqshband's Lives: Sufi Hagiography between Manuscripts and Genre 75
Shahzad Bashir

3 The Works of Ḥusayn Vāʿiẓ Kāshifī as a Source for the Study of Sufism in Late 15th- and Early 16th-Century Central Asia 98
Maria E. Subtelny

4 Ḥażrat Jīo Ṣāḥib: How Durrānī Peshawar Helped Revive Bukhara's Sanctity 119
Waleed Ziad

5 Valī Khān Tūra: A Makhdūmzāda Leader in Marghīnān during the Collapse of the Khanate of Khoqand 162
Kawahara Yayoi

6 Reliquary Sufism: Sacred Fiber in Afghanistan 191
R. D. McChesney

7 Sufism in the Face of Twentieth-Century Reformist Critiques: Three Responses from Sufi *Imāms* in the Volga-Ural Region 238
Allen J. Frank

8 **Sufism on the Soviet Stage: Holy People and Places in Central Asia's Socio-Political Landscape after World War II** 256
Eren Tasar

9 **Sufi Groups in Contemporary Kazakhstan: Competition and Connections with Kazakh Islamic Society** 284
Ashirbek Muminov

10 **The Biographical Tradition of Muḥammad Basharā: Sanctification and Legitimation in Tajikistan** 299
Jo-Ann Gross

Index 333

Acknowledgments

This volume presents ten papers with roots in a symposium on "Sufism and Islam in Central Asia" held at Princeton University on October 21–22, 2011. The symposium, supported by a generous grant from the family of Leon B. Poullada and sponsored by the Department and Program in Near Eastern Studies at Princeton University, was organized by the editors in conjunction with Professor Muhammad Qasim Zaman. It brought together scholars whose work has dealt with various aspects of the history and contemporary status of Sufi communities in diverse parts of Central Asia, from the 15th century to the 21st, with the aim of addressing a central and ongoing question in the study of Sufism (and of Central Asia): what is the relationship between Sufism as it was manifested in this region prior to the Russian conquest and the Soviet era, on the one hand, and the features of Islamic religious life in the region during the Tsarist, Soviet, and post-Soviet eras on the other, including some referred to and recognizable as "Sufi" activity as well as others not necessarily labeled as such. Sessions addressed issues of sources and interpretative strategies, realignments in Sufi communities and sources from the Russian to the post-Soviet period, and social, political and economic perspectives on Sufi communities.

The symposium marked an important step, we believe, in the development of scholarship on Sufism in Central Asia, and we are especially grateful to the Poullada family for supporting both the gathering itself and the preparation of this volume; the latter process was delayed by unavoidable personal and professional factors, and we are grateful also for the sponsors' patience during this extended delay. At the same time, the delay allowed, or prompted, a process of updating, rethinking, and reformulation affecting all the papers included here. Some were virtually rewritten, compared with their initial 'conference paper' iterations, and all were substantially revised, edited, reviewed, and revised again between 2015 and 2017. The Princeton gathering was the essential catalyst for setting this volume in motion, but the editors are also grateful to all the contributors for their patience, their openness to thinking anew, and above all, the extraordinary intellectual strength and substance they have brought to this project from its inception.

The original gathering involved lively discussions that regrettably could not be fully represented in this volume, beyond the incorporation of insights derived therefrom in the individual papers. It also involved invaluable comments by three discussants—specialists in Sufi history and literature, and in Muslim religious thought more broadly, elsewhere in the Islamic world—Zvi

Ben-Dor Benite, Dina LeGall, and Jawid Mojaddedi—whose contributions were of the utmost importance for all the participants, but are likewise not tangibly represented here. In addition, not all the participants were able to offer for publication the papers they presented; the line-up included Florian Schwarz, who presented an excellent analysis of a key Persian hagiographical work compiled in Bukhara in the late 17th century, the *Ṣamarāt al-mashā'ikh*, and Jun Sugawara, who explored *waqf* documents relating to multiple shrines in Kashghar, thus 'covering' the eastern part of Central Asia and balancing the geographical focus, in the papers included here, on the former Soviet Central Asia and Afghanistan. Allen Frank presented material from his then-forthcoming book, *Bukhara and the Muslims of Russia: Sufism, Education, and the Paradox of Islamic Prestige* (Leiden: Brill, 2012), and then decided, once preparation of the symposium volume was delayed, to offer a different paper for the volume, rather than repeat or summarize material presented in more depth in his book. In addition, we were happy to invite a contribution from Waleed Ziad, who attended the symposium as a doctoral candidate in the History Department at Yale University.

The editors would like to express their appreciation to all the participants and contributors to this volume for their fine scholarship, and to Şükrü Hanioğlu, Chair of the Department of Near Eastern Studies, Princeton University at the time of the symposium, and Cyrus Schayegh, Director of the Program in Near Eastern Studies at the time, for their support. We are also grateful to the two anonymous reviewers for Brill, whose comments and painstaking attention to the manuscript helped immensely to improve the volume, and to Patricia Radder and Kathy van Vliet for their support of the project. Special thanks go also to Paolo Sartori, editor of the *Handbuch der Orientalistik* series, for envisioning a place for the volume in this venue. We are grateful, lastly, to Rick Batlan for his help in solving multiple technical problems with the electronic files that yielded this book.

During the late stages of work on the volume, we learned the sad news of the death, on August 7, 2016, of Yuri Bregel, whose enormous contributions to the study of Central Asia underlie much of the work of all the contributors. We would like to dedicate this volume to his memory, as a small token of admiration and gratitude for his scholarly, and human, legacy.

Devin DeWeese
Indiana University

Jo-Ann Gross
The College of New Jersey

List of Figures and Maps

Figures

4.1 Spiritual and physical genealogy of Ḥażrat Jīo Ṣāḥib 125
4.2 Cross-section of the Principal Naqshbandī-Mujaddidī lineages of the Peshawar valley, late 17th–19th century 136
4.3 Maḥalla Fażl-i Ḥaqq, Yakātut gate 141
4.4 Portal of the *mazār* of Ḥażrat Jīo, Peshawar 142
4.5 *Mazār* of Ḥażrat Jīo, Peshawar 142
4.6 *Mazār* of Ḥażrat Jīo, Peshawar 143
4.7 Old tombstone, *Mazār* of Ḥażrat Jīo, Peshawar 143
4.8 Schematic depiction of Bukhara's religious institutions 146
4.9 Qarākol Gate, Bukhara 152
4.10 Genealogical tree of Ḥażrat Jīo Pishāvarī at Khānaqāh-i Ḥażrat Jīo, Peshawar, 2015 155
5.1 The Kīrgīl *mazār* (2014) 173
5.2 Shrine of Ulug' hazrat bobo (burial site of Valī Khān Tūra) 187
5.3 Decorated ceiling of the *chilla-khona* near the shrine of Ulug' hazrat bobo 188
6.1 The *Khirqat al-Nabī* as it appeared in the 1930s (*Sālnāma-yi Kābul*) 200
6.2 The *Khirqa* complex from the southeast showing the shrine and Aḥmad Shāh's tomb (*Sālnāma-yi Kābul*) 202
6.3 The *Khirqat al-Nabī* showing extensive renovations conducted under King Muḥammad Ẓāhir Shāh as it appeared after 2002 233
10.1 Front Portal, *Mazār* of Muḥammad Basharā 305
10.2 Reconstructed plan of the first stage of construction 307
10.3 Reconstructed plan of the third and final stage of construction 308
10.4 Mausoleum of Muḥammad Basharā 318

Maps

0.1 Early Modern Central Asia XVII
0.2 Post-Soviet Central Asia XVIII
4.1 Ḥażrat Jīo's *khānaqāh* at Yakātut gate 128

4.2 Location of *khulafāʾ* and *khānaqāhs* of Fażl Aḥmad Maʿṣūmī Pishāvarī ca. 1820 129
5.1 The Farghana valley in the second half of the 19th century as related to Valī Khān Tūra's *ghazavāt* 164
10.1 Location of the *Mazār* of Muḥammad Basharā in the Zarafshān valley, Tajikistan 304

Contributors

Shahzad Bashir
(Ph.D. 1998, Yale University) is Aga Khan Professor of Islamic Humanities at Brown University. He specializes in the intellectual and social history of Iran and Central and South Asia. He is the author of *Sufi Bodies: Religion and Society in Medieval Islam* (Columbia, 2011), *Fazlallah Astarabadi and the Hurufis* (Oneworld, 2005), and *Messianic Hopes and Mystical Visions: The Nūrbakhshīya Between Medieval and Modern Islam* (South Carolina, 2003). His is currently finishing a book entitled *Islamic Pasts and Futures: Conceptual Explorations* that proposes new ways for making Islam an object of historical inquiry.

Devin DeWeese
(Ph.D. 1985, Indiana University) is a Professor in the Department of Central Eurasian Studies at Indiana University. He is the author of *Islamization and Native Religion in the Golden Horde: Baba Tükles and Conversion to Islam in Historical and Epic Tradition* (Pennsylvania State University Press, 1994) and (with Ashirbek Muminov) of *Islamization and Sacred Lineages in Central Asia: The Legacy of Ishaq Bab in Narrative and Genealogical Traditions*, Vol. 1: *Opening the Way for Islam: The Ishaq Bab Narrative, 14th–19th Centuries* (Almaty: Daik-Press, 2013). His other publications on the religious history of Islamic Central Asia and Iran focus chiefly on problems of Islamization, on the social and political roles of Sufi communities, and on Sufi literature and hagiography in Persian and Chaghatay Turkic.

Allen J. Frank
(Ph.D. 1994, Indiana University) is an independent scholar based in Takoma Park, Maryland. His specialization is in Turkic manuscript sources on the history of Muslims in the Volga-Ural region and Central Asia. His major works include *Muslim Religious Institutions in Imperial Russia* (Brill, 2001), *Qurban-'Ali Khalidi, An Islamic Biographical Dictionary of the Eastern Kazakh Steppe* (co-editor), (Brill, 2005), *Tatar Islamic Texts* (Dunwoody Press, 2008), *The Cambridge History of Inner Asia: the Chinggisid Age* (co-editor) (Cambridge University Press, 2009), *Bukhara and the Muslims of Russia* (Brill, 2012), and *Sadwaqas Ghïlmani, Biographies of the Islamic Scholars of Our Times*, (co-editor), (Daik Press, 2015). His current research involves Kazakh Sufi hagiographies of the Stalin era.

Jo-Ann Gross
(Ph.D. 1982, New York University) is Professor of Middle Eastern and Central Asian History at The College of New Jersey. Her research focuses on the history of Sufism and shrine culture in Islamic Central Asia, and on Ismailism in Badakhshan. Her publications include *The Letters of Khwāja 'Ubayd Allāh Aḥrār and his Associates*, co-authored with Asom Urunbaev (Brill, 2002) and *Muslims in Central Asia: Expressions of Identity and Change* (editor), (Duke University Press, 1992). Her current research is a collaborative project, funded by a 3-year National Endowment for the Humanities Collaborative Research Grant, on the genealogical and documentary history of the Nizārī Ismāʿīlīs of Badakhshan in Tajikistan and Afghanistan, based on archival and field research she carried out between 2004–2016.

Kawahara Yayoi
(Ph.D. 2008, The University of Tokyo) is a research fellow at the Japan Society for the Promotion of Science. She specializes in the history of Central Asia, especially the khanate of Khoqand. She is a coeditor of *Muḥammad Ḥakīm khān, Muntakhab al-tawārīkh, I–II* (Tokyo, 2006–2009) and *Documents from Private Archives in Right-Bank Badakhshan (Facsimiles and Introduction)* (Tokyo, 2013–2015), and the author of *Private Archives on a Makhdūmzāda Family in Marghilan* (Tokyo, 2012) and "The Development of the Naqshbandiyya-Mujaddidiyya in the Ferghana Valley during the 19th and Early 20th Centuries," *Journal of the History of Sufism*, 6 (Paris, 2015).

R. D. McChesney
(Ph.D. 1973, Princeton University), Emeritus Professor at New York University, is the author of *Waqf in Central Asia* (1991), *Central Asia: Foundations of Change* (1996), and *Kabul Under Siege* (1999), and editor and co-translator of the eleven-volume *The History of Afghanistan: Fayż Muḥammad Kātib Hazārah's* Sirāj al-tawārīkh (Brill 2013–2016) He has also written many articles and book chapters on Afghan and Central Asian social history and is the founder and director of the Afghanistan Digital Library (https://afghanistandl.nyu.edu).

Ashirbek Muminov
(Ph.D. 1991, Institute of Oriental Studies, Saint Petersburg) is a Senior Researcher at the Research Centre for Islamic History, Art and Culture (IRCICA) in Istanbul. He has published monographs, catalogues and articles on Islam in Central Asia, including *The Hanafi Madhhab in the History of Central Asia* (Almaty, 2015, in Russian). He is currently preparing two books for publication: Saduaqas Ghīlmani. *Biographies of the Islamic Scholars of Our Times* (with Allen Frank and Aytzhan Nurmanova), and *Epitaphs of the Muslim*

Scholars from Samarkand of the 4th–8th/10th–14th Centuries: Cultural and Social Contexts (with Bakhtiyar Babadjanov, Lola Dodkhudoeva and Ulrich Rudolph).

Maria Subtelny
(Ph.D. 1979, Harvard University) is Professor of Persian and Islamic Studies in the Department of Near and Middle Eastern Civilizations, University of Toronto, where she has been teaching courses on the history of medieval Iran and classical Persian literature since 1984. Her publications include *Timurids in Transition: Turko-Persian Politics and Acculturation in Medieval Iran* (Brill, 2007); *Le monde est un jardin: Aspects de l'histoire culturelle de l'Iran médiéval* (Association pour l'Avancement des Études Iraniennes, 2002); and the chapter on "Tamerlane and His Descendants: From Paladins to Patrons," in vol. 3 of *The New Cambridge History of Islam* (Cambridge, 2010). She is currently working on an edition and translation of the *Akhlāq-i muḥsinī*, a Persian treatise on political ethics by the Timurid-era author Ḥusayn Vāʿiẓ Kāshifī.

Eren Tasar
(Ph.D. 2010, Harvard University) is Assistant Professor of History at the University of North Carolina at Chapel Hill. His first book, *Soviet and Muslim: The Institutionalization of Islam in Central Asia*, was published by Oxford University Press in December 2017. He has published articles and book chapters on aspects of Islam in Soviet Central Asia, and organized international conferences related to modern Central Asian history and Islamic Socialism.

Waleed Ziad
(Ph.D. 2017, Yale University) is Assistant Professor at Habib University in Karachi and was formerly an Islamic Law and Civilization Research Fellow at Yale Law School. He received his PhD with Distinction in History at Yale University, where his dissertation (*Traversing the Indus and the Oxus: Trans-regional Islamic Revival in the Age of Political Fragmentation and the 'Great Game', 1747–1880*, 797 pp.) was awarded the university-wide Theron Rockwell Field Prize. At the intersection of social history, religious studies, and anthropology, Ziad's research concerns the historical and philosophical foundations of Muslim revivalism in the 'Persianate' world. He is also currently completing a monograph on a pilgrimage site centered on a cave temple in the Sakra range in the Pakistan-Afghanistan frontier regions, which existed as a monetarily independent polity from the 4th–11th centuries. His articles on historical and ideological trends in the Muslim world have appeared in the *New York Times*, *International Herald Tribune*, the *Wall Street Journal*, *Foreign Policy*, *Christian Science Monitor*, and other international dailies.

Note on Transcription and Style

To the usual set of complications surrounding the consistent transcription of Central Asian names and technical terms rooted in multiple languages clothed in the Arabic script, the aim of this volume to bridge the divide between historical and contemporary perspectives adds still more complexity, largely because of the 20th-century crystallization of multiple 'national' languages in the region, written in varieties of the Cyrillic script, and the more recent adaptations of the Latin script as well. In specific terms, the present volume involves the use of sources in Persian, Darī, Chaghatay Turkic, Arabic, Pashto, and Russian, as well as in the Tajik, Uzbek (in Cyrillic and Latin scripts), Kyrgyz, and Kazakh national languages that took shape in Soviet times. It may help to clarify both the transcription principles adopted and some of the exceptions and inconsistencies allowed in our attempt to properly represent these many languages and alphabets.

For the transcription of Arabic and Persian, we have adopted the system used in the *International Journal of Middle East Studies* (*IJMES*); this includes the privileging of the tripartite Arabic vowel system for Persian contexts (on the assumption that contemporary Persian vowel quality in Tehran may be misleading for medieval and modern Tajik or Darī), but we have dispensed with strict consistency in rendering the same letters in different ways depending on the language context in which they appear: thus, in Persian environments, ث is "s̱", ذ is "ẕ", and ض is "ż", but in fully Arabic environments they are "th", "dh", and "ḍ", respectively. For Chaghatay Turkic, or other Arabic-script Turkic, consonants are rendered as in Persian, but vowels are assumed to reflect vowel-harmony, informed in particular cases by both medieval and modern languages, and distinguishing, on that basis, initial or medial "é" from "i" (both represented by ای- or -ی-), e.g., "bék" instead of "bik."

For Russian, a modified Library of Congress system is employed (but without the glides or brêves used for ю, я, or й).

The contemporary and Soviet-era national languages naturally present their own specific problems of transcription. Multiple systems have been proposed during the past two decades for rendering Cyrillic-script Turkic languages and Tajik, without any gaining widespread acceptance or significantly improving upon the pioneering transliteration tables assembled by Allworth in 1967. These tables provide the basis for the rendering of Cyrillic-script Kazakh in Ashirbek Muminov's contribution, and of Cyrillic-script Tajik in Jo-Ann Gross's study (alongside transcriptions from Arabic, Persian, and Russian). Occasional transcriptions from the Cyrillic Uzbek alphabet that was used through most of the 20th century appear alongside contemporary, post-independence Latin-script Uzbek in the contributions of Yayoi Kawahara and Eren Tasar (transcriptions from Cyrillic-script Kyrgyz also appear in Tasar's study, together with Cyrillic transcriptions, in Russian or Kyrgyz or Uzbek 'style,' of Arabic-script material that still circulated in Soviet-era Central Asia). At the same time, we have mostly opted for the standard forms of ethnonyms currently in use: thus "Uzbek" instead of "O'zbek," "Kyrgyz" instead of the older "Kirghiz" or Russian-based "Kirgiz," and "Tajik" instead of "Tojik." In the case of "Qazaq" and "Kazakh," however, both are employed, the former for contexts prior to the 1920s (in Allen Frank's contribution, for instance), and the latter reflecting the prevailing international standard at present (in Muminov's study).

The extensive presence, in these national languages, of names and terminology drawn from Arabic-script Islamic literary traditions on the one hand serves as a constant reminder of the pervasive indigenization of Muslim culture and religion throughout Central Asia, in the past and at present, but on the other hand entails the dual risk of obscuring significant distinctions (we may recall, for instance, the Sovietological conflation of *khoja*s and *ḥājjī*s) and masking important conceptual and terminological continuities across the supposedly firm barriers of 'modernity' and 'secularism.' With this in mind, the editors have encouraged contributors, where relevant, to use the forms of particular titles and terms found in the national languages, but to indicate their 'classical' Arabic-script equivalents as well.

For one term in particular we have purposefully rejected strict consistency in order to distinguish different connotations of the term: the technical transcription "*khwāja*" is used when the term is used as a title or honorific for particular individuals, while a form more closely indicative of actual pronunciation, "*khoja*," is used to refer to the familial groups claiming descent from specific saints of the past (often alongside contemporary 'national' forms, e.g., *xoʻja*, or *qozha*). On the other hand, for a small set of commonly occurring 'religious' or Sufi terms, we have tended to privilege a more rigorous transcription (Qur'ān, *ḥadīth, imām, qāżī, muftī, mullā, ʿulamā* or *ʿulamāʾ, murīd*), unless contributors have included explicit discussion of their usage.

A less rigorous rendering, on the other hand, has been adopted for most geographical names. Relatively well-known place-names, that is, are given without diacritics, but in forms that often do not reflect those used in the official or national languages of the countries in which the sites they designate are presently located, e.g., Bukhara (not Bukhārā or Bukhoro), Tashkent (not Tāshkand or Toshkent), Kashghar (not Kāshghar or Kashgar or Qäshqär or Kashi), Herat, Kabul, Qandahar, Peshawar, Khurasan, Kashmir, Farghana, Syr Darya, Amu Darya; Kazan is used instead of Qāzān, Qazān, or Kazanʹ. Diacritics are retained, however, for adjectival formations (Khurāsānī, Qandahārī, Kashmīrī, etc.), and in direct transcriptions from Arabic-script sources; diacritics are also retained for less familiar place names (e.g., Badakhshān, Ghaznī, Namangān, Marghīnān, Khwārazm). More broadly, we have not sought to eliminate or obscure what may be regarded as 'natural' inconsistencies (along the lines of "Qazaq" vs. "Kazakh") resulting from shifts in the prevailing 'official' archival languages (transcribing from Arabic-script Persian or Turkic in some cases but from Russian in others, e.g., "Namangān" vs. "Namangan," "Astarkhān" vs. "Astrakhan"), on the assumption that these will pose few problems for most readers.

It is hoped that the resulting mixture of rigor, accessibility, and contextual consistency will help familiarize the general reader with some of the complexities of Sufi religiosity in Central Asia, while also allowing those familiar with Central Asian languages to recognize indigenous terminology as encountered in multiple venues and forms.

Maps

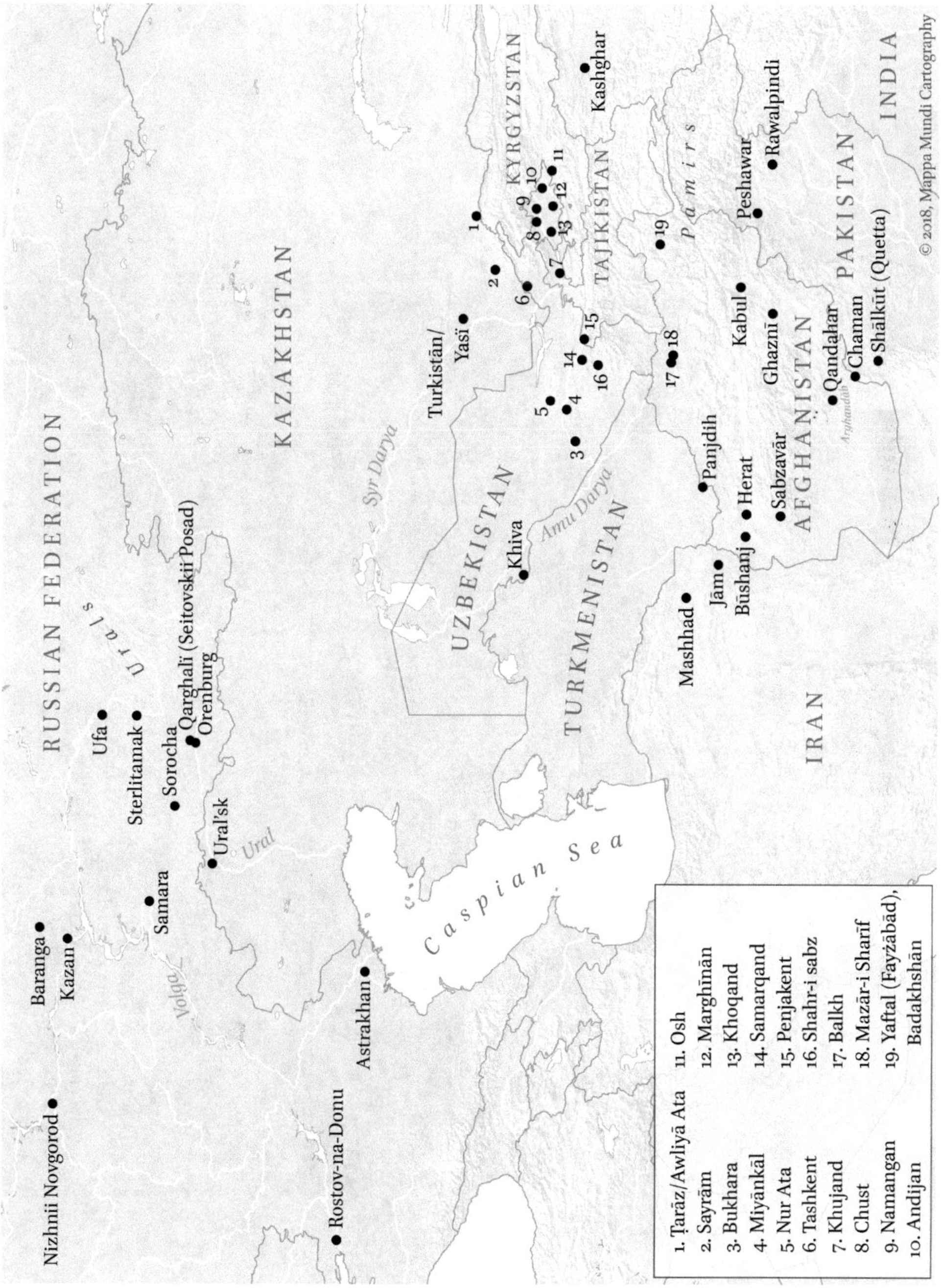

MAP 0.1 *Early Modern Central Asia*

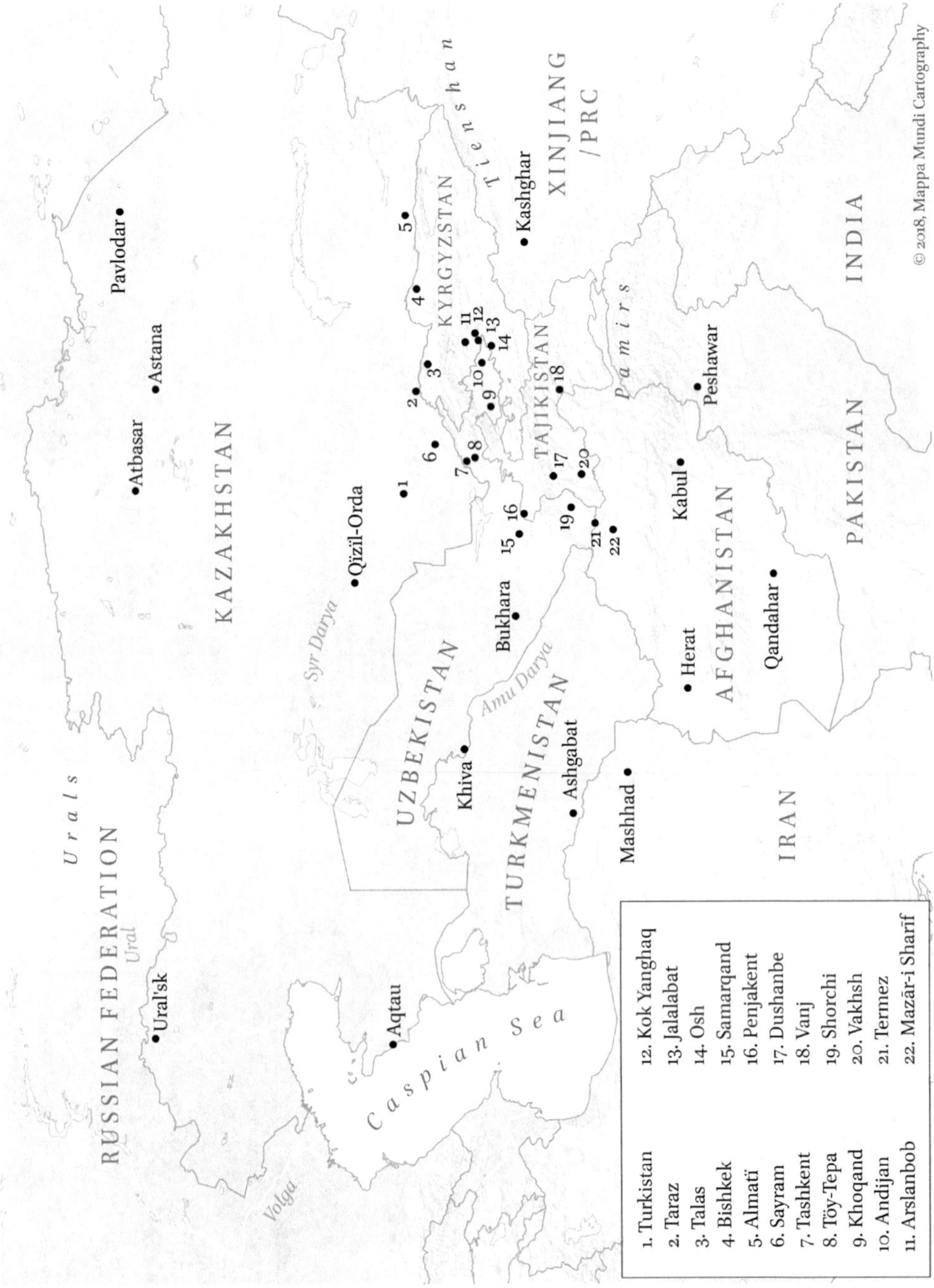

MAP 0.2 *Post-Soviet Central Asia*

Introduction

Devin DeWeese and Jo-Ann Gross

The Princeton symposium of 2011 that prompted the preparation of the papers presented here was framed around new approaches to and perspectives on the study of Sufism in Central Asia, and marked a distinctive moment in the development of scholarship on that broad subject: the two decades following the collapse of the Soviet Union brought increasing recognition of the inadequacy of the assessment of Sufism in the Soviet context advanced by Alexandre Bennigsen and his followers, and also witnessed a substantial growth in scholarly explorations focused on the history of Sufi groups in Central Asia before the Russian conquest. The Princeton conference was intended to link those two directions, providing a historically-grounded perspective on the continuation, or revival, of Sufi currents in Central Asia since the late Soviet period, reassessing our understanding of Sufism during the Soviet era itself, and treating the history of Sufi communities in Central Asia as a connected phenomenon, with continuities linking developments from the 15th century to the present alongside broad historical shifts in organization and structure, rather than as separate phases shaped entirely by political circumstances and framed in terms of political history.

The key assumption underlying the symposium was that any attempt to understand the contemporary roles of Sufi groups would have to be based on a deep historical understanding of the sort that is still being built for this field; it was also taken for granted that diverse perspectives, reflecting sources, historical patterns, and specific structures of Sufi organization evident in different parts of Central Asia, would be crucial to prepare the ground for addressing the problem, as would a broad chronological framework, to help ensure that common or widespread trends and specific, perhaps even unique, developments would neither mask one another nor fail to be recognized. These assumptions, in turn, reflect (if inversely) the lingering impact of the views and approaches of the Bennigsen school on thinking about Sufism in Central Asia, which lacked historical understanding, failed to draw upon comparative perspectives from elsewhere in the Muslim world, and adopted a quite narrow chronological framework for its focus—i.e., the Soviet era—which seemed open-ended in the early 1980s, but was soon provided with an end-point just 70-odd years later than its starting point.

 | DOI:10.1163/9789004373075_002

With these goals and frameworks in mind, we may offer a few general remarks, by way of contextualizing the study of Sufism in Central Asia, in order to frame the specific contributions to the present volume. There are, after all, compelling reasons to study the history of Sufi traditions in Central Asia. The region was home to many of the early 'foundational' saints, celebrated throughout the Muslim world, who—whatever their actual historical affiliations—were incorporated into the 'back-story' devised for Sufism by the 10th century. Prominent Sufi writers who shaped Sufi teaching and literary expression were active in Central Asia, and if we include Khurasan within that broader regional label—as makes sense through much of history, in political and cultural terms—their numbers grow dramatically. Central Asia was the birthplace of major Sufi orders: the internationally important Naqshbandiyya, the regionally prominent Yasaviyya, and the widely influential Kubraviyya are the best known, but other groups less prominent than these (in Central Asia, at least), such as the Chishtīs or the Shaṭṭārīs, also had roots in the region.

Particular periods in Central Asian history, moreover, provided the backdrop for the formative stages of several of these Sufi communities and, later, for classic examples of competitive rivalries among multiple strong Sufi groups, reflecting their expanded social profiles. We likewise find important cases of the intimate involvement of Sufis in political and economic affairs, or of Sufi lineages claiming credit for distinct patterns of Islamization, their claims often masking a process that ought to be thought of more in terms of establishing networks of personal and communal allegiance than in terms of 'preaching' Islam or Sufi doctrine. It is the social context, indeed, and the creation of religiously-defined sub-communities that cross class and ethnic boundaries (and compete for various constituencies), that ought to be understood as underlying the broad reach, and appeal, of Sufism in Central Asia. In much of the post-Mongol era, that is, the social and intellectual manifestations of Sufism shaped literary production, healing cultures, kinship structures, and architectural legacies, whether the *khānaqāh* or shrine or *madrasa*, throughout Central Asia. Sufism, indeed, shaped religious language and the intellectual formation of the *ʿulamā*, but also 'spoke to' the religious lives of the inarticulate and illiterate. Sufism's sources, moreover—above all hagiographical works—serve as an important window on social history, to balance the perspectives of court chronicles. The religious vision, or visions, they articulate played a role in shaping Central Asian society that was arguably more pervasive than that played by the voices of 'reform' or 'modernity, certainly in 'pre-modern' or pre-Soviet times, but in large measure also in Soviet times and at present, below the surface of the elites and globalization.

More broadly, the structures and practices associated with Sufi history in the region offer an excellent vantage point from which to restore 'religious life' to historical inquiry, by way of moving beyond the unhelpful dichotomy that relegates 'religion' to a 'pre-modern' past, or to a narrow slice of human activity defined by scriptural minimums. Sufi history allows us not only to appreciate the religious visions that shape societies, but to understand the multiple social structures through which Sufism, or 'religion' more generally, intersects with social history. At the same time, as Sufism is made the focus of historical investigation, its students must take stock of what this "-ism" encompasses in different times and different social contexts. The usual short-hand definition of Sufism as "Islamic mysticism," for instance, can interfere with recognizing its ethical, devotional, and communal dimensions, and with appreciating the ways in which both Sufi doctrine and Sufi social experience provide organizational and conceptual foundations for individual and communal experience, shaping perception as well as modes of negotiating life in social and psychological terms. Understanding these dimensions, however, requires an in-depth and deeply contextualized study of Sufi sources (rather than their dismissal or celebration as "mystical" and otherworldly).

In short, the study of Sufi traditions in Central Asia is an essential component of studying the history of Central Asia in general, and has much to contribute toward 'historicizing' the study of Sufism in the Muslim world at large. It is worth stressing, however, that the study of Sufism in Central Asia stands in a distinctive place relative to scholarship on Sufi traditions elsewhere: it began, in earnest, well after the formative early phases in the study of Sufism, and both the sources and structures of Sufi history in Central Asia remained outside the conversation that shaped the study of Sufism on a broader scale. The fact that the study of Sufism in Central Asia had its impetus in Sovietology left many unfortunate legacies, but with respect to the study of Sufism in the Muslim world at large, the late 'timing' of scholarship on Central Asia had various consequences, with many of them, ironically, positive.

To begin with, the study of 'Sufi history' has moved steadily away from various older assumptions that shaped the early study of Sufism, such as the notion of Sufism's extra-Islamic origins, or that of its fundamentally 'un-orthodox' character. Though elements of these paradigms lie poorly hidden in the narratives of the Bennigsen school, they had largely been abandoned in scholarship on Sufism by the time the study of Central Asian Sufi groups got underway. Similarly, the 'golden age' paradigm, in which the classic texts from the earliest phase of Sufi doctrinal exposition were contrasted with the 'debasement' and 'popularization' of Sufism in later times, was prominent in both Soviet and

Sovietological literature, but had mostly been abandoned before the serious study of Central Asian Sufi history began, leaving a smaller body of dross to wade through, or haul away, than specialists on other regions face. Aside from the Bennigsen narrative, and some older projections about Sufism in Central Asia (based chiefly in Turkish scholarship, with a focus on the Yasavī tradition), the problem with scholarship on Sufism in Central Asia was that there was relatively little of it, *not* that what did exist was bad.

Scholarship on Sufism, in general, has also moved away from the typologies and periodizations proposed in the classic work of Trimingham.[1] Though we still lack a suitable 'replacement' volume that goes beyond the potential 'information overload' to offer a comprehensive synthesis,[2] we have instead a growing body of specialized studies on particular times and places, of which the still-small but steadily expanding corpus of studies on Central Asian Sufi groups is part. Yet once again, starting late not only meant that scholarship on Sufism in Central Asia could avoid the pitfalls of those earlier assumptions and paradigms; it also meant that the field could benefit from the excellent work being produced on particular Sufi traditions and environments during the last two decades of the 20th century. It was particularly fortuitous that several outstanding specialists on Sufism in South Asia—Bruce Lawrence, Richard Eaton, Carl Ernst, Simon Digby—were producing important studies of 'their' region just as the study of the Central Asian context was beginning.

To be sure, the late start also meant that Central Asia's Sufi history remained out of the line of sight for scholars who shaped important developments in Sufi studies, some of which may need revision once the case of Central Asia

---

1 J. Spencer Trimingham, *The Sufi Orders in Islam* (Oxford at the Clarendon Press, 1971). Though pioneering in its attempt to engage with the organizational aspects of Sufism throughout the Muslim world, past and present, Trimingham's work offered only a variation on the 'golden age' paradigm, framing the development of Sufi communities in terms of three stages—which he termed *khānaqāh, ṭarīqa,* and *ṭā'ifa*—marked by decline from individual spiritual yearning to routinization and popularization, and posited as chronologically uniform in different regions (see pp. 102–104, where he indeed uses the terms "golden age" and "decay"); in addition, his specific treatment of Central Asian Sufi groups is full of errors and misinterpretations. Many of these flaws, and the uneven treatment of different parts of the Muslim world, were noted in early reviews of the book; see, for example, that of Simon Digby, in *Bulletin of the School of Oriental and African Studies*, 36/1 (1973), 136–139.

2 There have been, to be sure, important contributions in this direction, including Carl Ernst, *The Shambhala Guide to Sufism* (Boston: Shambhala, 1997); Ahmet T. Karamustafa, *Sufism: The Formative Period* (Berkely: University of California Press, 2007); Alexander Knysh, *Islamic Mysticism: A Short History* (Leiden: Brill Publishers, 2000); and Nile Green, *Sufism: A Global History* (West Sussex, UK: Wiley-Blackwell, 2012).

is considered in context. For example, important revisionist work on 18th-century Sufi networks and on 'neo-Sufi' movements[3] was not able to take stock of the trends outlined only recently in the case of Central Asian Sufi groups. Nevertheless, with regard to the narrower field of Central Asia itself, the late start for the study of Sufism in the region has been a net positive, overall, and an additional factor is worth noting as well. Scholarship on Central Asian Sufi groups came of age as Central Asia was 'opening up' as a result of the collapse of the Soviet Union; though circumstances have varied widely from country to country, there can be no doubt that post-Soviet times have provided increased opportunities for cooperation with scholars based in the region, and increased access to the legacies of Sufi thought, practice, and social organization, whether written or oral.

One of the chief attractions of scholarship on Sufi communities of Central Asia lies in the abundance of sources that remain largely untapped. This, of course, reminds us that the conclusions we draw about Sufi history must remain quite tentative unless and until we arrive at a more thorough assessment of the available sources. Yet despite the challenging agenda before us, it is important to acknowledge that much important and foundational work has been undertaken during just the past quarter-century. Indeed, the Princeton symposium itself stands as confirmation that the study of Sufi traditions in Central Asia has come into its own.

Thirty-odd years ago, that is, a bibliography of studies on Sufis of Central Asia would have been quite short, and skewed toward earlier periods than the one addressed in the present volume. Aside from scattered western studies focused on the pre-Mongol era,[4] or on individual figures of that era such as al-Ḥakīm al-Tirmidhī, Abū Saʿīd b. Abīʾl-Khayr, Aḥmad-i Jām, or Najm al-Dīn

3 See Nehemia Levtzion and John O. Voll, *Eighteenth-Century Renewal and Reform in Islam* (Syracuse: Syracuse University Press, 1987); R. S. O'Fahey and Bernd Radtke, "Neo-Sufism Reconsidered," *Der Islam*, 70 (1993), 52–87.

4 E.g., Paul Klappstein, *Vier turkestanische Heilige: ein Beitrag zum Verständnis dr islamischen Mystik* (Kiel, 1919; Inaugural-Dissertation zur Erlangung der Doktorwürde der hohen philosophischen Fakultät der Christian-Albrechts-Universität zu Kiel); F. Meier, "Ḫurāsān und das Ende der klassischen Ṣūfik," in *La Persia nel Medioevo* (Rome: Accademia Nazionale dei Linzei, 1971; Atti del Convegno Internazionale, Quaderno no. 160), 545–570; Jacqueline Chabbi, "Remarques sur le développement historique des mouvements ascétiques et mystiques au Khurasan, IIIe/IXe siècle–IVe/Xe siècle," *Studia Islamica*, 46 (1977), 5–72; idem, "Zuhd et soufisme au Khorasan au IVe/Xe siècle," in *La Signification du bas Moyen-Âge dans l'histoire et la culture du monde musulman (Actes du 8e Congrès de l'Union Européenne des Arabisants et Islamisants)*, ed. R. Mantran (Aix-en-Provence, 1978), 53–61; idem, "Réflexions sur le soufisme iranien primitif," *Journal asiatique*, 266 (1978), 37–55.

Kubrā[5]—most of which appeared only in the 1970s—and a similarly small body of publications on Central Asian Sufis of the Mongol and Timurid periods, such as Sayyid ʿAlī Hamadānī or Bahāʾ al-Dīn Naqshband,[6] one could point only to a few early studies of the Naqshbandī *khwāja* lineages of Eastern Turkistan,[7] and to a single European publication on a post-Timurid Sufi from

5 E.g., Bernd Radtke, *Al-Ḥakīm at-Tirmidhī—Ein islamischer Theosoph des 3./9. Jahrhunderts* (Freiburg: Klaus Schwarz Verlag, 1980; Islamkundliche Untersuchungen, Bd. 58); W. Ivanow, "A Biography of Shaykh Ahmad-i-Jam," *Journal of the Royal Asiatic Society*, 1917, 291–307; Fritz Meier, *Die Fawāʾiḥ al-Ǧamāl wa-Fawātiḥ al-Ǧalāl des Naǧm ad-Dīn al-Kubrā: eine Darstellung mystischer Erfahrungen im Islam aus der Zeit um 1200 n Chr* (Wiesbaden: Franz Steiner Verlag, 1957); idem, *Abū Saʿīd-i Abū l-Ḫayr (357–440/967–1049): Wirklichkeit und Legende* (Leiden: E. J. Brill, 1976; Acta Iranica troiseème série, Textes et Mémoires, vol. IV).

6 E.g., A. A. Hekmat, "Les voyages d'un mystique persan de Hamadān au Kashmir." *Journal asiatique*, 240 (1952), 53–66; J. K. Teufel, *Eine Lebensbeschreibung des Scheichs Alī-i Hamadānī (gestorben 1385): Die Xulāṣat ul-Manāqib des Maulānā Nūr ud-Dīn Caʿfar-i Badaxšī* (Leiden: E. J. Brill, 1962); Marijan Molé, "Autour du Daré Mansour: l'apprentissage mystique de Bahāʾ al-Dīn Naqshband," *Revue des études islamiques*, 27 (1959), 35–66; idem, "Quelques traités naqshbandis," *Farhang-i Īrān-zamīn*, 6 (1337/1958), 273–284; idem, "Les Kubrawiyya entre sunnisme et shiisme aux huitième et neuvième siècles de l'hégire," *Revue des études islamiques*, 29 (1961), 110–124; H. Beveridge, "The Rashahat-i-'Ainal-Hayat (Tricklings from the Fountain of Life)," *JRAS*, 1916, 59–75; Jean Aubin, "Un santon quhistānī de l'époque timouride," *Revue des études islamiques*, 35 (1967), 185–216; cf. the Persian article of Zeki Velidi Togan, "Gazan-Han Halil ve Hoca Bahaeddin Nakşbend" [the title appears in Turkish, but the article is in Persian], in *Necati Lugal Armağanı* (Ankara: Türk Tarih Kurumu Basımevi, 1968), 775–784. Here too may be noted Turkish scholarship on the legacy of Aḥmad Yasavī (typically relegated to the pre-Mongol era), beginning with Mehmed Fuad Köprülü, *Türk edebiyatında ilk mutasavvıflar* (Istanbul: Maṭbaʿa-yi ʿĀmira, 1918), which did not appear in Latin script until 1966, but was summarized in German and French (Theodor Menzel, "Köprülüzade Mehmed Fuad's Werk über die ersten Mystiker in der türkischen Literatur," *Kőrösi Csoma-Archivum*, 2 [1926–1932], 281–310, 345–357, 406–422; idem, "Die ältesten türkischen Mystiker," *ZDMG*, 79 [1925], 269–289; Lucien Bouvat, "Les premiers mystiques dans la littérature turque," *Revue du monde musulman*, 43 [1921], 236–282); see also Köprülü's "Orta-Asya Türk dervişliği hakkında bazı notlar," *Türkiyat mecmuası*, 14 (1964), 259–262, and Zeki Velidi Togan, "Yesevîliğe dair bazı yeni malûmat," in [*60 doğum yılı münasebetiyle*] *Fuad Köprülü Armağanı* (İstanbul: Osman Yalçın Matbaası, 1953), 523–529, as well as W. Gordlevsky, "Choğa Aḥmed Jasevi" [in German], in *Festschrift Georg Jacob*, ed. Theodor Menzel (Leipzig: Otto Harrassowitz, 1932), 57–67.

7 Henry Walter Bellew, "History of Kashghar," in Thomas Douglas Forsyth, *Report of a Mission to Yarkund in 1873 under Command of Sir T. D. Forsyth; With Historical and Geographic Information regarding the Possessions of the Ameer of Yarkund* (Calcutta, 1875), 106–213; "Epitome of the Memoirs of the Khojas," from *The History of the Khojas of Eastern-Turkistan, summarised from the Tazkira-i-Khwajagan of Muhammad Sadiq Kashghari*, ed. Robert Barkley Shaw, N. Elias (Supplement to the *Journal of the Asiatic Society of Bengal*, 66/1 (1897), 31–63); H. Beveridge,

the western part of Central Asia (one with Sufi ties, however, with the groups in Eastern Turkistan).[8] The list grows somewhat longer if we include Russian-language publications from Tsarist times,[9] though many of these were not easily accessible to western scholars, and from the Soviet period as well,[10]

"The Khojas of Eastern Turkestan," *Journal of the Asiatic Society of Bengal*, 71 (1902), 45–46; Martin Hartmann, "Ein Heiligenstaat im Islam: das Ende der Caghataiden und die Herrschaft der Choğas in Kašgarien," in Hartmann's *Der islamische Orient*, vol. I (Berlin: Wolf Peiser Verlag, 1905), pt. 6–10, 195–374; Saguchi Tōru, "The Revival of the White Mountain Khwājas, 1760–1820 (from Sarimsāq to Jihāngīr)," *Acta Asiatica*, 14 (1968), 7–20; Henry G. Schwarz, "The Khwajas of Eastern Turkestan," *Central Asiatic Journal*, 20 (1976), 266–296 (the latter study omits mention of the Khwājas' status as Naqshbandī Sufis).

8 Martin Hartmann, "Mešreb der weise Narr und fromme Ketzer: Ein zentralasiatisches Volksbuch," *Der islamische Orient: Berichte und Forschungen*, Band I (Berlin: Wolf Peiser Verlag, 1905), 147–193. The number may be doubled if we include the important article on Central Asian shrines by J. Castagné, "Le culte des lieux saints de l'Islam au Turkestan," *L'Ethnographie*, 46 (1951), 46–124.

9 Tsarist-era publications naturally include important material on Sufism in 19th-century Central Asia—e.g., N. Lykoshin, "Rol' dervishei v musul'manskoi obshchine tashkentskikh tuzemtsev," *Sbornik materialov dlia statistiki Syr-Dar'inskoi oblasti*, 7 (Tashkent, 1899), 94–115, followed by his "Ishany tashkentskie" (116–136) and "Perevod 'Risallia-i-tarikat'" (137–157); cf. N. Mallitskii, "Ishany i sufizm," *Sbornik materialov po musul'manstvu*, I, ed. V. I. Iarovogo-Ravskago (St. Petersburg, 1899), 85–99, and, in the same volume, E. T. Smirnov, "Dervishizm v Turkestane," 49–71—but occasionally dealt with earlier figures, e.g., N. Veselovskii, "Dagbid," *Zapiski Vostochnogo otdeleniia Russkogo arkheologicheskogo Obshchestva*, 3 (1889), 85–96; N. S. Lykoshin, transl., "Kodeks prilichii na Vostoke (Adab-ul-salikhyn). Sbornik Mukhammed Sadyk-i-Kashkari," *Sbornik materialov po musul'manstvu*, t. II, ed. V. P. Nalivkin (Tashkent, 1900), 21–86; N. S. Lykoshin, transl., *Divana-i-Mashrab: Zhizneopisanie populiarneishego predstavitelia mistitsizma v Turkestanskom krae* (Samarkand: Samarkandskii oblastnyi statisticheskii komitet, 1910); A. A. Semenov, "Bukharskii sheikh Bakha-ud-Din. 1318–1389. (K ego biografii). Po persidskoi rukopisi," in [*ash-Sharqīyāt*] *Vostochnyi sbornik v chest' A. N. Veselovskogo* (Moscow, 1914; Trudy po vostokovedeniiu, izdavaemye Lazarevskim institutom vostochnykh iazykov, vyp. 43), 202–211; idem, "Rasskaz shugnanskikh ismailitov o bukharskom sheikh Bekhā-ud-Dīne," *Zapiski Vostochnogo otdeleniia Russkogo arkheologicheskogo Obshchestva*, 22 (1913–14), 321–326 (not to mention V. A. Zhukovskii's studies of early Sufi literature).

10 From the Soviet period, on Sufism in post-Timurid Central Asia, may be mentioned V. L. Viatkin, "Ferganskii mistik Divana-i-Mashrab," in [*al-Iskandariyya*], *Sbornik Turkestanskogo Vostochnogo instituta v chest' professora A. È. Shmidta* (Tashkent, 1923), 24–34; idem, "Shaikhi Dzhuibari. I: Khodzha Islam," in [*'Iqd al-jumān*] *V. V. Bartol'du turkestanskie druz'ia, ucheniki i pochitateli* (Tashkent, 1927), 3–19; M. F. Gavrilov, *Sredneaziatskii poèt i sufii Khuvaido* (Tashkent: Obshchestvo po izucheniiu Tadzhikistana i iranskikh narodnostei za ego predelami, 1927); A. L. Troitskaia, "Zhenskii zikr v starom Tashkente," *Sbornik Muzeia antropologii i ètnografii AN SSSR*, 7 (1928), 173–199; A. A. Semenov, "Unikal'nyi

especially for works dealing with Central Asian Sufism after the Timurid period. Even the studies mentioned here, to be sure, were ignored in the deeply flawed and historically-uninformed literature produced by the Bennigsen school, but it was only in the second half of the 1970s and the early 1980s that the pioneering researches of Hamid Algar[11] and the late Joseph Fletcher[12] began to

---

pamiatnik agiograficheskoi sredneaziatskoi literatury XVI v.," *Izvestiia Uzbekistanskogo filiala AN SSSR*, 1940, No. 12, 54–62; 1941, No. 3, 37–48; P. P. Ivanov, *Khoziaistvo dzhuibarskikh sheikhov* (Moscow/Leningrad: Izd-vo AN SSSR, 1954); M. A. Salakhetdinova, "Sochinenie Mukhammed-Sadyka Kashgari 'Tazkira-i-khodzhagan' kak istochnik po istorii kirgizov," *Izvestiia AN KirgSSR*, seriia Obshchestvennykh nauk, t. I, vyp. 1 (Istoriia), 1959, 93–125; V. P. Iudin, "Izvestiia 'Ziia al-kulub' Mukhammad Avaza o kazakhakh XVI veka," *Vestnik Akademii nauk Kazakhskoi SSR*, 1966, No. 5, 71–76; A. Pulati and A. È.-A. Khatipov, "O traktatakh Makhdumi A'zama: Predvaritel'noe soobshchenie.," *Trudy Samarkandskogo Gosudarstvennogo universiteta*, 229 (1972; = *Voprosy istorii matematiki i astronomii*), 19–24; A. M. Mukhtarov, "Zhitie sheikha Khuseina—istochnik po istorii kul'turnoi zhizni kontsa XV—nachala XVI v." *Material'naia kul'tura Tadzhikistana*, 3 (1978), 242–246; I. Saidullaev, "Istoriko-literaturnoe proizvedenie 'Tazkirai Khodzhagan' Mukhammeda Sadyka Kashgari," *Izvestiia AN KazSSR*, seriia filologicheskaia, 1979, No. 1, 41–45. The work of Soviet-era ethnographers is also important for an understanding of Sufism and its legacies in Central Asia, and might have informed Sovietological studies, above all the publications of G. P. Snesarev, V. N. Basilov, and S. M. Demidov from the 1970s and '80s.

11 Hamid Algar, "Bibliographical Notes on the Naqshbandi Tariqat," in *Essays on Islamic Philosophy and Science*, ed. George F. Hourani (Albany: SUNY Press, 1975), 254–259; idem, "The Naqshbandi Order: A Preliminary Survey of its History and Significance," *Studia Islamica*, 44 (1976), 123–152 (a revised version of this seminal article was published as "A brief history of the Naqshbandî order," in *Naqshbandîs: cheminements et situation actuelle d'un ordre mystique musulman* [Actes de la Table Ronde de Sèvres, 2–4 mai 1985], ed. Marc Gaborieau, Alexandre Popovic, and Thierry Zarcone [Istanbul/Paris: Éditions Isis, 1990; Varia Turcica, v. 18], 3–44); idem, "Silent and Vocal *dhikr* in the Naqshbandī Order," *Akten des VII. Kongresses für Arabistik und Islamwissenschaft* (Göttingen, 15. bis 22. August 1974), ed. Albert Dietrich (Göttingen: Vandenhoeck & Ruprecht, 1976), 39–46; Hamid Algar, transl., *The Path of God's Bondsmen from Origin to Return* (*Merṣād al-ʿebād men al-mabdāʾ elāʾl-maʿād*), *A Sufi Compendium by Najm al-Dīn Rāzī known as Dāya* (Delmar, New York: Caravan Books, for Persian Heritage Series, 1982).

12 Joseph Fletcher, "Central Asian Sufism and Ma Ming-hsin's New Teaching," *Proceedings of the Fourth East Asian Altaistic Conference* (Taipei, 1971), 75–96; idem, "Confrontations between Muslim Missionaries and Nomad Unbelievers in the Late Sixteenth Century," in *Tractata Altaica: Denis Sinor sexagenario optime de rebus altaicis merito dedicata* (Wiesbaden, 1976), 167–174; idem, "The Naqshbandiyya and the *Dhikr-i Arra*," *Journal of Turkish Studies*, 1 (1977), 113–119; and his posthumously-published "The Naqshbandiyya in Northwest China," in Fletcher, *Studies on Chinese and Islamic Inner Asia*, ed. Beatrice Forbes Manz (Aldershot, Hampshire: Variorum, 1995), No. XI.

offer new starting points for understanding the history of Central Asian Sufi communities.

Since that time, the field has seen tremendous growth, represented by the publications of contributors to the present volume, and by those of others who were not able to join us at the Princeton symposium, including Bakhtiyar Babajanov, David Brophy, Stéphane A. Dudoignon, Hamada Masami, Anke von Kügelgen, Jürgen Paul, Alexandre Papas, Sawada Minoru, Maria Szuppe, Rian Thum, and Thierry Zarcone.[13] In addition, several recent dissertations, ranging from historical investigations based on archival research to anthropological

13 See, for example: Bakhtiyar Babajanov, "La naqshbandiyya sous les premiers Sheybanides," *Cahiers d'Asie centrale*, 3–4 (1997 = *L'Héritage timouride: Iran—Asie centrale—Inde, XVe–XVIIIe siècles*), 69–90; Baxtiyor M. Babadžanov, "Le renouveau des communautés soufies en Ouzbékistan," *Cahiers d'Asie centrale*, 5–6 (1998 = *Boukhara-la-Noble*), 285–311; David Brophy, "The Kings of Xinjiang: Muslim Elites and the Qing Empire," *Etudes orientales*, No. 25 (2008), 69–89; David Brophy, "The Oirat in Eastern Turkistan and the Rise of Āfāq Khwāja," *Archivum Eurasiae Medii Aevi*, 16 (2008–09), 5–28; Stéphane A. Dudoignon, "From Revival to Mutation: The Religious Personnel of Islam in Tajikistan, from De-Stalinization to Independence (1995–91)," *Central Asian Survey*, 30 (2011), 53–80; Anke von Kügelgen, "Die Entfaltung der Naqšbandīya Muǧaddidīya im mittleren Transoxanien vom 18. bis zum Beginn des 19. Jahrhunderts: Ein Stück Detektivarbeit," in *Muslim Culture in Russia and Central Asia from the 18th to the Early 20th Centuries*, vol. 2: *Inter-Regional and Inter-Ethnic Relations*, ed. Anke von Kügelgen, Michael Kemper, and Allen J. Frank (Berlin: Klaus Schwarz Verlag, 1998), 101–151; Hamada Masami, "Le pouvoir des lieux saints dans le Turkestan oriental," *Asie centrale, Annales. Histoire, Social Sociales*, 5–6 (2004), 1019–1040; Alexandre Papas, *Soufisme et politique entre Chine, Tibet et Turkestan: Etude sur les khwajas naqshbandis du Turkestan oriental* (Paris: Librairie d'Amérique et d'Orient, Jean Maisonneuve successeur, 2005); Jürgen Paul, *Die politische und soziale Bedeutung der Naqšbandiyya in Mittelasien im 15. Jahrhundert* (Berlin, 1991) and *Doctrine and Organization. The Khwâjagân-Naqshbandîya in the First Generation after Bahâ'uddîn, ANOR* 1 (Berlin/Halle 1998); (ANOR 1), 1–84; Sawada Minoru, "Three Groups of *Tadhkira-i khwājagān*: Viewed from the Chapter on Khwāja Āfāq," in *Studies on Xinjiang Historical Sources in 17–20th Centuries*, ed. James A. Millward, Shinmen Yasushi, and Sugawara Jun (Tokyo: The Toyo Bunko, 2010; Toyo Bunko Research Library 12), 9–30; Maria Szuppe, "Ādīna Muḥammad Qarātēgīnī et 'son maître': Transmission des écrits de la tradition *kubravi* tardive en Asie centrale dans un recueil manuscrit de Ferghana," *Studia Iranica*, 45 (2016), 221–244; Rian Thum, *The Sacred Routes of Uyghur History* (Cambridge: Harvard University Press, 2014); and Thierry Zarcone, "The Sufi Networks in Southern Xinjiang during the Republican Regime (1911–1949). An Overview," in *Islam in Politics in Russia and Central Asia: Early 18th to Late 20th Centuries*, ed. Komatsu Hisao and S. A. Dudoignon (London: Kegan Paul, 2001), 119–132.

studies resulting from ethnographic fieldwork,[14] add substantially to our understanding of the religious, intellectual, and social currents in Central Asia in which 'Sufism' manifested its multiple facets, from the 18th century into the 21st, and also suggest that the field's most notable growth, and most important contributions, are yet to come.

At the same time, one general lesson to be drawn from the important studies of the past quarter-century is that the sources and structures of Sufi history in Central Asia differ substantially by period. An integrated approach is necessary to reveal these contours, identifying continuities but sensitive to the often-shifting referents of some 'standard' Sufi terminology. We must abandon, indeed—or at least suspend—the idea that we can zero in on one figure or period, bringing untested assumptions based on other figures or other periods, and hope to make sense of things. This cannot mean that we avoid the specialized study of individual figures, groups, or periods; but it must mean that in undertaking those specialized studies, we attempt to contextualize them in terms of broader processes of Sufi history in Central Asia, our understanding of which must inevitably be refined by the same specialized studies.

This is in fact what the contributions to the present volume are attempting. The assembled studies are ordered roughly along chronological lines, in terms of their focus, with Devin DeWeese's survey of much of the period placed first. His essay explores the inadequacies and impact of the Bennigsen/Sovietological narrative, and addresses the shifting patterns in organizational structure and 'transmissional' history among Sufi communities from the 16th to 20th centuries. It attempts to tie the Tsarist and Soviet eras into the earlier history of Central Asian Sufism, and to point out some continuities, generally overlooked in the past, that help contextualize and explain some of the failings of the Sovietological study of Sufism. It also attempts to take stock of diverse manifestations of 'Sufi' activity, applying a degree of conceptual flexibility that expands the range of phenomena recognizable as rooted in Sufism.

14 E.g., Waleed Ziad, "Traversing the Oxus and the Indus: Trans-regional Islamic Revival in the Age of Political Fragmentation and the Great Game, 1747–1857," Ph.D. Dissertation, Yale University, 2017; James Robert Pickett, "The Persianate Sphere during the Age of Empires: Islamic Scholars and Networks of Exchange in Central Asia, 1747–1917," Ph.D. Dissertation, Princeton University, 2015; Daniel Beben, "The Legendary Biographies of Nāṣir-i Khusraw: Memory and Textualization in Early Modern Persian Ismāʿīlism," Ph.D. Dissertation, Indiana University, 2015; Benjamin Clark Gatling, "Post-Soviet Sufism: Texts and the Performance of Tradition in Tajikistan," Ph.D. Dissertation, The Ohio State University, 2012 (now published as Benjamin Gatling, *Expressions of Sufi Culture in Tajikistan* [Madison: University of Wisconsin Press, 2018]).

In the second study, Shahzad Bashir explores a theoretical framework for the utilization of Persian hagiographical works as sources on religious, and social, history. In so doing, he grapples critically with key questions that will confront anyone who seeks to interrogate the large body of hagiographical sources produced by and about Central Asian Sufis, as outlined briefly in DeWeese's article, in order to study the history of Sufi communities and of the Central Asian world they inhabited. His analysis outlines the inverse relationship, in the production and actualization of hagiographical materials, among four categories that aptly describe the conceptual bases for the scholarly investigation of such materials, namely (1) the individual manuscripts through which we most often encounter hagiographical sources, (2) the texts of which we too simplistically regard the manuscripts as 'copies,' (3) the narrative fund that migrates in and out of the written and oral venues of 'textual' production and transmission, and (4) the genre of 'hagiography' itself—which, despite our use of a term extrinsic to Muslim literary traditions to refer to it, does indeed correspond to a recognizable body of works with distinctive shared features and, in most instances, extended patterns of intertextual relationship. With its careful delineation of these four 'fields,' Bashir's essay has important implications for the agenda of our work in the study of Sufism, in which the 'study and publication of sources' is often seen as the crucial first step. There may be merit in this longstanding approach, but Bashir's caution against assuming that the classical critical edition is the best way to approach hagiographical sources of our period is well taken, and indeed it may be suggested that devising strategies for the optimum use of the large number of unpublished, unstudied, and still largely unknown hagiographical sources from Central Asia is one of the central problems of the field. At the same time, Bashir also stresses that 'publishing' texts does not absolve the student of Sufi history of the need to use manuscripts, which, Bashir notes, always promise additional information—to the attentive reader—beyond what can be conveyed in even the best critical edition.

Along the way, more broadly, Bashir offers frequent reminders of an essential feature of hagiographical materials that makes them indispensable for the historian; he underscores, that is, the essential humanity that underlies and infuses a genre that is still too often dismissed as 'other-worldly' or preoccupied with the divine rather than with human, and social, concerns. Noting that hagiographical narratives convey their central religious messages through "dramatizations of relationships between human beings," Bashir foregrounds the human and social context, which must draw the attention of the social historian, without losing sight of the religious discourse in which hagiographies are framed. His particular examples are drawn from the body of works focused on the seminal figure of Bahāʾ al-Dīn Naqshband (d. 791/1389), produced during the 15th century, which stand at the beginning of a long series of hagiographies that are yet to be 'unpacked,' in terms of their contents or their interrelationships or a host of other codicological, textual, and historical issues. In addition to the invaluable conceptual framework he builds for us to keep front and center as we explore Central Asian hagiographical literature, his work reminds us again that the lessons learned from grappling with 15th-century works are vital for understanding 19th- and 20th-century phenomena.

The third contribution, by Maria Subtelny, addresses another key aspect of the volume's project by exploring the reflection of Sufi ties, and Sufi ideas, in the diverse writings of Ḥusayn Vāʿiẓ Kāshifī (d. 910/1504–05), a major intellectual and literary figure of the late Timurid era. She thereby draws attention to the intellectual appeal, and reach, of Sufism during the 15th and early 16th centuries, doing so in the context of a specific individual whose own career effectively narrows the gap we still too often insert between the scholarly apprehension of Sufi ideas, and relationships, and the world of so-called 'popular' Sufism. Like Bashir's study, her article is at once a case study illustrating, in this instance, how attention to 'Sufism' as refracted in the life of a single individual can illuminate that individual's social environment as well, and a model of the issues and conceptual frameworks that can and should be kept in mind when exploring later periods that are still less well-studied than the 15th century. The pattern of scholarly 'overlap' evident in Kāshifī's writings, as multiple Islamic sciences (including especially those framed as the 'occult' or esoteric sciences), intellectual interests, and social bonds are cultivated in a single life, helps us to frame questions about who the 'Sufi' is, and how 'Sufism' manifests itself in both intellectual and social life, that will serve us well in sweeping away the paradigms and classifications that have straitjacketed our understanding of 17th-century, or 19th- and 20th-century, Central Asia.

Ironically, indeed, attention to 'intellectual Sufism' once all but drowned out interest in the social history of Sufism, in Sufism's 'formative' era, but the process of outlining the history of Sufi communal formations from the 12th century onward has sometimes left the impression that these groups' intellectual history is less compelling; Sufi intellectualism in the 17th or 18th century is a barely explored phenomenon, with the exception of a few notable figures (e.g., Mullā Ṣadrā or Shāh Valīyullāh Dihlavī), but it is safe to say that no Central Asian Sufis are among those. By showing the substance of Sufi- or Sufi-influenced literature, and the intellectual content of Timurid thought as permeated by Sufi ideas, teachings, and concepts, Subtelny not only suggests the range of intellectual and social enterprises that were touched by Sufism;

she reminds us that the history of Sufism may be found also in the lives of individuals who are not typically identified, first and foremost, as Sufis. At the same time, in the citations and manipulations of verse from Rūmī's *Maṡnavī* in multiple works of Kāshifī's *ouevre* we may find the beginnings of a thread leading directly to the practice of many Sufi groups in Central Asia (and elsewhere) in the 18th and 19th centuries, namely the adaptation of the *Maṡnavī* as a key medium for instruction and edification, often in congregational settings, and indeed as a feature of 'liturgical' use in Sufi circles.

Waleed Ziad's groundbreaking study, the fourth in the volume, explores the expansion of Sufi networks extending from Peshawar to Bukhara and beyond in the 18th and 19th centuries, focusing on the career of the Mujaddidī shaykh Miyān Fażl Aḥmad Maʿṣūmī, popularly known as Ḥażrat Jīo Ṣāḥib (1157–1231/1744–1816). This figure offers a prime example of a Sufi shaykh 'in motion,' both in his long-term trajectory from Sirhind, in India, the place of his birth and Sufi training, to Peshawar in the new Durrānī state of Afghanistan, and in what we may see as quite consequential 'side-trips,' to Bukhara, Kabul, and elsewhere in the lands of Mawarannahr, Khurasan, and Hindustan. These regions remained divided politically, but were becoming increasingly interconnected in economic, cultural, and religious terms. Indeed, Ḥażrat Jīo's travels and longer residencies alike helped knit these regions together, as he established personal relationships and social and institutional frameworks—successors, disciples, ruler-patrons, *khānaqāh*s—nearly everywhere he went, helping to forge what Ziad aptly refers to as a unified "sacro-cultural" zone. That zone extended even further through the shaykh's role as a religious 'magnet,' in effect, drawing followers from a much wider 'catch-basin' extending from other parts of India to Kashghar and Kazan. With this in mind, Ziad argues that the fact, and example, of Durrānī patronage—both that aimed directly at specific Mujaddidī Sufi leaders and that directed more broadly for the cultivation of educational and commercial institutions—launched a religious revival that radiated northward through Bukhara, into the steppe, and as far as the Volga valley, Siberia, and Xinjiang. Here, then, is yet another challenge to the Russocentric understanding of Muslim religious history in the Tsarist empire; and figures and institutions that we need not stretch at all to label "Sufi" are at the heart of it. At the same time, Ziad's study is both an excellent example of the new perspectives and new worlds that can be uncovered through extensive 'digging' in the manuscript collections, *khānaqāh* libraries, and private archives of this once-unified zone in south-central Eurasia—his study brings to light a wide array of previously unused and unknown local histories and biographies of Ḥażrat Jīo from collections in Uzbekistan, Afghanistan, and

Pakistan—and a reminder of how provisional our narratives of Sufi history in the region must remain until more such work is undertaken.

In contrast to Ziad's exploration of Naqshbandī-Mujaddidī networks across a broad region, the subject of Yayoi Kawahara's contribution, the fifth in the volume, may be regarded as one local manifestation of the Mujaddidī legacy in 19th-century Central Asia. Her study examines the social, political, and military roles of Valī Khān Tūra at the time of the fall of the khanate of Khoqand and the establishment of direct Russian rule in the Farghana valley. This figure's name is associated with a 'rebellion' that has been portrayed by some as part of a proto-nationalist 'liberation' struggle, but Valī Khān Tūra's role in this disturbance in itself suggests other, overarching issues, as does his community's evident respect and reverence for him. A descendant of the pivotal 16th-century Naqshbandī shaykh known as Makhdūm-i Aʿẓam, Valī Khān Tūra belonged to a 'Sufi family' with enormous prestige throughout Central Asia, and especially in the Farghana valley. His great-grandfather was also a disciple of a prominent 18th-century Mujaddidī shaykh, providing yet another 'injection' of Sufi prestige and authority, both hereditary and initiatic, into the lineage. This accumulated prestige was hardly the only thing at work in the violence that has drawn attention to Valī Khān Tūra, but it provides the subtext for the rich documentary sources explored by Kawahara, whether the materials from the private family archives of his descendants (which include hagiographies and legal documents), or, inversely, the Russian documents relating to his arrest, which give voice to Russian officials' fears and concerns about what his prestige might lead to. Perhaps the most vivid illustration, however, of what widespread local esteem for representatives of the phenomenon we refer to somewhat clinically as 'hereditary Sufism' might lead to is found in the seals and signs of the residents of Marghīnān, the native town of Valī Khān Tūra, on the petition for his release. The petition itself is marked by quite understated bureaucratic language, wielded by Central Asians who had been barely three years under Russian rule, and who were compelled to acquiesce in that fact, but who nevertheless professed 'public' responsibility for the well-being, and good behavior, of their saint.

A different configuration of the social, economic, political, and religious implications of sanctity is presented in the volume's sixth offering, Robert McChesney's in-depth study of the shrine housing the Prophet's Cloak (*khirqa-yi sharīf*) in Qandahar. Reviewing the history of the shrine from the second half of the 18th century down to the present, McChesney focuses most closely on the reigns of three Afghan rulers spanning the half century from 1880 to 1930. He uses documents relating to the shrine itself, local narrative histories, travel accounts, reports of British agents, and earlier studies of the architectural history of the site to explore, in effect, one major physical embodiment of sacrality in the social landscape of 19th- and 20th-century Afghanistan. As he outlines the economic underpinnings of the shrine and its wider economic functions, the shrine's resonances in Afghan politics, and the social and religious roles played by the shrine and its patrons—including the fascinating discussion of individuals seeking sanctuary (*bast*) at the shrine—one question naturally arises: where are the Sufis? They are in fact hard to find in this essay, under this name; indeed, the only person who figures prominently in the discussion and is identified as a "Ṣūfī" is a calligrapher and architect who worked at the Shrine of the Prophet's Cloak in the early 20th century. Yet the world of more explicitly 'Sufi' activity is never far away from the site itself. A Sufi *khānaqāh* was part of the shrine complex from its establishment in the 1770s; shrines celebrating not the Prophet's Cloak, but saints recognized as Sufis, are nearby in Qandahar. More broadly, virtually everything about this shrine is modeled, in effect, on features and practices first, and best, known in connection with the shrines of Sufi saints. Whether we focus on the shrine's 'theoretical' infrastructure in the form of the *waqfiyya*, its institutional infrastructure in the buildings and embellishments, the charitable economic provisions that linked the shrine to the local society's needs, the family lineage that managed the shrine and came to absorb both its resources and its sacrality, the wider social circles that visited the shrine or attended to its upkeep, or the rulers who invested in the shrine, we find patterns of religious and social activity that can best be understood on the basis of parallels known from shrines of saints more directly linked with Sufism. It is as if the relic, in the form of the Prophet's Cloak, is a substitute for the body of the Sufi saint; "reliquary Sufism" thus marks yet another conceptual expansion that may be helpful in understanding the overlapping worlds of Sufis, saints, and shrines.

It is routinely acknowledged, of course, that a 'Sufi shrine' may memorialize not only the place (or places) where a Sufi was buried, but a place where the saint 'merely' spent the night, visited, or experienced some vision or transformative grace. And by the same token, if we do not readily see figures identified as Sufis at the Shrine of the Cloak, we should remember that we may also rarely see such Sufis at the shrines of Sufis. Yet whatever is understood to make a particular site holy—and the presence of the cloak of the Prophet adds particular spiritual weight to the site in Qandahar—all such sites may harbor, or attract, different facets of Sufi religiosity, through the 'story' that explains the site's holiness, through rites performed at the site, or through the social ties of the personnel who staff the site. As McChesney rightly notes in his introduction, the precise identity of the 'thing' believed to sanctify a particular shrine is rarely determinative of the kind of religious practice undertaken there.

Arriving at an honest but flexible configuration of the 'overlap' between Sufism and shrine culture is indeed another key desideratum of the study of Sufism in Central Asia.

If 'Sufism' as typically understood seems somewhat attenuated in certain papers—assuming the form of an intellectual with interests that included, but were not limited to, Sufism in Subtelny's study, of a sacred family in Kawahara's, and of a shrine in McChesney's—it comes back fully, under the name of Sufism, in the seventh study—but with a surprising twist. Allen Frank's examination of three responses by Sufis, in the Volga-Ural region, to the critiques of Sufi practices leveled by some 'reformist' Muslims in the early 20th century offers multiple correctives to the camps and alignments we all too often resort to in trying to understand Muslim religious life in the Russian empire; not the least of these is the reminder that Sufis could be 'reformers' too. He reviews three examples of Sufi writers addressing the religious and social issues affecting Muslim society in Tsarist Russia in the first two decades of the 20th century: a local history and shrine-guide focused on Astrakhan, from 1907, a targeted Sufi critique of the practices of certain Sufis, from 1911, and another locally-based 'family history' from 1914. In each one, Frank finds combinations of subjects and ideas that at first glance seem incongruous, because they violate the strict delineations of political and religious 'sides' that recur in the scholarly literature on Muslim society in Russia, but rarely occurred in real life. One Sufi writer defends the practice of pilgrimage and simultaneously champions his vision of "progress," admiring along the way the Islamic piety and rectitude of a group that is typically characterized—in the standard narrative one can still find repeated today—as barely Muslim, the Qazaqs. Another engages in soul-searching and self-criticism, not in order to discredit or delegitimize Sufism, but in order to purify it, and to call those drawn to it to a higher aspiration. And a third writer recounts in depth the Sufi connections of his family, all the while evincing an almost nostalgic, and at times self-critical, acknowledgment that the formerly familiar structures and aims of Sufi life were changing, and were already not what they had been a few generations earlier. The question remains, for us, what particulars of Sufism's face in the decades after 1914 the latter author could have foreseen; answering this question is, after all, the task at hand. What we can be sure of, however, is that these writers were not the Sufis we find caricatured by the Jadīds, or later by Soviet antireligious activists; they were nevertheless Sufis who must be included within our emerging understanding of what Sufism was in Tsarist Russia, on the eve of the Soviet era.

A similarly sweeping rejection of the usefulness of some key categories long employed in discussing Muslim religious life in Central Asia, now fully within the Soviet era, is the hallmark of the eighth contribution, Eren Tasar's pathbreaking study of the continuing strength and resilience of what is plainly 'Sufi activity' in the 1940s and 1950s, after the era of the most intense antireligious attacks of the Soviet era. To say that Tasar turns upside down our previous narratives of Sufism, or of Islam more broadly, being driven underground, destroyed, or disappearing during the 1930s is perhaps an understatement. His study, firmly rooted in the documentary legacy of those tasked with 'managing' the expected, and desired, demise of religiosity in Central Asia, shows a remarkably vibrant religious world among Soviet Muslims, a world in which Sufism retained a quite public, and even 'official,' face. Beginning with a focused critique of the Bennigsen narrative, and thoughtfully problematizing the terminology of his documentary sources, Tasar reveals the continuing vigor of Sufi networks, in effect, through the hereditary lineage installed in the leadership of SADUM, the official Soviet administrative structure established, in the midst of the Second World War, to represent and control Islam in Central Asia. He next examines in depth one of the favorite subjects of the Bennigsen school, the case of the so-called "Hairy Ishans," offering a well-grounded refinement of some aspects of the old narrative, and overturning other parts. Finally, he explores the remarkable case of the hereditary lineage that managed to hold onto its traditional custody of a sacred well in the Farghana valley even as the site was turned into a Soviet health resort. The skill of the local *khojas* in negotiating, and in some cases flouting or circumventing, official opposition to their role is as remarkable as the odd stance of the Soviet governmental organs, which sought to desacralize the holy waters even as they officially sanctioned, through socialist science, their healing powers. One cannot read Tasar's study and ever again think in the same way as before about Islam, or Sufism, in Soviet Central Asia.

The ninth essay, by Ashirbek Muminov, squarely addresses the face of Sufism and the diversity of groups claiming the legacy of Sufism in contemporary Kazakhstan. He examines four types of currently-active Sufi groups, focusing on their ritual practices and on the relations among the groups: the Nashbandiyya-Mujaddidiyya-Ḥusayniyya, with an initiatic lineage traceable to pre-Soviet times; Qādirī groups among the Chechens whose forebears were deported to Kazakhstan under Stalin; a group calling itself the Jahriyya, linked to Ismatŭlla Maqsŭm, a *shaykh* who moved to Kazakhstan from Afghanistan in post-Soviet times; and miscellaneous Turkish Sufi communities that have sought affiliates in post-Soviet Kazakhstan. This classification of groups by initiatic or ethnic or national origin overlies other ways of grouping them (a principle relevant to earlier times as well). In terms of historical roots in Kazakhstan, for instance, the Naqshbandī and Qādirī groups each have an established heritage in Central Asia (one considerably longer than the other), while the Jahriyya and the various Turkish groups came to Kazakhstan only in the post-Soviet era. In terms of legal status, the first group has an active "spiritual and organizational center" and is officially registered; the Chechen Qādirī groups appear to be ethnically exclusive; the leader of the Jahriyya has been exiled and is now imprisoned, with the group's Sufi activities curtailed; and the educational endeavors, at least, of the Turkish groups—which all appear to mix a 'Sufi' profile with other activities—have likewise been suspended recently.

Muminov's research, based mainly on oral interviews and observations, counters the Bennigsen narrative by digging into the everyday practices and the social environment of Sufis today, revealing both the continuity of long-established Sufi communities in the history of Central Asian Sufism, in the case of the Naqshbandiyya-Mujaddidiyya—albeit with remodeled organizational structures, ritual practices, and 'transmissional' history—and the impact of more recent political developments in bringing the other groups to Kazakhstan: the Qādirī presence was tied to the upheaval of the Chechen deportation, while the Jahriyya and the Turkish groups were able to begin their activities in Kazakhstan only in the wake of the collapse of the Soviet Union (with their current precarious position reflecting the lingering political uncertainties of the post-Soviet era). Yet patterns long familiar from pre-Soviet Sufi communities, involving conflict, rivalry, and competition over leadership, succession, and practice—including the recurrent issue of the silent vs. vocal form of the Sufi *z̤ikr* and the other tensions these alternatives often represent—have emerged both between and within particular groups, as Muminov's research shows. More broadly, the face of 'Sufism' in present-day Kazakhstan, as sketched by Muminov, demonstrates the importance, if not the necessity, of on-the-ground historical and ethnographic work in 'Sufi' communities, which until recently was impossible to carry out—with adverse consequences for our understanding of Sufism.

Finally, the tenth contribution likewise pulls us into the post-Soviet present, although it is firmly moored in biographical and architectural foundations stretching back through much of the Islamic era. In rooting the current search for biographical traditions surrounding the figure of Muḥammad Bashārā in the shrine, in Tajikistan, to which his name is attached, Jo-Ann Gross explores the conundrum posed by a disconnect that is not uncommon in Central Asia, but is rarely so starkly presented as in the case of this figure. On the one hand, this architectural jewel of a shrine, featuring remarkable ornamentation and calligraphic carving as well as a striking harmonization with the environment in which it was built, suggests that the figure buried there must have been of enormous stature, to merit the devotion of such resources—both at the time of construction and afterwards, through the endowments that supported its maintenance and functioning—to his memorialization. On the other hand, aside from a passage in a 19th-century pilgrimage guide to Samarqand, practically nothing is known about him, and the usual kinds of sources in which we seek biographical details, or hagiographical narratives, about other saints—including those linked with much less impressive shrines—fail us in his case. The disconnect between a prominent, and well-cared-for shrine, and an obscure saint is interesting in its own right, but as Gross shows, shrine culture abhors a vacuum, and multiple 'experts' have emerged to provide a 'back-story' for both the shrine and the saint. Similar to McChesney's study of "reliquary Sufism," the 'overlap' between Sufism and shrine culture, in this case, consists of a long-established tradition of pilgrimage, the physical construction over time of the mosque/*khānaqāh*/mausoleum, and a multifaceted biographical tradition.

The main players in the creation of the 'back-story' for the saint are the editor/translator of a hagiographical text, published near the very beginning of the post-Soviet era (based on an earlier, as yet unidentified, 19th-century text), and the 'Salafī'-style proponents of purifying Tajik Islam, a more recent feature of the Central Asian landscape, as also seen in Muminov's study. The hagiography portrays Muḥammad Bashārā as a native of the region where his shrine now stands, who journeyed to meet the Prophet and adopt Islam, returned to his homeland to bring Islam there, and despite the martyrdom of many Muslims, finally won the conversion of the local infidels. It is replete with familiar hagiographical motifs and invites pilgrims to participate in the saint's blessedness at his shrine. The Salafī biographical offering rejects most of the hagiographical motifs, in the name of pinning down a 'historical' and demythologized *muḥaddith* of 8th century Basra named Muḥammad b. Bashshār, based on Arabic biographical and *ḥadīth* literature. It lays out a restrictive vision of 'proper' practice in visiting shrines, again based on a limited repertoire of *ḥadīth*s, but is in fact notable for stopping short of the total rejection of shrine culture featured in much Salafī literature. Despite this work's conditional validation of shrine culture, the two biographies devised for the shrine saint offer a good encapsulation of the religious choice facing Central Asian Muslims today. Yet much of the 'baggage' they carry as they face this choice is of Soviet manufacture, and not the least of this study's merits is the addition of Soviet archeologists and architectural historians to the company of blind men intent on describing this particular elephant. Their quarrels over the building's dating and 'original' purpose were ostensibly based on the firm scientific study of material culture, but one can also find more than a few signs that ultimately tenuous assumptions—about the figure believed to be buried there and about the religious lives of those who developed the shrine and patronized it—helped to shape their arguments about the site.

• • •

Taken together, these studies mark a new phase in the development of scholarship on Sufi traditions of Central Asia, expanding and deepening the source base, reconceptualizing basic frameworks for understanding Sufi history, and challenging received assumptions and narratives. It is hoped that this sort of approach to the study of Sufism in Central Asia—an approach freed from the constraints of the Sovietological framework in which the subject was initially considered—may contribute to the broader goal of restoring Sufism, and religious life in general, to historical inquiry, both by improving our understanding of the social structures through which 'religion' acts in historical terms, and by reminding us of the essentially religious visions that shape those social structures.

CHAPTER 1

Re-Envisioning the History of Sufi Communities in Central Asia: Continuity and Adaptation in Sources and Social Frameworks, 16th–20th Centuries

Devin DeWeese

It was evidently a 10th-century Sufi from what we may count as Central Asia who first formulated a brief saying, relevant for Sufi history, that became quite popular in later Sufi circles. Several 11th-century Sufi writers introduce that saying by explaining that someone once asked Abū'l-Ḥasan ʿAlī b. Aḥmad b. Sahl al-Būshanjī (d. 348/959), a Sufi and *javānmard* of Khurasan, about Sufism—straightforwardly using the term *al-taṣawwuf*, suggesting that in this case, at least, the term indeed referred to a distinct 'movement' which the writers, and arguably al-Būshanjī himself, understood, or wished to define, as a coherent phenomenon, and thus indeed suggesting 'Sufism' as a reasonable translation. Those writers affirm, further, that al-Būshanjī had replied, when thus asked, "Today Sufism is a name without a reality, but formerly it was a reality without a name."[1]

The saying is noteworthy, beyond its pithy symmetry and its touch of irony, for encapsulating a 'theory,' in effect, about the historical development and social manifestations of Sufism. It combines, that is, statements about both the past and present of Sufism as viewed from the 10th or 11th century. The second half of the saying asserts an essentially historical (if also partly metaphysical) proposition that became important to Sufis, namely, that despite the historical appearance of the term 'Sufism,' or of the designation 'Ṣūfī' applied to individuals, only some centuries after the time of the Prophet, the phenomenon

1 This is the version given in Abū'l-Ḥasan ʿAlī b. ʿUthmān Hujvīrī (d. 465–469/1072–77), *Kashf al-maḥjūb*, ed. Maḥmūd ʿĀbidī (Tehran: Surūsh, 1387/2008), 59 (referring to Abū'l-Ḥasan-i Fūshanja); cf. *The Kashf al-Mahjúb: The Oldest Persian Treatise on Sufiism by ʿAlí b. ʿUthmán al-Jullábí al-Hujwírí*, tr. Reynold A. Nicholson (London: Luzac and Company, 1936; E. J. W. Gibb Memorial Series, vol. XVII; repr. 1976), 44. Slightly different phrasing is given in the accounts of Būshanjī in Abū ʿAbd al-Raḥmān al-Sulamī (d. 412/1021), *Ṭabaqāt al-ṣūfiyya*, ed. Nūr al-Dīn Sharība (3rd printing, Cairo: Maktabat al-Khānajī, 1406/1986), 459, and in ʿAbdullāh Anṣārī Haravī (d. 481/1089), *Ṭabaqāt al-ṣūfiyya*, ed. Muḥammad Sarvar Mawlāʾī (Tehran: Intishārāt-i Tūs, 1362/1983), 498 (these authors mostly reflect Khurāsānī Sufi traditions and may have credited a Khurāsānī Sufi with a saying that had wider currency, and earlier origins).

 | DOI:10.1163/9789004373075_003

denoted by the term had indeed existed in the Prophet's time (and in fact had been initiated by him). The first half of the saying, meanwhile, makes an implicit critique of the character of what was, in al-Būshanjī's time, labeled 'Sufism,' after just another century or so had exerted its corrosive influence upon that phenomenon. The saying naturally evokes the notion of temporal decline from a purer, 'original' state, as well as "the tension between the ideals of mysticism and the realities of social practice."[2] But it also affirms, in effect, the historical proposition that what we call Sufism existed in its best and purest form when it did not (yet) bear that designation, and that the term 'Sufi' might now be applied to, or claimed by, groups or individuals regarded—by those concerned about 'genuine' propriety or spiritual virtue—as quite far away (and in a downhill direction) from that best and purest form.[3] In short, the saying combines a purposeful and self-conscious essentialization of 'Sufism' as a coherent phenomenon with an acknowledgement—though one fraught with disapproval—of historical change in the manifestations of that phenomenon. A social historian, or a historian of religion, will naturally be more interested in the social 'realities' underlying the names applied to the manifestations of Sufism, than in the 'reality' that al-Būshanjī had in mind; but he or she must also be constantly mindful that the forms in which 'Sufism' appears in one era may differ from the forms it takes in another, and, more broadly, that names or labels and their social referents are quite different things.

The point of recalling this saying here is not merely to evoke the distinction the saying encapsulates between scholarly approaches to Sufism that emphasize spiritual teaching and practice, or even Sufism's 'timeless essence,' and those that stress its social manifestations, insisting that Sufism is indeed a proper focus for historical study (though this distinction is worth noting);[4] nor is it merely to argue that, within the historical approach, the problem of names

2 Carl W. Ernst, *The Shambhala Guide to Sufism* (Boston/London: Shambhala Publications, 1997), 24–25, in a brief discussion about the appearance of such laments over the decline of Sufism nearly as early as the appearance of the term 'Sufism.'

3 The sentiment was framed in other terms in roughly the same era; the 10th-century Central Asian Sufi writer Abū Bakr b. Muḥammad al-Bukhārī al-Kalābādhī (d. 385/995), for instance, outlined the diminishing proportion of real spiritual virtue to pretense, affirming that in the end, "the meaning departed, and the name remained" (Abū Bakr al-Kalābādhī, *The Doctrine of the Ṣūfīs* [*Kitāb al-Taʿarruf li-madhhab ahl al-taṣawwuf*], tr. A. J. Arberry [Cambridge: Cambridge University Press, 1935], 3).

4 On the shift from the former to the latter in scholarship on Sufism, see the insightful comments in the introduction to the review essay of Dina LeGall, "Recent Thinking on Sufis and Saints in the Lives of Muslim Societies, Past and Present," *International Journal of Middle East Studies*, 42/4 (2010), 673–687.

and labels and their social referents must be kept constantly in mind in order to account for change in the organization and public profiles of Sufi communities (though this too is worth arguing). The point is, rather, to suggest that in reminding us both of the problem of names and labels, and of the historicity of Sufism's manifestations, this saying is helpful to keep in mind as we go about the long-overdue process of dismantling the legacies left by an unfortunate era in the study of Sufism in Central Asia—the era of Sovietology, as represented above all by the work of Alexandre Bennigsen and his associates.

The inadequacies of the Bennigsen narrative, after all, rest on a failure to grapple with the two central issues that are crystallized in this saying: first, the proponents of the Bennigsen narrative used names and labels imprecisely, and were thus often not quite sure what they might be talking about when they talked of Sufism; and second, its proponents either ignored historical changes in the social manifestations of Sufism, or concocted a version of the 'history of Sufism' that had no foundation in the actual sources (of which they appear to have been mostly unaware). In seeking to assess the status of Sufism in Soviet Central Asia, in short, the practitioners of the Sovietological enterprise failed to ask critical questions about the ways in which 'Sufism' manifested itself, and then created a narrative of Sufi history before the Soviet era, to serve as 'background' for the period of interest to them; but they got that earlier history profoundly wrong, and in so doing also misunderstood the contemporary era that was supposed to be their chief concern, with adverse consequences that linger to this day.

With this in mind, the aim of the present essay is to outline the problems with the Sovietological approach to Sufism in Central Asia, as reflected in the Bennigsen narrative and in its echoes, and to suggest some correctives that may be applied to assessments of Sufi activity in the Tsarist and Soviet eras on the basis of a better understanding of the sources and structures of Sufi history from earlier times—above all, the still-poorly studied era from the 16th through the 19th century. It will necessarily stop short of a full review of Sufi history in Central Asia, or of the sources that must be employed in exploring that history; but it will nevertheless assume that a positive answer is possible for two broader questions that can be broached, but not fully fleshed out, at this point. First, can we construct a historical narrative for Sufi communities, in this still poorly-studied era of Central Asian history, that takes stock of the distinctive features of this period, as contrasted with the preceding era, during which the major Sufi traditions took shape (from the 13th to 15th centuries), but also traces historical shifts, and regional and diachronic granularity, within the era as a whole, thus allowing us to recognize how different the face of 'Sufism' was in 1850 as opposed to 1550, or 1650, and in Khwārazm, for instance, or Kashghar, as opposed to Mawarannahr? And second, can we then use that historical narrative to aid us in bridging the seemingly greater epistemological gap posed by the Soviet era (or its equivalents elsewhere in the region), when the kinds of sources we have grown accustomed to using to explore Sufi history in earlier times seem to disappear, or at least become harder to find, and when various unreflective approaches and assumptions about what 'Sufism' must look like serve to steer our inquiry in unfruitful directions?[5] The importance of addressing these questions, in practical and substantive terms, is underscored by the inadequacies of the prevailing narrative, to which we may now turn.

Flaws in the Sovietological Narrative

The unhelpful approaches and assumptions characteristic of Sovietology's assessments of Sufism in Central Asia have their roots in the brief flurry of interest in 'Sufism in the USSR' during the 1970s and '80s, and in the way in which that interest skewed the study of Sufism and the questions asked about it. Those decades saw considerable discussion in Sovietological literature about the presumed role of 'Sufi orders' in the Soviet world, including Central Asia, complete with rather grandiose notions of these groups as militant, but clandestine, organizations that were biding their time, waiting for the opportunity to bring down the Soviet state; such was the basic premise underlying the publications on 'Soviet Sufism' by Bennigsen and his school, as reflected above all in his *Mystics and Commissars* (1985),[6] co-written with S. Enders

5 Attempting to answer the second question without posing the first can lead to problematical results; see, for example, the study of Thierry Zarcone, "Bridging the Gap between Pre-Soviet and Post-Soviet Sufism in Ferghana Valley (Uzbekistan): The Naqshbandī Order between Tradition and Innovation," in *Popular Movements and Democratization in the Islamic World*, ed. Masatoshi Kisaichi (London/New York: Routledge, 2006), 43–56, rich with information but flawed from the start by an analytical framework insisting on a clear and rigid distinction between 'high' and 'low' or 'elite' and 'popular' Sufism. For a more successful study that spans the pre- and post-Soviet periods, see Stephane A. Dudoignon, "From Revival to Mutation: The Religious Personnel of Islam in Tajikistan, from de-Stalinization to Independence (1955–91)," *Central Asian Survey*, 30 (2011), 53–80.

6 Alexandre Bennigsen and S. Enders Wimbush, *Mystics and Commissars: Sufism in the Soviet Union* (Berkeley/Los Angeles: University of California Press, 1985); see also Alexandre Bennigsen, "Official Islam and Sufi Brotherhoods in the Soviet Union Today," in *Islam and Power*, ed. Alexander S. Cudsi and Ali E. Hillal Dessouki (Baltimore: The Johns Hopkins University Press, 1981), 95–106; Chantal Lemercier-Quelquejay, "Sufi Brotherhoods in the USSR: A Historical Survey," *Central Asian Survey*, 2/4 (1983), 1–35; and Alexandre Bennigsen,

Wimbush. Already by the late 1980s, of course, it was realized that these expectations were fanciful, and attention shifted elsewhere; as a result, Sufism receded from scholarly attention, to the point that current discussions of 'Islam in Central Asia' either repeat the less extravagant characterizations of Sufism in the region advanced by the Sovietological school (on the apparent assumption that they might be true even if the wilder claims were not), or dismiss the importance of Central Asia's Sufi movements as part of the religious landscape of the region in Soviet and post-Soviet times.

Both the dismissal of Sufism's presence and impact in the Soviet era (and today), and the particulars of the Sovietological exaggerations about Sufis in the Soviet era, could be regarded as mere historical curiosities—artifacts of the Cold War—if they did not still stand in the way of a more sober, historically-grounded understanding of Sufism in Central Asia during the Soviet era, and before and after it. They do so in two ways: first, some specific constructions of Sufi history traceable to the Sovietological accounts remain current in popular and even scholarly literature about Central Asia; and second, the willful neglect of the kind of historical study that could have reminded scholars, even in Soviet times, that most of the Sovietological narrative was ludicrous, persists today.

The hallmarks of the broader Bennigsen narrative included, as noted, the supposedly inherent militancy of Sufism, as a focus for resistance against Russian and Soviet control; the clandestine nature, hierarchical structure, and tight organizational solidity of Sufi groups, as advantages in maintaining their activity despite Soviet repression; the inclusion of Sufi activity within the larger framework of the Sovietological category of 'unofficial' or 'parallel' Islam; the classification of Sufi groups according to historically prominent 'orders' or 'brotherhoods,' each assignable to a particular geographical stronghold (based,

---

"Sufism in the USSR: A Bibliography of Soviet Sources," *Central Asian Survey*, 2/4 (Dec., 1983), 81–107 (this list does not include the more numerous studies of Sufism in the North Caucasus, or the not-so-numerous discussions of the Volga-Ural region). See also Azade-Ayse Rorlich, "Islam and Atheism: Dynamic Tension in Soviet Central Asia," in *Soviet Central Asia: The Failed Transformation*, ed. William Fierman (Boulder, Colorado: Westview Press, 1991), 186–218 (esp. 191, and 201–203, "The Problem of Sufism"). Ironically, Bennigsen's focus on Sufis in the USSR appears to have been prompted by developments in the broader study of Sufism underway by the mid-1970s; Sufism is barely mentioned in Alexandre Bennigsen and Chantal Lemercier Quelquejay, *Islam in the Soviet Union* (New York: Praeger, 1967). For a broader discussion of the Bennigsen school in the context of Cold War politics, see now Artemy M. Kalinovsky, "Encouraging Resistance: Paul Henze, the Bennigsen School, and the Crisis of Détente," in *Reassessing Orientalism: Interlocking Orientologies during the Cold War*, ed. Michael Kemper and Artemy M. Kalinovsky (London/New York: Routledge, 2015), 211–232.

in fact, on the center of activity of the orders' eponyms), with order-based distinctions between 'centralized' and 'decentralized' brotherhoods;[7] a concomitant claim that shrines served as the organizational centers for the orders, alongside a broader assumption of a direct, zero-sum correlation between Sufi groups and particular shrines under their control; an utterly groundless historical narrative for particular Sufi orders and for Sufism in general; a stress on the 'mystical' and hence anti-clerical, anti-scholarly orientation of Sufism; a historically- and terminologically-confused insistence, nevertheless, on Sufism as a 'fundamentalist' current in Soviet Islam;[8] and a similarly paradoxical stance regarding the 'brand' of Islam represented by Sufism: in some contexts the Bennigsen narrative credits Sufism with keeping Islam in the Soviet environment not only pure, but alive, while in others the narrative adopts the Soviet characterization of Sufism as 'syncretic,' 'popular,' 'folk,' and rife with elements of belief and practice drawn from pre-Islamic traditions and thus extraneous to 'learned' Islam (if sometimes without acknowledging or recognizing the implications of these characterizations).

As noted, some elements of this basic narrative did shift, beginning with the notion of Sufi militancy, which gave way to claims that Sufism is inherently apolitical and peaceful. Such a shift in characterization, from one extreme generalization to its opposite, is in itself testimony to the ongoing impact of the Bennigsen narrative, first through specific elements that continue to shape discussion of Sufism in the former Soviet world—whether by repetition or by rejection—and second through the broader example, in effect, of framing a subject in the absence of serious discussion and without the use of actual sources.[9]

---

7 As an example of the over-classification and sheer overreach that marked the Bennigsen narrative, we are told, regarding 'decentralized' groups, "All Naqshbandi groups in Central Asia and the Caucasus belong to this category" (Bennigsen and Wimbush, *Mystics and Commissars*, 73).

8 Ignoring both the 'modern' character of fundamentalisms, and the historical and intellectual profile of what may reasonably be called Muslim fundamentalism, Bennigsen and Wimbush write that "Fundamentalism, in the context of the Russian/Soviet empire, is a desire to return to pure, unadulterated Islam, or in other words a rejection of *jadid* modernist trends" (*Mystics and Commissars*, 4), and insist that "in the Soviet Union fundamentalist and radical Sufi tendencies are often, but not always, in harmony" (4); elsewhere the latter softening is abandoned, as we read that "… in Kirghizia, in parts of Kazakhstan, and notably in Turkmenistan [!], Sufi orders represent the organised vanguard of unorganised fundamentalist dissent" (2), and as "fundamentalist Sufism in all of its many aspects" is framed as the central subject of the book.

9 For example, Bennigsen's certainty that Tsarist- and Soviet-era Sufi history was marked by the endurance of the great historical orders was, by the mid-1990s, superseded in some circles by a formulation that was equally misleading, though in different ways; and, like elements

The Sovietological study of Sufism was thus flawed in specific elements of its narrative, and in the way the subject was framed and approached; and in both ways, the legacy of Bennigsen's Sovietological study of Sufism in Central Asia continued well past the breakup of the Soviet Union, through the 1990s and into the 2000s. The discussion of Sufism in Yaacov Ro'i's *Islam in the Soviet Union*, from 2000, was rooted in Bennigsen's conceptual framework,[10] and numerous elements from the Bennigsen narrative were marshalled in a popular handbook on Central Asia published the same year.[11] The Bennigsen legacy

---

of the Bennigsen narrative, this new formulation was parroted by multiple authors (often without citation): "By the beginning of the twentieth century, the link between the dervish organizations and their original Sufi orders was recognizable only with difficulty. Sufism had degenerated into Ishanism, and every ishan of any reputation became in time the founder of a separate order. On the other hand, Ishanism, as a Central Asian variety of Sufism, had absorbed a large number of pre-Islamic beliefs and elements of ancient cults" (Igor Lipovsky, "The Awakening of Central Asian Islam," *Middle Eastern Studies*, 32/3 [July 1996], 1–21 [3–4]); "By the early twentieth century, the link with the original orders was recognizable only with difficulty in Central Asia, traditional sufism having been superseded rather by 'ishanism', with each *ishan* of repute becoming the founder of a separate order.... In many respects their beliefs and practices were essentially animistic rather than Islamic in origin, tracing back to the rituals of ancient local cults" (Yaacov Ro'i, *Islam in the Soviet Union: From the Second World War to Gorbachev* [London: C. Hurst & Co., 2000], 386–387); "Great Sufi orders such as the Naqshbandiya and Qadiriya were influential in Central Asia in the past, but even before the Soviet era they had for the most part been reduced to the level of 'ishanism' (a syncretic, popular form of mysticism, centered on local, often hereditary, spiritual leaders). In the twentieth century this form of worship continued to attract adherents, but was far removed from the esoteric doctrines and practices of classical Sufism" (Shirin Akiner, "The Contestation of Islam in post-Soviet Central Asia: A Nascent Security Threat," in *The Middle East's Relations with Asia and Russia*, ed. Hannah Carter and Anoushiravan Ehteshami [London: RoutledgeCurzon, 2004], 75–102 [88]).

10 Ro'i, *Islam in the Soviet Union*, especially 385–405; the discussion is complete with the fanciful geographical distribution of the orders (386) and the depiction of the 'Hairy Ishans' as "a radical branch of the Yasawiyya" (398).

11 See Giampaolo R. Capisani, *The Handbook of Central Asia* (London: I. B. Tauris, 2000), where we are reminded early on of the implications, for Soviet times, of the "ancient schism between official *mullahs* and the confraternity of *shaykhs*," the latter deriving their "legitimacy" from "having remained in the Islamic faith during the Soviet era" (89). Later we read, regarding Islam in Kyrgyzstan, that "the intermingling between Islam and nomadic shamanism led to the rise of heterodox practice, spread and supported by Dervish orders or Sufi brotherhoods, known generally as 'parallel' or 'popular' Islam. Even today Dervishes play an active role among this formerly nomadic population" (235). Of Islam in Turkmenistan we are told, "Sufi fraternities are strong and well established, *even if* a large section of the population practices the official religion, Hanafi Sunni Islam.... if active

is evident also in the widely-read works of Ahmed Rashid,[12] and even more scholarly studies published well into the 21st century reveal elements of the Bennigsen narrative still at work.[13] With one important exception,[14] more

---

Islamic practice has survived it has been mainly due to the parallel Islam of the Sufi, with its complex religious and behavioral system, influenced by shamanic elements of pre-Islamic nomadic traditions. Some of Sufism's most important aspects include the worship of 'saints,' and pilgrimage to sacred places. This played a decisive role in the preservation of religious sentiment during the Soviet era, when people could only worship in 'holy places,' after the great majority of mosques had been closed down" (156, italics mine). The familiar typology of nomadic vs. settled Islam appears in a discussion of Tajikistan, where a 'historical' generalization is invoked to explain a religious orientation: "According to some historians the non-migratory nature of Tajik communities, based on 'an oasis mentality,' favored the adoption of a strict orthodox interpretation of the religion. Unlike in traditionally nomadic countries like Kyrgyzstan and Turkmenistan, in Tajikistan the Dervish orders are not very prevalent. Veneration of *mazar* is secondary, and religious life is restricted mainly to the mosques" (202).

12 See Ahmed Rashid, *Jihad: The Rise of Militant Islam in Central Asia* (New Haven, Connecticut, and London: Yale University Press, 2002); though in some ways the heir, as its title suggests, to the 'Islamic threat to the USSR' genre, also shaped in large measure by Bennigsen and his school, Rashid's *Jihad* features a host of cliches about Sufism drawn from other sources (its "tolerance," its opposition to "intellectualism" and "the clergy," its special appeal to nomads), but nevertheless reverts to the Bennigsen narrative in its capsule 'history' of Sufi orders and its account of their geographical concentration in Central Asia (27–28, complete with the utterly unfounded primacy ascribed to the "Qadiriyya," which "moved to Central Asia, becoming particularly strong during the thirteenth century" [!]), and in its emphasis on the contribution of the "Sufi secret societies" in "the survival of Islam" during the Soviet period (40–41, crediting "the well-organized Sufi sects" with the clandestine publication of "samizdat literature, similar to the writings produced by Soviet dissidents in Russia"). See also Rashid's earlier work, *The Resurgence of Central Asia: Islam or Nationalism?* (London: Zed Books, 1994), where he cites *Mystics and Commissars* in asserting that Sufism, as a "flourishing underground movement," kept Islam alive in Central Asia (43).

13 See, for example, Adeeb Khalid, *Islam after Communism: Religion and Politics in Central Asia* (Berkeley/Los Angeles/London: University of California Press, 2007), which offers a quite good summary of Sufi history (10–11) and rightly notes the 'overlap' of Sufis and scholars in Central Asia (31), but reverts to elements of the Bennigsen model in discussing Sufism in Soviet and post-Soviet times (119–120). In concluding that "Post-Soviet Sufism is not a return to the past but the creation of something new" (120), Khalid seems to imply that this characterization could not apply to earlier eras, and to suggest that earlier Sufisms were timeless and impervious to change.

14 See the earlier work of Bruce G. Privratsky, *Muslim Turkistan: Kazak Religion and Collective Memory* (Richmond, Surrey: Curzon Press, 2001), which also touches on significant aspects of Sufism's legacies, but notes that they are rarely linked with the label of 'Sufism.'

nuanced appreciations of contemporary Sufism in Central Asia began to appear only in the second half of the 21st century's first decade, in the form of anthropological studies dealing with aspects of religiosity linked with the legacies of Sufism;[15] many of these, however, were no better historically informed than the writings of the Bennigsen school, which continue, down to the present, to shape discussions of contemporary Islam, and of Sufism in particular, in Central Asia, especially in works focused on politics and policy.[16] It is fair

15 E.g., Maria Elisabeth Louw, *Everyday Islam in Post-Soviet Central Asia* (London/New York: Routledge, 2007); Krisztina Kehl-Bodrogi, *"Religion is Not So Strong Here:" Muslim Religious Life in Khorezm after Socialism* (Berlin: Lit Verlag, 2008); Johan Rasanayagam, *Islam in Post-Soviet Uzbekistan: The Morality of Experience*. Cambridge: Cambridge University Press, 2010. The piecemeal dismantling of the Bennigsen narrative underway in these anthropological studies is a welcome development, but naturally reflects a narrower 'national' focus, in each case, that hampers the articulation of a replacement for the Sovietological vision as a whole. In addition, this process has led to the emergence of fragmentary narratives that replace only parts of Bennigsen's description (i.e., framing Sufism as 'local' or 'national' Islam, or as 'morality,' or—with closer links to the Bennigsen approach—as shrine-based religiosity), leaving others in place, though in some cases simply ignored.

16 That the problems of the Bennigsen school are not a thing of the past, but continue to shape assumptions and approaches regarding Sufism in Central Asia in the policy circles that largely continue the legacies of Sovietology, is clear from much of the discussion summarized in "Understanding Sufism and its Potential Role in US Policy," ed. Zeyno Baran (Washington, D.C.: The Nixon Center, 2004; *Nixon Center Conference Report*, March 2004), and from Martha Brill Olcott, "Sufism in Central Asia: A Force for Moderation or a Cause of Politicization?," *Carnegie Papers, Russian and Eurasian Program*, No. 84, May, 2007 (Washington, D.C.: Carnegie Endowment for International Peace, 2007). See also the Sovietological discussion of religion—now a quarter-century after the collapse of the USSR—in Annette Bohr, "Turkmenistan: Power, Politics and Petro-Authoritarianism" (London: Russia and Eurasia Programme of Chatham House/ Royal Institute of International Affairs, 2016), 49–53. In an article sprinkled with references to survey data on religiosity in various Central Asian republics (Reuel R. Hanks, "Islamization and Civil Society in Central Asia: Religion as Substrate in Conflict Management and Social Stability," in *Civil Society and Politics in Central Asia*, ed. Charles E. Ziegler [Lexington: The University Press of Kentucky, 2015], 59–79), the author expresses his astonishment that, among those surveyed in Uzbekistan, "When asked if Sufis qualify as Muslims, 79 percent were either unfamiliar with the term 'Sufi' or did not know" (68); this follows his citation of the same survey's 'discovery' that, when asked whether Sunnis counted as Muslims, 72 percent of Uzbeks surveyed "had not heard of Sunnis or did not know." The questions themselves are absurd, of course (and we would be foolish to seek clarification on the precise breakdown of those who did not know vs. those unfamiliar with the terms), but in the author's certainty about the significance of such data—and in his implication that

to say, more broadly, that Sovietological scholarship, represented chiefly, with regard to Sufism, by Bennigsen and his school, showcased its misunderstandings of religiosity, of Sufism, and ultimately of the Soviet experience itself, in its discussions of Sufism in Central Asia, leaving a host of misconceptions and flawed approaches that remain current in some circles even today.[17]

With regard to its construction of an image of Sufism in Soviet Central Asia, the Bennigsen school inevitably approached Sufism, and Central Asia, from the perspective of the broader analytical framework that characterized the Sovietological study of Islam in the USSR;[18] its approach to Sufism thus began with a host of flawed assumptions about religious life in the Soviet environment, but developed several more seriously problematical approaches,

---

more Uzbeks *should* have an opinion regarding Sufism because the tomb of Bahā' al-Dīn Naqshband, "founder of one of the largest Sufi orders in the Islamic world," is located near Bukhara, on the territory of Uzbekistan—we may find also a bit of terminological determinism at work, with an externally—and, we might add, Sovietologically—constructed image of 'Sufism' used as the gauge of public understanding, revealing, in the process, "an unparalleled ignorance among the Uzbek population about the basic characteristics of Islam, more than twenty years after independence from the Soviet Union" (68). Central Asian Muslims were once judged ignorant of Islam if they could not translate a Qur'anic *sūra* from Arabic; now they are expected to know how Bennigsen and other western specialists understood, and deployed, the term 'Sufi.' Ironically, a few pages later, the author stresses Sufism as a home-grown phenomenon in the region, observing that some Sufi orders "actually were founded in Central Asia itself," and insists that the influence of Sufism, and its "doctrines," continues to be strong, or is even growing, in Central Asia, its "tradition of tolerance" making it "a counterweight to the rigid doctrines of Wahabism [*sic*], Salafism, and other fundamentalist movements *founded outside the region*" (72, italics mine).

17 For an example of a recent work with more scholarly ambitions that is nevertheless shaped in many ways by the Bennigsen narrative, see Emily O'Dell, "Subversives and Saints: Sufism and the State in Central Asia," in *Islam, Society, and Politics in Central Asia*, ed. Pauline Jones (Pittsburgh, Pennsylvania: University of Pittsburgh Press, 2017), 99–126, 303–306 (notes). Combining a fixation on 'orders' with facile 'historical' narratives about them (constructed on the basis, now, of post-Soviet literature about Sufism, without attention to actual sources on the history of Central Asian Sufi communities), the article features other hallmarks of Sovietological scholarship as well, including the juxtaposition of Sufi vs. scholar, the assignment of Sufism to the realm of 'folk' traditions, the 'survivals' paradigm linking Sufi practices to "shamanism" and other pre-Islamic religions, and a wide range of specific errors and mischaracterizations; the author takes 'Sufism' as a given, fixed phenomenon (without defining it or acknowledging historical development), and indeed cites *Mystics and Commissars* without any hint that its presentation might warrant critical attention.

18 See my comments in "Islam and the Legacy of Sovietology: A Review Essay on Yaacov Ro'i's *Islam in the Soviet Union*," *Journal of Islamic Studies* (Oxford), 13/3 (2002), 298–330.

claims, and conclusions specifically in connection with Sufism. To begin with, Bennigsen was more familiar with the North Caucasus than with Central Asia, and he projected the picture of Sufi activity he and his colleagues had developed for the North Caucasus onto Central Asia, assuming that the 'brotherhoods' active in the latter region would naturally take the same form, and do the same things, as the militant, anti-Russian brotherhoods he described as active in the North Caucasus. This picture quite plainly did not fit Central Asia, in Soviet or pre-Soviet times; whether it fit the North Caucasus is not our concern here, but recently others have pointed out the many problems with the Bennigsen school's approach to that region as well.[19]

The attempted transference to Central Asia of assumptions and conclusions developed for the North Caucasus in fact points to a broader problem underlying the Bennigsen school's narrative about Sufism: it was not based on any serious attempt to understand the history of Sufi traditions in Central Asia in any period. *Mystics and Commissars* includes almost no references even to Tsarist-era literature on Sufism in the region, and the work's discussion of earlier history is utterly confused. Its focus, rather, was the supposed response of 'Sufi orders' to Soviet rule, with occasional reference to Tsarist-era Sufi activity as preparatory to anti-Russian and anti-Soviet activity. To be sure, the Bennigsen narrative was certain that Sufis were organized into 'orders,' and that these structures provided the framework in which Sufis pursued their anti-Soviet activities; but the orders were presented simply as a given, and indeed as static entities without significant historical change or development since the time of their 'founders.'

Despite Sovietology's many errors and blind spots regarding religion in the Soviet era, the lack of historical groundedness in the Bennigsen narrative about Sufism is in many respects the principal root of more insidious, and persistent, problems. Yet the ahistorical approach underlying the Bennigsen narrative is evident not only in its assumption of the static 'tradition' represented by the Sufi orders, or in its numerous specific errors regarding Sufi history, but also in its reconstruction of the past on the basis of claims about the Soviet era. The Bennigsen narrative, after all, was not only about the then-Soviet 'present:' it included a historical component that in fact lacked any foundation in actual sources on Sufi history, and was constructed instead by projecting claims

19 See Alexander Knysh, "Sufism as an Explanatory Paradigm: The Issue of the Motivations of Sufi Resistance Movements in Western and Russian Scholarship," *Die Welt des Islams*, 42 (2002), 139–173, and Michael Kemper, "How to Build a Sufi Empire? The Strategies of the Daghestani Shaykh Said-Afandi," in *Islam v mul'tikul'turnom mire: Musul'manskie dvizheniia i mekhanizmy vosproizvodstva ideologii islama v sovremennom informatsionnom prostranstve* (Kazan, 2014), 222–232.

about Soviet-era 'data' into the past (i.e., the geographical distribution of the orders, the role of Sufis in 'preserving' Islam and fighting infidels, etc.).[20] The point is that even when elements of the Bennigsen *narrative* have shifted—from Sufi militancy to Sufi pacifism, or from Sufism framed in terms of orders to Sufism framed in terms of 'ishanism'—the *approach* to Sufism that marked Bennigsen's school, and the entire Sovietological and post-Sovietological 'policy' enterprise, has remained much the same, involving the neglect of historical sources and patterns, reliance on Soviet and Soviet-trained 'experts,' the projection of contemporary concerns into the past, and a refusal to step outside the closed circle of Sovietological scholarship and its heirs.

More broadly still, and as a consequence of this inattention to historical developments, the Bennigsen narrative never actually grappled with what it was that made someone a Sufi (other than 'membership' in an 'order,' and, evidently, a 'mystical' outlook). Was it engaging in the practices of Sufis, or holding 'Sufi' ideas, or reading Sufi literature, or visiting Sufi shrines, or something else? And what, after all, were Sufi practices, ideas, books, or shrines, in the first place, and what made them peculiar to 'Sufism?' In failing to address these basic questions of names and labels, the Bennigsen narrative

20 For example, in its characterization of Central Asian Sufism during the era explored in the present volume, *Mystics and Commissars* stressed two elements in its assumptions about Soviet-era Sufis—their role in spreading and 'preserving' Islam, and their militant opposition to infidels—to 'explain' both the historical prominence of Sufis and their seeming disappearance at a certain point (a narrative with no resemblance to what actual sources show): "Sufi brotherhoods played a major role in the history of the area [Central Asia] by protecting Islam against the onslaught of the infidels and by conducting missionary work among the same infidels" (Bennigsen and Wimbush, *Mystics and Commissars*, p. 31). After mentioning the "long period of decline in all fields" in Central Asia beginning in the 17th century, the authors continue, "In the eighteenth century, before the arrival of Russians, no external danger threatened Islam, so that the Sufi brotherhoods lost their main *raison d'être* and followed the general decline" (31). This mis-characterization of a dynamic and turbulent era in Sufi history in Central Asia in fact parrots, without citation, the earlier work of Lemercier-Quelquejay, "Sufi Brotherhoods in the USSR" (1983), 23: "Sufi brotherhoods therefore played a major role in the history of the area by protecting Islam against the onslaught of the infidels, and by conducting missionary work among the same infidels.... In the 17th and 18th centuries, before the arrival of the Russians and with the exception of the Buddhist Jungars and Kalmyks, no external danger threatened Islam, so the Sufi *tariqa* [*sic*] lost their main *raison d'être* and followed the general decline." The historically and intellectually indefensible implication here, that Sufism emerged as a movement to fight infidels and "external dangers" to Islam, and withered in the absence of a suitable enemy, is echoed often in the Bennigsen narrative, but was plainly modeled on equally indefensible claims about Sufism's role in the Tsarist and Soviet eras.

in effect bypassed the implications of al-Būshanjī's aphorism, assuming that an essentialized 'reality' of Sufism—even if left undefined—was its subject, and ignoring the possibility that the names, labels, or social manifestations of Sufism in Central Asia might have undergone historical change—ironically, in an era—the seven Soviet decades—marked by little else *but* change, and dramatic change at that.

From this essentially ahistorical approach flowed numerous other problems in the Bennigsen narrative:

- It conveyed no sense of the substance or context of Sufi practice, offering virtually no discussion of the social framework for Sufi ritual and devotional ceremonies, or of the fate of the institution of the *khānaqāh*.[21] Discussion of the *ẕikr*, for instance, addressed the question of its silent or vocal character from the standpoint of 'security reasons' in Soviet times (i.e., groups supposedly switched to the silent *ẕikr* in order to conceal their practice from Soviet authorities), with no awareness of the longstanding polemics over the *ẕikr* in Central Asia, and with no attention to other well-known patterns of Sufi devotional and ritual practice.
- It essentially equated Sufism with any and all manifestations of what was referred to, in Soviet and Sovietological literature, as 'popular' or 'folk' or 'everyday' Islam, and especially with the visitation of saints' shrines, claiming that virtually all *ziyārat* was 'Sufi activity,' that shrines were 'Sufi centers,' and that shrines were thus the organizational linchpins of Sufi 'orders' (hence the simplistic equation of the shrine of an order's eponym with the 'center' or 'base' of the order).
- In so doing, it suspended the critical and indeed skeptical stance adopted in most western analyses of Soviet sources, and instead adopted wholesale the Soviet analysis of religion, including the two-tiered approach that divided elite, bookish, 'high' religion from the category of 'folk' or 'popular' religion, as well as the evolutionary models, the proliferation of -isms, and the notion of religious 'survivals' (*perezhitki*) that permeated the Soviet academic study of religion. In this analytical framework, Sufism was placed squarely on the

21 See the discussion of Sufi practice in the chapter on "The Inner Life of the Sufi Brotherhoods" (Bennigsen and Wimbush, *Mystics and Commissars*, 78–83). To their credit, the authors do discuss examples of what they call "funeral *zikrs*" and "medical *zikrs*," citing some Soviet ethnographic literature without following it too far into the discourse of "shamanism," yet insisting that when the *dhikr* becomes a "public" affair, it "loses its mystical religious character and becomes a folkloric survival" (81).

side of folk or popular religion, and was imagined as the central repository for survivals from pre-Islamic religion.[22]

– One consequence of this mode of analysis was the 'de-intellectualization' of Sufism, and the neglect of the literary venues in which Sufi doctrinal exposition, and the 'explanation' or justification of Sufi ritual and devotional practice, were undertaken. Instead of examining, or at least considering, the historical engagement of many Sufis with the full range of Islamic sciences, or the ongoing copying and reading of Sufi treatises into the Soviet era, the Bennigsen narrative identified Sufism with 'folk' religion, and 'intellectual Islam' with the writings of the Jadīds (whose critique of Sufi practices was uncritically assumed to be 'correct' and accurate); naturally this analytical stance rested also on the privileging of printed works over manuscript sources that characterized nearly all of the Sovietological study of Islam (and most scholarship on Tsarist-era Muslim culture in the Russian empire), but for the study of Sufism it meant that there was little awareness of, let alone any incentive to explore, the enormous literary and intellectual heritage of Central Asian Sufi communities.[23]

---

22 On this issue, see my discussion in "Survival Strategies: Reflections on the Notion of Religious 'Survivals' in Soviet Ethnographic Studies of Muslim Religious Life in Central Asia," in *Exploring the Edge of Empire: Soviet Era Anthropology in the Caucasus and Central Asia*, ed. Florian Mühlfried and Sergey Sokolovskiy (Münster: Lit Verlag, 2011; Halle Studies in the Anthropology of Eurasia, vol. 25), 35–58.

23 See my discussion in "It was a Dark and Stagnant Night ('til the Jadids Brought the Light): Clichés, Biases, and False Dichotomies in the Intellectual History of Central Asia," for *Journal of the Economic and Social History of the Orient*, 59/1–2 (2016), 37–92. The Bennigsen narrative regarding Sufism was built, naturally, atop a broader base of studies that, in discussions of the Tsarist era that was preparatory to Soviet times, focused almost exclusively on the 'modernizing' or 'reformist' Jadīds; inevitably, any approach to Sufism, and to religion in general, that assumes success on the part of the Jadīds (or of the Soviet state) in 'modernizing' (or, for that matter, entirely 'nationalizing') religious life (or in modernizing religion out of existence), and indeed any approach that posits 'modernity' as the chief, or only, intellectual and cultural equipment borne by Central Asians into the 20th and 21st centuries, will miss key continuities and adaptations in religious life in Central Asia, including Sufism and its fate in the region. At the same time, it must be noted that there is a good deal of internal contradiction and inconsistency (alongside the uncritical repetition noted earlier) in the Sovietological literature on Sufism. After framing "fundamentalist Sufism" in opposition to Jadīdism, as noted above, for instance, Bennigsen and Wimbush later dwell on identifying numerous Jadīds as Sufis (*Mystics and Commissars*, 38–39), then speak again of the Jadīds as representing the "liberal modernist trends" as opposed to the "conservative fundamentalist ones, as represented by the Sufi sheikhs" (45), and still later make the dubious claim (and lament the contrast) that "few

– At the same time, in part as a consequence of its relegation of Sufism entirely to the realm of 'folk' religion and intellectual backwardness, the Bennigsen narrative stressed Sufism's role as a force hostile to Soviet power (an agent, implicitly, of 'high' culture and intellectual modernity), to the point of conveying the impression that Sufism arose as an anti-Soviet—or, with a bit more historical depth, an anti-Russian—militant movement; indeed, Bennigsen and Lemercier-Quelquejay framed Sufi groups in the USSR as "ultra-conservative," as devoted to "traditional *jihad*," and as "tightly-knit religious organizations with a strong leadership and a disciplined apparatus," "well-suited to clandestine activity" and "a dangerous foe for the Soviet establishment."[24] The bubble that was over-inflated through this emphasis on Sufi militancy burst, as noted, by the late 1980s, as the Soviet world opened up and no Central Asian Sufi weapons of mass destruction were found; Sovietological hopes and fears turned away from Sufis and settled on 'Wahhābīs,' and only later on did the lingering legacies of Sovietology push some western analysts toward reviving interest in Sufis as representatives of peaceful, tolerant, non-threatening (to the independent Central Asian regimes) Islam.[25]

Soviet Muslims" remember the modernist Jadīds, while "almost everybody remembers and venerates the memory of Sufi leaders" who fought the Russians (106).

24 Alexandre Bennigsen and Chantal Lemercier-Quelquejay, "Muslim Religious Conservatism and Dissent in the USSR," *Religion in Communist Lands*, 6/3 (1978), 153–161 [158–159]. On the theme of militancy ascribed to Sufis by the Bennigsen school, see the discussion of Jeff Eden, "A Soviet Jihad against Hitler: Ishan Babakhan Calls Central Asian Muslims to War," *JESHO*, 59 (2016), 237–264 [241–246].

25 Both the lingering legacies of the Bennigsen narrative, and the continued appeal of ill-informed generalizations of the sort that served the Bennigsen approach, are evident in the following two passages, published a year apart, drawn from the literature on 'policy and terrorism.' First: "According to Bennigsen, the most significant of the Sufi brotherhoods was a secret society called the Naqshbandiya, a Freemason-style fraternity closely tied to the elite of Turkey, which had long-standing connections in Central Asia. The Naqshbandiya were especially strong in Chechnya, Dagestan, and parts of Central Asia, including southern Uzbekistan. 'The Naqshbandiya adepts have a long tradition of "Holy War" against the Russians' wrote Bennigsen. His conclusion was that nationalism in Central Asia was inextricably bound up with radical political Islam" (Robert Dreyfuss, *Devil's Game: How the United States Helped to Unleash Fundamentalist Islam* [New York: Metropolitan Books, 2005], 253). Second (with the shift to Sufism's potential as a counter to militancy): "Muslims in the Fergana Valley have traditionally followed Sufi teachings, which is [*sic*] a mystical and tolerant form of religious expression that does not lend itself well to support of extremism" (Christopher J. Fettweis, "The Fergana Valley," in *Flashpoints*

- Ironically, alongside the characterization of Sufism as a force necessarily hostile toward the Soviet state, and actually or potentially engaged in militant opposition against it—suggesting a fringe movement well outside the mainstream—the Bennigsen narrative also credited Sufism with keeping Islam as a whole alive in the Soviet era (in the process selling non-Sufi Muslims short). Chantal Lemercier-Quelquejay wrote, for instance, that "the fundamental role of Sufism in the Soviet Union is the preservation of the purity of Islam by providing the population with a minimal religious organization, without which the mass of believers would probably forget the faith of their ancestors ..."[26] This claim might please admirers of Sufism, with its link between Sufism and Muslim 'purity,' but one wonders what al-Būshanjī might have thought of it; in any case, the claim is misguided and misleading in many ways, but it is especially sobering to recall just how passive, ignorant, and negligent the "mass of believers" was imagined to be.
- A final aspect of the Bennigsen narrative's flawed character has to do with method, and sources: the narrative was constructed largely on the basis of attempting to read between the lines of anti-religious literature, or of press reports of the discovery and suppression of various religious activities. It must be stressed that such sources can indeed be read critically with profit, and can serve as important auxiliary sources on certain kinds of Sufi activities during the Soviet era. Often such accounts offer valuable information on the functioning of certain shrines, for example, and while activities at shrines, as noted, cannot automatically be equated with 'Sufi activity,' such accounts often attest to the continuation of devotional and ritual practices that may be understood as legacies of Sufi communities (whether hereditary or initiatic), or as 'tinged' with Sufi coloring. To properly assess such Soviet accounts, however, some broader familiarity with patterns of religious practice, and Sufi practice and organization, in Central Asia was needed, and this was precisely what was missing from the Bennigsen narrative, as a result of the resistance, on the part of its practitioners and consumers, against engaging with the pre-Soviet, and pre-Russian history of Sufi communities in the region, through the actual sources produced by those communities.

Such historical material, indeed, along with ethnographic accounts and the rich traditions of religious literature, popular religious tales, folklore, and epic narratives interwoven with religious themes and figures, was among the

in the War on Terrorism, ed. Derek S. Reveron and Jeffrey Stevenson Murer (New York: Routledge, 2006), 117–134 [122]).

26 Lemercier-Quelquejay, "Sufi Brotherhoods in the USSR," 30–31.

sources—many of them readily available—that could have informed the construction of the Bennigsen narrative, but these were not utilized at all—or, if some of them (chiefly ethnographic accounts) occasionally were cited, they were used uncritically, leaving the western specialists unwitting victims, and indeed promulgators, of the problematical and sometimes ideologically-driven analytical models embedded in the work of Soviet-era ethnographers. Similarly, another potential 'source' for informing an interpretation of Soviet-era reports about religious life—a historically grounded understanding of religious life in other Muslim societies—was applied to the Central Asian case only at the most superficial level.

The upshot is that the entire edifice of *Mystics and Commissars*, for instance, is best discarded, along with the other surveys produced in the same framework: these works' accounts of the history of particular traditions or of Sufism in general are unusable, their attempts to describe organizational frameworks are utterly unreliable, and their discussions even of Soviet-era phenomena[27] are so full of errors and misinterpretations that the entire corpus is now mostly useful as a cautionary tale of where and how scholarship can go so badly astray.

Replacing the Sovietological narrative will require in-depth study of the history of Sufi communities in Central Asia, based above all on the sources produced by those communities; these tasks cannot be taken up here in depth, but it may be helpful to consider the broad contours of that history, and those sources, by way of framing the era whose study is likely to be the most helpful for improving understanding of the Tsarist, Soviet, and post-Soviet periods.

Framing a Period of Sufi History and Its Sources

Sufis appeared in Central Asia by the 10th century—or earlier if we accept the existence of 'Sufism' before the appearance of that name—but their prominence in religious, social, and political life appears to have expanded significantly in the period after the Mongol conquest of the 13th century. From the 13th century through the 15th, moreover, the social roles, models of leadership,

27 Among the many errors that might be noted, the work's account of two supposedly Sufi groups active in the Farghana valley, the "Hairy Ishans" and the Laachi, are especially telling: Bennigsen and company declared both these groups to be "offshoots" of the Yasavī 'order' (implying some organizational continuity, among other things), and reveled in the charges of militant activity against them (Bennigsen and Wimbush, *Mystics and Commissars*, 12, 33–36, 68, 72, 146; cf. Lemercier-Quelquejay, "Sufi Brotherhoods in the USSR," 26–29). Not even the Soviet sources cited about these groups, however, claim that they were "Yasavī" groups. See now Eren Tasar's contribution to the present volume.

and organizational structures of Sufi communities were quite diverse, with the familiar features of the Sufi 'order' becoming dominant only toward the end of that period. The social profile of Sufi communities was far from static, however, due in part to competition among Sufi groups and other political and social factors; yet developments in Sufi organization—and nomenclature—after the 15th century remain poorly understood, largely because of broader trajectories of scholarly focus on Central Asia.

To some extent, that is, the study of Sufism in Central Asia reflects the broader pattern of scholarly attention to the region. Historical scholarship on Central Asia is relatively abundant for the pre-Mongol era, and remains substantial for the Mongol and Timurid periods, but drops off dramatically for the period from the 16th century to the 19th, rising again with the Russian conquest and the Tsarist and Soviet eras (for Eastern Turkistan, the curve is somewhat different, but the 16th and 17th centuries remain relatively poorly studied). In the case of scholarship on Sufism, the curve is somewhat different: despite the post-Timurid drop-off in scholarly attention, relatively more has been done on Sufi history in the 16th century, and, thanks to two seminal studies published 20 years ago,[28] some of the major developments of the 18th and 19th centuries have begun to draw attention. More work has also been done on the important Sufi currents active in Eastern Turkistan during the 17th and 18th centuries, though often in unfortunate isolation from studies on Sufi groups in the more westerly parts of Central Asia. This leaves the 17th century, in those westerly regions, as the major 'blank spot' with regard at least to the basic outlines of Sufi history in Central Asia; but in general it is fair to say that scholarship on Sufi

28 See Baxtiyor M. Babadžanov, "On the History of the Naqšbandīya Muǧaddidīya in Central Māwarā'annahr in the Late 18th and Early 19th Centuries," in *Muslim Culture in Russia and Central Asia from the 18th to the Early 20th Centuries*, ed. Michael Kemper, Anke von Kügelgen, and Dmitriy Yermakov (Berlin: Klaus Schwarz Verlag, 1996), 385–413, and Anke von Kügelgen, "Die Entfaltung der Naqšbandīya Muǧaddidīya im mittleren Transoxanien vom 18. bis zum Beginn des 19. Jahrhunderts: Ein Stück Detektivarbeit," in *Muslim Culture in Russia and Central Asia from the 18th to the Early 20th Centuries*, vol. 2: *Inter-Regional and Inter-Ethnic Relations*, ed. Anke von Kügelgen, Michael Kemper, and Allen J. Frank (Berlin: Klaus Schwarz Verlag, 1998), 101–151. On developments of this era, see also Jo-Ann Gross, "The Naqshbandīya Connection: From Central Asia to India and Back (16th–19th Centuries)," in *India and Central Asia: Commerce and Culture, 1500–1800*, ed. Scott C. Levi (New Delhi: Oxford University Press, 2007), 232–259, and Kawahara Yayoi, "On Private Archives Related to the Development of the Naqshbandīya-Mujaddidīya in the Ferghana Valley," in *History and Culture of Central Asia/Istoriia i kul'tura Tsentral'noi Azii*, ed. Bakhtiyar Babadjanov and Kawahara Yayoi (Tokyo: The University of Tokyo, 2012), 241–257.

communities in the region as a whole, through much of the past 500 years—despite enormous advances during the past two decades—remains at a quite basic level.

The overall lack of attention is not because of a lack of sources; primary sources are abundant for this period, but they still remain poorly known and largely untapped, and until quite recently none had been published. Rather, the lack of attention stems in part from an absurd historical narrative—of which the Sovietological 'back-story' for Sufism in Soviet Central Asia is a part—that assumes no significant historical development in the region between the beginning of the 16th century and the Russian (or Qing) conquest.

In fact, one of the key problems in dealing with this long period, both in general historical terms and in the specific case of the history of Sufi groups, is that it is set off chiefly by inattention, rather than by some overarching coherence or homogeneity. Beyond the broad chronological demarcations of the Uzbek conquest, the Russian conquest, the Soviet era, and the 'post-Soviet present'—historical markers that do not always serve as good dividing lines for understanding or even identifying important developments in indigenous culture and, especially, religious life—there are other recognizable beginnings and ends, and regional differences, in dynastic terms and in social and cultural terms, that inevitably affect our study of Sufi currents. I believe there *are* certain features, or trends, that set apart Central Asian Sufi groups, during the period from the 16th century through the 19th, from those that are familiar in earlier times, and that thus make it reasonable to adopt those chronological markers and to study the history of Sufi communities in that era together; but it would also make sense to distinguish the 16th century, roughly, as its own era, or to group it with the 17th century and set that unit apart from the major shifts underway during the 18th and 19th centuries. The point is that the work of making the case for periodizing Sufi history in Central Asia, and of arguing particular periods' importance for understanding the Soviet and post-Soviet eras, has barely begun, in part because that work depends upon the in-depth study of individual sources that remain poorly known, and upon completing the construction of a narrative of Sufi history in the region that remains, so far, fragmentary and ad hoc.

Such a narrative is needed, of course, to replace the facile Bennigsen narrative, and it is thus especially critical as 'background' for students focused on Soviet and contemporary developments; but the relative lack of attention to Sufi history in Central Asia from the 16th to 19th century also has adverse consequences for more serious scholarship on Central Asia and the Muslim world more broadly, and leaves some key developments in the social profile of Sufi communities unrecognized. It obscures, for instance, the very real, and significant, shifts in organizational structures, leadership models, and patterns of inter-communal relations characteristic of Sufi groups that set this period apart from the 'formative' era of the 13th–15th centuries. It also obscures, naturally, shifts *during* this long period itself, but in fact such shifts are often masked by the terminology in our sources—since the 'vocabulary' of Sufi organization, leadership, succession, and the master-disciple relationship remains relatively stable over many centuries—and interpreting the terminology requires familiarity with a broad range of sources from multiple periods. Taking stock of these shifts is often difficult, since it entails recognizing—perhaps less pessimistically than al-Būshanjī—that the social realities masked by the names in our sources may have changed substantially over the course of many centuries in which the same terminology is deployed. Ignoring these shifts, however, renders plausible, by default, a narrative that posits static and unchanging 'orders' as the definitive 'face' of Sufism (a narrative that is further undergirded by claims—by some Sufis, but also in some scholarship—of Sufism's immunity, in various respects, to change within historical time).

Inattention to Sufi history during this era obscures another significant development as well, in connection with the abundance of primary sources: the flourishing of hagiography. Indeed, a key point to note regarding the period from the 16th century to the 19th in Central Asia is that the Sufi hagiographical corpus both expanded and changed in this period; hagiography became cemented as a key venue through which Sufi communities envisioned their history—not by way of 'establishing a record,' but by way of asserting central elements of their self-identity, legitimation, and social 'outreach.' Hagiographical production became the key medium for articulating a vision of the continuities and authority of particular Sufi shaykhs and communities (as well as of disruptive 'interventions' by prominent figures); it naturally drew upon conventions and tropes developed in earlier times, and it would be naïve to suppose that the interpretative complexities posed by the genre changed entirely in this era, but hagiographical works from this period—whether works focused on individual Sufis or works dealing with dozens, or hundreds, of shaykhs—display important differences from earlier works, not the least of which is simply the abundance of hagiographies produced, especially during the 16th, 17th, and early 19th centuries. Nevertheless, the work of analyzing and even identifying these hagiographical sources has barely begun, and few from this period have been published; a thorough survey of the hagiographical corpus is sorely needed.

It must be emphasized, at the same time, that hagiographies are not the only sources that must be used in constructing a history of Sufi communities in this era. Doctrinal treatises, collections of ritual texts, and meditations on various kinds of Sufi insignia are important as well, and insofar as Sufis were prominent on the public stage, they appear regularly in chronicles; Sufi correspondence is another important genre, as are writings reflecting what we might understand as the 'auxiliary sciences' of Sufism. Through much of Sufi history, moreover, Sufi groups have produced their own 'documentary' legacy, in the form of specific authorizations and general licensures, and of *shajaras* and *silsila* charts. Despite the importance of such sources, however, hagiographies, during the period considered here, expanded beyond their didactic, exemplary, and devotional frameworks to serve the social and historical functions of defining and reinforcing the communal identities of Sufi groups, both across time and in particular regions, and often with a self-conscious focus on initiatic and/or hereditary lineage; they were adapted in these ways, moreover, for competitive purposes. At the very least, during this period, hagiographies make it possible to reconstruct skeletal histories of groups and lineages, and patterns of initiatic transmission and succession, but they usually offer much more than this, and extensive hagiographical production must itself be recognized as a distinctive feature of Sufi history in this era, and in this region.

A survey of hagiographical production in this broad period is beyond the scope of this essay, but the outlines are worth noting, by way of stressing both the abundance of sources, and the gaps in hagiographical 'coverage.' The 16th century[29] saw a remarkable flourishing of hagiographies produced in

29 For Mawarannahr in the 16th century, especially its first half, there is a somewhat larger body of scholarship touching on Sufis in Central Asia, beginning with the survey of Sufi history in Florian Schwarz, *'Unser Weg schliesst tausend Wege ein:' Derwische un Gesellschaft im islamischen Mittelasien im 16. Jahrhundert* (Berlin: Klaus Schwarz Verlag, 2000; Islamkundliche Untersuchungen, Bd. 226); see also idem, "Ohne Scheich kein Reich: Scheibaniden und Naqšbandīs in der Darstellung von Maḥmūd ibn Walī," in *Annäherung an das Fremde: XXVI. Deutscher Orientalistentag vom 25. bis 29.9.1995 in Leipzig, Vorträge*, ed. Holger Preissler and Heidi Stein (Stuttgart: Franz Steiner Verlag, 1998; *Zeitschrift der Deutschen Morgenländischen Gesellschaft*, Supplement XI), 259–267. For older studies, see Annemarie Schimmel, "Some Notes on the Cultural Activities of the First Uzbek Rulers," *Journal of the Pakistan Historical Society*, 8 (1960), 149–166; Ulrich Haarmann, "Staat und Religion in Transoxanien im frühen 16. Jahrhundert," *Zeitschrift der Deutschen Morgenländischen Gesellschaft*, 124 (1974), 332–369, R. G. Mukminova, "Dukhovenstvo i vakfy v Srednei Azii XVI veka," in *Dukhovenstvo i politicheskaia zhizn' na Blizhnem i Srednem Vostoke v periode feodalizma* (Bartol'dovskie chteniia, 1982) (Moscow: Nauka, 1985), 141–147, and, in the same volume, G. A. Dzhuraeva, "Mir-i Arab i politicheskaia zhizn' v Bukhare v XVI veke," 74–79, as well as the more recent work of Bakhtiiar Babadzhanov, "Mir-i Arab," *Kul'tura kochevnikov na rubezhe vekov (XIX–XX, XX–XXI vv.): Problemy genezisa i transformatsii (Materialy mezhdunarodnoi konferentsii g. Almaty, 5–7 iiunia 1995 g.)* (Almaty: Assotsiatsiia 'Rafakh,' Studiia 'Parallel'," Gosudarstvennyi muzei iskusstv im. A. Kasteeva, 1995), 88–102; B. Babadzhanov, "Iasaviia i Nakshbandiia v Maverannakhre:

Naqshbandī, Kubravī, and Yasavī lineages, focused above on particular 'nodes' in initiatic lineages; the Naqshbandī shaykh known as Makhdūm-i Aʿẓam (d. 949/1542) inspired several works,[30] as did the Kubravī shaykh Ḥusayn Khwārazmī (d. 958/1551),[31] while the chief sources from this era on Yasavī lineages were produced by a Central Asian who moved to Istanbul, the prolific Ḥazīnī.[32] For the second half of the 16th century, hagiographical works focused on claimants to the status of chief successor of Makhdūm-i Aʿẓam proliferate, with two or three iterations of a work focused on Luṭfullāh Chūstī (d. 979/1571),[33] and at least three major works inspired by the famous Jūybārī shaykhs of Bukhārā;[34] partisans of both these lineages continued the hagiographical tra-

---

iz istorii vzaimootnoshenii (ser. XV–XVI vv.)," in *Yäsaui Taghïlïmï* (Turkistan: "Mŭra" baspagerlĭk shaghïn käsĭpornï/Qoja Akhmet Yäsaui atïndaghï Khalïqaralïq Qazaq-Türĭk Universiteti, 1996), 75–96; and B. Babadjanov, "La naqshbandiyya sous les premiers Sheybanides," in *L'Héritage timouride: Iran—Asie centrale—Inde, XVᵉ–XVIIIᵉ siècles* (= *Cahiers d'Asie centrale*, 3–4 [1997], 69-90). Not directly concerned with Sufi communities, but noteworthy nonetheless for its use of many of the hagiographical sources noted here from the 16th and early 17th centuries, is Thomas Welsford, *Four Types of Loyalty in Early Modern Central Asia: The Tūqāy-Tīmūrid Takeover of Greater Mā Warā al-Nahr, 1598–1605* (Leiden: Brill, 2013).

30 B. Babajanov, "Biographies of Makhdūm-i Aʿẓam al-Kāsānī al-Dahbīdī, *Shaykh* of the Sixteenth-Century Naqshbandīya," *Manuscripta Orientalia*, 5/2 (1999), 3–8.

31 On this figure, see my "The Eclipse of the Kubravīyah in Central Asia," *Iranian Studies*, 21/1–2 (1988), 45–83, reprinted (with typographical corrections) in DeWeese, *Studies on Sufism in Central Asia* (2012), No. I.

32 Two of his works have been published: Hazini, *Cevâhiru'l-ebrâr min emvâc-ı bihâr* (*Yesevî Menâkıbnamesi*), ed. Cihan Okuyucu (Kayseri: Erciyes Üniversitesi, 1995); and Hazini, *Menbaʿu'l-ebhâr fî riyâzi'l-ebrâr*, ed. Mehmet Mâhur Tulum (Istanbul: Mehmet Ölmez, 2009).

33 See Bakhtiyor Babajanov, "Mawlānā Luṭfullāh Chūstī: An Outline of his Hagiography and Political Activity," *Zeitschrift der Deutschen Morgenländischen Gesellschaft*, 149/2 (1999), 245–270, and the earlier study of A. A. Semenov, "Unikal'nyi pamiatnik agiograficheskoi sredneaziatskoi literatury XVI v.," *Izvestiia Uzbekistanskogo filiala AN SSSR*, 1940, No. 12, 54–62; 1941, No. 3, 37–48 (the articles are based on two different manuscripts representing versions of a work focused on Chūstī).

34 See my discussion in "The Problem of the *Sirāj al-ṣāliḥīn*: Notes on Two Hagiographies by Badr al-Dīn Kashmīrī," in *Écrit et culture en Asie centrale et dans le monde turco-iranien, XIVᵉ–XIXᵉ siècles/Writing and Culture in Central Asia and the Turko-Iranian World, 14th–19th Centuries*, ed. Francis Richard and Maria Szuppe (Paris: Association pour l'Avancement des Études Iraniennes, 2009; *Studia Iranica*, Cahier 40), 43–92. See also my brief "Kašmiri, Badr-al-Din," *Encyclopaedia Iranica*, vol. XVI, fascicle 1 (New York: Encyclopaedia Iranica Foundation, 2012), 80–83; and for the most extensive overview of the Jūybārī *khwājas* and their legacy, see Bakhtyar Babajanov and Maria Szuppe, *Les*

ditions linked with these figures into the 17th century,[35] and the turn of the century saw not only a separate work written about yet another Naqshbandī shaykh of Bukhārā, Pāyanda Muḥammad Akhsīkatī (d. 1010/1601), but three works focused on two sons of Makhdūm-i Aʿẓam—Khwāja Muḥammad Amīn (subject of the *Jamarāt al-shawq*) and Khwāja Isḥāq (subject of the *Jalīs al-mushtāqīn* and the *Żiyāʾ al-qulūb*[36])—through whom long-lasting initiatic-cum-hereditary lineages would emerge in Eastern Turkistan. From late in the 16th century, finally, we have the *Az̤kār al-azkiyā*, a collective hagiography that deals with shaykhs of multiple *silsila*s, and is marked by a distinctive Central Asian 'geographical' vision in its coverage.

The 17th century yielded two major Yasavī hagiographies[37] and a large compendium, the *Jāmiʿ al-salāsil*, focused on a Kubravī successor of Ḥusayn

---

inscriptions persanes de Chār Bakr, nécropole familiale des khwāja Jūybārī près de Boukhara (London: School of Oriental and African Studies, 2002; Corpus Inscriptionum Iranicarum, Part IV, Persian Inscriptions down to the early Safavid Period; vol. XXXI: Uzbekistan).

35 One work focused on a disciple of Khwāja Muḥammad Islām Jūybārī has been published: Badr al-Dīn Badrī Kashmīrī, *Sirāj al-ṣāliḥīn*, ed. Sayyid Sirāj al-Dīn (Islamabad: Markaz-i Taḥqīqāt-i Fārsī-i Īrān va Pākistān, 1376/1997). In addition, a 17th-century Jūybārī hagiography has recently been published: Muḥammad Ṭālib b. Tāj al-Dīn Ḥasan Khwāja al-Ḥusaynī al-Ṣiddīqī, *Maṭlab al-ṭālibīn (matn-i ʿilmī-yi intiqādī)*, ed. Ghulām Karīmī and Érkin Mir-kāmilūf [i.e., Ghulam Kärimiy and Erkin Mirkamilov] (Tashkent: O'zbekiston Musulmonlari Idorasi, Movarounnahr Nashriyoti, 2012; Farhangistān-i ʿUlūm-i Jumhūrī-yi Uzbakistān/Instītū-yi Sharqshunāsī be-nām-i Abū Rayḥān Bīrūnī).

36 On this work, see V. P. Iudin, "Izvestiia 'Ziia al-kulub' Mukhammad Avaza o kazakhakh XVI veka," *Vestnik Akademii nauk Kazakhskoi SSR*, 1966, No. 5, 71–76; Z. N. Vorozheikina, "Doislamskie verovaniia kirgizov v XVI v. (Po rukopisi 'Ziia al-kulub')," in *Voprosy filologii i istorii stran sovetskogo i zarubezhnogo Vostoka* (Moscow, 1961), 182–189; and Joseph Fletcher, "Confrontations between Muslim Missionaries and Nomad Unbelievers in the Late Sixteenth Century," *Tractata Altaica: Denis Sinor sexagenario optime de rebus altaicis merito dedicata* (Wiesbaden: Harrassowitz, 1976), 167–174. On the subject of the work, see now Jeff Eden, "A Sufi Saint in Sixteenth-Century East Turkistan: New Evidence Concerning the Life of Khwāja Isḥāq," *Journal of the Royal Asiatic Society*, 3rd series, 25/2 (2015), 229–245.

37 See my "A Neglected Source on Central Asian History: The 17th-Century Yasavī Hagiography *Manāqib al-akhyār*," in *Essays on Uzbek History, Culture, and Language*, ed. Denis Sinor and Bakhtiyar A. Nazarov (Bloomington: Research Institute for Inner Asian Studies, 1993; Indiana University Uralic and Altaic Series, Vol. 156), 38–50, reprinted in DeWeese, *Studies on Sufism in Central Asia* (2012), No. III; and my "The Yasavī Order and Persian Hagiography in Seventeenth-Century Central Asia: ʿĀlim Shaykh of ʿAlīyābād and his *Lamaḥāt min nafaḥāt al-quds*," in *The Heritage of Sufism*, vol. III: *Late Classical Persianate Sufism (1501–1750), The Safavid and Mughal Period*, ed. Leonard Lewisohn and David Morgan (Oxford: Oneworld Publications, 1999), 389–414, reprinted in DeWeese,

Khwārazmī; an obscure Naqshbandī shaykh active in both Balkh and Bukhārā, Mullā Muḥammad Taytakī (d. 1056/1646) was the subject of another substantial work. A voluminous collective hagiography, the *Ṣamarāt al-mashā'ikh*, was produced at the end of that century, focused on shaykhs of the three major lineages active in the Bukharan oasis, for which it serves as a richly detailed source on local history and toponymy. From the beginning of the 18th century dates a hagiography focused on Ḥājjī Ḥabībullāh (d. 1111/1699–1700), the first Mujaddidī shaykh to establish himself in Bukhārā, a sign of important changes in the landscape of Sufism in Central Asia. The 18th century also saw the production of several examples of hagiographical works focused not on initiatic lineages, but on hereditary lines, focused on the descendants of several prominent Yasavī shaykhs as well as of Khwāja Aḥrār and Makhdūm-i A'ẓam; in the middle of that century, another large compendium, the work of Ṭāhir Īshān of Khwārazm, was produced, and the 18th century saw another burst of hagiographical production in Eastern Turkistan, within the rival Isḥāqī and Āfāqī lineages traced from Makhdūm-i A'ẓam, with works in both Persian and Chaghatay Turkic.[38]

Studies on Sufism in Central Asia (2012), No. IX. The work discussed in the latter article has been published in facsimile: Muḥammad 'Ālim Ṣiddīqī, *Lamaḥāt min nafaḥāt al-quds*, facs. ed. Muḥammad Nadhīr Rānjhā (Islamabad: Markaz-i Taḥqīqāt-i Fārsī-yi Īrān va Pākistān, 1406/1986).

38 See Martin Hartmann, "Ein Heiligenstaat im Islam: das Ende der Čaghataiden und die Herrschaft der Choǧas in Kašgarien," in Hartmann's *Der islamische Orient*, vol. I (Berlin: Wolf Peiser Verlag, 1905), pt. 6–10, 195–374; "Epitome of the Memoirs of the Khojas," from *The History of the Khojas of Eastern-Turkistan, summarised from the Tazkira-i-Khwajagan of Muhammad Sadiq Kashghari*, ed. Robert Barkley Shaw, N. Elias (Supplement to the *Journal of the Asiatic Society of Bengal*, 66/1 (1897), 31–63); Sawada Minoru, "Three Groups of *Tadhkira-i khwājagān*: Viewed from the Chapter on Khwāja Āfāq," in *Studies on Xinjiang Historical Sources in 17–20th Centuries*, ed. James A. Millward, Shinmen Yasushi, and Sugawara Jun (Tokyo: The Toyo Bunko, 2010; Toyo Bunko Research Library 12), 9–30; M. A. Salakhetdinova, "Soobshcheniia o kirgizakh v 'Khidaiat-name' Mir Khal' ad-Dina," *Izvestiia Akademii nauk Kirgizskoi SSR, Seriia Obshchestvennykh nauk*, tom III, vyp. 2 (1961), 133–140; Joseph Fletcher, "The Naqshbandiyya in Northwest China," in Fletcher, *Studies on Chinese and Islamic Inner Asia*, ed. Beatrice Forbes Manz (Aldershot, Hampshire: Variorum, 1995), No. XI (46 pp.); Isenbike Togan, "Chinese Turkestan," v, "Under the Khojas," *Encyclopaedia Iranica*, v, 474–476; David Brophy, "The Oirat in Eastern Turkistan and the Rise of Āfāq Khwāja," *Archivum Eurasiae Medii Aevi*, 16 (2008–09), 5–28; idem, "The Kings of Xinjiang: Muslim Elites and the Qing Empire," *Etudes orientales*, No. 25 (2008), 69–89; Alexandre Papas, *Soufisme et politique entre Chine, Tibet et Turkestan: Etude sur les khwajas naqshbandis du Turkestan oriental* (Paris: Librairie d'Amérique et d'Orient, Jean Maisonneuve successeur, 2005); my "The 'Competitors' of Isḥāq Khwāja in Eastern Turkistan: Hagiographies, Shrines, and Sufi Affiliations in the Late Sixteenth

In relative terms, the 17th and 18th centuries saw fewer hagiographies focused on individual shaykhs than were produced in the 16th century, but another flurry of hagiographical production came in the first half of the 19th century, tracing lines of succession to the important figure of Mūsā Khān Dahbīdī (d. 1190/1776), who combined a Mujaddidī *silsila* with natural descent from Makhdūm-i Aʿẓam; from the turn of the century, the *Taẕkira-yi Majẕūb Namangānī* traces rivalries among his successors, and no fewer than five important works were produced in the 1830s and 1840s, focused on those successors and on later figures in their lineages (of special importance among them are works entitled *Mirʾāt al-sālikīn* and *Mukāshif al-asrār*; one of the lineages reflected in these works can be traced down to the present[39]). The controversial figure of Islām Shaykh (d. 1222/1807) was the subject of two works, one in Turkic, by a disciple, and another in Persian, by one of his sons; and the middle of the 19th century yielded two major collective hagiographies, one completed around 1845 by Mīr Musayyab Bukhārī, the other in 1865 by a Muḥammad Sharīf Bukhārī. The early 20th century, finally, yielded a Turkic hagiography focused on Dūkchī Īshān, leader of the Andijan uprising of 1898, who also left his own quasi-autobiographical work in Turkic verse.[40]

The upshot is that more than 55 separate hagiographical works, many quite substantial, are known to survive as vitally important primary sources on Sufi communities of Central Asia from the first half of the 16th century to the beginning of the 20th; more may yet come to light, but it is already an impressive corpus, and among these works no more than seven have been published in some form, with most of them remaining not only unpublished, but quite

Century," in *Horizons of the World: Festschrift for Isenbike Togan/Hududü'l-Alem: İsenbike Togan'a Armağan*, ed. İlker Evrim Binbaş and Nurten Kılıç-Schubel (Istanbul: İthaki Press, 2011), 133–215; and, for the contemporary resonance of the works on these figures (and others), Rian Thum, *The Sacred Routes of Uyghur History* (Cambridge, Massachusetts: Harvard University Press, 2014).

39 See Bakhtiyar Babajanov, "Le renouveau des communautés soufies en Ouzbékistan," *Cahiers d'Asie centrale*, 5–6 (1998 = *Boukhara-la-Noble*), 285–311 [295–296], and Zarcone, "Bridging the Gap," pp. 45, 49–51. See now also the study of Ashirbek Muminov in the present volume.

40 The hagiography has been published: B. M. Babadzhanov, ed. and tr., *Manāqib-i Dūkchī Īshān: Anonim zhitiia Dūkchī Īshāna-predvoditelia Andizhanskogo vosstaniia 1898 goda* (Almaty: Daik-Press, 2004). On the work by Dūkchī Īshān, see Baxtiyar M. Babadžanov, "Dūkčī Īšān und der Aufstand von Andižan 1898," in *Muslim Culture in Russia and Central Asia from the 18th to the Early 20th Centuries*, vol. 2: *Inter-Regional and Inter-Ethnic Relations*, ed. Anke von Kügelgen, Michael Kemper, and Allen J. Frank (Berlin: Klaus Schwarz Verlag, 1998; Islamkundliche Untersuchungen, Bd. 216), 167–191.

poorly studied and, in some cases, barely known at all. This short outline, and these numbers, are themselves a sobering reminder of how much material remains to be assessed and digested, and of how incomplete our understanding of Sufism in Central Asia must remain until these sources are more thoroughly explored.

As a final general point with regard to the source base, however, it is important to note the shift in the kinds of sources available to us in more recent periods; and for these periods, without doubt the single most important development in scholarship on Sufism in Central Asia since the end of the Soviet era was the publication, in 2000, of the handlist of 'Sufi' manuscripts from the 18th, 19th, and 20th centuries preserved in the chief manuscript collection in Tashkent, at the Institute of Oriental Studies of the Academy of Sciences of Uzbekistan, the single largest repository of the manuscript heritage of Central Asia; though it does not cover the entire period of the 16th–19th centuries, the handlist brought to light dozens of previously unknown works, and in effect bore witness to the massive legacy of Sufi literary production—including hagiography—during the most recent periods of Central Asian history.[41] What it reveals, on the one hand, is an overall decline in hagiographical production: it was strong through the 18th century, and practically flourished again through the middle of the 19th, but during the second half of the 19th century, it appears to have waned noticeably. Explorations in still uncatalogued collections or in private manuscript libraries may alter this picture, and certain aspects of the hagiographical impulse clearly continued through this era, and indeed into the 20th century; but the decline in hagiographical production is balanced, in a sense, by another feature of the handlist, one that at first glance seems problematical, but in fact helps with the larger task of re-conceptualizing Sufism in the 19th and 20th centuries.

That feature is the handlist's inclusion of a large number of works that lie outside the classical genres of 'Sufi literature;' we might argue that some of the kinds of works included there stretch the limits of what can properly be called 'Sufi,' but in the end this is a good thing, insofar as this coverage shows not only the wealth of written material produced in Sufi circles of a type familiar from earlier times, but also the 'expansion,' or diffusion, of Sufi ideas, terms,

41 *Kratkii katalog sufiiskikh proizvedenii XVIII–XX vv. iz sobraniia Instituta Vostokovedeniia Akademiia Nauk Respubliki Uzbekistan im. al-Biruni*, ed. B. Babadzhanov, A. Kremer, and Iu. Paul' (Berlin: Das Arabische Buch, 2000), abbreviated KKSP; the work lists nearly 600 separate works, in over 2000 manuscripts or parts of manuscripts, thus expanding substantially the coverage of Sufi literature in the 11 volumes of the published catalogue of that collection.

practices, and perspectives on the world and on religious life into wider social circles. If we can argue that 'Sufi' rites were being adapted as communal and often 'public' rituals, in this era (see below), then the manuscript production showcased in the handlist shows us what 'Sufi literature' was becoming.

Alongside doctrinal treatises and works on longstanding issues of Sufi practice, such as the significance of the *khirqa*, the legitimacy of *samāʿ*, and the *ẕikr*, for example, we find genres not generally known from earlier times, whether the numerous craft *risāla*s that marked the sacralization of labor,[42] or *dāstān*s and *ḥikāyat*s recounting the exploits of 'pre-Islamic' prophets, members of the Prophet's family, or other early saints, and tales of 'mythic' figures invoked in ritual contexts, such as Bībī Seshanba or Bābā Burkh Dīvāna; all these are heavily infused with elements of Sufi doctrine and practice, and the same holds true for the proliferation of *shajara*s and *nasab-nāma*s and *silsila*s that simultaneously trace, and reimagine, initiatic and hereditary bonds across generations, and in some cases stake the identities of particular social groups (in both nomadic and sedentary contexts) on claims of descent from particular saints.

Also from this era, and similarly infused with Sufi teaching—though still in some ways distinct from specific organizational and ritual elements of Sufi life—are the many works focused on shrines, sometimes of individual saints but often of particular localities or entire regions, which are thus set off as sacred spaces, as ground hallowed by the presence of saints in their graves; we know 'classical' examples of shrine guides for the major cities of Bukhārā, Samarqand, Herat, and Balkh, produced from the 13th century to the 16th, but the 18th, 19th, and early 20th centuries saw the expansion and adaptation of this genre, yielding not only new iterations of works dealing with these cities, but new works on the holy shrines of Khwārazm, Sayrām, Osh and the Farghana valley, Tashkent, and Nur Ata, among others.[43] Also from this era date works focused on particular shrines or locally prominent saints, such as Qutham b. ʿAbbās in Samarqand, Maṣlaḥat al-Dīn Khujandī in Khujand, or Najm al-Dīn Kubrā in Khwārazm, each of whom is also the focus of hagiographical tales, recorded well into the Soviet era, that invest these localities'

42 See Jeanine Elif Dağyeli, *'Gott liebt das Handwerk:' Moral, Identität und religiöse Legitimierung in der mittelasiatischen Handwerks-risāla* (Wiesbaden: Reichert Verlag, 2011).

43 See my discussion in "Sacred History for a Central Asian Town: Saints, Shrines, and Legends of Origin in Histories of Sayrām, 18th–19th Centuries," in *Figures mythiques des mondes musulmans* (*Revue des mondes musulmans et de la Méditerranée*, 89–90), ed. Denise Aigle (Paris, 2000), 245–295. For the use of shrines in Soviet times to define the sacred topography of a newly re-envisioned (Soviet) Central Asia, see Eden, "A Soviet Jihad," 252–254.

sacrality, and security, in these saints. At the same time, just as shrine-focused practices, and literature, belong to a world shaped by Sufism, but not exclusive to Sufism, works dealing with dream interpretation or other occult sciences reflect intellectual traditions that often intersected with Sufism, but were far from the exclusive purview of Sufis;[44] these too reflect an intellectual and cultural world not readily 'accessed' through Russian sources or Jadīd literature, and though these kinds of works are distinct from what would be counted as 'Sufi literature' in earlier times, they nevertheless offer insight into important religious currents of the time, and cannot be excluded from the Sufi-shaped religious world of this era.

Following History and Hagiography into the Soviet Era

Taken together, these sources, and especially the shifts in their contours through the 19th century, reveal several developments that directly bear upon the narrative we can construct for 'Sufism' during the Tsarist and Soviet periods. To begin with, it must be kept in mind that the important and relevant changes in the profile of Sufi groups do not neatly follow the periodizations through which we typically structure the history of Central Asia in the 19th and 20th centuries: hagiographical production seems already to be tapering off prior to the Russian conquest, as noted, and often, in order to understand what Sufi groups were active, and where, during the Tsarist era, we must rely on the often faulty observations of travelers and officials, without a substantial body of indigenous sources as a control. Similarly, long before the Soviet and post-Soviet eras present us with often insurmountable problems in tracing specific Sufi *silsila* relationships of the kind that defined Sufi organization and identity in the 16th and 17th centuries, the nature and signification of those *silsila* relationships were changing substantially, leaving it essentially meaningless to identify particular Sufis in, or after, the Soviet era by assigning them to one of the classic orders; this appears to hold true for much of the Tsarist era, as well, although for much of the 19th century, it seems that the label 'Naqshbandī,' or 'Mujaddidī,' often did serve as a signifier of affiliation and identity in ways similar to what we find in earlier times.

---

44 For an insightful study of these traditions in 19th-century Central Asia, see Matthew Melvin-Koushki and James Pickett, "Mobilizing Magic: Occultism in Central Asia and the Continuity of High Persianate Culture under Russian Rule," *Studia Islamica*, 111 (2016), 231–284.

Consequently, the dates we use to demarcate Tsarist Central Asia from Soviet Central Asia, and Soviet from post-Soviet, are of little help in structuring a history of Sufism in Central Asia, or of developments in the social referents of the long-established names of 'orders;' no one can pretend to deny or underestimate the impact of major political and social changes entailed by these shifts, and signaled, at least in shorthand, by the familiar dates of 1917 and 1991, but it would be equally foolish to pretend that trends or developments underway or visible in 1915, or even 1885, were suddenly halted or rendered immaterial by the events of 1917, or 1928, or even 1938. Just as Soviet attitudes to religion or 'mysticism' or 'faith-healing' evident in the 1980s shaped, in part, some of the manifestations of the so-called 'revival' of Islam in late Soviet and post-Soviet times, the profile of 'Sufism' as it had developed by the second half of the 19th century did linger into the Soviet period, bringing with it patterns of religious behavior that were not automatically and finally extinguished by increasingly harsh Soviet anti-religious measures. We are only now beginning to realize, in fact, just how ineffective many of those were; and in any case, in a scholarly environment in which the crude and misleading 'measures' of religiosity framed during the Soviet era—by both Soviet and Sovietological writers—continue to shape discussion about the 'revival' of Islam in post-Soviet times, those interested in Sufism would do well to be skeptical of even the most basic claims about the Soviet era's impact on religiosity, Islam, or Sufi activity.

Before we try to assess 'policy impacts,' however, it is essential to be clear about the nature of the 'field' in which such impacts are imagined to have been felt. What is needed, that is, is a rethinking of the forms in which 'Sufi' activity may have manifested itself in the 19th, 20th, and 21st centuries, with the recognition that some of those forms may have followed developmental trajectories and timelines for which the blunt-instrument demarcations of major 'periods'—Tsarist, Soviet, post-Soviet—bear little specific significance. What is needed, in short, is a new conceptual framework, attentive to the shifting nature of the 'social terminology' of Sufi groups, that will provide better questions to ask of both long-known and newly-discovered data. Such a framework will naturally emerge in part against the backdrop of the failures of earlier approaches, i.e., through what the Sovietological narrative missed; and, more to the point, in order to avoid those failures, such a framework will necessarily have to be informed by patterns, personalities, conceptual complexes and religious idioms that can only be 'accessed' through earlier sources—whether the hagiographies that framed Sufi history from the 16th to 19th century, ongoing traditions of 'classical' Sufi doctrinal literature, or the other kinds of literary articulations of Sufism's place in Central Asian life and culture noted above. Central to that new analytical framework will be a re-imagining of what we mean by 'Sufism,' recognizing the pitfalls of remaining attached to certain assumptions that may seem to work for earlier periods, but undoubtedly entail multiple instances of misunderstanding for Central Asia from the 19th to 21st centuries.

Organizational Profiles

We need, first of all, to shed assumptions about the organizational profile characteristic of Sufi activity that foreground the so-called 'orders'—not merely because 'order' is a poor or misleading translation of the actual terminology (of *ṭarīqa* or *ṭarīq*, etc.), or because the 'structures' signaled by this terminology were nearly always more fluid and inchoate than is implied by the labels and by the evocations, in the labels, of vertical (i.e., diachronic) and horizontal (i.e., synchronic) stability, and continuity, but because the social realities underlying the names that had formerly been applied to 'orders' shifted—or, in other words, the meaning of those names was reconceptualized in several phases *within* Sufi communities themselves.

I have recently discussed some of the conceptual and organizational changes evident in Central Asian Sufi groups beginning in the 18th century,[45] noting the phenomenon of 'bundled *silsila*s' that decoupled initiatic transmission from communal structure, allowed the apparent (and rhetorically useful) continuation of initiatic labels that had no concrete social presence in communal terms, thereby masked the virtual disappearance of formerly important Sufi communities defined in terms of initiatic transmission (e.g., the Yasavī and Kubravī 'orders'), and accounted for the 'hybrid' designations that proliferate both in late hagiographical sources and in descriptions by Tsarist-era travelers, officials, and ethnographers. This phenomenon was already changing the social profile of Sufi groups before the Russian conquest, and its effects seem to be largely complete before the advent of Soviet power, yielding a religious landscape in which some Naqshbandī (and Naqshbandī-Mujaddidī) groups still maintained communal self-consciousness under those names—leaving the few initiatic lineages that can be traced from before the Russian conquest down to the present—while other 'Sufi' phenomena manifested themselves only outside the framework of the former 'orders,' in hereditary, public, 'cultural,' or other venues.

45 See my "'Dis-ordering' Sufism in Early Modern Central Asia: Suggestions for Rethinking the Sources and Social Structures of Sufi History in the 18th and 19th Centuries," in *History and Culture of Central Asia/Istoriia i kul'tura Tsentral'noi Azii*, ed. Bakhtiyar Babadjanov and Kawahara Yayoi (Tokyo: The University of Tokyo, 2012), 259–279.

Those other venues included four, in particular, that were missed by outside observers because of assumptions about what 'Sufism' ought to look like (such assumptions, it should be noted, sometimes operate well beyond Central Asia, in the study of the Muslim world more broadly, but they were particularly misleading in the hands of Sovietologists).

First, the assumption that Sufis have always and everywhere organized themselves into 'orders' led some scholars to ignore the maintenance of Sufi ritual and devotional practices in social settings not recognizable or definable as 'Sufi orders,' often involving entire villages or neighborhood communities; as I have suggested elsewhere,[46] such practices continued well into Soviet times (some descriptions date from the 1980s), and marked an ongoing 'public' manifestation of Sufi practice, but they came to be labeled—in Soviet scholarship and in its Sovietological refractions—not as Sufi rites, but as 'shamanism,' in line with the notion of religious 'survivals' noted above. Indeed, the 'diffusion' of Sufi rites into wider social circles has been part of Sufi history for centuries, but its consequences were particularly subject to misinterpretation in the Soviet context; Sovietologists were especially susceptible to uncritically accepting the re-labeling undertaken by Soviet ethnographers, because Sovietologists looking for signs of Sufi activity expected to find Sufi orders, and because the same Sovietologists were unacquainted with the pre-Soviet history of Sufi activity in the lands of the USSR.[47]

Second, a more widely-based assumption about Sufis—that they are everywhere and always on hostile terms with the learned 'doctors of the law'—led

46 See my "Shamanization in Central Asia," *Journal of the Economic and Social History of the Orient*, 57 (2014), 326–363.

47 Another phenomenon indicative of 'Sufi' legacies outside the framework of 'orders' in the 18th and 19th centuries, of less relevance for the landscape of Tsarist and Soviet Central Asia but with parallels to both the public diffusion of Sufi practices and the 'cultural' appeal of Sufism discussed below, is the widening use of the notion of Uvaysī saints to 'populate' shrines in Eastern Turkistan (a development with its own set of misinterpretations rooted in the assumption that the label "Uvaysī" must reflect an Uvaysī Sufi organization); see my discussion in "An 'Uvaysī' Hagiography from Eastern Turkistān: The *Tadhkira* of Quṭb al-Dīn 'Irāqī," in *Etudes orientales: Revue culturelle semestrielle* (Paris), Nos. 27–28 (2016), 15–86 (esp. 78–79), and see also the comments of David Brophy and Rian Thum in *The Life of Muḥammad Sharīf: A Central Asian Sufi Hagiography in Chaghatay*, tr. Jeff Eden, with an appendix by David Brophy and Rian Thum (Vienna: Verlag der Österreichischen Akademie der Wissenschaften, 2015; Veröffentlichungen zur Iranistik, No. 78), 59–64. See also the contribution of Jo-Ann Gross to the present volume, which explores the hagiographical 'back-stories' created for a saint linked with a shrine in Tajikistan, paralleling the 19th-century processes in Eastern Turkistan but without appeal to the Uvaysī principle.

observers to miss the confluence of Sufis and the *ʿulamā*, in concrete social and individual terms, that characterized Central Asia before, and to some extent during, the Soviet era. From at least the 17th century, that is (and in some cases earlier, though cases of hostility toward Sufis among certain groups of *ʿulamā* may be found more readily during and before the 16th century), it is safe to say that in Central Asia, the Sufis *were* the *ʿulamā*, and vice-versa; the opposition of these groups, *as* groups, that is described and assumed for other parts of the Muslim world, simply does not apply to Central Asia during the 17th, 18th, and 19th centuries.[48] There were, of course, certain kinds of dervishes, usually labeled Qalandars, who were reviled among the learned classes (including other Sufis), and who might be held up as the exception to the rule posited here, and the example of the antinomian Sufi known as Shāh Mashrab (d. 1711) likewise reminds us of the appeal of the rhetoric, at least, of playing fast and loose with the *sharīʿa* and with its learned upholders. But the fact remains that nearly all the Central Asian Sufis whose names and activities are recorded in locally-produced hagiographical sources from the 17th, 18th, and 19th centuries were to one degree or another steeped in traditional Muslim learning, often serving in capacities typically 'reserved' for the *ʿulamā*. Conversely, by far the majority of the learned class, active in the study of the Qur'ān and *ḥadīth*s, in juridical scholarship, or in practically any other branch of the Islamic sciences, also claimed one or more Sufi initiations, engaged in Sufi practices, and held a variety of ties and connections with the social reality of Sufi groups. This, after all, is part of the reason that Sufi thought and practice permeated all levels of Central Asian society in this era, and so heavily shaped the intellectual outlook and religious sensibility of the *ʿulamā*.

And again it stands to reason that this pattern might have continued into the Soviet era; yet assumptions rooted in superficial familiarity with circumstances elsewhere in the Muslim world, and with the mutual hostility and opposition imputed to the Sufis and the *ʿulamā* (or, worse still, with the simplistic relegation of the Sufis to the world of 'heterodoxy' frowned upon by the 'orthodox' *ʿulamā*) proved stronger, among Sovietologists, than any closer understanding of the Central Asian (or 'Russian Muslim') world that was, supposedly, their subject, leading the Sovietologists to miss some prominent Sufis of the Soviet era on the assumption that they belonged to (or had been drawn from) the *ʿulamā* and would thus brook no ties with Sufism. The 'dynasty'

---

48 See my discussion in "Sufis as the *ʿUlamā* in 17th-Century Central Asia: ʿĀlim Shaykh of ʿAlīyābād and Mawlānā Muḥammad Sharīf of Bukhārā," in *Sufis and Mullahs: Sufis and their Opponents in the Persianate World*, ed. Reza Tabandeh and Leonard Lewisohn (Irvine, California: Jordan Center for Persian Studies, forthcoming).

of Soviet-era leaders of the Tashkent religious board, the Babakhanovs, had Naqshbandī Sufi ties as well as hereditary links with several Sufis and jurists prominent in Central Asian religious history;[49] but Sovietologists seldom mentioned the Babakhanovs, or their powerful role in Soviet Central Asia, when discussing Sufism in the Soviet Union. The Babakhanovs were understood as 'clerics,' a category used by the Sovietologists to refer to members of the official Soviet religious establishments, but never to 'Sufis' (unless qualified as 'unofficial' clerics), who were by definition—for the Sovietologists—not part of anything 'official,' and not amenable to the *madrasa*-training that shaped the 'clerics' of Soviet Islam. The Sufis were expected to be 'unofficial' and 'unorthodox' as well; Islamic learning was not their scene.[50] By contrast, Soviet 'clerics' were understood as heirs, of sorts, to the *ʿulamā*, and a Sufi could be neither an *ʿālim* nor a 'cleric;' in the Sovietological narrative, moreover, the *ʿulamā* who staffed the Soviet religious boards were cast as heirs of the Jadīds, further distancing them from Sufis, who were, in this narrative, obscurantist targets of Jadīd scorn.

To be sure, another dichotomy was at work here, insofar as the Babakhanovs were understood to have been co-opted by the Soviet state, and were thus, in effect, collaborators. Sufis, by contrast, were portrayed (as noted) as Muslim purists, and as actually or potentially militant, but in any case as hostile to the Soviet state; and, once again, distinctions rooted in Sovietological categories that were in fact mostly meaningless in real time—co-opted lackeys of the Soviet regime vs. underground and possibly militant opponents who

49 On the Babakhanovs, see B. Babadzhanov, "Babakhanovy," in *Islam na territorii byvshei Rossiiskoi imperii: Èntsiklopeicheskii slovar'*, ed. S. M. Prozorov, vyp. 4 (St. Petersburg: 'Vostochnaia literatura,' 2003), 12–14, and now Eren Tasar, *Soviet and Muslim: The Institutionalization of Islam in Central Asia, 1943–1991* (Oxford: Oxford University Press, 2017).

50 The conceptual segregation of "Sufis" and "scholars" rests atop a broader segregation of "mysticism" from "scholarship," and atop other unhelpful dichotomies ("orthodox" vs. "heterodox," "elite" vs. "popular," etc.). In the practical context of manuscript catalogues—even the handlist noted above—this tendency masks the broad engagement of Sufis in multiple Islamic sciences; a work on astronomy, or medicine, for example, or even a work of *fiqh*, would typically be listed separately from a hagiography or a work on Sufi teaching or practice, even if the author of the 'scientific' work was, in social terms, a Sufi. The point is not to essentialize all writings by a Sufi as "Sufi literature," but to recognize the engagement of Sufis with intellectual pursuits not typically considered as part of a Sufi's concerns.

resisted that regime—got in the way of any sort of real understanding.[51] It is true, of course, that in time, with their official position in the post-war Soviet religious establishment, the Babakhanovs came themselves to emphasize their scholarly credentials (including their descent from a prominent Shāfiʿī jurist of Tashkent), to downplay their Sufi ties (again, whether hereditary or initiatic), and to turn in a distinctly scripturalist direction; but this is already a development of the second half of the Soviet era, reflecting their adoption of Soviet categorizations that in large measure paralleled those of the western Sovietologists.

In short, Sovietologists were looking for Sufis who stood apart from—in multiple ways—the 'clerical' class that served the Soviet religious establishments, and so they missed not only long-term patterns in Central Asian religious life of relevance to understanding 20th-century developments, but even the incorporation of Sufis into those Soviet religious boards (in positions of leadership, no less). This issue overlaps, of course, with the assumption that Sufis were necessarily militant and politically-driven opponents of the Soviet regime, an assumption rooted in the broader question of where to put 'Sufism' in political terms; we will return to this issue shortly.

As for the third venue in which 'Sufism' may be sought in the 19th and 20th centuries, the same assumptions about Sufi 'orders' that led Sovietologists to miss the maintenance and adaptation of Sufi rites in communal, and indeed public, settings, and to miss the considerable 'overlap' between the spheres of Sufis and scholars, also hindered recognition of one of the most obvious, and pervasive and persistent, frameworks in which Sufi identities were known

51 This dichotomy, and the myopia about the Babakhanovs, persisted even after Sovietologists were reminded that ʿAbd al-Raḥmān Rasūlī—the first *muftī* of another Soviet religious board, the one based in Ufa—was, like his father, a Muslim scholar with profoundly important Sufi affiliations; see Hamid Algar, "Shaykh Zaynullah Rasulev: The Last Great Naqshbandi Shaykh of the Volga-Urals Region," in *Muslims in Central Asia: Expressions of Identity and Change*, ed. Jo-Ann Gross (Durham, North Carolina: Duke University Press, 1992), 112–133, as well as Eden, "A Soviet Jihad," 246–249. Bennigsen and Wimbush did mention the Naqshbandī affiliations both of the Babakhanovs (*Mystics and Commissars*, 2, 44–45) and of the Rasulev father and son (38), but without letting this acknowledgment get in the way of the basic juxtaposition of Sufi vs. scholar, or of the oft-repeated claim that the leaders of "official Islam" were heirs to the modernist Jadīds. We might object that, whatever we might say about the Rasūlevs' 'mystical' inclinations, the Babakhanovs were decidedly "unmystical" in their religious orientation; in this case, of course, we are dealing with another unhelpful approach to "Sufism," one that defines it simply as "Islamic mysticism" and thereby downplays, or misconstrues, the ethical, intellectual, ritual, and above all social dimensions of what "Sufism" has been.

throughout the period we are focused on, from the 16th century through the Soviet era: heredity. Here again developments underway centuries earlier shaped 'Soviet Sufism' in ways that led Sovietologists to look for Sufism in the wrong places, and to miss it where it actually existed.

Communities that understood themselves as comprising, or as built around, the natural descendants of prominent Sufis dominate the social face of 'Sufism' in the 11th, 12th and 13th centuries; they existed alongside emerging 'orders,' framed in initiatic terms, through the 14th and 15th centuries, during which time we find *silsila*-based Sufi groups (and sometimes other kinds of Sufi groups) criticizing hereditary Sufi transmission, and doing so in order to claim a competitive advantage, but in the process attesting to the strength of the hereditary principle they sought to undermine. By the 16th and 17th centuries, the Sufi order conceived in terms of initiatic transmission was paradigmatic, but even during this classic age of Central Asian Sufi orders, hereditary transmission inevitably crept back into organizational structures and succession to leadership, though typically with the assurance that the inheriting son was also the disciple of his father, and not 'merely' his son. This is clear even within various groups classed as Naqshbandī, beginning with the Jūybārī shaykhs but continuing with the many other hereditary-cum-initiatic lines extending from Makhdūm-i Aʿẓam; at the same time, we find groups that maintained a hereditary identity linking them with a particular eminent Sufi saint of the past—e.g., the Aḥrārī families, or descendants of Sayyid Ata—but produced individuals inclined to establish initiatic ties with other Sufi lineages.

In addition, during this same period, as competition among several orders gave way to the increasing dominance of Naqshbandī groups, we find Sufi communities framed in terms of hereditary ties to saints of other 'orders'—above all Yasavī shaykhs—admitted corporately into a Naqshbandī initiatic framework, but with the provision that they could still engage in Sufi practices inherited from their Yasavī ancestors, even if those practices were not otherwise recognized as part of the Naqshbandī repertoire. We might be inclined to ask whether such practices, continued in such an environment, represented an 'authentic' or 'spiritually potent' ritual and devotional undertaking, or whether they became mere fossilized rituals maintained as a mark of kinship rather than of 'real' Sufi aspiration. In social terms, however, the difference does not really matter in the end, and our sources, at least, treat those practices—and those kinship identities—as something of social, religious, and indeed spiritual significance.

As the familiar structures and groups of the 16th and 17th centuries eroded during the 18th, heredity once again played a key factor in the identity of particular Sufi groups, both through the ongoing prominence of hereditary communities by now drawn under the Naqshbandī, or Naqshbandī-Mujaddidī organizational 'umbrella,' and through the apparent weakening of the solely initiatic bond as well. By the middle of the 19th century, most former initiatic labels—such as Kubravī, Yasavī (or its equivalents), Suhravardī, or Qādirī—can be found only in the 'bundled' contexts noted earlier, but labels for hereditary Sufi groups seem to proliferate, at least to judge from our sources' shorthand references to family groups such as the Shaykh Khāvand-i Ṭahūrīs, or Sayyid Atāʾīs, or Amīr Kulālīs, or Ṣadr Atāʾīs; we might object that these were 'only' social labels, or that members of these families were only rarely engaged with the 'spiritual' practices we expect of Sufi groups (a charge that was leveled against such hereditary groups, by their opponents, already in the 16th century), but these arguments not only run afoul of what our sources say—that members of these families did maintain and transmit the physical, ritual, and 'spiritual' trappings of Sufi activity—they also continue to steer us in the direction of an essentialized understanding of 'mystical Sufism,' a direction that yields not only the Bennigsen narrative, but a host of other assumptions that get in the way of a more historically-grounded understanding of the social, and human, reality of 'Sufism.'

In short, 'Sufism' became, in the period of concern here, of which the Soviet period is but one part, what it had often been through various historical periods: a family thing. It is, once again, often helpful to stress certain distinctions between spheres of activity that overlap with Sufi life, whether hereditary Sufism or communal ceremonies or shrine traditions, but it is also essential to be aware of the conceptual costs of making those distinctions too rigid;[52] likewise, it would be going too far to suggest that the era of Sufi 'orders' framed in terms of the *silsila* was an aberration in Sufi history, but it *was* a limited period that nevertheless cemented expectations—both in much Sufi literature and in western scholarship—about what 'Sufism' would look like, in social and organizational terms. In the Soviet context, important aspects of what may rightly be understood as Sufi activity were missed because of their frequently hereditary character, misleading those who expected to find 'Sufi orders' defined by traditional *silsila*s.

52 In this connection it may be noted that not all sacred descent groups in Central Asia need be linked with Sufism, though connections with Sufi saints, shrines, or practices are often prominent in the lore of such groups. For an overview of the growing literature on such 'holy families,' in the context of a case study, see Jeanine Elif Dagyeli, "By Grace of Descent: A Conflict between an *Īšān* and Craftsmen over Donations," *Der Islam*, 88 (2012), 279–307.

The fourth venue, finally, for manifestations of the emerging face of Sufism in this era, and one that must be kept in mind in connection with the cultural appeal of Sufism in late- and post-Soviet times, is the sphere of literary and cultural expression linked with the intellectual legacy of Sufism and of the Sufi-scholar overlap noted above. Students of Sufism are familiar with the famous dictum that Sufism is not to be found in books, a statement intended to distinguish the real and profound experiential aspect of Sufi disciplines from what can be described in language and in texts; yet in fact Sufi books have always been an avenue of access into the intellectual, ritual, devotional, and even social worlds of Sufism, even if a particular Sufi's life story, for instance, inevitably portrays him as eventually turning from the books to a real-life master. Whether we view that turning as paradigmatic and prescriptive, or as real and essential, we can nevertheless accept that Sufi literature of various kinds, and the broader cultural production linked with Sufi thought and practice (including oral and visual and musical venues), played important roles in shaping a public and social profile that was permeated by Sufism. We can leave aside for now some specific questions raised by this recognition—i.e., does someone who reads a Sufi text, or recites a Sufi litany, or listens to Sufi music, or ponders an element of Sufi teaching, or engages in a Sufi practice through imitation (rather than through initiatic transmission tailored by the wise guidance of a master) warrant characterization as a Sufi?—to acknowledge that even if the answer is no, such a person's experience stands, in some way, as evidence both of a 'presence' of 'Sufism' in his or her society, and of the participation of his or her society in 'Sufism.'

This is especially significant for contemporary Central Asia, insofar as approaching and engaging with Sufism (and with other aspects of Muslim religiosity) through books (or now through internet sites) appears to be a significant component of the late- and post-Soviet 'revival' of Sufi activity, as individuals with no direct tie with a Sufi master, or lineage, organized 'study circles' to explore Sufi literature (especially poetry). We might insist that participants in such activities were not actually Sufis, and that their 'freelancing' approach to Sufi intellectual or aesthetic experience amounts to dilettantism and runs counter to key principles of Sufi transmission and practice; but when we read, in earlier hagiographical sources, of similarly dilettantish engagements with Sufi teaching and practice (whether as a negative example, as a contrastive prologue to a more serious engagement, or as a positive model for external imitation leading to internal development), or of the central role played by the recitation of Sufi poetry or of other Sufi literature (including hagiography) in gatherings of 'real' Sufis—that is, Sufis organized the way we expect them to be—then we may be reminded that contemporary seekers may be no more diverse than those of earlier times. Once again, in any case, it behooves us to be more flexible in thinking about what constitutes 'Sufi activity,' lest we prematurely reject the importance, or validity, of practices, or practitioners, that may turn out to be a significant aspect of the emerging face of Sufism; to extrapolate from al-Būshanjī's dictum, what is called, or regarded as, Sufism may differ from one period to the next, and it is neither appropriate nor helpful for scholars to insist on overly exclusive definitions.

This leads, perhaps, to a broader question of historical and social importance. Is there a middle ground, a compromise of sorts, between insisting that *all* of these manifestations—publicly diffused Sufi practices, kinship groups rooted in Sufi identities, Sufi affiliations 'suspended' in favor of scholarly claims under conditions of Soviet rule, and the 'cultural' experience of Sufism—are 'Sufism,' on the one hand, and insisting that *none* of them are, outside the framework of the old initiatically-framed structures and transmissions of 'Sufi orders' rooted in the master-disciple relationship and the cultivation of contemplative 'mystical' endeavors? Addressing this question will no doubt require different approaches in different environments and periods, but precisely for this reason, it would be foolish to overlook the potential lessons of earlier examples of 'Sufi literature,' in all its diversity. In particular, this is where engaging with the kinds of sources through which we come to know the social profile of Sufis in earlier times—books constructed around hagiographical narratives written about, by, and for individuals who 'knew' not to look for Sufism in books—can be particularly illuminating.

The point is not that we can determine, or merely choose, a 'correct' answer to the question, "Who is a Sufi?" (whether more expansive, or more specific, than the one Bennigsen implicitly assumed, or simply different from it), and then on that basis more accurately assess the impact of 'Sufism' in Soviet or post-Soviet Central Asia. The problem is not merely one of information, or definition, or classification. The point, rather, is that understanding Sufism in Central Asia must inevitably be an extended process, involving both a critical eye and an openness to seemingly unconventional manifestations that may be counted as 'Sufism,' in addition to broader experience of, and exposure to, the diverse possibilities of 'Sufi' activity; that process necessarily demands conceptual flexibility and historically-grounded argumentation. The 'practice' of grappling with Sufi history, and Sufi life, through engagement with hagiographies and other kinds of 'Sufi literature' offers a foundation for embarking upon that process; but Sovietological training has never provided the would-be student of Central Asia with the proper conceptual or methodological tools even to notice, let alone to analyze or understand, the social and religious phenomena that might fall into the category of 'Sufism.' Sovietology's shortcomings in this regard are even more evident when we keep in mind al-Būshanjī's 'disconnect' between the name and the reality of 'Sufism.'

Political Patterns

Drawing on the historical profile of Sufi activity, by engaging with hagiographical sources, may also be helpful for putting in perspective the 'political' pressures placed on Sufi groups during the Soviet era. Much of the Bennigsen narrative, of Sufis as resisters against or opponents of the Soviet system, rested not merely on the legal framework of Soviet anti-religious activity, but also on a persistent (if vaguely drawn) counter-narrative, of a time in which Sufis wielded extensive political power in their own right, and shaped notions of legality and political legitimacy instead of being victimized by them. There is no denying the political 'clout' wielded by some prominent Sufis, or the writings of Sufis about *sharīʿa*-based notions of justice, in certain eras of Central Asian history; Sufis represented substantial constituencies with both social and economic (and sometimes even military) importance, and rulers were often careful to cultivate them, whether through various modes of patronage or through simply heeding their counsel.

It is sometimes overlooked, however, that this was a two-way street, and that rulers and political elites played important roles in shaping the framework in which Sufis could live and act in political terms. Such was the case in the 16th century, a time in which our hagiographical sources often insist that such-and-such a *sulṭān* was completely devoted to a particular Sufi shaykh, and did nothing without his blessing; this claim indeed seems to underscore the political influence of that Sufi shaykh, until, that is, we read a second or third account—and we may recall how works advancing such claims proliferated in that era—insisting that the same *sulṭān* was a devotee of a different shaykh, and did nothing without *his* blessing. We continue to find such claims through the 17th, 18th, and 19th centuries, and more often than not, they mask a political reality in which shaykhs and *sulṭān*s in fact needed each other, with each group seeking to manipulate and negotiate to its advantage; this in itself gave rulers and officials leverage over Sufi leaders, and vice-versa, but the overall balance seems to have shifted by the late 18th and 19th centuries, when tensions among Sufi groups were actively exploited by the *khān*s of the new 'tribal' dynasties as part of their efforts to strengthen central control.

Already in the early 18th century, the Ashtarkhānid ruler ʿUbaydullāh Khān (r. 1702–1711) sought and gained the support of the new Mujaddidī circle (established by Ḥājjī Ḥabībullāh) as he tried, in vain, to regain the prerogatives that had been lost to members of the tribal aristocracy and their allies among well-established 'native' Central Asian Naqshbandī groups.[53] The pattern of seeking political leverage through the patronage of these new Mujaddidī Sufi groups with roots outside Central Asia became even clearer as the tribal dynasties emerged in the latter 18th century, unable to appeal to the principle of Chinggisid legitimation—in decay already in any case—and hence in need of other sources of legitimacy. This has been demonstrated extensively, in Anke von Kügelgen's work, for the Manghït dynasty in Bukhara, where Shāh Murād (r. 1785–1800) sought to consolidate Manghït rule and to centralize power by neutralizing the locally entrenched opposition, including Sufi communities; von Kügelgen has discussed extensively how he supported shaykhs who took a hard line against the vocal *ẕikr*, symbolic of ritual innovations and moral degeneration, and thus claimed the mantle of 'reform,' directed against harmful innovations, as a way to undermine his opponents.[54]

Similar patterns are evident in the khanate of Khiva, under Muḥammad Raḥīm Khān (r. 1806-1825), and in the khanate of Khoqand, under ʿĀlim Khān (r. 1798–1809); the latter, in particular, gained a reputation for mocking fraudulent dervishes and exposing their 'innovations.' ʿĀlim Khān, we are told, suppressed "persons who falsely called themselves *sayyid-zādas* and *shaykh-zādas*;" he completely "uprooted" the practice, said to prevail "in Turkistān," of creating false shrines; he forced the "wealthy beggars," who begged despite their riches, to work as camel-drivers; and he assembled and examined all the "shaykh-makers" (*shaykh-tarāshān*), who "presented themselves as shaykhs, engaged in deceitful miracle-mongering (*karāmat-furūshī*), and led the Muslims astray into the path of corruption," honoring those whose deeds turned out to be in accord with the *sharīʿa* and forcing all the rest, through various unspecified torments, to repent of their ways.[55]

In each case, we see the emergence of the ruler, and the state, not merely as a utilizer, or exploiter, of religious legitimation, but as a factor in shaping the character of the Sufi practice that would be sanctioned as licit. That in turn involved rhetoric, and action, against the practices declared to be illicit, as

53 See my discussion in "'Dis-ordering' Sufism," 262–265.

54 See von Kügelgen, "Die Entfaltung."

55 Thus in a source from the 1840s; see Mukhammed Khakimkhan, *Muntakhab at-tavarikh*, facs. ed. prepared by A. M. Mukhtarov, kn. 2 (Dushanbe: Ilm, 1985), 424–425. See further, on ʿĀlim Khān's hostility toward certain Sufis, *Histoire de l'Asie Centrale par Mir Abdoul Kerim Boukhary*, ed. and tr. Charles Schefer (Paris: École des Langues Orientales Vivantes, 1876; repr. Amsterdam: Philo Press, 1970), tr., 211–212; text, 94–95.

maintained by the local Sufi groups targeted for marginalization; in Bukhara,[56] this meant the vocal *ẕikr*, or *jahr*, the subject of debates in earlier times that were now used for different goals. Those debates had already been realigned in communal terms: through the reconfiguration of Sufi communities themselves, the modes of *ẕikr* were by this time disputed between groups that were part of the Naqshbandī-Mujaddidī 'umbrella'—no longer, that is, between some Naqshbandī groups and a distinct Yasavī community. The social context for engagement in the *ẕikr* had expanded as well, through the process of ritual diffusion noted earlier, with the *ẕikr* adapted as a communal rite outside the framework of Sufis in the traditional *khānaqāh*. As a result, the *ẕikr*, and Sufi practice more broadly, were politicized, as rhetorical denunciations of the vocal *ẕikr*, and of the complex of other practices the vocal *ẕikr* came to symbolize (in part because of the wider public 'diffusion' noted above), were used by rulers intent on centralizing their control in order to condemn and undermine their opponents, and as actual practice of the vocal *ẕikr* was suppressed (or its practitioners exiled).

The pressure against the vocal *ẕikr*, however, inspired extensive efforts to collect and document defenses of the practice,[57] and ultimately the campaigns against it appear to have failed. Yet these attacks upon, and defenses of, the vocal *ẕikr* belong to a much longer pattern of contestations of Islamic practice, which go back well before the early 18th century, and continue down to the present; each era inevitably brought its own distinct political circumstances and social environment, but Mujaddidī attacks on the vocal *ẕikr* and practices linked with it reflect a tendency that was expressed in later times through Jadīdism, in the context of Tsarist rule, through Soviet antireligious efforts in the 20th century, and through 'Wahhābism' and Salafist currents in late Soviet and post-Soviet times. On the other side—and we should be careful about drawing the lines too starkly, in the early 19th century or today—we may locate not only explicit defenses of the vocal *ẕikr*, and those Mujaddidī shaykhs

56 The affirmation, in various sources (including the *Muntakhab al-tavārīkh*), that 'Ālim Khān adhered to the "*ṭarīqa-yi Jahriyya*," and indeed participated himself in vocal *dhikr* sessions under the leadership of a Naqshbandī shaykh who performed the *jahr*, may stand as another example of one side in a religious competition 'claiming' the ruler, but it is also a reminder that the labels "Jahriyya" and "Naqshbandī" had shifted somewhat in their referents. It also suggests that the vocal *dhikr* was not universally recognized as a symbol of innovation and moral degeneration (as it certainly was in Bukhara, in certain circles).

57 See B. M. Babadzhanov and S. A. Mukhammadaminov, eds., *Sobranie fetv po obosnovaniiu zikra dzhakhr i sama'* (*A Collection of Fatwas Legitimizing the Vocal Dhikr and Sama'*) (Almaty: Daik-Press, 2009).

who joined some earlier Naqshbandīs in acknowledging that the vocal *ẕikr* was licit, but also the broader pattern of 'resistance' to, or simple inattention to, the program of the Jadīds, and the continuation of these public aspects of religiosity through the Soviet period. Evidence of state support for 'traditional' Islam, in 'national' varieties, is a contemporary manifestation, but here again, both the state and various groups are contesting these issues.

The upshot, in any case, is that living in a political environment in which state officials and their supporters sought to coerce, curtail, or manipulate the activities of Sufis was not a new thing for Central Asian Sufis in the Soviet era; nor was ruthless action by political leaders, targeted against so-called religious frauds, including Sufi shaykhs, limited to the Soviet era (or the post-Soviet era, for that matter). Similarly, the politicization of matters of religious practice that we see reflected in the writings of members of the Soviet-era religious boards, and earlier in the program of 'reforms' advanced by the Jadīds, likewise had precedents (in the early 19th century, and in the early 18th century), both in terms of their specific targets, and in terms of their ultimate failure to dislodge many of the practices that remained public markers of Muslim religiosity in Central Asia (including shrine-centered rites and communal *ẕikr*s).

More broadly, the debates about the vocal *ẕikr*, and the political context in which they were conducted both in the early 18th century and in the early 19th, should remind us that the politicization of negotiations about religious propriety (involving issues of 'Sufi' practice) was already a factor in the history of Sufism before the Russian conquest, and continued to be afterwards, into the Soviet era. We thus go astray when we speak, for instance, about 'Soviet policy on Islam,' as if 'Islam' were a single uncontested thing, and, especially, as if Soviet policy did not inevitably interact differently with different visions of Islam, sometimes unwittingly, reflecting the views of some Muslims and thus strengthening them in some regards, but in any case, shaping the 'playing field' on which later iterations of those debates would be conducted. And today, in the wake of the Soviet era, multiple Central Asian governments have no doubt influenced the course of both popular and scholarly re-engagement with Sufism by embracing (and sometimes then dis-embracing) Sufism as a 'safe' or 'good' Islam that might guard regimes against perceived Islamist threats, and above all as a 'national' (or 'nationally appropriate') Islam that might provide a politically- and 'ethnically'-acceptable avenue toward a kind of connection with the Muslim past.

In any event, it should be clear that patterns of debate and discussion about the propriety of certain Sufi practices evident in the 18th and 19th centuries continued to inform religious debate and discussion through the Tsarist and Soviet eras, and today as well. But these patterns, as well as the intricacies of their politicization in different contexts, have been obscured in scholarship not only by inattention to the full range of sources from the 18th and 19th centuries, but by 'over-attention' to (and often uncritical admiration for) the representatives of just one side in those debates (whose views, and motives, in their actual complexity, are in fact more clouded than clarified by portraying them simply as forces of 'modernity'). Engagement with the history of Sufi groups, through sources they produced, would thus directly inform, and improve, discussions about 'religious policy' in both Soviet-era and contemporary Central Asia.

Sources, Methods, and Questions

As we unburden ourselves of a host of unhelpful approaches and assumptions (whether those 'baked into' the Sovietological narrative or others, outside it)—about Sufism and 'heterodoxy,' Sufism vs. the *'ulamā*, Sufism as filled with pre-Islamic 'survivals' or as thinly-veiled 'shamanism,' Sufism as a non-Islamic accretion onto a pure foundation of 'real' Islam, Sufism as involving solely 'ecstatic' or 'emotional' or 'mystical' religious styles, and so forth—and try to engage with Sufism as a social and 'public' phenomenon that can—and must—be the object of historical study, the question of sources again takes center stage. The rich source base produced within Sufi communities from the 16th century to the 19th presents not only a wealth of raw material, but a host of interpretative problems as well, and engaging with it fruitfully will demand a new appreciation of the 'output' of those we class as Sufis, in the present and in the past (whether they participate in Sufi practices, belong to Sufi organizations, claim Sufi kinship ties, revere a Sufi cultural legacy, or 'dabble' in Sufi doctrine), above all from the standpoint of what, precisely, those sources are about.

Indeed, a broader comment may be in order regarding the hagiographical works that must serve as the foundation for efforts to reconstruct the narrative of Sufi history in Central Asia: whatever these works' 'shortcomings' may be as sources on religious history, or on the history, in general, of Central Asia—whether those are judged from an older positivist standpoint found in dismissals of their 'fantastic' tales and miracles, or those rooted in suspicion of their formulaic character and their frequent rehearsal of stock narrative themes—it must first be recalled that despite common features, they are very different works, each reflecting a distinctive outlook and distinctive social and religious world, and it must then be acknowledged that they in fact offer, in many respects, unparalleled access into the constructed, negotiated, socially-embedded lives—that is to say, 'real' lives—of individuals and groups in the areas and times in which they were produced. They show us, in other words, a great many persons, of all walks of life, who were in some way engaged with the religious and social world of 'Sufism;' Sufis were not all they were, as is clear from the occupations and other activities they engaged in, and thus 'Sufi' was not the only name they bore, but each of them represents a decision to seek a connection with a Sufi shaykh (or with Sufi literature, or with a Sufi family, or with a Sufi shrine, etc.), no doubt for multiple reasons, and to make that connection a part of personal and social identity.

We may rightly ask many questions, based on the hagiographical sources that 'reveal' them—however coded and formulaic those 'revelations' may be—about the individuals identified as Sufis, the various social groups to which they belonged, the ways their Sufi activities shaped or intertwined with or 'sacralized' their other activities, their shifting connections during the course of their lives, their level of understanding of 'Sufi teaching' and the extent of their engagement in Sufi rites, and so forth; but we may not simply dismiss the hagiographical sources that mention them as irrelevant to our understanding of Central Asian life from the 16th through the 19th century, or, more to the point, as irrelevant to our understanding of contemporary Central Asians who are just a few generations removed from the subjects of some of those sources, their not-so-distant ancestors.

If a 16th-century work, that is, tells us of devotees of a particular shaykh from among the nomadic Türkmens or among villagers from the mountains near Ḥiṣār or among the urban elite of Samarqand, or if a 17th-century source tells us of *khalīfa*s of another shaykh among the Qazaqs or from towns of Miyānkāl, we are driven to ask what those relationships meant in terms of those individuals' lives (including the motivations behind establishing and maintaining them, and their impact in those individuals' own social circles), and what they meant in terms of knitting together diverse groups into new sorts of communities. Similarly, if a 19th-century hagiography tells us of disciples and successors of a Naqshbandī-Mujaddidī shaykh originating not only among the *'ulamā* of Bukhara or Khoqand, but among the Qïpchāq tribal groups of the Farghana valley, we must rightly consider what those affiliations might tell us about Qïpchāq life in that era, and about the consequences of a new kind of Sufi community that drew together Bukharans and semi-nomadic Qïpchāqs. We might begin by asking why a Qïpchāq 'tribesman' might have established such a bond (continuing traditional patterns of hereditary attachments, seeking a new network of social connections as tribal bonds frayed, enhancing access to urban markets, actualizing moral frameworks in a turbulent world, drawing closer to God, or a host of other reasons), but we must also consider the implications of the moments of encounter between our Qïpchāq and our Bukharan scholar/Sufi. We will also need to reflect on how those relationships might have set apart both the Qïpchāq and the Bukharan from others who maintained attachments to hereditary 'Sufi families' with different initiatic affiliations.

In any case, it is not only hagiographical works, but the wider world of 'Sufi literature' noted above, that might help us answer these questions; at the same time, we must recognize that the hagiographical sources that name our Qïpchāq and Bukharan devotees may give us only a name and a brief social descriptor, offering little specific help with those broader questions. Yet what must be underscored is that even by simply naming and identifying such individuals, the hagiographical sources demand that we pose such questions, and compelling us to ask them is in itself a key contribution of these works, and of that hagiographical corpus as a whole; knowing, for instance, that they at least paint a picture of persons from such diverse social groups being connected with a particular Sufi shaykh, we cannot *not* ask the implications of this information, however limited it may seem. And in asking those questions, we may even draw insights into the broader social and religious identities of the descendants of both the Qïpchāq and the Bukharan, who now call themselves Uzbeks, or at least learn to ask better questions about them (better, that is, than the questions posed by Sovietological 'nationalities' studies).

Indeed, we should recognize that learning to ask such questions about such individuals' lives in the 16th or 19th century, on the basis of the hagiographical sources we must interrogate in order to learn about 'Sufi history' in those times, may well help us to ask more fruitful questions about the here and now—questions that are better-informed, for being more deeply rooted in the kinds of patterns illuminated by such sources, and are more likely to make sense of 'modern' religious life as well. We go astray, to be sure, in assuming that hagiographical works and narratives of the sort we rely on to understand Sufi history through the 16th–19th centuries are entirely a thing of the past, but even those that are squarely rooted in, and focused on, earlier times command our attention for the present as well, insofar as they alone can acquaint us with the full range of social frameworks, conceptual encodings, and religious idioms comprising the 'language' of Sufism through the Soviet and post-Soviet eras.[58]

58 It should be stressed, indeed, that in addition to serving as the essential sources needed to understand the history of Sufi communities in Central Asia prior to the Tsarist and Soviet eras (and in addition to providing the stylistic and rhetorical foundations for hagiographical works that continued to be produced through those eras), hagiographical literature from the period discussed here is filled with religious narratives that have remained 'alive' through the Soviet and post-Soviet periods, chiefly in two ways. In some cases, hagiographical narratives recorded in these works stand as early versions of stories circulated in oral tradition well into the Soviet era and beyond, with versions recorded by Tsarist- and

Asking such questions, ultimately, is the way to connect the historical with the contemporary, and the failings of Sovietology should remind us that this process is best begun from the historical side; the responsibility of those moving from that historical side, however, and framing questions on the basis of what we learn from sources of various periods, is to not lose sight of the often uneasy relationship between names and realities—that is, between the names our sources deploy, and the social realities we seek, not entirely in vain, behind those names.

Bibliography

Akiner, Shirin. "The Contestation of Islam in post-Soviet Central Asia: A Nascent Security Threat." In *The Middle East's Relations with Asia and Russia*, ed. Hannah Carter and Anoushiravan Ehteshami (London: RoutledgeCurzon, 2004), 75–102.

Algar, Hamid. "Shaykh Zaynullah Rasulev: The Last Great Naqshbandi Shaykh of the Volga-Urals Region." In *Muslims in Central Asia: Expressions of Identity and Change*, ed. Jo-Ann Gross (Durham, North Carolina: Duke University Press, 1992), 112–133.

[ʿĀlim Shaykh ʿAlīyābādī]. Muḥammad ʿĀlim Ṣiddīqī. *Lamaḥāt min nafaḥāt al-quds*. Facs. ed. Muḥammad Naẕīr Rānjhā. Islamabad: Markaz-i Taḥqīqāt-i Fārsī-yi Īrān va Pākistān, 1406/1986.

Anṣārī Haravī, ʿAbdullāh. *Ṭabaqāt al-ṣūfiyya*. Ed. Muḥammad Sarvar Mawlāʾī. Tehran: Intishārāt-i Tūs, 1362/1983.

Babadjanov, B. "La naqshbandiyya sous les premiers Sheybanides." *Cahiers d'Asie centrale*, 3–4 (1997 = *L'Héritage timouride: Iran—Asie centrale—Inde, XVᵉ–XVIIIᵉ siècles*), 69–90.

Babadžanov, Baxtiyar M. "Dūkčī Īšān und der Aufstand von Andižan 1898." In *Muslim Culture in Russia and Central Asia from the 18th to the Early 20th Centuries*, vol. 2:

Soviet-era ethnographers (see, for instance, the 'legends' recorded, though typically analyzed within the framework of religious 'survivals,' in G. P. Snesarev, *Khorezmskie legendy kak istochnik po istorii religioznykh kul'tov Srednei Azii* [Moscow: Nauka, 1983]). More broadly, such narratives serve as typological and functional models for a host of Soviet-era 'miracle stories,' whether accounts of saintly healings or the familiar genre of stories about retribution for slights to a saint; such tales, recounting, for instance, the injuries, or worse, that befell officials who bulldozed a shrine, are at once admonitory and, in the Soviet context, subtly subversive, and they continue to provide a narrative framework in which many Central Asians make sense out of their religious history through the 20th century and into the 21st (for examples of such narratives, see Ulan Bigozhin, "Shrine, State, and Sacred Lineage in Post-Soviet Kazakhstan," Ph.D. Dissertation, Indiana University, Department of Anthropology, 2017).

Inter-Regional and Inter-Ethnic Relations, ed. Anke von Kügelgen, Michael Kemper, and Allen J. Frank (Berlin: Klaus Schwarz Verlag, 1998), 167–191.

Babadžanov, Baxtiyor M. "On the History of the Naqšbandīya Muğaddidīya in Central Māwarā'annahr in the Late 18th and Early 19th Centuries." In *Muslim Culture in Russia and Central Asia from the 18th to the Early 20th Centuries*, ed. Michael Kemper, Anke von Kügelgen, and Dmitriy Yermakov (Berlin: Klaus Schwarz Verlag, 1996), 385–413.

Babadzhanov, B. "Babakhanovy." In *Islam na territorii byvshei Rossiiskoi imperii: Èntsiklopeicheskii slovar'*, ed. S. M. Prozorov, vyp. 4 (St. Petersburg: 'Vostochnaia literatura,' 2003), 12–14.

Babadzhanov, B. "Iasaviia i Nakshbandiia v Maverannakhre: iz istorii vzaimootnoshenii (ser. XV–XVI vv.)." In *Yäsaui Taghïlïmï* (Turkistan: "Mŭra" baspagerlĭk shaghïn käsĭpornï/Qoja Akhmet Yäsaui atïndaghï Khalïqaralïq Qazaq-Türĭk Universiteti, 1996), 75–96.

Babadzhanov, B. M., ed. and tr. *Manāqib-i Dūkchī Īshān: Anonim zhitiia Dūkchī Īshāna-predvoditelia Andizhanskogo vosstaniia 1898 goda*. Almaty: Daik-Press, 2004.

Babadzhanov, Bakhtiiar. "Mir-i Arab." In *Kul'tura kochevnikov na rubezhe vekov (XIX–XX, XX–XXI vv.): Problemy genezisa i transformatsii (Materialy mezhdunarodnoi konferentsii g. Almaty, 5–7 iiunia 1995 g.)* (Almaty: "Assotsiatsiia 'Rafakh,' Studiia 'Parallel'," Gosudarstvennyi muzei iskusstv im. A. Kasteeva, 1995), 88–102.

Babadzhanov, B. M., and S. A. Mukhammadaminov, eds. *Sobranie fetv po obosnovaniiu zikra dzhakhr i sama' (A Collection of Fatwas Legitimizing the Vocal Dhikr and Sama')*. Almaty: Daik-Press, 2009.

Babajanov, B. "Biographies of Makhdūm-i A'ẓam al-Kāsānī al-Dahbīdī, *Shaykh* of the Sixteenth-Century Naqshbandīya." *Manuscripta Orientalia*, 5/2 (1999), 3–8.

Babajanov, Bakhtiyar. "Le renouveau des communautés soufies en Ouzbékistan." *Cahiers d'Asie centrale*, 5–6 (1998 = *Boukhara-la-Noble*), 285–311.

Babajanov, Bakhtiyor. "Mawlānā Luṭfullāh Chūstī: An Outline of his Hagiography and Political Activity." *Zeitschrift der Deutschen Morgenländischen Gesellschaft*, 149/2 (1999), 245–270.

Babajanov, Bakhtyar, and Maria Szuppe. *Les inscriptions persanes de Chār Bakr, nécropole familiale des khwāja Jūybārī près de Boukhara*. London: School of Oriental and African Studies, 2002; Corpus Inscriptionum Iranicarum, Part IV, Persian Inscriptions down to the early Safavid Period; vol. XXXI: Uzbekistan.

Baran, Zeyno, ed. "Understanding Sufism and its Potential Role in US Policy." Washington, D.C.: The Nixon Center, 2004; *Nixon Center Conference Report*, March 2004.

Bennigsen, Alexandre. "Official Islam and Sufi Brotherhoods in the Soviet Union Today." In *Islam and Power*, ed. Alexander S. Cudsi and Ali E. Hillal Dessouki (Baltimore: The Johns Hopkins University Press, 1981), 95–106.

Bennigsen, Alexandre. "Sufism in the USSR: A Bibliography of Soviet Sources." *Central Asian Survey*, 2/4 (1983), 81–107.

Bennigsen, Alexandre, and Chantal Lemercier Quelquejay. *Islam in the Soviet Union*. New York: Praeger, 1967.

Bennigsen, Alexandre, and Chantal Lemercier-Quelquejay. "Muslim Religious Conservatism and Dissent in the USSR." *Religion in Communist Lands*, 6/3 (1978), 153–161.

Bennigsen, Alexandre, and S. Enders Wimbush. *Mystics and Commissars: Sufism in the Soviet Union*. Berkeley/Los Angeles: University of California Press, 1985.

Bigozhin, Ulan. "Shrine, State, and Sacred Lineage in Post-Soviet Kazakhstan." Ph.D. Dissertation, Indiana University, Department of Anthropology, 2017.

Bohr, Annette. "Turkmenistan: Power, Politics and Petro-Authoritarianism." London: Russia and Eurasia Programme of Chatham House/Royal Institute of International Affairs, 2016.

Brophy, David. "The Kings of Xinjiang: Muslim Elites and the Qing Empire." *Etudes orientales*, No. 25 (2008), 69–89.

Brophy, David. "The Oirat in Eastern Turkistan and the Rise of Āfāq Khwāja." *Archivum Eurasiae Medii Aevi*, 16 (2008–09), 5–28.

[Bukhārī, 'Abd al-Karīm]. *Histoire de l'Asie Centrale par Mir Abdoul Kerim Boukhary*. Ed. and tr. Charles Schefer. Paris: École des Langues Orientales Vivantes, 1876; repr. Amsterdam: Philo Press, 1970.

Capisani, Giampaolo R. *The Handbook of Central Asia*. London: I. B. Tauris, 2000.

Dagyeli, Jeanine Elif. "By Grace of Descent: A Conflict between an *Īšān* and Craftsmen over Donations." *Der Islam*, 88 (2012), 279–307.

Dağyeli, Jeanine Elif. *'Gott liebt das Handwerk:' Moral, Identität und religiöse Legitimierung in der mittelasiatischen Handwerks-risāla*. Wiesbaden: Reichert Verlag, 2011.

DeWeese, Devin. "The 'Competitors' of Isḥāq Khwāja in Eastern Turkistan: Hagiographies, Shrines, and Sufi Affiliations in the Late Sixteenth Century." In *Horizons of the World: Festschrift for Isenbike Togan/Hududü'l-Alem: İsenbike Togan'a Armağan*, ed. İlker Evrim Binbaş and Nurten Kılıç-Schubel (Istanbul: İthaki Press, 2011), 133–215.

DeWeese, Devin. "'Dis-ordering' Sufism in Early Modern Central Asia: Suggestions for Rethinking the Sources and Social Structures of Sufi History in the 18th and 19th Centuries." In *History and Culture of Central Asia/Istoriia i kul'tura Tsentral'noi Azii*, ed. Bakhtiyar Babadjanov and Kawahara Yayoi (Tokyo: The University of Tokyo, 2012), 259–279.

DeWeese, Devin. "The Eclipse of the Kubravīyah in Central Asia," *Iranian Studies*, 21/1–2 (1988), 45–83, reprinted (with typographical corrections) in DeWeese, *Studies on Sufism in Central Asia* (2012), No. I.

DeWeese, Devin. "Islam and the Legacy of Sovietology: A Review Essay on Yaacov Ro'i's *Islam in the Soviet Union*." *Journal of Islamic Studies* (Oxford), 13/3 (2002), 298–330.

DeWeese, Devin. "It was a Dark and Stagnant Night ('til the Jadids Brought the Light): Clichés, Biases, and False Dichotomies in the Intellectual History of Central Asia," for *Journal of the Economic and Social History of the Orient*, 59/1–2 (2016), 37–92.

DeWeese, Devin. "Kašmiri, Badr-al-Din." *Encyclopaedia Iranica*, vol. XVI, fascicle 1 (New York: Encyclopaedia Iranica Foundation, 2012), 80–83.

DeWeese, Devin. "A Neglected Source on Central Asian History: The 17th-Century Yasavī Hagiography *Manāqib al-akhyār*." In *Essays on Uzbek History, Culture, and Language*, ed. Denis Sinor and Bakhtiyar A. Nazarov (Bloomington: Research Institute for Inner Asian Studies, 1993; Indiana University Uralic and Altaic Series, Vol. 156), 38–50; reprinted in DeWeese, *Studies on Sufism in Central Asia* (2012), No. III.

DeWeese, Devin. "The Problem of the *Sirāj al-ṣāliḥīn*: Notes on Two Hagiographies by Badr al-Dīn Kashmīrī." In *Écrit et culture en Asie centrale et dans le monde turco-iranien, XIVe–XIXe siècles/Writing and Culture in Central Asia and the Turko-Iranian World, 14th–19th Centuries*, ed. Francis Richard and Maria Szuppe (Paris: Association pour l'Avancement des Études Iraniennes, 2009; *Studia Iranica*, Cahier 40), 43–92.

DeWeese, Devin. "Sacred History for a Central Asian Town: Saints, Shrines, and Legends of Origin in Histories of Sayrām, 18th–19th Centuries." In *Figures mythiques des mondes musulmans* (*Revue des mondes musulmans et de la Méditerranée*, 89-90), ed. Denise Aigle (Paris, 2000), 245–295.

DeWeese, Devin. "Shamanization in Central Asia." *Journal of the Economic and Social History of the Orient*, 57 (2014), 326–363.

DeWeese, Devin. *Studies on Sufism in Central Asia*. Farnham, Surrey: Ashgate, 2012; Variorum Collected Studies reprint series.

DeWeese, Devin. "Sufis as the *ʿUlamā* in 17th-Century Central Asia: ʿĀlim Shaykh of ʿAlīyābād and Mawlānā Muḥammad Sharīf of Bukhārā." In *Sufis and Mullahs: Sufis and their Opponents in the Persianate World*, ed. Reza Tabandeh and Leonard Lewisohn (Irvine, California: Jordan Center for Persian Studies, forthcoming).

DeWeese, Devin. "Survival Strategies: Reflections on the Notion of Religious 'Survivals' in Soviet Ethnographic Studies of Muslim Religious Life in Central Asia." In *Exploring the Edge of Empire: Soviet Era Anthropology in the Caucasus and Central Asia*, ed. Florian Mühlfried and Sergey Sokolovskiy (Münster: Lit Verlag, 2011; Halle Studies in the Anthropology of Eurasia, vol. 25), 35–58.

DeWeese, Devin. "An 'Uvaysī' Hagiography from Eastern Turkistān: The *Tadhkira* of Quṭb al-Dīn ʿIrāqī." *Etudes orientales: Revue culturelle semestrielle* (Paris), Nos. 27–28 (2016), 15–86.

DeWeese, Devin. "The Yasavī Order and Persian Hagiography in Seventeenth-Century Central Asia: ʿĀlim Shaykh of ʿAlīyābād and his *Lamaḥāt min nafaḥāt al-quds*." In *The Heritage of Sufism*, vol. III: *Late Classical Persianate Sufism (1501–1750), The Safavid and Mughal Period*, ed. Leonard Lewisohn and David Morgan (Oxford:

Oneworld Publications, 1999), 389–414; reprinted in DeWeese, *Studies on Sufism in Central Asia* (2012), No. IX.

Dreyfuss, Robert. *Devil's Game: How the United States Helped to Unleash Fundamentalist Islam*. New York: Metropolitan Books, 2005.

Dudoignon, Stephane A. "From Revival to Mutation: The Religious Personnel of Islam in Tajikistan, from de-Stalinization to Independence (1955–91)." *Central Asian Survey*, 30 (2011), 53–80.

Dzhuraeva, G. A. "Mir-i Arab i politicheskaia zhizn' v Bukhare v XVI veke." In *Dukhovenstvo i politicheskaia zhizn' na Blizhnem i Srednem Vostoke v periode feodalizma* (Bartol'dovskie chteniia, 1982) (Moscow: Nauka, GRVL, 1985), 74–79.

Eden, Jeff. "A Soviet Jihad against Hitler: Ishan Babakhan Calls Central Asian Muslims to War." *JESHO*, 59 (2016), 237–264.

Eden, Jeff. "A Sufi Saint in Sixteenth-Century East Turkistan: New Evidence Concerning the Life of Khwāja Isḥāq." *Journal of the Royal Asiatic Society*, 3rd series, 25/2 (2015), 229–245.

Eden, Jeff, tr. *The Life of Muḥammad Sharīf: A Central Asian Sufi Hagiography in Chaghatay*; with an appendix by David Brophy and Rian Thum. Vienna: Verlag der Österreichischen Akademie der Wissenschaften, 2015; Veröffentlichungen zur Iranistik, No. 78.

Ernst, Carl W. *The Shambhala Guide to Sufism*. Boston/London: Shambhala Publications, 1997.

Fettweis, Christopher J. "The Fergana Valley." In *Flashpoints in the War on Terrorism*, ed. Derek S. Reveron and Jeffrey Stevenson Murer (New York: Routledge, 2006), 117–134.

Fletcher, Joseph. "Confrontations between Muslim Missionaries and Nomad Unbelievers in the Late Sixteenth Century." In *Tractata Altaica: Denis Sinor sexagenario optime de rebus altaicis merito dedicata* (Wiesbaden: Harrassowitz, 1976), 167–174.

Fletcher, Joseph. "The Naqshbandiyya in Northwest China." In Fletcher, *Studies on Chinese and Islamic Inner Asia*, ed. Beatrice Forbes Manz (Aldershot, Hampshire: Variorum, 1995), No. XI (46 pp.).

Gross, Jo-Ann. "The Naqshbandīya Connection: From Central Asia to India and Back (16th–19th Centuries)." In *India and Central Asia: Commerce and Culture, 1500–1800*, ed. Scott C. Levi (New Delhi: Oxford University Press, 2007), 232–259.

Haarmann, Ulrich. "Staat und Religion in Transoxanien im frühen 16. Jahrhundert." *Zeitschrift der Deutschen Morgenländischen Gesellschaft*, 124 (1974), 332–369.

Hanks, Reuel R. "Islamization and Civil Society in Central Asia: Religion as Substrate in Conflict Management and Social Stability." In *Civil Society and Politics in Central Asia*, ed. Charles E. Ziegler (Lexington: The University Press of Kentucky, 2015), 59–79.

Hartmann, Martin. "Ein Heiligenstaat im Islam: das Ende der Čaghataiden und die Herrschaft der Choğas in Kašgarien." In Hartmann's *Der islamische Orient*, vol. I (Berlin: Wolf Peiser Verlag, 1905), pts. 6–10, 195–374.

Hazini. *Cevâhiru'l-ebrâr min emvâc-ı bihâr* (*Yesevî Menâkıbnamesi*). Ed. Cihan Okuyucu. Kayseri: Erciyes Üniversitesi, 1995.

Hazini. *Menba'u'l-ebhâr fî riyâzi'l-ebrâr*. Ed. Mehmet Mâhur Tulum. Istanbul: Mehmet Ölmez, 2009.

Hujvīrī, Abū'l-Ḥasan 'Alī b. 'Uthmān. *Kashf al-maḥjūb*. Ed. Maḥmūd 'Ābidī. Tehran: Surūsh, 1387/2008.

Hujvīrī, Abū'l-Ḥasan 'Alī b. 'Uthmān. *Kashf al-maḥjūb. The Kashf al-Mahjúb: The Oldest Persian Treatise on Sufiism by 'Alí b. 'Uthmán al-Jullábí al-Hujwírí*. Tr. Reynold A. Nicholson. London: Luzac and Company, 1936; E. J. W. Gibb Memorial Series, vol. XVII; repr. 1976.

Iudin, V. P. "Izvestiia 'Ziia al-kulub' Mukhammad Avaza o kazakhakh XVI veka." *Vestnik Akademii nauk Kazakhskoi SSR*, 1966, No. 5, 71–76.

al-Kalābādhī, Abū Bakr. *The Doctrine of the Ṣūfīs* (*Kitāb al-Ta'arruf li-madhhab ahl al-taṣawwuf*). Tr. A. J. Arberry. Cambridge: Cambridge University Press, 1935.

Kalinovsky, Artemy M. "Encouraging Resistance: Paul Henze, the Bennigsen School, and the Crisis of Détente." In *Reassesing Orientalism: Interlocking Orientologies during the Cold War*, ed. Michael Kemper and Artemy M. Kalinovsky (London/New York: Routledge, 2015), 211–232.

Kashmīrī, Badr al-Dīn Badrī. *Sirāj al-ṣāliḥīn*. Ed. Sayyid Sirāj al-Dīn. Islamabad: Markaz-i Taḥqīqāt-i Fārsī-i Īrān va Pākistān, 1376/1997.

Kawahara Yayoi. "On Private Archives Related to the Development of the Naqshbandīya-Mujaddidīya in the Ferghana Valley." In *History and Culture of Central Asia/Istoriia i kul'tura Tsentral'noi Azii*, ed. Bakhtiyar Babadjanov and Kawahara Yayoi (Tokyo: The University of Tokyo, 2012), 241–257.

Kehl-Bodrogi, Krisztina. *"Religion is Not So Strong Here:" Muslim Religious Life in Khorezm after Socialism*. Berlin: Lit Verlag, 2008; Halle Studies in the Anthropology of Eurasia, Vol. 18.

Kemper, Michael. "How to Build a Sufi Empire? The Strategies of the Daghestani Shaykh Said-Afandi." In *Islam v mul'tikul'turnom mire: Musul'manskie dvizheniia i mekhanizmy vosproizvodstva ideologii islama v sovremennom informatsionnom prostranstve* (Kazan, 2014), 222–232.

Khalid, Adeeb. *Islam after Communism: Religion and Politics in Central Asia*. Berkeley/Los Angeles/London: University of California Press, 2007.

Knysh, Alexander. "Sufism as an Explanatory Paradigm: The Issue of the Motivations of Sufi Resistance Movements in Western and Russian Scholarship." *Die Welt des Islams*, 42 (2002), 139–173.

Kratkii katalog sufiiskikh proizvedenii XVIII–XX vv. iz sobraniia Instituta Vostokovedeniia Akademiia Nauk Respubliki Uzbekistan im. al-Biruni. Ed. B. Babadzhanov, A. Kremer, and Iu. Paul'. Berlin: Das Arabische Buch, 2000.

von Kügelgen, Anke. "Die Entfaltung der Naqšbandīya Muǧaddidīya im mittleren Transoxanien vom 18. bis zum Beginn des 19. Jahrhunderts: Ein Stück Detektivarbeit." In *Muslim Culture in Russia and Central Asia from the 18th to the Early 20th Centuries*, vol. 2: *Inter-Regional and Inter-Ethnic Relations*, ed. Anke von Kügelgen, Michael Kemper, and Allen J. Frank (Berlin: Klaus Schwarz Verlag, 1998), 101–151.

LeGall, Dina. "Recent Thinking on Sufis and Saints in the Lives of Muslim Societies, Past and Present." *International Journal of Middle East Studies*, 42/4 (2010), 673–687.

Lemercier-Quelquejay, Chantal. "Sufi Brotherhoods in the USSR: A Historical Survey." *Central Asian Survey*, 2/4 (1983), 1–35.

Lipovsky, Igor. "The Awakening of Central Asian Islam." *Middle Eastern Studies*, 32/3 (July 1996), 1–21.

Louw, Maria Elisabeth. *Everyday Islam in Post-Soviet Central Asia*. London/New York: Routledge, 2007.

Melvin-Koushki, Matthew, and James Pickett. "Mobilizing Magic: Occultism in Central Asia and the Continuity of High Persianate Culture under Russian Rule." *Studia Islamica*, 111 (2016), 231–284.

[Muḥamad Ḥakīm]. Mukhammed Khakimkhan. *Muntakhab at-tavarikh*. Facs. ed. A. M. Mukhtarov, kn. 2. Dushanbe: Ilm, 1985.

Muḥammad Ṭālib b. Tāj al-Dīn Ḥasan Khwāja al-Ḥusaynī al-Ṣiddīqī. *Maṭlab al-ṭālibīn (matn-i 'ilmī-yi intiqādī)*. Ed. Ghulām Karīmī and Érkin Mir-kāmilūf [i.e., Ghulam Kärimiy and Erkin Mirkamilov]. (Tashkent: O'zbekiston Musulmonlari Idorasi, Movarounnahr Nashriyoti, 2012; Farhangistān-i 'Ulūm-i Jumhūrī-yi Uzbakistān/ Instītū-yi Sharqshunāsī be-nām-i Abū Rayḥān Bīrūnī).

Mukminova, R. G. "Dukhovenstvo i vakfy v Srednei Azii XVI veka." In *Dukhovenstvo i politicheskaia zhizn' na Blizhnem i Srednem Vostoke v periode feodalizma* (Bartol'-dovskie chteniia, 1982) (Moscow: Nauka, GRVL, 1985), 141–147.

O'Dell, Emily. "Subversives and Saints: Sufism and the State in Central Asia." In *Islam, Society, and Politics in Central Asia*, ed. Pauline Jones (Pittsburgh, Pennsylvania: University of Pittsburgh Press, 2017), 99–126, 303–306.

Olcott, Martha Brill. "Sufism in Central Asia: A Force for Moderation or a Cause of Politicization?" *Carnegie Papers, Russian and Eurasian Program*, No. 84, May 2007 (Washington, D.C.: Carnegie Endowment for International Peace, 2007).

Papas, Alexandre. *Soufisme et politique entre Chine, Tibet et Turkestan: Etude sur les khwajas naqshbandis du Turkestan oriental*. Paris: Librairie d'Amérique et d'Orient, Jean Maisonneuve successeur, 2005.

Privratsky, Bruce G. *Muslim Turkistan: Kazak Religion and Collective Memory*. Richmond, Surrey: Curzon Press, 2001.

Rasanayagam, Johan. *Islam in Post-Soviet Uzbekistan: The Morality of Experience*. Cambridge: Cambridge University Press, 2010.

Rashid, Ahmed. *The Resurgence of Central Asia: Islam or Nationalism?* London: Zed Books, 1994.

Rashid, Ahmed. *Jihad: The Rise of Militant Islam in Central Asia*. New Haven, Connecticut, and London: Yale University Press, 2002.

Ro'i, Yaacov. *Islam in the Soviet Union: From the Second World War to Gorbachev*. London: C. Hurst & Co., 2000.

Salakhetdinova, M. A. "Soobshcheniia o kirgizakh v 'Khidaiat-name' Mir Khal' ad-Dina." *Izvestiia Akademii nauk Kirgizskoi SSR, Seriia Obshchestvennykh nauk*, tom III, vyp. 2 (1961), 133–140.

Sawada Minoru. "Three Groups of *Tadhkira-i khwājagān*: Viewed from the Chapter on Khwāja Āfāq." In *Studies on Xinjiang Historical Sources in 17–20th Centuries*, ed. James A. Millward, Shinmen Yasushi, and Sugawara Jun (Tokyo: The Toyo Bunko, 2010; Toyo Bunko Research Library 12), 9–30.

Schimmel, Annemarie. "Some Notes on the Cultural Activities of the First Uzbek Rulers." *Journal of the Pakistan Historical Society*, 8 (1960), 149–166.

Schwarz, Florian. *'Unser Weg schliesst tausend Wege ein:' Derwische un Gesellschaft im islamischen Mittelasien im 16. Jahrhundert*. Berlin: Klaus Schwarz Verlag, 2000; Islamkundliche Untersuchungen, Bd. 226.

Schwarz, Florian. "Ohne Scheich kein Reich: Scheibaniden und Naqšbandīs in der Darstellung von Maḥmūd ibn Walī." In *Annäherung an das Fremde: XXVI. Deutscher Orientalistentag vom 25. bis 29.9.1995 in Leipzig, Vorträge*, ed. Holger Preissler and Heidi Stein (Stuttgart: Franz Steiner Verlag, 1998; *Zeitschrift der Deutschen Morgenländischen Gesellschaft*, Supplement XI), 259–267.

Semenov, A. A. "Unikal'nyi pamiatnik agiograficheskoi sredneaziatskoi literatury XVI v." *Izvestiia Uzbekistanskogo filiala AN SSSR*, 1940, No. 12, 54–62; 1941, No. 3, 37–48.

Shaw, Robert Barkley, and N. Elias, eds. "Epitome of the Memoirs of the Khojas." In *The History of the Khojas of Eastern-Turkistan, summarised from the Tazkira-i-Khwajagan of Muhammad Sadiq Kashghari* (Supplement to the *Journal of the Asiatic Society of Bengal*, 66/1 (1897), 31–63.

Snesarev, G. P. *Khorezmskie legendy kak istochnik po istorii religioznykh kul'tov Srednei Azii*. Moscow: Nauka, 1983.

al-Sulamī, Abū 'Abd al-Raḥmān. *Ṭabaqāt al-ṣūfiyya*. Ed. Nūr al-Dīn Sharība. Third printing, Cairo: Maktabat al-Khānajī, 1406/1986.

Tasar, Eren. *Soviet and Muslim: The Institutionalization of Islam in Central Asia, 1943–1991*. Oxford: Oxford University Press, 2017.

Thum, Rian. *The Sacred Routes of Uyghur History*. Cambridge, Massachusetts: Harvard University Press, 2014.

Togan, Isenbike. "Chinese Turkestan," v, "Under the Khojas." *Encyclopaedia Iranica*, v, 474–476.

Vorozheikina, Z. N. "Doislamskie verovaniia kirgizov v XVI v. (Po rukopisi 'Ziia al-kulub')." In *Voprosy filologii i istorii stran sovetskogo i zarubezhnogo Vostoka* (Moscow, 1961), 182–189.

Welsford, Thomas. *Four Types of Loyalty in Early Modern Central Asia: The Tūqāy-Tīmūrid Takeover of Greater Mā Warā al-Nahr, 1598–1605*. Leiden: Brill, 2013.

Zarcone, Thierry. "Bridging the Gap between Pre-Soviet and Post-Soviet Sufism in Ferghana Valley (Uzbekistan): The Naqshbandī Order between Tradition and Innovation." In *Popular Movements and Democratization in the Islamic World*, ed. Masatoshi Kisaichi (London/New York: Routledge, 2006), 43–56.

CHAPTER 2

Naqshband's Lives: Sufi Hagiography between Manuscripts and Genre

Shahzad Bashir

Our ability to discuss the premodern religious history of Muslim Central Asia rests heavily on evaluating Sufi works belonging to many different genres that can be accessed only in manuscript form to this day. Surveying the state of the field, one can find numerous evocations of problems occasioned by this fact, including regrets regarding difficulty of access (particularly during the Soviet period), inadequacies of cataloguing and preservation, lack of proper scholarly care in dealing with works to be found in different versions, and the impropriety of drawing general conclusions when, very likely, much relevant material has yet to be consulted. These are all legitimate issues that must be emphasized for further work in the field. In this essay, I wish to contribute to the discussion regarding sources by examining the intellectual basis on which we are conditioned to think about the relationship between manuscripts and the literary texts they contain in the process of carrying out historiographical reconstruction. While work on texts and contexts continues apace, it is advisable to scrutinize the framework for analyzing the material artifacts that provide us access to the relevant history. Such deliberation enhances the value of our accounts of the Central Asian past by maximizing what we can glean from the sources.

When considering genres such as Sufi hagiography, we must, I suggest, self-consciously parse the form of textuality available to us into elements that have gone into its production. Doing this reveals specific questions for evaluating the texts as repositories of information. To this end, the ensuing discussion offers an interpretive scheme in which I propose distinguishing between four elements, nested within each other, that correlate between surviving manuscripts and hagiography as a prominent literary genre in Central Asia in the approximate period 1300–1700 CE. For purposes of illustration, I concentrate on works on Bahāʾ al-Dīn Naqshband (d. 791/1389), the eponym of the Naqshbandī chain of Sufi authority who is buried near Bukhara. Naqshband is an especially useful case because of his vast and varied posthumous footprint as a putative progenitor of socioreligious identities in Central Asia and beyond.

 | DOI:10.1163/9789004373075_004

When it comes to materials pertaining to Naqshband and similar figures, I suggest that we differentiate between the following elements: 1. The physical manuscripts that are unique witnesses from the times and places where they were produced; 2. The texts that are contained within these manuscripts, representing literary production attributable to authors and compilers; 3. A narrative fund consisting of the common set of stories and morals that is shared across hagiographical texts; and 4. Hagiography as a genre that encompasses the relevant material as a distinctive literary phenomenon. These four elements represent a methodological categorization for analytical purposes: I intend them as elements of a map used to make sense of a territory rather than a claim about the territory itself. My approach, described in greater detail below, derives from my struggles to make sense of hagiographical narratives and what I have learned from the work of other scholars.[1]

In addition to the focus on texts, my effort in this essay hypothesizes the historical relationship between literary artifacts and the sociointellectual world constituted by Central Asian Sufi communities. The categories I have created represent, simultaneously, my understanding of the surviving written materials and how I imagine the societies that gave rise to them. My interpretive rubric is an attempt to get out of the problematic bind that has led many modern readers to regard hagiographical literature as a mass of useless miracle mongering rather than proper history. I try to understand how these texts were meaningful for their original creators and then translate my comprehension into terms that we today regard as plausible representations of the past. This approach sidesteps the question of truth and falsity as it pertains to hagiographical representations while also respecting the sources' integrity and seeing them as critical resources for reconstructing their historical circumstances and the social imagination from which they derive. Work along these lines is necessary for fuller and better utilizations of hagiographical sources, with due attention to the literary and social complexities inherent in the materials. Below, I first describe my proposed interpretive scheme in summary, followed by detailed discussions of the four elements I have delineated above. In the process, I pay special attention to sources for the life of Bahāʾ al-Dīn Naqshband.

1 My understanding has been shaped by the effort to write a cultural history of the Persianate Sufi world during the 14th and 15th centuries CE (see Shahzad Bashir, *Sufi Bodies: Religion and Society in Medieval Islam* [New York: Columbia University Press, 2011]). For an earlier reflection on the use of hagiographical narratives for writing history see Jürgen Paul, "Hagiographische Texte als historische Quelle," *Saeculum*, 41 (1990), 17–43.

An Interpretive Paradigm

The stakes involved in my presentation bear repeating the truism that premodern hagiographical materials were produced by and for audiences other than us. The manuscripts we can read, and the texts contained in them, are social products of an alien historical context, which, moreover, is accessible to us only through these texts themselves. The information that the original authors and readers of premodern hagiography regarded as valuable differs very substantially from what we expect as the outcome of modern historiography. This variance is my point of departure for developing a scheme that allows us to historicize the material while remaining cognizant of our own commitments.

The process of creating the stories we wish to tell must begin by noting the special characteristics of manuscripts, the material artifacts without which we have no access to the worlds in question. When it comes to Sufi hagiography, distilling the contents of manuscripts into "critical editions" prized by traditional philologists is not the optimal way to approach the material. The notion of a critical edition has come under significant questioning in various fields in recent scholarship, following epistemological investigations of the premises on which it is based. The critical edition reflects an ideology of textuality that presumes a certain form of literary subjectivity as a universal. That is, the possibility of an authoritative critical edition presupposes that a text is always a product of authorial intent that is universal across time and space and that can be recovered through modern philological work. However, in historical terms, the process through which texts come into being is manifestly not the same for all of them; scholars have become increasingly sensitive to the fact that the form and the content of a text are interdependent in ways that are specific to genres.[2] Traditional critical editions create and erase information in equal measure since they marginalize incidental details in order to generate an authoritative version of the text. It is then problematic to regard "editing" as a single and uniform process that is identically appropriate for all premodern textual cultures and must remain the standard for processing manuscripts as the basis of historiographical work. Rather, for arenas such as Sufi hagiography, the surviving manuscripts must be treated as elements of an irreducible archive.

Moving a step beyond basic materiality, the manuscripts available to us contain hagiographical texts. We need to distinguish between manuscripts

---

2 For a summary treatment of recent scholarly trends in discussions of texts and editing, see David C. Greetham, *Theories of the Text* (New York: Oxford University Press, 1999).

and texts because, in the case of extended hagiography produced in Central Asia, we possess multiple works dedicated to the same figures, each of which usually survives in multiple manuscripts. The manuscripts vary among themselves, and the texts contain a further level of mutual difference. While the texts are framed differently, they contain much of the same didactic and narrative material. Reading across all that is available regarding a single figure (such as Naqshband) can produce a sense of déjà vu. However, the seemingly small differences between the manuscripts and the texts are a critical resource for mapping the dynamic sociohistorical situation that led to the production of the material artifacts. Each text represents the work of an author or compiler, who composed it while being cognizant of related predecessor and contemporary texts. Variation between the texts that is revealed through comparative study indexes the moving social world that underlay the production of the surviving textual corpus.

Repetition is a prominent feature of hagiographical works across the literature. The stories and morals one encounters in accounts of Naqshband, for example, are common enough to be found in narratives about other masters not connected to Naqshband's lineage. This fact leads me to posit the notion of a narrative fund, shared across time and space, from which Sufi authors drew while producing hagiographical texts and manuscripts. In addition to accounting for commonality, conceptualizing the presence of a narrative fund allows accounting for perpetual transferences between orality and literacy that are key to this form of narration. Hagiographical texts contain persistent references to compilers hearing reports from others, who are, themselves, said to have heard particular acts or miracles. Yet the written reports we possess conform to literary conventions, and within them we hear of stories being told to individuals and groups in oral form. Imagining a narrative fund that remains alive through oral-written transfers shows Sufis forming a world interconnected through the process of drawing upon a common set of stories and socioreligious ideals.

Ultimately, the hagiographical material I am considering constitutes a genre defined by characteristics that differentiate it from other literary forms. The genre exists across the oral-written divide and allows narratives of vastly different scales. It is distinguished by a set of mostly unstated rules regarding organization, progression of themes, and investment in religious, social, and political ideals. Hagiography is a capacious genre, such that works belonging to it share family resemblances rather than having been dictated to a single definitive pattern. It is also rooted in specific forms of sociality pertaining to the way Sufis imagined the ideal relationship between an all-powerful master and an acquiescent disciple. The genre's form has an ideological purpose that individual authors match to the task of advancing the interests of specific individuals and communities. Moreover, in context, hagiography competes with other genres such as the political chronicle, where the contestation between literary forms reflects how different powerholders opposed or accommodated each other in societies such as those of premodern Central Asia.

The progression across the four elements of hagiography that I have laid out leads us from the least to the most abstract category. Each of the four aspects becomes more visible as one reads further into the surviving archive. The more manuscripts we have read, the more we become aware of the texts, the narrative fund, and the overall genre instantiated in each surviving witness. While we must proceed from manuscript to genre as modern readers, the process of the production of these texts can be envisioned as working in reverse. Seen from that side, the manuscript comes into being as the result of a sociointellectual process tethered to the lives of the human subjects who are represented in the sources. From that point of view, hagiography as a genre is in the foreground since it is the mold that conditions the way lived human experience glides into linguistic form. This transmission is subject to evolving social conventions that determine the genre's contours. While the genre is an abstraction, it gives rise to the narrative fund of actual stories circulating in oral and written forms. Hagiographical texts signify a further narrowing of the selection, indicating the way generic patterns and stock stories found in the narrative fund come to represent the lives of specific Sufis. The manuscript is, then, the final product of the whole process since it constitutes a witness produced in a specific time and place.

Dividing the reading and production processes into four parts and positing them as inversions in the way I have suggested provides a multifaceted rubric for expanding the possibilities for what we can deduce from hagiographical materials. One key to the inversion is the fact that the two processes have opposing conditions of possibility: for us, the manuscript is the basis on which we infer the texts, the narrative fund, and the genre, while it is the genre and narrative fund that led to the formulation of the text that became material in the form of manuscript at some point in the past. It needs emphasis that, whether we approach the material from the side of reading or production, the four categories are thoroughly interdependent and are nested within each other. In expanding on the four categories with some examples, I proceed in the order from manuscript to genre since this progression pertains to our concrete access to the material. My conceptualization of the way the material was produced is hypothetical, having been gleaned from the process of reading the sources.[3] With all this in mind, let us now turn to more detailed discussions of the four proposed elements.

Manuscripts

At the level of manuscripts, the study of Sufi communities in Central Asia faces many of the same issues as other fields that depend on the understanding of premodern literary cultures. In cases where there is a single manuscript of a work that survives, determining how it should be read can be difficult because of uniqueness of the style, calligraphic hand, etc., and lack of supporting context. But equally significant complications surface when we have multiple manuscripts of a single work. As in the case of other premodern codices, simply reproducing multiple manuscripts without any editorial intervention does not further the cause of making the work better known. Reading manuscripts requires significant investments of time and effort, which only a few scholars have the luxury to make.

Manuscripts contain visual markings and physical contextual clues such as marginalia, dating, stamps, histories of travel, etc., that are either lost in the process of preparing the text for printed presentation, or have to be represented through cumbersome apparatuses. Furthermore, the preparation of editions requires decisions pertaining to the form of the modern book that sit awkwardly with respect to the evidence. For example, in the case where we have multiple manuscripts for a work, the two extreme options are either to have the main text consist only of material common to all manuscripts (that is, only that which overlaps in all instantiations), or to include all non-repetitive material that can be culled from the various witnesses. In both cases, the result is a new text, which dissembles from the contents of any one of the individual source manuscripts. In practice, of course, editors walk a middle line between these extremes, with the ending edition being a new text that is a product of their judgments.[4]

3 In thinking about how best to approach Sufi hagiographical texts I have benefitted from the perspective of the movement known as "genetic criticism." Most work in this vein has been concerned with modern European literary manuscripts but I find that some of the analytical issues that have guided it can help for other fields as well. For details of the history and practice of genetic criticism see Jed Deppman, Daniel Ferrer, and Michael Groden, eds., *Genetic Criticism: Texts and Avant-textes* (Philadelphia: University of Pennsylvania Press, 2004).

4 Looking to the future, texts published in an electronic format may have the ability to collate and maintain information from multiple manuscripts in a single interface. It remains to be seen whether Central Asian Sufi hagiography is of enough interest to scholars to warrant the expenditure of financial and technological resources that would be necessary to bring such

A kind of summary point for thinking about the difference between a manuscript and a printed edition is that a manuscript is a "situated" object whereas a printed edition comes to exist in numerous identical copies available to multiple readers simultaneously. Every manuscript is a unique product of a time and a place, whose traces it alone carries. We may not be able to decipher or recover a manuscript's originating situation but we can be certain that it was critical for the artifact to have come into being. A printed book that contains an edition, in comparison, bears different sorts of markings that pertain to the sociology of modern scholarship and book production. Ultimately, then, producing editions never fully absolves us from the necessity of learning about and utilizing manuscripts in our work. Even when we do rely on modern editions, including those with excellent references for variants among witnesses, we can be certain that looking at the manuscripts would yield additional information.[5]

Issues in the consideration of a single item are exemplified in a manuscript of a work dedicated to Bahā' al-Dīn Naqshband that is currently held at the Khuda Bakhsh Oriental Public Library in Patna, India. The manuscript makes no mention of the author but gives the name of the work contained within it as *Anīs al-ṭālibīn va ʿuddat al-sālikīn*.[6] As discussed below in greater detail, this name occurs at the head of numerous texts containing Naqshband's saintly life, and we must regard the manuscript as part of a class of texts. What is most interesting about the manuscript is that it states that ʿAbd al-Raḥmān Jāmī (d. 1492), famous poet and author of numerous Sufi works, transcribed the text, completing the task of copying on Jumādā 1, 856 (May 20, 1452).[7] Paleographical analysis assigns high probability to the idea that the handwriting matches that of other texts bearing Jāmī's name as the copyist. While the text follows the general sequence of topics as found in other versions of works that bear the

---

texts into existence. For examples of what may be possible in this sphere, see Jonas Carlquist, "Medieval Manuscripts, Hypertext and Reading: Visions of Digital Editions," *Literary and Linguistic Computing*, 19 (2004), no. 1, 105–118.

5 For an extended discussion of the significance of the difference between manuscripts and printed texts in the vein I am highlighting see Bernard Cerquiglini, *In Praise of the Variant: A Critical History of Philology*, tr. Betsy Wing (Baltimore: The Johns Hopkins University Press, 1999).

6 Anonymous, *Anīs al-ṭālibīn va ʿuddat al-sālikīn*, Ms. Persian 1377, Khuda Bakhsh Oriental Public Library, Patna, India, 1b.

7 Ibid., colophon (folios are not numbered).

same name, the specific materials contained here represent a selection that the editor of the manuscript has designated an abridgement (*khulāṣa*).[8]

Although it is impossible to be definitive about the authenticity of the attribution to Jāmī, this codex is nevertheless useful for the sake of illustrating the historiographical value of a manuscript. The most interesting aspect in this instance, however, is what the manuscript may convey about Jāmī rather than Naqshband, the work's ostensible subject. The date on the manuscript corresponds closely to the time at which Jāmī is thought to have joined a Naqshbandī circle in Herat, affiliating himself with Sufis among the scholarly classes.[9] The text contained in the manuscript matches what scholars have referred to as the shorter redaction of the work *Anīs al-ṭālibīn va ʿuddat al-sālikīn*.[10] The possibility that the attribution to Jāmī is authentic is corroborated by the fact that two other manuscripts of this redaction of *Anīs al-ṭālibīn*, now in Tashkent and St. Petersburg respectively, bear a genetic relationship to the text copied by Jāmī.[11]

In addition to the date, the contents of this version of the *Anīs al-ṭālibīn* provide contextual support for Jāmī having been the redactor.[12] For instance,

8 For details of these issues see the editor's introduction in ʿAbd al-Raḥmān Jāmī, *Khulāṣa-yi anīs al-ṭālibīn*, ed. Muḥammad Ẕākir Ḥusayn (Patna: Khuda Bakhsh Library, 1994), vii–xi.

9 See Hamid Algar, "Jāmī ii. and Sufism," *Encylopaedia Iranica*, q.v.; Ertuğrul Ökten, "Jāmī (817–898/1414–1492): His Biography and Intellectual Influence in Herat," Ph.D. dissertation, University of Chicago, 2007, 75–78. The original sources do not provide an exact date for Jāmī's affiliation to the Naqshbandiyya. Its placement in the early 1450s is a matter of reconstruction by modern scholars.

10 See Alexey Khismatulin, "Jāmī's Statement on the Authorship of the *Anīs al-ṭālibīn*," in *Jāmī and the Intellectual History of the Muslim World: The Trans-Regional Reception of ʿAbd al-Raḥmān Jāmī's Works, c. 9th/15th–14th/20th*, edited by Thibaut d'Hubert and Alexandre Papas (Leiden: Brill, forthcoming). I am grateful to Dr. Khismatulin for advance access to this work.

11 For the manuscript now in Tashkent see Devin DeWeese, "The Legitimation of Bahaʾ ad-Din Naqshband," *Asiatische Studien/Études Asiatiques* 60, no. 2 (2006), 274 (note 25). The manuscript in St. Petersburg is discussed in detail in Khismatulin, "Jāmī's Statement on the Authorship of the *Anīs al-ṭālibīn*," forthcoming.

12 Khismatulin's detailed consideration of manuscripts of this work differs from my interpretation on this score. He argues that the Patna manuscript is a kind of rough draft made by Jāmī early in life while the St. Petersburg manuscript, a fuller and correctly arranged version of the text, reveals that this work as well as the longer version of *Anīs al-ṭālibīn* were composed by Naqshband's disciple and famous author Khwāja Muḥammad Pārsā. He is said to have done so on the instigation of ʿAlā al-Dīn ʿAṭṭār (d. 1400), Naqshband's successor, who exercised authority over Pārsā after Naqshband's death. While a full

this rendering of Naqshband's life is a considerably more "rationalized" text than the longer versions; it would likely have appealed more to someone with a scholarly background. Its presentation of encounters between Naqshband and his associates has the tendency to remove incidental details and to concentrate on the point or moral of the story. Similarly, the arrangement of stories reflects choices of members of the scholarly class. In all redactions of *Anīs al-ṭālibīn*, the fourth section is dedicated to Naqshband's charismatic acts (*karāmāt*) and circumstances and effects (*aḥvāl va āsār*) associated with his life. In the shorter redaction, possibly copied by Jāmī and others, this section begins by noting the time when none of the scholars (*ʿulamā*) of Bukhara had attached themselves to Naqshband. One day, Naqshband exchanged pleasantries with a scholar named Ḥusām al-Dīn Khwāja Yūsuf (d. 768/1366–67) and his entourage in the street and later told his disciples that this man would be the first member of the scholarly class to attach himself to Naqshband's community.[13] The "miracle" then was that this is exactly what came to pass. In the published longer work also known as the *Anīs al-ṭālibīn*, which is based on comparing fourteen manuscripts, the fourth section begins with a story about Naqshband's miraculous knowledge about a disciple's movement, and the account of his encounter with Ḥusām al-Dīn occurs considerably later in the section.[14]

The variability between the contents and placements of stories relating to Naqshband in different hagiographical compilations is part of a general complex that I will discuss in the section on texts below. My exploration of specific details of the manuscript attributed to Jāmī's hand is admittedly a bare beginning of a worthwhile examination. However, my point is to illustrate why the "situatedness" of manuscripts is a matter of historiographical interest. If we

discussion of this argument is not germane to the topic of the present essay, I hesitate to concur because it requires us to presume many things about Jāmī's attitudes and scholarly practices, as well as the relationship between him and Pārsā and ʿAṭṭār. We generally have scant evidence for such matters concerning Sufi groups such as the early Naqshbandīs. My preference, then, is to take Khismatulin's detailed philological discussion as further evidence for the complicated relationship between manuscripts and texts when it comes to the hagiographical corpus connected to Naqshband (Khismatulin, "Jāmī's Statement on the Authorship of the *Anīs al-ṭālibīn*," forthcoming).

13 Jāmī, *Khulāṣa-yi anīs al-ṭālibīn*, 22–23; Khwāja Jalāl al-Dīn Muḥammad, *Anīs al-ṭālibīn va ʿuddat al-sālikīn*, Ms. e. 37, Bodleian Library, Oxford, 85b–86a. Khismatulin identifies this scholar as Khwājā Pārsā's paternal uncle, which is part of his argument that Pārsā was the text's author (Khismatulin, "Jāmī's Statement on the Authorship of the *Anīs al-ṭālibīn*," forthcoming).

14 Ṣalāḥ b. Mubārak Bukhārī, *Anīs al-ṭālibīn va ʿuddat al-sālikīn*, ed. Khalīl Ibrāhīm Ṣārīoghlū (Tehran: Kayhān, 1992), 162, 183–84.

take the scribal attribution seriously, it provides an important detail about Jāmī that corresponds to what we know from other sources about a critical juncture in his life. Expanding from this, the copying of a hagiography by someone like Jāmī may indicate that the reproduction of such texts was a pious exercise through which new initiates affirmed the group's understanding of its past. If we doubt the attribution of the manuscript to Jāmī, we arrive at the possibility of forgery and other equally interesting questions about the milieu in which the manuscript was produced. What circumstances may have led an author to sign the manuscript with Jāmī's name rather than his own? Undertaken in a comprehensive manner along these lines, the examination of incidental details in a significant number of hagiographical manuscripts adds to our understanding of Central Asian Sufi communities.

Texts

As the discussion so far indicates, the availability of multiple accounts of a single figure is a characteristic of Central Asian hagiography that is a major resource for understanding Sufi communities. Multiple versions of the life of a single figure raise evaluative challenges that have as much to do with assessing the positions of compilers and scribes as those of the saintly subjects. A prominent issue in this regard is the way specific texts are framed, including matters such as authorial intent, the relationship between the author and the subject(s), information regarding the text's sponsorship (that is, if the author claims to be writing based on someone's request), and the information we gather by comparing texts to note inclusions and exclusions. Central Asian texts of this nature include those dedicated to such major figures as Bahāʾ al-Dīn Naqshband, Sayyid ʿAlī Hamadānī (d. 1385),[15] Shāh Niʿmatullāh Valī (d. 1431),[16] Sayyid Muḥammad Nūrbakhsh (d. 1464),[17] Khwāja ʿUbaydullāh

15 See Devin DeWeese, "Sayyid ʿAli Hamadani and Kubrawi Hagiographical Traditions," in *Studies on Sufism in Central Asia* (Burlington, Vermont: Variorum, 2012).

16 See Jean Aubin, ed. *Matériaux pour la biographie de Shâh Niʿmatullâh Walí Kermânî* (Tehran: Institut Français d'Iranologie de Téhéran, 1956).

17 See Shahzad Bashir, *Messianic Hopes and Mystical Visions: The Nūrbakhshīya Between Medieval and Modern Islam* (Columbia: University of South Carolina Press, 2003).

Aḥrār (d. 1490),[18] Ḥusayn Khwārazmī (d. 1551),[19] Makhdūm-i Aʿẓam Kāsānī Dahbīdī (d. 1542),[20] and Khwāja Muḥammad Islām Jūybārī (d. 1563) and his influential descendants.[21]

To focus on Naqshband again, we can divide hagiographical notices on him into three categories that project different overall views of his life despite having much in common.[22] The categories are: 1. Works by disciples who were Naqshband's companions; 2. Extended collections of hagiographical stories produced in the first few generations after Naqshband's death; and 3. Subsidiary notices in later works by Naqshbandī authors as well as others who comment on Naqshband's life while pursuing other matters as their main intent.

The first category includes works such as Yaʿqūb Charkhī's *Kitāb-i maqāmāt va silsila-yi Naqshbandī*, and Khwāja Muḥammad Pārsā's *Risāla-yi qudsiyya*. In Charkhī's work, the figures of Naqshband and the author are inextricably interlaced and the narrative attempts to convey a sense for the master's charisma. Charkhī writes that he began to serve Naqshband after receiving an indication from God (*qabūl-i ilāhī*) while he was near the shrine of Sayf al-Dīn Bākharzī in Bukhara. Upon approaching, he found out that the master welcomed him because of his knowledge of the divine gift he had received. Subsequently, Charkhī was asked to undertake travel to spread the knowledge he had acquired. When he received the news of Naqshband's death while in Kīsh, he

18 See ʿĀrif Nawshāhī, ed., *Aḥvāl va sukhanān-i Khwāja ʿUbaydullāh Aḥrār* (Tehran: Markaz-i Nashr-i Dānishgāhī, 2001); Jo-Ann Gross, "Khoja Ahrar: A Study of the Perceptions of Religious Power and Prestige in the Late Timurid Period," Ph.D. dissertation, New York University, 1982.

19 See Devin DeWeese, "The Eclipse of the Kubravīyah in Central Asia," *Studies on Sufism in Central Asia* (Burlington, Vermont: Variorum, 2012), 25–34.

20 See Victoria R. Gardner, "The Written Representations of a Central Asian Sufi Shaykh: Aḥmad ibn Mawlānā Jalāl al-Dīn Khwājagī Kāsānī 'Makhdūm-i Aʿẓam' (d. 1542)," Ph.D. dissertation, University of Michigan, 2006 and Bakhtiyar Babadjanov, "Biographies of Makhdūm-i Aʿẓam al-Kāsānī al-Dahbīdī, Shaykh of the Sixteenth-century Naqshbandīya," *Manuscripta Orientalia* 5/2 (1999), 3–8.

21 See Florian Schwarz, *"Unser Weg schließt tausend Wege ein": Derwische und Gesellschaft im islamischen Mittelasien im 16. Jahrhundert* (Berlin: Klaus Schwarz Verlag, 2000). This work contains discussions of numerous masters and families.

22 For detailed considerations of the narratives and their underpinnings see DeWeese, "The Legitimation of Baha' ad-Din Naqshband" and Jürgen Paul, *Doctrine and Organization: The Khwajagan/Naqshbandiya in the First Generation after Baha'uddin* (Berlin: Das Arabische Buch, 1998).

became apprehensive that this would leave him bereft of direct instruction. But Naqshband then began to appear in his dreams to guide him.[23]

Cumulatively, Charkhī's work is a Sufi doctrinal tract concerned with ablutions, the performance of ritual prayer and *ẕikr*, and the general properties associated with Sufi saints (*awliyāʾ*). Naqshband occurs in the initial framing of the narrative and then at various points as an authoritative voice pronouncing on various matters. The work concentrates on providing a sense for the bond between Naqshband and his disciples rather than describing the circumstances of his life. A similar tendency is noticeable in the *Risāla-yi qudsiyya*, attributed to Khwāja Muḥammad Pārsā (d. 1420), another direct disciple. Pārsā's fame stems from his extensive literary output that evinces great knowledge of Islamic literature, including works by Sufis. This work does not contain a description of the personal relationship between the author and Naqshband; instead, Pārsā states at the very beginning that: "for the people of spiritual sight (*ahl-i baṣīrat*), the certitude that comes from ruminating on the discourse of this group [i.e. Sufis] is stronger and superior to the certitude that comes from seeing miraculous events (*khavāriq-i ʿādāt*)."[24] The author then follows this directive to the effect that the work consists of religious teachings coming from the mouths of Naqshband and others. Between Charkhī and Pārsā, we get the sense that preserving Naqshband's teachings, rather than giving a verbal portrayal of his physical presence in front of disciples, was the most pressing concern for his immediate disciples.

The second category of texts concerning Naqshband are collections with emphasis on stories of Naqshband's progress on the Sufi path, his becoming a great figure, and his interactions with a myriad of disciples. The most commonly found text of this type is the *Anīs al-ṭālibīn va ʿuddat al-sālikīn*, which exists in two redactions as I have described above. In the longer version, the author identifies himself as Ṣalāḥ b. Mubārak al-Bukhārī, who arrived in the service of Naqshband's disciple ʿAlā al-Dīn ʿAṭṭār (d. 1400) in the year 785/1383–84. He came to know Naqshband through the intermediacy of ʿAṭṭār, who asked him to collect materials about Naqshband after the great master had passed away in 1389. According to Bukhārī, Naqshband had interdicted the writing

23 Yaʿqūb Charkhī, *Kitāb-i maqāmāt va silsila-yi Naqshbandī*, Ms. e. 37, Bodleian Library, Oxford, 146b–147b. A version of this work has been published together with an Urdu translation: Yaʿqūb Charkhī, *Risāla-yi unsiyya*, ed. and tr. Muḥammad Naẕīr Rānjhā (Dera Ismail Khan, Pakistan: Maktaba Sirājiyya Khānaqāh-i Aḥmadiyya Saʿīdiyya, 1983).

24 Khwāja Muḥammad Pārsā, *Risāla-yi qudsiyya* (*Kalimāt-i Bahāʾ al-Dīn Naqshband*), ed. Aḥmad Ṭāhirī ʿIrāqī (Tehran: Kitābkhāna-yi Ṭahūrī, 1975), 3.

down of his life while he had been alive.[25] The shorter redaction of this work differs on the following points: it does not mention an author, presents the stories in a different arrangement, and omits some stories present in the longer version while also containing others that are not found in the work attributed to Bukhārī.[26]

As Devin DeWeese and Jürgen Paul have shown, the two redactions of *Anīs al-ṭālibīn* must be placed in the same textual field as two other surviving works that share much in common with them.[27] These are: the *Risāla-yi Bahā'iyya* attributed to Abū'l-Qāsim b. Muḥammad b. Mas'ūd Bukhārī, and the anonymous *Khavāriq-i Naqshband dar 'ilm-i sayr*.[28] When they speak in their own voices, the narrators of these compilations describe themselves as fulfilling requests made by Naqshband's disciples. Their choices to include or exclude materials, as well as the lessons they say must be learned from Naqshband's life, are thus tied to the interests of Naqshband's successors. These compilations are also the most extensive works on Naqshband's life. Their comprehensive approach, seemingly aimed at preserving all relevant details, is logical for those whose spiritual as well as sociopolitical impulses were geared toward a kind of "canonization" of the illustrious friend of God. These narratives have principally furnished the picture of Naqshband's life that we find in later pre-modern Sufi sources as well as in modern reconstructions.[29]

---

25 Bukhārī, *Anīs al-ṭālibīn va 'uddat al-sālikīn*, 66–67.

26 Khismatulin argues that "Ṣalāḥ b. Mubārak" is a pseudonym and that Khwāja Pārsā was the author of the *Risāla-yi qudsiyya* as well as both texts known as *Anīs al-ṭālibīn* (Khismatulin, "Jāmī's Statement on the Authorship of the *Anīs al-ṭālibīn*," forthcoming). Besides the issue that the evidence seems circumstantial rather than definitive, I am unsure about the analytical significance of regarding Pārsā as the author. Ultimately, the texts are quite different and indicate multiple verbal portraits of Naqshband irrespective of who created them. The textual diversity seems more consequential than purported authorship.

27 Cf. DeWeese, "The Legitimation of Baha' ad-Din Naqshband"; Paul, *Doctrine and Organization*.

28 Abū'l-Qāsim b. Muḥammad b. Mas'ūd Bukhārī, *Risāla-yi Bahā'iyya fī maqāmāt-i Hażrat Khwāja Bahā' al-Dīn*, Ms. 287.7/5 (Fārsī Taṣavvuf), Subhanullah Collection, Maulana Azad Library, Aligarh Muslim University, Aligarh, India, 1b–84a; Anonymous, *Khavāriq-i Naqshband dar 'ilm-i sayr*, Persian Ms. 844, Salar Jung Estate Library (Oriental Collection), Hyderabad, India, 1b–64b.

29 Two important works in this regard are 'Abd al-Raḥmān Jāmī, *Nafaḥāt al-uns min ḥażarāt al-quds*, ed. Maḥmūd 'Ābidī (Tehran: Intishārāt-i Iṭṭilā'āt, 1997), 389–394, and Fakhr al-Dīn 'Alī b. Ḥusayn Kāshifī Ṣafī, *Rashaḥāt-i 'ayn al-ḥayāt*, ed. 'Alī Aṣghar Mu'īniyān, 2 vols. (Tehran: Majmū'a-yi Mutūn-i Qadīm va Aḥvāl-i Dānishmandān va 'Irfānān, 1977), 1:95–101. To date, the most extensive account of Naqshband's life, written in a devotional

The third and last category of texts that deserves mention in this context includes works that are not devoted to Naqshband. Rather, they comment on him because of a relationship between him and other individuals who are the main subjects of the works. Perhaps the most important such work is Shihāb al-Dīn's *Maqāmāt-i Amīr Kulāl*, anchored in narratives about Sayyid Amīr Kulāl (d. 1370–71), who acted as Naqshband's master and whose legacy gave rise to a familial tradition that was a rival to Naqshband's disciples in Central Asia. This work was written by a great-grandson of Amīr Kulāl, likely contemporaneously with the production of works such as *Anīs al-ṭālibīn*. It presents Naqshband as a petulant and haughty disciple to Amīr Kulāl, reflecting both a probable constrained relationship between the master and disciple, and the rivalry between Amīr Kulāl's descendants and the Naqshbandīs as a group rapidly gaining influence in Central Asia during the 15th century.

Shihāb al-Dīn states that once while in Amīr Kulāl's company, Naqshband thought to himself that perhaps he was the closest disciple to the master. Just then Amīr Kulāl was presented a sheep and Naqshband reflected to himself that it would have been advantageous if another disciple, named Mawlānā ʿĀrif, had been present to prepare a meal from the animal. Intuiting the thought based on his insight into disciples' minds, Amīr Kulāl then asked Naqshband to call ʿĀrif to come to do the job. Naqshband objected that there was no way ʿĀrif could hear a call since he was in a village at quite some distance. When Amīr Kulāl insisted, Naqshband went outside and called the man three times. He appeared on the scene immediately, leading Amīr Kulāl to admonish Naqshband that the other man was closer to him and that it was better for him to concentrate on his own work and actions rather than setting up comparisons.[30] Similarly, in another story, Amīr Kulāl's foot once landed on Naqshband's head. This made the master proclaim that this meant that the rest of the world would come under Naqshband's feet. The narrator then interjects that from that moment on, Naqshband's star began to rise in the world.[31] In this instance, Naqshband's success is made contingent on Amīr Kulāl's approval, delivered in a way that demeans the disciple.

The three categories of texts, each with multiple manuscripts, that I have illustrated through reference to the life of Naqshband highlight the complexities involved in assessing materials associated with major Central Asian Sufi

---

rather than critical spirit, is Necdet Tosun, *Bahâeddin Nakşbend: Hayatı, Görüşleri, Tarîkatı* (Istanbul: İnsan Yayınları, 2002).

30 Shihāb al-Dīn, *Maqāmāt-i Amīr Kulāl*, Ms. C1562, Russian Academy of Sciences, Saint-Petersburg Branch, Institute of Oriental Studies, 25a–b.

31 Ibid., 33b.

figures. The various sources share much in common, and what appears to us today as repetition symptomizes continuities among the various works. However, authors also deploy the same morals and stories for divergent ends, allowing us to notice matters such as rivalries and shifts in ideologies and practices. In this material as elsewhere, the sources' contents provide information not simply through the plain linguistic meaning but via placement, inclusion and exclusion, and explicit and implicit ways in which the narrative leads from a story to its purported lesson. The multiplicity of categories and contents of works, together with the fact that these works exist in many manuscripts that differ from each other, make hagiographical literature a rich and intricate source base for writing Central Asian history.

Narrative Fund

To a large degree, the notion of a narrative fund is prefigured in what I have already said about the issue of internal variation between manuscripts and texts. At the base level, such a fund includes the collectivity of all that we can substantiate from different sources on Sufi figures and groups active in Central Asia. But it is important to theorize the presence of a narrative fund separately from manuscripts and texts for two interrelated reasons. First, the transition between the narrative fund and texts encompasses the very significant issue of transfers between oral narratives and written texts. And second, the narrative fund idea helps account for hagiography's nature as a highly stylized recounting of the past that conveys universal claims through the citation of particularities.

Hagiographical texts consist mainly of vignettes that narrate interactions between a saintly figure and a person or a group who receives teachings, censure, material rewards, or punishment. Whether represented as being customary or highly dramatic, these exchanges are narrated in the voices of individuals who purport to have observed the interactions in person. As in the case of *ḥadīth*, oral transmission is a central component in hagiographical stories' claims of truth and authenticity. What the reader experiences in these texts is not a seamless narrative of the life of a friend of God, but constant interjection of situational data, such as names of people and places and the circumstances of a given incident. The result is a text that comes across as trying to retain its oral antecedent as much as possible.

The privileging of the oral is central to hagiography and reflects the social context from which the texts originate, which they are attempting to represent, and in which they were utilized. The hagiographer's purpose is to take the reader to the saintly person's physical presence in specific moments in time. Hagiographical texts are not random conglomerations of vignettes but instantiations of a sophisticated form that aims to produce intimacy between the reader and the subject. They attempt to recreate, through text, the ideal relationship between master and disciple that is supposed to be based on love and the acknowledgement of total dependence in exchange for protection and spiritual as well as worldly provision. The preservation of the oral context within the literary form also renders the narratives readily consumable in later situations of personal contact. In effect, the preservation of the oral frame within written text allows it to be carried back seamlessly into live performance.

While a hagiographical text presents incidents in the life of a master as unique occurrences, reading multiple texts we see constant repetition of patterns. In fact, reading across the genre can be a tedious affair since one sees the same stories and lessons again and again. Although the material is repeated among texts, lineage groups, and large spans of time, it is domesticated to local contexts in each immediate case through citing names of witnesses and places. The evocation of orality in hagiography is thus not something to be taken on face value alone. Orality is a literary trope that allows hagiographical narrators to conjoin universal themes in the representation of saintly figures to the particularities of the lives of their immediate subjects. A given narrative's efficacy eventually depends on the hagiographer's skill in maintaining a balance between themes from the narrative fund on the one hand and quotidian details of a human life observed in the flesh on the other. Overemphasis on either side can dissipate the narrative's purpose since, on one side, a figure simply re-performing the acts of earlier exemplars begins to appear like an automaton, and on the other, a narrative about a human life pure and simple fails to advance the advertising and didactic purposes of the hagiographical text.

Considering extant Persian hagiographical literature from the 14th and 15th century as a narrative fund, I have elsewhere offered a cultural history of Sufi communities through a focus on topics that repeat most frequently in the stories. Bahāʾ al-Dīn Naqshband is a major figure in my account of this social world, appearing in discussions pertaining to the typical life-cycle of the Sufi master, and in miracles where the saint is able to be present in multiple locations at the same time, protects the bodies of disciples dedicated to him, and grants food and children to supplicants.[32] My work in this vein stemmed from observing that hagiographical narratives pay very close attention to corporeal matters that are, themselves, effects of an overall sociointellectual system centered on properties associated with the great Sufi masters. This approach led

32 Bashir, *Sufi Bodies*, 89–90, 171–72, 174–76, 196–97, 199–200.

me to suggest that the body was regarded as a doorway that connected apparent (*ẓāhir*) and hidden (*bāṭin*) aspects of reality that Sufis took for granted as constituting the structure of the cosmos. Within the details of the stories, I identified that hagiographical authors attend especially to rituals, social hierarchies, love and desire, and saints' ability to perform miracles. Rather than tracing matters within texts associated with a specific community, chapters on these topics in my book deliberately collate material from texts and paintings with diverse origins. My point in doing this was to argue that, taken as a narrative fund, hagiographical literature symptomizes a powerful social imagination that held sway over multiple spheres in premodern Central Asia and Iran. Sufi manuscripts and texts that survive for us are all anchored in this narrative fund common to the milieu across specific communities.

Positing the notion of a narrative fund as a distinct element within the context of hagiography highlights the combination of literary and social processes that form the backdrop for this type of material. The manuscripts and texts at our disposal are not products of scriptoriums geared toward producing philologically standardized versions of the life histories of Sufi masters. On the contrary, internal variation is fundamental to the social context from which these texts emerge and must be taken as a given for our analyses. However, these texts are not simply free-floating descriptions of individuals either. They are highly typological and attempt to tie individual lives to universalizing patterns. They draw on reservoirs of idealized lives ranging between *ḥadīth, sīra,* lives of prophets, and the constantly expanding repertoire of Sufi hagiography. The existing narrative fund of stories and morals validates the content of a given manuscript or work by providing the good tale that enlivens the storyteller's yarn and anchors it in the identitarian and sociocultural concerns of the historical setting.

Genre

As in the case of previous categories, the question of genre is prefigured in the issues I have discussed up to now. Some of what I have suggested under the rubric of the narrative fund clearly applies to the way we might define extended Sufi hagiography as a genre. However, I am making a distinction between the two categories to highlight hagiography's thematic characteristics at the most general level.

In the basic sense, Sufi hagiography is best described as an argument for sanctity made on behalf of a friend of God by her or his disciples. It is a close cognate to the genre of chronicle, replacing God's friend or the Sufi *silsila* for a royal personage or dynasty. It is highly didactic but its religious message is conveyed through dramatizations of relationships between human beings rather than direct exhortation involving God or other purely metaphysical beings. It also shares much in common with storytelling genres, intermixing prose and poetry in a way that is common for medieval Islamic belletristic literature.

Beyond these basics, it is significant to consider how a hagiographical narrative produces its distinctive affect that separates it from other genres. In my view, a large part of hagiography's narrative success derives from the tension inherent in bestowing intense glorification on the saintly figure, a subject whose claim to distinction is that s/he does not care to be glorified. This tension, which is endemic to Sufism as a religious system, generates compelling stories with multiple levels of meaning. It provides the narrator the opportunity to build any amount of dramatic description, which a properly prepared reader knows to understand both as straightforward portrayal and, simultaneously, its very antithesis. For instance, descriptions of Sufis' severe hardships and poverty imply both their proper choice and the fact that they are the ones who are truly rich because of the rewards they await based on their relationship with the divine. In the opposite vein, when subjects are described as powerful and resplendent in worldly ways, the reader is supposed to know that they really care not at all about such matters because of their dedication to religious aims. Neither outward poverty nor excessive worldly trappings are thus the true measure of a Sufi, although the hagiographical narrator is at liberty to use both to any extent for the sake of the narrative's efficacy.

The structure and the distribution of contents of the larger version of the *Anīs al-ṭālibīn va ʿuddat al-sālikīn*, a work dedicated to Naqshband that I have discussed above, further illustrate hagiography's qualities as a genre. The author, Ṣalāḥ b. Mubārak al-Bukhārī, claims to be working on the request of Naqshband's successors, who wished to preserve knowledge about him after his death. Disciples' desire for the master forms the genre's frame and determines the type of information to be included in it.[33] Subsequently, the work is divided into four very unequal parts. Bukhārī begins by defining the saint (*valī*) and sainthood (*valāyat*), citing Sufi theory as well as metaphors such as the notion that the acts and benefits that issue from the saint are like shadows cast by divine light when it shines on the saint's body.[34] The second section, which at ten percent of the work is about twice as long as the first, describes circumstances that prevailed before Naqshband's birth and what occurred in his childhood and youth. We hear about his ancestors and spiritual predecessors,

33 Bukhārī, *Anīs al-ṭālibīn va ʿuddat al-sālikīn*, 66.

34 Ibid., 71.

who legitimate him as someone destined for greatness before even being conceived in his mother's body. The key distinguishing feature of the material presented in this section is that Naqshband is not yet a Sufi master in his own right and receives direction from guides who are either living or appear to him in visions. The section ends by recounting Naqshband's initiation into the Khwājagānī chain of Sufi authority, a moment that is critical for establishing his socioreligious credentials.[35] Taken together, the first two sections of the work are, respectively, the theoretical and the historical bedrocks of hagiography as a genre.

The work's third section is about as long as the first two combined (fifteen percent of the text) and presents a summary picture of Naqshband's sayings and customary actions. The focus is on Naqshband's own person, describing his attitude to different types of people, his likes and dislikes, and aphorisms attributed to him.[36] The fourth section is the longest (about seventy percent of the work) and presents Naqshband as a religious and social commander working amongst disciples seeking his favor and guidance. This is where we see the saint in full bloom, acting to protect and provide for his followers while also admonishing and punishing his opponents.[37]

As this brief description of *Anīs al-ṭālibīn* illustrates, a hagiography's purpose is to create a time and a space for the subject whose argument for sanctity it wishes to push forward. The narrator accomplishes this through constant toggling between universal and particular references. At one level, every saintly life exhibits the same set of standard features, which the narrator substantiates in the theoretical sections and then deploys through invoking themes found in the narrative fund I have discussed above. The key sources for the hagiographical mold range between the Qur'ān, *ḥadīth*, and various genres of saintly lives such as prophets, Imāms, and earlier Sufis. A further "universalizing" element in these narratives is the use of Persian poetry, which has a distinctive voice of its own and works to imbue the narratives with emotion, passion, and hyperbole. While these elements are ubiquitous, they are thoroughly interlaced together with the quotidian and the particular pertaining to lived human experience. Incidental details of specific actions and encounters with named individuals are important for domesticating the generic stories. The resulting discourse is simultaneously an instantiation of a universal paradigm and the account of a life that is relatable to the reader's lived experience because of consistent appeal to humanizing details. In the final instance, hagiography as

35 Ibid., 79–115.

36 Ibid., 115–162.

37 Ibid., 162–386.

a genre constitutes a flexible framework that can be populated by stories traceable to the hagiographical narrative fund. Each hagiographical text is the actuation of a subset of possibilities allowed by the genre, placed in a determined sequence to further the saintly claim of a Sufi exemplar. And every manuscript we can scrutinize represents the instantiation of a text, the narrative fund, and the genre at a given time and place.

Conclusion

Sufi hagiographical works are among the most valuable resources we possess to understand premodern Central Asia. They provide information on topics such as biographies of major figures, the establishment and transformation of communities, the rise and evolution of intellectual trends, and Sufis' place among the society's elites. However, these works are very far from being transparent windows onto the past. They are effects of a social world that is encoded within hagiography as a literary form. To utilize these works for modern historiographical reconstruction requires that we unpack them to hypothesize the conditions that gave rise to them and to derive information from their contents, structures, and aporia. I have suggested that we evaluate hagiographical literature by treating manuscripts, texts, a narrative fund, and the literary genre as interrelated but distinguishable loci for analysis. My proposed disaggregation expands interpretive possibilities beyond what is deducible from straightforward perusal.

Examining materials that inform us about the life of Bahāʾ al-Dīn Naqshband illustrates the outcomes of my approach. Naqshband has been a subject for Sufi hagiographical narration for more than six centuries, from immediately after his death to our own day. For the premodern period, our primary material witnesses for claims about Naqshband's life are "manuscripts" that contain compilations of reports regarding his sayings and actions. Each of these manuscripts is a unique object marked by the times and places where it was produced and has been utilized over the centuries. All these objects have their own stories to tell that splice Naqshband's life to the lives of the objects' producers and users. A manuscript attributed to the hand of a specific person such as ʿAbd al-Raḥmān Jāmī informs us about how Naqshband's life story remained a potent example for those who attached themselves to his lineage.

In the centuries after Naqshband's death, his successors split into factions that competed among themselves as well as with other Sufi lineages. We can map this aspect of Naqshband's story by noting differences between compilations of anecdotes pertaining to Naqshband that sometimes vary by names and at others by versions assigned the same name. These are the hagiographical "texts" that I distinguish from the category of manuscripts. Among Sufis, the exemplarity of Naqshband's life rested in its similarity to the lives of others regarded as saints rather than his uniqueness. Virtually all reports describing his powers and attitudes can be found echoed in hagiographies devoted to other Sufis. Taken together, these stories constitute a "narrative fund" that we can conceptualize as an abstraction that was shared across the world of premodern Sufis. And finally, Naqshband's hagiography is almost all that we know about him: for historiographical purposes, the saint is coterminous with the changing and evolving narratives about his life found in our archive. The "genre" hagiography consists of the range of patterns and possibilities that instantiate the Sufi past. Manuscripts, texts, and the narrative fund subsumed under the genre are central to any claims we can make about premodern Sufi communities.

Naqshband is one among dozens of Central Asian Sufi masters who were made subjects of hagiographical narration by their followers. Stories about other figures sometimes intersect with those of Naqshband and his followers and at other times diverge in important ways. Multiply what I have said regarding Naqshband many times and we can have a sense for the wealth of information contained in hagiography. Imbued with religious ideology and miracles, hagiographical narratives become most valuable for our purposes when we see them as symptoms of social worlds rather than as straightforward statements informing us about what happened in the past. The interpretive scheme I have presented in this article aims at a systematic approach to this task.

Bibliography

Algar, Hamid. "Jāmī, ii. and Sufism." *Encylopaedia Iranica*, XIV, fasc. 5, 475–479.

Anon. *Anīs al-ṭālibīn va ʿuddat al-sālikīn*. Ms. Patna (India), Khuda Bakhsh Oriental Public Library, Persian 1377.

Anon. *Khavāriq-i Naqshband dar ʿilm-i sayr*. Ms. Hyderabad (India), Salar Jung Estate Library (Oriental Collection), Persian Ms. 844, ff. 1b–64b.

Aubin, Jean, ed. *Matériaux pour la biographie de Shâh Niʿmatullâh Walí Kermânî*. Tehran: Institut Français d'Iranologie de Téhéran, 1956.

Babadjanov, Bakhtiyar. "Biographies of Makhdūm-i Aʿẓam al-Kāsānī al-Dahbīdī, Shaykh of the Sixteenth-century Naqshbandīya." *Manuscripta Orientalia*, 5/2 (1999), 3–8.

Bashir, Shahzad. *Messianic Hopes and Mystical Visions: The Nūrbakhshīya Between Medieval and Modern Islam*. Columbia: University of South Carolina Press, 2003.

Bashir, Shahzad. *Sufi Bodies: Religion and Society in Medieval Islam*. New York: Columbia University Press, 2011.

Bukhārī, Abū'l-Qāsim b. Muḥammad b. Masʿūd. *Risāla-yi Bahāʾiyya fī maqāmāt-i Ḥażrat Khwāja Bahāʾ al-Dīn*. Ms. Aligarh (India), Aligarh Muslim University, Maulana Azad Library, Subhanullah Collection, 287.7/5 (Fārsī Taṣavvuf), ff. 1b–84a.

Bukhārī, Ṣalāḥ b. Mubārak. *Anīs al-ṭālibīn va ʿuddat al-sālikīn*. Ed. Khalīl Ibrāhīm Ṣārīoghlū. Tehran: Kayhān, 1371/1992.

Carlquist, Jonas. "Medieval Manuscripts, Hypertext and Reading: Visions of Digital Editions." *Literary and Linguistic Computing*, 19/1 (2004), 105–118.

Cerquiglini, Bernard. *In Praise of the Variant: A Critical History of Philology*. Tr. Betsy Wing. Baltimore: The Johns Hopkins University Press, 1999.

Charkhī, Yaʿqūb. *Kitāb-i maqāmāt va silsila-yi* Naqshbandī. Ms. Oxford, Bodleian Library, e. 37, ff. 145b–168b.

Charkhī, Yaʿqūb. *Risāla-yi unsiyya*. Ed. and tr. Muḥammad Naẕīr Rānjhā. Dera Ismail Khan, Pakistan: Maktaba Sirājiyya Khānaqāh-i Aḥmadiyya Saʿīdiyya, 1983.

Deppman, Jed, Daniel Ferrer, and Michael Groden, eds. *Genetic Criticism: Texts and Avant-textes*. Philadelphia: University of Pennsylvania Press, 2004.

DeWeese, Devin. "The Eclipse of the Kubravīyah in Central Asia." In DeWeese, *Studies on Sufism in Central Asia* (Burlington, Vermont: Ashgate, 2012), No. I.

DeWeese, Devin. "The Legitimation of Bahāʾ ad-Din Naqshband." *Asiatische Studien/Études Asiatiques*, 60/2 (2006), 261–305.

DeWeese, Devin. "Sayyid ʿAli Hamadani and Kubrawi Hagiographical Traditions." In DeWeese, *Studies on Sufism in Central Asia* (Burlington, Vermont: Ashgate, 2012), No. II.

Gardner, Victoria R. "The Written Representations of a Central Asian Sufi Shaykh: Aḥmad ibn Mawlānā Jalāl al-Dīn Khwājagī Kāsānī 'Makhdūm-i Aʿẓam' (d. 1542)." Ph.D. dissertation, University of Michigan, 2006.

Greetham, David C. *Theories of the Text*. New York: Oxford University Press, 1999.

Gross, Jo-Ann. "Khoja Ahrar: A Study of the Perceptions of Religious Power and Prestige in the Late Timurid Period." Ph.D. dissertation, New York University, 1982.

Jāmī, ʿAbd al-Raḥmān. *Khulāṣa-yi anīs al-ṭālibīn*. Ed. Muḥammad Ẕākir Ḥusayn. Patna: Khuda Bakhsh Library, 1994.

Jāmī, ʿAbd al-Raḥmān. *Nafaḥāt al-uns min ḥażarāt al-quds*. Ed. Maḥmūd ʿĀbidī. Tehran: Intishārāt-i Iṭṭilāʿāt, 1376/1997.

Khismatulin, Alexey. "Jāmī's Statement on the Authorship of the *Anīs al-ṭālibīn*." In *Jāmī and the Intellectual History of the Muslim World: The Trans-Regional Reception of ʿAbd al-Raḥmān Jāmī's Works, c. 9th/15th–14th/20th*, ed. Thibaut d'Hubert and Alexandre Papas (Leiden: Brill, forthcoming).

Muḥammad, Khwāja Jalāl al-Dīn. *Anīs al-ṭālibīn va ʿuddat al-sālikīn*. Ms. Oxford, Bodleian Library, e. 37, ff. 44b–144b.

Nawshāhī, ʿĀrif, ed. *Aḥvāl va sukhanān-i Khwāja ʿUbaydullāh Aḥrār*. Tehran: Markaz-i Nashr-i Dānishgāhī, 1380/2001.

Ökten, Ertuğrul. "Jāmī (817–898/1414–1492): His Biography and Intellectual Influence in Herat." Ph.D. dissertation, University of Chicago, 2007.

Pārsā, Khwāja Muḥammad. *Risāla-yi qudsiyya* (*Kalimāt-i Bahāʾ al-Dīn Naqshband*). Ed. Aḥmad Ṭāhirī ʿIrāqī. Tehran: Kitābkhāna-yi Ṭahūrī, 1354/1975.

Paul, Jürgen. *Doctrine and Organization: The Khwajagan/Naqshbandiya in the First Generation after Baha'uddin* (Berlin: Das Arabische Buch, 1998; *Anor*, 1).

Paul, Jürgen. "Hagiographische Texte als historische Quelle." *Saeculum*, 41 (1990), 17–43.

Ṣafī, Fakhr al-Dīn ʿAlī b. Ḥusayn Kāshifī. *Rashaḥāt-i ʿayn al-ḥayāt*. Ed. ʿAlī Aṣghar Muʿīniyān. 2 vols. Tehran: Majmūʿa-yi Mutūn-i Qadīm va Aḥvāl-i Dānishmandān va ʿIrfānān, 2536/1356/1977.

Schwarz, Florian. *"Unser Weg schließt tausend Wege ein": Derwische und Gesellschaft im islamischen Mittelasien im 16. Jahrhundert*. Berlin: Klaus Schwarz Verlag, 2000.

Shihāb al-Dīn. *Maqāmāt-i Amīr Kulāl*. Ms. St. Petersburg, Institute of Oriental Manuscripts, Russian Academy of Sciences, C 1562.

Tosun, Necdet. *Bahâeddin Nakşbend: Hayatı, Görüşleri, Tarîkatı*. Istanbul: İnsan Yayınları, 2002.

CHAPTER 3

The Works of Ḥusayn Vāʿiẓ Kāshifī as a Source for the Study of Sufism in Late 15th- and Early 16th-Century Central Asia

Maria E. Subtelny

The works composed by the Timurid-era preacher Kamāl al-Dīn Ḥusayn b. ʿAlī Vāʿiẓ, known as Kāshifī (d. 910/1504–05), may be viewed as a late medieval attempt to encompass the totality of religious, literary, scientific, and cultural knowledge in Persianate Central Asia at the turn of the 16th century. Kāshifī's works on subjects ranging from political ethics and Qurʾān commentary to astrology and spiritual chivalry earned him a tribute from the preeminent Timurid-era poet and patron ʿAlī-shīr Navāʾī, who referred to him in his *Majālis al-nafāʾis* as a polymath (*ẕū funūn*).[1] Although his works are compilative in nature, drawing heavily on earlier (often Arabic) authors, Kāshifī is very much present in them, and while synthesizing the works of his predecessors, he uses them as a springboard to demonstrate his own literary and rhetorical talents. His success was due to his ability to organize his material in a rational and economical fashion, and more important, to present it to a discerning Persian audience in an attractive literary formulation. Utilizing this approach, Kāshifī consciously created what might be termed the Persian equivalent of an Everyman's Library of his time.[2] This article will survey those works by Kāshifī that are concerned specifically with Sufism and the occult sciences that had traditionally been closely associated with Sufism. It may be inferred from the popularity of these works that the religio-ethical perspectives of Islamic mysticism, and esotericism more generally, were part and parcel of mainstream Persianate culture in the eastern Islamic world of his time.

Originally from Sabzavār (in the province of Bayhaq), Kāshifī moved to the Timurid capital, Herat, in 860/1456 after allegedly being summoned to the town in a dream vision by the recently deceased Naqshbandī Sufi master Saʿd

1 Alisher Navoiy, *Majolisun nafois: Ilmiy-tanqidiy tekst*, ed. Suyima Ghanieva (Tashkent: Uzbekiston SSR Fanlar akademiyasi nashriyoti, 1961), 143.

2 Maria E. Subtelny, "Husayn Vaʿiz-i Kashifi: Polymath, Popularizer, and Preserver," *Iranian Studies*, 36/4 (2003), 463.

 | DOI:10.1163/9789004373075_005

al-Dīn Kāshgharī.[3] Born in the 1420s, Kāshifī would have been in his thirties at the time. When he was named chief judge (*qāżī al-qużāt*) of the province of Bayhaq by the new Timurid ruler of Khurasan, Sulṭān-Abū Saʿīd (863–73/1458–69), he returned to Sabzavār for a time.[4] After Sulṭān-Ḥusayn-i Bāyqarā (r. 873–911/1469–1506) came to power in Khurasan, Kāshifī returned to Herat (possibly at his invitation), where he remained until his death in 910/1504–5.[5] In Herat, Kāshifī was patronized by Sulṭān-Ḥusayn and various members of the Timurid military elite, chiefly Mīr ʿAlī-shīr Navāʾī (d. 906/1501), to whom he dedicated a number of his works.

Kāshifī's popularity was acknowledged by the historian Khwāndamīr, who in his biographical entry on him in the *Ḥabīb al-siyar* (completed in Herat ca. 930/1524) stated that, as a Qurʾān exegete (*mufassir*), he had no equal in Khurasan in his day, and he noted his expertise in astrology (*ʿilm-i nujūm*) and epistolography (*inshāʾ*).[6] Khwāndamīr named seven of his works that he regarded as his best known. These were his lettrist commentary on the Qurʾān, *Javāhir al-tafsīr li-tuḥfat al-Amīr*, which was never completed;[7] another Qurʾān commentary entitled *Mavāhib-i ʿaliyya*;[8] the ʿAlid martyrology *Rawżat al-shuhadāʾ* (composed 908/1502–3), the work for which he is probably best known today;[9] *Anvār-i suhaylī*, a rendition of Naṣrullāh Munshī's Persian translation of the *Kalīla va Dimna* animal fables (commissioned by and dedicated

3 Fakhr al-Dīn ʿAlī b. Ḥusayn Kāshifī, "Ṣafī," *Rashaḥāt-i ʿayn al-ḥayāt*, ed. ʿAlī Aṣghar Muʿīniyān (Tehran: Intishārāt-i Bunyād-i Nīkūkārī-i Nūriyānī, no. 15, 2536/1977), vol. 1, 252–253.

4 Gottfried Herrmann, "Biographisches zu Ḥusain Wāʿiẓ Kāšifī," in *Corolla Iranica: Papers in Honour of Prof. Dr. David Neil MacKenzie on the Occasion of His 65th Birthday on April 8th, 1991*, ed. Ronald E. Emmerick and Dieter Weber (Frankfurt: Peter Lang, 1991), 93–94, 98–99.

5 Alisher Navoiy, *Majolisun nafois*, 143; Mīr Niẓām al-Dīn ʿAlī-shīr Navāʾī, *Majālis al-nafāʾis: Dar taẕkira-yi shuʿarāʾ-i qarn-i nuhum-i hijrī* (translated into Persian and expanded by Sulṭān-Muḥammad Fakhrī Harātī and Ḥakīm Shāh-Muḥammad Qazvīnī), ed. ʿAlī Asghar Ḥikmat (Tehran: Chāpkhāna-yi Bānk-i Millī-yi Īrān, 1323/1945), 93, 268; Herrmann, "Biographisches," 90.

6 Khwāndamīr, *Tārīkh-i Ḥabīb al-siyar fī akhbār afrād-i bashar*, ed. Jalāl al-Dīn Humāʾī (reprint ed., Tehran: Khayyām, 1362/1984), vol. 4, 345; also Khwāndamīr, *Khātima-yi Khulāṣat al-akhbār*, in Khwāndamīr, *Maʾāṣir al-mulūk, bi-żamīma-i Khātima-i Khulāṣat al-akhbār va Qānūn-i Humāyūnī*, ed. Mīr Hāshim Muḥaddiṣ (Tehran: Muʾassasa-yi Khadamāt-i Farhangī-yi Rasā, 1372/1994), 221.

7 Kamāl al-Dīn Ḥusayn b. ʿAlī Vāʿiẓ Kāshifī, *Javāhir al-tafsīr: Tafsīrī adabī, ʿirfānī, ḥurūfī, shāmil-i muqaddimaʾī dar ʿulūm-i qurʾānī va tafsīr-i sūrat-i Ḥamd*, ed. Javād ʿAbbāsī (Tehran: Mīrāṣ-i Maktūb, 1379/2000–2001).

8 Kamāl al-Dīn Ḥusayn b. ʿAlī Vāʿiẓ Kāshifī, *Mavāhib-i ʿaliyya yā Tafsīr-i ḥusaynī (bi-fārsī)*, ed. Muḥammad Rižā Jalālī Nāyinī, 4 vols. (Tehran: Iqbāl, 1317–29/1938–50).

9 Kamāl al-Dīn Ḥusayn b. ʿAlī Vāʿiẓ Kāshifī, *Rawżat al-shuhadāʾ*, ed. Āyatullāh Ḥājj Shaykh Abūʾl-Ḥasan Shaʿrānī (Reprint ed., Tehran: Intishārāt-i Islāmiyya, 1379/2000–2001).

to the Timurid amir Niẓām al-Dīn Shaykh Aḥmad Suhaylī, whose name is alluded to in the title);[10] a treatise on epistolography, entitled *Makhzan al-inshāʾ* (completed 907/1501–2 for ʿAlī-shīr Navāʾī and dedicated to Sulṭān-Ḥusayn);[11] a treatise on ethics and statecraft, entitled *Akhlāq-i muḥsinī* (composed in 907/1501–2 for the benefit of Sulṭān-Ḥusayn's son Abūʾl-Muḥsin Mīrzā);[12] and *Ikhtiyārāt al-nujūm* or *Lavāyiḥ al-qamar* (composed in 878/1473–74 for the Timurid *vazīr* Majd-al-Dīn Muḥammad Khwāfī), a work on elective astrology which appears to be the only book of Kāshifī's septet on astrology, *Sabʿa-yi kāshifiyya*, to have survived.[13]

As a professional preacher, or *vāʿiẓ*, Kāshifī achieved great renown among his contemporaries thanks to his beautiful voice, rhetorical skill, and ability to explain Qurʾānic verses and prophetic Traditions to his audience in an interesting and accessible manner.[14] The title *vāʿiẓ* denoted a free preacher as distinct on the one hand from the *khaṭīb*, who delivered the standardized sermon (*khuṭba*) in the mosque at the Friday prayer, and on the other from the street preacher, or *qāṣṣ*.[15] The *vāʿiẓ* was a learned individual whose sermons, delivered in sessions called *majālis al-vaʿẓ*, were on a sophisticated "academic" level.[16] Like the *khaṭīb* and the *qāṣṣ*, he was advised not to expound on theological questions in his sermons, but unlike the *qāṣṣ* he was not one to stir up confessional strife.[17] It is noteworthy that, from the earliest times in Muslim society, the *vāʿiẓ* had inclined toward asceticism and mysticism.[18] According

10 For which see Christine van Ruymbeke, *Kāshefi's Anvār-e Sohayli: Rewriting Kalila and Dimna in Timurid Herat* (Leiden: Brill, 2016).

11 For which see Colin Paul Mitchell, "To Preserve and Protect: Husayn Vaʿiz-i Kashifi and Perso-Islamic Chancellery Culture," *Iranian Studies*, 36/4 (2003), 488–494.

12 For a summary and discussion of the dating of this work, see Maria E. Subtelny, "A Late Medieval Persian *Summa* on Ethics: Kashifi's *Akhlāq-i Muḥsinī*," *Iranian Studies*, 36/4 (2003), 602–604.

13 For which see Sergei Tourkin and Živa Vesel, "The Contribution of Husayn Vaʿiz-i Kashifi to the Transmission of Astrological Texts," *Iranian Studies*, 36/4 (2003), 591–597.

14 Khwāndamīr, *Ḥabīb al-siyar*, vol. 4, 345; Khwāndamīr, *Khātima-yi Khulāṣat al-akhbār*, 221–22. See the comments of ʿUbaydullāh Aḥrār about the popularity of Kāshifī's sermonizing (*mawʿiẓa-yi vay maqbūl-i khavāṣṣ va ʿavāmm ast*) in Ṣafī, *Rashaḥāt*, vol. 2, 491.

15 See George Makdisi, *The Rise of Colleges: Institutions of Learning in Islam and the West* (Edinburgh: Edinburgh University Press, 1981), 217–218.

16 George Makdisi referred to the *vaʿẓ* as an "academic sermon" (see Makdisi, *Rise of Colleges*, 217).

17 Makdisi, *Rise of Colleges*, 218.

18 On this point see Johs Pedersen, "The Islamic Preacher: *wāʿiẓ, mudhakkir, qāṣṣ*," in *Ignace Goldziher Memorial Volume*, Pt. 1, ed. Samuel Löwinger and Joseph Somogyi (Budapest: Globus Nyomdai Műintézet, 1948), 238.

to the description of his duties provided by the 14th-century Egyptian/Syrian Shāfiʿī jurisconsult and preacher Tāj al-Dīn al-Subkī, the *vāʿiẓ* was to admonish people to perform their religious obligations, to put the fear of God into them, and to provide moral lessons by drawing on examples from the lives of Muslim saints.[19] A skilled orator, Kāshifī knew how to gauge his audience and he was not above employing some of the story-telling techniques of the professional story-teller (*qiṣṣa-khvān*). As he wrote in his *Futuvvat-nāma-yi sulṭānī*, the *vāʿiẓ* must be endowed not only with knowledge (*dānish*) but also with insight (*bīnish*) in order to enable him to judge his audience and what it is capable of understanding.[20]

Thanks to what must have been a prodigious memory, Kāshifī was able to draw on a vast reservoir of anecdotes and poetic citations that made his sermonizing sessions the biggest draw in Timurid Herat. He preached regularly on appointed days, holding sessions of admonition and moral counsel (*vaʿẓ va naṣīḥat*) at some of the most prestigious venues in the city. On Friday mornings he preached at a lodge (*khānaqāh*) called Dār al-sayāda in the central market of Herat that had been constructed expressly for him by Sulṭān-Ḥusayn and of which he had been appointed lodge master (*shaykh*).[21] On Fridays he preached at the congregational mosque of Mīr ʿAlī-shīr Navāʾī; on Tuesdays at the royal *madrasa-khānaqāh* complex of Sulṭān-Ḥusayn; and on Wednesdays at the local shrine of Abū'l-Walīd Aḥmad. Towards the end of his life he also preached on Thursdays at the tomb of the Timurid prince Sulṭān-Aḥmad Mīrzā. He apparently had a flair for the theatrical and would kiss the base of the *minbar*, or pulpit, before ascending to deliver a sermon; he would also clap his hands and stamp his feet while speaking, practices that, according to his son Fakhr al-Dīn ʿAlī Ṣafī (d. 939/1532–33), he discontinued on the advice, relayed to him obliquely, of the Naqshbandī shaykh of Samarqand, Khwāja ʿUbaydullāh Aḥrār, who regarded such gestures as heretical (*bidʿat*).[22] He likely made a compilation of his sermons, a supposition that appears to be supported by a reference

19 Makdisi, *Rise of Colleges*, 217.

20 Kamāl al-Dīn Ḥusayn b. ʿAlī Vāʿiẓ Kāshifī, *Futuvvat-nāma-yi sulṭānī*, ed. Muḥammad Jaʿfar Maḥjūb (Tehran: Intishārāt-i Bunyād-i Farhang-i Īrān, no. 113, 1350/1971), 303–304.

21 Herrmann, "Biographisches," 96–99; Khwāndamīr, *Khātima-yi Khulāṣat al-akhbār*, 192; and Khwāndamīr, *Maʾāṣir al-mulūk*, in Khwāndamīr, *Maʾāṣir al-mulūk, bi-żamīma-yi khātima-yi Khulāṣat al-akhbār va Qānūn-i Humāyūnī*, ed. Mīr Hāshim Muḥaddiṣ (Tehran: Muʾassasa-yi Khadamāt-i Farhangī-yi Rasā, 1372/1994), 174.

22 Ṣafī, *Rashaḥāt*, vol. 2, 491–492.

to his leafing through the pages of a *majālis-i vaʿẓ*, or sermonizing sessions, possibly his own, although this is by no means certain.[23]

A survey of a selection of Kāshifī's works will provide some indication of the status of Sufism in late Timurid Iran and Central Asia and the place it occupied in religious and literary culture.

Mavāhib-i ʿaliyya

Kāshifī's Qurʾān commentary in Persian, entitled *Mavāhib-i ʿaliyya*, is a short but highly effective, non-sectarian, confessionally mainstream Sufi commentary on the Qurʾān for a contemporary Timurid-era public. In the introduction to the work he states that he had originally been commissioned by Navāʾī to compose a lettrist Qurʾān commentary entitled *Javāhir al-tafsīr li-tuḥfat al-Amīr* ("The jewels of Qurʾān exegesis [presented] as a gift to the Amīr"). But seeing that it was going to take too long to complete all four projected volumes, in Muḥarram 897/November 1491, acting upon what he refers to as "an inspired hint from the Unseen" (*īmāʾ-i mulhim-i ghaybī*), Kāshifī abandoned the project,[24] and instead embarked on the composition of a shorter commentary, entitled *Mavāhib-i ʿaliyya* ("Gifts presented to ʿAlī-[shīr]")—a title that can also be interpreted to mean "Gifts from the supernal world"—which he completed in 899/1494.[25]

The popularity of this commentary, better known as *Tafsīr-i ḥusaynī* or *Tafsīr-i Kāshifī*, cannot be overstated. It is the most popular of Kāshifī's works, with 285 manuscript copies in Iran alone. Virtually every major manuscript repository in the world contains at least one copy. Characteristically accessible in style, it is based on citations from earlier exegetical works, especially esoteric Qurʾān commentaries, as well as from the works of theosophers and Sufi poets that Kāshifī refers to as "the Masters of Verification" (*arbāb-i taḥqīq*), a designation for esotericists of the highest order.[26] Kāshifī's idea of *tafsīr* is really *taʾvīl*,

23 ʿAbd al-Vāsiʿ Niẓāmī Bākharzī, *Maqāmāt-i Jāmī: Gūshahāyī az tārīkh-i farhangī va ijtimāʿī-yi Khurāsān dar ʿaṣr-i Tīmūrīyān*, ed. Najīb Māyil Haravī (Tehran: Nashr-i Nay, 1371/1992–93), 253. I have not been able to locate a manuscript copy of his collection of sermons.

24 At the time of writing the *Majālis al-nafāʾis*, that is, in 896/1490–91, ʿAlī-shīr Navāʾī stated that Kāshifī had completed only one volume of *Javāhir al-tafsīr* as far as the *Sūrat al-baqara* (the 2nd chapter of the Qurʾān); hence the commentary was essentially only on the *Fātiḥa* (see Alisher Navoii, *Majolisun nafois*, 143; Alīshīr Navāʾī, *Majālis al-nafāʾis*, 93).

25 Kāshifī, *Mavāhib-i ʿaliyya*, vol. 1, i–ii (author's introduction).

26 Kāshifī, *Mavāhib-i ʿaliyya*, vol. 1, ii (author's introduction). The term refers to those who, as a result of their spiritual attainments, can verify as to the reality of Truth and the truth of Reality. The use of the term actually went back to Ibn ʿArabī.

esoteric interpretation of the scriptural text on the basis of what he refers to as *ʿilm-i ladunī*, or divinely-inspired knowledge.[27]

The degree to which mystical or esoteric interpretations of the Qurʾān had become commonplace in Kāshifī's day may be gauged from an interesting anecdote related about Kāshifī in the *Maqāmāt-i Jāmī* ("The assemblies of Jāmī"). While leafing through the abovementioned compilation of sermons, Kāshifī reportedly hit upon a novel interpretation of the Qurʾānic verse "And a sign for them is the night: We withdraw therefrom the day [and behold they are plunged into darkness]" (Q 36:37). He states that he interpreted the word "day" (*nahār*) to signify "the light of being" (*nūr-i vujūd*) and night (*layl*) "the darkness of non-existence" (*ẓulmat-i ʿadam*), meaning that whenever God removed "the light of being" from people, they remained in "the darkness of non-existence." The next day, eager to present this interpretation to the great Sufi shaykh and Persian mystical poet ʿAbd al-Raḥmān Jāmī (d. 898/1492), he went to his house for an audience. Apparently reading his mind thanks to his powers of *firāsat*, or physiognomy, Jāmī pre-empted Kāshifī's presentation by asking him whether he had ever come across an interpretation of a Qurʾānic verse in any Qurʾān commentary he had studied that was not found in books written by the Sufis (*kutub-i qawm*). In other words, what Jāmī was suggesting was that Kāshifī's interpretation was not novel at all, but rather that it merely reiterated existing esoteric Qurʾān commentaries and Sufi epistemology as a whole, including the theosophical writings of Ibn ʿArabī, on whose works Jāmī had written commentaries.[28]

A great admirer of the 13th-century Persian mystic and poet Jalāl al-Dīn Rūmī (d. 672/1273), Kāshifī often cites from his *Mas̱navī* in the *Mavāhib-i ʿaliyya* as if it were an authoritative Qurʾān commentary. In fact, citations from Rūmī's *Mas̱navī* (or his *Dīvān*) may be considered a litmus test of the authenticity of Kāshifī's authorship of those works that have been put into question by some scholars. Even though the *Mas̱navī* may have been regarded in certain circles in its own day as an esoteric commentary on the Qurʾān, it was not universally acknowledged as such by the mainstream Sunni exegetical community.[29]

27 See Kristin Zahra Sands, "On the Popularity of Husayn Vaʿiz-i Kashifi's *Mavāhib-i ʿaliyya*: A Persian Commentary on the Qur'an," *Iranian Studies*, 36/4 (2003), 469–483.

28 Bākharzī, *Maqāmāt-i Jāmī*, 253.

29 According to a famous anecdote in the hagiographical work *Manāqib al-ʿārifīn*, Rūmī's son Sulṭān Valad responded to the charge some religious scholars were making that the *Mas̱navī* was being called the Qurʾān, by saying that the *Mas̱navī* was the commentary on the Qurʾān; see Shams al-Dīn Aḥmad Aflākī, *Manāqib al-ʿārifīn*, ed. Taḥsīn Yāzījī (reprint ed., Tehran: Dunyā-yi Kitāb, 1375/1996), vol. 1, 291; Shams al-Dīn Aḥmad-e Aflākī, *The Feats of the Knowers of God* (*Manāqeb al-ʿārefīn*), tr. John O'Kane (Leiden: Brill, 2002), 201.

Kāshifī's frequent citation of Rūmī's poetry not only enhanced his interpretations of Qur'ānic verses but also contributed to the extraordinary popularity of his commentary even in the Safavid period.

By way of illustration, in his commentary on Qur'ān 8:17, "You did not throw when you threw but it was God who threw" (*mā ramayta idh ramayta wa lākin Allāh ramā*), Kāshifī cites two verses from the *Masnavī* (in addition to Jāmī's *Nafaḥāt al-uns* and Ibn 'Arabī's *al-Futūḥāt al-makkiyya* in Persian paraphrase) to illustrate the idea that it was not Muḥammad's act (an allusion to Muḥammad's throwing a handful of pebbles or sand at the enemy before the Battle of Badr) but rather God acting through him. The verses are not consecutive but taken from two different books of the *Masnavī*. The first is from Book 2 (line 1,306):

> God said [in the Qur'ān]: 'You did not throw when you threw'
> God's actions have precedence over ours.

And the second is from Book 1 (line 616):

> If we shoot an arrow, it is not from us,
> We are just the bow and it is God who shoots the arrow.

These citations are followed by what appears to be a verse of Kāshifī's own composition, written in the metre of the *Masnavī*, in which he offers a suggestion of how to achieve an intuitive understanding of the meaning of Rūmī's words:

> Unless a person becomes overwhelmed (*maghlūb*) he will not understand [the meaning of] this,
> If you wish [to understand], you must make haste to that other (i.e., spiritual) side.[30]

In his commentary on Qur'ān 31:12, "We bestowed wisdom (*al-ḥikma*) on Luqmān," Kāshifī relates a number of tales about Luqmān, a legendary, Aesop-like figure from pre-Islamic times who was supposedly a black slave whose wisdom had been granted him from a divine source.[31] According to one such tale, which Kāshifī cites from Tha'labī's Qur'ān commentary, Luqmān had been sent, together with other slaves, to gather fruit from the master's garden.

30 Kāshifī, *Mavāhib-i 'aliyya*, vol. 2, 10 (*Sūrat al-anfāl*).

31 Kāshifī, *Mavāhib-i 'aliyya*, vol. 3, 444–445 (*Sūra Luqmān*).

His fellow slaves ate the fruit they were supposed to bring back to the master and blamed Luqmān. In order to counter the false accusation, Luqmān told his master to give everyone hot water to drink and then make them vomit the fruit by having them run around in a field. The one who threw up fruit would be the guilty party. In this way Luqmān was exonerated because he was the only one to vomit nothing but water.[32] To illustrate this Qurʾānic legend, Kāshifī cites Rūmī's take on it, which ends:

> Since Luqmān's wisdom can be demonstrated from this, then what must be the wisdom of the Lord of Existence!
> 'On the day when all things secret will be searched out,'[33] there will appear from you something latent, [the appearance of] which is not desired.
> When 'they will be given boiling water to drink,'[34] all the veils will be rent [revealing] that which is abhorrent.
> Whatever has been concealed will be made public, and whoever who has been deceitful will be disgraced.[35]

Kāshifī's citation of Rūmī's interpretation of the Qurʾānic verses and prophetic legend adds another dimension to his commentary by turning it into an admonition about the afterlife when, according to Islamic belief, people's true natures will be revealed on the Day of Judgement.[36]

Lubb-i lubāb-i maʿnavī

In a work entitled *Lubb-i lubāb-i maʿnavī* (also: *Lubb-i lubāb-i Masnavī*) ("The quintessence of [spiritual] meaning" or "The quintessence of the *Masnavī*"), completed in 875/1471, Kāshifī uses citations from Rūmī's *Masnavī* to illustrate the stages of the Sufi path. The work may have been modelled on the

32 The tale is taken from the "legends of the prophets" literature; see Abū Isḥāq Aḥmad ibn Muḥammad ibn Ibrāhīm al-Thaʿlabī, *ʿArāʾis al-majālis fī qiṣaṣ al-anbiyāʾ or "Lives of the Prophets,"* tr. William M. Brinner (Leiden: Brill, 2002), 588.

33 Qurʾān 86:9.

34 Qurʾān 47:15.

35 [Jalāl al-Dīn Muḥammad Rūmī al-Balkhī], *The Mathnawí of Jalálu'ddín Rúmí: Edited from the Oldest Manuscripts Available with Critical Notes, Translation, and Commentary*, ed. and tr. Reynold A. Nicholson, 8 vols. ([Cambridge]: Trustees of the E. J. W. Gibb Memorial, 1925–40), Book 1, lines 3,594–3,600.

36 See Sands, "On the Popularity," 478–479.

Kunūz al-ḥaqā'iq fi rumūz al-daqā'iq of Kamāl al-Dīn Ḥusayn Khwārazmī (d. 839/1435–36), which, like the *Lubb-i lubāb*, was based on a thematic arrangement of verses from the *Maṣnavī* according to particular topics related to Sufism and the Sufi path.[37] Kāshifī describes the *Lubb-i lubāb* as "selections from the selections of the *Maṣnavī*," that is, as an abridged version of his larger anthology entitled *Lubāb al-ma'navī fī intikhāb-i Maṣnavī*.[38] Kāshifī states that after he had compiled the anthology, some of his Sufi friends (*jamī' az rufaqā-yi ṭarīq*) asked him to compose a shorter work for the use of those just setting out on the spiritual path (*mubtadiyān-i ṭarīq-i ṭarīqat*) and those already on the way to the Truth (*sālikān-i manāhij-i ḥaqīqat*).[39] This signals that the work was intended for a general audience with an interest in Sufism, but a Sufism without the heavy physical and psychological commitments demanded of hardcore practitioners.[40]

Kāshifī refers to Rūmī as "the cream of the gnostic saints" (*ṣafvat al-awliyā' al-'ārifīn*), "the demonstrable proof of those who follow the Sufi path" (*burhān al-sālikīn*), "the tongue of the age" (*lisān al-zamān*), and "the master of the eternal Now" (*abū'l-vaqt*),[41] and he calls the *Maṣnavī* "the pages of the secrets of the Divine and the volumes of the knowledge of the Eternal."[42] Citing Rūmī's own characterization of the *Maṣnavī* as "the fundamentals of the fundamentals of the fundamentals of the Faith (*uṣūl uṣūl uṣūl al-dīn*) with respect to the unveiling of the secrets of Attainment and Certainty (*fī kashf asrār al-vuṣūl va'l-yaqīn*)," which contains allusions to works Rūmī claimed to supercede in his *Maṣnavī*, such as *Uṣūl al-dīn* (the title of many works on Ash'arī *kalām* and Ḥanafī jurisprudence) and *Kashf al-asrār* (the title of Maybudī's 12th-century

37 For Ḥusayn Khwārazmī's *Kunūz al-ḥaqā'iq*, which has not been published, see Devin A. DeWeese, "The *Kashf al-Hudā* of Kamāl ad-Dīn Ḥusayn Khorezmī: A Fifteenth-century Sufi Commentary on the *Qaṣīdat al-Burdah* in Khorezmian Turkic: Text Edition, Translation, and Historical Introduction," PhD diss. (Indiana University, 1985), 219–220, 223–224 and 560 (for manuscripts of the work).

38 I have not been able to locate a manuscript copy of this work, which may not actually be a separate composition.

39 Kamāl al-Dīn Ḥusayn b. 'Alī Vā'iẓ Kāshifī, *Lubb-i lubāb-i Maṣnavī*, ed. Naṣrullāh Taqavī (Qum: Bungāh-i Maṭbū'ātī-yi Afshārī, 1344/1965), 17.

40 The work was dedicated to an unnamed patron, whom Kāshifī refers to in the conclusion as *khwāja-i ṣāfī-dil-i ṣūfī-ṣifat*, who appears to have been a good poet (*khusraw andar shā'irī lālā-yi ū*) and a grandee who became a Sufi (*dar buzurgī rāh-i darvīshī girift*), and whose identity I will not speculate on at this time; see Kāshifī, *Lubb-i lubāb*, 469.

41 Kāshifī, *Lubb-i lubāb*, 17.

42 Kāshifī, *Lubb-i lubāb*, 29.

Sufi commentary on the Qurʾān),[43] Kāshifī amplifies the list by describing the *Maṡnavī* as "the texts of the elect" (*nuṣūṣ-i arbāb-i khuṣūṣ*)—an allusion to the *Naṣṣ al-nuṣūṣ* ("The text of texts"), a 14th-century commentary on Ibn ʿArabī's *Fuṣūṣ al-ḥikam* by Ḥaydar Āmulī; "the jewels of the secrets of the bezels" (*javāhir-i asrār-i fuṣūṣ*)—an allusion to Ibn ʿArabī's *Fuṣūṣ al-ḥikam* ("The bezels of wisdom") and possibly also to *Javāhir al-asrār va zavāhir al-anvār*, Khwārazmī's commentary on the *Maṡnavī*;[44] "the provision for the path of the Sufis" (*zād-i ṭarīq-i sālikān*)—an allusion to Sanāʾī's *Zād al-sālikīn*; and "the companion of the spiritual realization of the sincere" (*rafīq-i taḥqīq-i ṣādiqān*), an allusion to the *Ṭarīq al-taḥqīq*, a Sufi guidebook ascribed to Sanāʾī.[45] Kāshifī ends by saying: "May God give us to taste [this] purest wine of spiritual verities" (*raḥīq al-ḥaqāyiq*).[46] However, with this reference, Kāshifī has switched gears and is no longer referring to the *Maṡnavī* but to his own *Lubb-i lubāb*.

It is therefore misleading to call the *Lubb-i lubāb* simply an anthology of selections from Rūmī's *Maṡnavī*. It is much more than that, because what Kāshifī does is use selections from the *Maṡnavī* to illustrate the three stages of the Sufi path—*sharīʿat, ṭarīqat, ḥaqīqat*. As in the case of his Qurʾān commentary, he often does not cite consecutive verses from the *Maṡnavī*; rather, he chooses appropriate verses to illustrate a given concept or technical term from anywhere in the *Maṡnavī* and arranges them in such a manner that they appear to be consecutive. His ability to do this indicates that either he used a powerful search engine that located verses for him on a given topic, or else he had assimilated the *Maṡnavī* so completely that he was able to call up appropriate verses from the different books of the *Maṡnavī* from memory.

Since the Sufi novice (*sālik*) must first traverse the stages of *sharīʿat*, then acquire the attributes of those who follow the path of *ṭarīqat*, only after which can he attain the position of those who possess *ḥaqīqat*, Kāshifī explains that it was necessary for him to create three distinct chapters called "springs" (*ʿayn*) in

---

43 Rūmī, *Mathnawí of Jalálu'ddín Rúmí*, Book 1, p. 1.

44 See Kamāl al-Dīn Ḥusayn b. Ḥasan Khwārazmī, *Javāhir al-asrār va zavāhir al-anvār: Sharḥ-i Maṡnavī-i Mawlavī*, ed. Muḥammad Javād-Sharīʿat, vol. 1 (Isfahan: Muʾassasa-yi Intisharātī-yi Mashʿal-i Iṣfahān, 1360/1981). For a discussion of this work, which was well known in Timurid Herat, see DeWeese, "*Kashf al-Hudā*," 197, 219–222. Jāmī used it himself in compiling his *Nafaḥāt al-uns*.

45 Kāshifī, *Lubb-i lubāb*, 29. For *Ṭarīq al-taḥqīq* see Bo Utas, ed., *Ṭarīq ut-taḥqīq: A Sufi Mathnavi Ascribed to Ḥakīm Sanāʾī of Ghazna and Probably Composed by Aḥmad b. al-Ḥasan b. Muḥammad an-Naxčavānī* (Lund: Studentlitteratur, 1973).

46 Kāshifī, *Lubb-i lubāb*, 29. The word *raḥīq* occurs in the Qurʾān (Q 83:25) as a hapax legomenon. The phrase *raḥīq al-ḥaqāyiq* contains what I believe is an allusion to the *Kunūz al-ḥaqāʾiq* of Khwārazmī, for which see above, n. 37.

order for “the waters of these meanings (*maʿānī*) to flow forth.”[47] This division into “springs” appears to be an allusion to Rūmī’s description of the *Maṣnavī* in terms of Qurʾān 76:18:

> [It is] the garden of Paradise of the heart (*jinān al-janān*), having springs and trees, among them a spring (*ʿayn*) ‘called Salsabīl’ (*tusammā Salsabīlan*) by the travellers on this [spiritual] Path (*sabīl*).[48]

Kāshifī calls the first “spring” “the compendium of the ways of the Sharīʿa” (*sharīʿat*); the second “the treasury of the secrets of the Sufi path” (*ṭarīqat*); and the third “the dawning place of the lights of Truth” (*ḥaqīqat*). He further divides each “spring,” or chapter, into a number of “rivers” (*nahr*), each river being further subdivided into a number of “sprinklings” (*rashḥa*). Thus, the first “spring” on the ways of the Sharīʿa (*aṭvār-i sharīʿat*) is subdivided into seven “rivers,” the first being further subdivided into three “sprinklings,” the second into six, the third into two, the fourth into two, the fifth into two, the sixth into three, and the seventh into seven again.

In the first chapter on *sharīʿat*, Kāshifī presents key aspects of Islamic doctrine from a spiritual and moralistic rather than legalistic point of view. The subdivisions of the first “river” include the definition of faith (*īmān*), the profession of faith (*shahādat*), and worship (*ʿibādat*); those of the second “river” include ritual purity (*ṭahārat*), prayer (*namāz*), fasting (*rūza*), the duty of paying *zakāt*, the pilgrimage (*ḥajj*) and holy war (*jihād*); those of the third “river” include the meaning of divine destiny (*qażā va qadar*) and of predestination and free-will (*jabr va ikhtiyār*); those of the fourth “river” deal with knowledge (*ʿilm*) and the intellect (*ʿaql*); and the last “sprinkling” (*rashḥa*) deals with death and the afterlife. One can readily see that this first chapter is a kind of catechism. The difference is that each one of the items treated is illustrated by means of appropriate excerpts from the *Maṣnavī*, for which Kāshifī does not provide the exact references.

To illustrate the meaning of faith (*īmān*) Kāshifī quotes a number of consecutive lines from Book 5 of the *Maṣnavī* (lines 287–92) which end with a verse taken from another part of Book 5 (line 3,355):

47 Kāshifī, *Lubb-i lubāb*, 17–18. Lloyd Ridgeon has provided a full description of the organization and contents of the work; see Lloyd Ridgeon, “Naqshbandī Admirers of Rūmī in the Late Timurid Period,” *Mawlana Rumi Review*, 3 (2012), 160–163.

48 Rūmī, *Mathnawí of Jalálu’ddín Rúmí*, Book 1, p. 1.

> The [true] believer (*mu'min*) is he whose belief (*īmān*) amidst the ebb and flow [of fortune]
> Makes the infidel (*kāfir*) envious (*ḥasrat khvurd*).[49]

The last line triggers the anecdote Rūmī recounts in Book 5 (lines 3,356 ff.) about the Zoroastrian who was invited to accept Islam but declined because the only person he regarded as a genuine Muslim was the great 9th-century visionary Sufi, Bāyazīd Basṭāmī, and, not having the spiritual strength to attain to his level, he preferred not to accept the superficial faith of the Muslims he normally encountered, stating that for them "Muslim" was just a name with no meaning (*zānkeh nāmī bāshad va maʿnīsh nay*).[50]

To jump to the third and last "spring" on *ḥaqīqat*—this consists of three "rivers" that provide, in a nutshell, an overview of the most salient Sufi doctrines. The first "river" deals with the definition and characteristics of love (*ʿishq*). The second deals with such doctrines as visionary imagination (*mushāhada*), and the paired Sufi concepts of *qabż* and *basṭ*, and *qurb* and *vaṣl*. The third and last deals with gnosis (*maʿrifat*), the annihilation of the ego-self and the "abiding" in the Divine (*fanā va baqā*), and the goal of all Sufi spiritual exercises and visionary activity—unicity with the Divine (*tawḥīd*) and its four levels, which he refers to as *imtis̱ālī, istidlālī, ḥālī*, and *ẕū'l-jalālī*.[51] To illustrate the concept of *tawḥīd-i ḥālī*, Kāshifī cites Rūmī's take on the ancient Sanskrit tale of the elephant and the blind men, according to which the people who touched the elephant were not blind but rather tried unsuccessfully to determine the shape of the elephant in a darkened room. According to Rūmī's conclusion to the tale, if they had a candle (i.e., a spiritual guide like Rūmī or perhaps like Kāshifī himself) they would be able to attain holistic knowledge of the Divine.[52]

---

49 Kāshifī, *Lubb-i lubāb*, 40.

50 Kāshifī, *Lubb-i lubāb*, 40.

51 Kāshifī, *Lubb-i lubāb*, 388ff.

52 Kāshifī, *Lubb-i lubāb*, 463–464. For a discussion of the tale, see Maria E. Subtelny, "An Old Tale with a New Twist: The Elephant and the Blind Men in Rūmī's *Mas̱navī* and Its Precursors," in *No Tapping around Philology: A Festschrift in Honor of Wheeler McIntosh Thackston Jr.'s 70th Birthday*, ed. Alireza Korangy and Daniel J. Sheffield (Wiesbaden: Harrassowitz, 2014), 1–22.

Kāshifī's *Asrār-i qāsimī*

A work that demonstrates Kāshifī's preoccupation with esotericism is his *Asrār-i qāsimī*, which is an exposition of the occult sciences of *sīmiyā*, or letter magic, also known as *ʿilm-i ḥurūf*, and *rīmiyā*, or prestidigitation, also known as the science of conjuring (*ʿilm-i shuʿbadāt*).[53] *Sīmiyā* was regarded as a universal science, mastery of which allowed its practitioners to access and control reality through the power inherent in the letters (*ḥurūf*) of the Arabic alphabet.[54] The connection between Sufism and the occult sciences, lettrism in particular, was a long-standing one, as Sufis were the main practitioners of letter magic, which was also associated with the writing of talismans. According to Ibn ʿArabī, a lettrist grand master himself, "The science of letters is the science of the saints (*al-awliyāʾ*),"[55] the explanation for this being that the thaumaturgical gifts (*karāmāt*) of the Sufi masters were the result of divine inspiration, and not magic or sorcery in the conventional sense.[56]

Kāshifī's exposition of *sīmiyā* and *rīmiyā* is based on two Arabic works: *ʿUyūn al-ḥaqāʾiq wa īḍāḥ al-ṭarāʾiq* ("The sources of truths and the exposition of the methods [of attaining them]") by Abū'l-Qāsim Aḥmad al-Sīmāwī, also known as al-ʿIrāqī, a well-known author of mid-13th-century Mamluk Egypt, who wrote principally on alchemy; and a work entitled *Siḥr al-ʿuyūn*

53 Kamāl al-Dīn Ḥusayn b. ʿAlī Vāʿiẓ Kāshifī, *Asrār-i qāsimī*, Ms. Tehran, Majlis, 12559/2, p. 55; *Asrar-i qasimi*, Ms. Tehran, Majlis, 12568, p. 6. I have consulted manuscripts of the work rather than the Mumbai lithograph edition, which represents a later, Safavid amplification and elaboration of Kāshifī's original. Pierre Lory's groundbreaking article, "Kashifi's *Asrār-i Qāsimī* and Timurid Magic," *Iranian Studies*, 36/4 (2003), 531–41, is to be amended in many respects as it was based on the expanded version of the work represented by the Mumbai lithograph.

54 For letter magic, see Pierre Lory, *La science des lettres en islam* (Paris: Éditions Dervy, 2004), 37ff.; Manfred Ullman, *Die Natur- und Geheimwissenschaften im Islam* (Leiden: E. J. Brill, 1972), 361ff; and Matthew Melvin-Koushki, "The Occult Challenge to Philosophy and Messianism in Early Timurid Iran: Ibn Turka's Lettrism as a New Metaphysics," in *Unity in Diversity: Mysticism, Messianism and the Construction of Religious Authority in Islam*, ed. Orkhan Mir-Kasimov (Leiden: Brill, 2014), 250 (for a succinct definition).

55 For this famous formulation of Ibn ʿArabī's and its origin, see Denis Gril, "The Science of Letters," in Ibn al-ʿArabi, *The Meccan Revelations: Selected Texts of al-Futūḥāt al-Makkiya*, vol. 2, ed. Michel Chodkiewicz, tr. Cyrille Chodkiewicz and Denis Gril (New York: Pir Press, 2004), 123.

56 On the connection between Sufism and lettrism, see Ibn Khaldūn, *al-Muqaddima*, ed. ʿAbd al-Salām al-Shaddādī (Casablanca: Khizānat Ibn Khaldūn, Bayt al-Funūn wa'l-ʿUlūm wa'l-Ādāb, 2005), vol. 3, 116; and Ibn Khaldûn, *The Muqaddimah: An Introduction to History*, tr. Franz Rosenthal (New York: Pantheon Books, 1958), vol. 3, 167.

by a certain Abū ʿAbdullāh al-Maghribī, which Kāshifī says was also known as *Kitāb Ibn Ḥallāj*, and which I believe should be identified as *Kitāb Ibn al-Ḥājj* by the North African occultist Muḥammad Ibn al-Ḥājj al-Tilimsānī al-Maghribī (d. 737/1336), the author of *Shumūs al-anwār wa kunūz al-asrār*. Kāshifī explains that because the language and technical terminology employed in these Arabic works were too difficult, he translated them into Persian.[57]

Kāshifī states that he embarked upon his translation on the "order" of Amīr Sayyid Qāsim, the charismatic and controversial Sufi shaykh, better known as Qāsim-i Anvār (757–837/1356–1433), who had been active in early Timurid Herat.[58] As Qāsim-i Anvār would have been long dead by the time Kāshifī set about composing his *Asrār-i qāsimī* (the date usually given for completion of the work being 907/1501–2), the telepathic directive he received from him must be understood as a trope, and the title *Asrār-i qāsimī*, which alludes to Qāsim-i Anvār's name, can be interpreted to mean "The secrets authorized by Qāsim-i Anvār."

Kāshifī and his later Timurid-era contemporaries regarded Qāsim-i Anvār as a revered Sufi master, mystical poet, lettrist, and esotericist. Dawlatshāh included a separate notice on him in his anthology of poets, *Taẕkirat al-shuʿarā*, in which he referred to him as "the royal falcon in the atmosphere of *lāhūt* and the knower of this world and the supernal kingdom (*malakūt*)," and he made the interesting observation that anyone who met him, even those who may have been ill-disposed, came to believe in him to the point where most of the grandees and members of the military elite of Timurid Herat became his spiritual adherents (*murīdān*).[59] Navāʾī begins his *Majālis al-nafāʾis* with his biography and corroborates Dawlatshāh's remarks by stating that all the Chaghatayids—that is, Timurid princes and military commanders—were his devotees.[60] In later Timurid times he was regarded as a saint, and Navāʾī had

57 Kāshifī, *Asrār-i qāsimī*, Ms. Tehran, Majlis, 12559/2, p. 54; Kāshifī, *Asrār-i qāsimī*, Ms. Tehran, Majlis, 12568, p. 5. For these authors, see Ullmann, *Die Natur- und Geheimwissenschaften*, 391–392 and 235–236.

58 The *Asrār-i qāsimī* has sometimes incorrectly been described as having been dedicated to him, and some scholars have suggested he was a Safavid *amīr*, or military commander. My own identification of him as Amīr Abū'l-Qāsim, the marshall of the sayyids of Nishapur during the late Timurid period, is also to be corrected. See *Encyclopaedia of Islam*, 2nd ed., s.v. "Kās̲h̲ifī, Kamāl al-Dīn Ḥusayn b. ʿAlī" (by G̲h̲olam Hosein Yousofi); Lory, "Kashifi's *Asrār-i Qāsimi*," 531; and *Encyclopaedia Iranica*, s.v. "Kāšefi, Kamāl-al-Din Ḥosayn Wāʿeẓ" (by M. E. Subtelny).

59 Dawlatshāh Samarqandī, *Taẕkirat al-shuʿarā*ʾ, ed. Edward G. Browne (reprint ed., Tehran: Intishārāt-i Asāṭīr, 1382/2003), 346.

60 ʿAlī-shīr Navāʾī, *Majālis al-nafāʾis*, 6.

a building constructed in the garden of the Sufi lodge at Kharjird-i Jām where he finally settled and where his tomb was located.[61] Kāshifī quotes Qāsim-i Anvār's mystical poetry in several of his works. In the *Futuvvat-nāma-yi sulṭānī*, for example, he cites one of his poems to illustrate the meaning of the word "*darvīsh*" through the word's constituent letters.[62]

Futuvvat-nāma-yi sulṭānī

An important contribution to the understanding of the relationship between Sufism and Timurid society is Kāshifī's *Futuvvat-nāma-yi sulṭānī*, the title of which translates as "The book of spiritual chivalry relating to (or perhaps inspired by) the "Sultan [of Khurasan]," that is, ʿAlī Riżā, the eighth Shīʿī *imām*. In it he elaborates the ideals and practices of *futuvvat*, or spiritual chivalry, that blended Sufi esotericism with the ethics of manly virtue, or *javānmardī*, with particular regard to professional and craft guilds. The date of completion of the work is unknown, and the introduction does not mention the name of any of Kāshifī's usual patrons. Rather, Kāshifī states that the work was dedicated to the "servitors" of the shrine (*khuddām-i mazār*) of Imām Riżā at Mashhad, hence the allusion to the "Sultan of Khurasan." Nevertheless, the *Futuvvat-nāma-yi sulṭānī* does appear to be a work by Kāshifī, and, as mentioned earlier, one of the proofs of his authorship is his frequent citations in it from the *Maṡnavī* of Rūmī.[63]

The *Futuvvat-nāma-i sulṭānī* has been characterized as the most comprehensive medieval Persian treatise on *futuvvat*.[64] Written in a question and answer format, it sets out in great detail the moral qualities necessary for a *fatan*, or member of a *futuvvat* group, and explains the meaning of all the practices and rituals, especially those associated with initiation, stressing that they are all to be traced back to ʿAlī or some prophetic authority. Kāshifī provides long lists of moral qualities that are prerequisites for each aspect of the path of *futuvvat*.

61 Dawlatshāh, *Taẕkirat al-shuʿarāʾ*, 349.

62 Kāshifī, *Futuvvat-nāma-i sulṭānī*, 56–57. See Qāsim-i Anvār, *Kulliyāt*, ed. Saʿīd Nafīsī (Tehran: Kitābkhāna-yi Sanāʾī, 1337/1958), 335–336.

63 For a discussion of the attribution of the work and its authorship see Arley Loewen, "Proper Conduct (*Adab*) Is Everything: The *Futuwwat-nāmah-i Sulṭānī* of Husayn Vaʿiz-i Kashifi," *Iranian Studies*, 36/4 (2003), 544, n. 6.

64 Loewen, "Proper Conduct (*adab*) Is Everything," 544–545; and Lloyd Ridgeon, *Morals and Mysticism in Persian Sufism: A History of Sufi-futuwwat in Iran* (London: Routledge, 2010), 99–108.

For example, in answer to the question, "How many are the conditions of spiritual chivalry?" Kāshifī replies that there are 71, 48 of which must be present, and 23 of which must be absent. Of those which must be present are included: submission (*islām*), belief (*īmān*), intellect (*ʿaql*), knowledge (*ʿilm*), humility (*ḥilm*), asceticism (*zuhd*), abstinence (*varaʿ*), truthfulness (*ṣidq*), generosity (*karam*), manliness (*muruvvat*), and kindness (*shafaqat*). Among those which must be absent are acting contrary to the laws of the Sharīʿa (*mukhālafat-i sharʿ*), foul speech (*kalām-i mustaqbaḥ guftan*), gossiping (*sukhan-chīnī kardan*), excessive laughter (*bisyār khandīdan*), envy (*ḥasad burdan*), wine-drinking (*khamr khwurdan*), pederasty and adultery (*livāṭa va zinā kardan*), and associating with irreligious people (*bā mardum-i bad-maẕhab va bad- iʿtiqād muṣāḥabat namūdan*).[65] Finally, Kāshifī enumerates the various guilds and professions of his time, insisting that each aspect of a particular profession and even each implement used by a member of a profession or an artisan is infused with esoteric significance. In this way, the mundane activities even of wrestlers, plasterers, jugglers, and story-tellers are portrayed as sanctified actions, permeated with spiritual meaning and laden with salvific significance.

Crucially, Kāshifī incorporates a definition and discussion of Sufism in his exposition of *futuvvat*. In fact, it is difficult to distinguish between the two, but the explanation Kāshifī provides for the differences between them is illuminating:

> If asked: What is manly virtue (*muruvvat*)? Say: Manly virtue is a part of spiritual chivalry (*futuvvat*), just as spiritual chivalry is a part of the Sufi path (*ṭarīqat*).
>
> If asked: Since it is the basis of the Sufi path (*aṣl-i ṭarīqat*), why is this science called 'the science of spiritual chivalry' (*ʿilm-i futuvvat*) and not 'the Sufi path' (*ṭarīqat*)? Say: It is because not everyone possesses the power of endurance to tread the Sufi path (*ṭarīq-i ṭarīqat*), because the Sufi path means following the path of the Prophet and ʿAlī, step by step. And who has the power to do this except their Immaculate descendants? ... But whoever strives according to his spiritual concentration (*himmat*) and power (*quvvat*) will benefit from it.[66]

65 Kāshifī, *Futuvvat-nāma-i sulṭānī*, 26–27; Ḥusayn Wāʿiẓ Kāshifī Sabzawārī, *The Royal Book of Spiritual Chivalry* (*Futūwat nāmah-yi sulṭānī*), tr. Jay R. Crook (N.p.: Great Books of the Islamic World, 2000), 22–24.

66 Kāshifī, *Futuvvat-nāma-yi sulṭānī*, 29; Kāshifī, *Royal Book of Spiritual Chivalry*, 26.

Thus, conceding that not everyone is cut out for the Sufi path, Kāshifī explains that following the path of *futuvvat* is a respectable substitute to which anyone in society can aspire and from which anyone can derive spiritual benefit.

Membership in a chivalric order entailed initiatic rituals that were similar to those of Sufism. They comprised being dressed in the initiatic robe (*khirqa*), being girded with the initiatic belt (*shadd*), and taking the covenantal oath (*ʿahd*). Like many members of the Timurid religious intelligentsia and social elite of the time, Kāshifī belonged to the Sufi fraternity of the Naqshbandiyya. In Herat he had come under the influence of Kāshgharī's spiritual successor, ʿAbd-al-Raḥmān Jāmī, and was initiated into the Naqshbandī order. His son ʿAlī Ṣafī followed in his footsteps and composed a work entitled *Rashaḥāt-i ʿayn al-ḥayāt*, a hagiography of Naqshbandī shaykhs, chief among these being ʿUbaydullāh Aḥrār (d. 895/1490). Kāshifī also appears to have been a member of a chivalric order himself. In the *Futuvvat-nāma-i sulṭānī* he provides his chains of initiation (*asnād*) for various aspects of his *futuvvat* activities. First, he mentions his Sufi chain (*sanad*), which begins with his spiritual master, or "Master of the path" (*shaykh-i ṭarīqat*), Shaykh Nūr al-Dīn Aḥmad b. Muḥammad al-Qāyinī, and ends with ʿAlī and Muḥammad.[67] His chain (*sanad*) for the covenantal oath begins with his "Master of the covenant" (*pidar-i ʿahd Allāh*), Darvīsh Tāj al-Dīn ʿAlī Dihqān, the son of Mawlānā Luṭfullāh Nīshāpūrī, and ends with ʿAlī. His chain (*sanad*) for the initiatic girding begins with his "Master of the belt" (*ustād-i shadd*), Darvīsh Jamāl al-Dīn Salmān b. Darvīsh Bābākā, and ends with ʿAlī and Muḥammad, as well as with such historico-mythic figures as Abū Muslim Khurasānī and Sālmān Fārisī.[68]

The *Futuvvat-nāma-yi sulṭānī* summarizes the ethical code of behavior that marked the culture of spiritual chivalry: honesty, generosity, chastity, loyalty, and the maintenance of decorum (*adab*). Kāshifī's treatise on Ḥātim al-Ṭāyy, entitled *Risāla-yi ḥātimiyya*, which was devoted to a pre-Islamic figure proverbial for his generosity, further underscores the importance accorded generosity in the ethical code of *futuvvat*.[69] Sufism and *futuvvat* reinforced each other:

67 He must be the son of the well-known Ḥanafī jurist, preacher, and traditionist of Herat, Jalāl al-Dīn al-Qāyinī (d. 838/1434–45), for whom see Maria Eva Subtelny and Anas B. Khalidov, "The Curriculum of Islamic Higher Learning in Timurid Iran in the Light of the Sunni Revival under Shāh-Rukh," *Journal of the American Oriental Society*, 115/2 (1995), 218ff., 228. The other masters he subsequently enumerates have not been identified.

68 Kāshifī, *Futuvvat-nāma-yi sulṭānī*, 123–126. See also Ridgeon, *Morals and Mysticism*, 105–6.

69 Completed in 891/1486 and dedicated to the Timurid ruler Sulṭān-Ḥusayn. For a recent translation, see Lloyd Ridgeon, *Jawanmardi: A Sufi Code of Honour* (Edinburgh: Edinburgh University Press, 2011), 175–208.

without Sufism, *futuvvat* would lack its spiritual ethos, and without *futuvvat*, Sufism would remain isolated from a broader spectrum of society. Kāshifī's promotion of a kind of "lay Sufism,"[70] reinforced by the ethical perspective of *futuvvat*, contributed to the deepening of Muslim mores in late 15th and early 16th-century Central Asian society.

Epilogue

It is perhaps no wonder that, in post-Soviet Central Asia, Kāshifī's works are enjoying something of a renaissance. His *Futuvvat-nāma-yi sulṭānī* was published in Tajik Cyrillic script in Dushanbe in 1991, together with his *Akhlāq-i muḥsinī* and *Risāla-yi ḥātimiyya*.[71] In 2009, the Tajik National Encyclopedia again published the *Akhlāq-i muḥsinī*, together with the *Risāla-yi ḥātimiyya* (under the title *Sarguẕasht-i Ḥātim*).[72] In what can only be interpreted as a response to these Tajik cultural initiatives, in 2010 the National Encyclopedia of Uzbekistan published the facsimile of an early manuscript of the *Akhlāq-i muḥsinī* from the collection of the Al-Beruni Institute of Oriental Studies of the Academy of Sciences of Uzbekistan, together with an abridged Uzbek translation.[73] We can only hope this trend continues and more of Kāshifī's works are published for the wider audience for which they had originally been intended.

Bibliography

Aflākī, Shams al-Dīn Aḥmad-e. *The Feats of the Knowers of God (Manāqeb al-ʿārefīn)*. Tr. John O'Kane. Leiden: Brill, 2002.

Aflākī al-ʿĀrifī, Shams al-Dīn Aḥmad. *Manāqib al-ʿārifīn*. Ed. Taḥsīn Yāzījī. 2 vols. Reprint ed., Tehran: Dunyā-yi Kitāb, 1375/1996.

70 For an elaboration of this idea see Ridgeon, *Morals and Mysticism*, 108–116; and Ridgeon, *Jawanmardi*, 165–173.

71 Husayn Voizi Koshifī, *Futuvvatnomai sultonī—Akhloqi mūhsinī—Risolai Hotamiya* (Dushanbe: Adib, 1991).

72 *Akhloqi mūhsinī—Sarguzashti Hotam—Tūtinoma* (Dushanbe: Sarredaktsiyai Ilmii Ènsikopediyai Millii Tojik, 2009).

73 Husayn Voiz Koshifiy, *Akhloqi muhsiniy* (Uzbek title p.: *Yakhshi khulqlar*), facsimile ed. Bahrom Abduhalimov and Tursunali Quziev; tr. Mahmud Hasaniy and Asadali Hakimjonov (Tashkent: Uzbekiston Milliy Èntsiklopediiasi, Davlat ilmiy nashriyoti, 2010).

Akhloqi mūhsinī—Sarguzashti Hotam—Tūtinoma. Dushanbe: Sarredaktsiyai Ilmii Ènsikopediyai Millii Tojik, 2009.

Alisher Navoiy. *Majolisun nafois: Ilmiy-tanqidiy tekst.* [Chaghatay]. Ed. Suyima Ghanieva. Tashkent: Uzbekiston SSR Fanlar akademiiasi nashriyoti, 1961.

ʿAlī-shīr Navāʾī, Mīr Niẓām al-Dīn. *Majālis al-nafāʾis: Dar taẕkira-i shuʿarāʾ-i qarn-i nuhum-i hijrī* (translated into Persian and expanded by Sulṭan-Muḥammad Fakhrī Harātī and Ḥakīm Shāh-Muḥammad Qazvīnī). Ed. ʿAlī Asghar Ḥikmat. Tehran: Chāpkhāna-yi Bānk-i Millī-yi Īrān, 1323/1945.

Bākharzī, ʿAbd al-Vāsiʿ Niẓāmī. *Maqāmāt-i Jāmī: Gūshahāyī az tārīkh-i farhangī va ijtimāʿī-yi Khurāsān dar ʿaṣr-i Tīmūrīyān*. Ed. Najīb Māyil Haravī. Tehran: Nashr-i Nay, 1371/1992–93.

Dawlatshāh b. ʿAlāʾ al-Dawla Bakhtī-shāh al-Ghāzī al-Samarqandī. *Taẕkirat al-shuʿarāʾ*. Ed. Edward G. Browne. Reprint ed., Tehran: Intishārāt-i Asāṭīr, 1382/2003.

DeWeese, Devin A. "The *Kashf al-Hudā* of Kamāl ad-Dīn Ḥusayn Khorezmī: A Fifteenth-century Sufi Commentary on the *Qaṣīdat al-Burdah* in Khorezmian Turkic: Text Edition, Translation, and Historical Introduction." PhD diss., Indiana University, 1985.

Gril, Denis. "The Science of Letters." In Ibn al-ʿArabi, *The Meccan Revelations: Selected Texts of al-Futūḥāt al-Makkiya*. Vol. 2, ed. Michel Chodkiewicz, tr. Cyrille Chodkiewicz and Denis Gril (New York: Pir Press, 2004), 105–219.

Herrmann, Gottfried. "Biographisches zu Ḥusain Wāʿiẓ Kāšifī." In *Corolla Iranica: Papers in Honour of Prof. Dr. David Neil MacKenzie on the Occasion of His 65th Birthday on April 8th, 1991*, ed. Ronald E. Emmerick and Dieter Weber (Frankfurt: Peter Lang, 1991), 90–100.

Husayn Voizi Koshifī. *Futuvvatnomai sultonī—Akhloqi mūhsinī—Risolai Hotamiya*. Dushanbe: Adib, 1991.

Ibn Khaldūn, ʿAbd al-Raḥmān. *al-Muqaddima*. Ed. ʿAbd al-Salām al-Shaddādī. 5 vols. Casablanca: Khizānat Ibn Khaldūn, Bayt al-Funūn wa al-ʿUlūm wa al-Ādāb, 2005.

Ibn Khaldûn. *The Muqaddimah: An Introduction to History*. Tr. Franz Rosenthal. 3 vols. New York: Pantheon Books, 1958.

Kāshifī, Kamāl al-Dīn Ḥusayn b. ʿAlī, Vāʿiẓ. *Asrār-i qāsimī*. Ms. Tehran, Majlis, 12559/2.

Kāshifī, Kamāl al-Dīn Ḥusayn b. ʿAlī, Vāʿiẓ. *Asrār-i qāsimī*. Ms. Tehran, Majlis, 12568.

Kāshifī, Kamāl al-Dīn Ḥusayn b. ʿAlī, Vāʿiẓ. *Asrār-i qāsimī*. Lithograph ed., Mumbai: Fatḥ al-Karīm Press, 1302/1885.

Kāshifī, Kamāl al-Dīn Ḥusayn b. ʿAlī, Vāʿiẓ. *Futuvvat-nāma-yi sulṭānī*. Ed. Muḥammad Jaʿfar Maḥjūb. Tehran: Intishārāt-i Bunyād-i Farhang-i Īrān, no. 113, 1350/1971.

Kāshifī, Kamāl al-Dīn Ḥusayn b. ʿAlī, Vāʿiẓ. *Javāhir al-tafsīr: Tafsīrī adabī, ʿirfānī, ḥurūfī, shāmil-i muqaddimaʾī dar ʿulūm-i qurʾānī va tafsīr-i sūrat-i Ḥamd*. Ed. Javād ʿAbbāsī. Tehran: Mīrāṡ-i Maktūb, 1379/2000–2001.

Kāshifī, Kamāl al-Dīn Ḥusayn b. ʿAlī, Vāʿiẓ. *Lubb-i lubāb-i Maṡnavī*. Ed. Naṣrullāh Taqavī. Qum: Bungāh-i Maṭbūʿātī-yi Afshārī, 1344/1965.

Kāshifī, Kamāl al-Dīn Ḥusayn b. ʿAlī, Vāʿiẓ. *Mavāhib-i ʿaliyya yā Tafsīr-i ḥusaynī* (*bi-fārsī*). Ed. Muḥammad Riżā Jalālī Nāyinī. 4 vols. Tehran: Iqbāl, 1317–29/1938–50.

Kāshifī, Kamāl al-Dīn Ḥusayn b. ʿAlī, Vāʿiẓ. *Rawżat al-shuhadāʾ*. Ed. Āyatullāh Ḥājj Shaykh Abūʾl-Ḥasan Shaʿrānī. Reprint ed., Tehran: Intishārāt-i Islāmiyya, 1379/2000–2001.

Kāshifī Sabzawārī, Ḥusayn Wāʿiẓ. *The Royal Book of Spiritual Chivalry (Futūwat nāmah-yi sulṭānī)*. Tr. Jay R. Crook. N.p.: Great Books of the Islamic World, 2000.

Khwāndamīr, Ghiyās̱ al-Dīn b. Humām al-Dīn al-Ḥusaynī. *Khātima-i Khulāṣat al-akhbār*. In Khwāndamīr, *Maʾās̱ir al-mulūk, bi-żamīma-yi Khātima-yi Khulāṣat al-akhbār va Qānūn-i Humāyūnī*. Ed. Mīr Hāshim Muḥaddis̱. Tehran: Muʾassasa-yi Khadamāt-i Farhangī-yi Rasā, 1372/1994.

Khwāndamīr, Ghiyās̱ al-Dīn b. Humām al-Dīn al-Ḥusaynī. *Maʾās̱ir al-mulūk*. In Khwāndamīr, *Maʾās̱ir al-mulūk, bi-żamīma-yi khātima-yi Khulāṣat al-akhbār va Qānūn-i Humāyūnī*. Ed. Mīr Hāshim Muḥaddis̱. Tehran: Muʾassasa-yi Khadamāt-i Farhangī-yi Rasā, 1372/1994.

Khwāndamīr, Ghiyās̱ al-Dīn b. Humām al-Dīn al-Ḥusaynī. *Tārīkh-i Ḥabīb al-siyar fī akhbār afrād-i bashar*. Ed. Jalāl al-Dīn Humāʾī. 4 vols. Reprint ed., Tehran: Khayyām, 1362/1984.

Khwārazmī, Kamāl al-Dīn Ḥusayn b. Ḥasan. *Javāhir al-asrār va zavāhir al-anvār: Sharḥ-i Mas̱navī-i Mawlavī*. Ed. Muḥammad Javād-Sharīʿat. Vol. 1. Isfahan: Muʾassasa-yi Intisharātī-yi Mashʿal-i Iṣfahān, 1360/1981.

Koshifiy, Husayn Voiz. *Akhloqi muhsiniy* (Uzbek title p.: *Yakhshi khulqlar*). Facsimile ed. Bahrom Abduhalimov and Tursunali Quziev; tr. Mahmud Hasaniy and Asadali Hakimjonov. Tashkent: Uzbekiston Milliy Èntsiklopediiasi, Davlat ilmiy nashriyoti, 2010.

Loewen, Arley. "Proper Conduct (*Adab*) Is Everything: The *Futuwwat-nāmah-i Sulṭānī* of Husayn Vaʿiz-i Kashifi." *Iranian Studies*, 36/4 (2003), 543–570.

Lory, Pierre. "Kashifi's *Asrār-i Qāsimī* and Timurid Magic." *Iranian Studies*, 36/4 (2003), 531–541.

Lory, Pierre. *La science des lettres en Islam*. Paris: Éditions Dervy, 2004.

Makdisi, George. *The Rise of Colleges: Institutions of Learning in Islam and the West*. Edinburgh: Edinburgh University Press, 1981.

Melvin-Koushki, Matthew. "The Occult Challenge to Philosophy and Messianism in Early Timurid Iran: Ibn Turka's Lettrism as a New Metaphysics." In *Unity in Diversity: Mysticism, Messianism and the Construction of Religious Authority in Islam*, ed. Orkhan Mir-Kasimov (Leiden: Brill, 2014), 247–276.

Mitchell, Colin Paul. "To Preserve and Protect: Husayn Vaʿiz-i Kashifi and Perso-Islamic Chancellery Culture." *Iranian Studies*, 36/4 (2003), 485–507.

Pedersen, Johs. "The Islamic Preacher: *wāʿiẓ, mudhakkir, qāṣṣ*." In *Ignace Goldziher Memorial Volume*, Pt. 1, ed. Samuel Löwinger and Joseph Somogyi (Budapest: Globus Nyomdai Műintézet, 1948), 226–251.

Qāsim-i Anvār. *Kulliyāt*. Ed. Saʿīd Nafīsī. Tehran: Kitābkhāna-yi Sanāʾī, 1337/1958.
Ridgeon, Lloyd. *Jawanmardi: A Sufi Code of Honour*. Edinburgh: Edinburgh University Press, 2011.
Ridgeon, Lloyd. *Morals and Mysticism in Persian Sufism: A History of Sufi-futuwwat in Iran*. London: Routledge, 2010.
Ridgeon, Lloyd. "Naqshbandī Admirers of Rūmī in the Late Timurid Period." *Mawlana Rumi Review*, 3 (2012), 124–168.
[Rūmī, Jalāl al-Dīn Muḥammad al-Balkhī]. *The Mathnawí of Jalálu'ddín Rúmí: Edited from the Oldest Manuscripts Available with Critical Notes, Translation, and Commentary*. Ed. and tr. Reynold A. Nicholson. 8 vols. E. J. W. Gibb Memorial Series, n. s., 4.1–8. [Cambridge]: Trustees of the E. J. W. Gibb Memorial, 1925–40.
Ruymbeke, Christine van. *Kāshefi's Anvār-e Sohayli: Rewriting Kalila and Dimna in Timurid Herat*. Leiden: Brill, 2016.
Ṣafī, Fakhr al-Dīn ʿAlī b. Ḥusayn Kāshifī. *Rashaḥāt-i ʿayn al-ḥayāt*. Ed. ʿAlī Aṣghar Muʿīniyān. 2 vols. Tehran: Intishārāt-i Bunyād-i Nīkūkārī-i Nūriyānī, no. 15, 2536/1977.
Sands, Kristin Zahra. "On the Popularity of Husayn Vaʿiz-i Kashifi's *Mavāhib-i ʿaliyya*: A Persian Commentary on the Qurʾan." *Iranian Studies*, 36/4 (2003), 469–483.
Subtelny, Maria E. "Husayn Vaʿiz-i Kashifi: Polymath, Popularizer, and Preserver," *Iranian Studies*, 36/4 (2003), 463–466.
Subtelny, Maria E. "A Late Medieval Persian *Summa* on Ethics: Kashifi's *Akhlāq-i Muḥsinī*." *Iranian Studies*, 36/4 (2003), 601–614.
Subtelny, Maria E. "An Old Tale with a New Twist: The Elephant and the Blind Men in Rūmī's *Maṡnavī* and Its Precursors." In *No Tapping around Philology: A Festschrift in Honor of Wheeler McIntosh Thackston Jr.'s 70th Birthday*, ed. Alireza Korangy and Daniel J. Sheffield (Wiesbaden: Harrassowitz, 2014), 1–22.
Subtelny, Maria Eva, and Anas B. Khalidov. "The Curriculum of Islamic Higher Learning in Timurid Iran in the Light of the Sunni Revival under Shāh-Rukh." *Journal of the American Oriental Society*, 115/2 (1995), 210–236.
al-Thaʿlabī, Abū Isḥāq Aḥmad ibn Muḥammad ibn Ibrāhīm. *ʿArāʾis al-majālis fī qiṣaṣ al-anbiyāʾ or "Lives of the Prophets."* Tr. William M. Brinner. Leiden: Brill, 2002.
Tourkin, Sergei, and Živa Vesel. "The Contribution of Husayn Vaʿiz-i Kashifi to the Transmission of Astrological Texts." *Iranian Studies*, 36/4 (2003), 589–599.
Ullmann, Manfred. *Die Natur- und Geheimwissenschaften im Islam*. Leiden: E. J. Brill, 1972.
Utas, Bo, ed. *Ṭarīq ut-taḥqīq: A Sufi Mathnavi Ascribed to Ḥakīm Sanāʾī of Ghazna and Probably Composed by Aḥmad b. al-Ḥasan b. Muḥammad an-Naxčavānī*. Lund: Studentlitteratur, 1973; Scandinavian Institute of Asian Studies Monograph Series, no. 13.

CHAPTER 4

Ḥażrat Jīo Ṣāḥib: How Durrānī Peshawar Helped Revive Bukhara's Sanctity

Waleed Ziad

Introduction

This study introduces Ḥażrat Jīo Ṣāḥib Pishāvarī, a scholar-saint of the Naqshbandī-Mujaddidī Sufi *ṭarīqa*, who, through the 18th and 19th centuries, was instrumental in tying together the social fabric of the Peshawar valley and Bukhara.

His story is set against the backdrop of dramatic political and economic realignments in Mawarannahr, Khurasan, and Hindustan in the mid-18th century.[1] This period witnessed the fragmentation of the Safavid and Mughal empires and the Ashtarkhanid state, and the gradual encroachment of Imperial China, Russia, and Britain. In the midst of this crisis, the Afghan Durrānī empire managed to secure a tentative hold over a vast territory at the center of the Persianate world. For more than half a century, the Durrānīs were positioned at the center of a transregional domain of commodities and ideas.[2]

At this juncture, Sufi networks from Hindustan and Khurasan expanded their reach into Mawarannahr, as far as Kazan and Kashghar. Foremost among these were the successors of Shaykh Aḥmad Sirhindī (d. 1624), known as the Naqshbandiyya-Mujaddidiyya.[3]

---

1 The terms 'Hindustan,' 'Khurasan,' and 'Mawarannahr,' as per contemporary Persian sources, will be employed in lieu of terms such as Central Asia and South Asia, or Afghanistan and India, which represent later European conceptualizations of this region. 'Khurasan' encompasses modern day Afghanistan, north-western Pakistan, southern Turkmenistan, and north-eastern Iran.

2 Jos Gommans, "Mughal India and Central Asia in the Eighteenth Century: An Introduction to a Wider Perspective," *Itinerario*, 15 (01) (1991), 64–66.

3 Shaykh Aḥmad Sirhindī was known as the 'Mujaddid-i Alf-i Thānī', or reviver of the second Islamic millennium. Among his numerous intellectual contributions were reconciling *ḥaqīqa* (truth, or the Sufi mystical path) and *sharīʿa* (the divine path or divine law), systematizing Sufi meditative practices, and elaborating upon the doctrine of *waḥdat al-shuhūd* (unity of contemplative witnessing). Sirhindī's successors, the Naqshbandiyya-Mujaddidiyya (referred to, herein, as the Mujaddidiyya), had already established a presence in Khurasan

 | DOI:10.1163/9789004373075_006

One of Sirhindī's Sufi inheritors who emerged in the mid-18th century was the scholar-saint Miyān Fażl Aḥmad Maʿṣūmī, popularly known as Ḥażrat Jīo Ṣāḥib Pishāvarī.[4] He forged a network of institutions that spanned the region from Bukhara and the Farghana valley to Waziristan and Punjab, attracting a range of adherents from ascetics and celebrated *ʿulamā'*, to local rulers.

Primarily based on local histories and biographies of Ḥażrat Jīo, this study explores how local ruling elites from Hindustan, Khurasan, and Mawarannahr effectively entrusted the academic and social services sectors to Sufi lineages, whose popular authority appealed to both urban intelligentsia and tribal populations. These Sufi networks, in turn, were able to provide coherence to this politically fragmented region. Moreover, this study demonstrates that a half-century of urban renewal under the Afghan Durrānīs (ca. 1750–1800), within a decentralized, informal imperial structure, facilitated an academic and spiritual revival from Khoqand to Kazan. Through figures like Ḥażrat Jīo, the religio-academic milieu of Mughal Hindustan mediated through Durrānī Khurasan injected Mawarannahr with a new corpus of literature, epistemologies, and practices. In the case of Bukhara, it even helped invigorate an exceptional model of governance and sacred kingship reflecting Naqshbandī-Mujaddidī Sufi ethics.

This paper will begin by presenting an overview of the life and career of Ḥażrat Jīo. I will outline his journey from Sirhind to Peshawar and Bukhara, and the subsequent development of Sufi institutions and subsidiary *silsila*s along this route. I will next focus on two case studies of Peshawar and Bukhara, examining how Ḥażrat Jīo and his contemporaries contributed to what local sources refer to as the 'revival' of both regions.

Constructed Frontiers

This study challenges a key historiographical paradigm regarding the interconnectedness of what eventually came to be known as the 'Great Game' buffer states. Geographic conceptualizations of pre-colonial Mawarannahr, Khurasan, and Hindustan have been influenced by several assumptions rooted in colonial historiography.

---

and Mawarannahr by the mid-17th century. However, their institutions and networks most rapidly expanded in the late 18th century.

4 'Jīo' is an archaic term of respect often applied to saints from Punjab to the Peshawar valley, analogous to the Hindustani 'Jī'. 'Jīo' and 'Jī' can be applied interchangeably.

First, as Jonathan Lee points out, British imperial administrators defined the region based on several constructed frontiers. Following ancient Greek historiography, in the colonial consciousness the Amu Darya was conceived of as the "border between civilization and barbarism."[5] Mawarannahr, situated north of the Amu Darya, was imagined as the domain of lawlessness and despotic government.[6] Likewise, the Pashtun tribal belt, demarcating the limits of British India, was defined as another natural frontier. A second, related legacy of the 'Great Game' narrative views this period as one of academic and religious isolation and stagnation.

This compartmentalized viewpoint persists to date, overlooking complex relationships between urban and tribal spheres throughout the Persianate oecumene in the 18th and 19th centuries. Studies most often approach religious revival and activism in the Peshawar valley or Kabul as localized phenomena. More emphasis is placed on religio-political and military activism, than on the multivalent functions of religious institutions, and their pedagogies.[7]

This isolation paradigm has been challenged through studies of trans-regional economic interactions,[8] although linkages in the religio-academic domain have only begun to be investigated.[9] There are, in particular, a dearth of micro-historical studies tracing the contours of Sufi and *ʿulamāʾ* networks.

5 J. L. Lee, *The "Ancient Supremacy": Bukhara, Afghanistan and the Battle for Balkh, 1731–1901* (Leiden: Brill, 1996), xviii. The Amu Darya is referred to as the Oxus in British colonial sources, based on the classical Greek designation for the river.

6 Geoff Watson, "Images of Central Asia in the 'Central Asian Question' c. 1826–1885," in *Walls and Frontiers in Inner Asian History* (Silk Road Studies, VI), ed. Craig Benjamin and Samuel Lieu (Turnhout, Belgium: Brepols, 2003), 138.

7 See Senzil K. Nawid, *Religious Response to Social Change in Afghanistan, 1919–29: King Aman-Allah and the Afghan Ulama* (Costa Mesa, California: Mazda Publishers, 1999); Sana Haroon, *Frontier of Faith: Islam in the Indo-Afghan Borderland* (New York: Columbia University Press, 2007); Robert Nichols, *Settling the Frontier: Land, Law and Society in the Peshawar Valley, 1500–1900* (Karachi: Oxford University Press, 2001).

8 See Jos Gommans, *The Rise of the Indo-Afghan Empire: C. 1710–1780* (Leiden: E. J. Brill, 1995); Scott C. Levi, *The Indian Diaspora in Central Asia and Its Trade: 1550–1900* (Leiden: Brill, 2002); Wolfgang Holzwarth, "The Uzbek State as Reflected in Eighteenth Century Bukharan Sources," *Asiatische Studien*, 60/2 (2006), 321–353; Claude Markovits, *The Global World of Indian Merchants, 1750–1947: Traders of Sind from Bukhara to Panama* (Cambridge: Cambridge University Press, 2000); and Muzaffar Alam, "Trade, State Policy and Regional Change: Aspects of Mughal-Uzbek Commercial Relations, c. 1550–1750," *Journal of the Economic and Social History of the Orient*, 37/3 (1994), 202–227.

9 See, for example, the following studies on the transmission of the Naqshbandī-Mujaddidiyya into Mawarannahr: Jo-Ann Gross, "The Naqshbandiya Connection: From Central Asia to India and Back (16th–19th Centuries)," in *India and Central Asia: Commerce and Culture,*

In this respect, interrogating sources on Ḥażrat Jīo from both sides of the Amu Darya[10] is highly revealing.[11] Sources suggest that despite political

1500–1800, ed. Scott C. Levi (New Delhi: Oxford University Press, 2007), 232–259; Anke von Kügelgen, "Die Entfaltung der Naqšbandīya Muǧaddidīya im mittleren Transoxanien vom 18. bis zum Beginn des 19. Jahrhunderts: Ein Stück Detektivarbeit," in *Muslim Culture in Russia and Central Asia from the 18th to the Early 20th Centuries*, vol. 2: *Inter-Regional and Inter-Ethnic Relations*, ed. Anke von Kügelgen, Michael Kemper, and Allen J. Frank (Berlin: Klaus Schwarz Verlag, 1998), 101–151; Muḥammad Iqbāl Mujaddidī, "'Ālamī Satih par Silsila-yi Naqshbandiyya Mujaddidiyya kā Athr-o Rasūkh," in *Armaqān-i Imām Rabbānī, Vol. 2*, ed. Muḥammad Humāyūn Abbās Shams (Lahore: Sher-i Rabbānī Publishers, 2008), 69–81; and Devin DeWeese, "'Dis-ordering' Sufism in Early Modern Central Asia: Suggestions for Rethinking the Sources and Social Structures of Sufi History in the 18th and 19th Centuries," in *History and Culture of Central Asia/Istoriia i kul'tura Tsentral'noi Azii*, ed. Bakhtiyar Babadjanov and Kawahara Yayoi (Tokyo: The University of Tokyo, 2012), 259–279.

10 The earliest biographical accounts were compiled by two disciples, ʿAbd al-Raḥīm Pishāvarī and Ḥāfiẓ Muḥammad Saʿīd. Both accounts are copied in a larger manuscript located at the Khānaqāh-i Ḥażratkhayl established by Ḥażrat Jīo's grandsons at the village of Thana now in the Malakand Agency. The most comprehensive biography of Ḥażrat Jīo, however, is *Tuḥfat al-murshid*, written by Niẓām al-Dīn Balkhī Mazārī at the behest of Ḥażrat Jīo's son and *khalīfa*, Miyān Fażl-i Ḥaqq in the early 19th century; see Niẓām al-Dīn Balkhī Mazārī, *Tuḥfat al-murshid dar manāqib-i Quṭb-i Zamān Ghawth-i Jahān Ḥażrat Jīo Ṣāḥib Shāh Fażl Aḥmad Maʿṣūmī* (Lahore: Fayż-i ʿĀm, 1913). Imām Muḥammad Ḥusayn, a son of Ḥażrat Jīo's *khalīfa* among the Miyānkhayl Pashtuns, composed a second comprehensive biography of the *silsila, Rawżat al-awliyāʾ*, culminating with an entry on the author's father, Imām Muḥammad Riżā (Faqīr Ṣāḥib) of Zakori in Dera Ismail Khan; see Imām Muḥammad Jīo Ṣāḥib Zakorī, *Rawżat al-awliyāʾ fī aḥvāl-i aṣfiyāʾ* (Zakori, Dera Ismail Khan: Nījar Rūz Bāzār Press, 1333/1914–15). Another key source on Ḥażrat Jīo's lineage was written by ʿAbdullāh Jān Fārūqī Naqshbandī, a fifth generation descendant of Ḥażrat Jīo; *see* ʿAbdullāh Jān Fārūqī Naqshbandī, *Gulhā-i chaman* (Thana, Malakand Agency: Idāra-yi Naqshbandiyya Garhī Ḥażratkhayl, 1967). In addition, several biographical dictionaries, royal chronicles, and regional histories mainly of Bukhara, Khoqand, Herat, Badakhshān, Kazan, and Peshawar contain entries on the lineage. Several works of disciples from sub-lineages, in regions including Waziristan and Malakand, have also been published over the last century.

11 Sources employed in this study include works produced within Sufi orders (for instance, hagiographies, biographies, epistles, poetry, theological or cosmological works, or endowment deeds), Persian, Arabic, Turkic, Pushtu, and Urdu sources produced outside Sufi networks (e.g., city histories, biographical dictionaries, shrine catalogues, and royal chronicles), and British, Russian and French sources (such as administrative documents, travel accounts, and gazetteers). Sources produced with the Mujaddidī tradition are no doubt valuable, but have several limitations. Using them as historical tools requires an acute familiarity with forms and genres, cultural contexts, themes, narrative devices, and

dissolution, the region remained socially, culturally, and intellectually integrated. By establishing *khānaqāhs* and *madrasas*, the Mujaddidiyya in fact played a critical role in sustaining a Hindustan-Khurasan-Mawarannahr zone of exchange through textual production, networks of pilgrimage, trade, and literary exchange, and trans-regional structures of authority. Most significantly, we learn that a range of social currents in the urban and tribal spheres, generally treated as distinct moments in local histories—from those of the Akhund of Swat, the anti-colonial *mujāhid*, to Bukhara's 19th-century renaissance—actually formed part of an interconnected web of social-intellectual-religious movements.

Following Joseph Fletcher, this study demonstrates that religio-academic revival in Kazan, or the formation of autonomous Pashtun tribal zones under religious direction, cannot be understood apart from socio-political developments in greater Hindustan, and in turn, the Afghan Durrānī empire.[12] Drawing upon Jos Gommans' work on inter-regional trade, it further demonstrates that the Afghan empire was the fulcrum that facilitated north-south flows. Ḥażrat Jīo and other Mujaddidī Sufis, akin to Gommans' Shikārpūrī traders and *powindās*, were the agents of exchange.

functions. In fact, reading sources such as hagiographies against the grain is possible only after a longue durée survey of the Naqshbandī hagiographical literary tradition, and an appreciation for the *Sitz im Leben* of each respective text. It is further important to note that Sufi works rarely concern contemporary political realities. In any of these sources, selecting historically 'relevant' references has in past scholarship generated skewed representations of the Mujaddidī project. However, such sources can provide a detailed map of networks, and elucidate the types of debates and theological concerns circulating in the Persianate intellectual sphere, and the day-to-day mechanics of the network. British, Russian, and French sources from the 18th and the first half of the 19th centuries present yet another set of challenges, particularly since most visitors had only a rudimentary understanding of the religious and scholastic domain. Despite the shortcomings of each genre, collectively they can furnish a more sophisticated picture of the religious-scholastic domain.

12 See Joseph Fletcher, "Integrative History: Parallels and Interconnections in the Early Modern Period," in Fletcher, *Studies on Chinese and Islamic Inner Asia*, ed. Beatrice Manz (Hampshire: Variorum, 1995), No. X, and Robert D. Crews, *For Prophet and Tsar: Islam and Empire in Russia and Central Asia* (Cambridge, Massachusetts: Harvard University Press, 2006).

The Life of Ḥażrat Jīo Pishāvarī: Sirhind to Peshawar to Bukhara

Ḥażrat Jīo,[13] born into Shaykh Aḥmad Sirhindī's family in 1157/1744, was a product of the academically and spiritually active milieu of late Mughal Sirhind.[14] A cosmopolitan town on the Lahore-Delhi highway, Sirhind featured the shrine of Shaykh Aḥmad Sirhindī, along with his descendants and *khulafāʾ*. It also hosted a Mujaddidī academic complex, which for several generations served as a focal point for scholars. The city's *khānaqāh*s, mosques, and *madrasas* produced a large body of literature synthesizing pedagogies of multiple Sufi *silsila*s of Hindustan, Khurasan, and Mawarannahr.[15] The curriculum at these institutions balanced the esoteric and exoteric sciences, encompassing ethics, philosophy, cosmology, doctrine, and Qu'rānic exegesis, among other core disciplines. This was grounded in Shaykh Aḥmad Sirhindī's *Maktūbāt*, the seminal text of the Naqshbandī-Mujaddidī *ṭarīqa*, which stressed the interdependence of *sharīʿa* and Sufism in the journey towards spiritual advancement.[16]

Ḥażrat Jīo's father, Niyāz Aḥmad, was a poet and historian of repute and a descendent of Sirhindī's older brother.[17] Ḥażrat Jīo's mother, Dilras Begum, also considered a saint, was of both Mujaddidī and Sayyid descent. Nineteenth century Mujaddidī biographies sketch out interlocking physical and spiritual

13 Today Miyān Fażl Aḥmad is more popularly referred to by devotees as Jīo Bābā, and Ḥażrat Jī. Interview with the administrator at the *khānaqāh* and shrine of Ḥażrat Jīo, Peshawar, August, 2014.

14 Aḥmad Abu'l Khayr al-Makkī, *Hadiya-yi Aḥmadiyya* (Kanpur: Maṭbaʿ-i Niẓāmī, 1313/1895–96), p. 65; ʿAbdullāh Jān Fārūqī Naqshbandī, *Gulhā-i chaman*, 10.

15 Khwāja Muḥammad Iḥsān Mujaddidī Sirhindī, *Rawżat al-qayyūmiyya*, ed. Iqbāl Aḥmad Fārūqī (Lahore: Maktaba Nabawiya, 2002), 1, 96; Muḥammad Naẓīr Rānjhā, *Tārīkh-u Tażkira-yi Khānaqāh-i Sirhind Sharīf* (Lahore: Jamīʿat Publications, 2011), 121–137.

16 See Yohannan Friedmann, *Shaykh Ahmad Sirhindi: An Outline of His Thought and a Study of His Image in the Eyes of Posterity* (Montreal: McGill-Queen's University Press, 1971), and Arthur F. Buehler, *Revealed Grace: The Juristic Sufism of Ahmad Sirhindi (1564–1624)* (Louisville, Kentucky: Fons Vitae, 2011). The *Maktūbāt-i Imām Rabbānī* comprises 536 epistles on a broad range of topics. As Arthur Buehler explains, Sirhindī's concept of *sharīʿa* is a multivalent term encompassing outward acts of worship, faith, and the Sufi path.

17 Ḥażrat Jīo was the son of Niyāz Aḥmad (d. ca. 1764), son of Mīr Ṣafar (the author of *Maqāmāt-i Maʿṣūmī*), son of Ḥājjī Fażlullāh, son of Shaykh ʿAbd al-Qādir, son of Muḥammad Amīn, son of Shāh ʿAbd al-Razzāq, the elder brother of Shaykh Aḥmad Sirhindī. See Niẓām al-Dīn Balkhī Mazārī, *Tuḥfat al-murshid*, 3–6; Mīr Ṣafar Aḥmad Maʿṣūmī, *Maqāmāt-i Maʿṣūmī*, ed. Muḥammad Iqbāl Mujaddidī (Lahore: Ziyāʾ al-Qurʾān Publications, 2004), 1, 329–349.

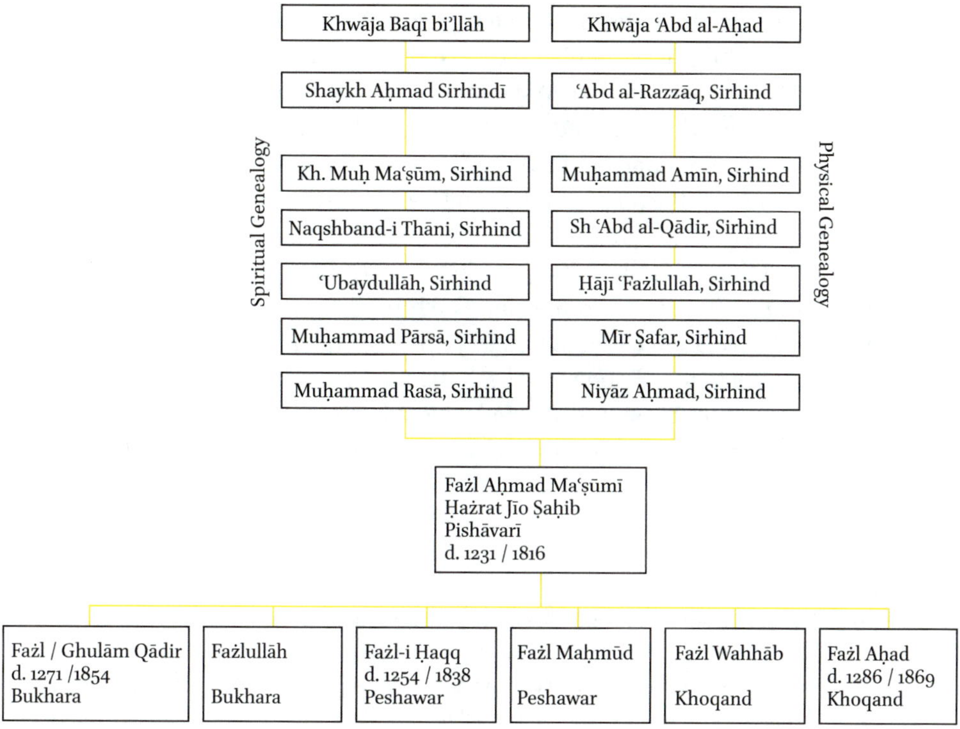

FIGURE 4.1 *Spiritual and physical genealogy of Ḥażrat Jīo Ṣāḥib*

genealogies, reinforcing Ḥażrat Jīo's connection to the Prophet Muḥammad and to Sirhindī.

For several years, Ḥażrat Jīo served his *pīr* and maternal grandfather, Muḥammad Rasā.[18] Under his instruction, Ḥażrat Jīo studied the revealed and rational sciences, including jurisprudence and scriptural study. He also received intensive training in Naqshbandī Sufi practices, such as engaging the *laṭā'if* (the subtle centers) through guided meditation, a subject on which

18 Shaykh Muḥammad Rasā was the *khalīfa* and son of Shaykh Muḥammad Pārsā, *khalīfa* of Muḥammad 'Ubaydullāh, *khalīfa* of Muḥammad Naqshband-i Thānī (father of Shaykh Muḥammad Pārsā), *khalīfa* and son of Khwāja Muḥammad Ma'ṣūm, *khalīfa* and son of Shaykh Aḥmad Sirhindī. The *Hadiya-yi Aḥmadiyya* records Shaykh Muḥammad Rasā's death in 1157/1743–44, which cannot be accurate given that Ḥażrat Jīo was born only one year earlier. It is also possible that Ḥażrat Jīo's *murshid* was instead Muḥammad Rasā's son, Aḥmad Rasā (d. 1174/1760). Muḥammad Rasā's daughter, Dilras Begum was Ḥażrat Jīo's mother. See Imām Muḥammad Jīo Ṣāḥib Zakorī, *Rawżat al-awliyā'*, 163.

he authored a short treatise in later years.[19] After the death of Muḥammad Rasā, for six months he studied the Chishtī and Qādirī *ṭarīqas* with Mīr Sayyid ʿAbdullāh Bukhārī, another Mujaddidī *pīr* based in Sirhind.[20] He obtained *ijāzas* (teaching licenses) and *khilāfat* from both teachers, and taught for several years at the *khānaqāh* in Sirhind.[21]

In the wake of the political crises and wars involving the Mughals, Durrānīs, Marathas, and Sikhs that unsettled Sirhind in the mid-18th century, the Mujaddidī Sufis and their disciples fled the city. Both Ḥażrat Jīo's father and brother were killed in battle against Sikh militias who eventually occupied Sirhind. Hagiographical stories imply that Ḥażrat Jīo, too, may have been directly threatened.[22] Some of the Mujaddidī Sufis resettled in Hindustanī towns, including Delhi and the Indo-Afghan state of Rampur. Many others were welcomed in Durrānī territories, such as Qandahar, Kabul, Peshawar, and Kashmir.

---

19 Miyān Fażl Aḥmad Maʿṣūmī, *Risāla*, Ms. Tashkent, IVANRUz, Inv. No. 2572/XXVI (ff. 571b–578b), dated 1235/1819–20. Activating the *laṭāʾif*, which correspond to points on the human body, through meditation is a core practice of the Naqshbandī *ṭarīqa*, and Shaykh Aḥmad Sirhindī is considered a pioneer in developing this science.

20 Mīr Sayyid ʿAbdullah Bukhārī was the disciple of Ḥażrat ʿAbd al-Aḥad (Miyān Gul), son of Muḥammad Saʿīd, son of Shaykh Aḥmad Sirhindī.

21 There are some discrepancies in the sources regarding Ḥażrat Jīo's *ijāzas*. First, the *Tuḥfat al-murshid* relates that he attained an *ijāza* only in the Naqshbandī *ṭarīqa* from Muḥammad Rasā, and in the Qādiriyya and Chishtiyya from ʿAbdullah Bukhārī. Both the *Rawżat al-awliyāʾ* and the *Makhāzin al-taqvā* imply that Ḥażrat Jīo was also given an *ijāza* in the Suhrawardī *ṭarīqa*. Second, while later biographies cite Muḥammad Rasā as Ḥażrat Jīo's direct *murshid*, two contemporary *ijāzatnāmas* cite Ḥażrat Jīo as the *khalīfa* of ʿAbdullah Bukhārī, who in turn is listed as the *khalīfa* of Muḥammad Rasā. See Aḥmad Abū'l-Khayr al-Makkī, *Hadiya-yi Aḥmadiyya*, 62–63; "*Shajara-yi Mujaddidiyya* of Fażl Aḥmad Maʿṣūmī," in *Risāla*, Ms. Islamabad, Kitābkhāna-yi Ganj-bakhsh, 3992 (pp. 110–14, n.d., early 19th c.), pp. 113–114; *Ijāzatnāma* and *Shajara-yi Mujaddidiyya* (citing ʿAbd al-Qādir, *khalīfa* of Fażl Aḥmad Maʿṣūmī), Ms. Islamabad, Kitābkhāna-yi Ganj-bakhsh, 8201 (ff. 258–261, n.d., early 19th c.); Mīr Ḥusayn b. Shāh Murād, *Makhāzin al-taqvā*, Ms. Tashkent, IVANRUz, Inv. No. 51 (ff. 1b–312b, undated), ff. 64b–65a; Niẓām al-Dīn Balkhī Mazārī, *Tuḥfat al-murshid*, 6–7.

22 Iqbāl Mujaddidī proposes that Niyāz Aḥmad was killed during the fourth Sikh invasion of Sirhind in 1764. This invasion was carried out in concert with the Marathas and devastated the city. Ḥażrat Jīo's brother, Shaykh Fażl Maʿṣūm, was killed in a later incident. See Niẓām al-Dīn Balkhī Mazārī, *Tuḥfat al-murshid*, 45; Mujaddidī, "ʿĀlamī Satih par Silsila-yi Naqshbandiyya Mujaddidiyya," 97; Mīr Ṣafar Aḥmad Maʿṣūmī, *Maqāmāt-i Maʿṣūmī*, 354; Imām Muḥammad Jīo Ṣāḥib Zakorī, *Rawżat al-awliyāʾ*, 166.

In the mid-1760s, Ḥażrat Jīo migrated to Peshawar[23] via Lahore, Sialkot, and Chhachh Hazara.[24] He was accompanied by his mother and surviving family members. He established himself at a humble mosque situated in Peshawar's Kākā Jamaʿdār quarter.[25] Here, he earned a favorable reputation amongst the people of the town by supplying vast quantities of free bread from his *langar*[26] during a harsh draught.

The biographies relate that during this time his circle of disciples grew exponentially, and he eventually inaugurated an independent *khānaqāh* near Yakātut gate in the southeast end of Peshawar (ca. 1770).[27] The new *khānaqāh* was in a neighborhood that eventually came to be known as Maḥalla Fażl-i Ḥaqq, after Ḥażrat Jīo's son Miyān Fażl-i Ḥaqq. In this *khānaqāh*, scholars from "Bukhara, Samarqand, Balkh, Kabul, Ghaznī, Herat, Kashmir, and Badakhshān, received initiation into the Naqshbandī-Mujaddidī *ṭarīqa*, and often returned to their homelands to propagate the teachings."[28]

In the mid-1770s, Ḥażrat Jīo embarked upon the first of five journeys to Bukhara, via the Khyber Pass, Kabul and Mazar-i Sharif, setting up *khānaqāh*s or teaching circles en route.[29] Upon arriving in Bukhara, he established a

---

23 The *Rawżat al-awliyā'* mentions that Ḥażrat Jīo spent 24 years in Sirhind in service of Muḥammad Rasā, followed by six months under ʿAbdullah Bukhārī. Iqbāl Mujaddidī more realistically proposes that he was forced to migrate with his entire family in 1764, upon the final sack and occupation of Sirhind by the Sikhs, as mentioned above.

24 He may have temporarily stayed in both locations, as many of his disciples hailed from Sialkot, and the biographies mention tribes in Chhachh Hazara among his followers. See Niẓām al-Dīn Balkhī Mazārī, *Tuḥfat al-murshid*, 5, and Imām Muḥammad Jīo Ṣāḥib Zakorī, *Rawżat al-awliyā'*, 163.

25 Situated in today's Darūgha *kachehrī*.

26 Soup kitchen, generally associated with a religious institution.

27 Interview with administrator of the *khānaqāh* and shrine, Peshawar, August 2014; Muḥammad Shafʿī Ṣābir, *Shakhṣīyāt-i sarḥad* (Peshawar: University Book Agency, n.d.), 65–66.

28 Imām Muḥammad Jīo Ṣāḥib Zakorī, *Rawżat al-awliyā'*, 166.

29 According to the *Tuḥfat al-murshid* and the *Rawżat al-awliyā'*, Ḥażrat Jīo made the journey four times, although an Appendix to the lithograph edition of the *Tuḥfat al-murshid* mentions five journeys. The exact route is not specified, but several sources indicate that he passed through the Khyber, Kabul, Aybak (Samangan), Kholm, Mazar-i Sharif, Balkh, Tashqurghan, and Ḥiṣar. Based on hagiographies, epistles, and chronicles, we can infer that he was based in Bukhara after ca. 1787 and in ca. 1799, and he returned from his last trip to Bukhara in 1814. He also left for Ḥajj during the reign of Amīr Ḥaydar (after 1800), but most probably was unable to complete the journey. See Niẓām al-Dīn Balkhī Mazārī, *Tuḥfat al-murshid*, 190; Imām Muḥammad Jīo Ṣāḥib Zakorī, *Rawżat al-awliyā'*, 166; Anke von Kügelgen, "Sufimeister und Herrscher im Zwiegespräch: Die Schreiben des

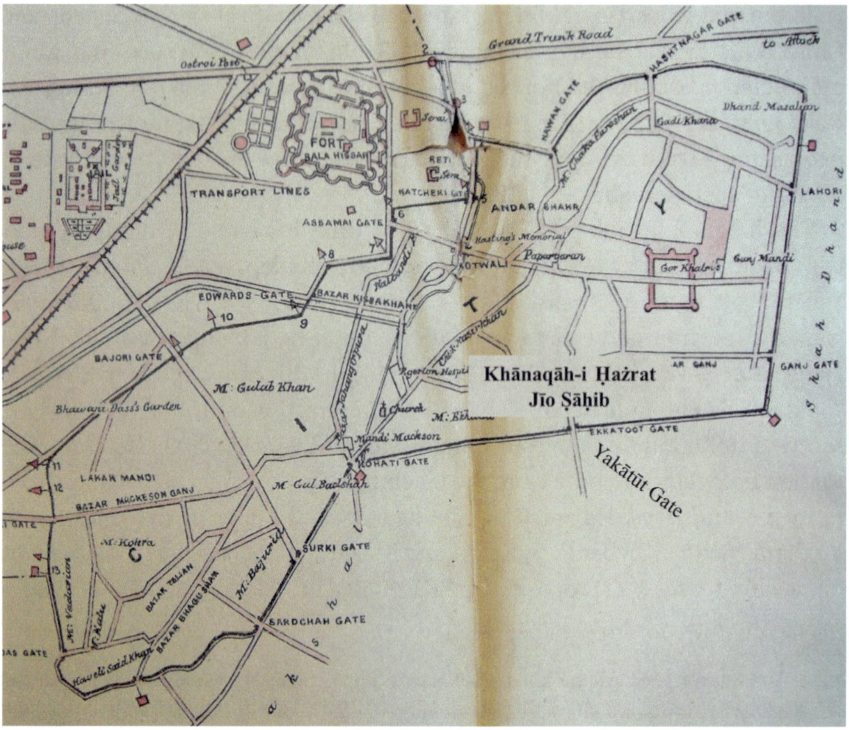

MAP 4.1 *Ḥażrat Jīo's* khānaqāh *at Yakātut gate*
Note: Map adapted from *The Thirty-Seventh Report of the Calcutta Corresponding Committee of the Church Missionary Society Being for the Year 1855* (Calcutta: Sanders, Cones & Co. 1856).

khānaqāh, where the celebrated khanate-builder of Bukhara, Shāh Murād (r. 1785–1800) and his son and successor Amīr Ḥaydar (r. 1800–1826), in addition to numerous *'ulamā'* and nobility, became his devoted disciples.

Faḍl Aḥmad aus Peschawar an Amīr Ḥaydar in Buchara," in *Muslim Culture in Russia and Central Asia*, vol. 3: *Arabic, Persian and Turkic Manuscripts (15th–19th Centuries)*, ed. Anke von Kügelgen, Aširbek Muminov, and Michael Kemper (Berlin: Klaus Schwarz Verlag, 2000), 231; William Moorcroft and George Trebeck, *Travels in the Himalayan Provinces of Hindustan and the Panjab; in Ladakh and Kashmir; in Peshawar, Kabul, Kunduz, and Bukhara: From 1819 to 1825* (London: J. Murray, 1841), vol. 2, 408.

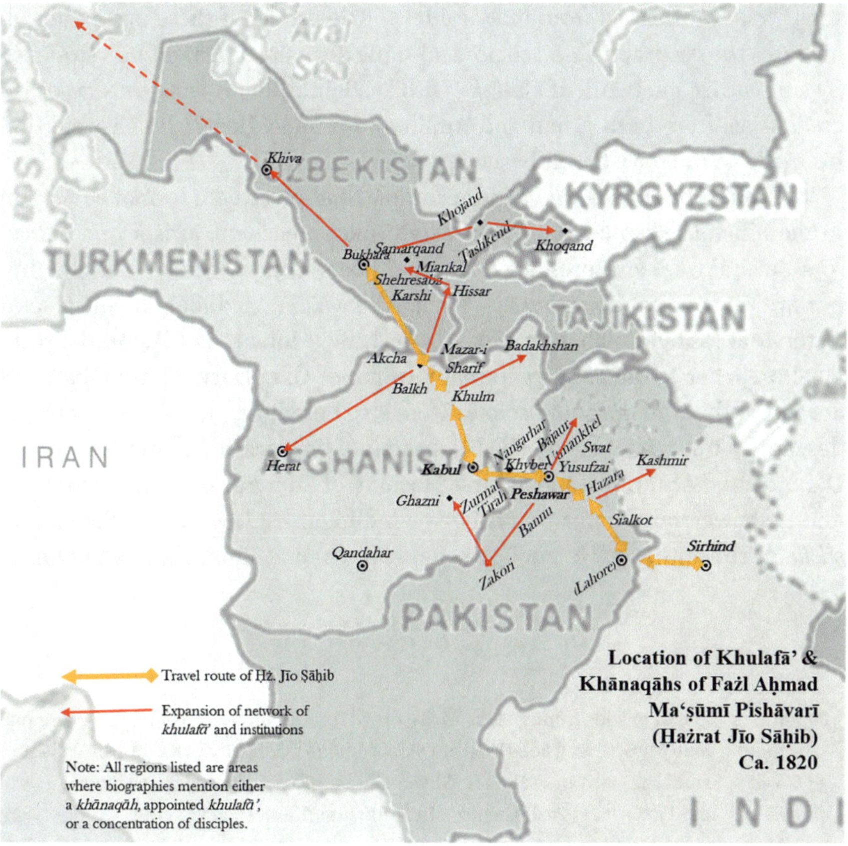

MAP 4.2 *Location of* khulafāʾ *and* khānaqāhs *of Fażl Aḥmad Māʿṣūmī Pishāvarī ca. 1820*

Khulafāʾ and Disciples

Contemporary biographies tell us that by the end of his life, Ḥażrat Jīo's disciples numbered in the thousands on both sides of the Amu Darya. The figure above traces Ḥażrat Jīo's travel route, and sheds light on how his network was able to permeate through and link together Khurasan and Mawarannahr.

From among his disciples, Ḥażrat Jīo appointed over 600 *khulafāʾ*, evenly divided between Mawarannahr and Khurasan, with several in the Punjab and other parts of Hindustan.[30] Of these, at least 128 names, including five of his

30 The exact number of disciples is uncertain, and there are discrepancies in the sources regarding the number of *khulafāʾ*. In a letter to Amīr Ḥaydar, Ḥażrat Jīo mentions appointing 800 *khulafāʾ* (Niẓām al-Dīn Balkhī Mazārī, *Tuḥfat al-murshid*, 144–145).

sons,[31] can be gleaned from biographies.[32] The profile of these appointees illustrates the geographic and socio-economic diversity of Ḥażrat Jīo's students. By cultivating a network of *khulafā'* with academic, literary and lineage-based credentials from both urban and rural backgrounds, Ḥażrat Jīo ensured that his *silsila* would have broad-based appeal.

The majority of his *khulafā'*, for example, had received a formal education in the religious sciences, and were established preachers, jurists, and educators. Several were also prolific writers and poets. Others were directors of important mosques and *madrasas*—such as Mawlānā Asadullāh, the instructor at the Madrasa-yi Kalābād in Bukhara, or Ḥāfiẓ Muḥammad ʿAẓīm, the principal preacher at the congregational mosque of Ganj Darvāzā in Peshawar.[33] Several of the *khulafā'* and disciples were also hereditary members of families descended from other established Naqshbandī lineages, including the Jūybārī, Dahbīdī, and Aḥrārī *khwāja* and the 'Hażarāt' of Shor Bāzār, Kabul, Qandahar, and Peshawar, reinforcing bonds between different sub-groups of the greater *silsila*.[34] The author of Ḥażrat Jīo's seminal biography, similarly, was a member

31 Ḥażrat Jīo had 10 sons from several wives, of whom four died at a young age. From one mother were Miyān Fażl Qādir (ʿAbd al-Qādir, Ghulām Qādir, Miyān Kalān, Miyān Ṣāḥib-i Kalān, Ṣāḥibzāda), Miyān Fażlullah (Miyān Ghulām Fażlullah, Khwāja Fażlullah, Miyān Ṣāḥib), and Fażl Aḥad (Fażl Aḥmad, Miyān Buzurg, Katta Ḥażrat). From another were Miyān Fażl-i Ḥaqq (Miyān Awliyā') and Fażl Maḥmūd (Miyān Valī). From a third mother, the daughter of Ḥażrat Jīo's *khalīfa* Qāżī Mīrzā Yaʿqūb from Miyānkāl, were Fażl Ṣiddīq, Fażl Ḥakīm, and Fażl Wahhāb. A fourth wife, who was a descendent of Ḥabībullāh Bukhārī, bore Miyān Fażl Karīm. Biographies do not mention who bore the 10th son, Fażl Ghafūr. See Niẓām al-Dīn Balkhī Mazārī, *Tuḥfat al-murshid*, 131–144; Imām Muḥammad Jīo Ṣāḥib Zakorī, *Rawżat al-awliyā'*, 214–215; von Kügelgen, "Sufimeister und Herrscher," 232–233; Maʿṣūmī, *Maqāmāt-i Maʿṣūmī*, 355–363; Abū ʿAbd al-Raḥmān ʿAbdullāh b. Muḥammad ʿĀrif al-Bukhārī, *Tārīkh al-Bukhārā wa tarjumāt al-ʿUlamā'* (Orenburg: Dīn va Maʿīshat Bāṣma-khānasi, 1908), 3–4.

32 Niẓām al-Dīn Balkhī Mazārī, *Tuḥfat al-murshid*, 131–170, 185–190; Imām Muḥammad Jīo Ṣāḥib Zakorī, *Rawżat al-awliyā'*, 215–217; Shāh ʿAbdullāh Badakhshī, *Armaqān-i Badakhshān* (Tehran: Bunyād-i Mawqūfāt-i Duktur Maḥmūd Afshār, 1385 H.Sh./2006–07), 111–113; Ṣābir, *Shakhṣīyāt*, 167–171; ʿAbd al-Ḥalīm Athār, *Rūḥānī Rābita aw Rūḥānī Tārūn* (Peshawar: University Book Agency, 2004), vol. 2, 780–783; Fikrī Saljūqī, *Risāla-yi mazārāt-i Harāt* (Herat: ʿAbd al-Ḥalīm Muḥammadī, 1386 H.Sh./2007–08), 249; *Shajaratnāma*, Ms. Central State Archives of the Republic of Uzbekistan, fond I-323, opis' 2, No. 90 (scroll, n.d., early 19th century).

33 Faqīr Muḥammad Āmir Shāh Qādirī, *Tazkira-yi ʿulamā' va mashā'ikh-i Sarḥad* (Peshawar: ʿAẓīm Publishing House, 1972), I, 128.

34 See the discussion on Peshawar and Bukhara below.

of the Anṣārī family of Mazar-i Sharif and son of the custodian of the shrine of Imām ʿAlī b. Abī Ṭālib.[35]

As with other Naqshbandī-Mujaddidī *silsilas*, the breadth of coverage and appeal of Ḥażrat Jīo's network was certainly enhanced given the varied socio-economic backgrounds of the *khulafāʾ*. They ranged from the rulers of Bukhara, to one of his principal Pashtun deputies, Imām Muḥammad Riżā, formerly a goat herder.[36]

Additionally, *khulafāʾ* came to Bukhara or Peshawar from neighboring towns, as well as rural and tribal regions. After initiation and intensive training, they often returned to their homelands to propagate the teachings through new *khānaqāhs*, *madrasas*, and mosques.[37]

Principal *khānaqāhs*, along with smaller regional institutions, became hubs for sub-*silsilas*. For example, the *khānaqāh* at Zakori in Dera Ismail Khan[38] appointed *khulafāʾ* across the Pashtun belt, between Dera Ismail Khan and Ghaznī, and into Bannu and Yusufzai territories.[39] Similarly, the Khānaqāh-i Ṣāḥibzāda, inaugurated by Ḥażrat Jīo's son Miyān Ghulām Qādir at Bukhara, appointed *khulafāʾ* in Tashkent, Kazan, and Siberia.[40]

Ḥażrat Jīo, too, had extended stays in cities, towns, and villages en route to Bukhara and Peshawar. These visits provided an opportunity to solidify and expand networks in each location. Biographies, as well his correspondence with Amīr Ḥaydar of Bukhara, specifically mention that he stayed in Kabul and Balkh, as well as at the pilgrimage sites of Mazar-i Sharif and at the shrine of Bahāʾ al-Dīn Naqshband outside Bukhara.[41]

---

35 Niẓām al-Dīn Balkhī Mazārī, *Tuḥfat al-murshid*, 2, 171–175; R. D. McChesney, *Waqf in Central Asia: Four Hundred Years in the History of a Muslim Shrine, 1480–1889* (Princeton: Princeton University Press, 1991), 250–251.

36 Imām Muḥammad Jīo Ṣāḥib Zakorī, *Rawżat al-awliyāʾ*, 228.

37 For example, Ākhūnd Jān Tāshkandī travelled from Tashkent with a group of companions to attend sessions at the *khānaqāh* in Bukhara. Many of the Pashtun *khulafāʾ* from tribal regions came to Peshawar, and eventually returned to administer their own institutions. See Imām Muḥammad Jīo Ṣāḥib Zakorī, *Rawżat al-awliyāʾ*, 169–170.

38 Dera Ismail Khan is an entrepot on the trading route between Multan and Ghaznī.

39 Fayżullāh Manṣūr, *Mihr-i ṣafā: Ḥażrat Pīr Muḥammad ʿAbd al-Laṭīf Zakorī Sharīf* (Lahore: Muslim League Writers Academy, 2004), 27–49.

40 Shihāb al-Dīn Marjānī mentions, for example, that Miyān Ghulām Qādir's grandson, Mullā Fayż Bakhsh, son of Miyān Quddūṣ, settled in Kazan; see Shihāb al-Dīn Marjānī, *Mustafad al-akhbār fī aḥvāl Qazān va Bulghār* (Kazan: Tipografiia Imperatorskago Universiteta, 1900), II, 257.

41 ʿAzīz al-Dīn Vakīlī Fūfalzāʾī, *Tīmūr Shāh Durrānī* (Kabul: Anjuman-i Tārīkh-i Afghanistan, 1333 H.Sh./1954–55), 274–275; Imām Muḥammad Jīo Ṣāḥib Zakorī, *Rawżat al-awliyāʾ*, 227–229.

As with other Mujaddidī *silsila*s, disciples could receive *khilāfat* in multiple *silsila*s from Ḥażrat Jīo upon mastery of the practices and knowledge associated with each order.[42] This phenomenon of 'bundled *silsila*s' was well established by the 18th century across Hindustan and Mawarannahr, and most Mujaddidī lineages, following Shaykh Aḥmad Sirhindī's example, imparted multiple *silsila*s to their students. Integrating multiple *silsila*s allowed for flexibility, enabling the Naqshbandiyya-Mujaddidiyya to incorporate an array of practices and philosophies. Moreover, bundled *silsila*s, as Devin DeWeese argues, helped bring formerly distinct Sufi communities based on *silsila* affiliation within the Naqshbandī-Mujaddidī umbrella.[43] This ultimately helped foster cohesive, transregional networks like that of Ḥażrat Jīo.

Peshawar

Turning to Peshawar, this section will explore how the city's distinctive position in the Durrānī empire allowed it to host a religio-academic infrastructure where ideas and pedagogies could gestate and travel northwards. The Durrānīs and their subsidiary polities assigned educational and religious as well as social services to Sufi-*ʿulamāʾ* networks such as the Mujaddidiyya with widespread legitimacy and several generations of experience. As these networks were strengthened, they extended their institutional reach and were able to provide mediational, academic, and commercial links between urban centers and tribal peripheries, and between the Durrānī empire and its neighboring polities.

---

42 Initiation into multiple *silsila*s was also common among other contemporary Sufi networks, notably the Qādiriyya, Chishtiyya, and Suhrawardiyya. *Pīrs* would be affiliated with multiple *silsila*s (with separate initiatory genealogies presented in their biographies), but one *silsila* would be generally designated as their primary affiliation. Niẓām al-Dīn Balkhī Mazārī provides us with the text of three *vaṣiyyat-nāma*s he received from Ḥażrat Jīo's son Miyān Fażl-i Ḥaqq, after completing the requisite course of studies for each *ṭarīqa*. Each was conferred as a separate written document. Similarly, an *ijāzat-nāma* template for Ḥażrat Jīo's *khalīfa* ʿAbd al-Qādir (presumably his son at Bukhara, Miyān Ghulām Qādir) specifies the Naqshbandī *ṭarīqa* only. An *ijāzat-nāma* conferred upon Amīr Ḥaydar, however, does not specify the *ṭarīqa* for which it is issued. See *Ijāzatnāma* and *Shajara-yi Mujaddidiyya*, pp. 260–261; von Kügelgen, "Sufimeister und Herrscher," Teil C–a Nr. 27, f. 56a; Niẓām al-Dīn Balkhī Mazārī, *Tuḥfat al-murshid*, 177–179.

43 DeWeese, "'Dis-ordering' Sufism," 268–269.

Given Peshawar's position as an important Mughal entrepôt, the Mujaddidī *ṭarīqa* was established there soon after its emergence in Sirhind.[44] Since Peshawar had not undergone the same depopulation and devastation as Kabul and Qandahar, respectively, in the 18th century, the *ṭarīqa* was able to gradually expand and mature. It was, therefore, able to leverage from the living legacies of such Sufi luminaries as Pīr Bābā Buner (d. 1583), Akhund Darvīzā (d. 1638), and Panjū Ṣāḥib (d. 1636).[45] Fortunately, even Nādir Shāh's invasion did not drastically destabilize the Peshawar valley.[46]

Particularly following the Durrānī occupation in 1747, the Peshawar valley greatly benefited from political turmoil in the Mughal empire. Sufis from across Hindustan, including many Mujaddidī Sufis, fled in waves and established themselves in both urban and tribal areas.[47] Aḥmad Shah Durrānī (r. 1747–1772) also provided land and stipends to local Sufis and *mullās* within the Peshawar valley to expand their own institutions.[48] Pīr ʿUmar of Chamkanni

---

44 Sayyid Ādam Binorī, a principal *khalīfa* of Shaykh Aḥmad Sirhindī, appointed several *khulafāʾ* who settled in the Peshawar region. Notable among them were Nūr Muḥammad Pishāvarī, Ḥājjī Bahādur of Kohat, and Ḥājjī Muḥammad Ismāʿīl Ghūrī Naqshbandī, who disseminated the Mujaddidī *ṭarīqa* in the Peshawar valley in the late 17th century. In addition, Ādam Binorī's *khalīfa* Shaykh Saʿdī Lāhūrī (based in Lahore) initiated several key religious leaders in Peshawar in the late 17th and early 18th centuries. Throughout the 17th and early 18th centuries, Lahore functioned as a base for the dissemination of the Mujaddidī *ṭarīqa* in the Peshawar valley and amongst the Pashtun tribes. See Ghulām Sarvar Lāhūrī, *Khazīnat al-aṣfiyā*, 2 vols. (Kabul: Anṣāri Kutub Khāna, 1994), I, 630–636, 647–657; ʿIjāz al-Ḥaqq Quddūsī, *Taẕkira-yi ṣūfiyya-yi Sarḥad* (Lahore: Markazī Urdu Board, 1966), 267, 369, 444; Ṣābir, *Shakhṣīyāt*, 29–43.

45 See, for example, the biography of the Chishtī *pīr* Panjū Ṣāḥib, *Tuḥfat al-awliyāʾ*, which highlights how 18th–19th century Sufis from the Peshawar valley conceived of themselves as following these and other earlier luminaries of the region. In fact, Panjū Ṣāḥib's shrine and adjacent mosque were expanded in the Durrānī period in 1798, indicating a renewed interest in Peshawar's earlier Sufi heritage. This shrine complex held a prominent place in the spiritual landscape of the Peshawar valley, serving as a pilgrimage site for all Sufi *silsilas*. See Mīr Aḥmad Shāh Riżvānī Pishāvarī, *Tuḥfat-i awliyāʾ* (Lahore: Maṭbaʿ-i Mufīd-i ʿĀm Press, 1321/1903–4), 45.

46 Nādir Shāh's forces occupied Peshawar, but allowed the Mughal governor Nāṣir Khān to retain his position as the governor of Peshawar and Kabul until 1748; see Ahmad Hasan Dani, *Peshawar: Historic City of the Frontier* (Peshawar: Khyber Mail Press, 1969), 117.

47 Mujaddidī, "ʿĀlamī Satih par Silsila-yi Naqshbandiyya Mujaddidiyya," 96–98.

48 Biographical dictionaries of the Peshawar valley also reference several Sufis and *ʿulamāʾ*, such as Shaykh Ḥabīb Ṣāḥib and Shāh ʿAbdullāh Biyābānī Nawshāhī, who settled in Peshawar after serving with the Durrānī armies, or relocated to Peshawar from Kabul and other parts of the Durrānī empire. See Sayyid Amjad Ḥusayn, *ʿĀlam Mayn Intikhāb*

(d. 1190/1776) near Peshawar, who famously blessed Aḥmad Shāh's invasion of Hindustan, was one such figure.[49]

The situation improved even further after the 1770s, when Aḥmad Shāh's successor, Tīmūr Shāh (r. 1772–1793), selected Kabul and Peshawar as his dual capitals. The sister cities profited from a rejuvenated north-south trade, and accordingly, land grants to Sufis increased considerably.[50]

Under the Durrānis, Ḥażrat Jīo acquired considerable regular revenue to finance his *khānaqāh*s and cover operating expenses. These included food distribution, stipends to teachers and families, lodging costs for students, and provisions for travelers and the needy.[51] From the "Bādishāhān-i Khurāsān", we are told, Ḥażrat Jīo received an annual stipend (in the form of *madad-i maʿāsh*) of 30,000[52] rupees in addition to 20,000 rupees in the form of *jāgīrs* (presumably converted *khāliṣa* lands).[53]

Peshawar (Peshawar: Dār al-Adab, 2003), 144; Quddūsī, *Tazkira-yi ṣūfiyya-yi Sarḥad*, 357–359.

49 Biographic dictionaries relate that when Aḥmad Shāh arrived in the Peshawar valley with the intent to occupy Hindustan, he first approached Muḥammad ʿUmar at Chamkanni, and accepted him as his *pīr*. On his return, Aḥmad Shāh granted vast amounts of land to the *pīr*, to the extent that until the 20th century his lineage reported the largest landholdings in the Northwest Frontier Province. See Ṣābir, *Shakhṣīyāt*, 61–62; Quddūsī, *Tazkira-yi ṣūfiyya-yi Sarḥad*, 454–455. Chamkanni is located 7 km. east of Peshawar, and served as a *sarai* for travelers on the principal highway between Hindustan and Khurasan.

50 The Durrānī nobility invested heavily in both Kabul and Peshawar. It was only at the turn of the century, in fact, with the Durrānī wars of the succession, the emergence of the Barakzais, and the Sikh occupation, that this period of unprecedented growth came to a halt. By the time Gopal Dās compiled *Tārīkh-i Pishāvar* (1878), the educational apparatus of Peshawar had all but disappeared; see Munshī Gopal Dās, *Tārīkh-i Pishāvar* (Lahore: Koh-i Nūr Press, 1878), 707–711.

51 The *Shakhṣīyāt-i Sarḥad* mentions that Ḥażrat Jīo was famous for distributing basic supplies to needy visitors, relating an instance in which he gave away his prayer mat and the shirt off his back to a needy traveler. Ḥażrat Jīo also assigned land to *ʿulamāʾ* and poets for their subsistence, and a disciple was specifically commissioned to issue grant documentation. ʿAbd al-Raḥīm Pishāvarī relates an instance when Ḥażrat Jīo issued a grant of land to a poet after being impressed by his verses. See Ṣābir, *Shakhṣīyāt*, 65–66; ʿAbd al-Raḥīm b. Khān Muḥammad Pishāvarī, *Taṣarruf-nāma*, Ms. Khānaqāh-i Ḥażratkhayl, Thana, Malakand Agency (13ff., n.d., mid 19th c), f. 3a.

52 Of this amount, 20,000 rupees had been directly allotted to Ḥażrat Jīo, while 10,000 rupees were allotted to Miyān Fażl-i Ḥaq by Maḥmūd Shāh Durrānī.

53 These villages were assigned to either Ḥażrat Jīo or to his sons, and included 12 villages in the Peshawar region, three villages in Doaba (the fertile triangle near the confluence of the Swat and Kabul rivers), and two villages in Jalalabad (to Ghulām Qādir and Miyān

Ḥāfiẓ Muḥammad Fāżil Khān, who travelled through Mawarannahr in 1812 with Mīr ʿIzzatullāh, pointed out that one of Balkh's profitable irrigation channels was named after Ḥażrat Jīo's son, Miyān Ghulām Qādir.[54] The income of the channel had been allocated by Maḥmūd Shāh Durrānī (r. 1801–3, 1809–1818) to the 'Ṣāḥibzādas of Sirhind'. Other Durrānī princes may have also financed Ḥażrat Jīo's activities, particularly since biographies mention that Shāh Shujāʿ, Ayyūb Shāh, Shāh Sulṭān ʿAlī, Shāhzāda-yi Jahān, Kāmrān and Zamān Shāh all regularly visited Ḥażrat Jīo for "*ziyārat* and *tavajjuh* (guided meditation) after evening prayers."[55]

The result of Durrānī investment and westward migration of the scholarly classes was the development of closely-knit networks of Sufi *silsila*s. Disciples set up *madrasa*s and *khānaqāh*s that provided esoteric and exoteric education, venues for theological debate and literary production and reproduction, and an array of basic social services. In these institutions, a range of philosophies and pedagogies from across Hindustan and Khurasan had the opportunity to coalesce, ready for onward travel to Mawarannahr's open markets.

The chart below is a representative cross-section of some of the principal Naqshbandī lineages of Peshawar and its environs that feature in biographical dictionaries.[56] It indicates the degree to which *silsila*s and popular sociopolitical movements were intimately connected.

Among Ḥażrat Jīo's disciples was ʿAbd al-Ghafūr (the 'Akhund of Swat'), the anti-colonial spiritual leader and de facto ruler of the Swat valley.[57] Incidentally,

---

Fażl-i Ḥaqq). See Niẓām al-Dīn Balkhī Mazārī, *Tuḥfat al-murshid*, 34–35; von Kügelgen, "Sufimeister und Herrscher," 247–248.

54 Ḥāfiẓ Muḥammad Fāżil Khān, *Tārīkh-i manāzil-i Bukhārā* (Srinagar: Centre of Central Asian Studies, 1981), 4, 27.

55 Imām Muḥammad Jīo Ṣāḥib Zakorī, *Rawżat al-awliyāʾ*, 188.

56 Many of these *pīr*s were also affiliated with other *ṭarīqa*s, notably the Qādiriyya and Chishtiyya.

57 Ākhūnd ʿAbd al-Ghafūr (d. 1295/1878), known as the Akhund of Swat, set up an independent polity at Swat under Sayyid Akbar Shāh in 1849. He assumed direct control after 1857. Ḥażrat Jīo was one of two *pīrs* from whom he derived his spiritual authority. In his early life ʿAbd al-Ghafūr was devoted to Ḥażrat Jīo, we are told, walking on foot from Swat to Peshawar to meet his teacher. The hagiographical entries mention that in one instance, in a state of ecstasy, ʿAbd al-Ghafūr disrupted meditative sessions and prayed out loud, and for this reason was asked by Ḥażrat Jīo to leave Peshawar. Afterwards, he was initiated by the Qādirī-Naqshbandī Shaykh Shuʿayb Tordher. The Akhund and Ḥażrat Jīo's family, however, maintained close relations for several generations and the Akhund provided land and security for the family in Malakand after they fled Peshawar in the 1830s. See Abdul Wadud, *The Story of Swat as Told by the Founder Miangul Abdul Wadud Badshah Sahib to*

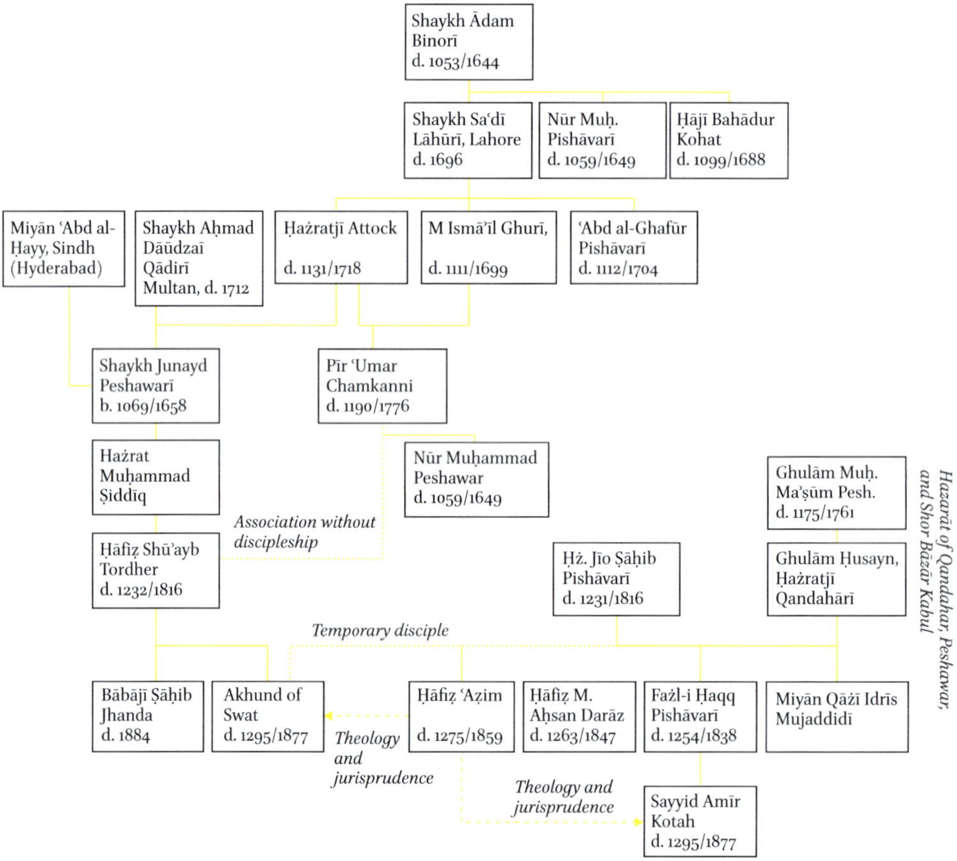

FIGURE 4.2 *Cross-section of the Principal Naqshbandī-Mujaddidī lineages of the Peshawar valley, late 17th–19th century*

another disciple and *khalīfa* was the Akhund's political rival, Sayyid Amīr al-ʿUs̱mānzāʾī (the 'Kotah Mullā'), who vied with the Akhund for influence over the valley.[58] Eventually, it was Ḥażrat Jīo's grandson, Fażl Hādī, a *pīr* in the Swat valley, who reconciled the two opponents.[59]

Muhammad Asif Khan (Peshawar: Ferozsons Limited, 1963), p. xlii; Quddūsī, *Taẕkira-yi ṣūfiyya-yi Sarḥad*, 551; ʿAbdullāh Jān Fārūqī Naqshbandī, *Gulhā-i chaman*, 60–61.

58 The 'Mullā of Kotah' (d. 1295/1877) was initiated into the Naqshbandiyya-Mujaddidiyya by Ḥażrat Jīo's son Fażl-i Ḥaqq. In 1827, at age 17, he joined Sayyid Aḥmad of Rai Bareilli in his campaigns against the Sikhs in the Peshawar valley. On this basis, he was later accused by detractors, including the Akhund of Swat, of being a Wahhābī. See Quddūsī, *Taẕkira-yi ṣūfiyya-yi Sarḥad*, 561–564; Ṣafīullāh Ṣāḥib, *Naẓm al-durrar fī sālik al-sayr* (Delhi: Maṭbaʿ al-Farūqī, n.d.), 9–10.

59 Ṣafīullāh Ṣāḥib, *Naẓm al-durrar*, 176.

Several *pīrs* from Peshawar of the 'Ḥażarāt' lineage were also appointed by Ḥażrat Jīo as *khulafāʾ*. The Ḥażarāt were another principal Mujaddidī lineage of the Durrānī empire based at Shor Bāzār, Kabul, as well as in Peshawar, Shikarpur, and Qandahar.[60] Like Ḥażrat Jīo, they were descendants of Shaykh Aḥmad Sirhindī, and claimed both hereditary and initiatic inheritance from him. They accordingly embodied greater sacred capital than solely initiatic lineages.[61]

Ḥażrat Jīo's *khulafāʾ* also included several prominent *ʿulamāʾ* of Peshawar, whose *madrasas* and mosques became affiliated with his *khānaqāh*.[62] Of note were Ḥāfiẓ Darāz (d. 1263/1847) and Ḥāfiẓ Muḥammad ʿAẓīm (d. 1275/1859), leading educators in Peshawar who attracted students from Mawarannahr

---

60 In particular, Ḥażrat Jīo's lineage was linked with that of Shāh Ghulām Muḥammad Maʿṣūm (Ḥażratjī Pishāvarī), the senior-most *pīr* of a Sufi network which included the Ḥażarāt of Shor Bāzār, Kabul, Sind, Yarkand, Qandahar, and other regions. While in Kabul, Ḥażrat Jīo also stayed in Shor Bāzār, and his disciples retained their association with the *khānaqāh* at Shor Bāzār over several generations. Additionally, two notable grandsons of Ḥażratjī Pishāvarī (Ḥażrat Mīr Muḥammad Shāh and Miyān Muḥammad Idrīs) were among Ḥażrat Jīo's *khulafāʾ* in Peshawar. Miyān Muḥammad Idrīs, known as Miyān Qāżī, held the office of *Qāżī al-qużāt* under the Durrānīs, and issued *fatwās* in support of Durrānī campaigns in Hindustan. He also directly participated in several campaigns. According to *Sirāj al-tavārīkh*, Miyān Qāżī's and Mīr Muḥammad Shāh's father, Miyān Ghulām Ḥusayn (Ḥażratjī Qandahārī), was the most celebrated Sufi *pīr* of Qandahar. Several members of the Barakzāʾī family, including Kohandil Khan, the ruler of Qandahar, were buried at his shrine. See Fayz Muhammad Katib Hazarah, *The History of Afghanistan: Fayz Muhammad Katib Hazarah's Siraj al-Tawārīkh*, tr. Robert D. McChesney and Mehdi M. Khorrami (Leiden: Brill, 2012), II, 197; Niẓām al-Dīn Balkhī Mazārī, *Tuḥfat al-murshid*, 156, 189; Shāh Muḥammad Fażlullāh, *ʿUmdat al-maqāmāt* (Hyderabad, Sindh: Nuʿmānī Publishers, 1355/1936–7), 189, 434; Shaykh ʿAbdullāh Ghulām ʿAlī Dihlavī, *Maqāmāt-i Maẓharī: Aḥvāl va malfūẓāt va maktūbāt-i Ḥażrat Mirzā Maẓhar Jān-i Jānān Shahīd*, tr. Muḥammad Iqbāl Mujaddidī (Lahore: Urdu Science Board, 2001), 49; Imām Muḥammad Jīo Ṣāḥib Zakorī, *Rawżat al-awliyāʾ*, 227–229, 238.

61 Mujaddidī Sufis who were hereditary descendants of sacred lineages (whether Sirhindī, Sayyid, or Aḥrārī *khwāja*) often had multiple initiations from both members of their immediate families, as well as from other Mujaddidī teachers. In such cases, as in the Ḥażarāt, members would evoke the authority of their biological lineage and often inherit their institutions and any underlying property, while claiming primary spiritual or scholastic allegiance to their initiatic lineage. In other words, the initiatic lineage would be more pronounced in their biographical genealogies.

62 A clearer understanding of the mode of affiliation between *khānaqāhs* and *madrasas* is required. For example, it is uncertain as to whether graduates of the *madrasas* were simultaneously attending Ḥażrat Jīo's *khānaqāh*, or whether the curriculum and pedagogy of the *madrasas* was influenced directly by Ḥażrat Jīo's Sufi teachings.

and Hindustan. They were appointed by Ḥażrat Jīo to deliver lectures at his *khānaqāh*s on Fridays and Thursdays, respectively.[63] Both were also among the key *ʿulamāʾ* who challenged the Mujāhidīn movement of Sayyid Aḥmad of Rai Bareilli (d. 1246/1831) in Peshawar. Ḥāfiẓ Darāz, in fact, wrote one of the earliest theological tracts refuting the extreme theological and political positions of Sayyid Aḥmad, and his ideologue, Shāh Ismāʿīl Dihlavī. Sayyid Aḥmad, in response, issued two letters to the "*ʿulamāʾ* of Peshawar"—specifically naming Ḥāfiẓ Darāz and Ḥāfiẓ Muḥammad ʿAẓīm—refuting their accusations in the late 1820s.[64]

Trade and Diplomacy

In parallel with furnishing an academic and religious foundation for Peshawar, Ḥażrat Jīo and his contemporaries also played critical roles in providing coherence to a region where governance was highly decentralized.

The archaeologist and traveler Charles Masson writes in his notes that caravans through the Khyber would be accompanied by Sufis who, acknowledged

63 Both were originally from Punjab, and settled in Peshawar under the Durrānīs. Ḥāfiẓ Muḥammad ʿAẓīm Ṣāḥib, designated as Baḥr al-ʿUlūm, was the *khaṭīb* at the congregational mosque and Dār al-ʿUlūm of Khwāja Maʿrūf (near Ganj Darvāza). The Akhund of Swat, Sayyid Akbar Shāh (ruler of Swat until 1857), and Sayyid Amīr of Kotah were among his students in the revealed and rational sciences. Ḥāfiẓ Muḥammad Iḥsan, known as Ḥāfiẓ Darāz, was another of Peshawar's renowned scholars, and his *madrasa* attracted students from Peshawar and its environs, Pashtun tribal areas, Samarqand, Bukhara, Herat, Kabul, Qandahar, and Ghaznī. Like Ḥażrat Jīo, he maintained close linkages with Mawarannahr's educators, and engaged in correspondence with Amīr Ḥaydar of Bukhara. See Qādirī, *Tażkira-yi ʿulamāʾ va mashāʾikh-i Sarḥad*, I, 122–138.

64 See Ḥāfiẓ Darāz Pishāvarī, *Risāla radd-i Wahhābiyyat*, Ms. Rotograph, Dr. Iqbal Mujaddidī Collection, R. No. 238.6 (14ff., 1250/1834–35, Original 1240/1824–25), ff. 1a–14a; Sayyid Aḥmad Shahīd, *Makātib-i Sayyid Aḥmad Shahīd* (photograph of manuscript), (Lahore: Maktaba Rashīdiyya, 1395/1975), ff. 115b–120a. Sayyid Aḥmad spearheaded an armed religio-political movement against the Sikh rulers of Punjab who had occupied the Peshawar valley in the 1820s. On account of this, he was initially supported by the religious and political elite in the Peshawar valley, and even briefly governed Peshawar in 1829–30. Sayyid Aḥmad was condemned by Ḥāfiẓ Darāz, Ḥāfiẓ Muḥammad ʿAẓīm, and others for his rejection of *madhāhib* (characterized as *zindīq*), his use of widespread violence against Muslims, and other heretical activities. Throughout the 19th century, the Mujaddidiyya in Hindustan and Khurasan remained among the most vehement theological opponents of 'Wahhābī'-oriented movements, which, like Sayyid Aḥmad, proscribed certain core Sufi practices.

by tribal authorities, could negotiate safe passage and tolls. In fact, he points out certain trade routes that could *only* be traversed by Sufi *pīrs*.[65] Likewise, Elphinstone notes a caravan from Kabul to Bukhara led by a "Sahebzadda of Sirhind."[66] While Ḥażrat Jīo's biographies do not explicitly mention commerce, several miracle stories involving the saint and his disciples are set against the backdrop of caravan journeys.[67] The stories imply that Ḥażrat Jīo, like the Jūybārī Sufis of Bukhara, engaged in trading activities.[68]

The routes traversed by Ḥażrat Jīo and his disciples constituted a central artery of the north-south trade through Russia, Mawarannahr and Hindustan. These were the very same highways traversed by the trans-regional Shikārpūrī merchant families discussed at length by Levi and Markovitz. Commercial and religio-academic travel and pilgrimage were, undoubtedly, linked. In fact, one of Ḥażrat Jīo's messengers between Peshawar and Bukhara was a Hindu merchant of Shikarpur.[69] Additionally, pilgrimage sites frequented by Ḥażrat Jīo and his disciples, such as those of Khwāja Bahā' al-Dīn Naqshband and 'Alī b.

65 Charles Masson, *Masson Collection: Papers of Charles Masson (1800–53)*, Ms. British Library, India Office Records and Private Papers, B98, 1828. (a), f. 24.

66 *Papers of Mountstuart Elphinstone: Accounts of Afghanistan and Central Asia, Etc.*, Ms. British Library, India Office Records and Private Papers, Eur F88/372, 1808, ff. 67–68.

67 We are told that when Ḥażrat Jīo initially travelled to Peshawar he was joined by the tribes of Chhachh-Hazara (near today's Attock), who became his followers. Although the biography is sparing in detail, it is possible that Ḥażrat Jīo was selected to lead a *powindā* caravan during its annual migration from the Hazara region into Khurasan. Mullā 'Abd al-Raḥīm Pishāvarī mentioned another instance in which Ḥażrat Jīo was traveling with a caravan from Peshawar to Kabul. Much to the author's surprise, the caravan was molested by Afghan tribesman. Mullā 'Abd al-Raḥīm pointed out that it was unusual that Afghans would trouble the caravan in the presence of the *pīr*. Shortly thereafter, a tribal leader arrived with a hundred horsemen to safely escort the caravan through the Khyber. In a later story, we are told that a *khalīfa* had been explicitly sent by Ḥażrat Jīo to lead a caravan into Hindustan. See 'Abd al-Raḥīm Pishāvarī, *Taṣarruf-nāma*, ff. 2a–2b.

68 See Audrey Burton, "Bukharan Trade 1558–1718," *Papers on Inner Asia*, 23 (Bloomington, Indiana: Research Institute for Inner Asian Studies, 1993), 25. Another possibility to consider is whether the *khānaqāh*s may have been deliberately promoted by local rulers as caravanserais. In the wake of political crisis in Khurasan and Mawarannahr in the early 18th century, and the invasion of Nādir Shāh, the caravanserai network facilitated by the courts at Delhi and Bukhara may have deteriorated. Masson mentions staying at several *khānaqāh*s and shrines en route between Hindustan and Kabul, including the *khānaqāh* of Chamkanni, then presided over by Pīr 'Umar's wife. See Charles Masson, *Masson Collection: Papers of Charles Masson (1800–53)*, Ms. British Library, India Office Records and Private Papers, E163, 1828. (b), 2.

69 Von Kügelgen, "Sufimeister und Herrscher," 232–233.

Abī Ṭālib at Mazar-i Sharif, hosted commercial fairs, which may have provided a venue for commercial activities.[70]

Ḥażrat Jīo's networks along this highway, and widespread spiritual authority, positioned him as a critical mediator between rulers, traders, religious figures, and even foreign agents.[71] Indeed, when both 'Great Game' players William Moorecroft and Alexander Burnes required safe passage into Mawarannahr, they were referred to Ḥażrat Jīo's son, Miyān Fażl-i Ḥaqq, on account of the fact that "the king of Bokhara and the chiefs of the Oxus … owned him as their spiritual guide." In fact, Miyān Fażl-i Ḥaqq provided Burnes with letters of introduction to five rulers, granting him access to a region where the English were regarded with great suspicion.[72]

Indeed, it is this combination of educational, economic, and diplomatic services which would have allowed the *silsila* ease of entry into Mawarannahr.

Bukhara

We now turn to Bukhara, Ḥażrat Jīo's second base of operations. Bukhara, like Peshawar, offered ample opportunities for scholars under the patronage of the Manghït khāns,[73] notably Shāh Murād (r. 1785–1800), who struggled to reassert Bukhara's position as the political and academic center of Mawarannahr.

---

70 In the early 19th century, the shrine of Khwāja Bahā' al-Dīn Naqshband hosted a weekly fair, where "horses, asses, and goods are put on sale;" see Meer Izzut-oollah, *Travels in Central Asia by Meer Izzut-Oollah in the Years 1812–13*, tr. Captain Henderson (Calcutta: Foreign Department Press, 1872), 58.

71 Von Kügelgen, "Sufimeister und Herrscher," 249–250.

72 See Moorcroft and Trebeck, *Travels*, II, 408, 440; Alexander Burnes, *Travels into Bokhara* (London: J. Murray, 1834), I, 106–107; Munshī Mohan Lal, *Travels in the Panjab, Afghanistan, Turkistan, to Balk, Bokhara, and Herat: And a Visit to Great Britain and Germany* (London: W. H. Allen and Co., 1846), 56. Burnes disposed of the letters prior to his journey, as he was informed by Mullā Najīb, who had traveled with Elphinstone into Kafiristan, that Fażl-i Ḥaqq was responsible for difficulties Moorcroft faced at Qunduz. Moorcroft's account makes no note of Fażl-i Ḥaqq's involvement in his detention at Qunduz, except that he was unable to secure a letter of recommendation from Fażl-i Ḥaqq in time as the latter had traveled to Bukhara.

73 The Manghïts effectively ruled as *atālïqs* (royal tutors) from 1747–1785, and assumed the title *khān* from 1785–1920.

FIGURE 4.3 *Maḥalla Fażl-i Ḥaqq, Yakātut gate*

Durrānī Khurasan served as an ideal springboard for these developments. With its age-old reputation as a seat of learning, Bukhara in the previous two centuries had cultivated a distinctive model of Chinggisid and Persian sacred kingship emphasizing personal commitments to mystical praxis, scholarship, and sober asceticism.

Several pre-Mujaddidī Naqshbandī lineages had historically dominated the religious and academic landscape of Bukhara. Notable among them were the

FIGURE 4.4 *Portal of the* mazār *of Ḥażrat Jīo, Peshawar*

FIGURE 4.5 Mazār *of Ḥażrat Jīo, Peshawar*

FIGURE 4.6 Mazār *of Ḥażrat Jīo, Peshawar*

FIGURE 4.7
Old Tombstone, Mazār *of Ḥażrat Jīo, Peshawar*

Jūybārī and the Dahbīdī *khwāja*.[74] As in Peshawar, however, the Naqshbandī-Mujaddidī *ṭarīqa* had been introduced to Bukhara within the first generation after Sirhindī. Ḥājjī Ḥabībullāh (d. 1111/1699–1700), a disciple of Shaykh Aḥmad Sirhindī's son, Khwāja Muḥammad Maʿṣūm, was one of the first to propagate the *ṭarīqa*. Nevertheless, the Mujaddidī *ṭarīqa* had difficulty in taking root for several reasons.[75]

First, the initial entry of the Mujaddidiyya placed the sub-order in direct conflict with Bukhara's entrenched religious elites. The Mujaddidiyya, as DeWeese explains, threatened to "realign" Mawarannahr's Sufi communities away from distinct localized lineages and communal structures towards transregional communities built around ritual practice and beliefs.[76]

Second, Mawarannahr suffered sustained political and environmental crises in the first half of the 18th century. The result was large-scale de-urbanization and the degeneration of the academic apparatus of Bukhara.

Then, in 1740, Nādir Shāh's occupation of Bukhara dealt a crippling blow to the Chinggisid Ashtarkhanid dynasty. The Ashtarkhanid khans, who controlled only the immediate environs of the city of Bukhara, were effectively replaced by their Uzbek *atālīq*s from the Manghït tribe.

The early Manghït rulers began to reconsolidate Bukhara's power, subdue recalcitrant tribes and provincial potentates, and rebuild and repopulate Bukhara. At this time, Bukhara's Sufis and *ʿulamāʾ* began receiving some renewed patronage. Many took the opportunity to travel from Bukhara (as well

74 The Dahbīdī Naqshbandīs were descended from the Naqshbandī luminary, Aḥmad Khwājagī Kāsānī, Makhdūm-i Aʿẓam (d. 1542). The Jūybārīs were descended from Muḥammad Islām Jūybārī (d. 1563), a disciple of Makhdūm-i Aʿẓam. The official position of *Shaykh al-Islām* of Bukhara was reserved for the Jūybārīs even under the Manghïts. See William Erskine, *Erskine Papers: Oriental Chronology and Geography*, Ms. British Library, India Office Records and Private Papers, Eur D 28, 1810, p. 140; Nikolaï Vladimirovitch Khanykov, *Bukhara, Its Amir and Its People*, tr. Baron Clement A. de Bode (London: J. Madden, 1845), 246.

75 According to the *Rawżat al-qayyūmiyya*, Ḥājjī Ḥabībullāh was dispatched to Bukhara by Sirhindī's son, Muḥammad Maʿṣūm to dispel criticisms of the Mujaddidī *ṭarīqa* that had already taken hold in Bukhara prior to his arrival. We are told that he faced fierce opposition, and was accused of blaspheming the Prophets. At one stage, a crowd of 12,000 gathered to apprehend him, eventually dispelled by the forces of the Ashtarkhanid ruler, ʿUbaydullāh Khān (r. 1702–11). See Khwāja Muḥammad Iḥsān Mujaddidī Sirhindī, *Rawżat al-qayyūmiyya*, II, 133–136. Devin DeWeese proposes that this may have represented a chapter of ʿUbaydullāh Khān's ongoing struggle against the tribal aristocracies, who were allied with the Jūybārī Khwājas.

76 DeWeese, "'Dis-ordering' Sufism," 263–265.

as Khoqand and Khiva) via the now reinvigorated trade routes to study with Mujaddidī *pīrs* and *ʿulamāʾ* in Durrānī territories.[77] After completing studies in Peshawar, Kashmir, or Kabul, they often returned to Bukhara. Concurrently, several Hindūstānī *pīrs* and *ʿulamāʾ* also travelled northwards and established *khānaqāh*s in Bukhara. Older *silsila*s in Mawarannahr were gradually subsumed under the Mujaddidiyya.[78]

However, according to Manghït histories, during the reign of Dāniyāl Atālïq (1758–85), the khanate of Bukhara once again began to crumble. Later chronicles describe a period of rampant corruption, with *madrasa*s having fallen into decay.

It is in this milieu that Ḥażrat Jīo came to Bukhara. He arrived two or three years after Shāh Murād's accession, and established himself at the historic Mīrakān mosque, in a quarter of the same name near Qarākūl gate.[79] The street hosting Ḥażrat Jīo's mosque and *khānaqāh* eventually became known as Guzar Miyān.[80]

It was here that he met the young ruler, Shāh Murād.

77 For example, Mūsā Khān, a Dahbīdī *khwāja* (d. 1190/1776), travelled to Durrānī Kashmir in the mid-18th century. There, he received an *ijāza* in the Mujaddidī *ṭarīqa* from Muḥammad ʿĀbid, a descendent of Sirhindī. Equipped with a new corpus of Naqshbandī-Mujaddidī teachings, he returned to Mawarannahr. After the 1770s, many Sufis from Mawarannahr came to Kabul to study at institutions, including the Masjid-i Uzbakān (where Khalīfa Niyāzqulī Turkmen received the Mujaddidī *silsila* from Fayż Khān Kābulī) and the Khānaqāh-i Mujaddidiyya-yi Shor Bāzār. See Nāṣir al-Dīn Ḥanafī al-Bukhārī, *Tuḥfat al-zāʾirīn* (Novaia Bukhara: 1910), 71–72; Crews, *For Prophet and Tsar*, 31–32.

78 Von Kügelgen, "Die Entfaltung," 142; Baxtiyor M. Babadžanov, "On the History of the Naqšbandīya Muğaddidīya in Central Māwarāʾannahr in the Late 18th and Early 19th Centuries," in *Muslim Culture in Russia and Central Asia from the 18th to the Early 20th Centuries*, ed. Michael Kemper, Anke von Kügelgen, and Dmitriy Yermakov (Berlin: Klaus Schwarz Verlag, 1996), 391–398.

79 Armenius Vambery mentions that at the time of his visit in 1863, Mīrakān was one of the four notable mosques of the city; see Armenius Vambery, *Travels in Central Asia* (Cambridge: Cambridge Scholars Press, 1864), 363–364. Khanykov lists "Mir Akan" as one of the eight principal "Maschidi Juma" mosques of the city (Khanykov, *Bukhara*, 103). Mīrakān was situated on the edge of Bukhara, at least a 25-minute walk from the Arg, near the Qarākūl Gate. This area hosted several *khānaqāhs* of several prominent 18th century Sufis of Bukhara. While neither Khanykov nor Vambery list the Mīrakān as a *madrasa*, the term *madrasa* is occasionally used in Persian sources in reference to Ḥażrat Jīo's *khānaqāh*.

80 Maqṣūd b. Naṣr Bukhārī, *Rivāyat al-quds*, Ms. Kamilxon Kattayev Library in Samarkand (430 pp., n.d.), p. 279.

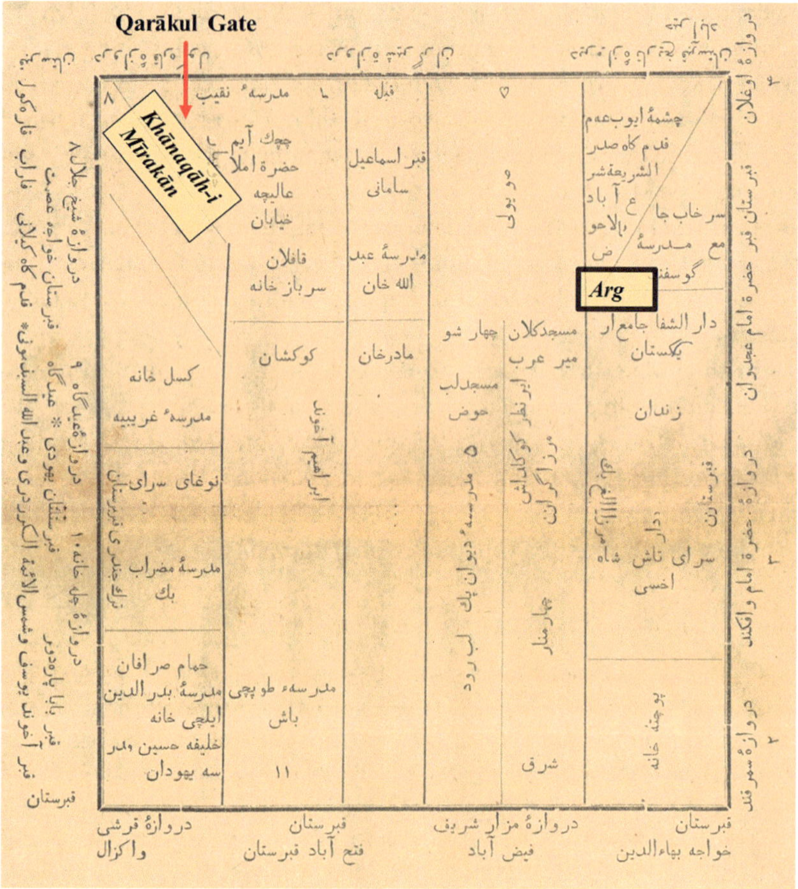

FIGURE 4.8 *Schematic depiction of Bukhara's religious institutions*
SOURCE: ʿABDULLĀH B. MUḤAMMAD ʿĀRIF AL-BUKHĀRĪ, *TĀRĪKH-I BUKHĀRĀ VA TARJUMĀT AL-ʿULAMĀʾ*, FIG. 1 (BETWEEN PP. 28–29)

Shāh Murād

Even prior to meeting Ḥażrat Jīo, Shāh Murād had been introduced to the Mujaddidī *ṭarīqa*. Offering an idealized depiction of the ruler, the Manghït royal chronicles and Mujaddidī hagiographies relate the following narrative.

From a young age, Shāh Murād had expressed a commitment to Sufism and religious scholarship, and first was initiated into the Mujaddidī *ṭarīqa* under Shaykh Ṣafar (d. ca. 1785).[81] After his initiation, the young prince sought only

81 Imām Muḥammad Jīo Ṣāḥib Zakorī, *Rawżat al-awliyāʾ*, 174–175; Mīr ʿAbd al-Karīm Bukhārī, *Tārīkh-i Bukhārā*, ed. Charles Shefer (Paris: L'Ecole des Langues Orientales Vivantes, 1876), 54–55; Mīr Ḥusayn b. Shāh Murād, *Makhāzin al-taqvā*, ff. 30b–31a.

the company of Sufis and *ʿulamāʾ*. Chronicles relate that he abandoned all trappings of royalty, and engaged in manual labor. According to one narrative, he purportedly refused to accept the mantle of kingship, until pressured by the community to assume the position and rectify the ills of his father's reign.[82]

Two or three years after his accession, in 1200/1787–8, Shāh Murād was initiated by Ḥażrat Jīo.[83] Shāh Murād, we are told, would attend Ḥażrat Jīo's assembly every morning and evening, spending several hours in the *khānaqāh*. The *Rawżat al-awliyāʾ* relates one instance in which, in his humility, the king waited his turn outside the *khānaqāh* to see the *pīr*.[84]

From the outset, the king was attentive to the *pīr*'s requests on matters of religion. In fact, on Ḥażrat Jīo's first visit to Bukhara, Shāh Murād convened a scholarly inquiry upon his request to rectify the methods of Qurʾānic recitation throughout the city. While this inquiry initially was unfavorably received by Bukhara's *ʿulamāʾ*, it would have established Ḥażrat Jīo's expertise in the religious sciences.

The Mujaddidī hagiographies go on to explain that eventually the young king excelled in *tavajjuh* (spiritual focus) and other practices. Consequently, he, and later his son Amīr Ḥaydar, were appointed amongst the *pīr*'s *khulafāʾ*, with permission to guide students on the Sufi path.[85] Cementing bonds yet further, Shāh Murād presented his daughter in marriage to Ḥażrat Jīo's son, Miyān Fażlullāh.[86]

The presence of Ḥażrat Jīo and his contemporaries amplified a pre-existing ethos of divinely-guided kingship in Bukhara. This was most directly evidenced through specific ideals of governance as expressed in the royal chronicles, and through Shāh Murād's conspicuous patronage of esoteric and exoteric education.[87]

---

82 Mīr ʿAbd al-Karīm Bukhārī, *Tārīkh-i Bukhārā*, 111–112.

83 Shāh Murād was also initiated by Jān Muḥammad Kulābī, the *khalīfa* of the Mujaddidī *pīr* Ṣūfī Allāh-yār. The *Makhāzin al-taqvā* relates Shāh Murād's early associations with Jān Muḥammad (Mīr Ḥusayn b. Shah Murād, *Makhāzin al-taqvā*, ff. 15a, 63b–65a).

84 Imām Muḥammad Jīo Ṣāḥib Zakorī, *Rawżat al-awliyāʾ*, 188–189.

85 Mīr Ḥusayn b. Shāh Murād, *Makhāzin al-taqvā*, ff. 63b–64a; Imām Muḥammad Jīo Ṣāḥib Zakorī, *Rawżat al-awliyāʾ*, 166–167; von Kügelgen, "Sufimeister und Herrscher," Teil C–a Nr. 28, 56a–58a.

86 Niẓām al-Dīn Balkhī Mazārī, *Tuḥfat al-murshid*, 135.

87 Shāh Murād also initiated judicial, fiscal, administrative, and legal reforms to strengthen the *sharīʿa* and "eliminate unlawful innovations." This entailed an emphasis on justice, by purging state-level corruption and preventing fraud in the marketplace through the appointment of *muḥtasib*s. Activities like gambling, alcohol, and tobacco were likewise purged. He repealed all taxes, duties, and tolls except *zakāt* and *ʿushr*, and actively promoted trade, enriching Bukhara as a commercial hub connecting Russia, China, and

Shāh Murād's support of Mujaddidī institutions certainly served his state-building aims. In addition, it was a means to legitimate his rule in Islamic terms, particularly since he, as a Manghït Uzbek, did not hail from a historically recognized Chinggisid lineage.

A Hybrid Model of Kingship

At the personal level, the king modeled himself in the image of the Sufi-scholar. He retained the habit of a dervish, wrote treatises, including a book on jurisprudence, and reserved only four *dirhams* a day for his family expenses. He even purportedly made himself accessible to the population, giving "audience daily to all comers."[88]

From Shāh Murād's reign onwards, a modified model of sacred kingship emerged. Conscious of their non-Chinggisid origins, the Manghïts synthesized Persianiate models and steppe traditions within a Mujaddidī ethical consciousness. They specifically alluded to the Mujaddidī conception of renewal of the *sharīʿa*, through a focus on both inner and outer dimensions of the faith. Later court chronicles often begin entries on the reign of Shāh Murād with the *ḥadīth* of *tajdīd* (referring to centennial renewal of the faith through a *Mujaddid*, or renewer).[89] Shāh Murād is referred to explicitly as the Mujaddid of the century. These chronicles present the reign of his father, Dāniyāl, as the

---

Khurasan. He also replaced the *darbār* with a council of 40 *ʿulamāʾ*. It is difficult to conclusively argue, however, that these reforms were directly influenced by Ḥażrat Jīo and his Mujaddidī contemporaries. After all, similar reforms were initiated at various stages of Bukhara's history with the aim of restoring order. More importantly, Ḥażrat Jīo's letters to Amīr Ḥaydar do not address issues of this nature. His correspondence deals mostly with matters of personal spirituality, methods of teaching Sufism, and mediation between subjects and the king. As von Kügelgen points out, Ḥażrat Jīo makes only generalized pleas to the king to establish justice and fairness, with occasional warnings that his rule should not contravene the *sharīʿa*. His letters are not specifically prescriptive. Ḥażrat Jīo's only specific recommendations to Amīr Ḥaydar concern the follies of over-taxation. For details see Mīrzā Shams Bukhārī, *Tārīkh-i Bukhārā, Khūqand va Kāshghar* (Tehran: Āyna-yi Mirāth, 1377 H.Sh./1998–99), 113; Erskine, *Erskine Papers*, pp. 138–139; von Kügelgen, "Sufimeister und Herrscher," 240–241.

88 Erskine, *Erskine Papers*, pp. 138–9; Mirzā Shams Bukhārī, *Tārīkh-i Bukhārā, Khūqand va Kāshghar*, 116.

89 This theme continues from Mīr Ḥusayn's *Makhāzin al-taqvā* in the early 19th century to Mīrzā ʿAbd al-ʿAẓīm Sāmī's histories from the late century; see Mīr Ḥusayn b. Shāh Murād, *Makhāzin al-taqvā*, ff. 2b–3a; Mīrzā ʿAbd al-ʿAẓīm Sāmī, *Tuḥfat-i shāhī*, Ms. Tashkent, IVANRUz, Inv. No. 2091 (298 pp., 1348/1929), ff. 58a–60b.

archetypal period of decline and disorder, in which a young prince meets a dervish. Shāh Murād assumes the throne, appropriately, in the year 1200, and revives the Sunna. The ideal king is still the Perso-Turkic empire builder, administrator and soldier. But to this is added the humble ascetic-scholar in the Mujaddidī tradition who walks with his head low, carrying a walking stick through the streets, gives daily lessons on exegesis and doctrine, and trains his own students in advanced Mujaddidī esoteric practices. He is the accessible supporter of the masses, the Sufi miracle worker (the dust of whose grave purportedly had healing qualities), and the magnanimous patron of *khānaqāh*s and *madrasa*s.[90] Concurrently, the Mujaddidīs embraced these Bukharan ideals of kingship and sainthood embodied by Shāh Murād. In hagiographies from Ḥażrat Jīo's and other lineages, Shāh Murād was represented as the exemplary dervish-sovereign conforming to a Sirhindīan model, and a benchmark for other contemporary rulers.

Patronage of *Khānaqāh* and *Madrasa*

Shāh Murād patronized education to such a degree that Bukhara was transformed into a regional seat of learning. Under his son, Amīr Ḥaydar, the city boasted 80 *madrasa*s with several thousand students supported by the state.[91]

---

90 Meer Izzut-oollah, *Travels in Central Asia*, 61. Khanykov refers to Shāh Murād as "Ishan-Morad-Bey" (Khanykov, *Bukhara*, 3), while Mīrzā Shams Bukhārī mentions that the people referred to him with the appellation 'Ḥażrat' (Mirzā Shams Bukhārī, *Tārīkh-i Bukhārā*, 116). Building on this model, Amīr Ḥaydar propagated a similar image. Contemporary travelers and chroniclers praise him for fasting every other day, keeping night prayer vigils, and delivering lectures on religious matters to hundreds of students, in addition to his knowledge of Sufism and adherence to the *sharī'a*. Both Shāh Murād and Amīr Ḥaydar were, henceforth, included in several hagiographies composed in Mawarannahr and Khurasan. This was highly unusual, particularly for Naqshbandī literature. Although Chinggisid khans of Bukhara were honored in Sufi hagiographies prior to this period, Shāh Murād and Amīr Ḥaydar are among the only contemporary rulers in Hindustan, Khurasan, or Mawarannahr to be awarded their own entries in hagiographies. See Ḥāfiẓ Muḥammad Fāżil Khān, *Tārīkh-i manāzil-i Bukhārā*, 37–38, 42–43; Nāṣir al-Dīn, *Tuḥfat al-zā'irīn*, 94–96; Maqṣūd b. Naṣr Bukhārī, *Rivāyat al-quds*, p. 287.

91 Estimates of the number of *madrasa*s and mosques varies. Mīr 'Izzatullāh claims there were 80 colleges in Bukhara as of 1812–13, containing 40 to 200 or 300 rooms each (Meer Izzut-oollah, *Travels in Central Asia by Meer Izzut-Oollah*, 63). Khanykov estimates between 180 and 200 *madrasas* in Bukhara under Amīr Naṣrullāh (r. 1826–1860), and the number of students enrolled at 15,000 to 16,000 (Khanykov, *Bukhara*, 294).

In particular, institutions associated with the Naqshbandiyya-Mujaddidiyya flourished.[92]

Shāh Murād provided generous support to Ḥażrat Jīo, his sons, and his *khulafā'* for their activities in Bukhara as well as in Peshawar and elsewhere. As with the Durrānīs, support came in the form of fixed monthly stipends, annual donations, direct gifts of land, and land revenue assignments, as well as charitable endowments assigned towards specific institutions. Ḥażrat Jīo and his sons received revenue from land in Bukhara, Kasbi, Balkh, and Qarshi, in addition to other regions.[93] They further expanded his capital through the purchase, sale, and lease of mills in Mawarannahr.[94]

Given the academic and economic opportunities created by the Shāh Murād, Ḥażrat Jīo was able to bring with him Sufis and scholars from Hindustan and Khurasan. It is noteworthy that while his disciples from these regions often settled in Mawarannahr, we do not hear of any of Ḥażrat Jīo's students from Mawarannahr moving permanently to Khurasan and Hindustan in the capacity of *khulafā'*—a trend all too common in the early part of the 18th century and before. Disciples from Mawarannahr, did, on occasion, join Ḥażrat Jīo in his journeys to Peshawar and stayed for extensive periods of time at his *khānaqāh*, only to return to teach in Mawarannahr.[95]

A shared Persian language, and its corresponding religio-cultural modalities and symbols, ensured that the authority of *khulafā'* from Hindustan and Khurasan could be recognized across Mawarannahr. Several *khulafā'* from the Punjab and Peshawar were appointed at Balkh, Samarqand, Bukhara, Aqcha,

92 As Jo-Ann Gross points out, Shāh Murād and Amīr Ḥaydar's "confluence of personal devotion, state-building, and Islamic legitimizing efforts" were vital factors in the expansion of the Mujaddidiyya in Mawarannahr (Gross, "The Naqshbandiya Connection," 249).

93 Niẓām al-Dīn Balkhī Mazārī, *Tuḥfat al-murshid*, 35; von Kügelgen, "Sufimeister und Herrscher," 245–249. Some of these lands were allotted by Amīr Ḥaydar. Both the Durrānis and the Manghïts provided land in the contested region of Balkh during periods of their respective control over the region. The Manghïts assigned the villages of Bakht-i Shāh and Dah-i Naw to Ḥażrat Jīo and Fażl-i Ḥaqq. It is noteworthy that these land grants to Ḥażrat Jīo and his sons were not impacted by political transitions.

94 A photograph of the epistle is provided in von Kügelgen, "Sufimeister und Herrscher," 346–47 (Teil C–a Nr. 93, ff. 118b–119a). We can also assume that other rulers of the Amu Darya regions who were counted among Ḥażrat Jīo's disciples, such as Mīr Muḥammad Murād Beg of Qunduz, would have provided similar support. The ruler of Badakhshān, Mīr Sulṭān Shāh, for example, patronized two *khulafā'* and family members of Ḥażrat Jīo, Mīr Aḥmad Ṣāḥib Mujaddidī, and Muḥammad Anwar. See Moorcroft and Trebeck, *Travels*, II, 447; Badakhshī, *Armaqān-i Badakhshān*, 111–113; (Meer Izzut-oollah, *Travels in Central Asia by Meer Izzut-Oollah*, 63).

95 Niẓām al-Dīn Balkhī Mazārī, *Tuḥfat al-murshid*, 175–180.

Khiva, and Khoqand. Remarkably, some of the Punjābī migrants were regarded as native saints of Mawarannahr within their lifetimes. Among them was Laʿl Beg Samarqandī, from Qaṣba Darvaysh, Punjab, whose grave, along with his son's, became revered shrines in Samarqand.[96] In regions where the Persian language was not commonly understood, securing a foothold could naturally be challenging. The *Tuḥfat al-murshid* relates the unfortunate story of Qāżī Ghulām Ḥusayn of Wazirabad, Punjab, who was appointed at Khiva. Distressed, he left soon after his arrival, as the people of Khiva could converse neither in Persian nor Hindūstānī.[97]

As Bukhara's *madrasa* and *khānaqāh* infrastructure rapidly developed, the Durrānī state began providing stipends for students to study there.[98] Elphinstone mentions that as of 1808, an extensive academic exchange existed between Peshawar and Bukhara.[99] Ḥażrat Jīo's institutions formed part of this exchange.

Eventually, Ḥażrat Jīo's *silsila* became deeply engaged with both Peshawar's (as discussed above) and Bukhara's Naqshbandī networks. The hagiographies of Ḥażrat Jīo and other Bukharan Sufis make it clear that he and his contemporaries perceived themselves as parts of an integrated Naqshbandī-Mujaddidī *silsila*. Consciously, they forged initiatory and marriage ties and absorbed practices and literature of their contemporaries.[100]

For example, Ḥażrat Jīo married into the family of Ḥabībullāh Bukhārī, and in 1814, his grandson, Miyān Fażl Raḥīm, was even buried in Ḥabībullāh's funerary complex.[101] This effectively generated interlocking lineages and sacred spaces with Bukhara's oldest Mujaddidī branch. Relations between Ḥażrat Jīo's lineage and the Dahbīdīs were particularly extensive. Hagiographies of both lineages treat the other with reverence, despite moments of serious

---

96 Niẓām al-Dīn Balkhī Mazārī, *Tuḥfat al-murshid*, 156.

97 Niẓām al-Dīn Balkhī Mazārī, *Tuḥfat al-murshid*, 188.

98 Mirzā ʿAbd al-Qādir Qādirī Kashmirī (quoted in ʿAzīz al-Dīn Vakīlī Fūfalzāʾī, *Durrat al-zamān fī tārīkh-i Shāh Zamān* [Kabul: Anjuman-i Tārikh-i Afghanistan, 1337 H.Sh./1958–1959], 403) mentions Zamān Shāh Durrānī providing stipends to students from the Durrānī empire to study at *madrasas* in Bukhara, notably the Kokaltāsh.

99 Elphinstone mentions that at the time of his visit, still more students were coming from Bukhara to Peshawar than vice-versa; see Mountstuart Elphinstone, *An Account of the Kingdom of Caubul, and Its Dependencies, in Persia, Tartary, and India: A View of the Afghaun Nation, and a History of the Dooraunee Monarchy* (London: R. Bentley, 1839), I, 301.

100 As von Kügelgen argues, the lack of an established hierarchy, the presence of local independent centers, and flexibility of practices were among the factors that facilitated the success of the Mujaddidiyya in Mawarannahr (Kügelgen, "Die Entfaltung," 145–147).

101 Niẓām al-Dīn Balkhī Mazārī, *Tuḥfat al-murshid*, 143.

FIGURE 4.9 *Qarākol Gate, Bukhara*

tension between disciples of Mūsā Khān Dahbīdī and Ḥażrat Jīo.[102] The *Tuḥfat al-murshid* also mentions that at least four of Ḥażrat Jīo's principal *khulafāʾ* in

102 For example, the Dahbīdī biography, *Rivāyat al-quds*, contains a brief entry on Ḥażrat Jīo (Maqṣūd b. Naṣr Bukhārī, *Rivāyat al-quds*, p. 279). Khumūlī relates that in 1805, several disciples of Ḥażrat Jīo informed Amīr Ḥaydar that Muḥammad Amīn (d. 1813), Mūsā Khān's successor at Dahbīd, was planning a revolt at Ḥiṣar. While Khumūlī does not substantiate

Bukhara were also initiated by Mūsā Khān Dahbīdī and his successors.[103] In one of his discourses, Ḥażrat Jīo in fact specifically praises the spiritual stature of Mūsā Khān, and the high caliber of his students.[104]

The 'Ṣāḥibzādas'

Two years after his departure from Bukhara, at age 84, Ḥażrat Jīo passed away in Peshawar (1231 or 1232/1816 or 1817). He and later his son Miyān Fażl-i Ḥaqq were buried near his *khānaqāh*.[105] After the death of Fażl-i Ḥaqq, his disciple Yār Muḥammad Khān Bārakzā'ī (governor of Peshawar and brother of the ruler of Kabul, Amīr Dost Muḥammad Khān) invested several thousand rupees in a permanent shrine.[106] Until today, the shrine complex is visited by devotees and those seeking physical or spiritual healing.[107]

With patronage from both sides of the Amu Darya, Ḥażrat Jīo's *silsila* rapidly spread across Mawarannahr and beyond. The story of his successors highlights the degree to which Sufi lineages such as Ḥażrat Jīo's integrated the regions north and south of the Amu Darya. His sons and grandsons—known as the *Ṣāḥibzādas*—were venerated as saints in Khurasan, Mawarannahr, Kazan, and beyond. They were referred to by a series of culturally specific appellations, including Ḥażratjī, Ṣāḥibzāda, Miyān Buzurg, Īshān Pīr, and Kattā Ḥażrat.

Alexander Burnes' 'Persian Secretary,' Mohan Lal, describes Ḥażrat Jīo's son, Miyān Fażl-i Ḥaqq, as the "murshid of all the Mawarannahr and Peshawer

---

the claim, he relates that later Muḥammad Amīn facilitated the capture of Ura Tepe by the Khan of Khoqand. See Mullā Jum'a-qulī Ūrgūtī "Khumūlī," *Tārīkh-i Khumūlī*, Ms. Tashkent, IVANRUz, Inv. No. 37/VI (ff. 133b–345b, dated 1278/1861), ff. 313a–314b.

103 Niẓām al-Dīn Balkhī Mazārī, *Tuḥfat al-murshid*, 152–170. Amīr Ḥaydar was eventually initiated by Muḥammad Amīn, the *khalīfa* of Mūsā Khān Dahbīdī (Khumūlī, *Tārīkh*, f. 328a).

104 Niẓām al-Dīn Balkhī Mazārī, *Tuḥfat al-murshid*, 99.

105 Niẓām al-Dīn Balkhī Mazārī, *Tuḥfat al-murshid*, 129.

106 Munshī Gopal Dās, in *Tārīkh-i Pishāvar* (1878) provides a "List of those Pilgrimage Sites and Mosques which the people of Peshawar Consider Blessed;" Ḥażrat Jīo's is one of 15 listed (Munshī Gopal Dās, *Tārīkh-i Pishāvar*, 148–149).

107 M. Zamān Khokar, who visited the *khānaqāh* on a pilgrimage journey through Pakistan's North West Frontier Province several decades ago, related that the shrine-*khānaqāh* complex was visited by the sick on Thursdays for its healing qualities. He added that it was famous for hosting *khatm-i Qur'ān* ceremonies attracting thousands; see M. Zamān Khokhar, *Peshawar Say Quetta Tak: Dāman-i Koh mayn Qadīmī Tārīkhī aur Ruhānī Maqāmāt* (Gujrat, Punjab: Yāsir Academy, 2003), 229. The annual death anniversary still draws pilgrims from across Pakistan and Afghanistan.

people."[108] Miyān Fażl-i Ḥaqq's progeny, likewise, were renowned among Pashtun tribes between Kabul and Peshawar. His principal son and successor, Fażl Hādī, was a well-regarded *pīr* in Swat and Jalalabad, and was held in esteem by the Akhund of Swat.[109]

Ḥażrat Jīo's son and successor in Bukhara, Miyān Ghulām Qādir (d. 1271/1855) established a second *khānaqāh* in the city in a district adjacent to Mīrakān. The *khānaqāh* was known as Khānaqāh-i Ṣāḥibzāda, and the district, likewise, came to be known as 'Ṣāḥibzāda.'[110] The Tatar 'reformer' Shihāb al-Dīn Marjānī (d. 1889), who received an *ijāzat-nāma* from him, relates that he was so highly celebrated that the majority of the city of Bukhara attended his funeral.[111]

Yet another son, Miyān Fażl Aḥad (d. 1869), was the progenitor of one the most influential Sufi families of the Khanate of Khoqand.[112] Several members of his family eventually settled in Kazan, while representatives of another branch of his *silsila* currently manage two central *khānaqāh*s in North Waziristan and the Malakand Agency.[113]

---

108 Munshī Mohan Lal, *Travels*, 56; Mohan Lal refers to him as a "Sayyid."

109 'Abdullāh Jān Fārūqī Naqshbandī, *Gulhā-i chaman*, 58–64; Fażl Hādī's nephew, Fażl Rashīd (b. Fażl Laṭīf b. Fażl-i Ḥaqq b. Fażl Aḥmad Ḥażrat Jīo), was later married to the Akhund's daughter.

110 'Abdullāh al-Bukhārī, *Tārīkh al-Bukhārā va tarjumāt al-'ulamā'*, 3–4, 15–16.

111 Ṣāliḥ b. Thābit, *Marjānī* (Kazan: Ma'ārif Maṭba'asi, 1333/1914–5), 71–72; Thierry Zarcone, "Le Qâdiriyya en Asie centrale et au Turkestan oriental," *Journal of the History of Sufism* (*Special Issue: The Qâdiriyya Order, dedicated to Alexandre Popovic*), ed. Thierry Zarcone, Ekrem Işin, Arthur Buehler, and Alexandre Popović, 1–2 (2000), pp. 322–325. Marjānī spent time in his service at his *khānaqāh*, and received both an *ijāzat-nāma* and *khaṭṭ-i irshād* from him. Ghulām Qādir also appointed *khulafā'* among the Volga Tatars, who carried the *silsila* into Siberia. Ṣāliḥ b. Thābit erroneously refers to Miyān Ghulām Qādir ('Abd al-Qādir) as the son of Niyāz Aḥmad Sirhindī.

112 Niẓām al-Dīn Balkhī Mazārī, *Tuḥfat al-murshid*, 136; Muhammad Yunus Djan Tashkandī, *The Life of Alimqul: A Native Chronicle of Nineteenth Century Central Asia*, tr. Timur K. Beisembiev (Richmond: Curzon Press, 2003), 21–22; Imām Muḥammad Jīo Ṣāḥib Zakorī, *Rawżat al-awliyā'*, 215; Timur K. Beisembiev, "Farghana's Contacts with India in the 18th and 19th Centuries (According to the Khokand Chronicles)," *Journal of Asian History*, 28/2 (1994), 127. Miyān Buzurg taught in Bukhara as of 1240/1825, but regularly travelled between Peshawar and Bukhara. He arrived in Khoqand ca. 1826, where he established an important *khānaqāh*, serving as a hub for a network of Sufis and *'ulamā'* in Farghana, Kashghar, and elsewhere. His cousin, Miyān Khalīl Ḥażrat (also a *khalīfa* of Ḥażrat Jīo), served as the ambassador of Khoqand to Russia as of 1842.

113 'Abdullāh Jān Fārūqī Naqshbandī, *Risāla-yi inkishāf* (Idak, North Waziristan: Idāra-yi Naqshbandiyya Ḥażratābād, n.d.), 73.

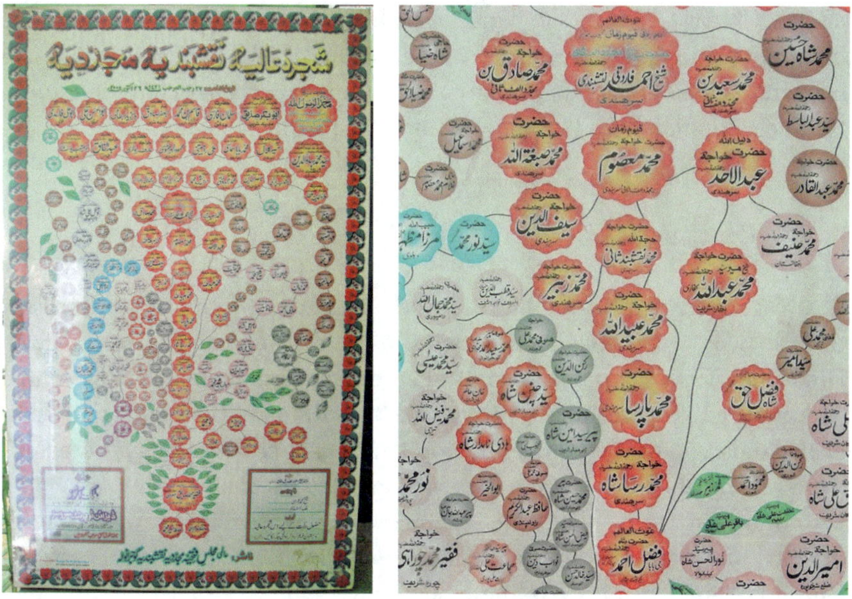

FIGURE 4.10 *Genealogical tree of Ḥażrat Jīo Pishāvarī at Khānaqāh-i Ḥażrat Jīo, Peshawar, 2015*

The genealogical tree depicted above is displayed in Ḥażrat Jīo's shrine and *khānaqāh* in modern day Peshawar.[114]

This image illustrates how distinct branches of the Mujaddidiyya are interconnected in the *silsila*'s consciousness even today, covering modern day Pakistan, Afghanistan, and India—with the lineage of Ḥażrat Jīo occupying a prominent place in the center. Other celebrated lineages depicted on this tree are those based at the Khānaqāh-i Shor Bāzār, Kabul, and the historic Khānaqāh-i Maẓhariyya at Delhi, where the Indian Muslim reformer Sir Sayyid Aḥmad Khan spent his youth. The *silsila* lines repeatedly intersect, reinforcing the connection to Shaykh Aḥmad Sirhindī. At the end of each *silsila* are green leaves representing living *pīr*s from North Waziristan to Sindh, indicating the *ṭarīqa*'s appeal in ethnically and culturally diverse regions, even today.

What stands out in this modern representation of Ḥażrat Jīo's *silsila* is the complete absence of Mawarannahr, representing the breaking of the historical chains that we have discussed. Determining how and when this occurred merits further research on the subsequent development of Ḥażrat Jīo's *khānaqāh*s

114 Muḥammad Masʿūd Aṣdaq Khān, *Shajara-yi ʿāliyya-yi ṭarīqa-yi Naqshbandiyya-yi Mujaddidiyya*. Gujranwala, Punjab: ʿĀlamī Majlis Fatḥiyya Mujaddidiyya Naqshbandiyya, 2000.

and sub-lineages. Aspects to consider include, among others, the fate of the *awqāf* after the fall of the Durrānīs, the impact of Sikh, British and Russian educational and economic policies, the ascendancy of vernacular literatures, the decline in north-south trade, and the articulation of colonial frontiers.

Conclusion

This case study of Ḥażrat Jīo's network illustrates the multiple processes through which the Mujaddidī network expanded its reach westward from Hindustan. With the breakdown of older empires, ruling households invited and financed trans-regionally recognized Sufis to revive the sacred and scholastic landscape of their emerging polities. In each new location, these Sufis were readily absorbed within the existing religious milieu. They generated institutional networks that were separate from the fiscal-military institutions of state, and possessed greater resilience and longevity. In this process, the Durrānī Afghan empire was the chief catalyst that allowed the Mujaddidī order re-entry into Mawarannahr and beyond.

As Sufi saints and jurists, Mujaddidī Sufis such as Ḥażrat Jīo assumed the role of arch-intermediaries in a dynamic and fragile environment. They were called upon to mediate between urban and tribal elites and subjects, antagonistic polities, colonial and local authorities, and agrarian and highland communities. Their institutions served as loci for trade, negotiation, and diplomacy, integrating regions north and south of the Amu Darya into a single sacro-cultural and economic zone.

Bibliography

ʿAbd al-Raḥīm b. Khān Muḥammad Pishāvarī. *Taṣarruf-nāma*. Ms. Khānaqāh-i Ḥażratkhayl, Thana, Malakand Agency (13ff., n.d., mid 19th c.).

Abdul Wadud. *The Story of Swat as Told by the Founder Miangul Abdul Wadud Badshah Sahib to Muhammad Asif Khan*. Peshawar: Ferozsons Limited, 1963.

ʿAbdullāh Jān Fārūqī Naqshbandī. *Gulhā-i chaman*. Thana, Malakand Agency: Idāra -yi Naqshbandiyya Garhī Ḥażratkhayl, 1967.

ʿAbdullāh Jān Fārūqī Naqshbandī. *Risāla-yi inkishāf*. Idak, North Waziristan: Idāra-yi Naqshbandiyya Ḥażratābād, n.d.

Abū ʿAbd al-Raḥmān ʿAbdullāh b. Muḥammad ʿĀrif al-Bukhārī. *Tārīkh al-Bukhārā wa tarjumāt al-ʿulamāʾ*. Orenburg: Dīn va Maʿīshat Bāṣma-khānasi, 1908.

Aḥmad Abū'l-Khayr al-Makkī. *Hadiya-yi Aḥmadiyya*. Kanpur: Maṭbaʿ-i Niẓāmī, 1313/1895–96.

Alam, Muzaffar. "Trade, State Policy and Regional Change: Aspects of Mughal-Uzbek Commercial Relations, c. 1550–1750." *Journal of the Economic and Social History of the Orient*, 37/3 (1994), 202–227.

Athār, ʿAbd al-Ḥalīm. *Rūḥānī Rābita aw Rūḥānī Tārūn*; 2 vols. Peshawar: University Book Agency, 2004.

Babadžanov, Baxtiyor M. "On the History of the Naqšbandīya Muğaddidīya in Central Māwarā'annahr in the Late 18th and Early 19th Centuries." In *Muslim Culture in Russia and Central Asia from the 18th to the Early 20th Centuries*, ed. Michael Kemper, Anke von Kügelgen, and Dmitriy Yermakov (Berlin: Klaus Schwarz Verlag, 1996; Islamkundliche Untersuchungen, Bd. 200), 385–413.

Badakhshī, Shāh ʿAbdullāh. *Armaqān-i Badakhshān*. Tehran: Bunyād-i Mawqūfāt-i Doctor Maḥmūd Afshār, 1385 H.Sh./2006–07.

Beisembiev, Timur K. "Farghana's Contacts with India in the 18th and 19th Centuries (According to the Khokand Chronicles)." *Journal of Asian History*, 28/2 (1994), 124–135.

Buehler, Arthur F. *Revealed Grace: The Juristic Sufism of Ahmad Sirhindi (1564–1624)*. Louisville, Kentucky: Fons Vitae, 2011.

Burnes, Alexander *Travels into Bokhara*. London: J. Murray, 1834.

Burton, Audrey. "Bukharan Trade 1558–1718," *Papers on Inner Asia*, 23 (Bloomington, Indiana: Research Institute for Inner Asian Studies, 1993).

Crews, Robert D. *For Prophet and Tsar: Islam and Empire in Russia and Central Asia*. Cambridge, Massachusetts: Harvard University Press, 2006.

Dani, Ahmad Hasan. *Peshawar: Historic City of the Frontier*. Peshawar: Khyber Mail Press, 1969.

DeWeese, Devin. "'Dis-ordering' Sufism in Early Modern Central Asia: Suggestions for Rethinking the Sources and Social Structures of Sufi History in the 18th and 19th Centuries," in *History and Culture of Central Asia/Istoriia i kul'tura Tsentral'noi Azii*, ed. Bakhtiyar Babadjanov and Kawahara Yayoi (Tokyo: The University of Tokyo, 2012), 259–279.

Elphinstone, Mountstuart. *An Account of the Kingdom of Caubul, and Its Dependencies, in Persia, Tartary, and India: A View of the Afghaun Nation, and a History of the Dooraunee Monarchy*. London: R. Bentley, 1839.

Elphinstone, Mountstuart. *Papers of Mountstuart Elphinstone: Accounts of Afghanistan and Central Asia, Etc.*, Ms. British Library, India Office Records and Private Papers, Eur F88/372, 1808.

Erskine, William. *Erskine Papers: Oriental Chronology and Geography*, Ms. British Library, India Office Records and Private Papers, Eur D 28, 1810.

Fayż Muḥammad Kātib Hazāra. *The History of Afghanistan: Fayz Muhammad Katib Hazarah's Siraj al-Tawārīkh*. Tr. Robert D. McChesney and Mehdi M. Khorrami. Leiden: Brill, 2012.

Fletcher, Joseph. "Integrative History: Parallels and Interconnections in the Early Modern Period." In Joseph Fletcher, *Studies on Chinese and Islamic Inner Asia*, ed. Beatrice Manz (Hampshire: Variorum, 1995), No. x, 1–35.

Friedmann, Yohannan. *Shaykh Ahmad Sirhindi: An Outline of His Thought and a Study of His Image in the Eyes of Posterity*. Montreal: McGill-Queen's University Press, 1971.

Fūfalzā'ī, 'Azīz al-Dīn Vakīlī. *Durrat al-zamān fī tārīkh-i Shāh Zamān*. Kabul: Anjuman-i Tārīkh-i Afghanistan, 1337 H.Sh./1958–59.

Fūfalzā'ī, 'Azīz al-Dīn Vakīlī. *Timūr Shāh Durrānī*. Kabul: Anjuman-i Tārīkh-i Afghanistan, 1333 H.Sh./1954–55.

Ghulām Sarvar Lāhūrī. *Khazīnat al-aṣfiyā*; 2 vols. Kabul: Anṣāri Kutub Khāna, 1994.

Gommans, Jos. "Mughal India and Central Asia in the Eighteenth Century: An Introduction to a Wider Perspective." *Itinerario*, 15 (01) (1991), 51–70.

Gommans, Jos. *The Rise of the Indo-Afghan Empire, c. 1710–1780*. Leiden: E. J. Brill, 1995.

Gross, Jo-Ann. "The Naqshbandiya Connection: From Central Asia to India and Back (16th–19th Centuries)." In *India and Central Asia: Commerce and Culture, 1500–1800*, ed. Scott C. Levi (New Delhi: Oxford University Press, 2007), 232–259.

Ḥāfiẓ Darāz Pishāvarī. *Risāla radd-i Wahhābiyyat*. Ms. Rotograph, Dr. Iqbāl Mujaddidī Collection, R. No. 238.6 (14ff., 1250/1834–35, Original 1240/1824–25).

Ḥāfiẓ Muḥammad Fāżil Khān. *Tārīkh-i manāzil-i Bukhārā*. Srinagar: Centre of Central Asian Studies, 1981.

Haroon, Sana. *Frontier of Faith: Islam in the Indo-Afghan Borderland*. New York: Columbia University Press, 2007.

Holzwarth, Wolfgang. "The Uzbek State as Reflected in Eighteenth Century Bukharan Sources." *Asiatische Studien*, 60/2 (2006), 321–353.

Ḥusayn, Sayyid Amjad. *'Ālam Mayn Intikhāb Peshawar*. Peshawar: Dār al-Adab, 2003.

Ijāzatnāma and *Shajara-yi Mujaddidiyya* (citing 'Abd al-Qādir, *khalīfa* of Fażl Aḥmad Ma'ṣūmī). Ms. Kitābkhāna-yi Ganj Bakhsh, Islamabad, 8201 (ff. 258–261, n.d., early 19th c.).

Imām Muḥammad Jīo Ṣāḥib Zakorī. *Rawżat al-awliyā' fī aḥvāl-i aṣfiyā'*. Zakori, Dera Ismail Khan: Nījar Rūz Bāzār Press, 1333/1914–15.

Khān, Muḥammad Mas'ūd Aṣdaq. *Shajara-yi 'āliyya-yi ṭarīqa-yi Naqshbandiyya-yi Mujaddidiyya*. Gujranwala, Punjab: 'Ālamī Majlis Fatḥiyya Mujaddidiyya Naqshbandiyya, 2000.

Khanykov, Nikolaï Vladimirovitch. *Bukhara, Its Amir and Its People*. Tr. Baron Clement A. de Bode. London, 1845.

Khokhar, M. Zamān. *Peshawar Say Quetta Tak: Dāman-i Koh mayn Qadīmī Tārīkhī aur Ruhānī Maqāmāt*. Gujrat, Punjab: Yāsir Academy, 2003.

Khwāja Muḥammad Iḥsān Mujaddidī Sirhindī. *Rawżat al-qayyūmiyya*, ed. Iqbāl Aḥmad Fārūqī. Lahore: Maktaba Nabawiya, 2002.

von Kügelgen, Anke. "Die Entfaltung der Naqšbandīya Muǧaddidīya im mittleren Transoxanien vom 18. bis zum Beginn des 19. Jahrhunderts: Ein Stück Detektivarbeit." In *Muslim Culture in Russia and Central Asia from the 18th to the Early 20th Centuries*, vol. 2: *Inter-Regional and Inter-Ethnic Relations*, ed. Anke von Kügelgen, Michael Kemper, and Allen J. Frank (Berlin: Klaus Schwarz Verlag, 1998; Islamkundliche Untersuchungen, Bd. 216), 101–151.

von Kügelgen, Anke. "Sufimeister und Herrscher im Zwiegespräch: Die Schreiben des Faḍl Aḥmad aus Peschawar an Amīr Ḥaydar in Buchara." In *Muslim Culture in Russia and Central Asia*, vol. 3: *Arabic, Persian and Turkic Manuscripts (15th–19th Centuries)*, ed. Anke von Kügelgen, Aširbek Muminov, and Michael Kemper (Berlin: Klaus Schwarz Verlag, 2000; Islamkundliche Untersuchungen, Band 233), 219–351.

Lee, Jonathan L. *The "Ancient Supremacy": Bukhara, Afghanistan and the Battle for Balkh, 1731–1901*. Leiden: Brill, 1996.

Levi, Scott C. *The Indian Diaspora in Central Asia and Its Trade: 1550–1900*. Leiden: Brill, 2002.

Manṣūr, Fayżullāh. *Mihr-i ṣafā: Ḥażrat Pīr Muḥammad ʿAbd al-Laṭīf Zakorī Sharif*. Lahore: Muslim League Writers Academy, 2004.

Maqṣūd b. Naṣr Bukhārī. *Rivāyat al-quds*. Ms. Kamilxon Kattayev Library in Samarkand (430 pp., n.d.).

Markovits, Claude. *The Global World of Indian Merchants, 1750–1947: Traders of Sind from Bukhara to Panama*. Cambridge: Cambridge University Press, 2000.

Masson, Charles. *Masson Collection: Papers of Charles Masson (1800–53)*, Ms. British Library, India Office Records and Private Papers, B98, 1828. (a).

Masson, Charles. *Masson Collection: Papers of Charles Masson (1800–53)*, Ms. British Library, India Office Records and Private Papers, E163, 1828. (b).

McChesney, R. D. *Waqf in Central Asia: Four Hundred Years in the History of a Muslim Shrine, 1480–1889*. Princeton: Princeton University Press, 1991.

Meer Izzut-oollah. *Travels in Central Asia by Meer Izzut-Oollah in the Years 1812–13*. Tr. Captain Henderson. Calcutta: Foreign Department Press, 1872.

Mīr ʿAbd al-Karīm Bukhārī. *Tārīkh-i Bukhārā*, ed. Charles Shefer. Paris: L'Ecole des Langues Orientales Vivantes, 1876.

Mīr Aḥmad Shāh Riżvānī Pishāvarī. *Tuḥfat-i awliyāʾ*. Lahore, Maṭbaʿ-i Mufīd-i ʿĀm Press, 1321/1903–4.

Mīr Ḥusayn b. Shāh Murād. *Makhāzin al-taqvā*. Ms. Tashkent, IVANRUz, Inv. No. 51 (ff. 1b–312b., undated).

Mīr Ṣafar Aḥmad Maʿṣūmī. *Maqāmāt-i Maʿṣūmī*, ed. Muḥammad Iqbāl Mujaddidī. Lahore: Ziyāʾ al-Qurʾān Publications, 2004.

Mīrzā ʿAbd al-ʿAẓīm Sāmī. *Tuḥfat-i shāhī.* Ms. Tashkent, IVANRUz, Inv. No. 2091 (298 pp., 1348/1929).

Mīrzā Shams Bukhārī. *Tārīkh-i Bukhārā, Khūqand va Kāshghar.* Tehran: Āyna-yi Mirāth, 1377 H.Sh./1998–99.

Miyān Fażl Aḥmad Maʿṣūmī. *Risāla.* Ms. Tashkent, IVANRUz, Inv. No. 2572/XXVI (ff. 571b–578b, dated 1235/1819–20).

Moorcroft, William, and George Trebeck. *Travels in the Himalayan Provinces of Hindustan and the Panjab; in Ladakh and Kashmir; in Peshawar, Kabul, Kunduz, and Bukhara: From 1819 to 1825.* London. J. Murray, 1841.

Muhammad Yunus Djan Tashkandī. *The Life of Alimqul: A Native Chronicle of Nineteenth Century Central Asia.* Tr. Timur K. Beisembiev. Richmond: Curzon Press, 2003.

Mujaddidī, Muḥammad Iqbāl. "ʿĀlamī Satih par Silsila-yi Naqshbandiyya Mujaddidiyya kā Athr-o Rasūkh." In *Armaqān-i Imām Rabbānī, Vol. 2*, ed. Muḥammad Humāyūn Abbās Shams (Lahore: Sher-i Rabbānī Publications, 2008), 69–81.

Mullā Jumʿa-qulī Ūrgūtī "Khumūlī." *Tārīkh-i Khumūlī.* Ms. Tashkent, IVANRUz, Inv. No. 37/VI (ff. 133b–345b, dated 1278/1861).

Munshī Gopal Dās. *Tārīkh-i Pishāvar.* Lahore: Koh-i Nūr Press, 1878.

Munshī Mohan Lal. *Travels in the Panjab, Afghanistan, Turkistan, to Balk, Bokhara, and Herat: And a Visit to Great Britain and Germany.* London: W. H. Allen and Co., 1846.

Nāṣir al-Dīn Ḥanafī al-Bukhārī. *Tuḥfat al-zāʾirīn.* Novaia Bukhara, 1910.

Nawid, Senzil K. *Religious Response to Social Change in Afghanistan, 1919–29: King Aman-Allah and the Afghan Ulama.* Costa Mesa, California: Mazda Publishers, 1999.

Nichols, Robert. *Settling the Frontier: Land, Law and Society in the Peshawar Valley, 1500–1900.* Karachi: Oxford University Press, 2001.

Niẓām al-Dīn Balkhī Mazārī. *Tuḥfat al-murshid dar manāqib-i Quṭb-i Zamān Ghawth-i Jahān Ḥażrat Jīo Ṣāḥib Shāh Fażl Aḥmad Maʿṣūmī.* Lahore: Fayż-i ʿĀm, 1913.

Qādirī, Faqīr Muḥammad Āmir Shāh. *Tazkira-yi ʿulamāʾ va mashāʾikh-i Sarḥad.* Peshawar: ʿAẓīm Publishing House, 1972.

Quddūsī, ʿIjāz al-Ḥaqq. *Tazkira-yi ṣūfiyya-yi Sarḥad.* Lahore: Markazī Urdu Board, 1966.

Rānjhā, Muḥammad Naẓīr. *Tārīkh-u Tazkira-yi khānaqāh-i Sirhind Sharīf.* Lahore: Jamīʿat Publications, 2011.

Ṣābir, Muḥammad Shafʿī. *Shakhṣīyāt-i Sarḥad.* Peshawar: University Book Agency, n.d.

Ṣafīullāh Ṣāḥib. *Naẓm al-durrar fī sālik al-sayr.* Delhi: Maṭbaʿ al-Farūqī, n.d. (late 19th c.).

Ṣāliḥ b. Thābit. *Marjānī.* Kazan: Maʿārif Maṭbaʿasi, 1333/1914–5.

Saljūqī, Fikrī. *Risāla-yi mazārāt-i Harāt.* Herat: ʿAbd al-Ḥalīm Muḥammadī, 1386 H.Sh./2007–08.

Sayyid Aḥmad Shahīd. *Makātib-i Sayyid Aḥmad Shahīd* (photograph of manuscript), Lahore: Maktaba Rashīdiyya, 1395/1975.

Shāh Muḥammad Fażlullāh. *'Umdat al-maqāmāt*. Hyderabad, Sindh: Nu'mānī Publishers, 1355/1936–7.

"*Shajara-yi Mujaddidiyya* of Fażl Aḥmad Ma'ṣūmī." In *Risāla*, Ms. Islamabad, Kitābkhāna-yi Ganj-bakhsh, 3992, (pp. 110–14, n.d., early 19th c.).

Shajaratnāma. Ms. Tashkent, Central State Archives of the Republic of Uzbekistan, fond I-323, opis' 2, No. 90 (scroll, n.d., early 19th century).

Shaykh 'Abdullāh Ghulām 'Alī Dihlavī. *Maqāmāt-i Maẓharī: Aḥvāl va malfūẓāt va maktūbāt-i Ḥażrat Mirzā Maẓhar Jān-i Jānān Shahīd*. Tr. Muḥammad Iqbāl Mujaddidī. Lahore: Urdu Science Board, 2001.

Shihāb al-Dīn Marjānī. *Mustafad al-akhbār fī aḥvāl Qazān va Bulghār*. Kazan: Tipografiia Imperatorskago Universiteta, 1900.

The Thirty-Seventh Report of the Calcutta Corresponding Committee of the Church Missionary Society Being for the Year 1855. Calcutta: Sanders, Cones & Co., 1856.

Vambery, Armenius. *Travels in Central Asia*. Cambridge: Cambridge Scholars Press, 1864.

Watson, Geoff. "Images of Central Asia in the 'Central Asian Question' C. 1826–1885." In *Walls and Frontiers in Inner Asian History* (Silk Road Studies, VI), ed. Craig Benjamin and Samuel Lieu (Turnhout, Belgium: Brepols, 2003), 141–158.

Zarcone, Thierry. "Le Qâdiriyya en Asie centrale et au Turkestan oriental." *Journal of the History of Sufism* (*Special Issue: The Qâdiriyya Order, dedicated to Alexandre Popovic*), ed. Thierry Zarcone, Ekrem Işin, Arthur Buehler, and Alexandre Popović, 1–2 (2000), 295–338.

CHAPTER 5

Valī Khān Tūra: A Makhdūmzāda Leader in Marghīnān during the Collapse of the Khanate of Khoqand

Kawahara Yayoi

This paper presents a case study of a family of shaykhs in Central Asia, exploring the role played by the leader of a Makhdūmzāda family—i.e., a family claiming natural descent from the prominent 16th-century Naqshbandī shaykh, Khwāja Aḥmad Kāsānī (d. 1542), who was widely known by his honorific title of Makhdūm-i Aʿẓam ("Great Master")—in Marghīnān, a prominent town of the Farghana valley, during the last years of the Khanate of Khoqand and the beginning of direct Russian rule in the region.[1] The leader in question, known as Valī Khān Tūra, was an influential shaykh, a spiritual guide of *murīd*s (disciples), as well as a prominent member of local society who was actively involved in public service. With the demise of the *khān*'s authority in Marghīnān, he became the virtual ruler of the region and raised a *ghazavāt* against Russian rule and its supporters. Although the *ghazavāt* was defeated, its collapse occasioning the official annexation to Russia of the entire territory of the Khanate of Khoqand, Valī Khān Tūra's authority and reputation in local society remained intact; indeed, two years after the defeat of his *ghazavāt*, when he was arrested in 1878 and imprisoned by the Russian authorities, the residents of Marghīnān successfully petitioned for his release, suggesting that Valī Khān Tūra was the closest thing to a 'popular leader' in Marghīnān during those times of violent political upheaval.

Valī Khān Tūra's reputation both drew upon, and enhanced, the status of his Makhdūmzāda family. Today in Marghīnān and its suburbs there are extant *mazār*s of this family, and their descendants possess numerous historical documents, such as genealogies, deeds, and hagiographies. The descendants have also maintained various legends concerning the family's origins. According to these sources, the family's ancestors became famous as miracle-performing

1 This work was supported by JSPS KAKENHI Grant Numbers JP25770254 and JP17J40138.

 | DOI:10.1163/9789004373075_007

saints and, being *sayyid*s, managed to gain official positions in the Khanate and accumulate copious amounts of wealth. The Makhdūmzāda lineage to which Valī Khān Tūra belonged is thus part of the broader phenomenon of hereditary Sufi communities and their multiple roles in local society.

Hereditary succession in the leadership of Sufi communities became quite common in Central Asia, as in other regions, and entailed not only the legitimation of particular shaykhs through genealogical connections with still earlier saintly ancestors, but the elaboration of broader genealogical frameworks linking prominent shaykhs and multiple groups that claimed descent from them; inheritance of the title "shaykh" thus carried the presumption, at least, that the shaykh possessed saintly spiritual powers by virtue of descent, and also had the authority to license *murīd*s as well as to hand down various properties and assets of the family/*ṭarīqa* group. The most salient examples of influential families of shaykhs are those of the Jūybārī family in Bukhara and the Isḥāqī and Āfāqī *khwāja* families in Kashghar. However, although the political activities of these families of shaykhs have received a relatively large amount of scholarly attention, the social aspects of their relations with local communities have not yet been sufficiently elucidated.

Many families of shaykhs also prospered and declined in the Farghana valley, where in the beginning of the 18th century the Uzbek Ming tribe established the Khanate of Khoqand. The most powerful families through the entire period of the Khanate were the "Makhdūmzādas," descended from the Naqshbandī shaykh Makhdūm-i Aʿẓam. Their predominance can be explained by the fact that the Farghana valley was Makhdūm-i Aʿẓam's birthplace and the region of the families' activities, located between Dahbīd, where numerous descendants of Makhdūm-i Aʿẓam lived around his *mazār*, and Kashghar. The Makhdūmzādas did not form a single, unified group, but rather consisted of various branches of different origins.

The purpose of this paper is to examine the social functionality of one of these Makhdūmzāda families, as an example of the wider phenomenon of families of shaykhs, by investigating their relationship with the local population. As noted, this particular Makhdūmzāda family had great influence in a major town of the Khanate of Khoqand, Marghīnān; the family claimed to be descended, in the maternal line, from Āfāq Khwāja (d. 1694), a religious and political leader in Kashghar (himself a great-grandson of Makhdūm-i Aʿẓam), and according to the legend recorded at Valī Khān Tūra's shrine (see below, pp. 176–177), the family migrated to Marghīnān from Kashghar in the first half of the 18th century. By the mid-19th century, the clan had grown to be one of the most influential families of shaykhs in Marghīnān. Several *mazār*s of

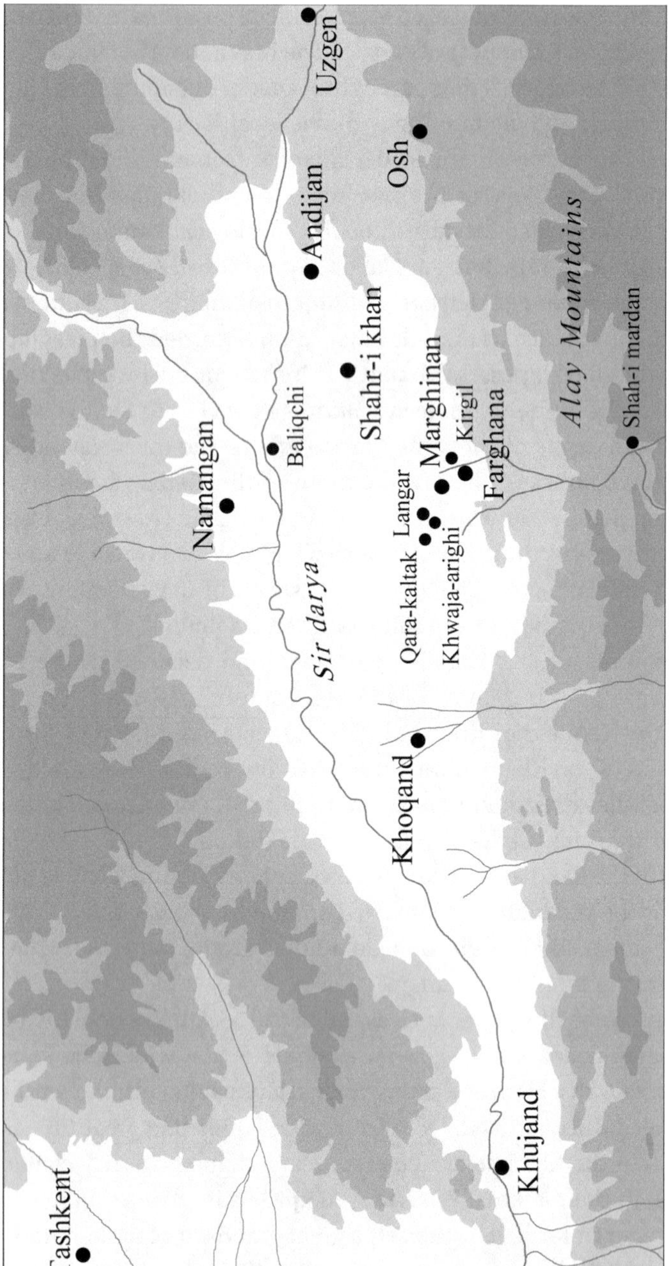

MAP 5.1 *The Farghana valley in the second half of the 19th century as related to Valī Khān Tūra's* ghazavāt

the family members in Marghīnān and in the region eastwards from it remain to this day.[2]

Regarding the history of the family, there are three groups of historical sources written from different viewpoints. The first group consists of historical texts compiled under Russian rule in the beginning of the 20th century. They depict at length how the influential shaykh of this family, Valī Khān Tūra, participated in the insurrection known as "the Rebellion of Fūlād Khān," which occurred in the late period of the Khanate of Khoqand, and which led the people of Marghīnān, under the banner of *ghazavāt*, against the Russian army that intervened to crush the rebellion. The second group comprises archival documents related to Russian imperial rule in Farghana Province after the annexation of the Khanate. They provide a detailed description of the arrest of Valī Khān Tūra by the Russian authorities, and offer a glimpse at the reaction it provoked among the people of Marghīnān. The third and final group consists of private documents currently held by the descendants of Valī Khān Tūra and his collateral relatives. The author collected copies of the latter documents from the owners during field research. They consist of hagiographies, genealogies, and legal documents (deeds), and constitute internal family documents that have been held for the purpose of securing the family's status, authority, and wealth.[3]

Based on these materials, the first part of this paper will re-examine the course of events during the *ghazavāt* and Valī Khān Tūra's role in it, and clarify what the populace in Marghīnān wanted to achieve and how Valī Khān Tūra became their leader. In order to clarify the social context of these events, the second part will explore the origins of this Makhdūmzāda family and the first half of Valī Khān Tūra's life, using privately-held historical documents and oral traditions to explain how the family's social status contributed to Valī Khān

2 The author expresses profound gratitude to Dr. Nadirbek Abdulahatov for his unreserved help and support during field research at these *mazārs*. This field research made it possible to examine the growth and development of the family, although at that time a lack of materials on Valī Khān Tūra's *ghazavāt* and on his later arrest did not allow for sufficient examination of his personality or of the relationship between his family and the local people. See Yayoi Kavakhara, "'Sviatye semeistva' Margelana v Kokandskom khanstve v XIX v.," *Mir Islama/Pax Islamica*, 4 (2010), 121–139.

3 As these privately held documents prove to be highly valuable for exploring the activities of families of shaykhs from the inside, but are rather difficult for researchers to access and use, the author published the texts with an introduction and facsimiles: Kawahara Yayoi, *Private Archives on a Makhdūmzāda Family in Marghilan* (Tokyo: TIAS: Department of Islamic Area Studies Center for Evolving Humanities, Graduate School of Humanities and Sociology, The University of Tokyo, 2012).

Tūra's role in the *ghazavāt*. The third part will analyze the post-*ghazavāt* assessments of his activities based on the archival documents related to his arrest, since Valī Khān Tūra's authority in Marghīnān should be seen in the context of his treatment after the arrest.

Valī Khān Tūra's *Ghazavāt*

The *Tārīkh-i ʿAzīzī* ("History of ʿAzīz") by Mullā ʿAzīz Marghīnānī[4] is a local history, written in Turkic, that provides a detailed eyewitness account of the situation in Marghīnān at the end of the Khanate of Khoqand; it also assiduously depicts the course of Valī Khān Tūra's *ghazavāt*. Marghīnān is a historic town located in the south of the Farghana valley. Although the capital of the Khanate was situated in the boom city of Khoqand, throughout the entire history of the Khanate, Marghīnān continued to be an important urban center, for which *ḥākims* were always appointed from among the *khān*'s most trusted relatives. In the *Tārīkh-i ʿAzīzī*, Valī Khān Tūra appears without any explanation of his parentage, suggesting that he was a well-known figure in the town.

The rebellion occurred against the background of political instability in the Khanate and aggression from Russia. In 1867, Russia established the Governor-Generalship of Turkestan in Tashkent, and the next year (1868), when the first Governor-General, von Kaufman, and Khudāyār Khān (r. 1845–1858, 1862–1863, 1865–1875) signed the protectorate treaty, the Khanate of Khoqand was put under the rule of the Governor-Generalship. Tribes within the Khanate rose in rebellion, followed by incessant uprisings. In 1875, the Qïrghïz, who had long nursed grievances over the exorbitant taxes and compulsory military service

4 Mullā ʿAzīz Marghīnānī, *Tārīkh-i ʿAzīzī*, Ms. Tashkent, Institute of Oriental Studies of the Academy of Sciences of the Republic of Uzbekistan (hereafter "IVANRUz"), No. 1108. Mullā ʿAzīz's family lived in Marghīnān for many generations; he himself had served as a scribe (*mīrzā*) at the governmental office of Marghīnān Province for 27 years before authoring this book. The book is believed to have been written no earlier than 1912; see T. K. Beisembiev, *Kokandskaia istoriografiia, issledovanie po istochnikovedeniiu Srednei Azii XVIII–XIX vekov* (Almaty: TOO 'Print-S', 2009), 131–132. This work was recently published with its facsimiles: Mulla Aziz bin Mulla Muhammadrizo Marg'inoniy, *Tarixi Aziziy*, ed. B. M. Bobojonov and I. A. Qayumova (Tashkent: O'zbekiston Respublikasi Oliy va O'rta-Maxsus Ta'lim Vazirligi Toshkent Davlat Sharqshunoslik Instituti huzuridagi Abu Rayhon Beruniy nomidagi Sharq Qo'lyozmalari Markazi, 2016). A part of this work roughly corresponding to one-fourth of the whole volume has been published in modern Uzbek transcription; see Muhammad Aziz Marg'iloniy, *Tarixi Aziziy* (*Farg'ona chor mustamlakasi davrida*), ed. Shodmon Vohidov and Dilorom Sangirova (Tashkent: Ma'naviyat, 1999).

levied on them by successive *khāns*, as well as over the loss of pastures due to the expansion of arable lands as a result of large-scale irrigation works, rose in rebellion in the east of the Farghana valley, led by Fūlād Khān (c. 1844–1876). The rebellion, aggravated by internal conflict within the *khān*'s family, spread throughout the valley. Von Kaufman sent the army to crush the uprising, and then, in 1876, completely annexed the Khanate of Khoqand.

A relatively large amount of research has focused attention on analyzing the rebellion from the historical perspective of the Russian annexation of Central Asia. The accounts can be roughly divided between two approaches, those that assess it as a national liberation movement of the Qïrghïz people against the oppression of the *khān* of Khoqand, and those that view it as a reactionary attempt to revive the Khanate.[5] However, in both cases, virtually no examination has been made of the role the people of the Khanate played in the rebellion. Such studies are based only on Russian historical documents related to the conquest of the Khanate of Khoqand, which mostly cover communications between von Kaufman and the *khān*, details of military affairs, the treatment of the ringleaders, and other such matters.

In early July 1875, the Qïrghïz at Uzgen enthroned as their ruler Mullā Isḥāq b. Ḥasan, under the name Fūlād Khān (the name actually borne by a grandson of the famous ʿĀlim Khān, who ruled the Khanate from 1799 until 1809); thereupon, under his authority, they raised a riot. Khudāyār Khān dispatched his chief retainer, ʿAbd al-Raḥmān Āftābachī, of Qïpchaq origin, to quell the uprising.[6] However, ʿAbd al-Raḥmān Āftābachī betrayed Khudāyār Khān and allied himself with the so-called Fūlād Khān; he confined Khudāyār's younger brother, Sulṭān Murād Bék, who was *ḥākim* of Marghīnān, and backed Khudāyār Khān's oldest son, Naṣr al-Dīn Bék, for the *khān*'s throne on July 24. Then Āftābachī seized the reins of power, proclaimed *ghazavāt* against Russia, and raised an army. Khasanov, who meticulously examined this uprising as a popular movement of the Qïrghïz, concluded that the slogan of *ghazavāt* was not seen among the Qïrghïz people, and that Āftābachī proclaimed it only in order to use the popular movement for his own purposes.[7] At about the same time, in Khujand, by then already annexed to Russia, a man named

5 V. M. Ploskikh, *Kirgizy i Kokandskoe khanstvo* (Frunze: Ilim, 1977), 309.

6 During Khudāyār Khān's first rule, while he was a child, the government was in the hands of the Qïpchaq warlord Musulmān-qūl. Although later Khudāyār Khān put Musulmān-qūl to death in order to regain the reins of power, he, by himself, brought up Musulmān-qūl's son, ʿAbd al-Raḥmān Āftābachī, and appointed him to high positions in his government.

7 A. Kh. Khasanov, *Narodnye dvizheniia v Kirgizii v period Kokandskogo khanstva* (Moscow: Glavnaia Redaktsiia Vostochnoi Literatury, 1977), 63–69.

ʿAbd al-Karīm also proclaimed himself *khān* and raised an army,[8] plunging the Farghana valley into greater chaos.

Regarding these events, particular interest arises from the Russian translation of five letters preserved in the archives from the period of Russian rule.[9] These letters were confiscated from Valī Khān Tūra upon his arrest in 1878. None of them is dated, but their contents describe the situation of July 1875 (these documents will be examined in the third part of this paper). One of the letters was sent by ʿAbd al-Karīm Khān from Khujand, and it reads thus:[10]

> I inform the honorable Seid-Mukhamed-Vali-Khan-Tiura (Sayyid Muḥammad Valī Khān Tūra) and Tanikul Dadkha (Tanīqul Dādkhwāh) of the following. On Monday, the 11th day of the month of Jumādā II,[11] all the people of Kokand, Khudzhent, Margelan, Sharikhan, Andizhan, Osh, the Sarts, the Tadzhiks, the Kipchaks, the Kirgiz unanimously elected me their *khan*. We, together with Abdulla-bek-menbashi (ʿAbdullāh Bék Mīngbāshī)[12] and Omir-bek-Parmanachi (ʿUmar Bék Parvānachī),[13] have come in several thousands to the border of Taglyk. Therefore, we request that you, Vali-Khan-Tiura, and Tanikul-Dadkha, as soon as you receive this letter, immediately join us.

The expressions are probably quite exaggerated, but similar content can be seen in letters from local people clearly stating that 7,000 people had gathered there for the purpose of undertaking *gazzat/gazavat* (*ghazā/ghazavāt*) against Russia. Moreover, letters from *kazi*s (*qāżī*s) plead for Vali-Khan-Tiura to

8 Mīrzā ʿĀlim Mushrif b. Mīrzā Raḥīm Tāshkandī, *Ansāb al-salāṭīn va tavārīkh-i khavāqīn*, Ms. Tashkent, IVANRUz, No. 1314, ff. 137b–138a. According to this manuscript, these events took place just before Khudāyār Khān fled to Tashkent (August 5).

9 Central State Archive of the Republic of Uzbekistan, *fond* I-1, *opis'* 29, *delo* 341, ll. 8–11.

10 Personal names in the letters are transcribed from the Russian translation, and the ordinary corresponding transcription from the Arabic spelling is shown in parentheses. The original letter is said to bear the seal of Seid Abdulkarem-Khan-Mukhamed (Sayyid ʿAbd al-Karīm Khān Muḥammad), the son of Sadyk-Khan-Seid-Mukhamed (Ṣādiq Khān Sayyid Muḥammad).

11 It must be dated in the year 1292 AH (hence July 14, 1875).

12 This may refer to ʿAbdullāh Bék Qïrghïz, one of Fūlād Khān's followers, later killed by supporters of Naṣr al-Dīn Khān; see Timur K. Beisembiev, *Annotated Indices to the Kokand Chronicles* (Tokyo: Research Institute for Languages and Culture of Asia and Africa, Tokyo University of Foreign Studies, 2008), 309.

13 This may refer to ʿUmar Bék, a Qïrghïz tribal chief who under Fūlād Khān became the ruler of Andijan; see Beisembiev, *Annotated Indices*, 329.

save and liberate the devout Muslims and the *sharigat* (*sharīʿat*) from Russian oppression. On the other hand, there are two letters in which the writers recount their dreams. One letter describes a dream in which Vali-Khan-Tiura, at the order of his late father, "Khazret Katep Padsha khodzha" (Ḥażrat Katta Pādshāh Khwāja), kills the Governor-General and other Russians; the other letter describes a dream in which the people of Marghīnān bless Vali-Khan-Tiura for the *gazavat*. Because the dreams of the saints were believed to have spiritual power, people often alluded to such dreams as reasons to prompt desired actions. It remains unclear what relations had existed before between ʿAbd al-Karīm and Valī Khān Tūra, who the "Tanikul-Dadkha" mentioned in the letter was, and when these letters were received by Valī Khān Tūra. There are also no extant records confirming that Valī Khān Tūra consented to the requests.

After von Kaufman recognized Naṣr al-Dīn Khān on August 4, Khudāyār Khān fled to Tashkent on August 5, and after a week he emigrated to Orenburg, in Russia. Although Āftābachī's army first intended to challenge the Russians near Khujand, the difference in military potential was obvious. On August 29, Khoqand surrendered without a fight, and, on September 8, Marghīnān did the same. On September 22, von Kaufman and Naṣr al-Dīn Khān concluded a treaty according to which the territory on the right bank of the Syr Darya, i.e., the northern half of the valley, was annexed to Russia as Namangan Province.[14] Marghīnān formally remained in the territories under the Khanate's rule, but Russia began to openly intervene in the city's affairs. Von Kaufman appointed a certain Āta-qul Bahādurbāshī to the post of Marghīnān's *ḥākim* and levied a fine on the residents for the riot. Meanwhile, Fūlād Khān and his followers continued their resistance around Andijan.[15]

According to Mullā ʿAzīz, the residents of Marghīnān, outraged by the fine, came together and pleaded to Valī Khān Tūra, saying,

> Āta-qul Bahādurbāshī has become a sidekick of unjust Russia and oppresses the Muslims. He levied and collected such an onerous fine. [The collected fine] was sent to Russia. And now he has levied yet another fine causing hardships on all Muslims and despising them, while his brutal servants terribly torment the people. Oh, Tūram! Now, there is no *pādshāh* who would understand the Muslims' pain, but you! Now, many have gathered at the palace (*orda*) [of Marghīnān]. Please, mount

14 Khasanov, *Narodnye dvizheniia*, 69–77.

15 Mullā ʿAzīz, *Tārīkh-i ʿAzīzī*, ff. 164a–b.

> your horse at once. Let us go with infantry and horsemen and kill him in the *ghazāt* [sic].[16]

Valī Khān Tūra tried to stop them. However, on the same day, the rebels killed Āta-qul Bahādurbāshī and looted the palace. They even plundered the house of Valī Khān Tūra; the violence was such that he barely escaped death himself. Nevertheless, as the townsmen could not believe that the people were able do this on their own, rumors circulated that it was Valī Khān Tūra who led the people to kill Āta-qul, plunder his house and the palace, and take back the collected fines.[17]

In this way, the people of Marghīnān defined the killing of the Russian-appointed *ḥākim* as a *ghazavāt* and began to extol Valī Khān Tūra as their leader, calling him *pādshāh*. Regardless of whether Valī Khān Tūra himself was proactive or not, petitions for *ghazavāt* continued to come from both inside and outside the town.

When, in October, Fūlād Khān took the situation in Marghīnān under his control, he appointed Valī Khān Tūra as the *ḥākim* of Marghīnān. The actual duties were entrusted to one of Valī Khān Tūra's *murīd*s. However, the previous *ḥākim* of Marghīnān, Sulṭān Murād Bék, backed with von Kaufman's support, set out to win Marghīnān back. Thus, Valī Khān Tūra was forced to confront Sulṭān Murād Bék. Valī Khān Tūra turned to the *qāżī*s for permission to capture Sulṭān Murād Bék. The *ʿulamā*, who accompanied him onto the battlefield in the suburb of Marghīnān, issued a *fatwā*, stating that "as the *bék* became a man of Russia, it is allowed to fight him."[18] At this point, Valī Khān Tūra became recognized as ruler not only by the rebels, but also by the *ʿulamā* of the town, and the *ghazavāt* against Russia also became a reality.

At that time, Valī Khān Tūra had about 20,000 troops, including reinforcements dispatched by Fūlād Khān, under his command. Following their attack, Sulṭān Murād Bék was captured and taken to Fūlād Khān. Fūlād Khān broke the *bék*'s seal in front of him and killed him.[19] This demonstrates that military affairs were, in fact, administered by Fūlād Khān. At the same time, Mullā ʿAzīz also provides an interesting insight into the relationship between the two

---

16 Mullā ʿAzīz, *Tārīkh-i ʿAzīzī*, ff. 164b–165a.

17 Mullā ʿAzīz, *Tārīkh-i ʿAzīzī*, ff. 165a–166a.

18 Mullā ʿAzīz, *Tārīkh-i ʿAzīzī*, f. 167a. The four *qāżī*s were: *qāżī-yi kalān*, *qāżī-yi ʿaskar*, *qāżī al-qużżāt*, and *qāżī-raʾīs*. They issued yet another *fatwā* stating, "As today is the day of the battle, it is allowed not to fast." Hence, the battle took place in the month of Ramadan of 1292 AH (October 1–30, 1875).

19 Mullā ʿAzīz, *Tārīkh-i ʿAzīzī*, ff. 167b–168a; Khasanov, *Narodnye dvizhenie*, 82.

leaders. In the middle of the battle with the Russian army, Fūlād Khān fell from his horse and broke his leg; later the wound worsened so much that he had to be carried in a cart, and so he visited Valī Khān Tūra, had the men take him off the cart, and expressed his respects on entering the house. There he received Valī Khān Tūra's prayer, and then left.[20] It thus appears that Fūlād Khān also recognized Valī Khān Tūra's religious authority.

Having gained momentum, Valī Khān Tūra's camp headed in the direction of Namangān to challenge the Russian army, and arrived at a place named Balīqchī in the environs of the Syr Darya. However, while the troops were resting on the bank of the river, the Russians crossed the river and made a surprise attack, which promptly ended with Valī Khān Tūra's complete defeat. Valī Khān Tūra himself only barely escaped together with his *vazīr* and servants. Thereafter, the Russian army completely crushed the uprising, and on February 19, 1876, the Khanate of Khoqand was annexed to the Russian Empire. The rebels were severely punished. Fūlād Khān was captured, brought before court-martial, and executed. He was charged with the killing of Sulṭān Murād Bék and other members of the *khān*'s family, and with mutiny against Russia. On the other hand, because ʿAbd al-Raḥmān Āftābachī did not oppose Russia, he was given a position in the Russian army and later moved to live in Orenburg.[21]

According to Mullā ʿAzīz, Valī Khān Tūra was a refugee for some time until he was eventually allowed by the head of the Marghīnān district, Békchūrīn (Bekchurin), to return home. His pardon was based on the rescript from Russia that prescribed that, with regard to high-ranking noblemen of the Khanate, investigations should be carried out with particular discretion, and they should not be executed. Valī Khān Tūra was married to a younger sister or a daughter of Khudāyār Khān and, therefore, was regarded as a son-in-law of the *khān*'s family.[22]

It can be seen that Valī Khān Tūra's *ghazavāt* lacked planning as well as military strength; in addition, the losses were tremendous. A contemporary of Mullā ʿAzīz, the Jadīd activist ʿIbrat, who bitterly criticized the uprising in his *Tārīkh-i Farghāna*, writes, "In Marghīnān, a madman named Valī Khān Tūra said that he was going to wage *ghazavāt* and meaninglessly devastated the people."[23] ʿIbrat might be right in placing the responsibility for the incident

---

20 Mullā ʿAzīz, *Tārīkh-i ʿAzīzī*, ff. 166a, 168b.

21 Mullā ʿAzīz, *Tārīkh-i ʿAzīzī*, ff. 174b, 176a–b; Khasanov, *Narodnye dvizhenie*, 88.

22 Mullā ʿAzīz, *Tārīkh-i ʿAzīzī*, f. 175a.

23 Isḥāq Khān b. Junaydullāh Khān Tūraqūrghānī, *Tārīkh-i Farghāna*, Ms. Dushanbe, A. Rudaki Institute of Language, Literature, Oriental Studies and Written Heritage, Academy of Sciences, Republic of Tajikistan, No. 1512, p. 150.

upon Valī Khān Tūra. However, Mullā ʿAzīz recounts the attitudes of the people of Marghīnān in a different way:

> Valī Khān Tūram was the head (*ṣāḥib*) of Marghīnān and held the reins of government. Among both the *ʿulamā* and the people, everyone obeyed Valī Khān Tūram. Once he produced a miracle. All Muslims believed his words that "If we fight against Russia in *ghazāt* [sic], God will bestow victory upon us Muslims," and everybody agreed that "Tūram says this because he is convinced of something. No wonder Tūram has victory in his hands." Those who did not have a horse bought a horse, armed themselves, and gathered around Tūram.[24]

Probably such sentiments were particularly popular because the people of Marghīnān did not directly feel sympathy either for Fūlād Khān's rebellion or for the feuds within the *khān*'s family. Mullā ʿAzīz describes Fūlād Khān as a man "who, although was a Muslim, became a beast-like creature, having killed many members of the *khān*'s family;" he describes ʿAbd al-Raḥmān Āftābachī as a man "who demolished the peaceful motherland and, though he had first confronted Russia, eventually ran away without even giving battle."[25] The people of Marghīnān wished to prevent a Russian invasion, but at the same time to maintain the existing order, and they saw Valī Khān Tūra as the figure that could be entrusted with both these tasks.

Valī Khān Tūra's Origins and the First Half of His Life as Seen from the Privately-Held Historical Documents

Out of all the historical writings on Valī Khān Tūra's *ghazavāt*, there is only one notation in the *Tārīkh-i ʿAzīzī* that refers to his origin. This is an episode describing a miracle of a saint identified as "*ṣāḥib* of the Kīrgīl *mazār*, namely ʿAbdullāh, or ʿĪbādullāh Khwān Khūjam Tūram [sic], or Valī Khān Tūram's father, Katta Tūram."[26] In other words, this record is no more than an ambiguous reference to the possibility that Valī Khān Tūra was a descendant of the saint entombed in the Kīrgīl *mazār*.

24 Mullā ʿAzīz, *Tārīkh-i ʿAzīzī*, ff. 173b–174a.

25 Mullā ʿAzīz, *Tārīkh-i ʿAzīzī*, ff. 170a, 171b.

26 Mullā ʿAzīz, *Tārīkh-i ʿAzīzī*, f. 121b. Regarding "Katta Tūram," as seen in the letters brought up in the previous section, "Katta Pādshāh Khwāja" would be a more correct naming. "*Katta*" means "big" and might have been simply added to express respect. On the miracle ascribed to ʿIbādullāh, see below, pp. 176–177, and p. 178, note 50.

FIGURE 5.1 *The Kīrgīl* mazār (2014)

The Kīrgīl (or Kirgil-ota) *mazār* is a large-scale saint's mausoleum still extant in Qirguli[27] district on the outskirts of Marghīnān. While conducting field research, the author learned that this mausoleum is considered to belong to ʿIbādullāh, a real person who lived during the time of the Khanate of Khoqand, and that Valī Khān Tūra was his grandson.[28]

This vague allusion to Valī Khān Tūra's origins is clarified somewhat in other kinds of sources that bear more directly on the history of his Makhdūmzāda family; accordingly, this second part of the paper examines the process of establishing the economic bases and the religious fame of the family, and the first half of Valī Khān Tūra's life, before the *ghazavāt*, based on historical materials

27 It is not certain how the place name written as "Kīrgīl" in historical materials became the current "Qirguli." In addition to the *Tārīkh-i ʿAzīzī*, the spelling "Kīrgīl sū" is seen in other sources, but the spelling reflecting the pronunciation of "Qirguli" is not seen in any historical material; see Beisembiev, *Annotated Indices*, 672.

28 Kavakhara, " 'Sviatye semeistva' Margelana," 131–137.

in possession of the descendants. In the background presented below, there are some key points that indicate how he showed leadership in the *ghazavāt*.

With regard to the materials directly relating to Valī Khān Tūra, there are legal documents (deeds) and hagiographies kept by his great-great-grandson, Mr. Rustamov. The collection numbers 24 documents in total; of these, 15 were issued during Valī Khān Tūra's lifetime, and the rest concern his legacy: two relate to the portion inherited by one of his sons, Sayyid Bāqir Khān Tūra, and 7 deal with the division of Sayyid Bāqir Khān Tūra's property. As for the hagiographies, there are two accounts in verse and two in prose, all of which are similar in content. One of the versions in verse carries the title *Rawżat al-ansāb* ("Garden of Genealogies"). It depicts events from before Valī Khān Tūra's birth until he turned 41, and almost all the notations are devoted to extolling his virtuous deeds and miracles, as well as to justifying his appointment as a successor by his father. In addition, there are genealogies certifying his status as a *sayyid*, decrees of the *khān*s on tax exemption, and a memorandum concerning a gift received from a *khān*, all in possession of other descendants of this family.[29]

Valī Khān Tūra was born circa 1813[30] to a prominent family of shaykhs in Marghīnān. His father, Pādshāh Khān Tūra, held the office of *shaykh al-islām*.[31] The *shaykh al-islām* was the highest religious dignitary in a city or province during the period of the Khanate of Khoqand, and the position was held exclusively by *sayyid*s. According to the *Rawżat al-ansāb*, Pādshāh Khān Tūra was the shaykh of all the people in *sharīʿa* and *ṭarīqa*, and had several thousand followers, *khalīfa*s and *murīd*s. The rulers and *amīr*s of the Khanate of Khoqand also received his guidance.[32] As the family claimed to be descended from Makhdūm-i Aʿẓam (this will be discussed later), the "*ṭarīqa*" mentioned here at least nominally should refer to the Naqshbandiyya, but the actual character of the Sufi identity, teaching, and practice entailed by Pādshāh Khān Tūra's role of shaykh in the *ṭarīqa* has not been made clear in any known sources. As with many other shaykhs of that time, he also gained fame as a saint. For example, the *Rawżat al-ansāb* mentions an episode in which he produced a miracle by healing a lame man so that the man could walk upright.[33] The *Rawżat al-ansāb* also describes a scene in which Pādshāh Khān Tūra was appointed by his father,

29 Kawahara, *Private Archives*, xv–xxvii.

30 He was 29 years old when Muḥammad ʿAlī Khān of the Khanate of Khoqand (r. 1822–1842) died; see Kawahara, *Private Archives*, 319, 377.

31 Kawahara, *Private Archives*, 231.

32 Kawahara, *Private Archives*, 284–285, 356–357.

33 Kawahara, *Private Archives*, 341–342, 393–394.

ʿIbādullāh Khwāja, as his successor, pushing aside the latter's two brothers,[34] suggesting that he inherited the shaykh's office from his father. ʿIbādullāh Khān's biography is unclear, but it is known that he died around 1810.[35] Pādshāh Khān Tūra must have begun functioning as an independent shaykh about that time as well.

This was the time when the Khanate of Khoqand was at the height of its prosperity. The Khanate of Khoqand in the 18th century had controlled almost all the territory of the Farghana valley, and in the beginning of the 19th century conquered the largest commercial city in the south of the Qazaq steppe, Tashkent. The reign of ʿUmar Khān (r. 1809–1822) even witnessed the revival of Timurid court literature.[36] ʿUmar Khān ordered the court poets to recite legendary genealogies identifying him a descendant of Bābur, the founder of the Mughal dynasty, and endeavored to strengthen his authority.[37] On the other hand, the shaykhs provided the *khān*s with religious support, and through building marital relations with the shaykhs, the *khān*s involved them with political activities at the very heart of government. In the 1810s, the office of *shaykh al-islām* in Khoqand was occupied by shaykhs of a Makhdūmzāda group belonging to a lineage different from that of the family in Marghīnān.[38]

As for Makhdūmzāda groups in Khoqand and Marghīnān, Valikhanov offers valuable information. He mentions the descendants of *khwāja* families in Kashghar as one of the prominent *sayyid* or *khoja* groups in Central Asia: Padshakhan-khodzha (Pādshāh Khān Khwāja) in Khoqand and Ibadulla-khodzha (ʿIbādullāh Khwāja) in Marghīnān. These *khoja*s owned extensive lands, had luxurious mansions, were very rich, and received offerings from the people of Kashghar; they had exclusive right to the title of "*tiuria*" (*tūra*).

34 Kawahara, *Private Archives*, 237, 391–392. The names of the brothers who were barred from succession are Raḥmatullāh and Khwāja Jahān.

35 Kawahara, *Private Archives*, 290, 359. ʿIbādullāh died shortly before Valī Khān Tūra's birth.

36 János Eckmann, "Çağatay Edebiyatının Son Devri (1800–1920)," *Türk Dili Araştırmaları Yıllığı Belleten 1963* (1964), 121–156.

37 Mīrzā Qalandar Isfaragī, *Shāh-nāma-yi ʿUmar-khānī*, Ms. St. Petersburg, Institute of Oriental Manuscripts of the Russian Academy of Sciences, No. C471, ff. 33b–34b.

38 During the reign of ʿUmar Khān, the position of Khoqand's *shaykh al-islām* was held by Maʿṣūm Khān, the father of Muḥammad Ḥakīm Khān (the author of *Muntakhab al-tavārīkh*); see Muḥammad Ḥakīm Khān, *Muntakhab al-tawārīkh, Selected History*, ed. Yayoi Kawahara and Koichi Haneda, vol. 2 (Tokyo: Research Institute for Languages and Culture of Asia and Africa, Tokyo University of Foreign Studies, 2006), 136–137.

Valikhanov also states that about 200 *tiuria*s live in Khoqand and Marghīnān.[39] His information is not correct in detail, but he is apparently talking about the Makhdūmzāda family of Marghīnān to which Valī Khān Tūra belonged.

Pādshāh Khān Tūra based his activities in Chubūrgān *maḥalla*, located next to the *madrasa* of Pādshāh Iskandar in the center of Marghīnān.[40] The family, in addition to a house and land with a stable, also owned garden land, an orchard, grassland, and farmland. In the deeds, this *maḥalla* is referred to as "maḥalla-yi Pādshāh Khān Tūra Shaykh al-Islām,"[41] which attests to the fact that this place was widely known as the center of his family's activities.

Nowadays, this place carries the name of "Jo'raxon Sultonov Street." Pādshāh Iskandar's *madrasa* has also survived until the present day. On the premises, there is a *mazār*, known as that of "Ulug' hazrat bobo," and a residence of Valī Khān Tūra's descendants. According to the descendants, the *mazār* is that of ʿIbādullāh's father, ʿAbdullāh. ʿAbdullāh is considered the founder of the family in Marghīnān, and at the *mazār*, legends about the history of ʿAbdullāh and numerous miracles produced by ʿIbādullāh are told.

> Abdulla (ʿAbdullāh) was a descendant of Maxdumi A'zam (Makhdūm-i Aʿẓam) and a *sayyid*. He was born to the daughter of Oppoq xo'ja (Āfāq Khwāja), who used to rule in Qashqar (Kashghar), and [her husband] Odilxon (ʿĀdil Khān), the son of Oppoq xo'ja's brother, Karomatulla (Karāmatullāh). After a political upheaval, Abdulla emigrated from Qashqar to India, where he became a *murīd* of Miyon Obid (Miyān ʿĀbid), a shaykh of the Naqshbandiyya-Mujaddidiyya. He miraculously healed a daughter of the Indian Emperor Avrangzeb (Awrangzīb) [or, according to a different version, of Ali Gavhar (ʿAlī Gawhar)] who was unable to walk because of disease. He then married her, and thus Ibodulla (ʿIbādullāh) was born. The princess soon died, and Abdulla, following Miyon Obid's order, moved together with his son to Marg'ilon for religious propagation. Abdulla occupied the position of *xatib* (*khaṭīb*) of a mosque. Besides Ibodulla, Abdulla also had a son named Rahmatulla (Raḥmatullāh) born to his wife from Marg'ilon.
>
> Ibodulla was a saint who performed many miracles. When preaching inside the mosque, he miraculously perceived that there was a man outside who had come late and hesitated to enter the mosque. He called him

39 Ch. Ch. Valikhanov, *Sobranie sochinenii v piati tomakh*, tom 3 (Alma-Ata: Glavnaia Redaktsiia Kazakhskoi Sovetskoi Ėntsiklopedii, 1985), 50, 182–184.

40 Kawahara, *Private Archives*, 240, 242, 244, 249, 253.

41 Kawahara, *Private Archives*, 239.

> in, saying "Enter!" (*Kirgil!*),[42] so the mosque became known popularly as "Kirgil-ota." At that time, Olimxon (ʿĀlim Khān) of the Khanate of Khoqand, in order to suppress the spread of pseudo-saints, subjected the saints to tests. The *xon* (*khān*) sent for Ibodulla and offered him pilaf cooked with cat's meat. Ibodulla exclaimed in sorrow, "Oh, sinful *xon*!" and stretched his hand out over the pilaf. Then, the cat, resurrected, jumped out from the pilaf, and ran away. The *xon* acknowledged the miracle. After the saint's death, his body, in accordance with his last will, was mounted on two camels and buried at the place where they stopped. Later, the whole region became known by the name of the *mozor* (*mazār*) as the *Kirgil/Qirguli* district.[43]

Such descriptions of origins and personal history constitute typical motifs in the hagiographies of saints; it is thus meaningless to inquire into their veracity. However, the very fact that Pādshāh Khān Tūra held the position of *shaykh al-islām* testifies that he was officially recognized as a *sayyid*. Although the genealogy of Valī Khān Tūra, both in the *Rawżat al-ansāb* and in the deeds, can be traced back only to ʿIbādullāh,[44] there are three extant genealogies that verify the *sayyid*-status of the descendants of a different lineage of this family, and their content almost completely coincides with the legends told at the *mazār*. Among these documents, a genealogy of Maḥmūd Khān Tūra, written in the 1960s during the Soviet period, deserves particular attention; Maḥmūd Khān Tūra is identified as a descendant of Valī Khān Tūra's older brother. This genealogy contains a notation asserting that ʿĀdil's mother was born of the same mother as one of Āfāq Khwāja's sons, named Khwāja Ḥasan,[45] who, with the demise of the Āfāqī *khwājas*, is said to have traveled through to India and then to have returned to Central Asia.[46] ʿAbdullāh's origin seems to be based or superimposed on the legend of Khwāja Ḥasan.

---

42 In Uzbek, "*kir-*" is a verb meaning "to enter", and "*-gil*" is the ending for the second person singular imperative.

43 From an interview with Mr. Rustamov, the great-great-grandson of Valī Khān Tūra, living at the shrine of Ulugʿ hazrat bobo, conducted in Uzbek. April 2003. During the interview at the Kirgil-ota *mazār* with the *mazār* custodian and descendant, Mr. Murtazaev, conducted in Uzbek, they told a similar legend. April 2003.

44 The genealogy is also cited in the eulogy for Valī Khān Tūra, though it omits many generations; see Kawahara, *Private Archives*, 348.

45 Kawahara, *Private Archives*, xii–xiv, 217–224.

46 On the legends related to Khwāja Ḥasan, see Kawahara Yayoi, "Tadhkira of Khwāja Ḥasan Ṣāḥibqirān: Study on a Private Manuscript in Ferghana Valley," *Journal of Asian and African Studies*, 71 (2006), 205–257.

On the other hand, saints' legends also seem to heavily reflect the epoch from which they originate. Miyān ʿĀbid (d. 1746), who appears in the legend, was a shaykh of the reformist Mujaddidī branch of the Naqshbandī order, who laid the very foundations of the tradition that later spread widely throughout Central Asia.[47] With the beginning of the 19th century, this branch actively began propagation in the Farghana valley as well.[48] The legend of ʿAbdullāh describes the historical events between the end of the 17th century and the first half of the 18th century, but insofar as the legend reflects the social situation no earlier than the 19th century, when the Mujaddidiyya had already expanded across the Farghana valley, and the symbolic genealogy that relates ʿUmar Khān to the Mughal emperors had already become known, there is a high probability that this legend describing the family's origins appeared as the result of the well-rooted establishment of the family in local society.

We do not know when the two *mazār*s mentioned above were constructed. Among the deeds related to the family's base in Chubūrgān *maḥalla*, not a single document refers to the existence of Ulugʻ hazrat bobo.[49] On the other hand, because Kirgil-ota is mentioned in the *Tārīkh-i ʿAzīzī*, it must have existed at the beginning of the 20th century, while historical works from the era of the Khanate of Khoqand do not contain any reference to it. Still, it is clear that Pādshāh Khān Tūra's father, ʿIbādullāh, was a real figure and was widely believed to be the saint entombed in the Kirgil-ota *mazār*. It is, after all, the miraculous resurrection of the cat by ʿIbādullāh, closely matching the story told at the shrine, that is recounted in the episode from the *Tārīkh-i ʿAzīzī* alluded to at the outset of this section.[50]

---

47 Baxtiyor M. Babadžanov, "On the History of the Naqšbandīya Muǧaddidīya in Central Māwarā'annahr in the Late 18th and Early 19th Centuries," in *Muslim Culture in Russia and Central Asia from the 18th to the Early 20th Centuries*, ed. Michael Kemper, Anke von Kügelgen, and Dmitriy Yermakov (Berlin: Klaus Schwarz Verlag, 1996), 391.

48 For details, see Kawahara Yayoi, "The Development of the Naqshbandiyya-Mujaddidiyya in the Ferghana Valley during the 19th and Early 20th Centuries," *Journal of the History of Sufism*, 6 (2015), 139–186.

49 With regard to Ulugʻ hazrat bobo, it is reported that the old building was demolished early in the Soviet period, but the shrine was reconstructed in 1976 (from the interview with Mr. Rustamov).

50 According to the *Tārīkh-i ʿAzīzī*, ʿĀlim Khān subjected the *ʿulamā*, *sayyid*s, and *shaykh*s to various tests and invited them to the *masjid* of the palace. He offered them pilaf cooked with cat's meat. Among them, the *ṣāḥib* of the Kīrgīl *mazār*, namely ʿAbdullāh, or ʿĪbādullāh Khwān Khūjam Tūram [sic], or Valī Khān Tūram's father, Katta Tūram stretched his hand out over the pilaf and exclaimed in sorrow, "Oh, how sinful!" Thereupon, the cat, resurrected, jumped out from the pilaf and ran away. ʿĀlim Khān expressed his apologies,

Valī Khān Tūra was thus born into an influential family that was already deeply rooted in local society. He had three older brothers, namely Īshān Khān, Tūra Jān Tūra, and Awliyā Khān.[51] It is reported that from his early childhood Valī Khān Tūra grew physically strong and was graced with outstanding learning abilities; at the age of four, it is said, he looked like a nine- or ten-year-old child.[52] When he turned 16 (ca. 1829), he devoted every day to practicing Sufism and spent all his time performing the *ẕikr*.[53]

When he was about 20 (ca. 1833), Valī Khān Tūra went on a pilgrimage to the Shāh-i Mardān *mazār* in the mountains to the south of Marghīnān.[54] This *mazār* is located next to a lake in the Alay mountains; the local people believe it to be the grave of ʿAlī b. Abī Ṭālib, and in the time of the Khanate of Khoqand, it was the most important sacred land in the Farghana valley.[55] In the following year (ca. 1834), Valī Khān Tūra reconstructed and broadened the road leading from Marghīnān to Shāh-i mardān, so that carriages could pass. As for the motive behind this instance of public service, the *Rawżat al-ansāb* mentions a revelation from his ancestor, ʿAlī, who appeared to Valī Khān Tūra in a dream, but there also might be a connection with irrigation projects vigorously promoted at that time by the *khān*s of Khoqand.[56] According to the author's fieldwork, other members of this family also worked on irrigation projects.[57] It seems that such public works were among the points of direct contact between society and the members of the family. In the course of the reconstruction, many residents of Marghīnān provided their support, and Valī Khān Tūra also produced multiple miracles.[58]

The historical documents do not provide any evidence that Valī Khān Tūra might have occupied an official post, as did his father. So how could he raise the funds needed to perform such public service? Clues may be found in the

---

asked for forgiveness, invited everyone to a feast with lawful food, gave them gifts of robes, renewed everyone's *ʿinayāt-nāma*s and sealed them, and asked them to pray for him. See Mullā ʿAzīz, *Tārīkh-i ʿAzīzī*, ff. 121a–b.

51 Kawahara, *Private Archives*, 287–290, 357–359.

52 Kawahara, *Private Archives*, 294, 361.

53 Kawahara, *Private Archives*, 300–301, 365–366.

54 Kawahara, *Private Archives*, 302–307, 367–369.

55 S. N. Abashin, "Shakhimardan," in *Islam na territorii byvshei Rossiiskoi imperii, Èntsiklopedicheskii slovar'*, vol. 2 (Moscow: Izdatel'skaia firma 'Vostochnaia Literatura' RAN, 1999), 109–111.

56 P. P. Ivanov, *Ocherki po istorii Srednei Azii (XVI-seredina XIX v.)* (Moscow: Izdatel'stvo Vostochnoi literatury, 1958), 181–182.

57 For details, see Kavakhara, "'Sviatye semeistva' Margelana."

58 Kawahara, *Private Archives*, 307–314, 370–374.

title deeds. Those issued during Valī Khān Tūra's lifetime show that for 47 years, he continued to obtain landed property. The properties mentioned in these deeds were mainly located in Marghīnān town and in the villages of Khwāja-arīghī, Langar, and Qarā-kaltak to the west of Marghīnān.[59] The sizes of the properties are not indicated, but the total value of the purchased plots corresponded to 531 *miṣqāls*[60] of Khoqand gold coins and 10 gold coins of the Russian Imperial period. For that time, it was quite a large-scale agricultural enterprise. Moreover, it is possible that the family received tax exemptions from the *khāns* of Khoqand for their business activities. A descendant of another lineage of the family still has in his possession two edicts certifying the recipient's tax exemption rights regarding *kharāj* and other taxes, on the basis of his status as a *sayyid*.[61] Pādshāh Khān Tūra and Valī Khān Tūra, who were officially-recognized *sayyids*, must have received similar certificates and must have enjoyed similar privileges in their management of the agricultural lands. Their accumulation of land must have had a substantial effect on the economic and material lives of the many peasants who worked on their lands.

The fact that Valī Khān Tūra was obtaining prodigious amounts of wealth is also obvious from his lavish spending. When he was 22 (ca. 1835), he laid out a large fruit garden in a place called Chārchaman.[62] There were four gates on the four sides of the garden and a pond in its center. Valī Khān Tūra often organized large-scale feasts in the garden. To these magnificent banquets were invited *qāżīs*, the *ʿulamā*, prominent scholars, shaykhs, noblemen, *amīrs*, rich merchants, *murīds*, and devotees (*mukhliṣ*) from all over Marghīnān. Later, when his son, Bāqir Khān Tūra, and his daughter, Pādshāh Āyim, were born, the celebration of each event was also held there (ca. 1846). About 1,500 carpets were laid in the garden, and the guests were presented with rich robes appropriate for the occasion.[63]

In 1842, when Valī Khān Tūra was 29, immense changes occurred in the Khanate of Khoqand. The city of Khoqand itself was conquered by the Amirate of Bukhara, and the ruler, Muḥammad ʿAlī Khān, and his family were killed. After three months, Shīr ʿAlī Khān, who came from a collateral lineage living

59 All of them now belong to the Qoʻshtepa District of Farghana Province.

60 At that time, 1 *miṣqāl* weighed 4.55 grams. However, as Document 4 is not a deed certifying a purchase of real property by Valī Khān Tūra himself, it is not included in assessing the total sum.

61 Kawahara, *Private Archives*, 228–229.

62 Document 9 presents a deed of the sale of farmland in the village of Chārchaman in Marghīnān district to Valī Khān Tūra, but the specific location of the village is unclear.

63 Kawahara, *Private Archives*, 314–316, 318, 329–338, 374–376, 385–390.

in exile with a Qïrghïz tribe, ascended the throne (r. 1842–1845), and the *khān*'s title passed over to his descendants. However, they did not have a firm base in Khoqand. The time of his and his descendants' rule was an age of turmoil and decay, as the Qïpchaq, Qïrghïz and other tribes gained more influence and grasped real power in the Khanate. According to the *Rawżat al-ansāb*, Shīr ʿAlī Khān dispatched his nephew to deliver his cherished prayer beads (*tasbīḥ*) as a gift to Valī Khān Tūra, inviting him to the palace for prayer.[64] Regarding the relations between the two, a memorandum issued by Shāh Murād Khān (r. 1862) to a member of the family, Sulṭān Khān Tūra, provides valuable insight.[65] According to the document, the *khān* sent a robe as a gift in appreciation of Sulṭān Khān Tūra's having dispatched his son to offer a prayer for the *khān*. Similar examples can also often be seen in the court documents of Khudāyār Khān.[66] The *khān*s customarily received prayers from the saints and heavily relied on their sacred powers. No doubt the episode involving the prayer for Fūlād Khān's wounded leg, noted in the previous section, should be understood in the same context. Moreover, according to the *Tārīkh-i ʿAzīzī*, Valī Khān Tūra was married to Khudāyār Khān's daughter or younger sister; Valī Khān Tūra's descendants report instead that one of his wives was a younger sister, (by the same mother) of Malla Khān (r. 1858–1862), who was Khudāyār Khān's paternal half-brother.[67] Such marital relationships with the rulers would have increased his authority in the community.

The *Rawżat al-ansāb* reports that when Valī Khān Tūra was 34 (ca. 1847), Pādshāh Khān Tūra made a will appointing Valī Khān Tūra as his successor, and transferred land to him;[68] the primary purpose in writing the *Rawżat al-ansāb* was to justify Valī Khān Tūra's succession. Seven years later (ca. 1855), when Valī Khān Tūra was 41, Pādshāh Khān Tūra died at the age of 82.[69] The assets left upon his death were divided among his four sons and one daughter. The main text of the *Rawżat al-ansāb* ends with the comment that Valī Khān Tūra freed many of the slaves he inherited, but his older siblings refused to do

64 Kawahara, *Private Archives*, 319–326, 377–382.

65 Kawahara, *Private Archives*, 230.

66 A. L. Troitskaia, *Katalog arkhiva kokandskikh khanov XIX veka* (Moscow: Izdatel'stvo 'Nauka,' Glavnaia Redaktsiia Vostochnoi Literatury, 1968), 418–420.

67 From the interview with Mr. Rustamov.

68 It is possible that the transference of land to Valī Khān Tūra certified by Document 3 (1839) might be relevant to this event; see Kawahara, *Private Archives*, 237–238, 338–341, 391–393.

69 Pādshāh Khān Tūra's tomb is located within the premises, to the south of Ulugʻ hazrat bobo.

so,[70] suggesting that there might have been some quarrel among the siblings over the inheritance.

There is no detailed information about Valī Khān Tūra's activities over the next 20 years, until he began the *ghazavāt* in 1875, but there are eight deeds drawn up during that period indicating that he continued to purchase numerous properties. It seems that while the Khanate of Khoqand was heading for decline, Valī Khān Tūra's influence over local society was, on the contrary, steadily increasing.

The Arrest and Release

In 1876, the Khanate of Khoqand was annexed to the Russian Empire, transformed into Farghana Province, and put under direct Russian military rule. Within two years, in 1878, Valī Khān Tūra was arrested in Marghīnān. Among the historical documents from the archives of the Farghana Military Governor's Office, there is a file entitled *Ob arestovanii Valikhan tiuri za politicheskuiu neblagonadezhnost'* ("On the arrest of Valī Khān Tūra for political disloyalty") that describes this event in detail. The file comprises original documents received by the second Military Governor of Farghana Province, Abramov, from the Governor-General of Turkistan and his office in Tashkent, as well as drafts of the documents sent to Tashkent. In the archive of the Turkestan Governor-Generalship, meanwhile, there is a corresponding file entitled *Perepiska s voennym gubernatorom Ferganskoi oblasti i drugimi o Valikhan-Tiure, arestovannym v g. Margelane za politicheskuiu neblagonadezhnost' i zakliuchenie ego v Tashkentskoi gorodskoi tiur'me* ("Correspondence with the Military Governor of Farghana and others about Valī Khān Tūra, arrested in Marghīnān for political disloyalty, and his confinement in Tashkent City Prison"); this file consists mainly of original documents received from Farghana and drafts of the documents sent from Tashkent.

The arrest was instigated by a telegram sent from Abramov to von Kaufman, which reads,

> Among the people who came from Kashgar, there is the famous Valikhan Tiura, who used to live in Margelan. This is a politically dangerous man, who has returned to his old pursuits again, agitating people. He is over 70 years old, so it is rather difficult to arrest him. I request permission to

70 Kawahara, *Private Archives*, 344–346, 395–397.

immediately send him to Tashkent. This extremely influential man possesses great power, and is obviously a detrimental figure.[71]

When the Khanate of Khoqand was defeated by Russian forces at Tashkent in 1865, many men who were formerly in Khoqand's army participated in Yaʿqūb Bék's government,[72] but after Yaʿqūb Bék died in 1877 and his government collapsed, many people who were connected with this government moved from Kashghar to Farghana.[73] It is quite possible that, after being pardoned, Valī Khān Tūra also first moved to Kashghar and then returned. Sentiments and attitudes among the migrants from Kashghar were a matter of great concern to Abramov, who aimed to promote social stability in the province. Valī Khān Tūra was suspected of being back to his "old pursuits," in other words plotting a new *ghazavāt*. Nevertheless, Abramov requested permission not for arresting him, but for deporting him to Tashkent, since Valī Khān Tūra was an extremely influential elderly man whose arrest might provoke local unrest.

However, von Kaufman's reaction exceeded even Abramov's request. In the blank margin of the telegram delivered to Tashkent, there is a hand-written note dated June 5 that reads, "To be immediately sent to Tashkent." On June 7, a telegram was sent to Abramov with the order to "send [him] to Tashkent for confinement."[74]

On receiving the telegram, on June 8, Abramov issued an order to the Chief of Police of Marghīnān City and had Valī Khān Tūra arrested. On the same day, Valī Khān Tūra was dispatched to Tashkent. He was delivered to Tashkent on June 11 and put into solitary confinement at the Tashkent City Prison. On June 12, the mayor of Tashkent officially reported the confinement to the Governor-Generalship.[75]

Shortly afterwards, the Governor-Generalship requested that Abramov send information related to the charges against Valī Khān Tūra.[76] However, prior to this, on June 20, Abramov had already sent five letters that had been confiscated from Valī Khān Tūra.[77] These five letters, which urge Valī Khān Tūra to

---

71 Central State Archive of the Republic of Uzbekistan, *fond* I-1, *opis'* 29, *delo* 341, l. 1.

72 Yasushi Shinmen, "Yākūbu begu seiken no seikaku ni kansuru ichi kousatsu (The Character of the Government of Yaqub Beg)", *Shigaku-zasshi* 97 (1987), 1–42.

73 The archive of Farghana Province contains many documents related to returnees from Kashghar; see, for example, Central State Archive of the Republic of Uzbekistan, *fond* I-276, *opis'* 1, *delo* 72, 326, 564, etc.

74 Central State Archive of the Republic of Uzbekistan, *fond* I-276, *opis'* 1, *delo* 324, l. 2.

75 Central State Archive of the Republic of Uzbekistan, *fond* I-276, *opis'* 1, *delo* 324, l. 3–6; *fond* I-1, *opis'* 29, *delo* 341, ll. 3, 5.

76 Central State Archive of the Republic of Uzbekistan, *fond* I-276, *opis'* 1, *delo* 324, l. 8.

77 Central State Archive of the Republic of Uzbekistan, *fond* I-1, *opis'* 29, *delo* 341, ll. 6–11.

begin *ghazavāt*, were noted above in Part 1. As already mentioned, the letters were written in 1875; therefore, they apparently could not be used as evidence of his guilt at the time of this arrest. After two months, in a dispatch dated August 20, the Governor-Generalship informed Abramov that, "Regarding Valī Khān Tūra, the Governor-General has ordered that he be kept confined in Tashkent City Prison until you decide that he can be released and allowed to return home, which probably should not happen within a year."[78] It seems that the Governor-Generalship did not admit the confiscated letters as evidence against Valī Khān Tūra, but rather respected Abramov's opinion that his presence might become a cause of political instability.

Meanwhile, on October 7, four Tashkent residents submitted a guarantee letter for Valī Khān Tūra's release on bail, addressed to the mayor of Tashkent. It reads:

> We, who signed and sealed [this document], namely Mullā ʿAbūl Qāsīm [sic] Bāy, son of Tāsh Bātur Bāy, ʿĪsā Bék, son of Sulṭān Bék, Mīr Yūnus Bāy, son of Mīr Kamāl Bāy, Muḥammad Yūsuf, son of Nūr Muḥammad Bāy, from Shaykhāvānd Ṭahūr district of Tashkent, will become guarantors for Valī Khān Tūra, son of Pādshāh Khān Tūra. We put seals [in promise] that the abovementioned guarantors will have him and other *tūra*s who are being searched for, should they appear in the province or in any different place, appear before any court.
>
> Muḥammad Yūsuf, son of Nūr Muḥammad Bāy, put his seal.
>
> Āqsaqāl Inʿām Khwāja of the Shaykhāvānd Ṭahūr district put his seal officially certifying [the identities of] these guarantors.
>
> Also, the Āqsaqāl of Bīsh Yagāch, ʿAzīz Khwāja, put his seal.[79]

Within just a week, on October 14, the Governor-Generalship informed Abramov that "He will be released on bail."[80] The relationships between the four guarantors and Valī Khān Tūra are unknown, but it is certain that he was released on bail based on this guarantee letter. On the day after receiving the notification, Abramov sent the news on to Marghīnān. After his release, Valī Khān Tūra probably stayed with his guarantors in Tashkent.

---

78 Central State Archive of the Republic of Uzbekistan, *fond* 1-276, *opis'* 1, *delo* 324, l. 10.

79 Central State Archive of the Republic of Uzbekistan, *fond* 1-1, *opis'* 29, *delo* 341, l. 13 (the original Turkic text is accompanied by a Russian translation).

80 Central State Archive of the Republic of Uzbekistan, *fond* 1-276, *opis'* 1, *delo* 324, l. 11 (Abramov received this dispatch on October 19).

Within several days, a petition was submitted, this time addressed to Abramov, which carried 15 seals and 51 signs of residents of Marghīnān.[81]

> To His Excellency, Military Governor Abrāmūf Tūra,
>
> Petition from residents and merchants of Marghīnān:
>
> Allow us to express our wishes regarding the affair. It seems that the people-loving Valī Khān Tūra, Pādshā [sic] Khān Tūra ūghūl, currently stays in Tashkent. This *tūra* himself is a good and honest man. Therefore, we, with hope, appeal to you. We beg you to accept our humble request and ask His Excellency, the highly esteemed Governor-General, to send this *tūra* to Marghīnān to his wife and children so that he could spend the winter in his native land and pray together with his children. In case some opposition movement against the order should arise from this *tūra* in the future, we, who signed and sealed [this petition], will take the responsibility. Your Excellency, you are a person of authority. For this, we put our signs and seals. October 24th, 1878. In God's will, we wish you good health.[82]

At least 22 of these 66 people carried the title of *èllīkbāshī*. Under Russian rule, *èllīkbāshī* meant "elector," i.e., a person who had the right to participate in the elections of *aqsaqal*s, chiefs of villages and districts. Considering the scale of the town of Marghīnān in those days, the fact that so many people signed the document must have had important meaning.[83] On December 10, Abramov sent notification to Marghīnān stating that the plan was to return Valī Khān Tūra to Marghīnān in two months.[84] Then, on February 19, 1879, Abramov officially requested that Valī Khān Tūra be acquitted and freed. Undoubtedly this petition relieved Abramov's concerns, because it must have been those who signed the petition who, in Abramov's words, constituted "forces under Valī Khān Tūra's influence." On February 28, the Governor-Generalship notified the mayor of Tashkent that von Kaufman permitted Valī Khān Tūra to return home, and the case apparently was closed.

---

81 However, the Russian translation of the document says that it carries 15 seals and 65 signs.

82 Central State Archive of the Republic of Uzbekistan, *fond* I-276, *opis'* 1, *delo* 324, ll. 14–15 (the original Turkic text is accompanied by a Russian translation).

83 The population of the *prigorod* (suburban district) of Marghīnān in 1909 was about 120,000 people. *Spisok naselennykh mest Ferganskoi Oblasti* (Skobelev: Tipografiia Ferganskago Oblastnogo Pravleniia, 1909), 102.

84 Central State Archive of the Republic of Uzbekistan, *fond* I-276, *opis'* 1, *delo* 324, l. 16.

Conclusion

Though Valī Khān Tūra's leadership may have been primarily based on the public service he performed, it was initially built on the foundations he laid using the property and the believers' community that he inherited from his father, Pādshāh Khān Tūra; it was backed, moreover, by his belonging to the lineage repeatedly sanctified through Makhdūm-i Aʿẓam, Āfāq Khwāja, and Awrangzīb, and through the fame of his saintly grandfather, ʿIbādullāh. Of course, the family's activities in Marghīnān cannot be traced back as far as the epoch of ʿAbdullāh, as the family legend maintains. Still, the *khāns* recognized their genealogy, built relations with them, relied on their sacred power, and in return supported their status and economic strength. The territorial range in which Valī Khān Tūra could directly use his influence was limited to Marghīnān, but this, on the contrary, made him the popular leader closest to the local people. In Marghīnān, the ideology of *ghazavāt* actualized only after Valī Khān Tūra joined the movement. Regarding this point, previous studies have clearly underestimated the significance of the *ghazavāt*.

We do not know whether Valī Khān Tūra really had in mind any plot of the sort that Abramov was concerned about. The sentiments and attitudes among the migrants from Kashghar are topics that need separate examination, but it appears that, in his governance, Abramov comprehended this clearly and allowed for the popularity and leadership of Valī Khān Tūra in local society. And the reality was that even though Valī Khān Tūra lost his *ghazavāt*, he never lost his influence.

Valī Khān Tūra died in 1306 AH (between September 9, 1888, and August 27, 1889), at around 75 years of age.[85] We lack any information about him after his release, but he must have spent the last ten years of his life without returning to "his old pursuits." Valī Khān Tūra is believed to be buried in his great-grandfather's shrine, that of Ulugʿ hazrat bobo, without a separate *mazār* constructed at the site.

During the author's field research in 2003, Ulugʿ hazrat bobo was flooded with pilgrims and worshippers who offered prayers for healing or pregnancy and were overwhelmed with exuberant energy and religious zeal, as befits the shrine of a saint. At the same time, in the descendants' residence area, there stood, awaiting partial renovation, the houses where Valī Khān Tūra once used to live. One of the buildings had been used as a "confinement for prayer" (*chilla-khona*); the ceiling was decorated in colors typical of mosques or palaces of the era of the Khanate of Khoqand, and the walls were covered with graffiti of Persian verse.

85 The fact that the deed relating to the division of his inheritance was made in 1308 AH also supports this conclusion; see Kawahara, *Private Archives*, 254–258, 346–350.

FIGURE 5.2 *Shrine of Ulug' hazrat bobo (burial site of Valī Khān Tūra)*
2003, BY YASUSHI SHINMEN

In one corner of this building, there remained a corpse-washing spot for washing the bodies of deceased family members before burial. The descendants did not seem to know much about Valī Khān Tūra's *ghazavāt*, but they

FIGURE 5.3 *Decorated ceiling of the* chilla-khona *near the shrine of Ulugʻ hazrat bobo (burial site of Valī Khān Tūra)*
2003, BY YASUSHI SHINMEN

said that, as a legend states, "When the Russian army annexed the Khanate of Khoqand, here in Marghīnān a great battle took place as well. Women and children ran in fear and confusion trying to escape. And then, when somebody said, 'The *tūra*'s place is protected by God, it must be safe there,' all gathered in his house, and the premises became flooded with people." It is quite possible that the sacredness of Ulugʻ hazrat bobo may originate not from Valī Khān Tūra's legendary grandfather, ʻAbdullāh, but rather from Valī Khān Tūra himself, who urged people to stand up and endeavored to protect them in the face of the Russian army.

Bibliography

Archival Sources

"*Ob arestovanii Valikhan tiuri za politicheskuiu neblagonadezhnost'* (On the arrest of Valī Khān Tūra for political disloyalty)." Central State Archive of the Republic of Uzbekistan, *fond* I-276, *opis'* 1, *delo* 324.

"*Perepiska s voennym gubernatorom Ferganskoi oblasti i drugimi o Valikhan-Tiure, arestovannym v g. Margelane za politicheskuiu neblagonadezhnost' i zakliuchenie ego v Tashkentskoi gorodskoi tiur'me* (Correspondence with the Military Governor of Farghana and others about Valī Khān Tūra, arrested in Marghīnān for political disloyalty, and his confinement in Tashkent City Prison)." Central State Archive of the Republic of Uzbekistan, *fond* I-1, *opis'* 29, *delo* 341.

Manuscripts and Published Works

Abashin, S. N. "Shakhimardan." In *Islam na territorii byvshei Rossiiskoi imperii, Èntsiklopedicheskii slovar'*, vol. 2 (Moscow: Izdatel'skaia firma 'Vostochnaia Literatura' RAN, 1999), 109–111.

Babadžanov, Baxtiyor M. "On the History of the Naqšbandīya Muğaddidīya in Central Māwarā'annahr in the Late 18th and Early 19th Centuries." In *Muslim Culture in Russia and Central Asia from the 18th to the Early 20th Centuries*, ed. Michael Kemper, Anke von Kügelgen, and Dmitriy Yermakov (Berlin: Klaus Schwarz Verlag, 1996), 385–413.

Beisembiev, Timur K. *Annotated Indices to the Kokand Chronicles*. Tokyo: Research Institute for Languages and Culture of Asia and Africa, Tokyo University of Foreign Studies, 2008.

Beisembiev, T. K. *Kokandskaia istoriografiia, issledovanie po istochnikovedeniiu Srednei Azii XVIII–XIX vekov*. Almaty: TOO 'Print-S', 2009.

Eckmann, János. "Çağatay Edebiyatının Son Devri (1800–1920)." *Türk Dili Araştırmaları Yıllığı Belleten 1963* (1964), 121–156.

Isfaragī, Mīrzā Qalandar. *Shāh-nāma-yi 'Umar-khānī*. Ms. St. Petersburg, Institute of Oriental Manuscripts of the Russian Academy of Sciences, No. C471.

Isḥāq Khān b. Junaydullāh Khān Tūraqūrghānī. *Tārīkh-i Farghāna*. Ms. Dushanbe, A. Rudaki Institute of Language, Literature, Oriental Studies and Written Heritage, Academy of Sciences, Republic of Tajikistan, No. 1512.

Ivanov, P. P. *Ocherki po istorii Srednei Azii (XVI-seredina XIX v.)*. Moscow: Izdatel'stvo Vostochnoi literatury, 1958.

Kavakhara, Yayoi. "'Sviatye semeistva' Margelana v Kokandskom khanstve v XIX v." *Mir Islama/Pax Islamica*, 4 (2010), 121–139.

Kawahara, Yayoi. "The Development of the Naqshbandiyya-Mujaddidiyya in the Ferghana Valley during the 19th and Early 20th Centuries." *Journal of the History of Sufism* 6 (2015), 139–186.

Kawahara, Yayoi. *Private Archives on a Makhdūmzāda Family in Marghilan*. Tokyo: TIAS: Department of Islamic Area Studies Center for Evolving Humanities, Graduate School of Humanities and Sociology, The University of Tokyo, 2012.

Kawahara, Yayoi. "Tadhkira of Khwāja Ḥasan Ṣāḥibqirān: Study on a Private Manuscript in Ferghana Valley." *Journal of Asian and African Studies*, 71 (2006), 205–257.

Khasanov, A. Kh. *Narodnye dvizheniia v Kirgizii v period Kokandskogo khanstva.* Moscow: Glavnaia Redaktsiia Vostochnoi Literatury, 1977.

Muhammad Aziz Marg'iloniy. *Tarixi Aziziy* (*Farg'ona chor mustamlakasi davrida*). Ed. Shodmon Vohidov and Dilorom Sangirova. Tashkent: Ma'naviyat, 1999.

Muḥammad Ḥakīm Khān. *Muntakhab al-tawārīkh, Selected History*. Ed. Yayoi Kawahara and Koichi Haneda. Vol. 2. Tokyo: Research Institute for Languages and Culture of Asia and Africa, Tokyo University of Foreign Studies, 2006.

Mulla Aziz bin Mulla Muhammadrizo Marg'inoniy. *Tarixi Aziziy*. Ed. B. M. Bobojonov and I. A. Qayumova. Tashkent: O'zbekiston Respublikasi Oliy va O'rta-Maxsus Ta'lim Vazirligi Toshkent Davlat Sharqshunoslik Instituti huzuridagi Abu Rayhon Beruniy nomidagi Sharq Qo'lyozmalari Markazi, 2016.

Mullā 'Azīz Marghīnānī. *Tārīkh-i 'Azīzī*. Ms. Tashkent, IVANRUz, No. 11108.

Ploskikh, V. M. *Kirgizy i Kokandskoe khanstvo*. Frunze: Ilim, 1977.

Shinmen, Yasushi. "Yākūbu begu seiken no seikaku ni kansuru ichi kousatsu (The Character of the Government of Yaqub Beg)." *Shigaku-zasshi*, 97 (1987), 1–42.

Spisok naselennykh mest Ferganskoi Oblasti. Skobelev: Tipografiia Ferganskago Oblastnogo Pravleniia, 1909.

Tāshkandī, Mīrzā 'Ālim Mushrif b. Mīrzā Raḥīm. *Ansāb al-salāṭīn va tavārīkh-i khavāqīn.* Ms. Tashkent, IVANRUz, No. 1314.

Troitskaia, A. L. *Katalog arkhiva kokandskikh khanov XIX veka.* Moscow: Nauka, Glavnaia Redaktsiia Vostochnoi Literatury, 1968.

Valikhanov, Ch. Ch. *Sobranie sochinenii v piati tomakh*, tom 3. Alma-Ata: Glavnaia Redaktsiia Kazakhskoi Sovetskoi Ėntsiklopedii, 1985.

CHAPTER 6

Reliquary Sufism: Sacred Fiber in Afghanistan

R. D. McChesney

The stories told of Sufi Islam in Central Asia usually focus on saintly personalities and the corporate entities (*ṭarīqa*, pl. *ṭarāʾiq, ṭuruq, ṭarīqāt*) to which they sometimes gave rise, the so-called 'orders' or networks, most prominently the Naqshbandī *ṭarīqa* and its affiliates—the Pārsāʾī, Anṣārī, Dahbīdī, Aḥrārī, Jūybārī, Mujaddidī, etc.—as well as the shrines associated with those groups. On the other hand, sacred relics and their shrines, the powers they were thought to possess, and the communities that arose around them have drawn little scholarly attention in comparison with the studies devoted to saintly personalities.

In Afghanistan, we find stories of various types of relics—heaven-sent stones,[1] saintly footprints (*qadamgāhs*), sites of visions (*naẓargāhs*), remnants of the Prophet Muḥammad's mantle or cloak (*khirqa-yi sharīf*), and the sacred hairs of his beard (*mū-yi mubārak*)—around which shrines have formed. In the case of the southern Afghan city of Qandahar (Kandahar), the cloak and the sacred beard hairs have produced shrines at different times. In this study I will focus on the *khirqa*, for which we have a considerable amount of information on its place in the social history of Qandahar, and refer only briefly to the appearance of the "beard hair" tradition and some of its ramifications. Rather than attempt a comprehensive treatment of the *khirqa*'s story, I will limit the discussion here to the half century, 1880–1930, represented by the regimes of three Muḥammadzāʾī *amīr*s, ʿAbd al-Raḥmān Khān (r. 1880–1901), his son, Ḥabībullāh Khān (r. 1901–1919), and his son Amānullāh Khān (r. 1919–1929). This period provides ample evidence of the multiple purposes these relics served, the function of the *khirqa* shrine in its local and regional context, and its social, political, and economic importance.

Little has been written about the religious policies of the first two of these *amīrs*. In light of the communications between the Islamic scholars of India and Afghanistan and the Islamic reform currents sweeping India during

1 Muḥammad Ṭāhir Balkhī b. Abīʾl Qāsim, *ʿAjāʾib al-ṭabaqāt*, Ms. Tashkent, Institute of Oriental Studies of the Academy of Sciences of Uzbekistan, Inv. No. 1993/1, f. 17b. An accessible source for the major urban shrines of Afghanistan is Nancy Hatch Dupree's *An Historical Guide to Afghanistan*, Revised and Enlarged (Kabul: Afghan Air Authority and Afghan Tourist Organization, 1977).

 | DOI:10.1163/9789004373075_008

this half century, especially those Islamic currents that arose as a result of the "back-to-a-simpler-purer-Islam" movements inspired by Sayyid Aḥmad Baralwī, it is difficult to imagine that all of the intellectual ferment there did not have an impact on Afghanistan. But there is little in the way of scholarly studies yet showing that it did. Hasan Kakar's classic study of the reign of ʿAbd al-Raḥmān Khān devotes only a few pages to the religious climate of the country.[2] His analysis focuses on the politics of religion. In discussing the government's policies towards the religious classes, he posits an enduring antagonism and contempt on the part of Amīr ʿAbd al-Raḥmān Khān for the clerics and Sufi leaders, a contempt that governed all his actions toward figures of the religious establishment, which included confiscating religious endowments, subjecting the *ʿulamā* to a licensing process, and executing any who opposed him. Asta Olsen, in a more detailed and analytic study, does not advance the argument much beyond Kakar's conclusions about the *amīr*'s anti-Shīʿī, anti-Wahhābī, and anti-Sufi policies and actions.[3] Both studies tend to draw sweeping conclusions from isolated incidents and rely heavily on the highly problematic "autobiography" of ʿAbd al-Raḥmān Khān.[4]

2 Hasan Kawun Kakar, *Government and Society in Afghanistan: The Reign of Amir ʿAbd al-Rahman Khan* (Austin: University of Texas Press, 1979), 147–163.

3 Asta Olsen, "The political use of Islam in Afghanistan during the reign of Amir Abdur Rahman (1880–1901)," in *Contribution to Islamic Studies: Iran, Afghanistan and Pakistan*, ed. Christel Braae and Klaus Ferdinand (Aarhus: The Danish Research Council for the Humanities, 1987), 59–114.

4 Sultan Mahomed Khan, *The Life of Abdur Rahman, Amir of Afghanistan*, 2 vols. (London: John Murray, 1900). This work, which has been enormously influential in the historiography of the country, was ostensibly based on what seems to have been the genuine work of ʿAbd al-Raḥmān, *Pandnāma-yi Dunyā wa Dīn* ("Advice for This World and the Next"), although that work is never specifically mentioned in *The Life*. The *Pandnāma* seems to have been only partially published by the *amīr*. The printed text (Kabul, 1303/1885–86) has 140 pages; see G.F. Girs, "Pervye pechatnye knigi Afganistana (istochnikovedcheskii obzor litografirovannykh izdanii XIX v. na dari i pushtu)," in *Pamiatniki istorii i literatury Vostoka. Period feodalizma* (Moscow: Nauka, 1986), 112–139. The printed text ends, moreover, with a complete sentence, but in the middle of a story; however, there is no collating word at the bottom of the last verso page, indicating that the lithographer, at least, had no more manuscript to work from. The first volume of the English translation is 295 pages and the *Pandnāma* corresponds only to the first 192. Besides the remaining 103 pages of the first volume, there are another 304 pages of the second volume of the English version for which no Persian original exists. It is possible that there was a manuscript from which Sultan Mahomed Khan worked, other than his own notes, but no reference is made to it, nor is one known to exist. The publisher, John Murray, believed that the first eleven chapters of the translation (ending on p. 292) represented the *amīr*'s own writing (see "Note by the Publisher," v–vi), the rest being from Sultan Mahomed Khan's own notes. The *Pandnāma* material actually corresponds only to the first

Recent work, such as that by Waleed Ziad, however, is beginning to reveal the intellectual currents flowing alongside, and often unrelated to, the political events that absorb so much of the literature.[5] In the case of ʿAbd al-Raḥmān Khān, the reality seems to have been far more complex than the literature yet shows. There can be little question about the *amīr*'s professed devotion to Islam even though there is scant evidence of his having fulfilled any of its formal requirements—*ḥajj*-pilgrimage, five-fold daily prayer, payment of *zakāt*, or observance of the Ramadan fast. His rhetoric in the hundreds of *farmāns* quoted in the *Sirāj al-tawārīkh* is redolent of piety and replete with Islamic references and terminology.[6] He always justifies his decisions as guided by God and the example of the Prophet Muḥammad. Moreover, he sponsored the building of the great ʿĪdgah Mosque and the Madrasa-yi Shāhī, and he patronized religious scholars with salaried positions, for which they were expected to show gratitude to him and support any requests of his for *fatwā*s or other endorsement of his policies. There is little question that he dealt harshly with anyone he considered an enemy, whether that person was a religious scholar, tribal leader, merchant, soldier, or ordinary civilian. But as we will see below, he backed the fiscal rights of religious figures and, rather than "confiscate" religious endowments, he set up a system of auditing to ensure that the rights of the endowed institutions were not usurped or violated by those who administered them. In the realm of spiritual inspiration, he cited his own dreams as explaining some decision or success he had achieved, but he tended to be highly skeptical of the claims of others to have had visions or dreams or to possess holy relics for which they thought they should be rewarded in some way.

His son and successor, Amīr Ḥabībullāh Khān, seems to have been far more credulous when it came to accepting the claims and representations of religious scholars and Sufi personalities, but also showed the same willingness

seven and one-half chapters. Sultan Mahomed Khan, in his introduction, says that he was depositing the original manuscript in the Oriental Reading Room of the British Museum (vii–viii); however, there is no evidence yet that he did so. Because of the assumed importance of this work in English a full analysis of it in light of what exists of the *Pandnāma* would seem to be an urgent desideratum. See further, on the question of authorship of the "autobiography," Hasan Kakar, *Afghanistan: A Study of Internal Political Developments* (Kabul, 1971), 217–220.

5 Waleed Ziad, "Transporting Knowledge in the Durrani Empire: Two Manuals of Naqshbandi-Mujaddidi Sufi Practice," in *Afghanistan's Islam: From Conversion to the Taliban*, ed. Nile Green (Berkeley: University of California Press, 2016), 105–128.

6 Fayż Muḥammad Kātib, *The History of Afghanistan: Fayż Muḥammad Kātib Hazārah's* Sirāj al-tawārīkh, 4 volumes in 11 (Leiden and Boston: Brill, 2013–2016), vol. 3 part 4, appendix 2, 1857–1879 and vol. 4, part 5, 2515–2551 for tables of all the *farmāns* and other documents issued by Amīr ʿAbd al-Raḥman Khān that are quoted in the work.

that his father had shown to invest in projects he thought would advance Islam in a more conventional way, like the multi-volume compilation of Ḥanafī legal material, *Sirāj al-aḥkām fī muʿāmalāt-i Islām*, or his rural project to spread basic Islamic teachings.[7]

Amīr Amānullāh Khān presents a somewhat more complex figure in terms of his projected self-image and the general perception of him both as *ghāzī*, for his securing Afghanistan independence from British control, and as social reformer. Scholars of his policies have emphasized his various efforts to weaken the power of Muslim leaders and focused less on how he tried to position himself as defender of Islam against the forces of unbelief.[8]

When it came to the sacred garment of the Prophet, all three rulers showed an outward devotion to its Qandahar shrine, but the devotion displayed by Amīr Ḥabībullāh Khān may have been the most unfeigned of the three, and certainly the record of his investments in the shrine far exceeds anything recorded about the patronage of the other two. But our story is not so much about the policies and actions of these three *amīrs* vis à vis the Prophet's cloak but rather the popular response to the relic and the comfort it offered to ordinary people oppressed by life's hardships and uncertainties, as well as the material benefit it offered the people most closely associated with it.

On the Mantle (*khirqa*) of the Prophet in Afghanistan

There are two known shrines of the *khirqa*, or fragments thereof, the more famous one in Qandahar and a more obscure one, whose origins are as yet unknown, in Herat.[9] In addition to the shrine of the sacred *khirqa*, there is also a mosque in Qandahar, the Masjid-i Jāmiʿ-i Mū-yi Mubārak (Congregational

7 Ibid., vol. 4, 1033–1034, 1096–1098.

8 See Leon Poullada, *Reform and Rebellion in Afghanistan, 1919–1929: King Amanullah's Failure to Modernize a Tribal Society* (Ithaca, New York: Cornell University Press, 1973), 119–130. See especially the more recent work of Senzil Nawid, *Religious Response to Social Change in Afghanistan 1919–29: King Aman-Allah and the Afghan Ulama* (Costa Mesa, California: Mazda Publishers, 1999), 119–130.

9 For a brief reference to the Herat shrine, see Nancy Hatch Dupree, *An Historical Guide to Afghanistan* (Kabul: Afghan Air Authority and Afghan Tourist Organization, 1977), 247. She was told the *khirqa* arrived there "about 500 years ago," brought by a "holy man." If approximately true, it would have placed the arrival during the height of Timurid glory in Herat, when other miraculous manifestations of saints were *au courant*, but then "500 years ago" is a time period not infrequently cited by an informant unwilling to admit ignorance about the actual age of some ancient site.

Mosque of the Blessed Strand), which serves as the repository and shrine for a single fiber of the Prophet's hair.[10] The two Qandahar sites of these sacred relics have contested histories and it is not my intent here to unravel the various narratives that have survived. Instead I will limit myself to eliciting the social history connected to these relics, specifically those aspects of it that have captured the attention of recorders of Afghan history and have been committed to writing. Clearly, when it is a question of belief, it is impossible to know what an artifact like the Prophet's mantle or a strand of the hair of his beard may mean to any one individual. The historical meaning that people attached to these sacred relics only manifests itself, however incompletely, through their actions as recorded in writing.

First, the presence in Qandahar of the cloak attributed to the Prophet deserves some background.[11] There are three main stories, each with its variants, that purport to tell how the *khirqa* came to Qandahar. All three credit Aḥmad Shāh Durrānī (r. 1747–1773), to whose reign the formation of the modern state of Afghanistan is generally attributed, for bringing the *khirqa* to Qandahar in 1768. The most fanciful story, and the one related by some Western journalists inquiring about the shrine and its meaning following the American and NATO occupation of Afghanistan in 2002, has Aḥmad Shāh going to Bukhara and then tricking the keepers of the *khirqa* into letting him take it away.[12] The second and more widely-held story connects the cloak with Aḥmad Shāh's confrontation and negotiation with Shāh Murād Bīy, then acting on behalf of his father, Dāniyāl Bīy, the Manghït *amīr* of Bukhara (r. 1758–1785).[13] The cloak was given to the Afghān, it is said, either to avoid a fight[14] or to settle the Amu Darya as the boundary between the kingdom of Qandahar and the emirate of Bukhara.[15]

10 Dupree, *Historical Guide*, 285.

11 I treat the Shrine of the Prophet's Cloak in more detail in a forthcoming comparative study of four Central Asian shrines—the Qandahar Shrine of the Cloak, the shrine of Abū Naṣr Pārsā in Balkh, the ʿAlid shrine at Mazār-i Sharīf, and Timur's tomb in Samarqand.

12 See Steve Inskeep, "The Cloak of the Prophet: Religious Artifact at the Heart of Former Taliban Stronghold," National Public Radio, January 10, 2002; Graeme Smith, "Prophet's cloak can't shelter Kandahar from terror," *Globe & Mail*, July 11, 2002; and "Mosques around the World" (http://famous-mosques-around-the-world.blogspot.com/2013/05/shrine-of-cloak.html).

13 See, e.g., Dupree, *Historical Guide*, 284; Fayż Muḥammad, *History*, vol. 1, 27.

14 J. L. Lee, *The 'Ancient Supremacy': Bukhara, Afghanistan & the Battle for Balkh, 1731–1901* (Leiden: Brill, 1996), 91.

15 Fayż Muḥammad, *History*, vol. 1, 27; Dupree, *Historical Guide*, 284; S. E. Grigoryev, "Afghan Historical Sources on the *Khirqa* of the Prophet Muhammad," *Manuscripta Orientalia: International Journal for Oriental Manuscript Research*, 8/2 (2002), 5–9; Fabrizio Foschini

The story has its earliest appearance in Sulṭān Muḥammad Bārakzāʾī's mid-19th-century *Tārīkh-i Sulṭānī*.[16] It was later embellished by adding a hair of the Prophet's beard to the gift of the Bukharan *amīr*.[17] The third story, and the one that seems to have more evidentiary weight behind it, because it was written by the *shāh*'s own chronicler, was recorded during the lifetime of Aḥmad Shāh (d. 1773). In this story, Bukhara is not involved at all and there is no evidence in this source, or in a contemporary one written in Lucknow, that Aḥmad Shāh ever set foot north of the Hindu Kush.[18] The cloak was in Yaftal (Fayżābād), Badakhshān, and on orders from the *shāh* one of his generals took it by force and brought it to the *shāh* in Kabul, whence it made its way to Qandahar.[19] How it got to Badakhshān in the first place also generated a number of different stories that cannot be dealt with here.

One of the economic resources of the shrine complex was created before the *khirqa* came to Qandahar. In 1755, Aḥmad Shāh ordered the construction of a new city in Qandahar to be modestly called "Noblest Aḥmad Shāh City" (*ashraf al-bilād-i Aḥmad Shāhī*). It was to replace the city of Nādirābād ordered built by its namesake, Nādir Shāh Afshār, after his conquest of the region in 1737. That in turn succeeded the old city of Qandahar, the site of which now lies to the west of the modern city. To support life in his new city, Aḥmad Shāh had a long trunk canal, called the Nahr-i Aḥmad Shāhī or Nahr-i Shāhī, excavated from the Arghandāb River, which flowed past the new city well to the northwest. The maintenance of it he assigned to members of his Durrānī confederation, a requirement that would come to be seen as an onerous burden. The canal, or some part of it—the exact details are uncertain—would be conveyed by Tīmūr Shāh, Aḥmad Shāh's son and successor, jointly with his brothers as an

and Bette Dam, "Under the Cloak of History: The Kherqa-ye Sharif from Faizabad to Kandahar," *Afghanistan Analysts Network*, 30 July 2014.

16 Sulṭān Muḥammad Khān Bārakzāʾī, *Tārīkh-i Sulṭānī* (Bombay, 1298/1881), 144. As it happened, Sulṭān Muḥammad Khān was writing in India during the time when the question of the limits of Afghan territory in the north was an issue of major concern to British policymakers worried about Russian expansion.

17 Dupree, *Historical Guide*, 285.

18 Imām al-Dīn Ḥusaynī, *Tārīkh-i Ḥusaynī* (henceforth *TH*), Ms. Kabul, Arshīf-i millī, No. 53/23 (dated 1213/1798–99); on the work, see Ch. A. Stori, *Persidskaia literature: Bio-bibliograficheskii obzor*, ed. and tr. Iu. È. Bregel', 3 vols. (Moscow: Glavnaia Redaktsiia Vostochnoi Literatury, 1972), vol. III, 1223.

19 Maḥmūd Ḥusaynī Jāmī, *Tārīkh-i Aḥmad Shāhī: Tārīkh-i tashkīl-i awwalīn ḥukūmat-i Afghānistān*, edited and annotated by Dr. Ghulām Ḥusayn Zargarī-nizhād (Tehran: Dānishgāh-i Tihrān, 1384/2005; henceforth *TAS*), 646.

endowment for the shrine-tomb-mosque-*madrasa-khānaqāh* complex, which Aḥmad Shāh had apparently planned and may have started building.

The Cloak at Qandahar

The earliest documented evidence of the *khirqa* in Qandahar is a *farmān* issued by Aḥmad Shāh and dated 26 Muḥarram 1183/1 June 1769, appointing a trustee (*mutawallī*) for the cloak and establishing certain conditions for its handling.[20] First, the box containing the cloak would remain locked, probably with a great iron padlock to which only the *mutawallī* would have a key. The box was never to be opened unless the sovereign ordered it. Later these conditions would be amplified by the further stipulation that anyone who wished to perform *ziyārat* (pilgrimage) to the cloak would have to perform it to the closed box.[21]

One last provision in Aḥmad Shāh's *farmān* of June 1769 was the appointment of a trustee. The man he chose was an Afghan, a member of the Yaʿqūbzāʾī clan of the Alkūzāʾī (Alikūzāʾī) tribe of the Durrānī confederation, Ākhūndzāda Ḥājjī ʿAbd al-Ḥaqq, son of Ḥājjī Mullā Shukr (or Shakar). The title *ākhūndzāda* indicates that he was from a line of scholars; it would eventually become the family name. Besides upholding Aḥmad Shāh's stipulations regarding the use and care of the *khirqa*, the *ḥājjī*'s responsibilities would soon come to include oversight of the financial resources of the *khirqa* complex. Aḥmad Shāh himself made no financial provisions for the cloak, although he probably let those close to him know his wishes.

---

20 ʿAzīz al-Dīn Wakīlī Fūfalzāʾī (Pūpalzāʾī), *Tīmūr Shāh Durrānī*, 2 vols. (Kabul: Anjuman-i Tārīkh, 1346/1967), vol. 1, 297. A photograph of a part of the *farmān* faces p. 297. This paper owes much to the incomparable work that ʿAzīz al-Dīn Wakīlī Fūfalzāʾī did in researching the history of the cloak. He worked at the shrine in Qandahar in the spring of 1962 and was given access to many if not most of the documents held at the shrine. Without his research and his reproduction of more than two dozen of these documents, this discussion of the cloak would not have been possible. He published his research in two editions, *Tārīkh-i khirqa-yi muʿaẓẓama-yi wāqiʿ dar Qandahār* which appeared serialized in *Āryānā* volume 23 (1965), 104–112, 133–147, 239–242, 399–405, 508–516, and 727–640 (*sic*, for 740), and volume 24 (1966), 72–79, 172–186, 326–338, 442–450, 533–542, and 626–629, and also appeared as a book, *Tārīkh-i Khirqat-i Sharīf* (Kabul: Islamic Research Institute, 1367/1988). He also included a summary of his findings in *Tīmūr Shāh Durrānī*, vol. 2, 294–301.

21 Fūfalzāʾī, *Tārīkh-i khirqa*, *Āryānā*, vol. 24, 184.

It was understood by the later author of the *Sirāj al-tawārīkh* that Aḥmad Shāh intended to have a single mausoleum built for both himself and the *khirqa*. The author, Fayż Muḥammad, recorded the observation of his patron, Amīr Ḥabībullāh Khān, who visited the mausoleum in 1907, that Aḥmad Shāh's tomb was not centered under the dome of the building. The tomb in the crypt and the cenotaph on the ground floor were both set to one side of the room as if awaiting the interment of something else to create a balanced symmetry. The *amīr* believed that this meant the mausoleum was also intended to house the *khirqa*, but that sacred garment was never placed there due to a *fatwā* from the *ʿulamā* forbidding its being moved "lest it become a plaything (*bāzīcha*) in the hands of rulers."[22] This begs the question as to where it was first housed before the complex was built. ʿAzīz al-Dīn Wakīlī Fūfalzāʾī believed it was housed in a small new mosque called Zāra Masjid near the home of Shāh Walī Khān Bāmīzāʾī on Bardarānī (or Bar-durrānī?) Street (*guzār-i Bardarānī*).[23]

Tīmūr Shāh, like his father, firmly believed in the efficacy of the *khirqa*. In the very short time he was in Qandahar, before moving the capital to Kabul in 1773, he devoted himself to giving the cloak and the commemoration of his father a more concrete reality. With all the construction that had gone on in the preceding four decades to make and then re-make the area as a political center, considerable design and construction expertise was available in Qandahar when he came to the throne, and he made good use of it. Fūfalzāʾī lists a number of the buildings in Qandahar designed and built by Qandahārī architects, and provides a genealogy of a family of Qandahārī builder-architects active under Tīmūr Shāh both in Qandahar and Kabul.[24] After the death of Aḥmad Shāh in 1773,[25] Tīmūr Shāh ordered the construction of a complex of buildings,

---

22 Fayż Muḥammad, *History*, vol. 1, 28. Fūfalzāʾī, *Tīmūr Shāh*, 297, drew on this account and added that it was Tīmūr Shāh's wish that the *khirqa* never be moved, and that he thus solicited a *fatwā* to that effect.

23 Ludwig Adamec, ed., *Historical and Political Gazetter of Afghanistan*, 6 vols. (Graz: Akademische Druck-u. Verlagsanstalt, 1972–1985), vol. 5 (Qandahar, henceforth *Gaz* 5), has a list compiled in 1880 of the quarters (*maḥallas*) of Qandahar, pp. 242–244. Five of them have the name "Badurani."

24 It is particularly regrettable that Fūfalzāʾī only rarely cites the source for his information and then without providing bibliographic information or page references. For more detail on the Qandahārī architects, see May Schinasi, *Kaboul 1773–1948: Naissance et croissance d'une capitale royale* (Naples: Università degli Studi di Napoli "L'Orientale," 2008), 45, and idem, *Kabul: A History* (Leiden: Brill, 2016).

25 TAS was in the best position to know when Aḥmad Shāh died and dates his death "Thursday, 2 Rabīʿ al-Awwal Lūy Yil (Dragon Year) 1186" (686). If it were not for the mixed Turkī-Hijrī system of dating, 2 Rabīʿ al-Awwal 1186 would correspond to June 3, 1772. In the

centered around his father's tomb and the *khirqa* shrine, that survives to the present. It includes, as separate structures in one enclosed area, the *khirqa* shrine, the tomb of Aḥmad Shāh, a Sufi hostel (*khānaqāh*), a cistern (*ḥawż*) and a *madrasa*-cum-congregational mosque. The combination tomb/shrine and *madrasa*/mosque was a traditional architectural form for more elaborate tomb sites.[26] The *khirqa* building was completed the first of Ramażān Pīchī Yil (Ape Year) 1190/October 14, 1776, and the tomb somewhat earlier.[27]

---

conventions of the time, however, the named duodecimal Turkī year was usually given the number of the Hijrī year in which Nawrūz (the vernal equinox, March 20–21), the beginning date for the Turkī year, fell. Lūy Yil 1186 thus began on 26 Dhū'l-ḥijja 1186, the last month of the Hijrī year. This meant that Rabīʿ al-Awwal, the third month of the Hijrī year, would have occurred in 1187, though it was called Lūy Yil 1186, and the obituary would have corresponded to the Common Era date of May 24, 1773. Some authoritative sources (e.g., *Encyclopaedia Iranica*, vol. 1, 548, and Christine Nölle-Karimi, *The Pearl in its Midst: Herat and the Mapping of Khurasan from the Fifteenth to the Nineteenth Centuries* [Vienna: Austrian Academy of Sciences Press, 2014], 304), however, give the date of Aḥmad Shāh's death as 1772. Others (C. E. Bosworth, *The New Islamic Dynasties* [New York: Columbia University Press, 1996], 341; Fūfalzā'ī, *Tārīkh-i khirqa, Āryānā*, vol. 23, 729) date his death 1773, although Fūfalzā'ī dates it the 20th of Rajab rather than 2 Rabīʿ al-Awwal. The duodecimal Turkī year naming system was used for some six centuries until it was abolished in Afghanistan under Amīr Amānullāh Khān in the 1920s. If we correlate the usage by al-Ḥusaynī with its use in the documents cited by Fūfalzā'ī and the later use by Fayż Muḥammad (early 20th century; see Fayż Muḥammad, *History*, vol. 3, appendix 9), we arrive at Lūy Yil as beginning in 1772 (since every twelve years there would be another Lūy Yil, Year of the Dragon). The obituary inscription inside Aḥmad Shāh's tomb only gives the Hijrī year 1186 (Dupree, *Historical Guide*, 283).

26 Major tomb/shrine sites that followed this pattern of development were the Shāh-i Zinda (see Roya Marefat, "Beyond the Architecture of Death: The Shrine of Shah-i Zindah in Samarqand," Ph.D. dissertation, Harvard University, 1991, 89) and the Gūr-i Mīr (see Lisa Golombek and Donald Wilber, *The Timurid Architecture of Iran and Turan*, 2 vols. [Princeton: Princeton University Press, 1988], vol. 1, 260–63) in Samarqand; the Chār Bakr complex at Bukhara (see Bakhtyar Babajanov and Maria Szuppe, *Les inscriptions persanes de Chār Bakr, nécropole familiale des* khwāja *Jūybārī près de Boukhara* [London: School of Oriental and African Studies, 2002; Corpus Inscriptionum Iranicarum, part IV, Persian Inscriptions down to the early Safavid Period, vol. XXXI: Uzbekistan], 30–34); and at Balkh, the tomb/shrine ascribed to a Naqshbandī saint, Abū Naṣr Pārsā (see R. D. McChesney, "Architecture and Narrative: The Khwaja Abu Nasr Parsa Shrine. Part 1: Constructing the Complex and Its Meaning, 1469–1696," *Muqarnas*, 18 [2001], 94–119).

27 Fūfalzā'ī, *Tīmūr Shāh*, 297. The fact that the asymmetrical placement of Aḥmad Shāh's grave in the mausoleum anticipated the never-effected interment of the cloak indicates the building was completed sometime probably well before the structure for the *khirqa*.

FIGURE 6.1 *The* Khirqat al-Nabī *as it appeared in the 1930s* (Sālnāma-yi Kābul).

In the same month that the *khirqa* shrine building was completed, Tīmūr Shāh, now campaigning from his new capital, Kabul, sent a *farmān* to the finance officials of Qandahar to provide stipends in the form of food rations for ten individuals associated with the new tomb complex whom Fūfalzā'ī identifies, apparently from the document he relied on, as "five scholars (*ʿulamā*) and five trustees (*mutawallīs*)," without naming them.[28] No endowment had yet been established and it is clear that the estate of Aḥmad Shāh had yet to be settled.

28 Two later *farmāns* (of February 1784 and March 1791) concerning the food rations for the ten men refer to a manual of instructions (*dastūr al-ʿamal*), which apparently no longer exists. The set of instructions appears to have dealt with the functions of all ten men, though only the "five *mutawallīs*" seem to have had assigned functions at the complex. The other five seem to have had no assigned function, and two of them, a *mullā-bāshī* and the manager (*amīn*) of the Sharīʿa Court of Qandahar, had other responsibilities. But at least part of their remuneration was seen as tied in some fashion to the complex.

The First Deed of Endowment (*waqfiyya, waqfnāma*)

The cost of building the complex—the tomb, the shrine building, and the mosque/*madrasa*—was probably taken from current revenues, but to ensure that it endured, Tīmūr Shāh and his six brothers, all heirs to Aḥmad Shāh's estate, endowed the shrine complex and the tomb of their father. The six years between completion of the complex and the promulgation of the endowment may have been required to probate the estate and secure the agreement of the six other sons,[29] Sulaymān, Iskandar, Parwīz, Dārāb, Shihāb, and Sanjar.

In the spring of 1962 when Fūfalzā'ī did his research at the shrine, the original endowment deed (*waqfiyya*) still existed in the hands of Ḥājjī 'Abd al-Razzāq Ākhūndzāda, a great-great-great grandson of the first *mutawallī*.[30] The initial capital of the endowment was the trunk canal, the Nahr-i Aḥmad Shāhī, built by Aḥmad Shāh to provide water to his new city. The endowment deed asserts that Aḥmad Shāh had paid for the canal with his own legal (*ḥalāl*) money and that it was the patrimony of his children. The canal is described in the deed as flowing from the Arghandāb River on a northwest to southeast course, then turning due east and terminating at Manzil Bagh. The latter was a garden estate that was built by Aḥmad Shāh and remained in royal hands well into the 20th century. The endowment included the water rights from the canal and the properties it served, but excluded certain estates in private hands or dedicated to some other purpose that depended on the canal's water.[31]

The original *waqfiyya* provided for the salary of the trustee named in Aḥmad Shāh's earlier *farmān*, Ḥājjī 'Abd al-Ḥaqq Ākhūndzāda, and instructed him to distribute daily servings of cracked wheat (*bulghur*) to the poor. Later *farmān*s

---

29 According to Fūfalzā'ī, *Tīmūr Shāh*, 29, the only reliable source for a list of the sons of Aḥmad Shāh is the endowment deed of 1196/1782, although he himself misstates the number of Tīmūr Shāh's brothers as five rather than the six listed in the deed and indeed by him on the same page.

30 In the forthcoming work mentioned above in note 11, I deal in more detail with the complex nature of the endowed property, the Nahr-i Aḥmad Shāhī and all the properties dependent upon it, as well as with the stipulations for maintaining it. However complicated the management of the endowment and the complex was, the fact that it has survived for a quarter of a millennium is some evidence of the ability of its managers to overcome the resistance, challenges, and outright efforts at usurpation that inevitably arose.

31 Fūfalzā'ī, *Tārīkh-i Khirqat*, 43–50. Perhaps as a reward for assisting in excavating the canal, Aḥmad Shāh allotted lands along it to fellow Durrānī chiefs, as well as certain administrative offices and the private household (*ḥaramsarāy*) (see *infra* note 45).

FIGURE 6.2 *The* Khirqa *complex from the southeast showing the shrine (right) and Aḥmad Shāh's tomb behind* (Sālnāma-yi Kābul).

would expand the distributions of the endowment to include a meal of lamb on Fridays (for the poor), as well as the daily (*sic*!) amount of fifty Tabrīzī *man*s of baked bread for the poor.[32] In addition, in 1776, six years before the *waqf* endowment was made, Tīmūr Shāh had issued a *farmān* assigning food rations to the ten individuals mentioned above.[33] The total of the daily stipend for the ten was to be "one *man* and ten seers of baked bread."[34] In 1782, these rations were now included within the endowment's distributions.

32 Ibid., 53.

33 Fūfalzā'ī, *Tārīkh-i Khirqa, Āryānā*, vol. 23, 172.

34 Fūfalzā'ī, *Tīmūr Shāh*, 297. The *man* was universally comprised of forty seers (*sīr*), so each person was entitled to five seers. The weight of the seer varied from region to region, but probably was in the neighborhood of 14–16 pounds avoirdupois. However, it should be noted that in Qandahar at this time the "Tabrīzī *man*" was current, and in Col. Henry Yule and A. C. Burnell, *Hobson-Jobson: A Glossary of Colloquial Anglo-Indian Words and Phrases, and of Kindred Terms, Etymological, Historical, Geographical and Discursive*, new edition, edited by William Crooke, 1886 (New Delhi reprint, 1986), 564, the "Persian Tabrizi *man*" is defined as seven pounds. Thus there are two *man*s in use, the one of forty seers and the Tabrīzī *man*, about half the weight of the seer. *Gaz* 5 (Qandahar) unfortunately does not give Qandahar weights in its introduction, but the weights for Kabul and Māzar-i Sharīf probably may be roughly extrapolated for Qandahar if we maintain a distinction between the *man* of forty seers and the Tabrīzī *man*. Thus the amount of baked bread each scholar was entitled to (i.e., some 70–80 pounds) meant they were also

Besides providing for the maintenance of the complex, the endowment provided life tenure for the staff—those in charge of the furnishings and building management; a stipend for the trustee of the cloak, Ḥājjī ʿAbd al-Ḥaqq Ākhūndzāda; and livings for professors at the *madrasa*. These stipends were considered as arising from the endowment, but the collections, processing, and distributions were clearly considered a government responsibility.

There is much more that could be said here about the economic underpinnings of the complex and its evolution through time, but since my focus will be limited to the fifty years represented by the reigns of the three *amīr*s, ʿAbd al-Raḥmān Khān, Amīr Ḥabībullāh Khān, and Amīr Amānullāh Khān, it is enough to say that the surviving *farmān*s pertaining to the shrine complex and issued by the Sadūzāʾī sovereigns—Tīmūr Shāh, Zamān Shāh, Maḥmūd Shāh, and Shāh Shujāʿ—and their Muḥammadzāʾī successors fully attest to the durability of the administrative dynasty of the Ākhūndzādas, notwithstanding recurrent political turmoil and regime change, and despite numerous challenges to the shrine administration; all of this is well documented for the period between the founding of the shrine complex in Qandahar in the early 1770s and the reigns of our three *amīr*s, beginning more than a century later. We turn now to this later period.

Privatizing Charitable Capital

One of the most significant social effects that the shrine complex, and indeed any endowed institution with a lengthy history, had was its effect on the managing family itself, in this case the Ākhūndzādas. Initially, appointment was a matter of prestige and honor, but once the role was routinized it became a struggle to maintain the position and thus its rewards. The financial benefits, though rarely emphasized in the documentary record, must have been a major attraction and they help determine who was seen as best fit to manage. Preserving the stipends and other perquisites of management meant constantly tending a network of relationships. Capital in land or improvements

---

redistributing the bread to their retainers. One issue throughout this first period under the Sadūzāʾī regimes is the stipend denominated in food grains, either in the form of baked bread (*nān-i pukhta*), as bulgur (*balqūr*), parched cracked wheat, or as unspecified cereal grains (*ghalla*). The assumption is that the recipients took *barāt*s or vouchers from the finance officials and either exchanged the vouchers for a discounted cash amount from brokers or presented the vouchers to government bakeries. None of this can be documented at this time, however.

is subject to the inevitable path of deterioration and depreciation from the moment of creation. An endowment is a kind of closed system that is expected to produce a certain output or yield with no further inputs of capital. But, from the moment of its creation, maintaining the expected output requires more input—labor or new capital. It is obviously essential to continually spend some of the yield of the capital on its own maintenance, and that reinvestment reduces the expected yield to the beneficiaries. In the case of the endowment of the *khirqa* shrine complex, continual inputs of labor were necessary for the maintenance of the irrigation system that formed the principal endowment capital of the shrine complex (shrine building, tomb building, and mosque/ *madrasa*). And the need for that labor generated resistance from those expected to provide it. The tools of coercion or influence were generally not in the hands of the shrine administrators, and the ability to overcome resistance, whether in compelling the Durrānī tribes living in Aḥmad Shāh's new city to provide free labor on the irrigation system, or to prevent unwarranted claims on the yield of the endowment, meant a continual interaction with those who commanded the forces of compulsion, i.e. those who had military and police power behind them. As these forces were often in flux in Qandahar, to maintain their positions and thus their incomes the shrine administrators had to be in regular and constant contact with whoever was perceived as holding predominant power. However, those who could deploy the forces of coercion, the governors and garrison commanders, were not entirely autonomous. They also had superiors to whom they had to answer and so, despite an assumed wish to maintain the integrity of the shrine and the sacred purpose supported by the endowment, they may not always have been able to give the shrine administrators their wholehearted backing.

As time passed, the personal interests of the Ākhūndzāda family probably began to take precedence—indeed if they had not always done so—over the institutional interests of the shrine. We have no way of knowing at this point how long the practice lasted of providing meals of bulgur and lamb, and the daily distribution of this seemingly enormous amount of bread. The tenor of the various *farmān*s reconfirming rights and the terms of the endowment emphasize the rights of the administrators to be paid rather than the rights of the beneficiaries, the poor and indigent, to be fed. Factors beyond the control of the administrators, notably drought, impacted their ability to meet the requirements of the endowment deed, and as the lands on which the endowment depended became less productive, as was inevitably the case, the chief trustee would have been forced to make changes in the distributions. The evidence we have suggests—and this would be perfectly reasonable—that the highest priority for ensuring the longevity of the family was ensuring the longevity of the shrine that gave the family its raison d'être, its fiduciary role. The perception of what constituted the wellbeing of the family seems to have evolved from enjoying high regard in the intellectual community to preserving the wealth gained through serving as managers and trustees of the shrine complex. We cannot be certain how the chief trustee, his family, and the wider circle of relatives were compensated after the documentation peters out on their role as trustees of the shrine. However, the very fact that the same family continued in authority indicates that their compensation must have been considered at least adequate and well worth protecting. Furthermore, we have signs that over the years the family had acquired certain fiscal privileges over and above any stipends associated with the shrine administration, privileges that the government felt compelled to reconfirm whenever the holder petitioned that those rights were being infringed upon. Stewardship of the shrine clearly brought with it opportunities for gaining certain monetary advantages, perhaps as a reward for services rendered at some point to a political figure in need of support. We are left with drawing inferences from what little textual evidence remains for the Ākhūndzāda family.

ʿAbd al-Raḥmān Khān and the Ākhūndzāda Family

Although ʿAbd al-Raḥmān Khān's first involvement with the *khirqa* shrine dates to the earliest days of his reign (see below), the first sign of his willingness to protect the fiscal rights of the family dates to the time shortly after he had returned from Rawalpindi where, following the Russian takeover of Panjdih, a very distant outpost claimed by the Afghans and now situated in southeastern Turkmenistan, an agreement of mutual defense had been reached with the British. That spring he had received a petition from a member of the Ākhūndzāda family concerning what he felt were violations of privileges he enjoyed. In Shaʿbān 1302/May-June 1885 the *amīr* sent a *farmān* to the police and postal station at Dih Ḥājjī, a village 28 kilometers southeast of Qandahar.[35] It said:

> To the postal service (*dākī*) of the police post (*tahāna*) at Dih Ḥājjī—Ghulām Jān Ākhūndzāda, ʿAṭā Muḥammad Bārakzāʾī, and Bahāʾ al-Dīn—may you all be well! Concerning requisitions in kind (*suyūrsāt*) on

35 Muḥammad Ḥakīm Nāhiż, *Qāmūs-i jughrāfiyāʾī-yi Afghānistān*, 4 vols. (Kabul: Anjuman-i Āryānā Dāʾirat al-Maʿārif, 1336/1957), vol. 2, 286 (henceforth *Qāmūs-i jughrāfiyā*).

> ʿAbdullāh Jān Ākhūndzāda of Mālikī Sūkhta,[36] specifically that portion of the requisitions on the aforementioned *ākhūndzāda* that is levied for the postal service, you are not to interfere with that person, but you are to leave him alone because the *ākhūndzāda* has been and is exempt from all requisitions. It is necessary for us to find another place for you to get your requisitions, and you are not to demand more (from him). Consider this settled and do not disobey.[37]

Dih Ḥājjī appears on the Soviet General staff map "Kandahar" (H-41-VI) as "Khadzhidih" (Ḥājjī Dih) lying west of the modern road heading toward Chaman and the border with Pakistan. The village of Mālikī Sūkhta could well be the same as one labeled "Sokhtaii Mukhammedkhak Akhund" lying just four kilometers to the west of Dih Ḥājjī on the same map. The police post would have served as a rest house for postal runners about a day's journey out of Qandahar. Such dak-posts, as well as customs posts (*bandar*s) with their garrisons of irregular troops (Sākhlū or *khāṣṣa-dār*s) were scattered around the country and were required to get their food supplies from the local populace, although a few cultivated the lands around their posts. All were obliged to pay for what they requisitioned, but since they had to eat and their own pay was sometimes slow in coming, the requisitions may often have been made with IOUs. Even if they were paid, the farmers were not always happy to have to sell to the government, particularly if payment was not immediately forthcoming, as we will see.

Although ʿAbdullāh Jān Ākhūndzāda is not identified here as connected in any way with the shrine, the fact that Fūfalzāʾī found this document at the shrine is some evidence that he may be the same ʿAbdullāh Ākhūndzāda who was the *mutawallī* mentioned in a December 1873 *farmān* issued by Amīr Shayr ʿAlī Khān in which his rights as chief trustee were confirmed against a counterclaim.[38]

ʿAbd al-Raḥmān Khān issued a similar edict in August of 1894 addressed to the clerk (*nawīsanda*) and the officer in charge (*żābiṭ*) of the customs post of

---

36 The adjective "*sūkhta*," which literally means "burnt," also has the meaning in Afghanistan of being exempt from certain taxes. See Mohammad Nasim Neghat, ed., *Qāmūs-i Darī-Inglīsī / Dari-English Dictionary* (Omaha: Center for Afghanistan Studies, 1993), s.v. (henceforth *Dari-English Dictionary*).

37 Fūfalzāʾī, *Tārīkh-i Khirqat*, 143.

38 Fūfalzāʾī, *Tārīkh-i Khirqat*, 102–103; facsimile on p. 105.

Takhta Pul, which also stood on the Qandahar-Chaman-Quetta road about 25 kilometers beyond Dih Ḥājjī in the direction of Chaman and Quetta (Shālkūt).[39]

> To Muḥammad Ibrāhīm Khān *żābiṭ* and Mīrzā ʿAlī Jān Khān *nawīsanda* at the customs post of Takhta Pul, may you enjoy good health! At this time Muḥammad Aslam Ākhūndzāda and ʿAṭā Muḥammad Ākhūndzāda of Ḥājjī Dih and Pāyanda Khayl Sukhta have stated, "Since ancient times we have been exempt from taxation so that *sūrsāt* (i.e., *suyūrsāt*) and *chighāt* requisitions were never levied on us. Now they are taking *sūrsāt* from us for the *khāṣṣa-dār*s (the irregular infantry) at Takhta Pul. Although they pay a fair price nevertheless it is a burden on us." Thus it is now decreed in writing that you should identify five other men from the tribes (from whom to levy the *sūrsāt*). You should be aware of anyone who has been annually exempted and wherever this is the case you should not impose demands. Wherever it is not the case, you should very carefully examine whatever the tribes show that pertains to these things. However it happens, you must not act for personal ends (*gharażdār nabāshīd*). You will pay for the grain for which you will get a voucher (*barāt*) and not consume God's creatures. The end. Consider this final (*tākīd bi-dāna(n)d*). Written Ṣafar al-Muẓaffar 1312/August 1894.[40]

Ḥājjī Dih and Dih Ḥājjī are unquestionably the same place, the former the Pashto form of the name, the latter the Persian. Pāyanda Khayl Sukhta cannot be identified yet, but obviously was in the requisitioning area of the Takhta Pul customs post.[41]

A year later in Ṣafar 1313/August 1895, Amīr ʿAbd al-Raḥmān Khān had occasion to warn off other officials attempting to collect taxes and fees from which the Ākhūndzāda family was exempt. This involved the village of Paymāl, probably the same as present-day Pīr Paymāl, a village just to the west-south-west of Qandahar City on the Arghandāb River.[42] The *farmān* reads:

---

39 This is the location of Takhta Pul (Bridge of Planks) on the "Afghanistan" 1:1,500,000 map (Albuquerque, New Mexico: Ayazi Publishing, 2001), and the USSR General Staff Map "Takhtapul" (H-41-XII). *Qāmūs-i jughrāfiyā*, vol. 1, 388 seems not to identify this Takhta Pul, but has one in the district of Arghastān east of Qandahar and far north of the location shown on the maps.

40 Fūfalzāʾī, *Tārīkh-i Khirqat*, 144.

41 There is "Payenda Kalay" briefly described in *Gaz* 5, s.v., which would have been roughly in the region serving Takhta Pul.

42 The village was the scene of fierce fighting on September 1, 1880 between the armies of General Frederick Roberts and Sardār Muḥammad Ayyūb Khān, son of Amīr Shayr ʿAlī

> To the officials and *maliks* of the village of Paymāl. May it be absolutely clear concerning Aḥmad Jān Ākhūndzāda and Ghulām Qādir Ākhūndzāda, *mutawallīs* of the blessed *khirqa* shrine who live in that village: they have a document sealed by a previous government that states that except for *māliya* (property tax) they are free from all other imposts such as *suyūrsāt* (requisitions) and the village fine for murder for which the people of that village have previously been billed. They therefore should not subject these *ākhūndzādas* to the *suyūrsāt* and other imposts and should collect the *māliya* from them in accordance with the official assessment. Know that this is final. Only. Written Saturday in Ṣafar 1313/ August 1895.[43]

It is probably fair to assume at this point that administration of the shrine was decidedly beneficial for the longevity of the Ākhūndzāda family. Not only did its members enjoy salaries for managing and maintaining the shrine as well as dealing with the government over infringement on the rights of the shrine, but they also seem to have been acquiring personal fiscal privileges that had nothing to do with the shrine. Resembling to some degree the "dynastic family" model proposed by George Marcus, the Ākhūndzādas did not so much "transform hereditary wealth into capital"[44] through the legal instrument of the trust as use the trust first to transform an appointed administrative position into a hereditary one, and then to acquire permanent personal fiscal privileges separate from those of the institution being managed.

With the privilege came responsibilities. The wider "family" included those religious scholars guaranteed food rations from the endowment income who, we might reasonably assume, passed those rights on to their heirs. In addition to looking after these individuals and all the other employees of the shrine complex, the trustees had to maintain close communication with those who had the power to interfere in and disrupt their administrations (the *amīr*, the governor, and fiscal officials). But there was a certain degree of mutual dependence. The shrine was a powerful Islamic symbol, and just as it was important for its managers to maintain good relations with those holding political power,

---

Khān. See (Lord) Frederick Roberts of Kandahar, *Forty-One Years in India*, 2 vols. (London: Richard Bentley and Son, 1897; henceforth "Roberts"), vol. 2, 362ff.; Howard Hensman, *The Afghan War of 1879–80* (New Delhi: Lancer, 2008; reprint of the London edition of 1881), 502ff.

43 Fūfalzā'ī, *Tārīkh-i Khirqat*, 143–144.

44 R. D. McChesney, *Central Asia: Foundations of Change* (Princeton: The Darwin Press, 1996), 75.

it was equally important for politicians to show their devotion to the shrine and to the Ākhūndzāda family.

While the above edicts suggest that the *amīr* was concerned with protecting rights acquired by the Ākhūndzāda family over the years, there is evidence that at the same time he was taking a harder line when it came to property rights that had been gradually acquired along the Nahr-i Aḥmad Shāhī, the great canal that provided the financial backbone of the shrine. We know that some of the lands watered by the canal were private, or already dedicated to some defined use, and were specifically excluded from the endowment deed of 1782.[45] Others, though not excluded from the *waqf* endowment, were bought and sold over the years to the point that their status as private lands was taken for granted.

The information that we have about the *amīr*'s policy regarding the lands watered by the Nahr-i Aḥmad Shāhī comes from quite a different source. Under the terms of the agreement by which the British backed ʿAbd al-Raḥmān Khān for the emirate throne in 1880, the British were allowed to maintain representatives at Kabul, Qandahar, and Herat. These representatives (*wakīl*s), also known as news writers (*wāqiʿa-nigār*s), were not Englishmen but Indian Muslims and were, for the most part, if not exclusively, Shīʿīs. Their responsibility was to gather information locally, as best they could, and file a weekly report. In the case of the Qandahar *wakīl*, the report was sent to the English commissioner of Baluchistan who resided in Shālkūt (Quetta). There the report was first translated into English and then handed to the commissioner. They were eventually published as *Kandahar Newsletters*. A newsletter dated August 31, 1885 from the British representative in Qandahar, Sayyid Mīr Hāshim, reported that he had heard that the *amīr* had ordered the confiscation of the lands and gardens watered by the "Shāhī Nahr," claiming the canal was crown property and people had no authority to take water from it. The news writer also noted that among those affected were "lands in the possession of the priests of the Khirka Sharif."[46] No further information is given as to how, or even whether,

---

45 Fūfalzāʾī, *Tārīkh-i Khirqat*, 49–50. These included properties for which their names tell us that they were garden estates or parks (*bāghs*)—Bāgh-i Dīwānkhāna (Chancellery Park), Bāgh-i Ḥaramsarāy (Harem Park), Anār Bāgh (Pomegranate Garden), Majlis Bāgh (Council Park), and Manzil Bāgh (Residence Park, constructed by Aḥmad Shāh for his own use). All but Anār Bāgh were likely to have been crown lands, or in the case of Bāgh-i Ḥaramsarāy and Manzil Bāgh, the private property of Aḥmad Shāh and his family.

46 Directorate of the Archives Department, Government of Baluchistan, *Kandahar Newsletters*, Quetta, Pakistan, 10 vols., Second Edition, 1990 (henceforth *Kandahar Newsletters*), volume 2, newsletter no. 30, 215.

those lands were ever reclaimed for the crown. If the British news writer's report was accurate, which should not be taken for granted given the constraints under which these representatives lived and their need to report something each week, the decree reflects the complicated nature of ownership and usage of the water rights of the canal. Given the otherwise consistent position of the *amīr* on the inviolability of property and fiscal rights, it is difficult to take the news writer's report too literally. In all probability, the *amīr* was concerned with governmental rights that had at one time existed but had been usurped over the course of time by private interests.

The Shrine as Sacred Space

The sacred relic and the shrine that housed it instantly became sacred space with associated powers. For Aḥmad Shāh, the hope was that the cloak itself would play a practical and utilitarian role to ensure his future victories and to protect him within its sacral aura and the blessings it was understood to give. Somewhat surprisingly he did not try to keep it in close proximity to his person wherever he went as, for example, the Ottoman sultan Aḥmad I (r. 1603–1617) did with the Prophet's mantle in possession of the Ottoman household.[47] Given the fact that cancer caused the Afghan *shāh* increasingly severe pain during the last four years of his life, it seems somewhat surprising that he did not keep the cloak with him. In fact, he might have done so, although the tradition is that it was housed in a new mosque built in his new city.

For Tīmūr Shāh, who did the most to give lasting form to the shrine complex and provide it with an enduring, if not unchallenged, endowment, the shrine was first and foremost a site for commemoration of his father, Aḥmad Shāh, whose tomb forms part of the complex. He apparently came to view or was compelled to see the *khirqa*-cloak as inextricably linked to his father's legacy. If there was any hint that he wanted to move the *khirqa* to Kabul when he decided to make that city his capital, such a desire has to be inferred from the reported disquiet about moving the cloak once it was in Qandahar. But the fact that he placed his father's grave off-center in the mausoleum suggests that he always intended the *khirqa* to remain in Qandahar. A controversy about moving it would be reflected in a reported *fatwā*, from the *ʿulamā* of Qandahar during Tīmūr Shāh's time, against its movement. Later still Amīr Ḥabībullāh

---

47 Nurhan Atasoy, "Khirḳa-yi Sharīf," *Encyclopaedia of Islam*, New Edition, V, 18–19.

Khān gave as a rationale for the *fatwā* the desire of the *ʿulamā* that the cloak not become "a plaything in the hands of sultans" (*bāzīcha-yi dast-i salāṭīn*).[48]

The shrine and its grounds evolved as a sacred space within the new cityscape of Qandahar (the Ashraf al-Bilād-i Aḥmad Shāhī) and offered very practical solutions to everyday problems, the first being physical sustenance. Tīmūr Shāh's endowment of the Nahr-i Aḥmad Shāhī and the agriculture it supported appears to have been deliberately made to address a real social problem, endemic hunger exacerbated by recurrent famine. There were many other choices he could have made for his endowment—stipends for *ʿulamā*, building maintenance, scholarships for students at the *madrasa* that was built at the complex, and salaries for their teachers. All of these would later be added. But instead he (and his brothers) chose to subsidize food. The 1782 deed of endowment mentions unspecified amounts of cracked wheat (*bulqūr*, bulgur) as the sole benefit from the endowment aside from administrative fees. By later *farmān*, the food to be distributed would also include the equivalent of 350 pounds per day of baked bread, and a meal of roast lamb on Fridays. It is difficult to imagine that this was a purely whimsical decision but must have been inspired by the real plight of the poor of the city.

Another very practical need that the shrine answered was the ultimate in protection, a kind of last resort against oppressive behavior by forces beyond the control of the individual. This was sanctuary, or at least the promise of sanctuary. The Persian (Darī) term for sanctuary in Afghanistan is *bast* and one "sits *bast*" (*bast nishīn gashtan*) or "chooses *bast*" (*dar bast guzīdan*). We know by the time of Amīr ʿAbd al-Raḥmān Khān that it was a well-established tradition, and that the shrine complex offered protection for individuals against forces that threatened them in some way. I have found only one report of the use of the shrine complex as a sanctuary that dates to a time before the reign of Amīr ʿAbd al-Raḥmān Khān, but it is a telling one and suggests that the tradition of sanctuary began with the founding of the shrine.

One of the two histories contemporary with the Sadūzāī period, Imām al-Dīn Ḥusaynī's *Tārīkh-i Ḥusaynī*, which was completed by 1798, never mentions the *khirqa* at all (the author was writing in Lucknow and there is no clear sign that he ever set foot beyond the Indus River), but at one point in his narrative he digresses a bit to write:

> They say that the Durrānīs and the descendants (*awlād*) of that sovereign (Aḥmad Shāh) have the following custom concerning the grave of that *shāh* in whom religion takes refuge, that when someone commits a

48 Fayż Muḥammad, *History*, vol. 1, 28. No such *fatwā* is known to survive.

> serious crime, anything other than murder, if he sits at the grave of that *pādshāh* he will be granted security from being killed and from (other) condign punishment (*siyāsat*). Consequently, many people, both high-born and low-, have sat at the head of that paradise-dwelling *pādshāh*, whether during the reign of the late Tīmūr Shāh or during that of Shāh Zamān—may his kingdom endure—and by the grace of God have found security and saved their own lives.[49]

Perhaps for the Durrānīs, it was the grave of Aḥmad Shāh that had the power to extend sanctuary, but it seems far more likely that it was the *khirqa* at the grave of Aḥmad Shāh that was seen to have that power. The reported reverence with which the cloak was greeted as it made its way from Badakhshān to Qandahar in 1768, leaving *qadamgāhs* (sites that became sacred as a result of its alighting there), would suggest that the cloak offered sanctuary by its very presence, however fleeting. It is not, however, until the reign of Amīr ʿAbd al-Raḥmān Khān that we find reported instances of specific sanctuary-taking as distinct from Imām al-Dīn Ḥusaynī's more general report. The fact that there are so many instances of *bast* under ʿAbd al-Raḥmān Khān's regime (1880–1901) may be taken as a sign of the effective extension of central state control to Qandahar associated with his reign, and the natural resistance to it. The problem for the outsider is that the evidence of sanctuary-seeking arises almost exclusively when the state becomes involved and creates a record of it. Everyday disputes in which sanctuary might have been sought—a wife from an abusive spouse, a debtor from a creditor, two lovers from an outraged spouse or an offended family or tribe, or an army deserter in protest of an officer's heavy handedness—might well have been resolved without Kabul's involvement or, more importantly, since almost all the records we do have involved the government in Kabul, i.e., the *amīr*, problems resolved locally have left almost no surviving record. The one exception is the weekly reporting of the British representative in Qandahar. His reports, no doubt largely based on hearsay, but still not easily dismissed, provide perhaps a more populist view of not only the use of the shrine as sanctuary but also its use in stirring sectarian sentiments. The records that do survive raise the possibility that beyond what was recorded, there was a hidden world of sanctuary-takers who achieved their ends without leaving a documentary trail.

People seeking sanctuary at the Shrine of the Cloak for whom records do exist took it for a number of different reasons. In some cases it was to protest what they felt was extortion on the part of tax officials. In a complicated case,

---

49 *TH*, 142–143.

dating to the spring of 1897, the chief finance officer (*sar daftar*) of Qandahar wrote to the *amīr* complaining about the poor performance of two men who held the tax concession for Qandahar's revenues. One of the illegal things they had done, he explains, was to charge the Hindus of Qandahar an excessive rate of taxation for the *jizya* (head tax on non-Muslims), levying 16 rupees per head, which was much higher than what had been agreed upon with the government. As a consequence, he notes, the Hindu merchants had taken *bast* at the Shrine of the Cloak.[50] How this was settled is hinted at in the explanation given by the concession-holders that commerce had increased considerably and the Hindus could well afford to pay the higher *jizya*. This may have been the same case reported in 1897 by the British representative, Dilawar Ali Shah, whose informants gave him a different story. They reported to him, and he passed it on in one of his newsletters, that the reason "fifty Hindu merchants" took sanctuary at the shrine was because they "were ordered to pay taxes in the coin of the realm instead of in Kabuli."[51] What he meant by "coin of the realm" is uncertain, but it probably referred to the Indian rupee. One must keep in mind that the phrase "coin of the realm" was not Dilawar Ali Shah's but that of his translator in Quetta. Since the Kābulī rupee was the coin of the Afghan realm, what Dilawar Ali Shah was most likely referring to was English coinage, i.e. the Indian rupee known in Afghanistan as the "*kalladār*" "*kāldār*," or "*chihra-shāhī*" (the "head" or "face" rupee with the English sovereign's image). The translator probably knew he could safely call the English rupee "coin of the realm" and not risk misleading his readership.

This was not the only case of Hindus taking sanctuary at the shrine. Sayyid Nūr Muḥammad Shāh Khān, the prime minister (*ṣadr-i aʿẓam*) for Amīr Shayr ʿAlī Khān, who was deceased by this time, had reportedly deposited 64,590 rupees with a Qandahārī Hindu moneychanger, Dīwān Shankū. In 1894, Sayyid Nūr Muḥammad's son sent the government documentation showing that this money was government money and so a bill was issued to the moneychanger. In July 1894, unwilling and probably unable to pay the sum, Dīwān Shankū took sanctuary at the shrine with his family. According to Fayż Muḥammad, he was tricked into leaving the shrine, at which point pressure was brought to bear and the money was collected from him and from his relatives.[52]

Another similar case, in which a Hindu banker took refuge at the shrine, dates to February 1895. The *amīr*, ʿAbd al-Raḥmān Khān, had been told that the banker was in possession of one lakh of rupees which had been deposited

---

50 Fayż Muḥammad, *History, tatimma* to vol. 3, 78.

51 *Kandahar Newsletters*, vol. 7, no. 3, 6.

52 Fayż Muḥammad, *History*, vol. 3, 1016.

with him by a now deceased sayyid. When he took sanctuary, his relatives were arrested, according to a report from the British representative, Dilawar Ali Shah. The British news writer was new to Qandahar at the time and was clearly intrigued by the power of the shrine to provide sanctuary. So he added a note to his report describing the function of the shrine, which he clearly had little understanding of. It is, he says (or as he was translated), "a Muḥammadan sanctuary in Kandahar and one who is involved (in a financial transaction) and is unable to pay the debt takes refuge in the shrine and is thus considered free from liability."[53] This was hardly the case, as the reported arrest of the banker's relatives indicates.

The question "whose shrine was it?" is implicit in one incident involving a Hindu refuge-seeker in the spring of 1903. A thief, identified as a Hindu, took sanctuary at the shrine. The news first reached the chief secretary (*mīr munshī*) of the governor. The religious loyalties of the secretary, Mīrzā Fayż Muḥammad, except for his being Muslim, unfortunately cannot be deduced from his name, or the incident might have had sectarian overtones. When he heard of the Hindu thief's taking refuge, he was heard to say with some exasperation, "This *dharamsāl* (i.e., *dharamshala*, a Hindu sanctuary) doesn't do the government any good." Some Afghans and Muḥammadzā'īs who overheard him were incensed and drew their swords to punish the insult of referring to the Shrine of the Cloak as a *dharamsāl*. With considerable difficulty, the *mīrzā* escaped and hid himself in the citadel. The governor suspended him from his duties awaiting orders from the *amīr* as to what to do with him. The *qāżī* of Qandahar also issued a decree pronouncing him an unbeliever (*kāfir*).[54] His ultimate fate is unknown.

The vast majority of sanctuary-seekers were Muslims, of course, and sometimes they crowded the place. The sanctuary or *ḥaram* area was fairly large and defined by the perimeter wall (*muḥawwaṭa*). Perhaps with some exaggeration, the British news writer, Dilawar Ali Shah, wrote in his twenty-fifth newsletter of 1895 of the crowd of people currently in sanctuary at the shrine complex:

> Were it not for the shrine of Khirka-i-Sharif, the local jails would have been full. Some 800–1,000 men are at present sheltering in the shrine pending the arrival of Sardar Nasralla Khan [second son of Amīr ʿAbd al-Raḥmān Khān] whom they contemplate petitioning on his arrival at Kandahar. Hindus and Musalmans take shelter in the shrine and, as already noted, the law cannot touch them so long as they remain there.

53 *Kandahar Newsletters*, volume 7, 6, newsletter no. 3.

54 *Kandahar Newsletters*, volume 10, "diary of 16 September 1903," 53–54.

> A few days ago the Governor posted orderlies on the gates of the shrine with orders to arrest anyone entering or issuing from the gates. As the general opinion was that the Governor's illness (a stroke) was due to this action, the orderlies were withdrawn.[55]

Sanctuary, however was by no means sacrosanct. The *amīr* had long since shown his willingness to violate the principle of absolute sanctuary. At the very outset of his reign in 1881 ʿAbd al-Raḥmān Khān confronted some enemies who took sanctuary at the shrine. That year he had to deal with one of the two most serious challenges to his claim to the throne, the counter-claim of his cousin, Sardār Muḥammad Ayyūb Khān, a son of the late Amīr Shayr ʿAlī Khān. The *sardar* had made his mark and enjoyed strong backing because of his military success against the British. The year before, he had led a force from his governorship at Herat to meet and defeat a British army at Maywand (Maymand), a village just west of Qandahar, on July 27, 1880.[56] Despite being repulsed in September by another British force, he took possession of Qandahar in the late autumn when the British withdrew their forces to India and gave up their plans to make Qandahar a British-backed princely state. From Kabul, ʿAbd al-Raḥmān had to confront Muḥammad Ayyūb before the latter could assemble forces in his turn to march against Kabul. In Qandahar, according to Fayż Muḥammad:

> One of the ulema, Akhūndzadah ʿAbd al-Rahim Kakari ... along with a few other ulema ... issued a fatwa which said "To support Sardar Muhammad Ayyub Khan is to aid the religion and to fight against Amir ʿAbd al-Rahman Khan and his troops is to preserve the Shariʿah of the Lord of the Prophets because the English have named him amir while Sardar Muhammad Ayyub Khan knotted the sacred garment of jihad and triumphed over the English army at the battle of Maymand and scattered it."[57]

But in the subsequent confrontation at Qandahar, ʿAbd al-Raḥmān prevailed in battle against Muḥammad Ayyūb and, according to his problematic autobiography, he dealt swiftly with those who had the temerity to pronounce him a *kāfir*:

---

55 *Kandahar Newsletters*, volume 7, 46–47.

56 Roberts, *Forty-One Years*, vol. 2, 334.

57 Fayż Muḥammad, *History*, vol. 3, 381–382. See Kakar, *Afghanistan*, 71–80 for a much more detailed account of the confrontation.

> One of the priests who had accused me of infidelity, named Abdul Rahim Akhund, Kakar (a tribe of Kandahar) had hidden himself under the Prophet's robe. I ordered that an impure-minded dog such as he should not remain in that sacred sanctuary; he was accordingly pulled out of that building, and I killed him with my own hands.[58]

By 1895 the *amīr*, not having forcibly removed anyone else to that point—although cutting off food and water to those taking refuge was not unheard of—decided to set limits on sanctuary-taking. In that year, confronted with a group of sanctuary-seeking Qandahar officials who had reportedly swindled the government out of hundreds of thousands of rupees, or so it was claimed by someone sent from Kabul to investigate corruption, the *amīr* issued a decree setting new policy on taking sanctuary. Asserting that corrupt officials were polluting the shrine by seeking sanctuary there, he ordered them removed by force and then set limits on legitimate sanctuary-seeking. Henceforth, he wrote:

> I inform the people of Qandahar that if there is a problem among them, other than a governmental issue, and they should take refuge at the Holy Cloak so that perhaps their adversary, out of regard for the cloak's sanctity, will forgive them, that's fine and there is no barrier to entering within the walls of the Cloak. But if tax assessors or collectors, murderers, fornicators, traitors, or violators of the Shariʿah or governmental regulations should enter and take sanctuary with the Cloak, they should be expelled forthwith and held to account, in accordance with the Holy Law, and whatever is required after a review of their account books.[59]

And from that point on, at least as long as he lived (until October 1901), those who were excluded from the protection of sanctuary by the terms of his decree were forcibly removed or in some cases starved out.

58 Sultan Mahomed Khan, *The Life of Abdur Rahman*, vol. 1, 216. One is uncertain what weight to put on this as it does not appear in the published *Pandnāma* (which stops at a point corresponding to p. 192 of *The Life of Abdur Rahman*). Mahmud Tarzi, who was a teenager in Qandahar at the time and whose family would be expelled from Afghanistan by ʿAbd al-Raḥmān, conjures up this episode in his reminiscences written in 1933 in a thoroughly melodramatic fashion complete with dialogue and vivid butchery. See Mahmud Tarzi, *Reminiscences: A Short History of an Era (1869–1881)*, edited by Wahid Tarzi, Afghanistan Forum, Occasional Paper No. 36, March 1998, 30–31.

59 Fayż Muḥammad, *History*, vol. 3, 1088–1089.

The British news writer in Qandahar, Mīr Hāshim, relates that forcible removal from the shrine was not unheard of even long before the *amīr*'s 1895 policy. Ten years earlier, he reported:

> Since the time of Ahmad Shah, the Khirka Sharif at Kandahar has been bast (place of refuge) for the people of Afghanistan. Anyone, though guilty of a heinous offense punishable with death, who entered the Khirka Sharif was safe and would not be brought out by order of any Governor. Lately however the present Governor accused a Sahibzada of retaining the property of Syed Nur Muhammad's son and the Sahibzada took bast in the Khirka Sharif yet the Governor sent 15 orderlies and had him forcibly removed thence and beaten with about 300 sticks until he fainted. There were one or two hundred people present but none dared utter a word. The people are all complaining and the leading men say among themselves that they had suffered enough from worldly troubles but that now their religion was also interfered with.[60]

Amīr ʿAbd al-Raḥmān Khān himself was involved in a personal case of sanctuary-seeking that was not covered by either of the two situations his proclamation foresaw. It involved his brother-in-law, Shāhzāda Jahāngīr Khān, the son of Mīr Jahāndār Shāh, father of the *amīr*'s first wife, Bībī Jān, who bore him no surviving children. Shāhzāda Jahāngīr Khān had been forced into internal exile in Qandahar from his homeland of Badakhshān because of an uprising there against the *amīr*. He came to suffer from mental illness and in May of 1899 became so deranged that his wife and children took refuge at the shrine to escape him. The *amīr* was surprisingly compassionate in his response, instructing the governor of Qandahar not to treat his brother-in-law as a madman (which would have meant incarceration), but to try and find some cure. Nor was he to suspend his stipend nor that of his brothers, who also had been removed from Badakhshān, "lest they be demeaned and embarrassed."[61]

That same year, the British news writer reported in May that so many "refugees from justice" had taken sanctuary at the shrine that the *amīr* ordered them forcibly removed. Fayż Muḥammad did not report that particular *farmān*, but cites one issued in July that was certainly connected to the same episode of *bast*-taking. A collector reported to the *amīr* that a massive bill for taxes owed

---

60 *Kandahar Newsletters*, volume 2, newsletter 36, 9 November 1885. This has some of the same features of the case involving Sayyid Nūr Muḥammad Khān mentioned by Fayż Muḥammad; see note 49.

61 Fayż Muḥammad, *History*, vol. 4, 295.

by tax concessionaires and sent from the Bureau of Audits was driving guarantors of the concessionaires to take sanctuary in the Shrine of the Cloak. Administrative policy required that any person applying for a government position where some fiduciary responsibility was involved (and this included tax concessionaires) had to provide guarantors in the event of defaulting on sums they owed. The *amīr* responded to the report in an explosion of fury blaming the governor, the chief finance officer, and the collector for giving concessions out to people who were not of sufficiently high birth, did not have the financial resources in the event they were unable to make good on their contractual obligations, or did not have well-heeled guarantors behind them. He vowed that if they (the governor, chief finance officer, and collector) did not collect those arrears themselves, he would take it from them and their families. We are told that on receipt of this menacing decree, "the Qandahar officials became fearful, forsook their personal agendas, undertook to collect the arrears, gathered the bulk of them, and deposited them in the treasury."[62]

Financial reasons or abuse of some sort were by no means the only reasons for taking sanctuary. In May of 1896, some soldiers from the Herati Regular Infantry Regiment stationed in Qandahar took refuge at the shrine. Some of them had fallen in love with three "beardless" youths who were bandsmen (*muzīkchīs*) in the regiment. When jealousy arose over the affections of these boys and fighting erupted among the soldiers, the regimental commander, Brigadier Muḥammad Ṣādiq Khān, transferred the bandsmen to the Nūrzāʾī Regular Infantry Regiment, which enraged their lovers, and they managed to incite twenty-two officers of the regiment to mutiny against the brigadier. They probably had other grievances as well, for in a cathartic moment of rage they assaulted the brigadier with sticks and stones as well as verbal abuse. But then, "having released the knot of indignation and anger from their hearts by this loutish behavior," chastened and fearing retribution, the mutineers took sanctuary at the shrine. One of the men involved in the mutiny, who had not joined the others taking *bast* at the shrine, went to the governor and got him and other officials to go to the shrine and try to persuade the men to leave. When they asked the sanctuary-sitters why they had taken refuge, they were ashamed of the real reason for their uprising against Brigadier Muḥammad Ṣādiq Khān and so they told the officials that he had treated them badly and that they were rioting against his oppression. On receiving a report of their claim, the *amīr* ordered the brigadier, his officers, and the mutineers to come to Kabul. Eventually, the brigadier was cleared of the charge of oppressive behavior and restored to his unit; some of the troublemakers were executed,

62 Ibid., 331–332.

and the rest had their eyes put out and were paraded in chains to Turkistan and Herat to serve as examples of the fate of soldiers who mutinied.[63]

Sometimes it was only thought necessary to threaten *bast* to achieve some purpose. On at least one occasion the threat of seeking sanctuary at the *khirqa* shrine was used only as a pretext to attain another goal. During the latter part of Amīr ʿAbd al-Raḥmān Khān's reign and through much of Amīr Ḥabībullāh Khān's, the government followed a policy of encouraging immigration (*hijrat*) from British India by Pashtun tribes and settled them primarily on Hazāra lands. Hazāras would continually appeal to the *amīr*s about the unjustified confiscation of their lands for the *muhājir*s, but to little effect. One of the chief administrators of this policy of resettlement was the *qāżī* of Qandahar, ʿAbd al-Shakūr Khān, the son of the governor of Herat, Qāżī Saʿd al-Dīn Khān, and a member of the Bārakzāʾī tribe of which the Muḥammadzāʾī were a branch. According to Fayż Muḥammad, himself Hazāra and no admirer of Qāżī ʿAbd al-Shakūr, the *qāżī* devised the plan of having the *muhājir*s complain to the *amīr* that he (the *qāżī*) was oppressing them by not giving them the Hazāra lands they were entitled to, and that they were going to have to take sanctuary at the Shrine of the Cloak unless something was done. The *qāżī* thought, according to Fayż Muḥammad, that such a complaint would discredit any Hazāra appeals against his settlement of *muhājir*s on their lands, and would make it seem as if he, the *qāżī*, were protecting the Hazāras.[64]

Amīr Ḥabībullāh Khān, in this as in other policies of his father, was inclined to take each case on its own merits. One such involved a kebab seller, Ghulām, working on the street in Qandahar. A sudden burst of snapping and sizzling sounds caused by his sprinkling water on his roasting kebabs startled a string of passing camels and they stampeded, injuring the chief finance officer (*sar daftar*) of the province, a Hindu named Dīwān Nand Laʿl, who was just then walking through the market. Ghulām claimed the angry Dīwān Nand Laʿl cursed him, a Muslim, and that this amounted to a violation of the Sharīʿa. Then in a confrontation in the *sar daftar*'s office, the kebab-seller in turn cursed the Hindu by saying, "I'll see you ride a cow." Considering this to be blasphemy against his religion, the chief finance officer complained to the governor, who ordered the kebab-seller arrested. The chief finance officer, who had powerful Muslim allies, denied that he had cursed Ghulām, and the latter, fearing punishment, took sanctuary at the *khirqa* shrine and appealed to the *amīr*. Having considered the case, Amīr Ḥabībullāh Khān, on August 2, 1904, ordered that Ghulām be fined 5,000 rupees for his anti-Hindu remarks, but he

63 Fayż Muḥammad 3, 1214; *tatimma*, 2.

64 Ibid., 4, 756.

was not forcibly ejected from the shrine. Instead, the governor was to make sure he had no food or water, and, when he eventually came out, to collect the fine from him.[65]

Royal Patronage of the Shrine: The Contributions of Prince Naṣrullāh Khān

Royal involvement with the shrine was by no means limited to issues of sanctuary. Whenever the royal person or a member of the royal family, or in later times, the presidents of the Democratic Republic or the Islamic Republic of Afghanistan, visited Mazār-i Sharīf, Herat, or Qandahar it was de rigeur and symbolic of a commitment to Islam for them to perform *ziyārat* by visiting and praying at the respective shrines of Ḥażrat ʿAlī, Khwāja ʿAbdullāh Anṣārī, and the Cloak of the Prophet, and sometimes to make a substantial gift or initiate some building project.

Although there is no record that Amīr ʿAbd al-Raḥmān Khān made any investments in the Shrine of the Cloak or its administration, other than granting certain tax exemptions to the Ākhūndzāda family, his second son, Prince Naṣrullāh Khān, undertook some work during a brief stay in October 1895. We noted above that some people had taken sanctuary at the shrine in expectation of his arrival and the opportunity to put their cases before him, but we never learn the outcome.

The prince had spent the previous six months traveling to England and touring London and the countryside, then traveling to France and Italy, visiting Paris, Marseilles, Naples, and Rome before departing for Karachi on a British vessel.[66] He was heading back to Kabul via Karachi, Shālkūt (Quetta), Qandahar, and Ghaznī at the time he stopped to perform *ziyārat* at the shrine.

65 Ibid., 907–908.

66 Prince Naṣrullāh Khān's trip, the first official mission by an Afghān to Europe, was at the invitation of the English government, which had hoped to convince Amīr ʿAbd al-Raḥmān Khān himself to make the trip, and then, when he refused, citing health reasons, to persuade his eldest son and likely successor, Sardār Ḥabībullāh Khān, to take his father's place. When his father gave excuses for him, the English government finally had to settle for Sardār Naṣrullāh Khān. The journey is covered in detail in Fayż Muḥammad, *History*, vol. 3 (see index under "Naṣr Allāh Khān, Sardār and Prince, son of His Majesty, Amīr ʿAbd al-Raḥmān Khān"). See also Ludwig Adamec, "Mission of an Afghan Prince to London: Nasrullah Khan's Visit to Britain as Reflected in the Press," The Afghanistan Forum, Occasional Paper No. 33 (New York, November 1994).

Fayż Muḥammad provides three brief notices of what the prince intended to do or was persuaded to do during the few days he spent in Qandahar:

1) On Tuesday, the tenth of Jumadi al-Awwal (sic)/29 October, (the prince) expressed an interest in expanding the western courtyard of the Blessed Cloak's precincts which had been originally built in a rather constrained way. So he ordered Hajji Asad Khan to buy, with the agreement and the approval of their owners, all the serais and houses which adjoined the Cloak and abutted its walls, to include them within the (shrine's) area and so add to it. (Hajji Asad Khan) was also (ordered) to install a silver screen (*panjarah*) around the chest in which the Blessed Cloak is stored and to make arrangements for fine carpets for the shrine floor. At the very outset of the work, he was (also ordered) to spend a sufficient sum for the shrine's hostel (or soup kitchen, *langar-khāna*). The prince himself, having decided to leave for Kabul, fixed Manzil Bagh (the garden-estate built by Aḥmad Shāh) as his (first) stop.[67]
2) Meanwhile, the noble Sardar Nasr Allah Khan, after giving the order to expand the area of the Holy Cloak, the cost of which was 5,000 rupees from the government treasury and a little something from his own pocket for some food for beginning the work, pitched his tent outside Qandahar at Manzil Bagh. On Wednesday, the eleventh of Jumadi al-Ula/30 October, … the prince, who had struck his tent at Manzil Bagh for the move to Kabul, at 7:00 A.M. returned to the city after sending his party on to the stopping place at Qalʿa-i Aʿzam. He performed the pilgrimage rites (at the Shrine of the Cloak), then turned his reins from the city toward the aforementioned *qalʿa*, and left the city at 10:00 A.M.[68]
3) Also at this time … five crystal chandeliers which the laudable felicity-consorting prince had instructed Colonel Ghulam Rasul Khan, the ambassador of this government (in Calcutta), to send to Qandahar to hang in the domed mausoleum of the Blessed Cloak (also) arrived and were installed inside the mausoleum.[69]

---

67 Fayż Muḥammad, *History*, vol. 3, 1157.

68 Ibid., 1160.

69 Ibid., 1185. In photographs dating prior to 1934 (see the annual *Sālnāma-yi Kābul*, 1313/1934, facing p. 120), a chandelier hangs in the entryway of the shrine, and inside the shrine five elaborate chandeliers may be seen, one at each corner of the room and a larger one in the ceiling's center. These were probably the gift of Prince Naṣrullāh Khān. Recent photographs (courtesy of Open Jirga) show very different chandeliers.

Contributions to the Shrine: Amīr Ḥabībullāh Khān's Qandahar Projects

On May 21, 1907, Amīr Ḥabībullāh Khān arrived in Qandahar and took up residence at Manzil Bāgh,[70] a park not just for royal stays now but used as well as a guest house for visiting dignitaries.[71] According to Fayż Muḥammad, the *amīr* stayed for 27 days before departing for Herat. It was a busy four weeks. Besides honoring various citizens, looking after the military garrison, and drafting letters to the viceroy in India concerning the troublesome Zakha Khayl Afrīdī tribe, the *amīr* spent considerable time planning and ordering the rebuilding of infrastructure. Fūfalzā'ī found a detailed account, written by a certain Mīr Muḥsin Āqā-yi Pishīnī, of the *amīr*'s projects inspired by his May-June stay in the city. Although he provides no indication of where or if the account was published, he does relate that the author died on 17 Shawwāl 1341/June 2, 1923 and is buried in Qandahar, giving us a terminus ad quem for the description of the projects. According to Fūfalzā'ī, Mīr Muḥsin Āqā was a scholar and a fine calligrapher (although he does not include him in his biography of Afghanistan's calligraphers).[72] He was also the first cousin (*pasar-i kākā*) of Shāh ʿAbd al-ʿAẓīm Pishīnī, known as "Shāh Āqā-yi Qalʿa-yi Qāżī" of Kabul, obviously a figure of renown.[73] Mīr Muḥsin Āqā's eyewitness account, as summarized by Fūfalzā'ī, is detailed and well worth giving verbatim:

70 Fayż Muḥammad, *History*, vol. 4, p. 1150.

71 When C. E. Yate arrived in Qandahar in April 1893, en route to Herat as border commissioner to try and settle Afghan-Russian disputes over water rights and then to assume the position of consul-general in Mashhad, he was put up in Qandahar at Manzil Bāgh and left the following description of it. "The Bagh-i-Manzil, which had been assigned to me as my residence during my stay, was a new garden-house constructed by order of the Amir [ʿAbd al-Raḥmān Khān] just behind the village of Deh Khojah, the scene of our sortie during the siege of 1880. The house itself was a large square building. The lower storey consisted of vaulted kitchens and servants' rooms. Mounting the stairs, we found ourselves in a huge hall, in the shape of a Maltese cross, with a small room at each corner and another room above each of those again. The garden was full of apricot, peach, pomegranate, and quince trees, giving a green and pleasant prospect, while a cuckoo was calling loudly, and there were lots of small birds around, giving life to the place." Lt-Col. C[harles] E[dward] Yate, *Khurasan and Sistan* (Edinburgh and London: William Blackwood and Sons, 1900), 3.

72 ʿAzīz al-Dīn Wakīlī Fūfalzā'ī, *Hunar-i khaṭṭ dar Afghānistān dar dū qarn-i akhīr* (Kabul: Anjuman-i Tārīkh-i Afghānistān, 11 Mīzān 1342 [October 1, 1963]).

73 Fūfalzā'ī, *Tārīkh-i Khirqat*, 104, note.

> (after long honorifics) Sirāj al-Milla wa'l-Dīn (Amīr Ḥabībullāh Khān) was always spending large sums on improving royal structures of the country. As soon as he came to Qandahar (in 1907) he undertook many projects that need to be mentioned here. First he rebuilt the walls of Qandahar that over the course of time had been breached here and there so that they would be pristine and beautiful and the envy of the world. Other projects were [whether new or renovated are not always clear]: the citadel (Arg), the *salāmkhāna* (reception hall), the Burj Palace and a new palace (*kūtī*) in the citadel, as well as flowerbeds (*guldānī*), and fountains (*fawāra-hā*). He completely refurbished the bazaars and holy places. For example, he expanded the courtyard of the Shrine of the Cloak, buying up courtyard houses (*sarāy*s) to the east and bringing them within its perimeter. He built vestibules (*dālān-hā*) on its south side and he appointed an imam, muezzin, custodial staff, professor, and students. He expanded the footprint of Masjid-i Jāmiʿ-i Shāh, which had been built by Aḥmad Shāh, by adding purchased and crown land to its north. The northern vestibules of the latter mosque he (also) completely rebuilt. He purchased, for a high price, *sarāy*s that stood to the northwest of the Masjid-i Jāmiʿ-i built by the late Sardār Kuhandil Khān, thereby doubling the size of the mosque and its grounds, and made the Pātāb Canal flow through the middle of its ground. He built 200 shops, which in fact formed a long bazaar, to cover the expenses (of the Sardār Kuhandil Khān Friday Mosque) and he placed the hair of the Prophet in (the mosque). He rebuilt the ʿUṣmānābād Mosque located in Shikārpūr Bazaar and other mosques. He built Kūhkarān Palace (*ʿimārat-i kūhkarān*) and a new palace (*kūtī*) in Manzil Bāgh which is adorned with a royal throne. (Other projects were the palaces of) Kūtī Yakhchāl and Kūtī Sarband and the cleaning of canals as well as road building and street cleaning. He also had the Nahr-i Sirājiyya trunk canal dug from the Helmand River, which, over the course of four years, employed 8,000 men before it was finished. It is one of the great public works of the Sirājī period and one of the fine results of his trip during which he left some major public work at every stop. The trunk canal project was largely carried through by the governor Sardār Muḥammad ʿUṣmān Khān.[74]

Mīr Muḥsin Āqā's account, however valuable, raises many questions. Obviously all this work did not occur during the 27 days the *amīr* stayed in Qandahar. Some of it was begun while he was in Qandahar, some started after he had

74 Ibid., 104–106.

left, and some did not begin until years after he was there. The only thing one can say for certain is that the work had at least begun by the time Mīr Muḥsin Āqā died in 1923 and probably before Amīr Ḥabībullāh Khān's death in February 1919.

It may be possible to document the *amīr*'s plans for the shrine through a series of photographs that represent it in its "before" state and then modern photographs which possibly give an idea of Amīr Ḥabībullāh Khān's plan of work and the resulting changes that dramatically altered the architecture of the place. But this must be taken as very tentative. My conclusions rely on the biographical information about the man identified as the chief architect chosen by Amīr Ḥabībullāh Khān to do the work and on some assumptions about the dates of the photographs.

In 1907, the *amīr* took one of his photographers, ʿAbd al-Ṣamad, on his circuit of the country. Some of the photographs were published in *Sirāj al-akhbār* six years after the fact.[75] One of the photographs taken of the shrine, which we might date to this trip, bears the caption "photo by ʿAbd al-Ṣamad."[76] I believe these photographs, although they could have been taken after 1907 (but before 1913), show the shrine and its related buildings in the state in which Amīr Ḥabībullāh Khān found them. Fūfalzāʾī, without providing any source for this information, tells us that when the *amīr* reached Herat he sent back to Qandahar a group of artisans led by one Ṣūfī ʿAbd al-Ḥamīd, a noted calligrapher and architect. Ṣūfī ʿAbd al-Ḥamīd was from the Khwānchīzāʾī clan of the Bārakzāʾī and was a native of Qandahar; he had gone with his family at the age of nine to Herat, where he received his education and training. The problem in accepting at face value what Fūfalzāʾī says here is that in another of his works, *Hunar-i khaṭṭ dar Afghānistān*, Fūfalzāʾī provides a relatively lengthy biography of Ṣūfī ʿAbd al-Ḥamīd[77] revealing that when Amīr Ḥabībullāh Khān visited Qandahar, Ṣūfī ʿAbd al-Ḥamīd was just 16 years old. There Fūfalzāʾī says that Ṣūfī ʿAbd al-Ḥamīd was summoned to Qandahar from Herat in 1327/1909, two years after the *amīr*'s visit, for architectural work rebuilding Manzil Bāgh. Then he says "after finishing work on the throne (*takht*) of Manzil Bāgh, the interior of the dome of the *khirqa* shrine building and the shrine of the Prophet's hair (Sardār Kuhandil Khān's congregational mosque) were repainted and given new inscriptions (*naqqāshī wa khaṭṭātī*) by him."[78] In Qandahar, he also was

---

75 *Sirāj al-akhbār*, vol. 3 (1913), no. 18, 5 and no. 20, 6.

76 *Sirāj al-akhbār*, no. 3 (1913), no. 18, 5.

77 Fūfalzāʾī, *Hunar-i khaṭṭ*, 46–47.

78 Ibid., 46. Dupree (*Historical Guide*, 284) attributes the covering of the shrine in polychrome tile to Amīr Ḥabībullāh Khān and the actual tile produced to a "master tilemaker" named Nīk Muḥammad.

asked to copy out the Mughal-era inscription at the Forty Steps site (*riwāq-i chihil zīna*, a veranda or porch situated high on a mountainside adjacent to the ancient city site of Qandahar) and his transcription was sent to Kabul.[79]

Ṣūfī ʿAbd al-Ḥamīd had many other skills that were useful to the government. Under Amīr Amānullāh Khān (r. 1919–1929), he was sent to Balkh in 1339/1920–21 to inspect the irrigation system and survey it into *paykāls*, a unit of some 90 or 120 acres depending on the type of *paykāl* in question.[80] He also introduced the people of Balkh to the principles of surveying, according to Fūfalzāʾī.[81] In 1342/1923–24, he spent another eleven months in Balkh and drew up a detailed map of the region and compiled a book of its geography, which he submitted to the Ministry of Education. When he returned to Kabul he was named chief of animal husbandry (*raʾīs-i tarbiya-yi ḥayawānāt*). There he spent the rest of his life in work involving calligraphy—at the mint, at the various government presses, and in creating inscriptions like those on Masjid-i Kārīz Mīr,[82] which was built at the order of His Majesty Muḥammad Ẓāhir Shāh. After a long and illustrious career in government service he died on June 6, 1962.[83]

The work attributed to Ṣūfī ʿAbd al-Ḥamīd on the Shrine of the Cloak by Fūfalzāʾī, painting the interior and adding calligraphic inscriptions, does not help explain the dramatic change in the appearance of the shrine building, which is visible in a comparison of the building as it appeared in the photos published in 1913 and in more recent images. The plain stucco exterior has been completely covered with a facing of ceramic tile, which was apparently installed during the reign of Muḥammad Ẓāhir Shāh. A plaque with his

79 Fūfalzāʾī, *Hunar-i khaṭṭ*, 46. The original inscription commemorated Bābur's conquest of Qandahar on the 13th of Shawwāl 928/5 September 1522; see Dupree, *Historical Guide*, 288–289.

80 R. D. McChesney, *Waqf in Central Asia: Four Hundred Years in the History of a Muslim Shrine, 1480–1889* (Princeton, New Jersey: Princeton University Press, 1991), 280–281.

81 Fūfalzāʾī, *Hunar-i khaṭṭ*, 46.

82 This is apparently the same site as a model farm built by the king. See Nancy Hatch (Dupree) and Ahmad Ali Kohzad, *An Historical Guide to Kabul* (Kabul: The Afghan Tourist Organization, 1965), 134. Ludwig W. Adamec, *A Biographical Dictionary of Contemporary Afghanistan* (Graz, Austria: Akademische Druck-u. Verlaganstalt 1987), 6, provides less and slightly different information from British sources about Ṣūfī ʿAbd al-Ḥamīd, dating his birth to 1887 rather than 1889. The British were unaware of his work in Qandahar but say he came to Kabul in 1913 from Herat and was employed in the arms factory (part of the Kabul Workshops). Then in 1929 he was appointed to the "Department of Contracts, Government Printing Office" (Maṭbaʿa-yi Nūt wa Ṣukūk, according to Fūfalzāʾī, *Hunar-i khaṭṭ*, 46).

83 Fūfalzāʾī, *Hunar-i khaṭṭ*, 47.

name but without a date or indication of just what he was responsible for was installed on the east façade of the building. A likely date for the work would be sometime in the late 1960s or early 1970s. Fūfalzāʾī, writing in 1965 or 1966, records,

> At the present time, at the order of his Majesty (Muḥammad Ẓāhir Shāh), it is planned (*dar naẓar ast*) to encase the box holding the *khirqa* in fine precious marble of Afghanistan. Likewise, the historic building is to be expanded and renovated in a modern form (*bi-shakl-i ʿaṣrī*).[84]

Perhaps the tile work, presumably replacing Amīr Ḥabībullāh Khān's tile work, was deemed to modernize the building.

We know of one other small addition made to the shrine, the sheathing in silver of the panels of the door leading to the innermost sanctum where the cloak was kept. This is attributed to Khūshdil Khān Lūynāb, who was the governor of Qandahar under both Amīr Ḥabībullāh Khān and Amīr Amānullāh Khān. An inscription on the door reads "During the sultanate of the Lamp of the Nation and the Religion (Amīr Ḥabībullāh Khān), this was a gift of Khūshdil Khān Lūynāb presented in 1336 (1917–18)."[85] According to Dupree, in 1974, a "splendid new door inlaid with lapis lazuli, Shah Maqsudi travertine, and chased silver inlaid with gold was installed."[86] Did this replace Khūshdil Khān Lūynāb's door or was it installed in another location?

Amīr Amānullāh Khān and the Shrine

Amīr Ḥabībullāh Khān's son and successor, Amīr Amānullāh Khān (r. 1919–1929), whose poorly thought-out social reforms produced a strongly negative reaction in the country, used the shrine as a backdrop for affirming his commitment to Islam and Islamic ways while seeking to overturn, in the views of his detractors, some of the most cherished institutions of Afghān society. He made several visits to Qandahar and on those occasions took the opportunity to make a speech or deliver a homily at the mosque of the complex, advocating the strengthening of Islam through reform. This was not a welcome sound to the ears of those in charge of the shrine or the religious leaders of the city. Qandahar, home to some of the most conservative *ʿulamā* of Afghanistan, had already expressed its opposition, long before he first visited, to his introduction

84 Fūfalzāʾī, *Tārīkh-i khirqa, Āryānā*, vol. 24, 542.

85 Ibid., 541.

86 Dupree, *Historical Guide*, 284.

of a constitutional monarchy in 1920.[87] On the 19th of Mīzān 1304 (October 12, 1925), in the wake of the Mangal rebellion in Khūst of 1924 and all the disquiet among tribes and Sunni religious leaders that lay behind it, Amānullāh came to Qandahar and delivered a speech "on the plaza" (*maydān*) of the congregational mosque of the Shrine of the Cloak as well as three homilies from the pulpit of the mosque on successive Fridays (30 Mīzān, 7 ʿAqrab, and 14 ʿAqrab 1304/October 19, 26, and November 2, 1925) in which he attempted to garb his various reform proclamations (*niẓāmnāmas*) in Islamic dress.[88]

Then again, when he set out for Europe in 1928, an act that proved fatal to his emirate, he arrived in Qandahar on the eighth of Qaws 1306/November 30, 1927. During the eight days he spent there, on two successive Fridays (the 10th of Qaws and the 17th/December 1 and 8) he performed *ziyārat* to the cloak and offered up special prayers calling for restoration of the rights of the Islamic world and Afghanistan. Then after receiving the prayers of the *mutawallī* and staff of the shrine for a safe journey, he set off on his twelve-country tour of the Middle East and Europe.[89] On his return, he reached Qandahar on the fifth of Saraṭān 1307/June 26, 1928, driving a new yellow Rolls-Royce boat-tail roadster given to him by the British government. He stopped at the shrine and again performed *ziyārat* of the *khirqa*.

He would have one more chance to pay his respects but it would not be as *amīr* of Afghanistan. Ousted from Kabul in January 1929 by the Tājīk leader, Ḥabībullāh Khān Kalakānī, Amānullāh Khān tried to rally forces in Qandahar. Despite various groups swearing their allegiance, he convinced himself he did not have the means to fight the Tājīk and on the sixth of Ḥamal 1308/March 26, 1929, he performed his last *ziyārat* and then bade farewell to the shrine and to Afghanistan.[90]

The Shrine as Sectarian Flashpoint

Despite the apparent ecumenism of the shrine when it came to offering protection, it was also, contrarily, a focal point for sectarian hatred. Anti-Shīʿism

87 Nawid, *Religious Response*, 80–81.

88 Fūfalzā'ī, *Tārīkh-i Khirqat*, 114–117 gives the gist of the speech and fuller texts of the homilies. See also Nawid, *Religious Response*, 126, who dates one speech in Qandahar to November 9, 1925. There is a problem with the dates that are given by Fūfalzā'ī if they were to fall on Fridays. The online "Afghan Calendar Converter" places all these dates on Wednesdays. I have used the converter to render all the Gregorian dates.

89 Fūfalzā'ī, *Tārīkh-i Khirqat*, 128–129.

90 Ibid., 131–133.

in the cities of Afghanistan, most notably in Kabul, Qandahar, and Herat, was a fact of life from 1737 onwards, after Nādir Shāh Afshār planted communities of Iranian soldiers and bureaucrats in those cities, groups that came to be known generically as "Qizilbāsh" ("redheads" a term dating back to the rise of the Ṣafavid dynasty in Iran at the beginning of the 16th century) and "Fārsīwān" ("Persian-speaking"). The situation was probably exacerbated by the fact that members of the Qizilbāsh community often held high positions in the central and provincial tax-collecting bureaucracies. On occasion, sparked by a viral rumor of some Shīʿī outrage (generally unfounded), there would be a spasm of violence against the Qizilbāsh or Fārsīwān community, which would wrack a town for a short period and then die down. But the embers of hatred never completely died out. The kinds of rumors that would light the fire were those things that involved violations of honor (notably sexual) or less commonly, some supposed supernatural immunity enjoyed by Shīʿīs. In times of stress, the *khirqa* shrine became the launch pad for Sunnī attacks on the city's Shīʿī community. It appears that the shrine itself had little appeal for the Qizilbāsh Shīʿīs, perhaps because the Sunnīs used it to kindle the flames of sectarian violence, often implicitly supported by the government. Or perhaps it was because Shīʿīs of Afghanistan had their own shrines commemorating the figure of ʿAlī b. Abī Ṭālib at Sakhī in Kabul and at the ʿAlid *rawża* at Mazār-i Sharīf.

According to the British representative Mīr Hāshim in his report of 1881 or 1883[91] (the story does not appear in Afghan sources), it was the custom at the time to remove the cloak from the shrine and parade it outside on special occasions to the holiday prayer grounds (the ʿĪdgāh). In this instance, the cloak was apparently taken out in celebration of the *ḥajj*-pilgrimage, although exactly why it was taken out is not explained. The report reads (in its English translation):

> The day that the Holy Cloak was taken to Idgah, Mulla Takhmir stood on the roof of the mausoleum and, in the presence of the Governor and the Sepah Salar (field marshal) and the whole population called out in a loud voice that Farsiwans are the same as Faringhies and Hindus and

91 There is a small dating problem here since the *Kandahar Newsletters*, volume 1, 109 and 112 give the impossible correspondence of 3 Dhū'l-ḥijja to October 26, 1883. But if it had been 3 Dhū'l-ḥijja then that would have only corresponded to the year 1881 (3 Dhū'l-ḥijja = October 27, 1881). Probably the Dhū'l-ḥijja date should be treated as the correct one and October 5 or 6, 1883 as the correct correspondence, not October 26.

> are Kafirs. This sort of speech is likely to provoke disturbances in the country.[92]

In the following week's newsletter, the representative reported on the latest cholera epidemic that was afflicting Qandahar and reveals how such moments also released sectarian hatreds:

> Not a single Farsiwan was attacked (by the cholera epidemic) and the Afghans prepare to make this a pretext for fighting the Farsiwans. This is the result of the Governor's want of resolution in not having Mulla Takhmir punished for denouncing the Farsiwans as Kafirs on the day the Holy Cloak was taken out.[93]

The Shrine's Power of Blessing

Besides offering sanctuary and serving to excite sectarian hatreds, the Shrine of the Cloak was viewed as a source of blessings (*barakāt*). One such blessing, which would last through all eternity, was obtained by burial within the perimeter of the shrine. Fūfalzā'ī tells a poignant story about an earlier governor of Qandahar, Sardār Muḥammad Amīn Khān. He was a devoted servant of the *mutawallī* and staff of the shrine, and in his last will and testament, he asked to be buried beneath a downspout from the roof of the shrine so that rain water running off the roof would continually freshen his grave with the blessings of the shrine. Unfortunately for him, on June 6, 1865 when he was killed in Kalāt to the northeast of Qandahar and his body was brought back to the city, no one there at the time knew his will and testament, and he was buried within the shrine's precincts but in the eastern part of the grounds near the entry vestibule (*dālān*), far from the downspout.[94]

There can be little doubt, even though records are nonexistent, that the shrine was frequented by people seeking blessings for all the reasons that shrines are revered—to alleviate or reverse infertility, poverty, and illness. Having a child blessed at the shrine would protect it from the evil eye. To have one's prayer beads blessed or purchased there or to have a gift blessed at the shrine before giving it, all these things made the shrine invaluable to Qandahar society.

92 *Kandahar Newsletters*, volume 1, newsletter no. 41 (October 26, 1883), 109, 112.

93 *Kandahar Newsletters*, volume 1, newsletter no. 42 (November 5, 1883?), 111–112.

94 Fūfalzā'ī, *Tārīkh-i Khirqat*, 140.

Sometime in 1899, the chief fiscal officer (*sar daftar*) of Qandahar, Ghulām Muḥammad Khān Wardak was reportedly collecting sums of money and goods from people who had been newly appointed as revenue agents before allowing them to take up their duties. At some point he began to fear the consequence should the *amīr* find out, and so he wrote the *amīr* an exculpatory note in which he explained about some 6,000 rupees he could not otherwise account for, claiming they had been given him as a gift. He asked if he could use the money to buy some farmland to provide food for himself and his family or whether he should deposit it in the treasury. The *amīr* (ʿAbd al-Raḥmān Khān) had long since established a strict policy about officials taking gifts and not notifying him and so was deceived by the *sar daftar*'s representations and, unusual for him, granted his request to buy some land with the 6,000 rupees. Thereupon, says Fayż Muḥammad,

> Thankful for this favor, he went to the precincts of the Holy Cloak with his wife and son and there offered up prayers for the perpetuity of the government and its authority and for the long life of His Majesty. He had the following items blessed at the shrine: a piece of finely embroidered silk turban cloth, two (women's) gold-thread skull caps, one set of prayer beads of Shāh Maqṣūd stone (a type of serpentine), and one finely embroidered silk handkerchief, and sent them to His Majesty. He also reported the prayers that he had offered.[95]

The Hair of the Prophet

Since the relic of the Prophet's hair is sometimes associated with the *khirqa* shrine complex, a note about its problematic existence is in order. Today, the mosque constructed by Kuhandil Khān (d. 1855), which stands along the same main north-south axis as the *khirqa* shrine, is known as Jāmiʿ-i Mū-yi Mubārak, the Friday Mosque of the Blessed Hair of the Prophet. In the 20th century, the sacred stories of the shrine and the Prophet's hair became so intertwined that when Nancy Dupree recorded the story of the mosque's relic, what she heard was that the hair was given to Aḥmad Shāh by the *amīr* of Bukhara at the same time as the cloak.[96]

This would seem at first blush to be a credible account for the hair's existence in Qandahar were it not for the fact that in the latter years of the 19th century

95 Fayż Muḥammad, *History*, vol. 4, 262.

96 Dupree, *Historical Guide*, 285.

several claims of possessing the genuine hair of the Prophet were made and discredited. These episodes would seem to make it clear that no such tradition then existed in Afghanistan or in Qandahar. The sudden emergence of claims in 1898–99 suggests that news had quickly spread that the Prophet's hair might be a valuable commodity, but the news of the *amīr*'s reaction to the stories was slower to circulate. Amīr ʿAbd al-Raḥmān Khān, who was highly skeptical of any stories involving the supernatural, except the significance of his own dreams, dismissed the claims with contempt but not without allowing the proponents the chance to prove the hairs' authenticity.

Three of the stories involved the Ottoman sultan ʿAbd al-Ḥamīd purportedly giving hairs of the Prophet to men who had made the pilgrimage to Mecca. When these men petitioned the court to come to Kabul and, one assumes, receive some hoped-for reward, the answers they received were not just disappointing but humiliating. The *amīr* dealt summarily with their requests, treating their claims with utter contempt and sarcastically suggesting they use the hair "to get your daily bread."[97]

But the incident that elicited the *amīr*'s greatest disdain, and for which he devised a foolproof method of debunking all such claims, involved a group of *muhājir*s, responding to the *amīr*'s opening up of Hazāra lands to new settlement by Afghāns from India. Thirty households of Achakzāʾī tribesmen entered Afghanistan at Kadanāy, southeast of Qandahar, at the end of October 1899, claiming to have with them the "blessed hair." The governor, *qāżī*, and chief financial officer then organized an elaborate welcoming ceremony, built a small annex at the Shrine of the Cloak to house the hair, and then escorted it into the city with great pomp. When he heard of this, the *amīr* denounced them in a long and lacerating diatribe for showing so little common sense. He asked them whether they had tested the hair, for, as everyone should know, the Prophet's body cast no shadow and therefore his hair should likewise cast no shadow. He cited as his authority for this the 15th-century Ṣūfī poet and saint, Mawlawī ʿAbd al-Raḥmān Jāmī but notably failed to say in which of Jāmī's numerous works this information was to be found. Further, he added, the Prophet was so pure that the wings of flies could not brush his body. Therefore, they were to pour syrup around the hair and see if flies were attracted. If not, and if the hair cast no shadow, then it was genuine and worthy of all reverence.[98] Needless to say, this test squelched the hopes pinned on possession of the hair.

---

97 Fayż Muḥammad, *History*, vol. 4, 159–160, 259–260, 296, 391, 393.

98 Fayż Muḥammad, *History*, vol. 4, 375–376. It is uncertain which of Jāmī's works was being referred to here. The debate about whether the Prophet Muhammad cast a shadow remains a lively one among both scholars and ordinary believers. See, e.g., https://islamqa

Nonetheless, the allure of the relic persisted. As noted earlier, Amīr Ḥabībullāh Khān was much more drawn to relic worship and the connection of sacred objects and saintly individuals to the unseen world than was his father, Amīr ʿAbd al-Raḥmān Khān. Mīr Muḥsin's account, as cited by Fūfalzāʾī, gives us some evidence that the tradition of the hair dates only to 1907, with the renovation of the congregational mosque built by Sardār Kuhandil Khān.

As for providing sanctuary or conferring blessings, the Mū-yi Mubārak Mosque (Sardār Kuhandil Khān's mosque of the sacred hair) has left no record that it enjoyed the same spiritual and worldly powers as the *khirqa* shrine, or at least no such record has yet come to light. Nor, aside from the reference to work ordered by Amīr Ḥabībullāh Khān, was it seen as a fit object of royal patronage. In the 1950s and 1960s, *Afghanistan News*, a monthly English-language publication coming out of the Afghan Embassy in London that was intended to showcase Afghanistan's progress in various fields, often had a section devoted to promoting tourism in one area or another of the country. For Qandahar, while the tomb of Aḥmad Shāh and the *khirqa* shrine are both mentioned as sights to see,[99] the Mū-yi Mubārak Mosque with its namesake relic perhaps seemed just slightly too bizarre to draw to foreigners' attention, and it is never mentioned.

Conclusion

In a world of arbitrary power, where ethnic, religious, and class identities were so crucial to one's expectations of life, shrines were understood to provide access to help beyond what could be negotiated personally with the government, with one's family and friends, with one's neighbors, or with one's enemies. In Qandahar, where there were important shrines to Sufi saints (for example, those of Ḥażrat Jī Bābā, where Sardār Kuhandil Khān, the builder of the Kuhandil Khān Mosque and long-time governor of Qandahar, is buried along with three of his full brothers and two of his half-brothers, and the Bābā Walī shrine, a saint claimed by Sikhs as well as Muslims[100]), none were more important than the Shrine of the Cloak.

.info/en/75395 or simply search the internet for "did the Prophet Muhammad cast a shadow?"

99 *Afghanistan News*, volume 2, no. 16 (December 1958), 13. Also *Visit Afghanistan*, a supplement to *Afghanistan News* (undated), 34.

100 Information on both saints may be had by Googling them by name and adding "Kandahar."

FIGURE 6.3 *The* Khirqat al-Nabī *showing extensive renovations conducted under King Muḥammad Ẓāhir Shāh as it appeared after 2002*
CREDIT: REZA KATEB

Not just a last resort for the downtrodden, the shrine also served the powerful as an instrument of policy. Ultimately, a ruler with the self-assurance of ʿAbd al-Raḥmān could do as he liked when it came to respecting *bast* at the shrine. Yet even he generally acknowledged it and tried to shape a policy with regards to its use. His successors seemed to want to identify themselves with the shrine as publicly as possible in order to bolster their credentials as Muslims, Amīr Ḥabībullāh Khān by lavish spending on the shrine in order to counter his reputation as playboy and flaunter of the Sharīʿa, and Amīr Amānullāh Khān, in hopes of offsetting the largely hostile response in the countryside to his social reforms, by making frequent appearances at the shrine to deliver the Friday homily (*khuṭba*) and then to invoke its power in a last-ditch but futile effort to hold on to his emirate.

Later rulers would continue to try to tap the power of the shrine to bolster their Islamic credentials, but the written accounts of the shrine would shift away from the powers in Kabul and back to the story of the Ākhūndzāda family.

Bibliography

Adamec, Ludwig W. *A Biographical Dictionary of Contemporary Afghanistan*. Graz, Austria: Akademische Druck-u. Verlaganstalt, 1987.

Adamec, Ludwig W., ed. *Historical and Political Gazetteer of Afghanistan*. 6 vols. Graz: Akademische Druck-u. Verlaganstalt, 1972–1985; vol. 1: Badakhshan; vol. 2: Farah; vol. 3: Herat; vol. 4: Mazar-i Sharif; vol. 5: Kandahar; vol. 6: Kabul.

Adamec, Ludwig. "Mission of an Afghan Prince to London: Nasrullah Khan's Visit to Britain as Reflected in the Press." The Afghanistan Forum, Occasional Paper No. 33 (New York, November 1994).

Afghanistan News, volume 2, no. 16, 12–13.

Atasoy, Nurhan. "Khirḳa-yi Sharīf," *Encyclopaedia of Islam*, New Edition, v (Leiden: Brill, 1986), 18–19.

Babajanov, Bakhtyar and Maria Szuppe. *Les inscriptions persanes de Chār Bakr, nécropole familiale des* khwāja *Jūybārī près de Boukhara*. London: School of Oriental and African Studies, 2002; Corpus Inscriptionum Iranicarum, part IV, Persian Inscriptions down to the early Safavid Period, vol. XXXI: Uzbekistan.

Balkhī, Muḥammad Ṭāhir b. Abī'l-Qāsim. *'Ajāib al-ṭabaqāt fī bayān 'ajā'ib al-'ālam*. Ms. Tashkent, Institute of Oriental Studies of the Academy of Sciences of Uzbekistan, Inv. No. 1993/I (ff. 1b–219a, copied in 1236/1820–21); described in *Sobranie vostochnykh rukopisei Akademii nauk Uzbekskoi SSR*, vol. I, ed. A. A. Semenov (Tashkent: Izdatel'stvo Akademii nauk UzSSR, 1952), 299, No. 686. On the work, see C. A. Storey, *Persian Literature: A Bio-bibliographical Survey*, vol. II, part 1 (London, 1958), 138–139.

Calmard, Jean. "Bast." *Encyclopaedia Iranica*, vol. III (1989), 856–858.

Churās, Shāh Maḥmūd. *Tārīkh*, ed. O. F. Akimushkin. Moscow: Nauka, 1976.

Davidovich, E. A. *Materialy po metrologii srednevekovoi Srednei Azii*. Moscow: Nauka, 1970.

Dupree, Nancy Hatch. *An Historical Guide to Afghanistan*. Kabul: Afghan Air Authority and Afghan Tourist Organization, 1977.

(Dupree), Nancy Hatch Wolfe, and Ahmad Ali Kohzad. *An Historical Guide to Kabul*. Kabul: The Afghan Tourist Organization, 1965.

Fayż Muḥammad Kātib Hazāra. *Sirāj al-tawārīkh*. 3 vols. in 2. Kabul: Maṭba'a-yi Dawlatī, 1331/1913–1333/1915.

Fayż Muḥammad Kātib. *The History of Afghanistan: Fayż Muḥammad Kātib Hazārah's* Sirāj al-tawārīkh [Vols. 1–3]. Ed. and tr. R. D. McChesney and M. M. Khorrami. 3 vols. in 6. Leiden: Brill, 2013.

Fayż Muḥammad Kātib. *The History of Afghanistan: Fayż Muḥammad Kātib Hazārah's* Sirāj al-tawārīkh [conclusion (*tatimmah*) of vol. 3 and vol. 4]. Ed. and tr. R. D. McChesney and M. M. Khorrami. *Tatimmah* and volume 4 in five parts. Leiden: Brill, 2016.

Foschini, Fabrizio, and Bette Dam. "Under the Cloak of History: The Kherqa-ye Sharif from Faizabad to Kandahar." *Afghanistan Analysis Network*, 30 July 2014.

Fūfalzā'ī, 'Aziz al-Dīn Wakīlī. *Hunar-i khaṭṭ dar Afghānistān dar dū qarn-i akhīr*. Kabul: Anjuman-i Tārīkh-i Afghānistān, 11 Mīzān 1342 [October 1, 1963].

Fūfalzā'ī (Pūpalzā'ī), 'Aziz al-Dīn Wakīlī. "Tārīkh-i khirqa-yi mu'aẓẓama-yi wāqi' dar Qandahār." *Āryānā*, vol. 23 (1343–44/1965), 104–112, 133–147, 239–242, 399–405, 508–516, 727–640 (*sic*-740); vol. 24 (1344–45/1966), 72–79, 172–186, 326–338, 442–450, 533–542, 626–629.

Fūfalzā'ī (Pūpalzā'ī), 'Aziz al-Dīn Wakīlī. *Tīmūr Shāh Durrānī*. Vol. 1 (of 2). Kabul: Anjuman-i Tārīkh, 1346/1967.

Fūfalzā'ī (Pūpalzā'ī), 'Aziz al-Dīn Wakīlī. *Tārīkh-i khirqa-yi sharīfa*. Kabul: Markaz-i taḥqīqāt-i 'ulūm-i Islāmī, 1367/1988.

Girs, G. F. "Pervye pechatnye knigi Afganistana (istochnikovedcheskii obzor litografirovannykh izdanii XIX v. na dari i pushtu)." In *Pamiatniki istorii i literatury Vostoka. Period feodalizma* (Moscow: Nauka, 1986), 112–139.

Golombek, Lisa, and Donald Wilber. *The Timurid Architecture of Iran and Turan*, 2 vols. Princeton: Princeton University Press, 1988.

Grigoryev, S. E. "Afghan Historical Sources on the *Khirqa* of the Prophet Muhammad." *Manuscripta Orientalia: International Journal for Oriental Manuscript Research*, 8/2 (2002), 5–9.

Hensman, Howard. *The Afghan War of 1879–80*. London, 1881; repr. New Delhi: Lancer, 2008.

al-Ḥusaynī *al-munshī* al-Jāmī, Maḥmūd b. Ibrāhīm. *Tārīkh-i Aḥmad Shāhī*. Facs. ed. A. Saidmuradov. 2 vols. Moscow, Nauka, 1974.

Ḥusaynī, Imām al-Dīn. *Tārīkh-i Ḥusaynī*. Ms. Kabul, Arshīf-i millī, No. 53/23 (dated 1213/1798–99). Ref: Storey/Bregel', III, 1223.

Ḥusaynī Jāmī, Maḥmūd. *Tārīkh-i Aḥmad Shāhī: Tārīkh-i tashkīl-i awwalīn ḥukūmat-i Afghānistān*, edited and annotated by Dr. Ghulām Ḥusayn Zargarī-nizhād. Tehran, Dānishgāh-i Tihrān, 1384/2005.

Inskeep, Steve. "The Cloak of the Prophet: Religious Artifact at the Heart of Former Taliban Stronghold." National Public Radio, January 10, 2002.

Kakar, Hasan Kawun. *Government and Society in Afghanistan: The Reign of Amir 'Abd al-Rahman Khan*. Austin: University of Texas Press, 1979.

Kandahar Newsletters. Directorate of the Archives Department, Government of Baluchistan, *Kandahar Newsletters*. Quetta, Pakistan, 10 vols.; Second Edition 1990.

Lee, J. L. *The 'Ancient Supremacy': Bukhara, Afghanistan & the Battle for Balkh, 1731–1901*. Leiden, Brill, 1996.

Marcus, George, with Peter Dobkin Hall. *Lives in Trust: The Fortunes of Dynastic Families in Late Twentieth-Century America*. Boulder, Colorado: Westview Press, 1992.

Marefat, Roya. "Beyond the Architecture of Death: The Shrine of Shah-i Zindah in Samarqand." Ph.D. dissertation, Harvard University, 1991.

Masson, Charles. *Narrative of Various Journeys in Balochistan, Afghanistan and the Panjab Including a Residence in Those Countries from 1826 to 1838*. 3 vols. London: Richard Bentley, 1842; repr. Delhi: Munshiram Manoharlal Publishers, 1997.

McChesney, R. D. "Architecture and Narrative: The Khwaja Abu Nasr Parsa Shrine. Part 1: Constructing the Complex and Its Meaning, 1469–1696." *Muqarnas*, 18 (2001), 94–119.

McChesney, R. D. *Central Asia: Foundations of Change*. Princeton, New Jersey: The Darwin Press, 1996.

McChesney, R. D. *Waqf in Central Asia: Four Hundred Years in the History of a Muslim Shrine, 1480–1889*. Princeton, New Jersey: Princeton University Press, 1991.

Nāhiż, Muḥammad Ḥakīm. *Qāmūs-i jughrāfiyā'ī-yi Afghānistān*. 4 vols. Kabul: Anjuman-i Āryānā Dā'irat al-Ma'ārif, 1336/1957.

Nawid, Senzil. *Religious Response to Social Change in Afghanistan 1919–29: King Aman-Allah and the Afghan Ulama*. Costa Mesa, California: Mazda Publishers, 1999.

Neghat, Mohammad Nasim, ed. *Qāmūs-i Darī-Inglīsī / Dari-English Dictionary*. Omaha, Nebraska: Center for Afghanistan Studies, 1993.

Nölle-Karimi, Christine. *The Pearl in its Midst: Herat and the Mapping of Khurasan from the Fifteenth to the Nineteenth Centuries*. Vienna: Austrian Academy of Sciences Press, 2014.

Olesen, Asta. "The political use of Islam in Afghanistan during the reign of Amir Abdur Rahman (1880–1901)." In *Contributions to Islamic Studies: Iran, Afghanistan and Pakestan*, ed. Chirstel Braae and Klaus Ferdinand (Aarhus: The Danish Research Council for the Humanities, 1987), 59–114.

Poullada, Leon B. *Reform and Rebellion in Afghanistan, 1991–1929: King Amanullah's Failure to Modernize a Tribal Society*. Ithaca, New York: Cornell University Press, 1973.

Roberts, (Lord) Frederick, of Kandahar. *Forty-One Years in India*. 2 vols. London: Richard Bentley and Son, 1897.

Schinasi, May. *Kaboul 1773–1948: Kaboul 1773–1948: naissance et croissance d'une capitale royale*. Naples: Universita degli Studi di Napoli "L'Orientale," 2008.

Sirāj al-akhbār. 7 vols. 1911–1918.

Storey/Bregel': Ch. A. Stori. *Persidskaia literature: Bio-bibliograficheskii obzor*, ed. and tr. Iu. È. Bregel', 3 vols. Moscow: Glavnaia Redaktsiia Vostochnoi Literatury, 1972.

Sultan Mahomed Khan, ed. *The Life of Abdur Rahman, Amir of Afghanistan*. 2 vols. London: John Murray, 1900; Elibron Classics reprint, 1905.

Sulṭān Muḥammad Khān Bārakzā'ī. *Tārīkh-i Sulṭānī*. Bombay, 1298/1881.

Tarzi, Mahmud. *Reminiscences: A Short History of an Era (1869–1881)*. Ed. Wahid Tarzi. East Hampton, New York: Afghanistan Forum, Occasional Paper No. 36, March 1998.

Yate, Lt-Col. C[harles] E[dward]. *Khurasan and Sistan*. Edinburgh and London: William Blackwood and Sons, 1900.

Yule, Col. Henry, and A. C. Burnell. *Hobson-Jobson: A Glossary of Colloquial Anglo-Indian Words and Phrases, and of Kindred Terms, Etymological, Historical, Geographical and Discursive*; new edition, ed. William Crooke, 1886; repr. New Delhi, 1986.

Ziad, Waleed. "Transporting Knowledge in the Durrani Empire: Two Manuals of Naqshbandi-Mujaddidi Sufi Practice." In *Afghanistan's Islam: From Conversion to the Taliban*, ed. Nile Green (Berkeley: University of California Press, 2016), 105–128.

Maps

Ayazi: "Afghanistan" map, 1:1,500,000. Albuquerque, New Mexico: Ayazi Publishing, 2001.

Soviet General Staff: USSR, General'nyi Shtab (Afghanistan Series 1:200,000)
"Lashkargakh" (H-41-V)
"Kandagar" (H-41-VI)
"Takhtapul'" (H-41-XII)

CHAPTER 7

Sufism in the Face of Twentieth-Century Reformist Critiques: Three Responses from Sufi *Imāms* in the Volga-Ural Region

Allen J. Frank

Historians writing on religious and social reform in the Muslim communities of late Imperial Russia and its protectorates generally focus on rationalist and modernist discourse within these societies. They typically depict the ideas of modernist Europhile intellectuals and Islamic reformists as the sole ideological engines of reform, and have accepted uncritically much that reformists have written about Sufism, which they see as antithetical to "reform." This paper examines the writings of a group of Sufi authors from the early 20th century that might broaden our understanding of "reform" and its relationship to Sufism, and also considers how "reformist" trends affected Sufism itself at that time. These authors help to illustrate some of the problems with received classifications of Muslim intellectual currents in the early 20th century, such as "reformism," Jadīdism, "modernism," and "conservatism." Their writings demonstrate that adherence to one or more of these currents by no means excluded adherence to another. The handful of scholars who have addressed Sufism in the Volga-Ural region have, on the whole, not challenged reformist depictions of Sufism as opposed to "reform," focusing rather on the 19th century, or, when dealing with the 20th, describing Sufi accommodation with Islamic modernism and reformism.[1] The tendency to associate reform exclusively with Islamic modernists in part derives from the emphasis on the use of Jadīd source materials in studying Muslim society in the late imperial period. These sources include journals and newspapers, which generally fall

1 Hamid Algar, "Shaykh Zaynullah Rasulev: the Last Great Naqshbandi Shaykh of the Volga-Urals Region," in *Muslims in Central Asia: Expressions of Identity and Change*, ed. Jo-Ann Gross (Durham, North Carolina: Duke University Press, 1992), 112–133; more recently a number of important studies of Sufism in the Volga-Ural region have emerged, including Michael Kemper, *Sufis und Gelehrte in Tatarien und Baschkirien: der Islamische Diskurs unter Russischer Herrschaft* (Berlin: Klaus Schwarz Verlag, 1998), and Diliara Usmanova, *Musul'manskoe "sektanstvo" v Rossiiskoi imperii* (Kazan: Fän, 2009).

 | DOI:10.1163/9789004373075_009

into the category of polemical works serving a political agenda, particularly for the period between the 1905 and 1917 revolutions and the Russian Civil War.

This article examines the responses, two in printed texts and one in manuscript form, written between 1907 and 1914 by three Sufi *imāms* who can be considered staunch partisans of social and political reform, but who also looked at the process of reform critically, and in ways distinctive from those adopted by the reformists. They include two printed works, the first, a history of Astrakhan, by Jahānshāh b. ʿAbd al-Jabbār al-Nīzhghārūṭī al-Ḥājjītarkhānī, printed in Astrakhan in 1907, and the second, a critique of Sufi ethics by Īshān Muḥammad-Ḥarrāṣ Āydārōf al-Qārghālī, published in Sterlitamak in 1911; the third account appears in a manuscript history by Aḥmad al-Barāngavī, devoted to a family of scholars from the village of Baranga, in Vyatka Province, entitled *Tārīkh-i Barāngavī*, and composed in 1914. The existence of the first two works in print should demonstrate that the printing press was not the exclusive domain of Islamic modernists and reformists, and that a wide variety of political ideas could be disseminated in print, to include Jadīd ideas, reactionary works, as well as Sufi debates. While particularly effective for disseminating political ideas, print itself among Muslims in Russia (as among non-Muslims) should be seen as politically diverse. Similarly, while the sacred significance of manuscripts for Muslims in the Volga-Ural region and Siberia has been discussed to some degree,[2] their significance, alongside printed formats, as a medium for expressing political ideas has generally been discounted. However, the *Tārīkh-i Barāngavī* itself demonstrates that manuscripts could be and were circulated as a polemical medium, including as a means of challenging printed Jadīd texts.

There has been a tendency, particularly in Tatar historiography, but also in Turkish and Western scholarship, to retrospectively equate Jadīdism with "Reform," a catch-all term to include Islamic reformism (including Salafist orientations), educational reform, and Europhilic modernism, and to link it with "intellectuals," supposedly distinct from the *ʿulamā*.[3] It is increasingly clear that Islamic scholars at the time distinguished the varying currents, and looked

---

2 Al'frid Bustanov, *Knizhnaia kul'tura Sibirskikh musul'man* (Moscow: Izdatel'skii dom Mardzhani, 2013); Allen J. Frank, *Bukhara and the Muslims of Russia: Sufis, Education, and the Paradox of Islamic Prestige* (Leiden: Brill, 2012), 125–129.

3 For examples of these approaches, see Damir Iskhakov, *Fenomen tatarskogo dzhadidizma: vvedenie k sotsiokul'turnomu osmysleniiu* (Kazan: Iman, 1997); Radik Salikhov, *Tatarskaia burzhuaziia Kazani i natsionalnye reformy vtoroi poloviny XIX—nachala XX v.* (Kazan: Master Lain, 2001); Alexandre Bennigsen and Chantal Quelquejay, *Les mouvements nationaux chez les musulmans de Russie* (Paris: Mouton, 1960).

at them separately and critically. Indeed, in a variety of manuscript sources by both Sufis and rationalist *ʿulamā*, Jadīdism is understood much more narrowly than most scholars today would define it. Historians such as Qurbān-ʿAlī Khālidī, Muḥammad-Fātiḥ al-Īlmīnī, and Aḥmad al-Barāngavī all referred to Jadīdism as *uṣūl-i jadīd*, the New Method, and were unanimous in describing it exclusively as an educational method that was in their view not particularly innovative, effective, or popular. It is evidently on a similar basis that the influential Naqshbandī shaykh Zaynullāh Rasulev (1833–1917) is described as a supporter of Jadīdism, when we know that he was also an unabashed critic of Islamic reformism, specifically of the Wahhābī current, strongly denouncing Ibn Taymiyya's critique of Sufism and attacks on pilgrimage and shrine veneration.[4] There is evidence of other Sufis, too, endorsing various aspects of the reform program, such as the editors of the progressive newspaper *Fiker* who praised a certain Muḥammad-īshān as a "servant of the nation" for blessing the inaugural issue of the publication.[5]

Certainly, Islamic reformists formed a powerful intellectual current in Russia and if not critical of Sufism and Sufis per se, they nevertheless denounced practices associated with Sufism, particularly shrine veneration and pilgrimage. Shihāb al-Dīn Marjānī wrote critiques of pilgrimage in Kazan, particularly associated with the cult of Qāsim Shaykh al-Qazānī.[6] He also wrote a treatise critiquing the region's most influential shrine catalogue and sacred history, the *Tavārīkh-i Bulghāriyya*. The Jadīd journalist Ẓāhir Bigiyev wrote critiques of shrine veneration in Astrakhan, and an extensive denunciation of the veneration of the tomb of Shaykh Bahāʾ al-Dīn Naqshband in Bukhara. The theologian Riżāʾ al-Dīn b. Fakhr al-Dīn wrote rather admiringly of Muḥammad-ʿAlī al-Ẓāhir al-Witrī, a late 19th century Arab critic of the veneration of Bahāʾ al-Dīn Naqshband, and wrote extensively on the issue of sainthood and saint veneration.[7] Farit Iakhin, in his survey of the Ural'sk Muslim press from 1905 to 1907, identifies the criticism of Sufism and *īshāns* as one of the major *leitmotifs* in a wide range of reformist and modernist publications.[8]

4 Allen J. Frank, *Tatar Islamic Texts* (Hyattsville, Maryland: Dunwoody Press, 2008), 89–90, 93–123.

5 R. U. Amirkhanov, *Tatarskaia demokraticheskaia pechat'* (Moscow: Nauka, 1988), 138–139.

6 Allen J. Frank, "Qāsim Shaykh al-Qazānī: a Muslim Saint in Tatar and Bulghar Tradition," *Asiatische Studien/Études Asiatiques*, 58/1 (2004), 115–129.

7 Frank, *Bukhara and the Muslims of Russia*, 172–173; Agnes Nilüfer Kefeli, *Becoming Muslim in Imperial Russia: Conversion, Apostasy, and Literacy* (Ithaca, New York: Cornell University Press, 2014), 225.

8 Farit Iakhin, *Tatarskaia literatura periodicheskoi pechati Ural'ska (1905–1907)* (Kazan: Tatarskoe Knizhnoe Izdatel'stvo, 1992), 107–115.

Sufis in the Volga-Ural region responded to different aspects of these critiques, and in varying ways acknowledged that the social significance of the *ṭarīqat* had changed or was changing in the early 20th century. At the same time, they might also defend specific practices while at the same time embracing various aspects of social and political changes. None of the responses addressed here can by any stretch be placed into the simple category of "reaction," but are rather nuanced assessments made in the context of broad social change.

Jahānshāh al-Ḥājjītarkhānī's Defense of Pilgrimage

The *imām* and Sufi Jahānshāh b. ʿAbd al-Jabbār al-Nīzhghārūṭī al-Ḥājjītarkhānī was the author of a treatise titled *Tārīkh-i Astarkhān*, published in Astrakhan in 1907.[9] He was born in 1881 and is thought to have come from the village of Shubino, in Nizhnii Novgorod Province. Toward the end of the 19th century he was already established in Astrakhan, where he studied under ʿAbd al-Wahhāb b. ʿAlī (d. 1899), a scholar and Sufi shaykh in that city. ʿAbd al-Wahhāb himself studied the exoteric sciences under ʿUbaydullāh b. Subḥān-qul al-Qazānī (d. 1853) and ʿAbd al-Raḥīm Ḥażrat. But he also was licensed in Sufism by Maḥmūd al-Dāghistānī (d. 1877), an influential Khālidī-Naqshbandī shaykh active in the Astrakhan region. Jahānshāh's own relationship to the *ṭarīqat* is unclear. He identifies ʿAbd al-Wahhāb as his "master" (*ūstāz*), which may suggest a Sufi relationship, although such a relationship is not explicitly stated in his work. We do know that he served as the *imām* of Astrakhan's Kriushin Mosque. In 1910 he left Astrakhan for Kiev, to become *imām* of a mosque there. In the 1920s he corresponded extensively with Akhmetzian Mustafin (1902–1986) who was also from Shubino, and who was to serve as an *imām* in Moscow in the 1980s. Jahānshāh was arrested in 1937, and is thought to have died in the Arkhangel'sk region.[10]

Jahānshāh's concept of social and political progress (*taraqqī*), which he firmly placed within an Islamic framework characterized by the expansion of

9 This work was discussed in Allen J. Frank, "Muslim Sacred History and the 1905 Revolution in a Sufi History of Astrakhan," in *Studies on Central Asian History in Honor of Yuri Bregel*, ed. Devin DeWeese (Bloomington, Indiana: Indiana University, Research Institute for Inner Asian Studies, 2001), 297–317.

10 Il'ia Zaitsev, "Zhigansha Abduljabbarov," in *Islam v Povolzh'e: Èntsiklopedicheskii slovar'* (Moscow-Nizhnii-Novgorod: ID Medina, 2013), 10.

the *sharīʿa* in Muslim society, has been discussed elsewhere,[11] and may be simply summarized here. In his history Jahānshāh addresses several themes. The first of these is the advent of "freedom" (*ḥurriyyat*) and "progress" (*taraqqī*) following the 1905 Revolution. Jahānshāh is particularly critical of tsarist autocracy and of the Russian Orthodox Church. He discusses the gradual enserfment of the Russian peasantry beginning in the 16th century, and dismisses the abolition of serfdom in 1861 as a half-measure that nevertheless left Russia and Turkey as the only countries in Europe without "freedom," clearly implying a lack of parliamentary representation. He endorses "progress" in other ways, including the study of secular subjects, but nevertheless emphasizes that European sciences and their fruits originated in the ʿAbbāsid period, and should be considered the fruits of all mankind. At the same time, he takes to task Polish Muslims for abandoning Islamic culture and imitating Europeans, and holds up Qazaqs as the example for Muslims to follow, pointing to their devotion to Islamic education and the *sharīʿa*. In effect, he reverses the typical Jadīd depiction of the Europeanized Polish Tatars as a model for Russian Muslims, and of the Qazaqs as ignorant and superstitious.

At the same time, while endorsing modernist education, parliamentary democracy, and social progress, Jahānshāh frames the history of the city of Astrakhan itself in sacred terms, and above all links its holiness with the tombs of dozens of "great shaykhs and mighty saints." In fact, he provides us with the most complete listing of saints and their tombs in the lower Volga region, that alone making his history an important source for Muslim hagiolatry in Russia. Following his list of saints and their tombs, he reflects on the significance of saints for the Muslim community, and on the shortcomings of Muslims in sufficiently venerating them:

> May they [the saints] all intercede for us. O dear brothers! Reflect on these saints. At one time they too renounced this world, like us. We must take a lesson from them. If one reflects [on it], then one must take a lesson from everything. The day will come when we will lie beneath the ground. This is because the cemetery is every person's place of residence. It must be respected. Not taking the cemetery into account is the worst sort of ignorance. Let us write histories as best we can and may our brothers profit. May they endeavor to look after the cemeteries and make them pleasant. So many other nations honor and venerate their cemeteries, and they make them into an earthly paradise. But the deeds and interactions of us Muslims are so regrettable by comparison. Does God Almighty give us

11 Frank, "Muslim Sacred History," 303–306.

> thought? There are so many saints buried in Astrakhan; do our countrymen have no thought of them? We Muslims need to look after the noble mausoleums of these saints, show them to our brothers, attain happiness up until the Resurrection, and appoint caretakers. [...] This is because [the caretakers] invite mercy in this world and are dear to God. The saint is above all for them. If an impropriety is committed, the shifting of that saint from his grave is sure to take place. Later, if blessings and bounty will not be offered up to the land, that is the reason. Currently, common people persist in their heedlessness, and because they have no scholarly or spiritual knowledge they do not distinguish, and are unaware of, the deeds that surely bring wisdom. They submit their souls to their senses and think in opposition to belief.[12]

This remarkable passage demonstrates that at least for Jahānshāh, and no doubt for other figures of the time, ideas of social and political progress and shrine veneration were closely linked, insofar as he calls for social and religious investment in the shrines themselves as an element of moral reform. At the same time, it shows that for Sufi scholars such as Jahānshāh there was no necessary reliance on Islamic reformism and rationalism in their understanding of progress. In this regard it is important to recognize that the relevance of defending of shrine pilgrimage and hagiolatry in Russia was an enduring feature of Islamic discourse in Russia through the 20th century, and remains so today.[13]

By fusing a defense of hagiolatry with an endorsement of political engagement, "progress," and elements of secular education, and then linking these political and educational reforms with the implementation of the *sharīʿa* in Muslim society, Jahānshāh demonstrates that modernists were not the sole constituency for many types of political change endorsed by the Jadīds. Soviet historians of the Tatar press have commented on the care Jadīds took not to offend their co-religionists by refraining from adopting a broad anti-clericalism. The assiduousness of the Jadīd writers also demonstrates the existence of a political constituency that supported the reform program, while defining the community in specifically religious and sacred terms—including shrine pilgrimage—as Jahānshāh's example demonstrates.

---

12 Jahānshāh al-Nīzhghārūṭī, *Tārīkh-i Astarkhān*, 49–51.

13 For an example of a treatise defending hagiolatry and shrine pilgrimage see Valiulla khazret Iakupov, *O pomoshchi dusham umershikh* (Kazan: Iman, 2005); cf. also Frank, *Tatar Islamic Texts*, 195–209.

Īshān Muḥammad-Ḥarrāṣ al-Qārghālī and the Moral Reform of Sufism

Sufi writings as such in late Imperial Russia have received little scholarly attention, but appear to have been influenced by attacks against Sufis and Sufism evident among Islamic reformists and modernists in Russia. At the same time, Sufis in Russia were also influenced more broadly by currents of thought within Sufism itself. As Devin DeWeese has argued on the basis of Central Asian sources, by the 18th century the older organizations derived from *silsila*-based Sufi communities were beginning to break down, and this phenomenon continued well into the 20th century. In particular, he refers to the "bundling" of *silsila*s, in which communal identity might be "de-coupled" from communal organization.[14] Although still poorly documented, there is evidence from within Sufi communities that there was also an emerging willingness to deemphasize communal identity, pointing to a more universal concept of Sufi affiliation, and at the same time to criticize certain Sufis, and specific Sufi practices, as unethical and at odds with the moral principles of Sufism. A case in point is a Turkic treatise from Khiva entitled *Khalvat-i ṣūfīhā*, compiled in 1813, which contains both these features.[15]

In this regard, a printed treatise by a Sufi in Orenburg province, Īshān Muḥammad-Ḥarrāṣ Āydārōf al-Qārghālī, entitled *Īshānlargha khiṭāb!*, reveals both internal debates over Sufi ethics and responses to external criticisms, particularly from the Jadīds. Although there is no additional biographical information in the text about the author, it is possible that he was Kharis Akhmetdzhanovich Aidarov (as his name appears in Russian sources), who was born in 1869 in Qarghalï (Seitovskii Posad in Russian sources), who served as *imām* in the village of Gabdrafiq, in Orenburg Province, as of 1902, and in 1907 became *imām* in the Bashkir settlement of Sorocha, in eastern Samara Province.[16]

---

14 Devin DeWeese, "'Dis-Ordering' Sufism in Early Modern Central Asia: Suggestions for Rethinking the Sources and Social Structures of Sufi History in the 18th and 19th Centuries," in *History and Culture of Central Asia/Istoriia i kul'tura Tsentral'noi Azii*, ed. Bakhtiyar Babadjanov and Kawahara Yayoi (Tokyo: The University of Tokyo, 2012), 268–269.

15 Baxtiyar M. Babadžanov, "Xalwat-i ṣūfihā (The Religious Landscape of Khorezm at the Turn of the 19th Century)," in *Muslim Culture in Russia and Central Asia*, vol. 3, *Arabic, Persian, and Turkic Manuscripts (15th–19th Centuries)*, ed. Anke von Kügelgen, Aširbek Muminov, and Michael Kemper (Berlin: Klaus Schwarz Verlag, 2000; Islamkundliche Untersuchungen, Band 233), 162–163.

16 Denis Denisov, "Kharis Akhmetzhanovich Aidarov," in *Islam na Urale: Èntsiklopedcheskii slovar'* (Moscow-Nizhnii Novgorod: ID Medina, 2009), 30.

Critiques of Sufism and Sufis materialized at different levels in the Volga-Ural region in the 19th and early 20th centuries. On the one hand, theologians writing early during the Islamic revival, around the turn of the 19th century, such as ʿAbd al-Raḥīm al-Bulghārī al-Utïz-Imäni and Abū'l-Nāṣir al-Qūrṣavī, who later became anointed as heralds of Islamic reformism in Russia, were strongly influenced by Sufi concepts and ethical models. The most prominent reformist-oriented Tatar and Bashkir scholars in the late 18th and 19th centuries had an ambivalent relationship with Sufism, particularly those who had studied in Bukhara, such as ʿAbd al-Raḥīm al-Bulghārī al-Utïz-Imäni, Abū'l-Nāṣir al-Qūrṣavī, and Shihāb al-Dīn Marjānī.[17] In his theological writings Qūrṣavī was in many respects influenced by Sufi ethics and concepts, and certainly cannot be considered "anti-Sufi" in a Salafist mode. At the same time, Islamic reformists, particularly those influenced by Ibn Taymiyya and other Salafists, became increasingly critical of the theological foundations of Sufism itself. As the currency of Islamic reformism increased in the second half of the 19th century, reformist theologians such as Marjānī and Riżāʾ al-Dīn b. Fakhr al-Dīn nonetheless remained circumspect in their criticisms of Sufism as a whole, suggesting that it retained some vigor and influence in Muslim society. If theologians were careful in the criticism of Sufism, they were far more willing to criticize Sufis abstractly, and in this regard a common theme was to emphasize the decline of Sufism by contrasting the holiness of its earliest adherents with the decadence and corruption of its modern-day practitioners. In this manner a critic could praise the foundations of Sufism, while deploring Sufism as it was currently practiced. For example, Marjānī wrote approvingly of the earliest Sufis, but was critical of the Sufis of his time, denouncing the immoral behavior of *īshāns*. Utïz-Imani was not necessarily a critic of Sufism as such, but rather denounced "false Sufis" and the greed he saw among Sufis. At the same time, in a treatise on ethics entitled *al-Sayf al-Ṣāʾim*, he emerges as a strong proponent of asceticism, and cites as his exemplars early Sufi figures such as Ḥasan Baṣrī (642–728 CE) and Ibrāhīm b. Adham (d. 777–778 CE) to demonstrate that asceticism (*zuhd*) and scrupulousness (*iḥtiyāṭ*) are integral aspects of Sufism in general, and of the Naqshbandiyya in particular (he draws these examples, further, from the *Maktūbāt* of the 17th century Indian

17 Cf. Nathan Spannaus, *Islamic Thought and Revivalism in the Russian Empire: an Intellectual Biography of Abū Naṣr Qūrṣāwī (1776–1812)*, Unpublished Ph.D. Dissertation, McGill University, 2012, 178–193; ʿAbd al-Raḥman-ḥażrat ʿUmarī, "Taṣavvufgha naẓarī," *Marjānī*, (Kazan: Maʿārif maṭbaʿasī, 1333/1915), 495–497; A. N. Iuzeev, "Tatarskie mysliteli kontsa XVIII–XIX vekov o sufizme," in *Idel buyïncha sufiychïlïq: tariykhï häm üzenchälekläre/ Sufizm v Povolzh'e: istoriia i spetsifika* (Kazan: Iman, 2000), 29–36.

Naqshbandī Aḥmad Sirhindī, confirming his familiarity with and respect for Sufi literature).[18]

In the case of the Jadīds we can begin so see a shift towards a more integral critique of Sufism, following now-familiar Salafist lines. A case in point are the writings of Ẓāhir Bigiyev, who was a reformist *imām* in Rostov-na-Donu from a Mishar family. He was also the author of a travelogue of Central Asia, compiled in 1893, but published posthumously in 1908. The work has been discussed in some detail elsewhere,[19] but here it suffices to point out that the focus of the work was a virulent criticism of Sufism and hagiolatry in Bukhara, stressing the lack of rational and scientific basis for both. However, we also see in the work a critique of a specific Sufi figure, the Tatar *muftī* Sirāj al-Dīn al-Bukhārī al-Ṣārātāghī, an influential Sufi and scholar in Bukhara who was quite advanced in years when Bigiyev met him, and who had been a *murīd* of one of Bukhara's most influential Sufis in the Manghït era, Niyāz-Qulī al-Turkmānī.

In the Jadīd press we see even more pointed critiques of "īshānism," combining the *ad hominem* attacks on Sufis evident in some degree in the works of Marjānī, and to a greater extent in the writing of Utïz-Imäni, while emphasizing the rationalism of the Jadīds. To this, we can add a third influence, the anti-clericalism of the Russian leftist press. This combination of critiques would persist in the works of Jadīd authors during the early Soviet period.[20] In his study of the Tatar press in Ural'sk, Farit Iakhin argues that a critique of Sufism was a central aspect of the Jadīd political program. For example, the Cossack *ākhūnd* Aḥmad-Farīd Shīrvānī, who was an *imām* to Muslim communities within the Ural Cossack Host,[21] composed a series of essays in the Russian press between 1902 and 1904 identifying Sufism as a feature of Muslim culture responsible for dividing Russian and Muslim communities, evidently a matter particularly relevant to the Cossack environment.[22] Blaming *īshāns* for the supposed "backwardness" of Muslims in Russia was a common leitmotif in the Turkic-language Jadīd press of Ural'sk, as well. A variety of Jadīd writers

18 Kemper, *Sufis und Gelehrte in Tatarien und Baschkirien*, 186–189.

19 Frank, *Bukhara and the Muslims of Russia*, 163–169.

20 See Dzhamaliutdin Validov, *Ocherk istorii obrazovannosti i literatury tatar* (Moscow-Petrograd: Gosudarstvennoe Izdatel'stvo, 1923); Zarif Mozaffari, *Işannar-dərvişlər* (Kazan: Janalif, 1931).

21 On this figure see Allen J. Frank, *Muslim Religious Institutions in Imperial Russia: the Islamic World of Novouzensk District and the Kazakh Inner Horde, 1780–1910* (Leiden: Brill, 2001), 110, 306; Iakhin, *Tatarskaia literatura*, 11.

22 Iakhin, *Tatarskaia literatura*, 108.

attacked the behavior and hypocrisy of Sufis, with Gabdulla Tuqay going so far as to call them "the microbes of the nation."[23]

Muḥammad-Ḥarrāṣ al-Qārghālī's treatise contains many of the features discussed in the critiques of Sufis and *īshāns* mentioned above. However, throughout his treatise, beginning on the title page, he refers to himself as a Sufi and *īshān*, and, as the title indicates, he appeals directly to Sufis. As he refers repeatedly to "we *īshāns*" in the treatise, it can be considered, at least in part, an internal critique. Muḥammad-Ḥarrāṣ explains his motives for writing the work as follows:

> I had been giving a lot of thought intending to write a treatise entitled "Attention *Īshāns*!" This is because deeds violating the true path are often heard about and witnessed among our *īshāns*. Among our *īshāns* there are those who are learned and erudite, but they are so few as to be counted on one's hands, and most of us are in a detestable state. They are given the title "*īshān*," and many *īshāns* came from Bukhara. Since most of our scholars studied there, obtained learning, and came back, they gave their names to the Sufi brotherhoods. In these times, the offenses that were committed under the names "brotherhood," "Sufism," and "*īshāns*" were numerous. Especially among our Qazaq and Bashkir brothers, we ignorant *īshāns* have multiplied. It has been heard that in the position of *īshān* [*īshānlïq*] there are those who have committed dishonorable and bad deeds. These actions, of course, are being done in the shadow of ignorance. In order to be saved from these circumstances, it was considered necessary to explain what is Sufism, what is the *sharīʿa*, [and] what is the *ṭarīqat*, and [to provide] some of the biographies of the illustrious *shaykhs*.

While the author's discussion of these three elements—*sharīʿa, ṭarīqat*, and the biographies of *shaykhs*—fits firmly in a Naqshbandī tradition, as do the authorities he cites, Muḥammad-Ḥarrāṣ also moves beyond the authority of the *silsila* by leaving out his own, seeming to base the authority of a true Sufi on the moral example provided by the earliest Sufis, and defining *ṭarīqat* and *sharīʿa* as elements of Sufism based ultimately on *ḥadīth*. In particular, he connects the *ṭarīqat* with ethical norms and ethical behaviors. He cites as authorities for this interpretation the *ḥadīths* of the Prophet Muḥammad and the *Maktūbāt* of the Imām-i Rabbānī, i.e. Aḥmad Sirhindī. At the same time, he contrasts the

23 Iakhin, *Tatarskaia literatura*, 108–113.

ideal of the *ṭarīqat* with a number of practices which he believed contradicted these norms:

> We are egotistical, thinking we are better than one another, when we reach our place, being praised for revelations and miracles, at assemblies engaging in sophistry and telling tales of the Israelites, and misleading the people. As far as they can, under any circumstances, they bind the people to [their] sides and they fill their [own] pockets. Externally they sell Sufism with huge turbans, and red, green, and white *chapāns*, and they make a show of the *ṭarīqat*. Internally, it is quite something else. Is it right to drive away or take each other's *murīds*, to pit one's own path against another's, [or] to send someone who left one's own *shaykh* to another's?[24]

Muḥammad-Ḥarrāṣ̱ is also critical of the behavior of Sufis in the Qazaq environment, particularly criticizing the way the Qazaqs' kinship affiliation was causing divisions among Sufis, rather than uniting them on the basis of ethical behavior and shared ethical norms:[25]

> Especially these days we [Sufis] have been increasing among our Qazaq brothers. They buy the rank of *īshān* and *shaykh* for money after spending three months in Khiva, Urgench, Bukhara, and Tashkent, and then come back. They open *khānaqāhs* and gain great repute, and they amass a lot of property. This is because 30, 40, or a hundred people come for the same purpose, driving livestock. If there are a lot of people, such a large amount of livestock flows in. That is why it seems so festive. He gathers [*murīds*] and opens up [a *khānaqāh*]. When he says, "Let me start it in a festive manner," it turns into a fight. According to what they say, the fighting starts like this: One of them obtained the rank of *īshān* from Khiva, and returned; intending to assemble his related clan [*qardāsh rūghïn jïyūb*], and open a *khānaqāh*, he specified a time. They assembled at the appointed time and he opened his *khānaqāh*. Those close to the new

---

24 Muḥammad-Ḥarrāṣ̱ Āydārōf al-Qārghālī, *Īshānlargha khiṭāb!*, 8.

25 The practice of Sufis attracting *murīds* from specific kinship groups is documented for a number of Qazaq nomadic communities; see Allen J. Frank, "Sufis, Scholars and Divanas of the Qazaq Middle Horde in the Works of Mäshhür-Zhüsip Köpeyulï," in *Islam, Society and States across the Qazaq Steppe*, ed. Niccolò Pianciola and Paolo Sartori (Vienna: Verlag der Österreichischen Akademie der Wissenschaften, 2013; Österreichische Akademie der Wissenschaften, Philosophisch-Historische Klasse, Sitzungsberichte, 844. Band), 213–232.

īshān admonished those close to the other *īshān*. "Our person returned. Let's raise up our own." At that time the other *īshān*'s *murīd*s came, and, saying, "You were our *īshān*'s *murīd*," they argued and raised their voices and started fighting.[26]

Much of the treatise is also devoted to asceticism, and to a critique of concern for worldly goods, which Muḥammad-Ḥarrās̱ considers to be rampant among Sufis.

If some of Muḥammad-Ḥarrās̱'s themes constitute a continuation of ideas current in Sufi discourse from the 18th and early 19th centuries, such as the defense of asceticism articulated in the works of ʿAbd al-Raḥīm al-Utïz-Imānī or the nascent concept of Sufi universalism—the deemphasizing of distinctions based on *silsila*, doctrine, practice, and "traditional" communal identifications—as expressed in *Khalvat-i ṣūfīhā*, his work also reflects the atmosphere of Muslim social and political reform that characterized the decade before 1917. For example, in an account of a Bashkir village in which he contrasts an "old *īshān*" with a "young *īshān*," Muḥammad-Ḥarrās̱ invokes the generational conflict of that decade. In this anecdote Muḥammad-Ḥarrās̱ depicts the old *īshān* as afflicted with the sort of greed criticized elsewhere in the work. By contrast he extols the young *īshān*'s devotion to raising the level of education in his community, and his service to the nation (*millat*). This young *īshān* establishes *waqf*s to fund the *maktab*, and generally serves the community to obtain the village's appointment to serve as its *imām*, thereby joining the teaching of esoteric learning with exoteric learning, which Muḥammad-Ḥarrās̱ emphasizes elsewhere in his account. He concludes this account by asking rhetorically whether the actions of the young *īshān* do not in fact correspond to the *ṭarīqat* and *sharīʿa* themselves. He adds that evidence for the need to establish *waqf*s can be found in such authoritative texts as the *Mukhtaṣar* and the *Hidāya*, and points out that all the *madrasa*s in Bukhara are themselves supported by *waqf*s, as are the city's *mudarris*es.[27]

Īshānlargha khiṭāb! presents us with an example of how Sufi communities in Imperial Russia were able to adapt long-standing internal debates about Sufi communal organization to the political circumstances of reformism. There is nothing necessarily "traditional" about Muḥammad-Ḥarrās̱' arguments, which reveal ongoing internal debates about changing affiliations in Sufi communities. Like Jahānshāh al-Nīzhghārūṭī, Muḥammad-Ḥarrās̱ is able to orient these debates within the larger current of reformism, in which Jadīdism, which is

---

26   Muḥammad-Ḥarrās̱ Āydārōf al-Qārghālī, *Īshānlargha khiṭāb!*, 8–9.
27   Muḥammad-Ḥarrās̱ Āydārōf al-Qārghālī, *Īshānlargha khiṭāb!*, 21–22.

not even mentioned in his treatise, formed one element. At the same time, the work demonstrates that *ad hominem* denunciations of Sufi immorality were not only part of Jadīd discourse, but more importantly, were part of Sufi discourse in this period.

Aḥmad b. Ḥāfiẓ al-Dīn al-Barāngavī and the Evolution of Sufism

One of our most important sources for the social history of the *ʿulamā* in imperial Russia is the *Tārīkh-i Barāngavī*, a 221–folio manuscript compiled in 1914 by Aḥmad b. Ḥāfiẓ al-Dīn al-Barāngavī (1877–1931), an *imām* in the village of Baranga, located in Vyatka Province, and today located in the Republic of Mari El.[28] The *Tārīkh-i Barāngavī* in large measure examines the relationship between Muslim scholars in Russia and the religious environment of Bukhara. Specifically, Aḥmad al-Barāngavī provides extensive biographies of his father Ḥāfiẓ al-Dīn b. Naṣr al-Dīn (1827–1918), a prominent scholar and Sufi who studied extensively in Bukhara from 1849 until 1863. Aḥmad also includes a substantial amount of biographical information on his uncle Burhān al-Dīn b. Naṣr al-Dīn, who studied in Bukhara during roughly the same period as did Ḥāfiẓ al-Dīn. Aḥmad also includes an extensive autobiography, in which he discusses at length his years in Bukhara from 1901–1905. For Aḥmad, Sufism remained a topic of sustained interest in his history, in particular the evolution of Sufism's social role both in Russia and Bukhara.

An important feature of Aḥmad's narrative is the long-standing multigenerational relationship between his own family and a family of Sufis in Bukhara. His grandfather, Naṣr al-Dīn b. ʿAbd al-Salām, had studied with the Naqshbandī-Mujaddidī shaykh Jalāl al-Dīn Khiyābānī (1785/86–1870/71) by correspondence at some point before 1849, and although the two never met face-to-face, Naṣr al-Dīn swore allegiance (i.e., "gave the *baʿyat*") to and "was accepted" by Khiyābānī.[29] When Naṣr al-Dīn's sons, Ḥāfiẓ al-Dīn and Burhān al-Dīn, came to Bukhara in 1849, they both approached Jalāl al-Dīn to become his *murīds*. He accepted Burhān al-Dīn, but rejected Ḥāfiẓ al-Dīn. Ḥāfiẓ al-Dīn then was accepted by another shaykh, ʿAbd al-Karīm al-Shahrisabzī (1795/96–1864/65), better known as Īshān-i Pīr, a *murīd* of the Indian shaykh Ghulām ʿAlī-Shāh al-Dihlavī.

28 For a description of the manuscript and a discussion of its place in the Islamic historiography of Imperial Russia see Frank, *Bukhara and the Muslims of Russia*, 20–26.

29 *Tārīkh-i Barāngavī*, Ms. Manuscript Institute of Tatarstan, 39/34 (henceforth: TB), ff. 21a, 143a.

Aḥmad provides a substantial amount of biographical information on these two figures, including their *silsila*s, which are firmly bound to Naqshbandī-Mujaddidī lineages (in Khiyābānī's case, via the Central Asian shaykh Mūsā Khān al-Dahbīdī, and in Īshān-i Pīr's case, directly through Indian shaykhs). While Aḥmad's careful transmission of Mujaddidī *silsila*s seems to suggest that such lineages dominated affiliation within Sufi communities at that time, it appears that the sort of "bundling" of *silsila*s described by DeWeese for the 18th and 19th centuries was under way among Tatar *murīd*s in Bukhara by the mid-19th century. In this regard, in addition to his Naqshbandī-Mujaddidī lineage, Aḥmad tells us that Khiyābānī also licensed Ḥāfiẓ al-Dīn in the Kubravī initiatic lineage.[30] His father was also an Uvaysī Sufi as was his master, Īshān-i Pīr, concerning which Ahmad writes:

> Our father was an Uvaysī (*uvaysī al-mashrab*), just as the Holy Īshān-i Pīr was an Uvaysī. Even though every Sufi returns to the same origin, every *ṭarīqat* has its particular prayers and litanies [*awrād wa ẕikrlarī*], and conventions [*istilāḥlarī*]. And also, a *ṭarīqat* will have a *khatm* that it recites at a time designated specifically for itself; for example, the *khatm-i khwāja* and the *khatm al-Imām Rabbānī*. [This *khatm*] consists of one *wird*. I think that this *khatm* is a tradition from the Prophet Muhammad (peace be upon him), or it was suggested by God to one of the *shaykhs*. Or else people like Khiẓr (peace be upon him) taught it. For example, it could be the result of various important commands or it was performed to rectify a shortcoming that was omitted or that appeared, and it corresponded to a desire [*murād*], and it was recommended to the friends [*yārānlarïna*] because of such commands, and it benefited them, and it was preferred for that *ṭarīqat*. In that way, each of them is from the prophets and each one is within the teaching and responsibility [of the *ṭarīqat*]. In that regard they have people say, for example, "In the footsteps of Jesus" and "in the footsteps of Muḥammad." They call such a person "*Muḥammadī al-mashrab*" or "*ʿĪsavi al-mashrab*."[31]

In this account, in explaining his father's multiple Sufi affiliations, Aḥmad seems to be minimizing ritual and doctrinal differences between the orders.

Aḥmad also alludes to a sense of obligation among Tatar and Bashkir students in the mid-19th century to find a Sufi master in Bukhara:

30 TB, f. 99b.

31 TB, f. 101b.

> Although he accepted a handshake from Shaykh Jalāl al-Dīn al-Khiyābānī (who had rejected my father out of doubt) and was accepted into the *ṭarīqat*, he was not assiduous. He was most likely involved in formal lessons. In that era, just as today, because there was the practice that travelers to Bukhara, especially students from Russia, would enter the Sufi discipline with one of the *īshāns*, it is possible that Burhān al-Dīn also was compelled to enter the *ṭarīqat*. This being the case, behind the backs of the Russian students, the Bukharans would always be saying things like "infidels."[32]

We know that scholars in Russia, when sending their students to Bukhara, would explicitly encourage them to "clasp hands" with a Sufi shaykh. Even the reformist Shihāb al-Dīn Marjānī studied Sufism under two shaykhs in Bukhara, ʿUbaydullāh b. Niyāz-Qulī al-Turkmānī (d. 1852) and ʿAbd al-Qādir b. Niyāz-Aḥmad Fārūqī (d. 1855), obtaining a *khaṭṭ-i irshād* from the latter. While at that time Marjānī probably had not yet fully developed his reformist ideas, this still gives some indication of the pressure to study under a Sufi shaykh. Aḥmad himself, upon arriving in Bukhara in 1901, came under some pressure from his father to embark upon the Sufi path. He explains that his father had suggested he take advantage of their family connections. He provided him with a blessing (*tabarruk süz*) and directed him to find the sons or grandsons of Jalāl al-Dīn al-Khiyābānī or Īshān-i Pīr. Eventually he found a grandson of Īshān-i Pīr, Maḥmūd b. Īshān-i Pādishāh Yaḥyā, and became his *murīd*.[33]

While assiduous in documenting his father's Sufi connections, and looking critically at his uncle Burhān al-Dīn's devotion to the Sufi path, Aḥmad himself appears to have lacked his father's zeal, and provides only the barest information on his own experience as a *murīd*, and on his own Sufi master Maḥmūd. Aḥmad clearly suggests that Sufism as a type of fashion was in decline in comparison with its heyday in the mid-19th century, when there was pressure on Tatar and Bashkir students in Russia to study Sufism. Nevertheless, Aḥmad does not refer to any external disparagement of Sufis, including from Jadīds, and his critical view appears to derive from an internal dynamic already well underway during his father's time in Central Asia.

32 TB, f. 35a.

33 TB, ff. 203a–204a.

Conclusion

The three examples discussed above demonstrate that at the beginning of the 20th century some Sufis in the Volga-Ural region, far from being sclerotic or politically reactionary, were fully invested in various aspects of religious and political reform. In this regard, religious and social ideas collectively understood as "reform" were by no means exclusive to modernist and reformist critics of Sufism. Among some Sufis in the Volga-Ural region, Sufi ideas did not necessarily originate in or derive authority from European ideas, but instead derived from internal Sufi dynamics that that were underway already in the previous centuries, and were applied to the economic and political circumstances of early 20th-century Russia. Similarly, Sufis were sufficiently self-confident in their own intellectual milieu to engage in self-criticism, and to recognize the social evolution of Sufism in Muslim life, while also proposing far-reaching moral reformism. The history of Sufi ideas and communities in Russia in the early 20th century remains poorly understood, in large measure due to the influence of modernist and reformist descriptions and assumptions, and due to the suppression of Sufi communities beginning in the 1930s. Nevertheless, we can glimpse, in these examples of the evolution of Sufi thought, an alternative to the received modernist and reformist narratives of "progress" and social evolution in 20th-century Muslim society in Russia.

Bibliography

ʿAbd al-Raḥman-ḥażrat ʿUmarī. "Taṣavvufgha naẓarī." In *Marjānī*, ed. Shahar Sharaf (Kazan: Maʿārif maṭbaʿasī, 1333/1915), 495–497.

Aḥmad b. Ḥāfiẓ al-Dīn al-Barāngavī. *Tārīkh al-Barāngavī*. Ms. Manuscript Institute of Tatarstan, 39/34.

Algar, Hamid. "Shaykh Zaynullah Rasulev: The Last Great Naqshbandi Shaykh of the Volga-Urals Region." In *Muslims in Central Asia: Expressions of Identity and Change*, ed. Jo-Ann Gross (Durham, North Carolina: Duke University Press, 1992), 112–133.

Amirkhanov, Ravil' U. *Tatarskaia demokraticheskaia pechat'*. Moscow: Nauka, 1988.

Babadžanov, Baxtiyar M. "Xalwat-i ṣūfihā (The Religious Landscape of Khorezm at the Turn of the 19th Century)." In *Muslim Culture in Russia and Central Asia, vol. 3, Arabic, Persian, and Turkic Manuscripts (15th–19th Centuries)*, ed. Anke von Kügelgen, Aširbek Muminov, and Michael Kemper (Berlin: Klaus Schwarz Verlag, 2000; Islamkundliche Untersuchungen, Band 233), 113–217.

Bennigsen, Alexandre and Chantal Quelquejay. *Les mouvements nationaux chez les musulmans de Russie*. Paris: Mouton, 1960.

Denisov, Denis. "Kharis Akhmetzhanovich Aidarov." In *Islam na Urale: Èntsiklopedicheskii slovar'* (Moscow-Nizhnii Novgorod: ID Medina, 2009), 30.

DeWeese, Devin. "'Dis-Ordering' Sufism in Early Modern Central Asia: Suggestions for Rethinking the Sources and Social Structures of Sufi History in the 18th and 19th Centuries." In *History and Culture of Central Asia/Istoriia i kul'tura Tsentral'noi Azii*, ed. Bakhtiyar Babadjanov and Kawahara Yayoi (Tokyo: The University of Tokyo, 2012), 259–279.

Frank, Allen J. *Bukhara and the Muslims of Russia: Sufism, Education and the Paradox of Islamic Prestige*. Leiden: Brill, 2012.

Frank, Allen J. *Muslim Religious Institutions in Imperial Russia: the Islamic World of Novouzensk District and the Kazakh Inner Horde, 1780–1910*. Leiden: Brill, 2001.

Frank, Allen J. "Muslim Sacred History and the 1905 Revolution in a Sufi History of Astrakhan." In *Studies on Central Asian History in Honor of Yuri Bregel*, ed. Devin DeWeese (Bloomington: Indiana University, Research Institute for Inner Asian Studies, 2001), 297–317.

Frank, Allen J. "Qāsim Shaykh al-Qazānī: a Muslim Saint in Tatar and Bulghar Tradition." *Asiatische Studien/Études Asiatiques*, 58/1 (2004), 115–129.

Frank, Allen J. "Sufis, Scholars and Divanas of the Qazaq Middle Horde in the Works of Mäshhür-Zhüsip Köpeyulï." In *Islam, Society and States across the Qazaq Steppe*, ed. Niccolò Pianciola and Paolo Sartori (Vienna: Verlag der Österreichischen Akademie der Wissenschaften, 2013; Österreichische Akademie der Wissenschaften, Philosophisch-Historische Klasse, Sitzungsberichte, 844. Band), 213–232.

Frank, Allen J. *Tatar Islamic Texts*. Hyattsville, Maryland: Dunwoody Press, 2008.

Iakhin, Farit. *Tatarskaia literatura periodicheskoi pechati Ural'ska (1905–1907)*. Kazan: Tatarskoe Knizhnoe Izdatel'stvo, 1992.

Iakupov, Valiulla khazret. *O pomoshchi dusham umershikh*. Kazan: Iman, 2005.

Iskhakov, Damir. *Fenomen tatarskogo dzhadidizma: vvedenie k sotsiokul'turnomu osmysleniiu*. Kazan: Iman, 1997.

Iuzeev, A. I. "Tatarskie mysliteli kontsa XVIII–XIX vekov o sufizme." In *Idel buyïncha sufiychïlïq: tariykhï häm üzenchälekläre/Sufizm v Povolzh'e: istoriia i spetsifika* (Kazan: Iman, 2000), 29–36.

Jahānshāh b. ʿAbd al-Jabbār al-Nīzhghārūṭī al-Ḥājjītarkhānī. *Tārīkh-i Astarkhān*. Astrakhan: Taraqqī Maṭbaʿasī, 1907.

Kefeli, Agnes Nilüfer. *Becoming Muslim in Imperial Russia: Conversion, Apostasy, and Literacy*. Ithaca, New York: Cornell University Press, 2014.

Kemper, Michael. *Sufis und Gelehrte in Tatarien und Baschkirien: der Islamische Diskurs unter Russischer Herrschaft*. Berlin: Klaus Schwarz Verlag, 1998.

Mozaffari, Zarif. *Işannar-dərvişlər*. Kazan: Janalif, 1931.

Muḥammad-Ḥarrāṣ Āydārōf al-Qārghālī, *Īshānlargha khiṭāb!* Sterlitamak: Nur, 1911.

Salikhov, Radik. *Tatarskaia burzhuaziia Kazan i natsionalnye reformy vtoroi poloviny XIX—nachala XX v.* Kazan: Master Lain, 2001.

Spannaus, Nathan. *Islamic Thought and Revivalism in the Russian Empire: An Intellectual Biography of Abū Naṣr Qūrṣāwī (1776–1812)*. Unpublished Ph.D. Dissertation, McGill University, 2012.

Usmanova, Diliara. *Musul'manskoe "sektanstvo" v Rossiiskoi imperii*. Kazan, Fän, 2009.

Validov, Dzhamaliutdin. *Ocherk istorii obrazovannosti i literatury tatar*. Moscow-Petrograd: Gosudarstvennoe Izdatel'stvo, 1923.

Zaitsev, Il'ia. "Zhigansha Abduljabbarov." In *Islam v Povolzh'e: Èntsiklopedcheskii slovar'*, (Moscow-Nizhnii-Novgorod: ID Medina, 2013), 10.

CHAPTER 8

Sufism on the Soviet Stage: Holy People and Places in Central Asia's Socio-Political Landscape after World War II

Eren Tasar

After violently attempting to liquidate all traces of religion during periods of the 1920s and 1930s, the Soviet state normalized church-state relations at the height of World War II. For the USSR's predominantly Muslim regions, and especially Central Asia, this meant that the many religious figures who had survived persecution were able to openly reassert themselves as sources of sacred authority in communities (and sometimes across regions). This paper argues that the moderate political climate of the postwar years facilitated new patterns of interaction between Sufi communities and state institutions. The postwar landscape created expansive opportunities for master-disciple networks, as well as lineage-based groups, to seamlessly integrate themselves into a variety of Soviet institutions and settings. The Soviet state's antireligious mission notwithstanding, multiple niches emerged in the cities and countryside for figures and sites associated with Sufism to thrive next to, and sometimes inside, state enterprises. This suggests that far from surviving exclusively as an underground phenomenon, Sufism comprised an organic component of the region's social and political life.

Scholarship on Sufism in Soviet Central Asia has remained limited in quantity, due undoubtedly to the dearth of available source material. This helps to explain why the Cold War-era writings of Alexandre Bennigsen and his students have continued to enjoy exceptional influence in framing discussion of the topic. An almost exclusive reliance on Soviet propaganda and social science literature concerning the USSR's Muslims, and a tendency to lump the Caucasus and Central Asia together, ranked as the twin hallmarks characterizing this body of literature. During the Afghan War, Bennigsen became interested in delineating the Soviet state's political vulnerabilities. His *Mystics and Commissars* (coauthored with Enders Wimbush) portrayed Sufism as a potential weapon, capable of undermining the Communist state from within. Its key argument was that "by their very survival, the [Sufi] brotherhoods have demonstrated that radical puritanism, even in its most fanatical and unyielding forms, can resist and indeed prosper under Soviet pressure without losing

 | DOI:10.1163/9789004373075_010

a single element in its creed, ritual, or way of life."[1] Bennigsen thus posited Sufism as a guarantor of Islam's survival in hostile conditions, comparable "to the first years of the Chagatay Khanate in Central Asia, whose Mongol rulers had in the beginning a strong-anti-Islamic attitude."[2] For him, Sufism's naturally clandestine nature enhanced its potential disruptiveness to the political system.[3] More recent contributions have ensured the survival of Bennigsen's basic framework for understanding Sufism in Central Asia in the decades of Soviet history following the Cultural Revolution of 1928–32 and the Great Terror of 1937–38.[4] A case in point is Yaacov Ro'i's exhaustively researched *Islam in the Soviet Union*, which analyzes Soviet policies toward Islam after World War II. Despite the wealth of empirical detail it provides, Ro'i's treatment of Soviet Sufism as a variety of "non-conformist Islam" leaves Bennigsen's conclusions unchallenged, especially given the author's assumption "that the *tariqas* were closed societies into which the adept was accepted after a ritual of initiation and remained under the control of his master ..."[5] By contrast, the analysis in this paper demonstrates that Sufism was anything but a clandestine phenomenon in the USSR.

The Bennigsenian analysis was not revisited until Devin DeWeese offered the first paradigm for understanding Sufism in Central Asia that was that not tied to the impact of Soviet policies and ideology. DeWeese charted significant social transformations in the organization and practice of Sufism since the 18th century, demonstrating that these shifts were of a social, rather than ideological, nature, and that they could not be conveniently tied to important dates

1 Alexandre Bennigsen and S. Enders Wimbush, *Mystics and Commissars: Sufism in the Soviet Union* (Berkeley, California: University of California Press, 1985), 112.

2 Alexandre Bennigsen, "Official Islam and Sufi Brotherhoods in the Soviet Union Today," in *Islam and Power*, ed. Alexander S. Cudsi and Ali E. Hillal Dessouki (Baltimore, Maryland: Johns Hopkins University Press, 1981), 104.

3 Alexandre Bennigsen, "Unrest in the world of Soviet Islam," *Third World Quarterly*, 10/2 (April 1988), 770–786. Bennigsen even cited an "authoritative" Soviet source assigning culpability to "Sufis" in the *Zheltoqsan* riots of December 1986, in which Kazakh protests at the removal of Party leader Dinmukhammet Qonaev led to mass violence.

4 Marie Broxup, "Political Trends in Soviet Islam after the Afghanistan War," in *Muslim Communities Reemerge: Historical Perspectives on Nationality, Politics, and Opposition in the Former Soviet Union and Yugoslavia*, ed. Edward Allworth (Durham, North Carolina: Duke University Press, 1994), 304–321 (esp. 312); Sergei Poliakov, *Everyday Islam: Religion and Tradition in Rural Central Asia*, ed. and trans. Martha Brill Olcott and Anthony Olcott (Armonk, New York: M. E. Sharpe, 2002).

5 Yaacov Ro'i, *Islam in the Soviet Union: From World War II to Perestroika* (London: C. Hurst & Co./New York: Columbia University Press, 2000), 389.

in political history, such as the Bolshevik Revolution of 1917. Most relevant for the present analysis is DeWeese's argument that Sufi "brotherhoods," which Bennigsen viewed as rigidly hierarchical (and therefore potent) organizations, did not exist in the way that much of the literature has assumed. From the early 19th century onward, Sufism was better described as an amalgam of saintly and scholarly lineages associated with multiple Sufi traditions (what DeWeese terms "bundled *silsilas*") and, of course, sacred spaces. The diffusion of Sufi practices from a relatively organized structure of master-disciple relationships into a decentralized forum of communal religious life and practice ranks as the most important change in Central Asian Sufism, one that started before the Soviets came to power and continued under their rule.[6]

Following DeWeese, the present discussion resituates the social life of Sufi communities in the Soviet political context, without, however, unwarrantedly privileging the Party-state's impact on religious life. To do so would inevitably lead to the trap of "link[ing] Sufism to dying pre-modern enclaves in modernizing states," and tying its fate solely to a backward countryside untouched by modernization.[7] In fact, Sufi responses to the modern state's centralizing reach have been diverse across the 20th-century Muslim world, from active participation in politics,[8] to avoidance of involvement with the state as a survival strategy,[9] to redefinition of the very concept of Sufism in response to fundamentalist, reformist, and secular postcolonial critiques of mysticism.[10] An examination of Sufi communities in Soviet Central Asia offers examples of all these strategies to some degree, suggesting that Sufism in the region needs to be placed in a broader Islamic, rather than solely Soviet, comparative framework.

Although such a comparative analysis will not be undertaken here, this paper departs from the standard Bennigsenian narrative by treating Sufism as an integral participant in social, political, and economic life, not as a besieged

6 Devin DeWeese, "Shamanization in Central Asia," *Journal of the Economic and Social History of the Orient*, 57/3 (2014), 326–363. DeWeese confronts the longstanding Soviet scholarly assumption that all or most religious change in Central Asia could be attributed to the growing influence of "shamans."

7 Julia Day Howell and Martin van Bruinessen, eds., *Sufism and the 'Modern' in Islam* (New York: I. B. Tauris, 2007), 12 (editors' introduction).

8 Brian Silverstein, "Sufism and Modernity in Turkey: From the Authenticity of Experience to the Practice of Discipline," in *Sufism and the 'Modern' in Islam*, ed. Howell and van Bruinessen, 39–60.

9 Matthjis van den Bos, *Mystic Regimes: Sufism and the State in Iran, from the Late Qajar Era to the Islamic Republic* (Leiden: Brill, 2002).

10 Itzchack Weismann, "Sufi Fundamentalism between India and the Middle East," in *Sufism and the 'Modern' in Islam*, ed. Howell and van Bruinessen, 115–128.

entity barely surviving in a circumscribed Islamic sphere. When mass violence ceased to figure as a policy measure of the Soviet state, opportunities emerged for a multitude of figures and sites popularly revered as "holy" to become a central presence: master-disciple networks affiliated with the Naqshbandī and Qādirī traditions, as well as shaykhs at the shrines of Sufi saints, became more visible than before. In contrast to the portrait painted by Bennigsen, these figures did not operate in a clandestine realm beyond the state's reach. Communist bureaucrats were acutely aware of the whereabouts of shrines and Sufi masters, and even selected a family rooted in a long Naqshbandī lineage to run Central Asia's sole legal muftiate. Through three case studies, this paper will demonstrate the radically varied forms of engagement with Soviet institutions that Sufi communities could experience in the postwar years. The case studies presented here are, first, the region's legally recognized muftiate (known in Russian as *Sredneaziatskoe Dukhovnoe Upravlenie Musul'man*, or SADUM); second, the 1952 trial of figures officially identified as members of the Qādirī order in the Farghana valley; and third, a state-funded health resort built around a holy spring in southern Kyrgyzstan, effectively run by the extended family of a Sufi shaykh. Taken together, these cases suggest that the Soviet state's undeniable hostility toward Sufism—which Bennigsen's source-base emphasized to the exclusion of all else—does not tell the whole story.

Evidence of the Party's exceptionally moderate posture toward Islam in the 1940s and 1950s abounds in several newly declassified archival collections in the region. These records stem, for the most part, from the state body charged with regulating Islam and numerous other religions, the Council for the Affairs of Religious Cults (CARC). Through its representatives in Central Asia's republics and provinces, CARC not only advanced the moderate line toward religion within the Party-state, but also meticulously recorded quantitative and qualitative data concerning Muslim life in the region. In an irony of fate, the Council's bureaucrats—almost all of them Communist functionaries—have bequeathed to historians a unique body of documentation for the study of Islam, albeit one harboring methodological limitations and challenges.

Sufism in Soviet Central Asia

Because figures and sites associated with Sufism permeated the Central Asian landscape, they inevitably stood to lose the most from concerted antireligious initiatives, and to gain the most from periods of relative moderation. The maintenance of master-disciple networks required a degree of mobility that only political stability could allow; the systematic, district-by-district roundups of religious figures practiced during the Great Terror forced many into hiding (in most cases by adopting "socially useful professions," though this tactic rarely fooled intelligence operatives).[11] At the height of the Terror, for example, Ziyovuddinkhon Bobokhonov (SADUM's *muftī* from 1958–1982) abandoned his post as a *madrasa* teacher to become a gardener in a local collective farm in the hope of evading arrest.[12] This ploy did not prevent his incarceration by the NKVD several months later.[13] In Uzbekistan alone, Shoshana Keller estimates that "more than 14,000 Muslim clergy were arrested, killed, exiled from their homes, or driven out of the USSR" during the Cultural Revolution and Great Terror.[14]

An unintended consequence of Stalin's normalization of religious policy in 1943–44 was the full-fledged blossoming of Muslim life.[15] With the country's attention fixated on the existential struggle with Nazi Germany, antireligious fervor was hard to come by at any level of Communist officialdom. In these conditions, illegal mosques and prayer groups reopened *en masse* across the five republics.[16] Communities quickly reoccupied abandoned mosque structures as well as those confiscated by collective farms during previous decades for use as storage, stables, livestock shelters, as well as cinemas and other "cultural-enlightenment institutions."[17] As shrines concurrently began to attract

11 BM JT 1516 / 1 / 44 / 27 (April 5, 1955).

12 Ashirbek Muminov, "Shami-damulla i ego rol' v formirovanii 'Sovetskogo Islama.'" R. S. Khakimov and R. M. Mukhametshin, eds., *Islam, identichnost' i politika v postsovetskom prostranstve: materialy mezhdunarodnoi konferentsii 'Islam, identichnost' i politika v postsovetskom prostranstve—sravnitel'nyi analiz Tsentral'noi Azii i Evropeiskoi chasti Rossii' 1–2 aprelia 2004 g.* (Kazan: Master Lain, 2005), 231–247.

13 O'zR MDA r-2456 / 1 / 166 / 7 (June 12, 1954).

14 Shoshana Keller, *To Moscow, Not Mecca: the Soviet Campaign against Islam in Central Asia, 1917–1941* (Westport, Connecticut: Praeger, 2001), 241.

15 Stalin's religious reforms reflected paramount sensitivity to the domestic and international ramifications of Soviet treatment of the Russian Orthodox and Catholic Churches inside the USSR, and cannot be reviewed in detail here. For a more detailed discussion of the reforms' impact upon Islam, see Eren Tasar, "Soviet Policies Toward Islam: Domestic and International Considerations," in *Religion and the Cold War: A Global Perspective*, ed. Philip E. Muehlenbeck (Nashville, Tennessee: Vanderbilt University Press, 2012), 158–181.

16 In 1945, for example, CARC enumerated 130 illegal mosques in Kyrgyzstan's Osh province alone. In smaller settlements, the average attendance at these mosques at each of the five congregational prayers ranged from 25–30, while in the cities the average exceeded 100. KR BMA 2597 / 1s / 20 / 19 (March 10, 1951).

17 KR BMA 2597 / 1s / 1 / 3 (July 10, 1945); 2597 / 2s / 8 / 2 (May 24, 1946); 2597 / 1s / 47 / 87 (January 20, 1956). The latter citation identifies 1934–1938 as the most intensive period of confiscations.

greater and greater numbers of pilgrims on the two *ʿeid*s, so too did figures traditionally associated with sacred space reappear across the countryside. The catch-all category of "wandering *mullā*s" (Russian, *brodiachye mully*), so prevalent in official correspondence, in fact referred to a striking array of religious character types, ranging from Sufi *ishan*s making rounds of the communities in which their disciples resided;[18] to *mullā*s performing routine rites (funerals, marriages, name-giving ceremonies) in remote, high-altitude, and/or semi-nomadic settlements tied to the seasonal migration schedules of collectivized ranches; to *duvonas* (*dīvānas*), *maddohs* (*maddāḥs*), *qalandar*s, and other varieties of holy fool.[19] By the conclusion of World War II, then, the Central Asian countryside was alive with religious activity: at shrines, mosques, and on the roads connecting towns and cities.

Though the sources testify to what may legitimately be called a postwar resurgence of Islam, they pose particular challenges for the analysis of Sufism. Although Soviet bureaucrats referred extensively to master-disciple networks and individual *ishan*s sought out by people for blessings, they almost never spoke of Sufism (Russian, *sufizm*) explicitly, and rarely when discussing a shrine or figure did they specify the tradition in question.[20] This constitutes a significant handicap for the historian endeavoring to utilize their output, since precisely what an individual bureaucrat (or his Muslim informants) intended to convey by using the word *ishan* does not always emerge from the archival sources.[21] To add more complexity to the issue of terminology, officials apparently distinguished between "Sufism" and "*ishanizm*."[22] A legitimate criticism

18 The term *ishan* used here reflects standard academic usage. *Eshon*, the spelling used by SADUM's staff that reflects the term's pronunciation in certain parts of Central Asia, has been retained, however, when the sources give it as a part of a figure's name or title.

19 KR BMA 2597 / 1s / 4 / 220 (1947); 2597 / 1s / 10 / 23–24 (April 15, 1949).

20 In fact, in parts of Kyrgyzstan and Tajikistan, the word *sufi* referred to the prayer call reader, generally known as the *muʾadhdhin* (muezzin) in much of the Muslim world, while the corresponding term in high-altitude regions of Kyrgyzstan such as Naryn was *sopu*.

21 In the Russian imperial tradition, the words *ishan* and *murīd* brought to mind images of holy warriors in the Caucasus, as memorialized in Tolstoy's masterpiece, *Hajji Murad*. A CARC bureaucrat in Kyrgyzstan regurgitated this Tsarist conceptual framework in unadulterated fashion when he asserted that "*ishanizm* and *miuridizm* rank among the most reactionary strands of the Islamic faith, and therefore the activities of various *ishan*s merit exceptionally vigilant attention." KR BMA 2597 / 1s / 37 / 18 (September 1, 1954).

22 When questioned by his superiors in Moscow about the existence of Sufism in Central Asia, CARC's representative for Kyrgyzstan had the following to say: "Among the Uzbek population, staff members of mosques who recite the call to prayer, who hold some authority in matters of faith with respect to the believing rank and file, but who claim

of the present analysis of Sufi communities, therefore, is that it necessitates a healthy dose of extrapolation from an indubitably problematic (and biased) source base, generated by bureaucrats with little regard for the complexities of Islamic or Central Asian terminology.

However, if one is to speak at all of Sufism as an historically-rooted phenomenon in Central Asia, one must assess the existence, and evolution, of Sufi "communities" by utilizing admittedly arbitrary criteria. The sources available to the historian for the study not only of Islam, but of the region's Soviet-era social history more generally, make this arbitrariness unavoidable. This especially applies to the period after the Terror, for, as DeWeese points out, it does not appear that the prism most conventionally employed for the analysis of Sufism, the "order," existed in widespread form at any point in the postwar decades. References to master-disciple networks and *ishan*s, which appear frequently in the documentation, are therefore treated here as representative of Sufism in Soviet conditions, as is the extended family of dynastic Sufi shaykhs discussed in this article, with the caveat that the term "Sufi" is intended less as a distinctive label and more as a reference to a coherent set of rituals, figures, and sites.

Sufi figures in this general meaning abounded across Central Asia, from the Tian Shan's remote hamlets to the Farghana valley's agricultural plains. Hakim Akhtiamov, CARC's representative in Kyrgyzstan from 1945 to 1960, noted the preponderance of "dervishes (*qalandar*s), *ishanizm*, and *miuridizm* in Jalalabat province" i.e., the Kyrgyz SSR's portion of the Farghana valley.[23] *Ishan*s regularly crossed into the republic from other parts of Central Asia. In areas of southern Kyrgyzstan, they "secretly" came from Andijan and Khoqand to see their *murīds*.[24] Across Kyrgyzstan's mountainous Ysyk Köl and Tian Shan provinces, the sons of a certain Moldo Nur Batmusa exercised considerable influence. This person had apparently studied in Qarategin (Tajikistan) and brought back with him a copy of the *Maẓhar-i kull*, a Sufi work from the early 17th century, by a certain Mawlānā Jāmī b. Kamāl al-Dīn al-Qarātegīnī, regarded as sacred

much less knowledge of religion than *imāms*—these individuals the Uzbeks refer to as SUFIS, while the Tatars call them MUAZINS. As for the emergence of Sufism and *dervishizm*, these do not exist in the form of separate groups. As for *ishanizm*, it is a survival [*perezhitok*] that holds some currency among Muslims." KR BMA 2597 / 1s / 4 / 344 (September 23, 1947).

23 KR BMA 2597 / 1s / 16 / 25 (April 27, 1950).

24 KR BMA 2597 / 1s / 42a / 95–6 (April 10–12, 1954).

by the population.[25] CARC's inspector for Tajikistan estimated that Eshon Ibrohimkhon of the Vakhsh valley (near Dushanbe) commanded 200–250 disciples; one of his *murīds*, Mahmudkhon Qori, enjoyed a regional reputation in his own right.[26] Members of the Uzbek Laqay tribe had a special reputation for providing disciples to *ishans*, especially in the valleys surrounding Dushanbe.[27] Noting their widespread influence in parts of southern Tajikistan, CARC's representative wrote that "although the majority of the authentic *ishans* have now died, their uneducated sons now avail themselves of their prestige."[28] Although *ishans* were to be found across the region, Akhtiamov pointed to their complete absence among the Dungan (Hui) and Uyghurs, two ethnic groups that had migrated from or fled neighboring Xinjiang at various points of the 20th century.[29]

These and other references by Soviet bureaucrats to *ishans* (and shrines) undermine Bennigsen's emphasis on the secrecy and implacable anti-Soviet hostility of Sufi communities. The latter proved themselves able and willing to adapt to changing political conditions, from the Great Terror (which many apparently survived) to the postwar era. Far from constituting an artifice reflecting Islam's unchanging essence, Sufism sought out—and successfully held on to—niches in the Soviet landscape.

The Central Asian Muftiate (SADUM)

The implementation of Stalin's religious reforms with respect to Islam entailed creating legally recognized Muslim organizations, or muftiates. The Central Asian muftiate was, during the postwar years, a body at once Soviet and Islamic, with Naqshbandī roots. For reasons that remain unclear, Uzbekistan's

25 KR BMA 2597 / 1s / 29 / 175 (December 31, 1953). Written in 1604, this work is an account of the basic principles of Islam; in the official correspondence it is referred to as "*Mazar Kul*," and is erroneously identified as an Arabic-language translation of a Persian treatise. This mysterious text was guarded jealously by an *abïstay* or holy woman named Ku Batyr. She hid it so fastidiously that CARC's local representative never succeeded in locating the manuscript. The *Maẓhar-i kull* and its author are discussed in Maria Szuppe, "Ādīna Muḥammad Qarātēgīnī et 'son maître': Transmission des écrits de la tradition *kubravi* tardive en Asie centrale dans un recueil manuscrit de Ferghana," *Studia Iranica*, 45 (2016), 221–244.

26 BM JT 1516 / 1 / 33 / 7 (October 21, 1954).

27 BM JT 1516 / 1 / 59 / 3 (December 1957).

28 BM JT 1516 / 1 / 32 / 58 (January 8, 1954).

29 KR BMA 2597 / 1s / 12 / 80 (December 19, 1949).

government recommended an old family, the Bobokhonovs, to run SADUM. The first generation of its leadership attempted to institutionalize Sufism through two strategies: first, by filling the body's ranks with Bobokhonov family members and their disciples; and second, by depriving regional *ishan*s of any authority in the running of the legally sanctioned mosques under SADUM's control. Inadvertently, then, the Party-state placed an extended network of master-disciple relationships, with an old and influential Naqshbandī family at its center, at the core of the limited legal breathing room it granted Islam in an atheist society.

Historical evidence remains scarce surrounding the circumstances of SADUM's creation. The Bobokhonov family had deep roots in the city of Tashkent.[30] Eshon Bobokhon, the first *muftī*, was arrested twice during the years leading up to the war, in 1937 and 1940, but on both occasions the authorities "abandoned his case."[31] He received a summons in early 1943 from the head of Uzbekistan's Supreme Soviet, Yoldosh Okhunboboyev, who instructed him to author a petition, on the establishment of a muftiate, to Mikhail Kalinin, head of the USSR Supreme Soviet. The future *muftī* and a group of *ʿulamā* sent the letter on July 12, 1943. In short order the Uzbek government

---

30 In his 1889 encyclopaedia, the Russian Orientalist N. S. Lykoshin wrote the following entry on Abdulmajidkhon, father of SADUM's first *muftī*, Eshon Bobokhon: "Mulla Abdulmajidkhon ibn Yunuskhon khoja Ishan lives in the Sabzor district of the Parchibob *mahalla*, eighty years of age. He belongs to the Naqshbandī brotherhood, is considered an educated *mullā*, engages in agriculture, and is financially well provided for. The ranks of his *murīd*s in the city of Tashkent exceed 400 people. The *ishan* received the *fātiḥa* (blessing) from the Bukharan scholar Mian G'ulomqodir (also known as Sahibzoda). In all the *ishan* has prepared fifteen deputies. Among them the best known live in Tashkent: *imām* Ali khoja Ishan (Parchibob mahalla), Siddiq Qori (Halimkup mahalla), Horun khoja Ishan (Rabot mahalla), Jalil khoja Ishan. The majority of the *ishan*'s *murīd*s live in Zangi Ota and Karamurt in Tashkent province and in the city of Sayram. The *ishan* is a relative of Muhiddin hoji, the *qāżī* of the city of Tashkent. The *ishan*'s oldest son is married to Muhiddin hoji's daughter. Mulla Abdulmajidkhon is the most esteemed cleric of the city. He claims a reputable *shajara*, demonstrating the roots of his line in the luminaries of Islam—something he is exceedingly proud of. For his property he pays 100 rubles tax annually. Every Friday morning a prayer takes place in the Parchibob mosque with 20–30 people participating. The *ishan* is a *mudarris*—the director of the Moy-i Muborak madrasa." Amirsaidkhan Usmankhodzhaev, *Zhizn' muftiev Babakhanovykh: sluzhenie vozrozhdeniiu Islama v Sovetskom Soiuze* (Nizhnyi Novgorod: Medina, 2008), 26–27.

31 He later related that his interrogator cried to him: "You shall fizzle out in this prison!" Whereupon the future *muftī* responded: "Everything in this world happens according to the will of Allah. I entrust myself to the Almighty and the fate He has prepared for me." Ibid., 36.

conveyed an invitation to Eshon Bobokhon to meet with Stalin in the Kremlin.[32] Following the audience, SADUM's founding *qurultoy* took place in Tashkent on October 20, 1943, attended by 160 Islamic scholars from the region.[33] The *muftī* used this inaugural confidence to place fellow *'ulamā*—revered scholars, disciples, and relatives—at the organization's helm.[34] Like him, all possessed some historical connection to the Naqshbandī historical tradition. If this common Sufi heritage registered on Soviet bureaucrats' radar, they made no mention of it.

Master-disciple networks bound the first generation of SADUM's leadership closely together and, from the available evidence, appear to have contributed to the organization's stature in Muslim communities. Many senior figures claimed *murīds* or disciples. The first *muftī*, Eshon Bobokhon, visited southern Kyrgyzstan in 1952 to hold meetings with his *murīds* "on the pretext of vacationing in Jalalabat," according to one report.[35] CARC received reports of a well-known *ishan* named Hamdon Qori, who resided in the village of Chinoz outside of Tashkent, calling upon the *muftī*.[36] Eshon Murod khoja Solihkhojayev, who ran the organization's central apparatus from 1945–1947, attempted to kiss the *muftī*'s feet on one occasion, hinting at a master-disciple bond.[37] Abdullojon Kalonov, who would become *qāżī* of Tajikistan and a prominent figure in the 1970s, was a *murīd* of SADUM's first *qāżī* in the republic, Bashirkhon tora Ishaqii.[38] The sources speak overwhelmingly concerning the authority enjoyed by one figure in particular: the *qāżī* of Kyrgyzstan

32 Ibid., 41–42.

33 O'zR MDA r-2456/1/184/59 (November 15, 1956).

34 He placed his son (and *muftī* from 1957–1982), Ziyovuddinkhon, in charge of SADUM's administration in the Uzbek SSR, and the esteemed Naqshbandī master Olimkhon tora Shokirkhojayev (concerning whom more below) at the helm of the muftiate's administration in Kyrgyzstan. Murod khoja Solihkhojayev, a disciple of Eshon Bobokhon, initially took charge of the central apparatus, while another Naqshbandī, Anna Eshonlar, became SADUM's *qāżī* for Turkmenistan. Shamsuddinkhon Bobokhonov, *Shaykh Ziyovuddinkhon ibn Eshon Bobokhon: ma'naviyat va ibrat maktabi* (Tashkent: Ozbekiston Milliy Entsiklopediyasi, 2001), 41; O'zR MDA r-2456/1/184/60 (November 15, 1956). On the other hand, a distinctly non-Sufi, non-Naqshbandī Islamic scholar, Shafoat hoji Kholiqnazarov of Osh, was handed responsibility for the muftiate's central finances, until his ouster in a 1947 power struggle.

35 KR BMA 2597 / 1S / 25 / 236 (December 25, 1952).

36 KR BMA 2597 / 1S / 4 / 219 (1947).

37 KR BMA 2597 / 1S / 2 / 62–63 (October 3, 1947).

38 O'zR MDA r-2456 / 1 / 211 / 14 (October 10, 1957).

from 1943 to 1962, Olimkhon tora Shokirkhojayev.[39] According to CARC in Uzbekistan, he "has a large number of disciples ... some of whom work as staff in the [registered] mosques of the Kyrgyz SSR."[40] His influence extended into both the registered mosques controlled by SADUM, as well as circles beyond the muftiate's control. Immediately after the founding *qurultoy* in 1943, the former made a tour of Kyrgyzstan's Talas province, perhaps even on his way back home from Tashkent, spreading the word that people could open mosques without state permission.[41] On numerous occasions CARC in Kyrgyzstan informed Moscow that he appointed unregistered disciples as his deputies

39 Kyrgyz, *Alïmkan toro Shakir kojo ulu*; Russian, *Alimkhan tiura Shakirkhodzhaev.* His father emigrated to the northern Kyrgyz city of Tokmuk from Chust, in the Farghana valley's Namangan region, in the last quarter of the 19th century and maintained a significant following of *murīds* in the northern provinces of Frunze and Ysyk Köl. Olimkhon tora lived with his father in Mecca for five years in his youth, studying in many of the city's madrasas. Upon returning to Turkestan he enrolled in a madrasa in Andijan, and after completing his education in 1911 taught at a madrasa in Tokmuk. During the 1916 rebellion, he fled to Kashgaria, returning after one year to Andijan, where he taught up to 1923. Until his appointment to the post of *qāżī* in 1943 he continued his educational activities while serving as *imām* in Tokmuk. Unlike many other highly-placed figures in SADUM, who were incarcerated during the Great Terror of 1937–1938, he was arrested in 1935 for "anti-Soviet agitation." As with his future colleagues, though, the authorities released him after a few months "for lack of evidence of a crime." He was fluent in Arabic, Persian, and a number of Turkic languages, but, like the majority of the region's religious figures at this time (and certainly like all of SADUM's leadership), he knew no Russian and could not read the Cyrillic script. Olimkhon tora had two brothers whose fates differed radically from his. One of them, Jabborkhon, remained in Mecca when Olimkhon and his father returned to Turkestan in the first decade of the 20th century, and from there emigrated to Turkey to study medicine. Jabborkhon would have returned home, had his father not died at Sayram in southern Kazakhstan on his way to Mecca to fetch him. He served as a doctor in the British army during World War II. A third son, Alikhon, fled to Kulja in northwestern Xinjiang after the Bolsheviks came to power, became foreign minister of the short-lived Republic of East Turkestan in the 1940s, and later returned to live in Tashkent, officially barred from traveling abroad. KR BMA 2597 / 1s / 1 / 169 (March 11, 1947). Alikhon still resided in Uzbekistan in 1975, when Ziyovuddin qori, then the *muftī*, mentioned his poor health in a Friday sermon and asked those present to pray for his recovery. Ziyovuddin qori paid tribute to Alikhon, noting the important role he played in educating young *imāms*, and "his organization of the Xinjiang Muslim army, which sought to defend Muslims from the Chinese yoke." O'zR MDA r-2456 / 1 / 570 / 28 (December 5, 1975).

40 O'zR MDA r-2456 1 / 184 / 36 (December 7, 1956).

41 KR BMA 2597 / 1s / 7 / 113 (June 2, 1948).

in spite of repeated warnings.[42] So elevated was Olimkhon tora's reputation that upon the first *muftī*'s death in 1957, he was one of two individuals widely considered as a potential candidate to assume control.[43] The *muftī*'s son and successor until 1982, Ziyovuddinkhon, regarded him as a threat until his ouster by CARC in 1962.[44] Though Ziyovuddinkhon and his associates would come to eschew the Sufi associations of their fathers, during the 1940s and 1950s, SADUM's inner corridors remained a staunchly Naqshbandī setting.

A likely reason for this eschewal, and all but disavowal, of Sufism was that centralization and control at the local level constituted the leadership's highest priority throughout SADUM's fifty-year history. By 1947, the muftiate sought direct administrative authority over the handful of legalized mosques in Central Asia. This put the body in direct conflict with figures beyond its aegis who possessed linkages with Sufi lineages and practices. Here it bears emphasizing that for local communities, the opening of these mosques carried overwhelming significance. They constituted the only space in which large numbers of Muslims could openly congregate without fear of official retaliation. Moreover, in the Soviet era (as in other periods), Central Asian mosques fulfilled important social functions, such as distributing bread to the poor.[45] It therefore comes as no surprise that communities did not lightly consent to handing over control of their mosques' finances, staffing, and operation to a distant, alien Islamic bureaucracy such as SADUM. For one, no such body had existed in the region before. More importantly, the landscape featured *ʿulamā*—almost all referred to as *ishan*s—who naturally emerged as obvious candidates for leadership in these newly legalized mosques. Thus the opening of a SADUM-run mosque often represented the imposition of the Bobokhonov family's authority over one or more local master-disciple networks. In other words, the muftiate was mapping out its own network upon the stage of officially approved religiosity.

These confrontations could get messy. The case of the registered mosque in Kok Yanghaq (Kyrgyz, Kök Jangak), a mining town in southern Kyrgyzstan, illustrates the muftiate's agenda particularly well. Here, SADUM first installed an *imām* over the wishes of local *ishan*s, then attempted to remove him from office. Upon his arrival in 1947, Mutigulla Asadullin, the *imām*, encouraged

42 KR BMA 2597 / 1s / 1 / 104 (August 12, 1946); 2597 / 1s / 1 / 170 (March 11, 1947); 2597 / 1s / 10 / 145 (November 2, 1949).

43 KR BMA 2597 / 1s / 66 / 146 (October 22, 1957); O'zR MDA r-2456 / 1 / 207 / 72 (October 16, 1957).

44 O'zR MDA r-2456 / 1 / 211 / 6–7 (October 10, 1957).

45 KR BMA 2597 / 1s / 77 / 51 (February 22, 1960).

local miners to perform as many of the daily prayers as possible at home rather than coming to the mosque. He also discouraged them from memorizing long Arabic prayers, suggesting a shorter prayer instead.[46] These pronouncements resulted in a sharp decrease in the number of Muslims coming to congregational prayers on days other than Friday: on average five to eight old men showed up, a very modest figure even for the dawn prayer in the Farghana valley in the 1940s.[47] Outraged by these apparently unprecedented changes, a local master named Eshon Mullo Murod Ortiqov (Russian, Artykov) arranged for Daujanov, chairman of the mosque's executive committee and one of his disciples, to compile a petition with twenty signatures requesting that SADUM remove Asadullin.[48] In a climate of palpable tension, Daujanov even interrupted the *imām* during one of his Friday sermons, virtually an unthinkable occurrence in Central Asia. Daujanov and Ortiqov began spreading rumors that Asadullin was a devil and that God would not accept prayers recited under his *imām*ship.[49] The exasperated miners rallied around Asadullin. At a spontaneously organized community meeting inside the mosque on July 29, 1947, the community fired Daujanov from his position on the executive committee *viva voce*.

SADUM did not take long to respond. Asadullin had already received a written warning from the *muftī*'s son and *qāżī* of Uzbekistan, Ziyovuddinkhon, demanding that he recant some of the more controversial positions in his sermons. Specifically, he encouraged the *imām* to attract as many believers to the mosque as possible so as to maximize donations. Now, the muftiate dispatched the Naqshbandī master and *qāżī* of Kyrgyzstan, Olimkhon tora Shokirkhojayev, to personally oversee Asadullin's removal and the installment of a new *imām*.

46 As transcribed from Cyrillic, *Rabbana 'atina fi al-dunya hasanatan wa fi al-akhirati hasanatan wa qina 'adhab al-nar, bi rahmatika ya arham al-rahimin.* (O Lord! Give us what is good in this life and in the next, and save us from the Hellfire, with your mercy.).

47 By way of comparison, an average of 500 people attended the dawn prayer at the Ravat Abdullokhon mosque (at the foot of the holy mountain in Kyrgyzstan known as the Throne of Solomon) on a daily basis during the 1940s. KR BMA 2597 / 1s / 4 / 217 (March–April 1947). In district centers in the south i.e., small towns, the corresponding numbers for the morning prayer ranged from 18–100. KR BMA 2597 / 1s / 7 / 51 (March 30, 1948).

48 According to Soviet legislation on religion, every house of worship required a functionary, an executive committee in charge of finances, and a committee of twenty original signatories requesting permission to open a prayer house. The chairman of the executive committee often exercised considerable influence in the workings of mosques. Clashes between these chairmen and *imāms* occurred frequently, especially in the 1970s and 1980s.

49 KR BMA 2597 / 1s / 10 / 82 (August 5, 1949).

Accusations leveled at Asadullin included responsibility for the low numbers of Muslims attending the mosque, disrespect for holy sites and saints, "nationalism," and being "the ladies' *imām*" (*khatunlar imami*) due to his efforts to encourage women to attend congregational prayers. Despite his best efforts to silence Asadullin's supporters, the *qāżī* failed to implement the *imām*'s removal. The muftiate's only remaining recourse was to appeal to CARC for assistance. When the bureaucrats launched an inquiry, however, they received a petition signed by 438 residents of Kok Yanghaq, praising Asadullin and requesting that he be allowed to stay. In these circumstances, CARC decided to take no action and Asadullin remained in his position until at least 1959.[50]

Although the archival record leaves numerous frustrating gaps, the basic trajectory of this episode is not hard to reconstruct. Rather than selecting a figure from the local community, SADUM appointed an outsider, Asadullin, to serve as *imām* in the newly legalized mosque. Asadullin's unconventional pronouncements (for Central Asia in the 1940s, at least), not to mention his very presence, infuriated at least one prominent local *ishan*. Confronted with this conflict, SADUM's chief concern was not the anger of a local Sufi figure, but rather the financial implications of low attendance at the mosque. The *ishan*'s complaints took on new significance, however, when the community dramatically fired Daujanov of its own volition. SADUM now attached symbolic significance to this seemingly obscure mosque: Olimkhon tora made the multiday journey from northern Kyrgyzstan to resolve the conflict—at the time a trek across unpaved roads through high-altitude passes.[51] (The willingness of such a high-profile figure to make such an arduous journey merely to resolve a staffing problem suggests that the *ishan* may have had links either to the Bobokhonov family or to Olimkhon tora.) The Kok Yanghaq episode thus sheds light on two aspects of SADUM's relations with Sufi figures beyond its administrative reach. First, it had no qualms about ignoring or trampling over their authority as a means of establishing control. Second, the muftiate attached some importance to a sense of Sufi propriety. The organization apparently encouraged its appointees to challenge local authority figures. But it was another thing entirely when communities did so at their own initiative. This represented an affront both to the organization's pretensions to absolute administrative control, and to the hierarchical master-disciple bonds comprising its structure.[52]

---

50 The text of the petition is in KR BMA 2597 / 1s / 10 / 86–99 (May 13, 1949) and in Russian translation in ll. 81–85.

51 The mountainous highway linking the republic's north and south did not yet exist.

52 A more straightforward interpretation, and in fact the one advanced by CARC bureaucrats, is that SADUM's sole interest in the mosque concerned control over money and

The Kok Yanghaq episode's viscerality characterized much of SADUM's confrontation with numerous ʿulamā embedded in Central Asia's villages and small towns. During the 1940s and 1950s, this attempt to override local authority networks largely failed. Only from the mid-1950s, with Ziyovuddinkhon's rise and subsequent election to the office of *muftī*, did the organization pursue the more productive strategy of co-opting and integrating these figures.[53] This outcome illustrates the possibilities for Islam, and with it Sufism, to evolve and expand at a time when the state exhibited little interest in religion generally. Not only did the muftiate have political room to assert its authority throughout the region, but religious figures and communities enjoyed the latitude to offer resistance.

The 1953 Jalalabat Trial

If SADUM's history in the decade after World War II represents a relative absence of state interference into Sufism, then the postwar trial of over a dozen alleged Sufi *khalīfas* offers a striking contrast. Held in the southern Kyrgyz city of Jalalabat in August 1953, the trial focused on individuals identified as members of the "Hairy *Ishan*" sect (Uzbek, *chachlik ishanlar*; Russian, *organizatsiia "Volosatykh ishanov"*) of the Qādirī order. Prosecutors employed vocabulary hearkening back to Soviet campaigns against Christian "sectarians," making it nearly impossible to contextualize the proceedings' reference to the Qādiriyya. The "Hairy *Ishan*" designation, similarly, appears arbitrarily, on the basis that the accused "wrapped themselves in torn clothes, grew long hair on their heads and beards, and referred to themselves as the people of the hairy *ishan, Chachlyk Ishan*."[54] Anti-religious proceedings are a problematic source for acquiring insight into Sufism, and the trial records offer no background on the groups' composition; prosecutors took it as a matter of course that they existed in the form of sects. Nevertheless, as the only court case explicitly targeting Sufism in the Farghana valley in the decade following World War II, the proceedings merit analysis balanced with a healthy dose of scrutiny.

---

donations. This explanation does not account for the involvement of senior SADUM figures—the *muftī*'s son and the *qāżī* of Kyrgyzstan—or for the relatively small size of Kok Yanghaq's Muslim community compared to other registered mosques.

53 Eren Tasar, *Soviet and Muslim: The institutionalization of Islam in Central Asia, 1943–1991* (New York: Oxford University Press, 2017), 167–172.

54 KR BMA 2678 / 1 / 4 / 39 (August 1953).

Employing antireligious xenophobia from the Great Terror, prosecutors accused the men involved of forming a "nationalist" and "anti-Soviet organization." The trial proceedings paint a portrait of reactionary young men roaming the Central Asian countryside in a conscious, clandestine effort to arouse anti-Soviet sentiment, all in the service of a future Islamic state (referred to in the documentation as *Musulmanabad*). At first glance, the proceedings appear to support Bennigsen's conclusions concerning both the hostility of Sufi figures toward the Soviet state as well as official xenophobia about Sufism.

Held on August 10–12, 1953, the trial centered around the "anti-Soviet" activities of a group of Hairy *Ishans* in the Farghana valley, the majority of them from Uzbekistan's Andijan Province. This group's alleged ringleader, a descendant of wealthy landowners named Tursunboy Madaripov (b. 1889), had been labeled a *kulak* in 1931 and consequently lost all his property. He assumed leadership of the "sect" in 1936, upon the arrest of his master (*pir-ishan*), Abdumutolib Satyvaldiyev, and 32 other members of the organization.[55] Madaripov organized a meeting of *khalīfa*s in Andijan in 1941 at which he allegedly set out four objectives: to attract new recruits from social groups alienated by Soviet policies; to conduct anti-Soviet agitation; to encourage the population to abstain from joining the Soviet Army on religious grounds; and to collect donations for the Hairy *Ishan* organization. The *khalīfa*s received orders to travel far and wide to instruct the sect's *murīd*s in implementing these objectives.[56] Under interrogation, one of Madaripov's disciples stated that he had preached "the creation in Central Asia of a Muslim state called *Musul'manabad* … only Muslims would be allowed in it, and upon its creation the Muslims would have a high standard of living."[57] In 1943 Madaripov was sentenced to five years in prison for refusing to serve in the army, but in 1949 he recommenced his illegal activities. At yet another 1951 meeting in Andijan, he instructed his *khalīfa*s to conduct agitation against the Soviet elections being held that year. The

55 According to the only other reference to this trial on record, those arrested were executed in 1938; see Satïbaldï Mambetaliev, *Sufizm jana anïn Kïrgïzstandagï akïmdarï* (Frunze: Kyrgyzstan, 1972), 43–54.

56 The use of the words *khalīfa* and *murīd* is enigmatic. Madaripov "kept in touch with the *murīd*s through the *khalīfa*s. He did everything through the latter." (l. 57) The proceedings also contain references to female disciples (*miuridka*) (l. 26).

57 KR BMA 2678 / 1 / 4 / 47 (August 1953). Yet another told interrogators: "Turnboy *ishan* said that in conversation with others it is necessary to propagandize the lifestyle of the associates of an *ishan* (*khalīfa*s and *duvona*s). He said that by tormenting themselves in this world and abstaining from all the good things of the world, *khalīfa*s and *duvona*s devote their existence to the service of God and their *ishan* and therefore in the next life they will arrive directly into Heaven." Ibid., l. 52.

arrests of Madaripov and a circle of his *khalīfa*s followed between August and November 1952. They were sentenced to 25 years in prison.[58]

The proceedings would seem to support Bennigsen's theses regarding Sufism in Central Asia: that Sufi communities stood in hostile opposition to the Soviet state, and that the Party feared Sufism as a political force. Yet the trial's exceptionally strange timing suggests otherwise. Whereas the 1940s witnessed relative indifference toward Islam on the part of the Soviet state, exceptional and even active moderation characterized the period from roughly 1951 until Khrushchev's antireligious campaign of 1959–1964. Moreover, no perceptible shift in Soviet religious policy generally accompanied Stalin's death earlier that year.[59] Scholars widely regard the Party Central Committee's Decree of November 10, 1954, "On Mistakes in the Conduct of Scientific-Atheistic Propaganda among the Population," as signaling the heyday of official laxity toward religion across the country.[60] Broader currents in Soviet society thus point to the summer of 1953 as an unusual moment for inaugurating a crackdown, especially given that the alleged crimes of the accused largely took place in the 1920s and 1930s. Of course, even at the best of times, individual crackdowns on religious figures and shrines, virtually always at the initiative of zealous district Party functionaries, were not unusual.[61] These instances of antireligious activism, however, do not paint a convincing portrait of widespread repression against Islam any more than the trial proceedings reliably indicate the existence of a Sufi conspiracy to overthrow the state. Since a wave of comparable trials did not occur in Central Asia at this time, one may plausibly view Jalalabat as a local episode with local roots, and comfortably dismiss Bennigsen's suggestions concerning Sufi conspiracies.[62]

---

58 The main proceedings are in KR BMA 2678 / 2s / 7 / 2–68 (August 12, 1953).

59 M. V. Shkarovskii, *Russkaia pravoslavnaia tserkov' pri Staline i Khrushcheve: gosudarstvenno-tserkovnye otnosheniia v SSSR v 1939–1964 gg.* (Moscow: Krutitskoe Patriarshee Podvor'e, Obshchestvo liubitelei tserkovnoi istorii, 1999).

60 Nathaniel Davis, *A Long Walk to Church: a contemporary history of Russian Orthodoxy* (Boulder, Colorado: Westview, 1995), 30.

61 For example, throughout the early 1950s officials at the State Security Ministry branch in Uzbekistan's Namangan province regularly crossed into Kyrgyzstan and imposed restrictions on a shrine near Jalalabat, Shoh Fozil. These restrictions most often involved road closures but on occasion included arbitrary detention of drivers transporting pilgrims. KR BMA 2597 / 1s / 21 / 39 (October 1, 1951); 2597 / 1s / 49 / 59 (November 9, 1954).

62 If a short-lived wave of detentions and trials targeting Sufism did occur in Central Asia in 1953–54, then surely the CARC documentation would offer some indication. The only way to know for sure, however, is to consult the KGB archives of the various Central Asian republics. These remain closed to researchers.

A more revealing context for understanding this trial is the broader bureaucratic analysis of Islam crystallizing during this decade. Detailed reports emerged of *duvonas* engaging in "charlatanism" and "trickstering," and in one case even coming back from the dead.[63] In 1952, eye-catching rumors reached CARC of a clandestine sect known as the *Lohochi*, which allegedly engaged in sexual orgies after ecstatic evenings of drum-beating and chanting, and required adepts to drink their master's urine.[64] It later emerged that details about the *Lohochi* had been poorly substantiated, deriving from local gossip obtained by CARC's provincial representative.[65] Nevertheless, the timing of these rhetorical formulations concerning Sufi fanaticism, taken together with the 1953 Jalalabat trial, points to new official awareness of Sufism as a distinct phenomenon.[66] This awareness did not translate into a bureaucratic or even verbal assault against Sufi communities until Khrushchev's antireligious campaign.

In fact, the testimony suggests that the accused enjoyed a remarkable degree of unhindered mobility in postwar Central Asia, and exerted little or no effort to conceal their community's existence. Madaripov's *khalīfas* traveled from collective farm to collective farm over the years without getting arrested. On these trips, they conducted community rites such as the *jahr*, collective *zikr* (referred to in the proceedings as *zikr-suhbat*), *mavludi sharif*, and group readings of the *Hikmat*[67] and the writings of the 19th century Uzbek poet Majzub Namangani.[68] As for the gatherings Madaripov organized with his *khalīfas*, these "illegal meetings" took place "on the pretext of conducting religious rites, during the course of which they not only conducted anti-Soviet indoctrination, but also received instructions concerning the organization of anti-Soviet agitation among the surrounding population, as well as the preparation of potential

63 KR BMA 2597 / 1s / 15 / 158–160 (November 3, 1950).

64 KR BMA 2597 / 1s / 42a / 49 (June 14, 1954).

65 KR BMA 2597 / 1s / 25 / 309 (February 3, 1953). Given the duration and geographical diversity of reports about the *Lohochi*, however, it is likely that the "sect" did exist in some form.

66 As I have argued elsewhere, CARC's preoccupation during these years with the categories of fanaticism, charlatanism, and isolation from society tacitly served to justify its dramatic support for Muslim figures and institutions it considered "authentically" Islamic i.e., SADUM's hierarchy and even the many unregistered mosques staffed by *imāms, adhan* readers, and other relatively "stationary" figures. Tasar, *Soviet and Muslim*, 132–138.

67 Devin DeWeese discusses Soviet uses of this term in a recent contribution. See his "Ahmad Yasavi and the *Divan-i-Hikmat* in Soviet scholarship," in *The Heritage of Soviet Oriental Studies*, ed. Michael Kemper and Stephan Conermann (London: Routledge, 2011), 262–290.

68 His *Tazkirat ul-avliyo*.

murīds."[69] (This implies that few obstacles existed to unregistered religious figures conducting rites, a theme that emerges repeatedly in CARC's documentation as well.) One of the *khalīfas*, A. Ermatov, had evaded a 1943 draft call from the Soviet military authorities in Osh merely by traveling a short distance to the mountainous Kyrgyz town of Arslanbob, where he later joined the Hairy *Ishans*. He was left untouched until his 1952 arrest—that is, for almost an entire decade—despite the fact that he presumably merited intense official monitoring, having been imprisoned from 1936 to 1939 for anti-Soviet agitation, and briefly incarcerated yet again in 1943 for refusing to join the army.[70] Another *khalīfa*, Mamasiddiq Alikhonov (b. 1911), was imprisoned from 1943–1949 for refusing to serve in the army, yet immediately came to Madaripov's side upon his release.[71] Moreover, the arrested *khalīfas* hailed from different corners of the Farghana valley—one even came from the city of Turkistan, site of the mausoleum of Khoja Aḥmad Yasavī, in southern Kazakhstan—suggesting the ability to travel back and forth to Madaripov's bases in Andijan, Arslanbob, and perhaps elsewhere on "religious business."[72]

All of this points to a panorama of religious life strikingly similar to the setting in which SADUM operated. With the state's attention focused elsewhere, breathing room existed in Muslim life for old relationships to come back to life and new networks to coalesce. Large and noisy rites took place in collectivized state farms without attracting the attention of authorities. Madaripov's *khalīfas*, who were apparently unemployed, traveled frequently through the countryside without being detained, despite the fact that many had criminal records. One of the few examples of hardline anti-Sufi activism in postwar Central Asia, the 1953 Jalalabat Trial, ends up offering little evidence of an antagonistic relationship between Sufi communities and the Soviet state. Quite the contrary: the Hairy *Ishans* made themselves at home in the most widespread Soviet institution in the USSR, the collective farm, and moreover did so, apparently, without undergoing any harassment. Although, like any Soviet source concerning religion, the trial proceedings leave many questions unanswered, at a minimum they demonstrate that Sufi communities beyond SADUM found more than one niche for themselves in the postwar sociopolitical landscape.

69 KR BMA 2678 / 1s / 4 / 41 (August 10–12, 1953).
70 Ibid., l. 49.
71 KR BMA 2678 / 2s / 7 / 29 (August 10–12, 1953).
72 Ibid., ll. 20–23.

Hazrat Ayub and the Jalalabat Resort

SADUM and the Jalalabat Trial represent two radically different settings. The former case illustrates the possibilities for bureaucracy with Naqshbandī historical roots to assert authority over religious life. The latter offers a reminder that the Party's antireligious orientation could, even in the early 1950s, manifest itself in action against Sufi communities. Hazrat Ayub, a holy spring in the middle of a state health resort (Russian, *sanatorii*) outside of Jalalabat city, combines elements of both cases. Here, a descent group claiming sacred lineage (Persian, *khwāja*; Uzbek, *khoja*) with Naqshbandī roots oversaw pilgrimages to the spring, while coming to assume almost total control over the resort's daily operations.[73] Soviet officialdom—the resort administration, Jalalabat's urban Party and government authorities, and CARC—attempted to bar pilgrims from coming to the spring, but took no direct action against the *khojas* until Khrushchev's antireligious campaign. Hazrat Ayub thus points to the impressive influence unregistered religious figures (i.e., those not employed by SADUM) could acquire within a Soviet institution, even when officialdom appreciated the scope of their activities and the depth of their influence.

The site's history is closely intertwined with a community of Naqshbandī *khojas*. Its name originates in a legend, according to which the Prophet Job (Ayyūb, Uzbek Ayub) first bathed in the springs as a cure for leprosy.[74] Hazrat Ayub once housed the mausoleum of an unidentified saint. Local authorities demolished this structure when they built the Jalalabat Resort around the springs in the 1920s.[75] They sought to take advantage of the springs' salubrious mineral properties, which health officials apparently acknowledged, while desacralizing the site for the benefit of modern Soviet citizens. When planners arrived to survey the site, however, they encountered a large number of *khoja* families residing around the springs and facilitating pilgrimage rites for visitors. They claimed descent from an Arab saint who had arrived in the region eight centuries earlier.[76] Both the Khoqand khans and the Russian

73 On the *khojas* see Devin DeWeese, "The Politics of Sacred Lineages in 19th century Central Asia: descent groups linked to Khwaja Ahmad Yasavi in shrine documents and genealogical documents," *International Journal of Middle East Studies*, 31/4 (1999), 507–533; his "Foreword," in *Islamizatsiia i "sakral'nye" rodoslovnye v Tsentral'noi Azii: nasledie Ishak Baba v narrativnoi i genealogicheskoi traditsiiakh, tom 2*, ed. Ashirbek Muminov, Anke von Kügelgen, Devin DeWeese, and Michael Kemper (Almaty: Daik Press, 2008), 6–33.

74 The site was also referred to as Ayub Buloq (Job's spring) and Ayub Payghambar (Prophet Job).

75 KR BMA 2597 / 1s / 15 / 157 (November 3, 1950).

76 The document lists his name as "Zimnun-il'-Kiori." KR BMA 2597 / 1s / 4 / 220 (1947).

colonial authorities permitted them to control Hazrat Ayub.[77] When construction of the resort reached completion in 1928, however, the *khojas* were denied access to the grounds. They responded by opening 14 teahouses (*choykhona*) immediately outside the front gate, where they conducted healing rites on sick pilgrims and accepted the meat of sacrificed animals.[78] During Stalin's collectivization drive inaugurated the same year, authorities shut down these teahouses and collectivized the *khojas*. A decade later, in 1939, a Party decree on the abuse of state property led to their forced relocation to two collective farms three kilometers from the shrine.[79] This removal came to a halt, however, with the onset of World War II in 1941: a sizeable number of *khoja* families remained next to the shrine; the others eschewed participation in collectivized agriculture, instead walking back and forth to the springs every day to service pilgrims.[80] By 1946, when they first appear in CARC's documentation, 72 of these *khoja* families resided next to or near Hazrat Ayub. They openly ran one teahouse, which served as a reception area for pilgrims.[81] In addition to their saintly lineage, the *khojas* claimed Naqshbandī lineage. Their ranks included disciples of Olimkhon tora Shokirkhojayev.[82] Very likely, some of them regarded Eshon Bobokhon as a master as well: in 1946, Eshon Murod khoja Solihkhojayev, head of SADUM's central apparatus and a disciple of the *muftī*, spent 22 days as a guest of the *khojas* at Hazrat Ayub.[83]

Although CARC's documentation does not focus on the *khojas*' role as Sufis, it suggests that, throughout the 1950s, they exercised a degree of control over the site comparable to the pre-Bolshevik era, enjoying nearly absolute authority in regulating pilgrimage traffic and rites. According to CARC, the *khojas* "propagandized" and "popularized" the cult of holy water to enhance their own esteem. As a rule, all pilgrims bathed in the springs, drank the water and rubbed it on their faces, soaked their clothes in it, and brought containers back home. In addition, many female pilgrims took handfuls of mud from underneath the

77 Khudoyor, the last khan of Khoqand, sent a deputy (*mutavallī*) to the shrine, whom the *khojas* subsequently evicted. The Tsarist Russians "used the springs for only 3–4 months, while the *khojas* remained in charge for the remainder of the year." Ibid., l. 220.

78 Bringing such meat to the caretakers of shrines was and remains a common feature of Central Asian shrine pilgrimage, especially on the two *ʿeids*.

79 Postanovlenie VKP/b/ i SNK SSSR ot 27 maia 1939 goda "O merakh khrany obshchestvennykh zemel' kolkhozov ot razbazarivaniia."

80 In 1948–1949, 60–70% of the relocated *khojas* (150–200 people) engaged in no agricultural work at the two collective farms. KR BMA 2597 / 1s / 11 / 31 (March 28, 1949).

81 This account is in KR BMA 2597 / 1s / 4 / 220–221 (1947).

82 KR BMA 2597 / 1s / 1 / 85 (June 1, 1946).

83 KR BMA 2597 / 1s / 4 / 221 (1947).

trees growing around the spring and rubbed it on their eyes and faces, doing the same to their children as well.[84] Access to the springs could be secured only through the *khojas*. In 1951, CARC's representative in Jalalabat province reported that "although the resort is a state enterprise, nevertheless the [*khoja*] shaykhs sit on the road leading to it and around the springs, relating various old wives' tales to visitors, accepting donations, and conducting sacrificial rites."[85] These shaykhs also set up a small bazar outside the grounds, where they sold jugs for pilgrims to take water home.[86] Between July–August 1950 over 500 cows and goats were sacrificed at a dedicated enclosure inside the resort under the *khojas*' supervision; in August and September the following year, pilgrims killed 5–10 animals per day.[87] By the mid-1950s, the *khojas* were conducting sacrifices in the courtyards of their homes, located on the resort grounds.[88] Through their lineage and affiliation with Hazrat Ayub, these shaykhs commanded enormous reverence. When a new spring was uncovered at the site in 1952, a *khoja* named Momin Ibragimov installed himself in front of it to control access and block "strangers" from approaching. In fact, pilgrims referred to the new spring as "Momin Buloq" (Mumin's spring).[89] In an extreme case, one pilgrim reportedly knifed his wife to death for refusing to believe that one of the shaykhs could cure her barrenness.[90] Thus, the *khojas* permeated the site as a component of the springs' sacred aura, and did so, moreover, openly within the limited confines of a state enterprise.

Together with the appropriation of space nominally under the state's control for sacred purposes, the *khojas* gradually filled most of the resort's employment vacancies as well. As a low-level government (rather than Party) body, the administration undertook no measures to screen its applicants for ideological suitability, hiring the nearest available labor instead. In 1951, CARC's local representative first noticed that 16 *khojas*—ten men and six women—had found employment there, though his proposal to replace them with ethnic Russians went nowhere.[91] By the next year this list had grown to 22 individuals, "either formally employed by the resort or unemployed but residing on the

84 KR BMA 2597 / 1s / 25 / 220–221 (December 25, 1952).
85 KR BMA 2597 / 1s / 18 / 55 (March 27, 1951).
86 KR BMA 2597 / 1s / 19 / 48 (November 15, 1951).
87 KR BMA 2597 / 1s / 21 / 41 (October 1, 1951).
88 KR BMA 2597 / 1s / 62 / 105 (February 25, 1958).
89 KR BMA 2597 / 1s / 25 / 222 (December 25, 1952).
90 KR BMA 2597 / 1s / 42a / 118 (April 10–12, 1954). The man was sentenced to ten years in prison.
91 KR BMA 2597 / 1s / 21 / 41 (October 1, 1951).

resort grounds." Mullo Toshkhoja Saidkamolov, identified as the "chief shaykh," held no position at the complex, but his son-in-law worked in the kitchen. The *khojas* labored mostly as gardeners, store staff, and construction workers, though one, Obid Roziqov, directed the complex's school for children;[92] it transpired that both he and another *khoja* employed by the procurement department belonged to the Communist Party.[93] Two others, including a *qori* (Qur'ān reciter), worked in the mud therapy section (*griazolechebnitsa*). Mamarasul, a *khoja* employed as groundskeeper, "wanders the resort's alleys and demands donations from passers-by."[94] By the mid-1950s, some had secured jobs for their children as well.[95] A 1956 count revealed 17 *khojas* living within the resort grounds, "either as family members of resort employees or on the pretext of occupying insignificant positions," as well as 27 other shaykhs (*sheikhstvuiushchikh lits-khodzhei*) at a nearby collective farm.[96] These reports demonstrate that aside from a narrow stratum of administrators removed from the realities of daily operation, all substantive interaction with visitors rested squarely in the *khojas*' hands. Like SADUM, the resort was an institution at once Soviet, Islamic, and Sufi.

Local government left Hazrat Ayub alone entirely during the first half of the 1950s, CARC's meticulous documentation of the shaykhs' activities notwithstanding. The resort administration had no incentive to crack down on pilgrimage rites, since such bodies were not charged with conducting antireligious propaganda. Administrators actually stood to benefit from the large number of visitors conducting pilgrimage by classifying them as "patients." Rising numbers of visitors were due to the enormous popularity of shrine pilgrimage in the Farghana valley during 1950s, a phenomenon that engendered little or no restriction at the local government level. Even the Throne of Solomon, a holy mountain inside the city of Osh (some 50 miles south of Jalalabat) visited by over 100,000 pilgrims on 'Eid ul-Adha in 1954 and 1955, did not witness any interference by the Osh Party committee until 1958.[97] Thus, the resort administration's indifference to religious life on its grounds, coupled with the general

92 KR BMA 2597 / 1s / 25 / 220–221 (December 25, 1952).

93 KR BMA 2597 / 1s / 62 / 106 (February 25, 1958). Roziqov's name appears in the 1952 report referenced in the previous footnote without any mention of his Party affiliation. As this 1958 report refers to him as a Party member, he presumably became a Communist at some point after 1952, i.e., while he was serving as a shaykh and schoolteacher at Hazrat Ayub.

94 KR BMA 2597 / 1s / 25 / 220–221 (December 25, 1952).

95 KR BMA 2597 / 1s / 47 / 109 (January 27, 1956); 2597 / 1s / 62 / 106 (February 25, 1958).

96 KR BMA 2597 / 1s / 55 / 168–169 (March 12, 1957); 2597 / 1s / 62 / 4 (July 10, 1957).

97 Tasar, *Soviet and Muslim*, 231–239.

climate of moderation toward Islam (combined with indifference or ineptitude at the local government level), ensured that the resort communicated with its "patients" almost exclusively through a Naqshbandī descent group.

Official responses changed in 1956, not because this year carried particular significance for religious policy, but because the rising number of pilgrims began to confront administrators with logistical difficulties. By this year, the visitor count during the summer months (when long-distance pilgrimage usually occurred) exceeded average occupancy rates by a factor of three.[98] Some guests complained about the bloodiness and goriness of animal sacrifice, while others protested that the pilgrims made too much noise and ruined their vacations.[99] The Jalalabat police department responded by setting up posts on the road leading to the resort and turning away cars that appeared to carry large numbers of pilgrims.[100] These measures reduced the number of pilgrims at the resort, but, as CARC lamented, did not serve the goals of scientific atheism, since the cars merely turned around and headed to the Throne of Solomon.[101] Moreover, this police presence did nothing to reduce visitation statistics: between August 15-September 10, 1957, a record 700–800 pilgrims were present at the resort at any given time.[102] The following summer, 400 new pilgrims arrived every day.[103] In one striking episode, 20 cargo trucks loaded with pilgrims arrived at Hazrat Ayub in procession, bringing eleven lambs with them. Again, the police responded by blocking access to pilgrims, but taking no action against the *khojas*.[104] According to the resort's chief doctor, the area's police captain did even this much reluctantly, while administrators lacked the resources to launch a struggle on their own.[105] Thus, local government struck out sporadically at pilgrims in extralegal fashion by denying Soviet citizens access to two public goods: the road leading to the resort, and the springs. Yet

98 The major shrines along the Kyrgyz-Uzbek border in the Farghana valley—the Throne of Solomon, Shoh Fozil, Arslanbob Ota, Shohimardon, and Hazrat Ayub—all experienced the most intensive pilgrimage during the period from May to September, and most especially in August.

99 On 'Eid ul-Adha in 1959, when many of the *khojas* had been forcibly removed from Hazrat Ayub, the resort's chief doctor, Nadezhda Antonovna Frolkina, commented: "This is the first holiday ever when we are working without pilgrims and our guests are able to relax peacefully." KR BMA 2597 / 1s / 83 / 201 (May 22, 1959).

100 KR BMA 2597 / 1s / 55 / 171 (March 12, 1957); 2597 / 1s / 56 / 160 (January 19, 1956).

101 KR BMA 2597 / 1s / 62 / 185 (February 23, 1957).

102 KR BMA 2597 / 1s / 62 / 105 (February 25, 1958).

103 KR BMA 2597 / 1s / 100 / 36 (January 12, 1963).

104 KR BMA 2597 / 1s / 62 / 105 (February 25, 1958).

105 KR BMA 2597 / 1s / 81 / 34 (April 3, 1959).

neither at any point before 1959 did the *khojas* experience pressure, nor did Hazrat Ayub attract the attention of local Party organs. This represents tacit acceptance of their central role at the resort.

Among the many insights offered by Hazrat Ayub, the site most pressingly demonstrates that the sociopolitical constraints of Soviet Central Asia did not necessarily force Sufi communities into the "underground." At the Jalalabat resort, Sufism and officialdom consciously coexisted. Both the Soviet state and an old Naqshbandī descent group made their presence felt at this institution, in different ways but certainly in equal measure. Despite their sacred lineage and status, the *khojas* fulfilled functions that existed in some form at all Soviet resorts: the Jalalabat resort was therefore no less a state enterprise than thousands of other such institutions across the USSR. Moreover, the *khojas* were very much on the radar screen of local government, which, when necessary, communicated its displeasure in a manner reflecting the decade's moderate climate. Thus, even in an openly antireligious political setting, impressive scope existed for Sufism to penetrate Soviet institutions, at least until the changes of 1959 rendered this pattern of coexistence politically untenable.

Conclusion

The three cases discussed in this article combine elements of official indifference toward religion and anti-Islamic activism to portray a picture of fluidity and ambiguity in the socio-political landscape of Muslim life during the 1940s and 1950s. Room existed in this landscape for radically different outcomes, depending on the context in question. Yet consistently, Sufi communities emerge as skilled negotiators, balancing the political possibilities of the postwar era with the Party-state's ongoing commitment to extirpating religion.

The objective of this analysis has been less to combat Bennigsen's emphasis on the antagonism separating Soviet bureaucrats from the Sufi communities under their rule, than to contextualize that antagonism. Antireligious sentiment within the Party-state did not translate, in the postwar years, into a climate of widespread repression. Sufi communities, ranging from the centralized bureaucracy represented by SADUM, to fluid and mobile groups like the Hairy *Ishans*, to established descent-based communities such as the Jalalabat *khojas*, all moved through the landscape of Central Asia in the 1940s and 1950s with an air of confidence that, in retrospect, seems remarkable. The central ambiguity of religious policy during these years—the combination of indifference and moderation toward religion exhibited by a Party-state avowedly opposed to religion—engendered substantial breathing room for these communities to carve niches for themselves in Soviet Central Asia's socio-political life.

Without doubt, Khrushchev's antireligious campaign reduced the scope of this process of exploration and co-existence. SADUM lost much of the administrative clout and authority it had enjoyed throughout the 1950s, especially when it came to regulating the affairs of mosques (like the one in Kok Yanghaq) at the local level.[106] Trials of religious figures, and presumably Sufi masters with them, increased in number, with lasting consequences for religious policy in the 1970s and 1980s.[107] A public declaration issued by Kyrgyzstan's Communist Party openly targeted Hazrat Ayub's *khojas*; subsequently the most prominent shaykhs at the resort were fired and/or forcibly exiled from the grounds.[108] The moderation of the 1950s was a thing of the past.

Yet despite the dramatic (though largely nonviolent) character of Khrushchev's assault on Islam, the emergence of Sufi communities as participants in the Soviet landscape during the postwar decades forms an integral component of the larger narrative of Central Asia's Sovietization. This process, whereby Central Asia moved from being a periphery of the Soviet empire to a fully organic component—culturally, socially, and politically—of the USSR, had as much to do with the unintended consequences of Soviet policies as with deliberate policymaking. The ambiguities of religious policy during the 1940s and 1950s are a case in point. Much like all other Soviet citizens, postwar Sufi communities found creative ways to make sense of their place in a society that had renounced mass violence against its own people, and to contribute to it as full-fledged members in spirit and in deed.

Bibliography

Archives

BM JT: Boigonii Markazii Jumhurii Tojikiston (Central Archive of the Republic of Tajikistan).

KR BMA: Kyrgyzstan Respublikasi Borborduk Mamlekettik Arkhivi (Central State Archive of the Kyrgyz Republic).

106 Tasar, *Soviet and Muslim*, 214–225.

107 Ibid., 202–207.

108 KR BMA 2597 / 1s / 83 / 174 (December 12, 1958); 2597 / 1s / 83 / 201 (May 22, 1959); 2597 / 1s / 100 / 36 (January 12, 1963).

O'zR MDA: O'zbekiston Respublikasi Markaziy Davlat Arxivi (Central State Archive of the Republic of Uzbekistan).

Secondary Sources

Bennigsen, Alexandre. "Official Islam and Sufi Brotherhoods in the Soviet Union Today." In *Islam and Power*, ed. Alexander S. Cudsi and Ali E. Hillal Dessouki (Baltimore, Maryland: Johns Hopkins University Press, 1981), 95–106.

Bennigsen, Alexandre. "Unrest in the World of Soviet Islam." *Third World Quarterly*, 10/2 (April 1988), 770–786.

Bennigsen, Alexandre, and S. Enders Wimbush. *Mystics and Commissars: Sufism in the Soviet Union*. Berkeley, California: University of California Press, 1985.

Bobokhonov, Shamsuddinkhon. *Shayx Ziyovuddinxon ibn Eshon Boboxon: ma'naviyat va ibrat maktabi*. Tashkent: Ozbekiston Milliy Entsiklopediyasi, 2001.

van den Bos, Matthjis. *Mystic Regimes: Sufism and the State in Iran, from the Late Qajar Era to the Islamic Republic*. Leiden: Brill, 2002.

Broxup, Marie. "Political Trends in Soviet Islam after the Afghanistan War." In *Muslim Communities Reemerge: Historical Perspectives on Nationality, Politics, and Opposition in the Former Soviet Union and Yugoslavia*, ed. Edward Allworth (Durham, North Carolina: Duke University Press, 1994), 304–321.

Davis, Nathaniel. *A Long Walk to Church: a contemporary history of Russian Orthodoxy*. Boulder, Colorado: Westview, 1995.

DeWeese, Devin. "Ahmad Yasavi and the *Divan-i-Hikmat* in Soviet scholarship." In *The Heritage of Soviet Oriental Studies*, ed. Michael Kemper and Stephan Conermann (London: Routledge, 2011), 262–290.

DeWeese, Devin. Foreword to *Islamizatsiia i "sakral'nye" rodoslovnye v Tsentral'noi Azii: nasledie Ishak Baba v narrativnoi i genealogicheskoi traditsiiakh*, tom 2, ed. Ashirbek Muminov, Anke von Kügelgen, Devin DeWeese, and Michael Kemper (Almaty: Daik Press, 2008), 6–33.

DeWeese, Devin. "The Politics of Sacred Lineages in 19th century Central Asia: descent groups linked to Khwaja Ahmad Yasavi in shrine documents and genealogical charters." *International Journal of Middle East Studies*, 31/4 (1999), 507–533.

DeWeese, Devin. "Shamanization in Central Asia." *Journal of the Economic and Social History of the Orient*, 57/3 (2014), 326–363.

Howell, Julia Day, and Martin van Bruinessen, eds. *Sufism and the 'Modern' in Islam*. New York: I. B. Tauris, 2007.

Keller, Shoshana. *To Moscow, Not Mecca: the Soviet Campaign against Islam in Central Asia, 1917–1941*. Westport, Connecticut: Praeger, 2001.

Mambetaliev, Satybaldy. *Sufizm jana anyn Kyrgyzstandagy akymdary*. Frunze: Kyrgyzstan, 1972.

Muminov, Ashirbek. "Shami-damulla i ego rol' v formirovanii 'Sovetskogo Islama.'" In *Islam, identichnost' i politika v postsovetskom prostranstve: materialy mezhdunarodnoi konferentsii 'Islam, identichnost' i politika v postsovetskom prostranstve—sravnitel'nyi analiz Tsentral'noi Azii i Evropeiskoi chasti Rossii' 1–2 aprelia 2004 g.*, ed. R. S. Khakimov and R. M. Mukhametshin (Kazan: Master Lain, 2005), 231–247.

Poliakov, Sergei. *Everyday Islam: Religion and Tradition in Rural Central Asia.* Ed. and trans. Martha Brill Olcott and Anthony Olcott. Armonk, New York: M. E. Sharpe, 2002.

Ro'i, Yaacov. *Islam in the Soviet Union: From World War II to Perestroika.* London: C. Hurst & Co./New York: Columbia University Press, 2000.

Shkarovskii, M. V. *Russkaia pravoslavnaia tserkov' pri Staline i Khrushcheve: gosudarstvenno-tserkovnye otnosheniia v SSSR v 1939–1964 gg.* Moscow: Krutitskoe Patriarshee Podvor'e, Obshchestvo liubitelei tserkovnoi istorii, 1999.

Silverstein, Brian. "Sufism and Modernity in Turkey: from the Authenticity of Experience to the Practice of Discipline." In *Sufism and the 'Modern' in Islam*, ed. Julia Day Howell and Martin van Bruinessen (New York: I. B. Tauris, 2007), 39–60.

Szuppe, Maria. "Ādīna Muḥammad Qarātēgīnī et 'son maître': Transmission des écrits de la tradition *kubravi* tardive en Asie centrale dans un recueil manuscrit de Ferghana." *Studia Iranica*, 45 (2016), 221–244.

Tasar, Eren. *Soviet and Muslim: The Institutionalization of Islam in Central Asia, 1943–1991.* New York: Oxford University Press, 2017.

Tasar, Eren. "Soviet Policies Toward Islam: Domestic and International Considerations." In *Religion and the Cold War: Global Perspective*, ed. Philip Muehlenbeck (Nashville, Tennessee: Vanderbilt University Press, 2012), 158–181.

Usmankhodzhaev, Amirsaidkhan. *Zhizn' muftiev Babakhanovykh: sluzhenie vozrozhdeniiu Islama v Sovetskom Soiuze.* Nizhnyi Novgorod: Medina, 2008.

Weismann, Itzchack. "Sufi Fundamentalism between India and the Middle East." In *Sufism and the 'Modern' in Islam*, ed. Julia Day Howell and Martin van Bruinessen (New York: I. B. Tauris, 2007), 115–128.

CHAPTER 9

Sufi Groups in Contemporary Kazakhstan: Competition and Connections with Kazakh Islamic Society

Ashirbek Muminov

Introduction

By the time of the collapse of the Soviet Union (1917–1991), many researchers believed that Sufi communities had not survived the Soviet era in Kazakhstan.[1] However, in 1998 Bakhtiyar Babajanov was able to identify a Naqshbandī-Mujaddidī-Ḥusaynī Sufi brotherhood in the village of Qŭsshï-Ata in the Türkïstan district (*audan* in Kazakh, *raion* in Russian) in southern Kazakhstan. In particular, he confirmed the existence of a line of succession through ʿAbd al-Vāḥid-Shaykh (Äbduluakhit Sheykh) Mamadshukurov (1885–1967), and described the main stages of his life, his followers, and the ritual life of this group.[2] Archival sources are now available on the Soviet-era history of this group, and among them is the report of the commissioner for religious affairs indicating that the "keeper of the mausoleum of Khwāja Aḥmad Yasavī (in Kazakh, Qozha Akhmet Yasaui) used to go together with pilgrims to the house of Äbduluakhit Sheykh, where they took an oath of loyalty (*bayʿat*) to Äbduluakhit Sheykh Mamadshukurov and became his students (*murīd*)."[3] In addition, it has become possible to clarify the date of Äbduluakhit Sheykh Mamadshukurov's death (April 1, 1967).[4] This is strong evidence that the traditional practice of

1 It should be noted that this dismissal of Sufism in Kazakhstan may be the result of a bias against the depth or strength of Islam among the Kazakhs; some researchers (e.g., Martha Brill Olcott, *The Kazakhs* [Stanford: Hoover Institution Press, 1995]) believe that Islam in Kazakhstan has "shallow roots" or is "superficial."

2 B. Babadjanov, "Le renouveau des communautés soufies en Ouzbékistan," *Cahiers d'Asie centrale*, 5–6 (1998), 285–304.

3 Report of the Chairman of the Council for Religious Affairs in Iuzhnaia Kazakhstanskaia Oblast' under the Council of Ministers of the USSR, A. Iuldashev (1947): South Kazakhstan Regional State Archive. Fond 1353, *opis'* 2, *stopka* 4, *kniga* 28, p. 93.

4 Aynŭr Äbdïräsïlqïzï, "Qazaqstandaghï Muzhaddidiya-Khusayniya Aghïmï zhäne Abd al-Vakhid shaykh," *Bulletin of the National Center of Archaeography and Source Studies*, 2 (2012), 36–44; Ashirbek Muminov, "From Revived Tradition to Innovation: Kolkhoz Islam in the

 | DOI:10.1163/9789004373075_011

initiating others into the Sufi path continued in the Soviet era. This paper aims to further expand the study of Sufism in modern Kazakhstan by examining the connections between historical Sufi groups such as the Naqshbandī-Mujaddidī-Ḥusayniyya, present-day Sufi groups, and new post-Soviet Sufi movements.

Modern Sufi Groups

There are currently four main Sufi groups in Kazakhstan. First, there is the aforementioned Naqshbandiyya-Mujaddidiyya-Ḥusayniyya. Its spiritual and organizational center is in the village of Qŭsshĭ-Ata, located 15–17 km southeast of the city of Türkĭstan. Here, in a private house, the sons of Äbduluakhit Sheykh Mamadshukurov gather their father's followers twice a year—during a *mawlid/maulĭt* and at the beginning of the holy month of Ramadan. The total number of followers is approximately 1500 people. In Türkĭstan district, the *qalpe* (*khalīfa*) and leader of the entire organization is the youngest son of Äbduluakhit Sheykh Mamadshukurov, Naṣīr al-Dīn (Näsĭrĭdin) Ishan Abduvoitov (b. 1951). "*Khalīfas*" run the regional organizations of this Sufi group. For example, the *qalpe* of Kazakhstan is Qŭrban-Älĭ (Qurbān-ʿAlī) Akhmetov. The organization is officially registered in Taraz city (Zhambĭl *oblast'*) as "Islam Shapaghatĭ." There are additional members of this group throughout Central Asia, mainly in Uzbekistan.[5]

The second one that has survived the Soviet period consists of Chechen Qādirī Sufi groups. The Chechens were resettled to Kazakhstan by Stalin in 1944. In 1957, the majority of the Chechens returned to their homeland in the Caucasus. However, in 1995, war broke out in Chechnya. The war was accompanied by a large loss of life, the destruction of towns and villages, and the collapse of the economy, which triggered a large-scale migration of refugees from Chechnya to other post-Soviet states, particularly Kazakhstan, where many

Southern Kazakhstan Region and Religious Leadership (through the Cases of Zhartĭ-Töbe and Oranghay since the 1950s)," in *Allah's Kolkhozes: Migration, De-Stalinisation, Privatisation and the New Muslim Congregations in the Soviet Realm (1950s–2000s)*, ed. Stéphane A. Dudoignon and Christian Noack (Berlin: Klaus Schwarz Verlag, 2014), 307–366 [309, 330–331].

5 B. Babadzhanov, "Khusainiia," in *Islam na territorii byvshei Rossiiskoi imperii: Èntsiklopedicheskii slovar'*, ed. Stanislav M. Prozorov, 1 (Moscow: Izdatel'skaia firma "Vostochnaia literatura" RAN, 2006), 431–432.

Chechens have relatives.[6] According to historian Zharas Èrmekbayev, the exact number of Chechens is difficult to determine because many family members move between Chechnya and Kazakhstan, but according to official statistics from 2009, there were 31,431 persons of Chechen descent in Kazakhstan, or 0.2% of the population.

The Sufi following of Kunta Ḥājjī (Kishiev, d. 1867), within the Qādirī brotherhood, became the largest Sufi group in Chechnya; at present around 60% of Chechens are affiliated with it. The major mosque of the Chechens in Astana is named after Shaykh Kunta Ḥājjī (Sheykh Kunta Qazhï). Many Chechens, and above all the followers of Vis Ḥājjī Zagiev (d. 1973), live together, as before, in the villages of Krasnaia Poliana, Arbuzinka, and Petrovka, located not far from Astana, the capital of Kazakhstan, in the Sandïq-Tau *audan* of Aqmola *oblast'*; today they number approximately 1,500.[7] They follow the religious practice of Vis Ḥājjī, who is also called the "Atbasar Shaykh," because he began his preaching in the environs of the town of Atbasar. Vis Ḥājjī's grave is located in Arbuzinka, and is a place of pilgrimage (Chechen *zerat*) for his *murīd*s. His immediate master (*ustaz*) was Dada Aḥmad, who received his training from Shaykh Chim-mirza, a successor of Kunta Ḥājjī. In the 1950s, during the exile in Kazakhstan, Vis Ḥājjī informed the *murīd*s of Chim-mirza that he had established direct contact with the teacher, Kunta Ḥājjī in the spiritual world, and that Kunta Ḥājjī had revealed to him the true meaning of his teaching, entrusting him with the mission of preaching the "pure path."[8]

The remaining two Sufi groups in contemporary Kazakhstan, the Jahriyya and a number of modern Turkish groups, have appeared recently in the post-Soviet era.

The Jahriyya, are the followers of Äbdïlghappar Maqsŭm-ŭlï, better known as "Ismatulla Maqsŭm."[9] Ismatulla Maqsŭm arrived in Kazakhstan from Afghanistan, where he lived in the city of Mazār-i Sharīf. The group linked with him became widespread in Kazakhstan in the mid-1990s. It was first seen in the town of Qarasu in the Almatï *oblast'* of Kazakhstan. In the late 1990s, this group was banned because it operated mosques and madrasas but was not

6 See Zharas A. Èrmekbaev, *Chechentsy i ingushi v Kazakhstane: Istoriia i sud'ba* (Almaty: Daik-Press, 2009).

7 Oral communication from Ruziia Islamovna Qamarova (b. 1965), an expert on local history and ethnography, Astana, 26 January 2015.

8 Mikhail Roshchin, "Chechenskii sufizm v period deportatsii: vozniknovenie virda Viskhazhi," http://www.kavkazoved.info/authors/mihail-roschin.html.

9 I.e., the name ʿIṣmatullāh, with the Kazakh adaptation of the title *makhdūm* ~ *makhzūm*, "master."

registered with the Spiritual Administration of the Muslims of Kazakhstan (SAMK). Ismatulla Maqsŭm was expelled from Kazakhstan. Then, in 2000, this Sufi group resumed its activities in the "Mamïr" micro-district in the city of Almatï. According to researchers, this group had approximately a thousand members in Almatï, led by Ismatulla Maqsŭm's *khalīfa*, Narïm-bay Razbek-ŭlï (d. 2014).

The Jahriyya has repeatedly tried to register officially with Kazakhstani authorities. The group also attempted but failed to open a charity named "Shakärïm;" it then registered a public association called "*Senïm. Bïlïm. Ömïr*" ("Belief, Knowledge, Life"), which had 17 branches and 16 offices in Kazakhstan. The main bases of the group are in the cities of Astana, Almatï, Ural'sk, and Türkïstan. Approximately 1500 people belong to the group, which is significantly involved with popular media: the musical group "Yasaui" is sponsored by the organization, as was a publication of poetry attributed to Qozha Akhmet Yasaui. On 18 October 2011, however, Ismatulla Maqsŭm and his chief assistants were given long prison sentences for "forming a criminal gang," and also for "extremism, illegally depriving persons of their freedom, and treating alcoholism and drug addiction by methods harmful to people's health," as well as for other criminal offenses.[10]

The fourth category of Sufis active in post-Soviet Kazakhstan consists of several modern Turkish Sufi groups. Their main activities are in the educational sphere. The modern Turkish Sufi groups do not emphasize *silsila*s in their teaching. Instead, they communicate through modern mass media, particularly print media. They have also opened schools, which again do not emphasize the transmission of knowledge from individual master to individual student, but from teachers—in the modern sense—to students. They have opened 28 high schools as well as two Kazakh-Turkish universities: The University of Foreign Languages and Business, and Süleyman Demirel University in Almatï.[11]

---

10 Nazira Narimbet, "Prigovor sufiiam ostalsia v sile." http://rus.azattyq.org/content/kazakh_sufism_ismatulla_abdigappar_sayat_ibraev/24569795.html.

11 Bayram Balci, *Missionnaires de l'Islam en Asie centrale: Les écoles turques de Fethullah Gülen.* (Paris: Maisonneuve and Larose, 2003); B. Balci, "Fethullah Gülen's Missionary Schools in Central Asia and their Role in the Spreading of Turkism and Islam," *Religion, State and Society*, 31 (2003), 151–177; Thierry Zarcone, "Bridging the Gap between Pre-Soviet and Post-Soviet Sufism in Ferghana valley (Uzbekistan): The Naqshbandi Order between Tradition and Innovation," in *Popular Movements and Democratization in the Islamic World*, ed. Masatoshi Kisaichi (London and New York: Routledge, 2006), 43–56.

Among the current Turkish groups, we can identify the following:

1. The Süleymenshïler, named after Turkish Sufi Süleyman Hilmi Tunakhan (1888–1959). This is an influential religious organization with a pan-Turkic orientation. A characteristic feature of this organization is its affiliates' strict adherence to Islamic law, when compatible with a secular way of life;
2. The Osman Topbashshïlar, who distribute the works of the Turkish Shaykh Osman Nuri Topbash (b. 1942);
3. The Ïqïlasshïlar, named after the Ïqïlas uaqïfï (Ihlas Vakfı), who are led by Osman Karabıyık (Hakikat Kitabevi Vakfı);
4. Two groups of Nurshïlar: the Oqŭshïlar (Okuyucular grubu) and the Yazıcılar (Yazıcılar grubu), who promote the *Risala-yi Nur*;
5. The Fetkhullashïlar (Gülen hareketi), named after Fethullah Gülen (b. 1941);
6. The Makhmŭdshïlar, named after the Äziz Makhmŭd Qŭdayï (1541–1628) *waqf* (Aziz Mahmûd Hüdâyi Vakfı).[12]

Tracts on Turkish Sufi thought are available in a variety of books, including the Russian-language magazine *Zolotoi Rodnik* and the Kazakh-language magazine *Rakhmet Samalï*.

The Question of Continuity (*silsila*)

The group of Äbduluakhit Sheykh Mamadshukurov continues the traditions of the local Mujaddidī–Ḥusaynī group, which is a branch of the Naqshbandiyya. The second component (Ḥusayniyya) in their title comes from the name of a famous Bukharan shaykh in the first half of the 19th century, Khalīfa Ḥusayn. The line of succession of ʿAbd al-Vāḥid-Shaykh Mamadshukurov is believed to be as follows: Aḥmad Sirhindī, the "*mujaddid-i alf-i thānī*" (d. 1034/1624) → Sayyid Muḥammad → Shaykh ʿAbdullāh → Mawlānā Miyān ʿĀbid-Shaykh → Muḥammad Mūsā-Khān Dahbīdī (d. 1190/1776) → Khalīfa Ṣiddīq (d. 1210/1795) → Khalīfa Ḥusayn (d. 1250/1835) → Khalīfa ʿAbd al-Sattār b. Khalīfa Ḥusayn → Khalīfa Muḥammad Ṣāliḥ → Khalīfa Muḥammad-Amīn → Khalīfa ʿAbd al-Vāḥid Turkistānī (Äbduluakhit Sheykh, d. 1967).

---

12 Oral communication from journalist Mŭkhan Isakhan (b. 1978), in which he outlined this classification of Turkish groups, Almatï, summer 2011.

Äbduluakhit Sheykh studied with the Bukharan Sufi master (*ustāẕ*) Muḥammad-Amīn, after which he returned to his own town, Ura-Tobe. Muḥammad-Amīn was a shaykh from the Naqshbandī-Mujaddidī *ṭarīqat* during the reign of the Bukharan Amir ʿAbd al-Aḥad (r. 1885–1910). Muḥammad-Amīn always avoided political involvement and maintained a conformist stance. Following the example of his teacher, Äbduluakhit Sheykh avoided involvement in politics, particularly in the early Soviet era, and tried to keep his religious activities from affecting his students and relatives. Äbduluakhit Sheykh managed to avoid reprisals in the Soviet era and adapted to new political conditions quickly.

According to his descendants, Äbduluakhit Sheykh accepted a very limited number of students and limited his instruction to teaching them about the *ẕikr*. He focused on teaching concentration (*tavajjuh*) on special "points" (*laṭāʾif*) located in different parts of the chest during *ẕikr*; this is the same sort of *ẕikr* ritual seen in other branches of the modern Ḥusayniyya.

Before Äbduluakhit Sheykh's death in 1967, he appointed as his successor (*khalīfa*) Qārī ʿAbdullāh (Qori Abdullo) from Tashkent, who had lived with Äbduluakhit Sheykh for 33 years. Qārī ʿAbdullāh was arrested on several occasions, although he was set free every time, on the condition that he would not recruit any more students. He died in Tashkent in 1976. Despite the authorities' ban, Qārī ʿAbdullāh managed to teach a few students who moved to other areas of Kazakhstan, to the Farghana valley, to Tashkent and other cities of Uzbekistan, and even to Russia. However, during the life of Qārī ʿAbdullāh, fear of the authorities prevented his disciples from writing *irshād-nāmas* in the traditional form; instead, they only transmitted this knowledge orally. Qārī ʿAbdullāh persistently warned his followers about the threat of arrest and recommended that they have no more than two or three students. Among Qārī ʿAbdullāh's followers, the most authoritative was Hazrat Ibrohim Mamatqulov, who lived in Qoqand and died in 2009.[13] Before his death, Ibrohim Hazrat gave permission orally to Qŭrban-Älĭ Akhmetov for the leadership of the portion of his community in Kazakhstan; indeed, 95% of his followers in Kazakhstan accepted the leadership of Qŭrban-Älĭ as their *pīr/pĭr*. A small group of *murīds/mürĭtter* remained with Näsĭrĭdin Ishan, whom Qŭrban-Älĭ now refers to as "self-proclaimed."[14]

---

13 B. Babadzhanov, "Ibrakhim-khazrat," in *Islam na territorii byvshei Rossiiskoi imperii: Èntsiklopedicheskii slovar'*, ed. Stanislav M. Prozorov, 1 (Moscow: Izdatel'skaia firma "Vostochnaia literature" RAN, 2006), 155–156.

14 Oral communication from Tŭrghanqŭlov Tangzharĭq Qasĭmqŭlŭlĭ (b. 1980), an expert on local history, Taraz, December 2014; interview by the author with Näsĭrĭdin Ishan Abduvoitov, in the village of Qŭsshĭ Ata, summer 2011.

The second group discussed above—the Chechen Qādiriyya—is less well known. We do not know of the names and lineages of the Qādirī groups in Kazakhstan. The SAMK (Spiritual Administration of the Muslims of Kazakhstan) has had a deputy *muftī* from the Chechen community since 2000, named Shaykh al-Islam Muḥammad Ḥusayn Alsabekov.

The Jahriyya is a more curious case. Ismatulla Maqsŭm has never stated his Sufi lineage. He has only stated that his ancestors are from the Qïzïl-Orda region and were members of the Junior Horde who moved to Afghanistan to escape the Bolsheviks. The basic doctrine of Ismatulla Maqsŭm centers on Maqsŭm's special mission to Kazakhstan: his followers believe that he came to Kazakhstan to revive Islam, based on a revelatory dream (*ayan*). Members of this group argue that they are following the true cultural legacy of the Kazakhs as demonstrated by Qozha Akhmet Yasaui and Shakärïm Qŭdayberdiyev (1858–1931). In 2005, the SAMK issued a *fatwā* that disapproved of the doctrine of Ismatulla Maqsŭm, calling it inappropriate according to the *sharīʿa*.

Sufi Practices

One distinctive feature of the Naqshbandī-Ḥusaynī group is the silent *ẕikr* (*ẕikr-i khafī*). After becoming initiated (*bayʿat, qol beru*), a *murīd* begins his individual development (*vaẓīfa*) with *ẕikr* and supplementary prayers (*navāfil*). For example, the followers of Qŭrban-Älï Akhmetov rise in the morning and perform a "*shukr-i vużu*'" (two *rakʿats* after ablutions), then do *tasbīḥ istighfār*—saying "*astaghfir Allah al-ʿAzim*"—at the end of a supplication (*duʿā*)—"*al-ladhī lā ilāha illāhu, al-Ḥayy al-Qayyūm, wa aṭūbu ilayhi.*" Early in the morning in addition to the "*bāmdād*" prayer, they perform the "*tahajjud*" prayer, which consists of two cycles of two *rakʿats* (four *rakʿats* in total). During the fourth *rakʿat*, after reciting the Fātiḥa *sūra*, they add a recitation of the Ikhlāṣ *sūra* to the orthodox sequence of *namāz*. After this, they perform the silent *ẕikr*.

The *ẕikr* is performed by the members of the group by reciting "Allāh" 101 times while concentrating on different parts of their bodies. Each of the following parts of the body is a locus of concentration in order:

1) *qalb/qalïb* (the lower left side of the chest);
2) *rūḥ/rukh* (the lower right side of the chest);
3) *sirr/sïr* (the upper left side of the chest);
4) *khafī/qŭpïya* (the upper right side of the chest);
5) *akhfā/aqpa* (the center of the chest),

Finally, the last stage of the *ẕikr* is the *nafʿ-i iṡbāt*, in which the performer of the *ẕikr* (in Kazakh, *zĭkĭrshĭ*) recites the words, in Persian, "*nishastagī jāyam qabram, pūshīdagī libāsam kafanam, giriftagī nafas-i man ākhir-i anfās-i man ast*" ("the place I sit is my grave, the clothes I put on are my shroud, the breath I have taken is the last of my breaths"), and, taking a deep breath, says "*Khudāvandā: maqṣūd-i man tū-yī, riżā-yi man tū-yī*" ("O lord, my goal is You, my satisfaction is You"), followed by the phrases, "*lā nīst ilāha hīch maqṣūdī illā'llāh juz' ẕāt-i pāk*" (a hybrid Arabic-Persian exclamation that "I have no goal other than the pure essence of God"), and "*lā maqṣūdī illā'llāh*" ("I have no goal but God"). Only after saying the phrase "*muḥammadun rasūlallāh*" does the *zĭkĭrshĭ* exhale. The *zĭkĭrshĭ* then starts the cycle over again but begins by concentrating on his *akhfā*, going through the parts of his chest and the *nafʿ-i iṡbāt* again.

The collective rituals of the Ḥusayniyya include:

1) *Mawlid/Maulĭt*: On the Prophet's birthday (*mawlid*), the students go to Äbduluakhit Sheykh's house. Here, they perform the "Mawlid al-Nabī" ritual. In this ritual, the shaykh reads stories and poetry about the Prophet, including sections of the Qur'ān. After this, the shaykh recites supplications for the Prophet. All of this is performed according to a textual tradition. Finally, the celebrants have a ritual feast (*Qŭday tamaq*).
2) *Khatm-i Qur'ān/Qatĭm Qŭran*: This ritual, a recitation of the Qur'ān, is performed at the start of Ramadan in the house of Äbduluakhit Sheykh.
3) *Majlis/Mäzhĭlĭs*: This is simply an assembly where Shaykh Qŭrban-Älĭ Akhmetov's *murīds* have the opportunity to meet with him and ask questions.

It should be noted that due to the difficulties of the Soviet era, followers (*pĭradar*) of this path are not clear on the history of the Ḥusayniyya. However, we know that after the death of Hazrat Ibrohim Mamatqulov, Shaykh Qŭrban-Älĭ Akhmetov took over the group's operations in Kazakhstan.

A distinctive feature of Ismatulla Maqsŭm's group is the vocal *ẕikr*, also known as the *ẕikr-i jahr*.[15] These rituals are usually carried out on Thursday or Friday nights in the *khānaqāh* (also called the *zĭkĭr-khana* or the

15 B. Babadzhanov, "Zikr dzhakhr i sama': sakralizatsiia profannogo ili profanatsiia sakral'nogo?," in *Podvizhniki Islama: Kul't sviatykh i sufizm v Srednei Azii i na Kavkaze*, ed. S. N. Abashin and V. O. Bobrovnikov (Moscow: "Vostochnaia literatura" RAN, 2003), 237–250; B. Babadzhanov, "O vidakh zikra dzhakhr sredi bratstv Tsentral'noi Azii," in *Istoriko-kul'turnye vzaimosviazi Irana i Dasht-i Kipchaka v XIII–XVIII vv.: Materialy mezhdunarodnogo Kruglogo stola* (Almaty: Daik-Press, 2004), 133–157.

zhahr-khana). The *zĭkĭr* ceremony begins with a sermon by Ismatulla Maqsŭm, which describes the Day of Judgment (*Aqĭret Kün*) or different stories from the life of the Prophet, his Companions, or famous Sufi shaykhs. Ismatulla Maqsŭm then claims that the only way of salvation has been shown by the saint Äzret/Khazret/Hazret Qozha Akhmet Yasaui, whom he characterizes as having reached perfection or the sixth stage of the mystical path.

Researchers have found only three or four types of *zĭkĭr* practiced by the followers of Ismatulla Maqsŭm. It consists of moving the head from right to left while saying "Hu-Hu, Ḥayy." There is a large emphasis on breathing techniques, which can help the *murīd* reach an ecstatic trance, known as a *ḥāl*.

3. The Chechen Qādirī groups also perform the vocal *ẕikr*.

Researchers have not yet studied the *ẕikr* practices of the Turkish-influenced groups in Kazakhstan.

Sufi-State Relations in Kazakhstan

The relationship of these various Sufi groups and the Kazakhstani state depends on two factors: the post-Soviet Muftiate, and the lack of formal church-like structures in which Sufism could be institutionalized. One legacy of the Soviet era in Kazakhstan is the state-sponsored Islamic bureaucracy known as the Spiritual Administration of the Muslims of Kazakhstan (SAMK). The SAMK is charged with ensuring the registration of all mosques, religious schools, presses, and other organizations. The relationship between the Sufi groups and the SAMK is not stable since the emergence of a charismatic Sufi leader would present an alternative Islamic authority in Kazakhstan. SAMK is thus always on alert for new charismatic leaders. This concern clearly underlies the *fatwā* issued by SAMK in 2005, noted above, that declared the doctrine of Ismatulla Maqsŭm to be contrary to the *sharīʿa*.

Some observers consider Sufism to be a possible counterweight to Islamic fundamentalism in Kazakhstan. In this regard, the experience of Uzbekistan is instructive. At the dawn of independence, Sufism was seen as the spiritual heritage of Uzbekistan, as the foundation for national revival, and as an aspect of Islam able to resist political Islamic ideologies, such as Wahhabism, Salafism, and Hizb al-Tahrir. However, after the 600th anniversary of the birth of Khwāja Aḥrār, the official attitude toward Sufism began to change. During this anniversary, the political roles of past Sufis such as Khwāja Aḥrār were publicized, and the Uzbekistani authorities became wary of Sufism.[16]

16 B. Babadzhanov, "Andizhanskoe vosstanie 1898 goda: 'dervisheskii gazavat' ili natsional'no-osvoboditel'noe dvizhenie?", *Özbekiston tarikhi*, 2001, № 2, 25–30; № 4, 61–67.

Sufis in Kazakhstan also participate in the debate over "traditional Islam" vs. "non-traditional Islam," and use the rhetoric of "traditional Islam" to justify their practices and ideologies. For example, Sufi groups argue that figures promoted as part of Kazakh history, such as Qozha Akhmet Yasaui, were Sufis. This is the way Ismatulla Maqsŭm linked his new philosophy to Qozha Akhmet Yasaui. Turkish Sufi groups often attempt to link their practices to historical Turkic groups emerging from Türkĭstan.

Kazakhstani authorities also focus on the ethnic dimensions of Sufi groups. Chechen groups are seen as closed to outsiders due to their cautious attitude toward state authorities. The Ḥusayniyya is often considered by Kazakhstani authorities to be "Uzbek" or "foreign": the commissioner for religious affairs in the South Kazakhstan *oblast'* argues that the followers of Äbduluakhit Sheykh are Uzbeks and Tajiks, for which reason they are viewed with suspicion and thought to represent possibly problematical "Uzbek" influences.

Conflicts within and between Sufi Groups

A split emerged in the Naqshbandiyya-Mujaddidiyya-Ḥusayniyya after the death of Hazrat Ibrohim Mamatqulov (1937–2009). In the 1950–1970's Mamatqulov was a student of the leaders of this group, Äbduluakhit Sheykh Mamatshukurov (d. 1967) and Qārī ʿAbdullāh (d. 1976). He then became a leader of this group. He lived in Tashkent until 1984, when he moved to his home village of Aqqorghan (in the Farghana valley). He claimed he had more than 20,000 followers (*murīd, mukhlis*). However, after his death, a schism between Näsĭrĭdin Ishan and Qŭrban-Älĭ Akhmetov emerged in Kazakhstan. Both claimed to be the *ishan* of the group. Qŭrban-Älĭ is by birth a member of the Kazakh Sabïlt *qozha* (*khoja*) group, which dwelled in the village of Shïghïrïq in the environs of Toy-Tepa (in Tashkent *oblast'*). In the early 1970s, with the support of Abdulla Qazhï Zholdasov, he enrolled in the Mīr-i ʿArab *madrasa* in Bukhara, and upon graduation he established himself in Qoylïq *raion* (southwest of Tashkent). It was there that he became acquainted with Ibrohim Hazrat in the early 1980s, and became his follower (*qol berdĭ*).[17]

The followers of Qŭrban-Älĭ Akhmetov abandoned the traditional Sufi clothing (a white robe with leather boots) and began wearing jeans and sneakers. Qŭrban-Älĭ has many followers in different cities of Kazakhstan, including Qïzïl-Orda, Taraz, and Astana, and has four wives. He is actively engaged in the publication of books and journals of religious content, and in the organization

17 Oral communication from the former SAMK functionary (cleric) Abdulla Qazhï Zholdasov (b. 1944), Shïmkent, December 2014.

of various assemblies and conferences.[18] By contrast, Näsïrïdin Ishan has followers only near Türkïstan and in Almatï, and has lived modestly in his home village.

In Uzbekistan, a different split emerged: rather than a fight over the title of *ishan*, separate *khalīfa*s were declared for several cities and towns, where communities linked to Ibrohim Hazrat survived and continued to exist illegally. The announcement of a new *ishan* is expected in the future. The main contender for the position of *ishan* is Naqshbandī Shaykh Dust-Muhammad Tursunov (born in 1935 in the area of Shorchi in Surkhandarya). He has received the backing of several *khalīfa*s in Uzbekistan, most notably ʿAbdusalāmov-Ghiylānī. He is well-versed in *fiqh*. Dust-Muhammad Ishan strongly criticizes other Naqshbandī shaykhs as well as Hazrat Ibrohim. He is not alone in his criticism of Hazrat Ibrohim: several other Naqshbandī shaykhs in Uzbekistan are also critical of Hazrat Ibrāhīm.

There is also a connection between the Naqshbandiyya and Ismatulla Maqsŭm's group. The group of ʿĀdil-Khān-Qārī Salāmov (1928–2009) in the city of Andijan occupied an intermediate position between the two groups. ʿĀdil-Khān received instruction (a) in the Ḥusayniyya from Qārī ʿAbdullāh, a student of Äbduluakhit Sheykh, and (b) in the *ẕikr-i jahr* from Muḥammad Sharīf Ḥiṣārī from Tajikistan. After the death of ʿĀdil-Khān, four students of his emerged: ʿAbd al-Bāqī ʿAbduraḥmānov in Namangan, and three persons in Andijan—ʿAbd al-Quddūs, ʿIzzatullāh-Qārī and Sāyib-Jān-Qārī. The latter group counts approximately 500 people as members. Rather than performing the silent *ẕikr*, they perform the *ẕikr-i jahr*, albeit in a manner different from that of the group of Ismatulla Maqsŭm.[19]

Some observers believe there is a fierce rivalry between the Ḥusayniyya and the group of Ismatulla Maqsŭm. However, Qŭrban-Älï claims that God has cut off the path of the Yasaviyya, saying that "The Yasavī path has come to an end" because "God closed that path" (*Yasaui zholï toqtap qaldï, Allah ol zholdï zhaptï*), and that God "developed the Naqshbandī path" (*Naqshbandiding zholïn damïttï*).

18 Among his recent publications, which appeared following his return to Kazakhstan in 2013 from a forced emigration to a series of Muslim countries, may be noted the following three: Khazretï Sheykh Qŭrbanälï Akhmed, *Namaznama* (Almatï, 2013); idem, *Ïlïmge ïlesu* (Almatï, 2014); idem, *Rukhnama* (Almatï, 2014).

19 See H. Yoldāshkhojayev, *Tariqatchilikning zamānaviy korinishlari* (Tashkent: Tāshkent Islām Universiteti, 2010).

Salafī Hostility to Sufism

Representatives of the Salafīs in Kazakhstan can be regarded as hardline opponents of Sufi groups. Salafīs and other reformers strongly condemn Sufi teachings and practices such as the veneration of shaykhs, the visitation of shrines and other sacred sites, etc. These features are regarded by fundamentalists as polytheism (*shirk*) and innovation (*bid'a*). Salafīs call themselves representatives of "traditional Islam" or "orthodox Islam." They regard the Sufis as contradicting the oneness of God (*tawḥīd*) and "pure Islam." Local Ṣalafīs are supported by many foreign charities and organizations in their fight against Sufi groups, such as "Istilah," "Tayba," and the "Committee of the Muslims of Asia."[20] Salafists in Kazakhstan include the students of the schools of 'Abdulkhalīl 'Abdudzhabbarov (with the nickname "Khalīl"), Toirdzhon Ibragimov, Rinat Zeynullin (with the nickname "Abū Muḥammad"), Dilmurat Makhamadov, Nazratullah Abdulqadirov (with the nickname "Abū Maryam"), Uktam Zaurbekov, and Darïn Mubarov.

The 'Nationalization' of Sufi Heritage

Many Kazakhs make pilgrimages to the graves of eminent Muslim figures, including Kazakh military heroes and saints. Historically, these pilgrimages have largely been unorganized and decentralized. However, in February 1997, Qïdïrälï Tarïbayev founded a pilgrimage-based Islamic group called Ata Zholï (also known as Aq Zhol and Orda). Qïdïrälï announced that he had had a prophetic dream (*ayan*) in which his Kazakh ancestors told him that Kazakhs should return to their ancestral way of practicing Islam. This meant that believers should travel to the tombs of saints, where they would communicate with the spirits of the saints (*äuliye*, i.e., *awliyā*) and ancestors (*aruaq, arwāḥ*) and receive their blessings (*bata, Fātiḥa*). Pilgrimage routes were developed in the regions of Almatï, Zhambïl, South Kazakhstan, and Qïzïl-Orda, and the group incorporated several travel companies. In addition, members of this group published biographies of saints. Thousands of people from all regions of Kazakhstan and even bordering regions of the Russian Federation went on pilgrimages with this group, which operates solely in Kazakh.[21]

---

20 See Dina Wilkowsky, *Arabisch-islamische Organisationen in Kasachstan: Exogener Einfluss auf die islamische Erneuerung, 1991–2007* (Berlin: Verlag Hans Schiler, 2009).

21 Aitzhan Nurmanova, "Pilgrimages to Mazars in Contemporary Kazakhstan—The Processes of Revivalism and Innovation," in *Mazar: Studies on Islamic Sacred Sites in*

Qozha Akhmet Yasaui is an increasingly important figure in post-Soviet Kazakhstan. He is regarded as the founder of "traditional Islam" in Kazakhstan, and of "Kazakh spirituality," and acts as a synecdoche for a Kazakh understanding of Islam. Recently, top Kazakhstani officials were told to create a national ideology and Kazakh oral tradition around Qozha Akhmet Yasaui, Abay Qŭnanbayev (1845–1904). It is unclear what role Yasavī's Sufi legacy will play in this ideology, but there may be other, less official evocations of that legacy on a national scale. On an expedition to Qostanay, Northern Kazakhstan, and Aqmola in 2008, we recorded stories from local informants. Some of these stories described individuals referred to as "*pĭradar*" who obtained that title by making a pilgrimage to the shrine of Qozha Akhmet Yasaui, in southern Kazakhstan, and being initiated by Sufi shaykhs on their trip. However, this topic remains to be explored, as textual evidence for this practice is lacking.

Conclusion

Four factors will influence the subsequent development of Sufism in Kazakhstan. The first factor is the opposition to Sufism by Salafīs and other fundamentalist groups. Second is the fear of the authorities that Sufi groups will become politicized, which is already visible in the confrontation between the group of Ismatulla Maqsŭm and the Kazakhstani state. Ismatulla Maqsŭm is currently imprisoned and his followers have become hostile toward the Kazakhstani state. It appears that the group of Qŭrban-Älĭ Shaykh has been maintained as a counterweight against other fundamentalist groups. The third factor is the degree of rivalry and cooperation between the various Sufi movements, which may take an ethnic form. For example, as mentioned above, some Kazakhs see the Ḥusayniyya as an "Uzbek" group. Ismatulla Maqsŭm attempted to present himself as purely Kazakh, which may irritate other Sufi groups, while the Qādiriyya is a purely Chechen phenomenon.

The fourth and final factor is the perception of Sufism by non-Sufis as the spiritual heritage of Kazakhstan and Sufism's influence on the art and culture of Kazakhstan.

The reformation of Sufi groups in Kazakhstan is only just beginning. The future may very well see an intensification of Sufi activity in Kazakhstan.

Central Eurasia, ed. Sugawara Jun and Rahile Dawut (Tokyo: Tokyo University of Foreign Studies, 2016), 63–72.

Bibliography

Äbdĭräsĭlqïzï, Aynŭr. "Qazaqstandaghï Muzhaddidiya-Khusainiya Aghïmï zhäne Abd al-Vakhid shaykh." *Bulletin of the National Center of Archaeography and Source Studies*, 2 (2012), 36–44.

Akhmed, Khazretĭ Sheykh Qŭrbanälĭ. *Ĭlĭmge ĭlesu*. Almatï, 2014.

Akhmed, Khazretĭ Sheykh Qŭrbanälĭ. *Namaznama*. Almatï, 2013.

Akhmed, Khazretĭ Sheykh Qŭrbanälĭ. *Rukhnama*. Almatï, 2014.

Babadjanov, B. "Le renouveau des communautés soufies en Ouzbékistan," *Cahiers d'Asie centrale*, 5–6 (1998), 285–304.

Babadzhanov, B. "Andizhanskoe vosstanie 1898 goda: 'dervisheskii gazavat' ili natsional'no-osvoboditel'noe dvizhenie?" *Ozbekiston tarikhi*, 2001, № 2, 25–30; № 4, 61–67.

Babadzhanov, B. "Ibrakhim-khazrat." In *Islam na territorii byvshei Rossiiskoi imperii: Èntsiklopedicheskii slovar'*, ed. Stanislav M. Prozorov, I (Moscow: Izdatel'skaia firma "Vostochnaia literatura" RAN, 2006), 155–156.

Babadzhanov, B. "Khusainiia." In *Islam na territorii byvshei Rossiiskoi imperii: Entsiklopedicheskii slovar'*, ed. Stanislav M. Prozorov, I (Moscow: Izdatel'skaia firma "Vostochnaia literatura" RAN, 2006), 431–432.

Babadzhanov, B. "O vidakh zikra dzhakhr sredi bratstv Tsentral'noi Azii." In *Istoriko-kul'turnye vzaimosviazi Irana i Dasht-i Kipchaka v XIII–XVIII vv.: Materialy mezhdunarodnogo Kruglogo stola* (Almaty: Daik-Press, 2004), 133–157.

Babadzhanov, B. "Zikr dzhakhr i sama': sakralizatsiia profannogo ili profanatsiia sakral'nogo?" In *Podvizhniki Islama: Kul't sviatykh i sufizm v Srednei Azii i na Kavkaze*, ed. S. N. Abashin and V. O. Bobrovnikov (Moscow: "Vostochnaia literatura" RAN, 2003), 237–250.

Balci, Bayram. "Fethullah Gülen's Missionary Schools in Central Asia and their Role in the Spreading of Turkism and Islam." *Religion, State and Society*, 31 (2003), 151–177.

Balci, Bayram. *Missionnaires de l'Islam en Asie centrale: Les écoles turques de Fethullah Guelen*. Paris: Maisonneuve and Larose, 2003.

Èrmekbaev, Zharas A. *Chechentsy i ingushi v Kazakhstane: Istoriia i sud'ba*. Almaty: Daik-Press, 2009.

Interview by the author with Näsĭrĭdin Ishan Abduvoitov (b. 1951), in the village of Qŭsshï Ata, summer 2011.

Ismatulla Maqsŭm. *Qŭran sïrlarïnïng älĭppesĭ*. Almatï: Alash, 2004.

Ismatulla Maqsŭm. *Zhariya zĭkĭrdĭng dälelĭ*. Almatï: Alash, 2006.

Iuldashev, A. Report of the Chairman of the Council for Religious Affairs in Iuzhnaia Kazakhstanskaia Oblast' under the Council of Ministers of the USSR, (1947): South Kazakhstan Regional State Archive. Fond 1353, *opis'* 2, *stopka* 4, *kniga* 28, p. 93.

Muminov, Ashirbek. "From Revived Tradition to Innovation: Kolkhoz Islam in the Southern Kazakhstan Region and Religious Leadership (through the Cases of Zhartï-Töbe and Oranghay since the 1950s)." In *Allah's Kolkhozes: Migration, De-Stalinisation, Privatisation and the New Muslim Congregations in the Soviet Realm (1950s–2000s)*, ed. Stéphane A. Dudoignon and Christian Noack (Berlin: Klaus Schwarz Verlag), 307–366.

Narimbet, Nazira. "Prigovor sufiiam ostalsia v sile." 2012. http://rus.azattyq.org/content/kazakh_sufism_ismatulla_abdigappar_sayat_ibraev/24569795.html.

Nurmanova, Aitzhan. "Pilgrimages to Mazars in Contemporary Kazakhstan—The Processes of Revivalism and Innovation." In *Mazar: Studies on Islamic Sacred Sites in Central Eurasia*, ed. Sugawara Jun and Rahile Dawut (Tokyo: Tokyo University of Foreign Studies, 2016), 63–72.

Olcott, Martha Brill. *The Kazakhs*. Stanford: Hoover Institution Press, 1995.

Oral communication from journalist Mŭkhan Isakhan (b. 1978), Almatï, summer 2011.

Oral communication from Ruziia Islamovna Qamarova (b. 1965), Astana, 26 January 2015.

Oral communication from the former SAMK functionary (cleric) Abdulla Qazhï Zholdasov (b. 1944), Shïmkent, December 2014.

Oral communication from Tŭrghanqŭlov Tangzharïq Qasïmqŭlŭlï (b. 1980), Taraz, December 2014.

Roshchin, Mikhail. "Chechenskii sufizm v period deportatsii: vozniknovenie virda Viskhazhi." 2012. http://www.kavkazoved.info/authors/mihail-roschin.html.

Wilkowsky, Dina. *Arabisch-islamische Organisationen in Kasachstan: Exogener Einfluss auf die islamische Erneuerung, 1991–2007*. Berlin: Verlag Hans Schiler, 2009.

Yoldāshkhojayev, H. *Tariqatchilikning zamānaviy korinishlari*. Tashkent: Tāshkent Islām Universiteti, 2010.

Zarcone, Thierry. "Bridging the Gap between Pre-Soviet and Post-Soviet Sufism in Ferghana valley (Uzbekistan): The Naqshbandi Order between Tradition and Innovation." In *Popular Movements and Democratization in the Islamic World*, ed. Masatoshi Kisaichi (London and New York: Routledge, 2006), 43–56.

CHAPTER 10

The Biographical Tradition of Muḥammad Bashārā: Sanctification and Legitimation in Tajikistan

Jo-Ann Gross

As scholarship on shrines and shrine culture in Central Asia has advanced in recent years, we have come to appreciate the diverse nature of the construction of Islamic sacred space, and the process whereby spiritual, social, and political meanings are attributed to sacred places and the eminent figures associated with them.[1] This study explores how two orally transmitted textualized

Note: I am grateful to Bahriddin Aliev, who accompanied me on my first visit and several subsequent trips to the shrine of Muḥammad Bashārā in Mazār-i Sharīf, and to Imom Shamsiddin, both of whom generously shared their knowledge about the village and the history and culture of the *mazār* and assisted me with sources, including obtaining a rare copy of the *Risolai Khoja Muhammad Bashoro*. For feedback on earlier drafts and written and oral comments offered, I thank Bahriddin Aliev, Devin DeWeese, Robert McChesney and Amineh Mahallati.

1 See especially the works of Devin DeWeese, "Sacred History for a Central Eurasian Town: Saints, Shrines, and Legends of Origin in Histories of Sayrām, 18th–19th Centuries," *Revue des mondes musulmans et de la Méditerranée*, 89/90 (1999), 245–295; DeWeese, "Sacred Places and 'Public' Narratives: The Shrine of Aḥmad Yasavī in Hagiographical Traditions of the Yasavī Sufi Order, 16th–17th Centuries," *Muslim World*, 90/3–4 (2000), 353–376; Robert McChesney, *Waqf in Central Asia: Four Hundred Years in the History of a Muslim Shrine, 1480–1889* (Princeton, NJ: Princeton University Press, 1991); McChesney, "Society and Community: Shrines and Dynastic Families in Central Eurasia," in R. D. McChesney, *Central Asia: Foundations of Change* (Princeton, NJ: Darwin Press, 1996), 69–116, McChesney, "Architecture and Narrative: The Khwaja Abu Nasr Parsa Shrines. Part I: Constructing the Complex and its Meaning, 1469–1696," *Muqarnas*, 18 (2001), 94–119, and "Architecture and Narrative: The Khwaja Abu Nasr Parsa Shrine. Part 2: Representing the Complex in Word and Image, 1696–1998," *Muqarnas*, 19 (2002), 78–108; Marcus Schadl, "The Shrine of Nasir-i Khusraw: Imprisoned Deep in the Valley of Yumgan," *Muqarnas*, 26 (2009), 63–93. For studies of shrines in Xinjiang, see Rahila Dawut and Rachel Harris, "Mazar Festivals of the Uyghurs: Music, Islam and the Chinese State," *British Journal of Ethnomusicology*, 11/1(2002), 101–118; Hamada Masami, "Islamic Saints and their Mausoleums," *Acta Asiatica: Bulletin of the Institute of Eastern Culture*, 34 (1978), 79–98; Alexandre Papas, "Les tombeaux de saints musulmans au Xinjiang: Culte, réforme, histoire," *Archives de sciences sociales des religions*, 142 (2008), 47–62; Shinmen Yasushi, "The History of the Mausoleum of the Aṣḥāb al-Kahf in Turfan," *Memoirs of the Research Department of the Toyo Bunko* (Tokyo: Toyo Bunko), 61(2004), 83–104; Sawada Minoru, "Tarim Basin Mazârs: A Fieldwork Report," *Journal of the History of Sufism*, 3 (2001),

 | DOI:10.1163/9789004373075_012

traditions inform the personhood, sanctify the memory, and authenticate the exemplary status of Muḥammad Bashārā, the saint who is believed to be buried in the *mazār* named after him located in the Zarafshān valley of Tajikistan in the village of Mazār-i Sharīf.[2]

My focus on the biographies created for Muḥammad Bashārā presumes the social and territorial importance of the shrine structure itself, which I discuss along with the narrative traditions. The chronological dimensions of the study stretch from the time of the Prophet Muḥammad and the first generations of his followers, to the construction of the shrine from the 11th or 12th century to the 14th century, to the biographical accounts either recorded in the 19th century, perhaps, and then revived in post-Soviet times, or constructed in the post-Soviet period, out of Arabic biographical dictionaries with their own long trajectory of memorialization.

The two biographical modes connect with long stretches of historical imagination in which the modern nation state of Tajikistan played no role, with some biographical frameworks deeply rooted in local soil, while others are drawn from far away. The first text is a hagiographical work, likely of 19th-century provenance, titled *Risolai Khoja Muhammad Bashoro* (Pers. *Risāla-yi Khwāja Muḥammad Bashārā*).[3] The *Risāla*, transcribed into Tajik (Cyrillic alphabet) from a privately held Persian manuscript, was prepared by Kobilboy Jum'aev and published in 1993, soon after the dissolution of the Soviet Union in 1991 and at the height of hostilities during the civil war in Tajikistan that followed.[4] The second work, *Muhammadi Bashoro*, was authored and

39–61; Jun Sugawara, "Mazar Legends in the Kashghar Region," in *Islamic Sacred Places in Central Asia: The Ferghana Valley and Kashghar Region* (Nara: The Nara International Foundation, Commemorating the Silk Road Exposition, 2007), 67–78.

2 Until the 19th century the village in which the shrine is located was known by its Soghdian name, Runj, or Khoja Runj, which later became Mazori Sharif.

3 *Risolai Khoja Muhammad Bashoro* (Pers. *Risāla-yi Muḥammad Bashārā*), prepared by Kobilboy Jum'aev (Khujand: Kitobi Tojikiston 1993). When quoting directly from interviews conducted in Tajik language or texts written in Tajik, or when citing contemporary Tajik personal names, I will use Tajik transliteration, and when appropriate, I will add the Persian or Arabic in parentheses. In cases where the original text was written in Persian or Arabic, I use standard Persian or Arabic transliteration.

4 The civil war in Tajikistan took place from 1992 to 1997. I have been unable to locate a copy of the Persian manuscript. It is likely that multiple variants of these oral traditions exist, in addition to written versions held in the hands of local families. Kobilboy Jum'aev, who comes from a religious family in the village of Mazār-i Sharīf and was living in Tashkent during the period of my research, apparently had access to one of them. *Risolai Khoja Muhammad Bashoro* is a modest pamphlet-type publication of 45 pages, of a sort that proliferated in the

published in Tajik in 2004 by Zainularabi Shamsiddin and Saidakbari Najibullo, two students who, at the time, were studying in The Islamic University of Imom Tirmizi (*Doneshgohi Islomi Imom Tirmizi*) in Dushanbe.[5] In contrast to the *Risāla, Muhammadi Bashoro* was published at a time when the war recovery, nation-building, and re-formation of Islamic identity in the Republic of Tajikistan were well under way. The latter work challenges the historical veracity of the *Risāla-yi Muḥammad Bashārā* and presents evidence from *ḥadīth* literature and Arabic biographical and historical works to legitimate and traditionalize the legacy of Khwāja Muḥammad Bashārā as the 8th–9th-century *muḥaddith* named Muḥammad b. Bashār b. ʿUthmān Qaysānī Baṣrī. The authors cite *ḥadīths* attesting to his birth in Basra in 167/782, his death in 242/866, and his role as a transmitter of *ḥadīths* and teacher (*ustod*) of the Central Asian scholar Muḥammad b. Ismāʿīl al-Bukhārī, author of the *Ṣaḥīh al-Bukhārī*.[6]

The two biographical works represent variant textualized conceptions of Muḥammad Bashārā published and disseminated in post-Soviet Tajikistan during a period when long-hidden manuscripts and documents, preserved mostly by private families under Soviet rule, began to resurface. As such, they not only serve to sanctify and memorialize the life and deeds of Muḥammad Bashārā; the biographies also represent distinct currents in post-Soviet Tajikistan regarding Islamic religiosity and perceptions of the sacred past, specifically the contrast between "traditional" Muslim religiosity and an increasingly dominant scripturalist/Salafi religiosity.[7] As several recent studies have demonstrated, a renewed Islamic textual tradition and religious discourse has emerged in

post-Soviet period (copies were distributed locally at shrines and sold in city and town bookstores and kiosks).

5 Zaynularabi Shamsiddin and Saidakbari Najibullo, *Muhammadi Bashoro* (Dushanbe: Arzhan, 2004). According to Epkenhans, The Islamic University of Imom Tirmizi was first established in 1992, as the educational branch of the Tajik Muftiate; see Tim Epkenhans, "Muslims without learning, clergy without faith: Institutions of Islamic learning in the Republic of Tajikistan," in *Islamic Education in the Soviet Union and its successor states*, ed. M. Kemper, R. Motika, and S. Reichmuth (London/New York, Routledge, 2010), 321. The name was later changed to Imami A'zam Abu Hanifa when it came under the supervision of the Ministry of Education. See Tim Epkenhans, "Defining normative Islam: some remarks on contemporary Islamic thought in Tajikistan—Hoji Akbar Turajonzoda's *Sharia and society*," *Central Asian Survey*, 30 (2011), 95, note 32.

6 *Muhammadi Bashoro*, 5.

7 Although the development of Islamic thought in early post-Soviet Tajikistan, and more recently, is of interest, as is current state policy regarding Islamic practices and the banning of Islamic political parties, they are beyond the scope of this paper.

post-Soviet Tajikistan that seeks to establish a narrow textual basis of spiritual authority (Qur'ān and *ḥadīths*) through the publication of such works.[8] What is of particular interest to this study are the distinctive approaches to creating an explanatory account of the personhood of Muḥammad Bashārā, the contrasting authorial intentions, and the internal dialogue between the two works.[9]

The *mazār* of Muḥammad Bashārā is only vaguely known outside of Tajikistan and is omitted from the standard Islamic architecture surveys published in the West. Yet the building exhibits some of the finest decorative features in Central Asia. The rich ornamentation and fine artisanship of the building's construction, together with its ideal location facing a stream to

8 This is especially the case for Sufi texts. See Benjamin Clark Gatling, "Post-Soviet Sufism: Texts and the Performance of Tradition in Tajikistan," unpublished Ph.D. Dissertation, The Ohio State University, 2012. Gatling's analysis of the reconstruction of "Jununī's legacy and spiritual authority through the narrative performance of historical legends and memorates associated with his life" is a case in point. In his dissertation he argues that "traditionalization" is a key component of contemporary Islam in Tajikistan, and that the present requires some form of "sacred historical legitimation" (Gatling, 98 and 248). Also see Tim Epkenhans, "Defining Normative Islam," 81–86; Epkenhans, "Muslims Without Learning, Clergy Without Faith," 313–348; Parviz Mullojonov, "The Islamic Clergy in Tajikistan Since the End of the Soviet Period," in *Islam in Politics in Russia and Central Asia (Early Eighteenth to Late Twentieth Centuries)*, ed. Stephane A. Dudoignon and Hisao Komatsu (New York: Kegan Paul, 2002), 221–250. For related discussions of post-Soviet Islam and Sufism in Uzbekistan, see Bakhtiyar Babadjanov, "Debates over Islam in Contemporary Uzbekistan: A View from Within," in *Devout Societies vs. Impious States? Transmitting Islamic Learning in Russia, Central Asia and China, through the Twentieth Century*, ed. Stephane A. Dudoignon (Berlin: Klaus Schwarz Verlag, 2004), 39–60; Bakhtiyar Babadjanov, "Muhammadjan Hindustani (1892–1989) and the Beginning of the 'Great Schism' among the Muslims of Uzbekistan," in *Islam in Politics in Russia and Central Asia (Early Eighteenth to Late Twentieth Centuries)*, ed. S. A. Dudoignon and K. Hisao (London: Kegan Paul, 2001), 195–219, and Johan Rasanayagam, *Islam in Post-Soviet Uzbekistan: The Morality of Experience* (Cambridge: Cambridge University Press, 2011).

9 Talal Asad's concept of Islam as a "discursive tradition" is particularly relevant here. Talal Asad, "The Idea of an Anthropology of Islam," reissued by Duke University Press in *Qui Parle*, 17/2 (Spring/Summer, 2009), 20. The article was originally published in the Occasional Paper Series sponsored by the Center for Contemporary Arab Studies, Georgetown University, 1986. Nile Green centers his study, *Sufism: A Global History*, on the notion of collective tradition, the importance of links to the past and the ways discourse "shape[s] other people's actions through their imitation of the exemplary models it provided." See Nile Green, *Sufism: A Global History* (West Sussex, Great Britain, Wiley-Blackwell, 2012), 6. See also the study by Ron Sela of the legendary biographies of Timur (mainly written in the early 18th century): Ron Sela, *The Legendary Biographies of Tamerlane: Islam and Heroic Apocrypha in Central Asia* (Cambridge/New York: Cambridge University Press, 2011).

the front and tucked into the mountains, suggest a well-planned settlement and a level of prosperity befitting the burial place of a saint of significant stature and prestige.[10] We would expect such a saint and his mausoleum to be noted in the Persian biographical writings (*tadhkiras*) and regional histories of the early modern period. Yet the only reference to the *mazār* or to Muḥammad Bashārā, to our knowledge, is found in the *Samariyya*, a 19th-century pilgrimage guide to Samarqand written by Abū Ṭāhir Khwāja Samarqandī. Samarqandī includes the following passage on "The Noble Mazār of Khwāja Muḥammad Bashār," in which he dates the construction of his *qabr* and a *khānaqāh* to 764/1362:[11]

> It is located in the mountainous dependency of Samarqand. He is mentioned in the *Taḥqīqāt* of Abū'l-Qāsim Samarqandī, and he was among the *tābiʿīn* (Followers of the Prophet Muḥammad).[12] His *mazār* is located in the town (*qaṣabche*) of Panjikant, which is under the authority (*maḥkūmāt*) of Samarqand. In 764 [1362 CE] the shaykhs of the *mazār* built a long grave (*qabr-i ṭūlānī*) above his tomb (*marqad*) and a noble *khānaqāh* on that land. His *mazār* is about eleven *farsang*s from Samarqand. One *ʿazīz* said, 'I made many pilgrimages (*ziyārāt*) to the great *mazār*s of Mawarannahr, but I never saw such a bountiful *mazār* as the *mazār* of Khwāja [Muḥammad Bashār].[13]

The architectural history sheds some light on the origins and uses of the *mazār* of Muḥammad Bashārā and the attraction it still holds today as an important

---

10 The decorated front portal of the shrine features carved terracotta with polychromatic tiles and blue-glazed bricks. Also notable are the corner decorative terracotta cylinders joined without mortar and covered in intricate carving. Khmel'nitskii notes that the portal reflects the transition that was taking place from a monochrome to polychrome style. "The major part of its decoration was executed in carved terracotta in its natural golden-yellow hue, but the tympanum of the arch is surfaced with majolica tiles of turquoise and blue with a delicate design, and the rectangles of the decorative panels, the bands with Arabic inscriptions and embellishments, are executed in carved terracotta and framed by blue glazed bricks." Sergei Chmelnizkij [Khmel'nitskii], "The Mausoleum of Muhammad Bosharo," *Muqarnas*, 7 (1990), 27.

11 Kobilboy Jum'aev incorrectly records the date as 714 AH on the inside cover (copyright page) of *Risalai Khoja Muhammad Bashoro*. For further discussion of this issue, see 362–363.

12 As discussed below, the authors of *Muhammadi Bashoro* reject this chronology and assert instead that he was from the "*tabaa Tobe'in*," or Successors of the Followers of the Prophet.

13 Abū Ṭāhir Khwāja Samarqandī, *Samariyya*, in *Qandiyya va Samariyya*, ed. Īrāj Afshār (Tehran: Mu'assasa-yi Farhangī-yi Jahāngīrī, 1367/1988), 193.

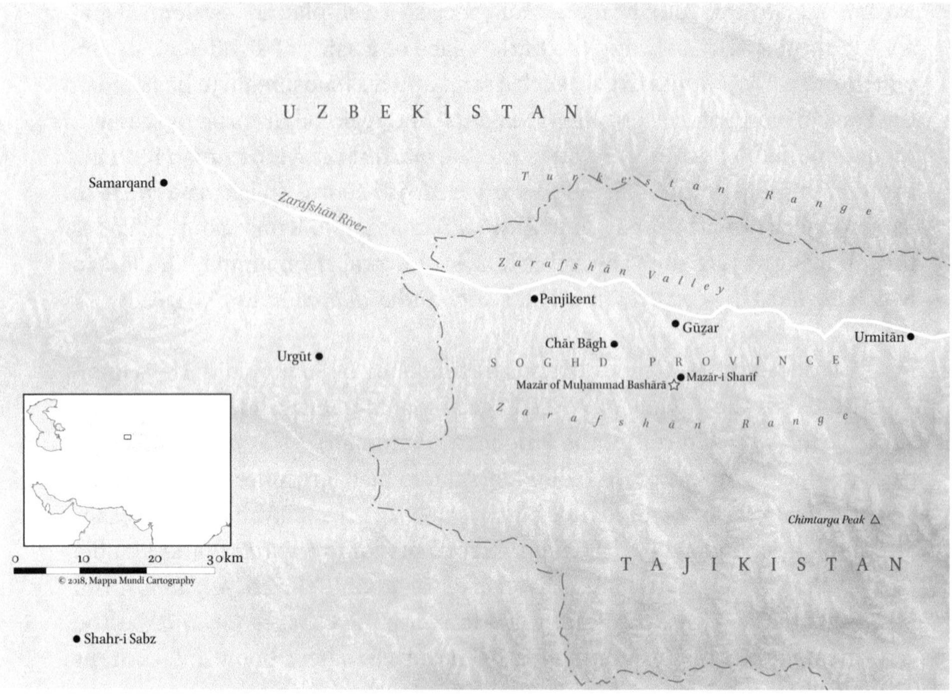

MAP 10.1 *Location of the* Mazār *of Muḥammad Bashārā in the Zarafshān Valley, Tajikistan*

pilgrimage site, although there is a disconnect between the appraisal of the site and the structures by Soviet architectural historians and archeologists and a plausible history of the site, including the social, economic and political significance of the site as evidenced in the largely unanalyzed documentary legacy, and the biographical traditions that are the major focus in this paper. The first in-depth architectural study of the shrine was published in 1958 by L. S. Bretanitskii, who "hypothesized that the portal of the mausoleum (one of the most beautiful in all Central Asia, it bears the original construction date of 1342–43) was erected later than the main structure, which he attributed to the late eleventh or early twelfth century."[14] His work was followed

14 Sergei Chmelnizkij [Khmel'nitskii], "The Mausoleum of Muhammad Bosharo," *Muqarnas*, 7 (1990), 23, discussing L. S. Bretanitskii, "Ob odnom maloizvestnom pamiatnike Tadzhikskogo zodchestva," *Materialy i issledovaniia po arkheologii SSR*, 66 (1959), 325–357. Bretanitskii dates the portal to 743/1342–43, as does Khmel'nitskii. Although there is agreement among scholars on the portal date of 743/1342–43, it may be possible to read the

FIGURE 10.1 *Front portal,* Mazār *of Muḥammad Bashārā*
GROSS 2010

date either as 743/1342–43 or 943/1536, since without dots, the number could read *tis*ʿ (9) or *sab*ʿ (7). Burchard Brentjes' brief article follows Bretanitskii and describes the shrine as a remarkable example of pre-Timurid Central Asian architecture: Burchard Brentjes, "Das Grabmal des Muḥammad Boššaro—Ein Vorläufer Timuridischer Baukunst," *Ibn Ḫaldūn unde seine Zeit*, ed. D. Sturm (Halle: Martin-Luther Universität, 1983), 17–23.

by V. L. Voronina and K. S. Kriukov in 1978. Voronina and Kriukov concluded that the mausoleum was built in two stages: the left wing was built first, and therefore is the oldest section (constructed in the 11th or 12th century); and the central part, the right wing, and the portal were built sometime later.[15] The most recent architectural study on the shrine is by S. Khmel'nitskii in 1990.[16] He refutes a number of the earlier findings of Bretanitskii, Voronina and Kriukov, in particular their view that the building was a combined mosque-mausoleum.[17] Khmel'nitskii maintains that the mausoleum of Muḥammad Bashārā was constructed in three stages, reflecting its evolution from a mosque built in the 13th century to a mausoleum in the 14th century.[18] According to his theory, "the first stage of construction was the central part of the building, constructed as a central-domed mosque with the entrance opposite the *miḥrāb* on the northwest side [see figure 10.2]."[19] He asserts, moreover,

> Not until the eleventh century, when Sufism began to spread in Central Asia, were the graves of honored spiritual masters transformed into sanctuaries (*mazar*). But the prohibition against praying on graves remained in force, and in order to resolve this contradiction a room for prayer

---

15 Bretanitskii, "Ob odnom maloizvestnom pamiatnike Tadzhikskogo zodchestva," 325–357; V. L. Voronina and K. S. Kriukov, "Mavzolei Mukhammeda Bosharo," in *Drevnost' i srednevekov'e narodov Srednei Azii* (*Istoriia i kul'tura*) (Moscow: Nauka, 1978), 58–68; Chmelnizkij [Khmel'nitskii], "The Mausoleum of Muhammad Bosharo," 29.

16 Chmelnizkij [Khmel'nitskii], "The Mausoleum of Muhammad Bosharo," 23–34, also published in Russian as S. Khmel'nitskii, "Mavzolei Muhammada Bashoro," *Izvestiia Akademii nauk Tadzhikskoi SSR*, Seriia Vostokovedenie, istoriia, filosofiia, 2/18 (1990), 28–35. Further references in this study will be to the English publication in *Muqarnas* and will use the standard transliteration of his name as Khmel'nitskii.

17 Khmel'nitskii, "Mausoleum," 29. Khmel'nitskii qualifies this by stating that the "appellation 'mosque-mausoleum' used by Bretanitskii, Voronina, and K. Kriukov for this building is incorrect, unless it is constructed as meaning that the building was first a mosque and only later a mausoleum."

18 See Khmel'nitskii, "Mausoleum," 29–30 for his refutation of Bretanitskii's analysis, which dates the building to the 11th or early 12th century and considers the construction of the mausoleum and the mosque to have taken place at the same time.

19 Khmel'nitskii argues that it would be highly unusual for a *miḥrāb* to be found in a mausoleum or burial site in this region. He considers the attempt to resolve this problem to be what led to the development of two-chambered mausoleums containing a *ziyāratkhāna* connected to the mortuary chamber (*gūrkhāna*), as is the case of the shrine of Muḥammad Bashārā. Khmel'nitskii writes, "The function of the central, square part of the edifice can be established without a doubt by the presence of the mihrab that is so strikingly set off and by the orientation of the whole toward the southwest (the qibla)—this structure was clearly built to be a mosque …" See Khmel'nitskii, "Mausoleum," 28–29.

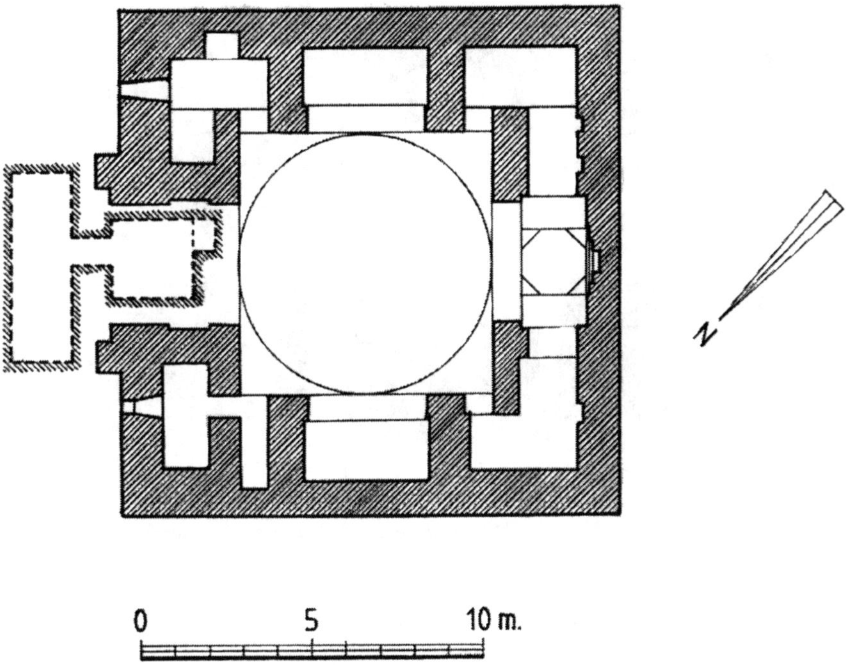

FIGURE 10.2 *Reconstructed plan of the first stage of construction*
KHMEL'NITSKII, 1990

(*ziaratkhana*), a memorial mosque connected to the mortuary chamber (*gurkhana*), began to appear.[20]

Sometime later, according to Khmel'nitskii, an unidentified man of apparent eminence was buried in an underground crypt "at the threshold of the mosque."[21] Two wings were later added to the original mosque, first the right wing that included the long grave (*qabr-i ṭūlānī*) (conceivably that of Muḥammad Bashārā) built over the tomb (*marqad*) and the *khānaqāh* reported by Samarqandī to have been built in 764/1362 (see figure 10.3). We know from the documentary record that the builder of the *qabr* and *khānaqāh* was Mawlānā Akram, who served as *mutawallī*, as did his descendants at least up to the 19th century.[22]

20 Khmel'nitskii, "Mausoleum," 29. Khmel'nitskii's statement regarding the force of "prohibitions" about praying at graves reveals the Sovietological argument he makes about architectural developments based on his notion of when Sufism arrived in the region.

21 Ibid., 31.

22 Mawlānā Akram built a *dakhma* (tomb) inside the *khānaqāh* for the burial of his own relatives. Extant legal documents I collected, which date as late as the 19th century, reaffirm

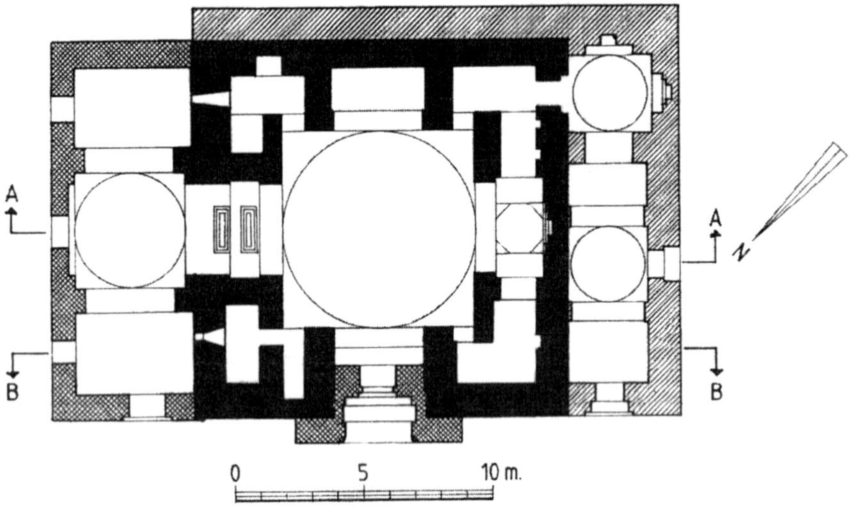

FIGURE 10.3 *Reconstructed plan of the third and final stage of construction*
KHMEL'NITSKII, 1990

The earliest known document pertaining to the shrine of Muḥammad Bashāra is an order (*ḥukm*), dated Rajab 829/1426, issued by Nāṣir al-Dīn Khwāja Ṣadr, confirming the reappointment of Shaykh Abū'l-Qāsim as *mutawallī* of the shrine of Muḥammad Bashārā.[23] It states that Shaykh Abū'l-Qāsim, in

the right of Akram's descendants (*awlād*) and relations (*'aqribān*) to be buried there. See also *Muhammad Bashoro*, 29. In an interview in May 2010 with Imom Shamsiddin, *mutawallī* of the shrine, he told me, "The *saghona*, called *dakhma*, located inside the *mazor* and now behind a wooden screen, holds the bones of *mutawallis*, shaykhs, and servants of the *mazor* and there is a special *saghona* for women ... There is a story about Ustod Akram, who worked in this mausoleum. According to the story, he died in Jamoat Sujina and was buried there. His grave still exists and is built of stone. People still visit that place. He is buried in a ravine, in the village of Dashte Malla."

23 Institute of History, Academy of Sciences of the Republic of Tajikistan, Inv. 2157. The original document is 19 x 12.3 centimeters and bears two seals of Nāṣir al-Dīn Khwāja Ṣadr. During the Soviet period, beginning in 1959, archaeologists, ethnographers and historians participated in annual expeditions in Tajikistan to collect manuscripts, epigraphic materials, and other aspects of material culture. Historian Ahror Mukhtarov played a leading role in these expeditions and published extensively on the sources he and his teams found. In 1962, he acquired 20 documents in the village of Mazār-i Sharīf relating to the history of the *mazār* of Muḥammad Bashārā. In his 1963 expedition to Ayni, Uroteppe and Penjikent and the cities of Samarqand, Bukhara and the Nurata region of the Uzbek SSR,

accordance with documents issued from the former *ṣadr*, had inherited the post of *mutawallī* and is reappointed to that post to manage the *waqf* revenues from donations and agricultural properties (*nudhūrāt va zirāʿāt*) for four named purposes: first, the repair of the mosque, second, for travellers and pilgrims, third, for the *mutawallī*, and fourth, for the maintenance of the *mazār*. The subsequent record of documentary evidence related to the administration establishes the interest of political authorities in *waqf* rights and the claim of one family to the trusteeship (*tawliyat*) of *the mazār*, namely that of the builder and likely the first *mutawallī*, Mawlānā Akram. Such evidence substantiates the existence of a well-endowed shrine that enjoyed the broad support of rulers, local figures and the populace at large over a period of five centuries.[24] Although extant documents related to the *waqf* and administrative history of the *mazār* do not solve the mystery of the identity of Muḥammad Bashārā or the original construction of the mosque and its transformation, they

his team acquired 375 documents dating from the 15th to the 20th century, 40 of which were acquired in Mazār-i Sharīf itself and were thus directly related to the history of the *mazār*. See A. M. Mukhtarov, "Khronika polevykh raboty otriiada sektora, Istorii srednikh vekov (1963–1973)," *Arkheologicheskie raboty v Tadzhikistane* 13 (Dushanbe: Donish, 1973), 241–242. Between 1975 and 1987, historians A. Yegani and O. D. Chekhovich published 17 of the documents collected by Mukhtarov (with Russian synopses and a selection of facsimiles) in a series of 4 articles: A. A. Egani and O. D. Chekhovich, "Regesty sredneaziatskikh aktov 1973, Series 1," *Pis'mennye pamiatniki Vostoka, Istoriko-filologicheskie issledovaniia* (Moscow, 1981), 44–49, 56–57, 305–336; "Regesty sredneaziatskikh aktov 1974, Series 2," *Pis'mennye pamiatniki Vostoka, Istoriko-filologicheskie issledovaniia* (Moscow, 1982), 36, 47–48, 50, 270, 305–306, 310, 315; "Regesty sredneaziatskikh aktov 1976–1977, Series 3," *Pis'mennye pamiatniki Vostoka, Istoriko-filologicheskie issledovaniia* (Moscow, 1984), 109–110 and 352–353; "Regesty sredneaziatskikh aktov 1978–1979, Series 4," *Pis'mennye pamiatniki Vostoka, Istoriko-filologicheskie issledovaniia* (Moscow, 1987), 36, 47–48, 50, 270, 305, 306, 310, 315. This important documentary record is stored in the archive of the A. Donish Institute of History, Archaeology and Ethnography of the Academy of Sciences of the Republic of Tajikistan, but it unfortunately remains inaccessible to scholars. I have heard rumors that an original *waqf* deed exists, but I am unaware of any formal record of it.

24 In addition to the above-mentioned documents, the authors of *Muhammadi Bashoro* include 12 unpublished Persian documents in their study, transcribed into Tajik, along with a sample of four facsimiles. During field research in 2004, I located 46 unpublished documents (purchase deeds, *waqf-nāmas*, and a variety of decrees, including *ḥukms* and *yarliqs*) in a nearby village, with dates ranging from 1562 to the 19th century (many of the later documents are undated fragments), five of which are among those included by Shamsiddin and Najibullah.

provide important clues about the local and regional significance of the shrine. When considered along with the extraordinary craftsmanship of the architectural and decorative features of the building, aside from what we know based on the architectural history, the documentary record indicates a significant investment on the part of local rulers, a strong popular attachment to the memory of Muḥammad Bashārā, and a long-term interest on the part of political authorities in the administration of the shrine and in the dynastic family (or families) of *mutawallīs* and *ṣadrs* who administered the shrine and developed their own bases of power and prestige. Thus, as we will see below, while there is a paucity of clear evidence about the inhabitant of the shrine, the biographical traditions are pegged to the shrine itself.

The Biographical Tradition of Muḥammad Bashārā

Despite the paucity of contemporary historical references, a rich oral, and, of late, newly textualized tradition exists surrounding Muḥammad Bashārā; it links him with the shrine as a migrant Islamizing figure, a common feature in accounts of saintly foundational figures in Central Asia and elsewhere in the Islamicate world. In 2004, the *imām* of the *mazār* of Muḥammad Bashārā recited the following verses to me from a handwritten booklet:

> We wandered in the mountains and valleys
> And have seen a hundred Caesars, Alexanders, and Dariuses.
> The *chashma hayvon* (spring of life) that Khizr (Khiżr) desired
> We saw in Khoja Muhammadi Bashoro.
> We found our homes in the far regions of the world
> And saw many sacred shrines.
> The light that recalls the purity of the Kaaba (Kaʿba)
> We saw in Khoja Muhammadi Bashoro.[25]

The verses recount the journey of a people through the mountains and valleys of pre-Islamic history, passing the Roman, Greek, and Persian patriarchs. Khiżr,

25 Imom Shamsiddin, interview by Jo-Ann Gross, Mazār-i Sharīf, May 2004. Shamsiddin and Najibullo include a similar poem in *Muhammadi Bashoro*, noting that "in popular oral literature (*adabiyoti shifohii mardum*; Pers. *adabiyāt-i shifāhī-yi mardum*) these kinds of 2-*bayt* quatrains (*du-baytiyu ruboihoi; dū-baytīhā-yu rubāʿīhā*) about this *mazār* are widespread" (*Muhammadi Bashoro*, 19–20). These sacred places are pivotal in *Risolai Khoja Muhammad Bashoro*, as will be discussed below.

the immortal servant of God, teacher of Moses, and symbol of God's mercy, drank from the water of life and wished for the sacred spring. The divine inspiration that is known to have embodied the spring is also seen in Muḥammad Bashārā. The first verse links the *jāhiliyya* period of wandering to Khiżr's role in the creation of the life-giving spring and to the blessed figure of Muḥammad Bashārā.[26] The second verse describes the settlement of this people in distant lands marked by numerous shrines, and distinguishes the pure light of the sacred House of God (*Baytullah*), the Kaʿba, the symbolic pole of the *umma*, the object of Muslim pilgrimage (*ḥajj*), as the light seen in Khwāja Muḥammad Bashārā. The two verses thus create a spiritual geography that links the holy city of Mecca and the Abrahamic tradition to this shrine, and in so doing they establish a cultural genealogy that both sanctifies the village and narrows the historical distance between the mausoleum of Muhammad Bashārā and the Kaʿba of Mecca.[27]

Muhammad Bashārā: Warrior Saint and Friend of the Prophet

The *Risolai Muhammad Bashoro* (Pers. *Risāla-yi Muḥammad Bashārā*) is an Islamization narrative composed in rather common rhymed Persian verse and based on regionally circulated oral tradition (*ḥikāyāt*). It is difficult to ascertain how much liberty the copyist took with regard to the transcription of the Persian into Tajik without a copy of the original text in our possession, but there are many examples where the correct meter (*ʿarūż*) has been obscured or eliminated, likely due to an incorrect reading of the Persian script. It is notable, however, that the editor includes a passage on the copyright page that is nearly identical to the passage in the *Samariyya* quoted earlier, albeit with some significant errors and additions, as follows:

> This history was written in the month of Safar in the year 1400.[28] The *mazor* of the abundant traces of Muhammadi Bashoro is located in the mountainous dependency of Samarqand, and that *muhaddis*[29] was from

26 According to Imam Shamsiddin, the name of the two springs that flow near the shrine are Minsaqi Ashob and Chashmai Niyat. Interview by Jo-Ann Gross in Mazār-i Sharīf, May 2004. Similarly, Shamsiddin and Najibullo refer to them as Chashma Minsāq and Chashma Niyyat. *Muhammadi Bashoro*, 4–5.

27 The *mazār* of Muḥammad Bashārā as a "second Kaʿba" will be discussed in the context of the *Risolai Muhammadi Bashoro*.

28 The date of 1400 is incorrect, since the *Samariyya* is a 19th-century pilgrimage guide. See Jürgen Paul, "Histories of Samarqand," *Studia Iranica* 22 (1993): 82–97.

29 The *Samariyya*, based on the so-called *Taḥqīqāt* of Abū'l-Qāsim Samarqandī, does not refer to "Khwāja Muḥammad Bashār" as a *muḥaddith*. It does, as noted earlier, describe

> the *toba'a tobi'in* (Arabic, *al-Tābiʿ al-Tābiʿīn*), (Successors of the Followers of the Prophet).[30] His *mazor* is located in the district (*muzojoti*)[31] of Panjakent, which is the suburb of Samarqand. In 714[32] the shaykhs of the *mazor* of the *ishon* built a noble (*oli*) *khonaqo* above his tomb (*marqad*), which made a long mark on the ground (*ki nishoni tuloni bar zamin dosht*).[33] His *mazor* is 11 farsangs from Samarqand.

This acknowledgement of Bashārā's position as a *muḥaddith* is external to the hagiography itself, although there is one comment within the *Risāla* about Khoja Bashārā's knowledge of *ḥadīth*.[34] Rather, the *Risāla* relates the tale of Muḥammad Bashārā, who lived with his father, mother, six brothers and a sister in a fortress of unbelievers (*qal'ai mardi kuffori*) with many servants and relatives.[35] One son was known by the name of Muḥammad[36] and he knew "everything from the earth to the celestial sphere" (*az falak to arz*).[37] One night he dreamed he was walking in a garden when a throne (*takht*) appeared from the sky on which the Prophet was seated.

> The light from his face spread to the world,
> Khoja felt a fondness in his breast for him.
> He laid his head on his chest,
> And bowed sincerely to the man's [Muḥammad's] feet.

Muḥammad Bashārā as "among the *Tābiʿīn*" (Arabic, *tābiʿūn*; Followers of the Prophet), but not the *tābiʿ al-Tabiʿīn* (Successors of the Followers of the Prophet), as do the authors of *Muhammadi Bashoro*. For my translation of this passage in the *Samariyya*, see above, page 353.

30 Interestingly, this conflicts with the narrative in the *Risāla*, in which Muḥammad Bashārā travels to Medina and becomes a follower of the Prophet Muḥammad. On the other hand, Kobilboy's version corresponds to the chronology put forward by the authors of *Muhammadi Bashoro*, who identify him as the historical figure "Muhammad ibn Bashor ibn Usmon ibn Saison" from Basra, who was born in 167 AH/782 AD.

31 The term used in the *Samariyya* is *qaṣabche* (town).

32 The date in the *Samariyya* is 764.

33 The sentence from the *Samariyya* reads: "In 764 the shaykhs of the *mazār* built a long grave (*qabr-i tūlānī*) above the tomb (*marqad*) and a noble *khānaqāh* on that land." *Samariyya*, 193.

34 *Risāla*, 79.

35 The text reads that his father had seven sons. *Risāla*, 3.

36 Later in the narrative when Muḥammad Bashārā meets the Prophet in Medina, the Prophet tells him, "My name is a gift for you. All who were present congratulated him. Because you are my namesake, your trouble and suffering have come to an end." *Risāla*, 14.

37 *Risāla*, 3.

> His Majesty placed him close to himself,
> And said to his companions (*ashob*),
> "This kind young man (*javoni mehrubon*) is our friend (*yor*),
> Because he is a faithful one (*vafodor*) of our religion."[38]

When Bashoro awoke from his dream he was a changed man. He tore his coat to pieces and put his face to the ground with overwhelming desire to meet the Prophet in Medina.[39] He asked God for a meeting with Mustafo [Muḥammad] and washed his face with his tears. Seeing him crying, his father became angry since his son "always kept his secret (*rozi*) hidden."[40] He told his sons to go hunting, but the Khoja didn't bring anything back for his father and he became angry. Finally, he ordered his sons to follow him to find out his secret. "In the morning, the Khoja went to the field, as Moses went in his time to Mt. Sinai, and his six brothers followed him. All the animals gathered around him, like the wolf, sheep, deer, tiger and lion. Making a shadow on his head, the hoopoe, nightingale and homa circled around him and bowed to his feet.[41] Each one was telling its story."[42]

After the sons reported what they had observed, his father told them of his "unusual and fearful dream" that his son would turn to the religion of Muḥammad and make a *fitna*.[43] So the father ordered his sons to kill him to prevent him from returning from Medina to conquer them with a great army.[44] The Khoja's beautiful sister, a follower of the true faith, warned him and implored him to run away immediately to Kufa and Baghdad. When he asked her what to bring with him she told him to bring water, as God had told her in a dream. "There is a spring in the west of Mazor.[45] Other rivers envy it for its

38 *Risāla*, 4. Dreams of Muḥammad are common in many accounts of religious experience and conversion. See John Renard, *Friends of God: Islamic Images of Piety, Commitment, and Servanthood* (Berkeley and Los Angeles: University of California Press, 2008), 70–77.

39 *Risāla*, 4.

40 Ibid., 6.

41 Although the primary meaning of the scene is Bashārā's benevolence and kindness to the animals, as opposed to his brother's intention to kill them for game, it brings to mind 'Aṭṭār's *Manṭiq al-ṭayr* (*Conference of the Birds*) when the birds of the world gather around the hoopoe, who is about to lead them on their journey through the seven valleys to find the Simorgh, or the "secret" of divine Love.

42 *Risāla*, 5–7.

43 Ibid., 7.

44 Ibid., p. 7.

45 The name "Mazor" is a notable self-referential allusion to the future shrine of Muḥammad Bashārā.

water. Khiżr dreams of seeing this spring. You should search for it in the mountains and villages." He took the jug of water, tearfully left behind his devoted sister, and set out for Medina. After three days he arrived in Baghdad, where he found everyone to be upset and heard fearful stories about Muḥammad, a prophet in Medina who had a mighty *mard* (man) named Murtazo Ali (Murtażā ʿAlī), who turns mountains to dust when in battle.[46] The Khoja continued his journey to Medina to meet the army of the Prophet in Uhlud [sic, for Uḥud],[47] and was so overwhelmed by his strong desire that he lost consciousness.[48] Finally, a soldier brought him to Medina, where he was accepted by the Prophet; his dream had come true.[49] The Khoja presented the Prophet and his companions with the jug of water, which Muḥammad and his companions drank, and miraculously the water never ran out (a common Sufi topos). The Khoja served the Prophet in his house and "learned the *sharīʿa* and ways to read the Qurʾān,"[50] but his heart was sad since his sister remained in their father's fortress. When he finally told the prophet Muḥammad about his

46 *Risāla*, 11.

47 The famous Battle of Uḥud took place in 3/625, when the Muslim forces led by Muḥammad were defeated by the Meccans under the military command of Abū Sufyān.

48 *Risāla*, 12. A fascinating discovery is the existence of a parallel tale studied by Devin DeWeese, the tale of Jānbāz. I am grateful to him for sharing his findings with me in advance of his article's publication. Based on a 19th-century Turkic manuscript from Xinjiang, China, the tale describes "Khūja Muḥammad Bashshārī" as a Companion of the Prophet who travels to Mecca with his jug of water, meets the Prophet, and sets out with Jānbāz, the *ʿalam-dār*, to fight the infidels. The characters in the *Risāla* are transposed. Jānbāz, a native of Vanj (in Tajikistan) on the upper Amu Darya River (known as the Panj River) is the one who dreams of meeting the Prophet and whose brothers and father turn against him. In contrast to the story in the *Risāla*, Jānbāz is the martyred Companion of the Prophet and *ʿalam-dār* rather than Sīnā Ibn al-Ḥarb. The unlikely appearance of parallel Islamization narratives in northwest China and the Zarafshan valley suggests a dynamic movement of people, ideas, and oral/textual traditions about such warrior saints, one Persian and the other Turkic. Interestingly, as DeWeese notes, Vanj seems to have been imagined to be "somewhere between Samarqand and Penjikent, or the mountains along the Zarafshān valley," although the end of the story is "transposed to western Xinjiang." What is notable about this *tadhkira*, moreover, is that it combines a shrine catalogue with a narrative of Islamization and holy war, similar to DeWeese's earlier study on Sayrām. See Devin DeWeese, "The Tale of Jānbāz Khoja: Pilgrimage and Holy War in a 19th-Century *Tadhkira* from Xinjiang," in *Mazar: Studies on Islamic Sacred Sites in Central Eurasia*, ed. Sugawara Jun and Rahile Dawut (Tokyo: Tokyo University of Foreign Studies, 2016), 227–252; cf. DeWeese, "Sacred history for a Central Asian Town."

49 *Risāla*, 12.

50 Ibid., 14–15.

family and his sister's strong faith and kindness, Muḥammad ordered him to return to conquer the infidels (*kuffor*) in Mawarannahr. He offered to join the Khoja with an army of a thousand men and the pronouncement of a hundred *du'o* for his success, or Muḥammad would give him the great heroic conqueror and *ʿalam dor* (standard-bearer, *Pers. ʿalam-dār*), Sinoi ibni Harb [Abū Sufyān b. Ḥarb].[51] The Khoja chose the *ʿalom dor* of the Muslim army, and they set off to Mawarannahr with the jug of water. With the help of Sīnā Ibn al-Ḥarb, the Khoja fought the infidels in city after city. He wrote a letter (*noma*) for each city, writing about hell and paradise and the Messenger of God who is a healer of sickness and pain and has an incalculable army.[52] They arrived in Samarqand, where the "Sho" was one who also loved the Prophet. The Khoja brought them the message of the Prophet and taught the people Islam and each of them took a sip of water from the jug. Finally, they reached Penjakent and Sujina,[53] where the Khoja attacked a fortress close to a river. Penjakent became illuminated from the *karamat* of the Khoja and he ordered another fortress to be burned. When he arrived in Sujina he found four female followers of the Prophet and forty people from the fortress of Chahorbog who accepted Islam and joined his army.[54] The infidels decided to fight the Khoja and his army, rejecting his message. When he arrived in Ghuẕar where his father's citadel was located, one of his brothers recognized him and ran to his father. The Khoja and his supporters debated how they would respond, but decided in the end to fight his father. In contrast to the beginning of the narrative, when the six brothers found Khoja peacefully conversing with the animals rather than hunting them, in battle the Khoja became "like a lion-hunter, his roar was like the tiger's rumble in the forest" and he killed hundreds of infidels in a minute.[55]

The narrative continues, describing the "bazaar of death" and strong resistance of the infidels, as well as the martyrdom of many believers. They fought for three days and nights, but the believers were defeated, just as the Muslim army was defeated at the Battle of Uḥud in 3/625. With sadness and pain, they rested close to the mountain and offered prayers to God, thinking about

51 Despite the phonological gap between "Sino" and "Abū Sufyān," I believe the reference is to the latter. It is odd, however, that the narrative places Abū Sufyān, who was Muḥammad's opponent at the Battle of Uḥud, in the position of standard-bearer (*ʿalam-dār*) of the Khoja's army of Islam, although Abū Sufyan did become a chief commander after the conquest of Mecca and his conversion.

52 *Risāla*, 17.

53 Sujina is located close to Penjakent in present-day Sughd Province.

54 *Risāla*, 21. See note 63 below on the significance of the number 40.

55 Ibid., 24–25.

Mustafo [Muḥammad]. They returned to Mussemo Mountain to rest, but were anxious the entire night and only slept a few hours.[56] During his sleep, Sīnā Ibn al-Ḥarb dreamed that his body was cut into two, which he related to the Khoja in the morning. During battle that day Sīnā Ibn al-Ḥarb was indeed martyred, as he had foreseen in his dream.[57] The Khoja saw that he had been cut in two by the sword. "He shed so many tears that a tree grew out of the earth from his tears."[58] Then four men (*chor mardi*) came from the East with two camels,[59] one for each side of his severed body, and they loaded the body and guided the camels to a fortress close to the river named "Raboti Khoja" [sic. Rabaṭ] and buried him there.[60]

On the third day, Khoja again took his place on the battlefield, dressed in military armor. "He attacked like a wild elephant," killing each infidel one by one, but he remained alone and sorrowful and retreated to a nearby mountain to rest with his companions, while the infidels followed, shooting arrows close behind him. Due to God's intervention, the mountain bent down and became even with the ground so that he was able to flee to safety, to the astonishment of the unbelievers (*kofiron*), and then the mountain returned to its previous form.[61] When Khoja was free from harm, he ran for help to a mountain named "mehrob" (*miḥrāb*), but "it was not *mehrob* but rather *ihrom* (*iḥrām*)."[62] Alone,

56 *Risāla*, 27.

57 In the tale of Jānbāz, it is he who dreams of his martyrdom and whose body is split in two by the infidels, rather than Sīna Ibn al-Ḥarb. As in the story of Muḥammad Bashārā, two camels were brought to carry the body, but in the *tadhkira* a white and a red camel carry the two halves of his body to separate places.

58 *Risāla*, 29.

59 Ibid., 29.

60 Ibid., 30.

61 Ibid., 31. Chahor.

62 *Risāla*, 32. The mountain above the shrine in Mazār-i Sharīf is known today as Chilmehrob (Forty *Mihrāb*). The standard definition of *miḥrāb* is the marking place (usually a niche in the wall of the mosque) for the direction of prayer towards Mecca, to the Kaʿba. Forty is a significant number in the Islamic tradition. For example, Muḥammad was 40 when he received his first revelation; Muḥammad fasted for 40 days in the cave; Muḥammad had 40 followers; and the spiritual retreat practiced by Sufis is 40 days long. Subsequent verses in the *Risāla* name the sacred points in the vicinity that are part of the *ziyārat* that pilgrims perform to this day—visiting the tree that grew from Bashārā's stick, drinking from the sacred spring, touching or kissing the stone onto which Bashārā is believed to have tied his horse, and the *naqsh* (footprint) of Bashārā left on a stone—all common topoi in hagiography. If we trust the copyist's transcription, the narrator tells us that the mountain is not "mehrob" but rather is "ihrom" (*iḥrām*), which is the sacred condition in which a pilgrim must enter Mecca to perform the *ḥajj*. Some four pages later, we are told

tired and suffering, he cried and lamented, asking why he was suffering such injustice and cruelty. Then he arrived at the opening of a cave through which he passed to another mountain, and there he laid his stick on the ground and went to sleep.[63] A large green tree grew from his stick and a spring (*chashma*) appeared.[64] After performing his ablutions and praying through the night, his horse, which had disappeared in battle, returned to him and laid its head at his feet.[65] Thanking God, he rode to the top of the mountain, where he tied his horse to a stone he found with a hole in it. Following this, the narrator inserts a comment about the *naqsh* of Muḥammad Bashārā and invites his readers to visit his grave, which is considered to be a "second Kaʿba."

> The mark (*naqsh*) of his hands and foot, indeed, *ba Khudo*,
> His mark will remain there until the Day of Judgment.
> If you do not believe these words,
> Go to that mountain and see for yourself.
>
> A sign (*ʿalomat*, Pers. *ʿalāmat*) of that king (*sho*) is on the stone,
> One by one, one by one,
> On *ʿIdi Qurbon* (*Eid-i Qurbān*) on the side of that mountain,
> His followers come from everywhere.
>
> They are looking at the mark of his foot in the stone,
> Come and kiss the mark.
> His mausoleum (*turbat*) is near this mountain,
> It is considered the second Kaʿba and is full of light.[66]

---

that Muḥammad Bashārā's *turbat* (mausoleum) located near the mountain is considered to be a second Kaʿba (Risāla, 36). Thus, the sacred sanctuary of the territory in which Muḥammad Bashārā performed his deeds as an Islamizer and as a Friend of the Prophet and the Four Companions, and the *turbat* in which he is buried, are spiritually connected with the sacred sanctuary, the Kaʿba in Mecca, and embodies this spiritual state of purity.

63 *Risāla*, 33.

64 *Risāla*, 33.

65 Ibid., 34.

66 Ibid., 35–36. Thierry Zarcone discusses the prevalence of "second Meccas" and "second Kaʿbas" at shrines in Central Asia and Eastern Turkestan, including those of Aḥmad Yasavī in Turkistan, Kazakhstan, Bahā' al-Dīn Naqshband in Bukhara, Takht-i Sulaymān (Throne of Solomon) in Osh, Kyrgyzstan, and the *mazār* of Tuyoq Khojam in Turfan, Northern Xinjiang (known as the *mazār* of the Seven Sleepers, or *Aṣḥāb al-Kahf*); see Thierry Zarcone, "Pilgrimage to the 'Second Meccas' and 'Kaʿbas' of Central Asia," in *Central Asian Pilgrims: Hajj Routes and Pious Visits between Central Asia and the Hijaz*, ed. Alexandre

FIGURE 10.4 *Mausoleum of Muḥammad Bashārā*
GROSS, 2010

The story returns to the 7th century, as Bashārā turned to God and dreamed that Muḥammad and his four Companions (*chahor yor*) came to the Mountain of Forty Ihrom (*Kuhi Chihil Ihrom*) to help him fight the final battle.[67] The mountain was like heaven; "violets were everywhere, springs were streaming to each river," "beautiful flowers were like the face of a fairy," "morning birds were singing, hyacinths were like lover's curls, and colorful lions and tigers were coming to lay their heads at his [the Khoja's] feet."[68] The Khoja prayed to see the Prophet, and when he saw the Prophet in his dream and told him what happened, Muḥammad told him not to worry because "four of my friends (*yoron*) will be your friends."[69] And when he awoke, the four suddenly appeared. "In the morning, they went to the infidels from the mountain to the fortress, and when the infidels saw the Murtazo (Murtażā ʿAlī), they all shook like a willow tree."[70] The infidels lost their power and were amazed, while ʿAlī took out his sword and "roared like thunder in the spring."[71] The Companions joined in a bloody battle and the next day the infidels came to the Khoja weeping and asking for forgiveness. They all became Muslims and welcomed him to his father's fortress, where he was reunited with his faithful sister. The four Companions of the Prophet celebrated with them and returned to Medina in the morning. The Khoja built a mosque, instructed the populace, read the Qurʾān, performed prayers, and devoted himself completely to God, and everyone became Muslims and his followers.[72]

The last sections of the narrative concern the Khoja's devotion, the recognition he received for his knowledge of *ḥadīth*, the sanctification of the landscape, which was like the garden of paradise, and his death and burial place. As noted above, this is the only place in the *Risāla* where Bashārā's knowledge

Papas, Thomas Welsford, Thierry Zarcone (Berlin: Klaus Schwarz Verlag, 2012), 251–277. For a discussion of the Kaʿba in the Islamic mystical tradition see Maria E. Subtelny, "Templificatio hominis: Kaʿba, Cosmos, and Man in the Islamic Mystical Tradition," in *Weltkonstruktionen: Religiöse Weltdeutung zwischen Chaos und Kosmos vom Alten Orient bis zum Islam*, ed. P. Gemeinhardt and A. Zgoll, *Orientalische Religionen der Antike* 5 (Tübingen: Mohr Siebeck, 2010), 195–222.

67 *Risāla*, 36.

68 *Risāla*, 36–37.

69 *Risāla*, 38–39. The "friends" are the Companions of the Prophet and the first four caliphs, Abū Bakr, ʿUmar, ʿUthmān, and ʿAlī.

70 *Risāla*, 39.

71 *Risāla*, 40.

72 *Risāla*, 42–43.

of *ḥadīth* (*hadis-i Rasul*) is acknowledged.[73] Once again, as the narrator does numerous times throughout the story, he highlights the sacred quality of the water and springs, their connection with the performance of ablutions and prayer, and the merit one achieves from it, since drinking it is equal to performing the *ḥajj*:

> Mustafa said, 'If someone drinks from this spring or someone performs ablutions, if he performs a prayer after ablutions, his worship will be equal to a *hojji*'s pilgrimage. If he performs another three prayers after washing, he can be an *imom* (prayer leader).' These merits all belong to the Khoja. There is no other sacred spring like this.[74]

It should be noted that although many of the discussed narrative themes in the *Risāla* resonate with similar themes in a variety of Sufi narratives (especially conversion narratives) in Central Asia, there is no overt mention in the *Risāla* of Sufism or of Muḥammad Bashārā's role as a Sufi figure per se.[75]

In the concluding section of the *Risolai Khoja Muhammad Bashoro*, on the death of "Khoja Muḥammad," the narrator locates his grave to the west of the spring (*chashma*). "The king of Rūm saw him in his dream, he built his *khonaqo* (*khānaqāh*) with a *turbat* (mausoleum)."[76]

> The roof of the *khonaqo* is so close to the sky,
> Angels come and kiss its threshold (*oston*).
> Kings make the pilgrimage to his grave,
> They gave 700 *mans* as *waqf* land for its benefit.[77]

---

73 Ibid., 43. Although it is impossible to know, this may have been inserted into a later version of the tale since it seems out of character with the rest of the narrative.

74 Ibid., 44.

75 The presence of a *chillakhāna* and *khānaqāh* suggest Sufi practice at the shrine. As noted earlier, Abū Ṭāhir Khwāja Samarqandī dates the construction of the *khānaqāh* to 764/1362. See note 23. There is a *qabr* inside the shrine that is popularly believed to belong to the grandson of Khwāja ʿUbaydullāh Aḥrār. In my interview with Imom Shamsiddin in May 2004, he told me that the grandson of Aḥrār "bequeathed in his will that he wanted to be buried in this holy threshold (*oston*) … because Muḥammad Bashoro was the *ustod* of Imom Bukhori and he had great authority as a Muslim leader."

76 Ibid., 45.

77 *Risāla*, 44. This is a rare but significant reference to the material world of charitable endowments that supported the *mazār*.

In the last few verses of the text, the narrator, who is either the original recorder/compiler of the story or a copyist at some later date, writes about himself, stating that he is "from that place" (i.e., Mazār-i Sharif), is waiting at his (Bashārā's) door with longing, and is the "servant of his servants" whose heart was "wounded from the wheel of fortune;" his skirt became like a red tulip from his tears, and his heart burned like no one has ever seen due to his grief.[78]

The last verses read:

> He wrote some incorrect words in the notebook [*daftar*],
> He put his feelings [in] there.
> Please forgive him for mistakes,
> Sometimes he lost consciousness (*muddadte raft khush az sar*).[79]
>
> Forgive him because he was distracted,
> His heart was broken in this world.
> Recite a *du'o* with sincerity,
> Recite, There is no god but God (*Lo iloha illalloh*).[80]

Muhammad Bashoro: Eighth-Ninth-Century Muḥaddith from Basra

The anonymous orally-circulated "traditional" poetic hagiography described above is set in Medina and the Zarafshān Valley and alternates temporally between the 7th-century Prophetic Age and an ambiguous present. The locus of spiritual authority, devotion and piety is Muḥammad, the Messenger of God, and through him Muḥammad Bashārā as a "friend" of the Prophet.[81] Spiritual rather than historical continuity defines the narrative, the sacred memory of Bashārā, and the sacralized landscape of his *mazār*. In contrast, *Muhammadi Bashoro* is a scripturalist account of Muḥammad Bashārā written by two students from the Islamic University in Dushanbe. It is divided into four sections, as follows: 1) Summary View of the Life and Time of Muḥammad Bashārā (Taj. *Nazari Ijmolie ba Zindagi va Ruzgori Muhammadi Bashoro*); 2) Documents of the *Mazār* of Muḥammad Bashārā (Taj. *Sanadhoi Mazori Muhammadi*

78 It is unclear whether the original author wrote these words, or a copyist at some later date.

79 This may refer to the state of Sufi contemplation (*murāqaba*), although it is unclear from the simple language used here.

80 *Risāla*, 46.

81 Bashārā's individual relationship with the Prophet is inherently predicated on his friendship with God.

Bashoro);[82] 3) Some Noble *Ḥadīth*s Related by Muḥammad b. Bashshār (*Yakchand Hadisi Sharif bo Rivoyati Muhammad ibn Bashshor*);[83] 4) Pilgrimage Guide (*Rohnamoii Zoiri*).[84] The locus of spiritual authority in this work is the Prophetic tradition. The authors have a didactic purpose, which is to provide a scripturalist (Salafi) explanation that legitimates Khwāja Muḥammad Bashārā as an eminent historical figure who was born in Basra in 167/782 and died at the age of 85 in 252/866. Unlike the *Risolai Muhammad Bashoro*, the authors have no interest in the legendary tales of Bashārā's dreams of and encounter with the Prophet Muḥammad, his heroic battles fought against the infidels in Mawarannahr, the paradisiacal sacred landscape of the *mazār* of Bashārā, or the concept of the shrine as a "second Kaʿba."—although they too seek an explanation about the figure buried in the *mazār*. Rather, Shamsiddin and Najibullo challenge the historical veracity of the legendary tales as well as the passage in the *Samariyya*, which describes Muḥammad Bashārā as among the *tābiʿīn* (Followers).[85] Instead, they offer what they consider to be the authoritative biography about Muḥammad Bashārā, constructed on the basis of *ḥadīth* and *sīra* literature. Secondary authorial intentions are to provide readers with documentary evidence dating from the 16th century that records an enduring Islamic history of the *mazār* as a religious institution, and to provide "legally sound" guidance on shrine visitation for pilgrims in post-Soviet Tajikistan, based on a selection of *sūras*, *ḥadīth*s, and sayings of eminent Sufis—and in doing so—they recognize the long-established and current practice of pilgrimage to the shrine.[86]

82 The section entitled "Documents of the Mazor of Muhammadi Bashoro" (*Sanadhoi Mazori Muhammadi Bashoro*) was compiled by Eshoni Saidhaydar from the village of Mazār-i Sharīf and includes Tajik translations of twelve Persian documents that were noted earlier in this study. They include the appointment and claims to the position of *mutawallī* and *imām*, funding for the renovation of the shrine, burial rights of the descendants of Mavlānā Akrām, the builder of the shrine, and three photographs of original documents recovered from the village of Mazār-i Sharīf.

83 The third section, "Several Noble *Ḥadīth*s Reported by Muḥammad b. Bashshār" (*Yakchand Hadisi Sharif bo Rivoyati Muhammad ibni Bashoro*) is composed of 14 *ḥadīth*s reported by Bashārā, in Tajik translation from the Arabic, including the *Sahehi al-Bukhori* (*Ṣaḥīḥ al-Bukhārī*), *Sunani Tirmizi* (*Sunān at-Tirmidhī*), *Sahehi Muslim* (*Ṣaḥīḥ Muslim*), *Sunani Ibni Moja* (*Sunān Ibn Mājah*) and *Sunani Dorami* (*Sunan al-Dārimi*), *See Muhammadi Bashoro*, 35–45.

84 *Muhammadi Bashoro*, 46–55.

85 We discuss this issue earlier on p. 303.

86 The focus of my discussion is the biographical tradition in the first section. However, the composite aspect of the text merits further study in comparison to earlier composite

In the beginning of the text, Shamsiddin and Najibullo remark that most of the stories about the life of Muḥammad Bashārā, i.e. those in the *Risolai Muhammadi Bashoro*, contradict one another; they thus reject them as "superstitious nonsense" as so many Islamic reformists of the past have done, going back to Ibn Taymiyya. They point to the numerous errors in the published *Risāla*, particularly with regard to rhyme and rhythm, and how they can lead to a misunderstanding of meaning.[87] They question Muḥammad Bashārā's dreams on historical grounds, asserting that Bashārā's life did not coincide with the lives of the Companions (*sahobagon*; Arabic *al-ṣāḥāba*) of the Prophet, since "Muhammad ibn Bashor" was not alive during the time of the Prophet or the four Companions,[88] concluding that, "the idea noted in this article [the Risola] is far beyond reality."[89] Similarly, the authors do not consider the passage in the *Samariyya* to be accurate, since Shamsiddin and Najibullo determine his lifetime to have been during the caliphate of al-Mahdī (r. 775–785) and his education to have taken place during the rule of al-Mahdī's son, Hārūn al-Rashīd (r. 796–809). Therefore, Abū Ṭāhir Samarqandī's statement that Muḥammad Bashārā was among the *tābiʿīn* is not true, since "he did not live during the lifetime of any of the companions (*sahobagon*) of the Prophet Muḥammad."[90]

They attribute Samarqandī's "error" to the tradition that Bashārā studied near "Yahyoi Katton" (Yaḥyā al-Qaṭṭān), one of the followers of the Prophet.[91] They note instead, "It is related from Ibn Khuzayma (Abū Bakr Muḥammad b. Isḥāq bin Khuzayma)", "I heard Bundor (Muhammadi Bashoro) say, 'I studied for twenty years near Yahyoi Katton (Yaḥyā al-Qaṭṭān) and if he had lived longer my knowledge would have increased'."[92]

In the main section of interest to this study, the authors provide evidence from *ḥadīth* literature and Arabic biographical literature that Khwāja Muḥammad Bashārā is the *muḥaddith* Muḥammad b. Bashār b. ʿUthmān

works on Sufis, shrines, and exemplary Islamic figures in Central Asia, as well the production of religious texts in post-Soviet Tajikistan.

87 This point is well taken regarding the many errors throughout the narrative, although knowledge of Persian would alert an informed reader. As mentioned earlier, the person who transcribed the text from the Persian manuscript may have had trouble reading Persian script and apparently was unfamiliar with the principles of *ʿarūż* poetic rhythm.

88 *Muhammadi Bashoro*, 6.

89 *Muhammadi Bashoro*, 5.

90 *Muhammadi Bashoro*, 6.

91 Ibid., 7. The authors cite al-Khaṭīb al-Baghdādī's *Tārīkh-i Baghdād* for this information.

92 Ibid., 6–7.

b. Qaysānī Baṣrī, with the nickname (*laqab*) al-Bundār.[93] The introductory quotation to their book is a *ḥadīth* from the *Tahdhīb al-tahdhīb* of Ibn Ḥajar al-ʿAsqalānī (printed in Arabic, then in Tajik translation), as follows.

> Bundor wrote a letter to me and in that letter he reported (*zikr mikard*) the chain of transmission of *ḥadīth* (*isnodi hadis*). If he (al-Bukhori) had no confidence in him then he would not report the *hadis*. He (Muhammad ibni Bashshor) was in the fourth station of al-Bukhori's [Imām al-Bukhārī's] shaykhs and he knew many *hadis*, and whatever had come to him from his knowledge of *hadis* (*ʿilmi hadis*) was not available from others.[94]

In discussing his name, the authors state that the Arabic-language sources compiled by the "*taba'a tobe'in*" say that his name is "Muḥammad ibn Bashor ibn Usmon ibn Saison from Basra who was born in 167 AH/782 AD. His *kunya* was Abubakr (Abū Bakr) and his *nasab* (patronymic) was Abdi (ʿAbdī)."[95] Concerning the *takhalluṣ* of Muḥammad, which is "Bashoro" or "Bashshor," the authors list a number of definitions given in the *Lughatnāma* of Dihkhudā, including the meaning of "Bashor" as "a lake in Basra," which they contend supports the fact that "Muhammadi Bashor came from Basra and that he received his name of Bashshor after the lake."[96] They state, furthermore,

> Of course, the challenging question is, is Muhammadi Bashshori Basri the Muhammadi Bashoro who is buried in Mazori Sharif or not? Undoubtedly there are conflicting thoughts when answering this question. But without hesitation, one can state that Muhammadi Bashshor is Muhammadi Bashoro who is buried in Mazori Sharif. First because the name Muhammad specifies it. Second, in the Arabic sources about the taba'a tobe'in (Arabic, *tābiʿ al-Tabiʿīn*) he is mentioned as Muhammadi Bashshor and only in the Persian sources (even though they mistakenly

93 Regarding the name "Bundār," the authors explain that Bashārā received his *laqab* Bundor, which means "tradesman of valuables and jewelry," "because he learned all the *ḥadīth*s of Basra and the *ḥadīth*s of the Prophet, which had great value for Muslims" (*Muhammadi Bashoro*, 6–7). Ibn Ḥajar's (d. 852/1449) work is an abbreviated version of al-Mizzī's *Tahdhīb al-kamāl*.

94 *Muhammadi Bashoro*, 3.

95 *Muhammadi Bashoro*, 8.

96 *Muhammadi Bashoro*, 8.

> report that he is from the *taba'a* (*tobe'in*) is he remembered as Muhammadi Bashoro. Third, the date of Muhammadi Bashshor's death is mentioned in the Arabic sources, but the exact location of his grave in Basra or in an Arab land (*volodi Arab*) is not specified. Fourth, only in the Islamic community of "*Ajamu Arab*" (*ʿajam*, meaning non-Arab) were such mausolea (*oromgohon*, i.e., *ārāmgāhs*) of well-known people as Muhammadi built, and Muhammadi Bashoro is on the list of those. Fifth, it becomes clear that the name "Bashshor" changed over time to "Bashoro." However, it should be clear for readers that we said Muhammadi Bashoro, which is derived from the Arabic sources as Muhammadi Bashshor.[97]

Shamsiddin and Najibullo note that Muḥammad Bashārā received his education in Basra and began to report *ḥadīths* from the age of 18.[98] The authors also establish that "Muhammad ibni Bashshor" was the teacher (*ustod*) of the renowned Central Asian legal scholar and author of the *Ṣaḥīḥ al-Bukhārī*, Muḥammad b. Ismāʿīl al-Bukhārī (194–256/810–870). "It is important to mention that the shrine of the renowned *imom* of the Islamic world, al-Bukhori, is located in the village of Hartang near Samarqand, and in the historical sources the relation of these two blessed *imoms* [Muḥammad b. Bashār and al-Bukhārī] is that of master and student (*ustod va shogird*)."[99] "In the *Tahzib ut-tahzib* (*Tahdhīb al-tahdhīb*), 'Zuhro' said that Imom Bukhori (Imām al-Bukhārī) told 205 *ḥadīths* from Muhammad ibn Bashor and 164 from Imom Muslim (Imām Muslim), but another source from our period mentions that he told 211, Imom Muslim (Imām Muslim) told 441, Imom Tirmizi (Imām Tirmidhī) told 525, Nasoi (Imām Aḥmad al-Nasāʾī) told 214, Abudovud (Ābū Dāvūd) told 85, Ibn Moja (Ibn Māja) told 279, Imom Ahmad (Imām Aḥmad) told 7, and Dorami (Dāramī) told 7 *ḥadīths* from Muhammad ibn Bashshor."[100] Shamsiddin and Najibullo include a table that lists those scholars who reported widespread *ḥadīths* from Muḥammad Bashārā in the "*Sihohi Sitta*" (*al-Ṣiḥāḥ al-sitta*, or "The Six Authentic Books of *Ḥadīth*"), which includes al-Bukhārī with 207, Imām Muslim with 438, Imām Muḥammad Tirmidhī with 495, Imām Aḥmad al-Nasāʾī with 199, Ābī Dāvūd with 78, and Ibn Māja with 275.[101]

---

97 *Muhammadi Bashoro*, 8–9.

98 For a discussion of *ḥadīths* about his early collecting and recitation and of them, see *Muhammadi Bashoro*, 8–11.

99 Ibid., 6.

100 Ibid., 9–10.

101 *Muhammadi Bashoro*, 12–13.

Soviet-era architectural historians sought to explain the origins, construction and uses of the shrine complex of Muḥammad Bashārā, particularly the presence of the *mihrāb*, whereas the two contrasting biographical works seek to explain the personhood of Muḥammad Bashārā, the sacred figure believed to be buried in the shrine. There is no material evidence at the shrine itself that identifies the figure buried there, a common feature of shrine culture in Central Asia, and in the greater Islamicate world. The attribution of personhood in these cases often appears in local (oral) tradition, textualized in the form of hagiography, and often adopted by authors of pilgrimage manuals and sometimes in historical chronicles. The *Risolai Khoja Muhammad Bashoro*, and *Muhammadi Bashoro* reveal variant conceptions of Muḥammad Bashārā in post-Soviet Tajikistan, and distinct currents of Islamic religiosity and perceptions of the sacred past. Yet, close analysis of the two texts reveals more than a simple differential in the personhood of Muḥammad Bashārā and the streams of religiosity they represent. The internal dialogue between the two works reveals a degree of ambiguity in their attempts to explain, give meaning to, and, in the case of *Muhammadi Bashoro*, grapple with, the ever-present popularity of shrine culture and pilgrimage in the local landscape in conjunction with a new awareness of Islamic identity. Shamsiddin and Najibullo's biography of Muḥammad Bashārā (as an 8th–9th-century *muḥaddith*) valorizes Arabic over Persian sources, and seeks an explanation based on the highly respectable (if historically problematic) Arabic *ḥadīth* and biographical tradition. Yet they must acknowledge—indeed, they cannot deny—the persistence of shrine culture, and the specific popularity of pilgrimage to the *mazār* of Bashārā, albeit on a conditional basis, by including, at the end of their work, a guide to "correct" practice.

Conclusion

The texts discussed in this paper represent two distinct literary forms within the biographical tradition in Central Asia: a poetic ahistorical Sufi-influenced hagiographic tale of a warrior Islamizing saint and the sacralized landscape of his shrine on the one hand, and a historicized biography (with pilgrimage guide) about a traditionalist scholar of Basra and his mausoleum on the other. Both biographical representations engage with the sacred past through oral traditions (local tales and *ḥadīths*) preserved and passed down through a process of transmission over time, and both construct links with the Prophet Muḥammad and espouse universal Islamic values, although spiritual rather than historical/scripturalist continuity defines the narrative of the *Risāla*. In

Muhammadi Bashoro, in contrast, "authentic" chains of transmission (*ḥadīths*) connect Muḥammad Bashārā to the Islamic community of the 8th–9th century and to important *ḥadīth* scholars, including al-Bukhārī.

On the copyright page, Kobilboy draws attention to the historical Muḥammad Bashārā and his *mazār* by paraphrasing (and misstating) details from Samarqandī's *Samariyya*.[102] Significantly, he refers here to Bashārā as a *muḥaddith* (which Samarqandī does not), making a point to preface the hagiographical narrative with an acknowledgement of his legal stature, since in the *Risāla-i Muḥammad Bashārā*, Bashārā's status as *muḥaddith* is extraneous. Muḥammad Bashārā meets the Prophet in his dream, is accepted by him as a friend (*yār*), and fulfills his duty to carry out holy war in Mawarannahr for the sake of Islam with the help of Abū Sufyān and the Companions of the Prophet. The editor's attribution of Bashārā's status as a *muḥaddith* is not at odds with his sacred heroic status as an Islamizer, the miraculous acts he performed, or the construction of and reverence to the shrine in Mazār-i Sharīf where he was buried. On the contrary, the *Risolai Khoja Muhammad Bashoro* was intended to reach a local audience familiar (or soon to be familiar) with the sacred landscape in which the shrine exists. It textualizes and legitimizes oral traditions about Bashārā and gives meaning to the practice of pilgrimage (*ziyārat*) to his *mazār*, inside of which is not only the *qabr* of Muḥammad Bashārā, but a stunningly beautiful *mihrāb*, a *saghāna* (burial chamber) containing the graves of *mutawallīs*, shaykhs and servitors of the shrine, two majolica tombs believed to belong to the builders of the mausoleum, the grave of a young unidentified girl, and another grave considered to belong to a grandchild of Khwāja ʿUbaydullāh Aḥrār, the well-known late 15th century Naqshbandī Sufi *pīr* buried outside Samarqand.

Both texts seek an explanation for the person buried in the Mazār-i Sharīf shrine. On the one hand, the *Risāla* sanctifies the shrine and its surroundings through Bashārā's exemplary deeds and miraculous events, as one chosen by Muḥammad to bring Islam to the region, while the authors of *Muhammadi Bashoro* establish Bashārā's position as an 8th-century *muḥaddith* based on the Qur'ān and *ḥadīths*. The *Risolai Muḥammad Bashoro* and *Muḥammadi Bashoro* thus represent contrasting religious discourses, i.e. "traditional" and scripturalist Muslim religiosity. Considered together, they speak to the discursive

102 It is possible that Jum'aev may have used another local text for this passage which misquoted the original text of the *Samariyya*. He fails to attribute the text to Samarqandī, or to name it; he incorrectly dates his unnamed source (apparently the *Samariyya*) to the month of Safar in 1400; and he incorrectly dates the construction of the *khānaqāh* to be 714 instead of 764.

concept of Islam in Central Asia, and when viewed in the context of post-Soviet Tajikistan, they offer valuable evidence on the contemporary creation and re-creation of the legacy of Muḥammad Bashārā, and the ways in which authors utilize rhetoric in the ongoing process of Muslim identity formation. There is no definitive answer to the question of whether the figure buried in the shrine in Mazār-i Sharif is indeed the *muḥaddith* Muḥammad b. Bashār b. ʿUthmān b. Qaysānī Baṣrī who was born in Basra in 167/782. However, the endeavor to preserve, memorialize and re-create the legacy of Muḥammad Bashārā is evident not only in the maintenance of his *mazār* in Mazār-i Sharīf and the lively traffic of pilgrims who make the *ziyārat* to it, but also, as this study demonstrates, through the production of texts that authenticate distinctive biographical traditions for present and future generations.

Bibliography

Asad, Talal. "The idea of an anthropology of Islam." Occasional Paper Series, Washington, D.C.: Center for Contemporary Arab Studies, Georgetown University, 1986. Reprinted by Duke University Press in *Qui Parle* 17/2 (Spring/Summer 2009), 1–30.

Babadjanov, Bakhtiyar. "Debates over Islam in Contemporary Uzbekistan: A View from Within." In *Devout Societies vs. Impious States? Transmitting Islamic Learning in Russia, Central Asia and China, through the Twentieth Century*, ed. Stephane A. Dudoignon (Berlin: Klaus Schwarz Verlag, 2004), 39–60.

Babadjanov, B., and M. Kamilov. 2001. "Muhammadjan Hindustani (1892–1989) and the Beginning of the 'Great Schism' among the Muslims of Uzbekistan." In *Islam in Politics in Russia and Central Asia* (*Early Eighteenth to Late Twentieth Centuries*), ed. S. A. Dudoignon and K. Hisao (London: Kegan Paul), 195–219.

Brentjes, Burchard. "Das Grabmal des Muḥammad Boššaro—Ein Vorläufer Timuridischer Baukunst." In *Ibn Ḫaldūn unde seine Zeit*, ed. D. Sturm (Halle: Martin-Luther Universität, 1983), 17–23.

Bretanitskii, L. S. "Ob odnom maloizvestnom pamiatnike Tadzhikskogo zodchestva." *Materialy i issledovaniia po arkheologii SSR*, 66 (1959), 325–357.

Chmelnizkij [Khmel'nitskii], Sergei. "The Mausoleum of Muhammad Bosharo." *Muqarnas*, 7 (1990), 23–34.

Dawut, Rahila and Rachel Harris. "Mazar Festivals of the Uyghurs: Music, Islam and the Chinese State." *British Journal of Ethnomusicology*, 11/1(2002), 101–118.

DeWeese, Devin. "Sacred History of a Central Eurasian Town: Saints, Shrines, and Legends of Origin in Histories of Sayrām, 18th–19th Centuries." *Revue des mondes musulmans et de la Méditerranée*, 89/90 (1999), 245–296.

DeWeese, Devin. "Sacred Places and 'Public' Narratives: The Shrine of Aḥmad Yasavī in Hagiographical Traditions of the Yasavī Sufi Order, 16th–17th Centuries." *Muslim World*, 90/3–4 (2000), 353–376.

DeWeese, Devin. "The Tale of Jānbāz Khoja: Pilgrimage and Holy War in a 19th-Century *Tadhkira* from Xinjiang." In *Mazar: Studies on Islamic Sacred Sites in Central Eurasia*, ed. Sugawara Jun and Rahile Dawut (Tokyo: Tokyo University of Foreign Studies, 2016), 227–252.

Dudoignon, Stephane A. "Local lore, the transmission of learning, and communal identity in late-20th-century Tajikistan: the *Khujand-Nāma* of ʿĀrifjān Yaḥyāzād Khujandī." In *Devout societies vs. impious states? Transmitting Islamic learning in Russia, Central Asia and China, through the twentieth century*, ed. S. A. Dudoignon (Berlin: Klaus Schwarz, 2004), 213–241.

Dudoignon, Stephane A. "From revival to mutation: the religious personnel of Islam in Tajikistan, from de-Stalinization to independence (1955–91)." *Central Asian Survey*, 30/1 (2011), 53–80.

Egani, A. A., and O. D. Chekhovich. "Regesty sredneaziatskikh aktov." *Pis'mennye pamiatniki Vostoka, Istoriko-filologicheskie issledovaniia 1973*, Series 1 (Moscow, 1981), 47–57, 305–335.

Egani, A. A., and O. D. Chekhovich. "Regesty sredneaziatskikh aktov." *Pis'mennye pamiatniki Vostoka, Istoriko-filologicheskie issledovaniia 1975*, Series 2 (Moscow, 1982), 34–51, 266–317.

Egani, A. A., and O. D. Chekhovich. "Regesty sredneaziatskikh aktov." *Pis'mennye pamiatniki Vostoka, Istoriko-filologicheskie issledovaniia 1976–77*, Series 3 (Moscow, 1984), 105–110, 321–361.

Egani, A. A., and O. D. Chekhovich. "Regesty sredneaziatskikh aktov." *Pis'mennye pamiatniki Vostoka, Istoriko-filologicheskie issledovaniia 1978–79*, Series 4 (Moscow, 1987), 57–63, 294–330.

Epkenhans, Tim. "Defining Normative Islam: Some Remarks on Contemporary Islamic Thought in Tajikistan—Hoji Akbar Turajonzoda's *Sharia and Society*." *Central Asian Survey*, 30 (2011), 81–86.

Epkenhans, Tim. "Muslims Without Learning, Clergy Without Faith: Institutions of Islamic Learning in Tajikistan." In *Islamic Education in the Soviet Union and Its Successor States*, ed. Michael Kemper, Raoul Motika and Stefan Reichmuth (New York: Routledge, 2010), 313–348.

Gatling, Benjamin Clark. "Post-Soviet Sufism: Texts and the Performance of Tradition in Tajikistan." Unpublished Ph.D. Dissertation, The Ohio State University, 2012.

Gatling, Benjamin Clark. "Historical Narrative, Intertextuality, and Cultural Continuity in Post-Soviet Tajikistan." *Journal of Folklore Research*, 53/1 (Jan.–Apr. 2016), 41–65.

Green, Nile. *Sufism: A Global History*. West Sussex: Wiley-Blackwell, 2012.

Gross, Jo-Ann. "Foundational Legends, Shrines and Isma'ili Identity in Tajik Badakhshan." In *Muslims and Others in Sacred Space*, ed. Margaret Jean Cormack (Oxford/New York: Oxford University Press, 2014), 164–192.

Gross, Jo-Ann. "The Motif of the Cave and the Funerary Narratives of Nāṣir-i Khusrau." In *Orality and Textuality in the Iranian World: Patterns of Interaction across the Centuries*, ed. Julia Rubanovich (Leiden: Brill, 2015), 130–168.

Gross, Jo-Ann. "Multiple Roles and Perceptions of a Sufi Shaykh: Symbolic Statements of Political and Religious Authority." In *Naqshbandis: Cheminements et situation actuelle d'un ordre mystique musulman*, ed. Marc Gaborieau, Alexandre Popovic, and Thierry Zarcone (Istanbul/Paris: Editions Isis, 1990), 109–121.

Hamada Masami. "Islamic Saints and their Mausoleums." *Acta Asiatica: Bulletin of the Institute of Eastern Culture*, 34(1978), 79–98.

Khmel'nitskii, Sergei. "Mavzolei Muhammada Bashoro." *Izvestiia Akademii nauk Tadzhikskoi SSR*, Seriia Vostokovedenie, Istoriia, Filosofiia, 2/18 (1990), 28–35.

Louw, Maria Elisabeth. *Everyday Islam in post-Soviet Central Asia*. London: Routledge, 2007.

Marefat, Roya. *Beyond the Architecture of Death: The Shrine of Shah-i Zinda in Samarqand*. Costa Mesa, California: Mazda Publishers, 1997.

McChesney, Robert. *Waqf in Central Asia: Four Hundred Years in the History of a Muslim Shrine, 1480–1889*. Princeton: Princeton University Press, 1991.

McChesney, Robert. "Architecture and Narrative: The Khwaja Abu Nasr Parsa Shrine. Part 1: Constructing the Complex and its Meaning, 1469–1696." *Muqarnas*, 18 (2001), 94–119.

McChesney, Robert. "Architecture and Narrative: The Khwaja Abu Nasr Parsa Shrine. Part 2: Representing the Complex in Word and Image, 1696–1998." *Muqarnas*, 19 (2002), 78–108.

al-Mizzī, Yūsuf b. al-Zakī ʿAbd al-Raḥmān. *Tahdhīb al-kamāl fī asmā al-rijāl*. Vol. 1 and 24. Beirut: Mu'assasat al-Risāla, 1992.

Mock, John. "Shrine Traditions of Wakhan Afghanistan." *Journal of Persianate Studies*, 4 (2011 = Special Issue on the Pamir, ed. Jo-Ann Gross), 117–145.

Mukhtarov, A. M. "Khronika polevykh rabot otriiada sektora Istorii srednikh vekov (1963–1973)." *Arkheologicheskie raboty v Tadzhikistane*, 13 (Dushanbe: Donish, 1973), 241–242.

Mullojonov, Parviz. "The Islamic Clergy in Tajikistan Since the End of the Soviet Period." In *Islam in Politics in Russia and Central Asia (Early Eighteenth to Late Twentieth Centuries)*, ed. Stephane A. Dudoignon and Hisao Komatsu (New York: Kegan Paul, 2002), 221–250.

Papas, Alexandre. "Les tombeaux de saints musulmans au Xinjiang: Culte, réforme, histoire." *Archives de sciences sociales des religions*, 142 (2008), 47–62.

Paul, Jürgen. "Histories of Samarqand." *Studia Iranica*, 22 (1993), 82–97.

Paul, Jürgen. "Hagiographic Literature in Persia and Central Asia." *Encyclopaedia Iranica*, 11, no. 5 (2002), 536–539.

Rasanayagam, Johan. *Islam in Post-Soviet Uzbekistan: The Morality of Experience*. Cambridge: Cambridge University Press, 2011.

Renard, John. *Friends of God: Islamic Images of Piety, Commitment, and Servanthood*. Berkeley and Los Angeles: University of California Press, 2008.

Risolai Khoja Muhammad Bashoro. Prepared by Jum'aev Kobilboy. Khujand: Kitob, 1993.

Samarqandī, Abū Ṭāhir Khwāja. *Samariyya*. In *Qandiyya va Samariyya*. Edited by Īrāj Afshār. Tehran: Mu'assasa-yi Farhangī-yi Jahāngīrī, 1367/1988.

Sawada Minoru. "Tarim Basin Mazârs: A Fieldwork Report." *Journal of the History of Sufism*, 3 (2001), 39–61.

Sela, Ron. *The Legendary Biographies of Tamerlane: Islamic and Heroic Apocrypha in Central Asia*. Cambridge/New York: Cambridge University Press, 2011.

Schadl, Marcus. "The Shrine of Nasir-i *Khusraw*: Imprisoned Deep in the Valley of Yumgan." *Muqarnas*, 26 (2009), 63–93.

Shamsiddin, Zaynularabi and Saidakbari Najibullo. *Muhammadi Bashoro*. Dushanbe: Arzhan, 2004.

Shinmen Yasushi. "The History of the Mausoleum of the *Aṣḥāb al-Kahf* in Turfan." *Memoirs of the Research Department of the Toyo Bunko*, 61 (2004), 83–104.

Subtelny, Maria E. "Templificatio hominis: Kaʿba, Cosmos, and Man in the Islamic Mystical Tradition." In *Weltkonstruktionen: Religiöse Weltdeutung zwischen Chaos und Kosmos vom Alten Orient bis zum Islam*, ed. P. Gemeinhardt and A. Zgoll (Tübingen: Mohr Siebeck, 2010; *Orientalische Religionen der Antike*, 5), 195–222.

Subtelny, Maria E. "The Islamic Ascension Narrative in the Context of Conversion in Medieval Iran." In *Orality and Textuality in the Iranian World: Patterns of Interaction across the Centuries*, ed. Julia Rubanovich (Leiden: Brill, 2015), 93–129.

Sugawara Jun. "Mazar Legends in the Kashghar Region." In *Islamic Sacred Places in Central Asia: The Ferghana Valley and Kashghar Region* (Nara: The Nara International Foundation, Commemorating the Silk Road Exposition, 2007), 67–78.

Voronina, V. L., and K. S. Kriukov. "Mavzoleii Mukhammeda Bosharo." In *Drevnost' i srednevekov'e narodov Srednei Azii (Istoriia i kul'tura)* (Moscow: Nauka, 1978), 58–68.

Zarcone, Thierry. "Pilgrimage to the 'Second Meccas' and 'Kaʿbas' of Central Asia." In *Central Asian Pilgrims: Hajj Routes and Pious Visits between Central Asia and the Hijaz*, ed. Alexandre Papas, Thomas Welsford, Thierry Zarcone (Berlin: Klaus Schwarz Verlag, 2012), 251–277.

Index

Prepared by John Dechant

ʿAbbāsid Caliphate 242
ʿAbd al-Ghafūr, the Ākhūnd of Swat 135–136, 138n
ʿAbd al-Karīm Khān (Khujand, 1875) 168–169
ʿAbd al-Raḥmān Khān 191–193, 203, 205–207, 209, 211–217, 219–220, 220n, 230–233
Äbduluakhit Sheykh *see* Mamadshukurov, Äbduluakhit Sheykh
Abramov, Aleksandr Konstantinovich 182–186
Abū Muslim Khurāsānī 114
Abū Saʿīd b. Abī'l-Khayr 5
Āfāqī *khwājas* 44, 163, 177
Afghanistan 13, 15, 17, 119n, 153n, 192, 194, 195, 199n, 206n, 207n, 211, 213, 216n, 217, 220, 222, 226–228, 231–232, 286, 290
Āftābachī, ʿAbd al-Raḥmān 167
Aḥmad-i Jām 5
Aḥmad of Rai Bareilli *see* Baralwī (Bareilli), Sayyid Aḥmad
Aḥrārī *khwājas* 55, 130, 137n, 191
Aḥrār, Khwāja ʿUbaydullāh 44, 84–85, 100n, 101, 114, 292, 320n, 327
Akhlāq-i muḥsinī 100, 115
Akhmetov, Qŭrban-Älĭ 285, 289–291, 293
Akhsīkatī, Pāyanda Muḥammad 43
Ākhūnd Darvīzā 133
Ākhūndzāda family 197, 201, 203–209, 220, 233
alchemy 110
ʿAlī b. Abī Ṭālib 112–114, 131, 139–140, 179, 220, 228, 314, 319
ʿAlī b. Mūsā al-Riżā 112
ʿĀlim Khān 60, 61n, 167, 177, 178n
Almatĭ (Almaty) 287
Amānullāh Khān 191, 194, 199n, 203, 225–227, 233
Amīr Kulāl 88
Amīr Kulālī family 56
Amu Darya 121–122, 129, 140, 150n, 153, 156
Āmulī, Ḥaydar 107
Andijan 45, 168, 169, 262, 266n, 271, 274, 294
Anīs al-ṭālibīn va ʿuddat al-sālikīn 81–83, 86–88, 92–93
Anṣārī, ʿAbdullāh 220
Anṣārī family 131, 191
Aqcha 150
Arghandāb River 196, 201, 207
Arslanbob 274, 279n
Asadullin, Mutigulla 267–269
Ashtarkhanids 119, 144
Asrār-i qāsimī 110–112
Astana 286–287, 293
Astrakhan 16, 239–243
astrology 98–100
Ata Zholĭ 295
Atbasar Shaykh *see* Zagiev, Vis Ḥājjī
ʿAṭṭār, ʿAlāʾ al-Dīn 82n, 83n, 86
awliyāʾ *see* saint, sainthood
Awrangzīb 176, 186
Aybak 127n

Babakhanov family *see* Bobokhonov
Bābur 175, 225n
Badakhshān 122n, 127, 150n, 196, 212, 217
Bākharzī, Sayf al-Dīn 85
Balkh 44, 47, 127, 131, 135, 150, 195n, 199n, 225
Baluchistan 209
baraka 229
Bārakzāʾī tribe 137n, 219, 224
Baralwī (Bareilli), Sayyid Aḥmad 136n, 138, 192
Baranga 239, 250
Barāngavī, Aḥmad 239–240, 250–252
Bashārā, Muḥammad 18–19, 299–328
Bashkir 244–245, 247, 249, 251–252
Baṣra 19, 301, 312n, 321
Baṣrī, Ḥasan 245
Baṣrī, Muḥammad b. Bashār b. ʿUthmān Qaysānī 19, 301, 321–328
bast 15, 211–213, 217–219, 233
Basṭāmī, Bāyazīd 109
Bayhaq 98–99
Bāyqarā, Sulṭān-Ḥusayn 99–101, 114n

Bennigsen, Alexandre, and the Bennigsen school of studies on Soviet Islam 1, 3–4, 8, 10, 17–18, 23–37, 39, 54n, 56, 58–59, 256–259, 263, 271–272, 280
Bībī Seshanba 47
Bigiyev, Ẓāhir 240, 246
Binorī, Sayyid Ādam 133n, 136f
biography *see* hagiography
Bobokhon, Eshon 264–265, 276
Bobokhonov family 53–54, 264, 267, 269
Bobokhonov, Ziyovuddinkhon 260, 265n, 267–268, 270
Britain 119, 220n
British Empire 156, 194, 205, 209, 215, 219, 225n, 227
British imperial agents, administrators, and policymakers 14, 121, 196n, 209–210, 212–214, 217, 228
Bukhara 13, 30n, 42–44, 47, 60–61, 64–65, 75, 83, 85, 119, 120, 122n, 123–124, 125f, 127–128, 130–131, 132n, 138n, 139–141, 144–154, 163, 180, 195, 196, 199n, 230, 240, 245–252, 264n, 288n, 289, 293, 308, 317n
Bukhārī, Abū'l-Qāsim b. Muḥammad b. Mas'ūd 87
Bukhārī, Mīr Sayyid 'Abdullāh 126, 127n
Bukhārī, Muḥammad b. Ismā'īl 301, 322n, 324–325, 327
Bukhārī, Ṣalāḥ b. Mubārak 86–87, 92
Bundār/Bundor *see* Baṣrī, Muḥammad b. Bashār b. 'Uthmān Qaysānī
Burnes, Alexander 140, 153
Būshanjī, Abū'l-Ḥasan 'Alī 21–22, 33, 36, 40, 58–59

Caucasus 25n, 26n, 31, 256, 261n, 285; *see also* Chechens/Chechnya, Dagestan
CARC *see* Council for the Affairs of Religious Cults
Chamkanni 133, 134n, 136f, 139n
Charkhī, Ya'qūb 85–86
Chechens/Chechnya 17, 18, 35n, 285–286, 290, 292–293, 296
Chhachh Hazara 127, 139n
China 119, 147n, 314n
Chishtīs 2, 126, 132n, 133n, 135n
Chūstī, Luṭfullāh 42
Council for the Affairs of Religious Cults (CARC) 259–263, 265–267, 269, 272n, 273–279

Dagestan 35n
Dāghistānī, Maḥmūd 241
Dahbīdī *khwājas* 130, 144, 145n, 151, 191
Dahbīdī, Mūsā Khān 45, 145n, 152–153, 251, 288
Dāniyāl Atalïq 145, 148
Delhi 124, 126, 139n, 155
Dera Ismail Khan 122n, 131
dhikr see ẕikr
Dih Ḥājjī 205–207
Dilras Begum 124, 125n, 127
Dūkchī Īshān 45
Durrānī, Aḥmad Shāh 133–134, 195–201, 202f, 204, 210–212, 221, 223, 230, 232
Durrānī Empire 13, 119–120, 123, 126, 132–135, 137, 141, 145, 150–151, 156
Durrānī, Maḥmūd Shāh 134n, 135, 203
Durrānī, Tīmūr Shāh 134, 196, 198, 200–203, 210–212
Dungan 263
Dushanbe 115, 263, 301, 321

Eastern Turkistan 6–7, 38, 43, 44, 51n, 317n; *see also* Xinjiang
Elphinstone, Mountstuart 139, 140n, 151

Farghana valley 14, 17, 35n, 37n, 38n, 47, 64, 120, 162–168, 175, 178–179, 180n, 182–183, 259, 262, 266, 268, 270, 271, 274, 278, 279n, 289, 293
Fārisī, Salmān 114
Fārsīwān *see* Qizilbāsh
fatwā 137n, 170, 193, 210, 211, 215, 290, 292
Fayżābād 196
Fetkhullashïlar 288
Fiker (newspaper) 240
fiqh 53n, 106, 125, 136f, 294
Fūfalzā'ī, 'Azīz al-Dīn Wakīlī 197n, 198, 199n, 200–201, 206, 222, 224–226, 227n, 229, 232
Fūlād Khān 165, 167–172, 181
Fuṣūṣ al-ḥikām 107
Futuvvat-nāma-yi sulṭānī 101, 112–115

Ghaznī 127, 131, 138n, 220
Great Game 120–121, 140
Gülen, Fethullah 287n, 288

Ḥabībullāh Khān 191, 193, 194, 198, 203, 210
ḥadīth 19, 52, 89, 91, 93, 100, 247, 301–302, 312, 319–320, 322–327
Ḥāfiẓ Darāz 136f, 137–138
Ḥāfiẓ Muḥammad ʿAẓīm 130, 137, 138
Ḥāfiẓ Muḥammad Fāżil Khān 135
Ḥāfiẓ Muḥammad Saʿīd 122n
hagiography 2, 11–14, 18–19, 40–52, 53n, 57–59, 63–65, 75–95, 99, 111, 114, 120, 122–124, 126–127, 129–135, 137, 139, 146–147, 149, 151–152, 162, 165, 174–175, 177, 247, 250–251, 295, 299–304, 312, 316, 321, 326–328
hagiolatry 242–243, 246
Hairy Ishans 17, 27n, 37n, 270–271, 274, 280
ḥajj 108, 127n, 193, 228, 311, 316n, 320
Ḥājjī Ḥabībullāh 44, 59, 130n, 144, 151
Ḥajjītarkhānī, Jahānshāh b. ʿAbd al-Jabbār al-Nīzhghārūṭī 239, 241–243
Hamadānī, Sayyid ʿAlī 6, 84
Ḥanafī jurisprudence 106, 114n, 194
Ḥaydar, Amīr (Manghït) 127n, 128, 129n, 131, 132n, 138n, 147–150, 152n, 153n
Hazāras 219, 231
Ḥażarāt 130, 137
Ḥażrat Jīo Ṣāḥib *see* Maʿṣūmī, Miyān Fażl Aḥmad
Ḥażratjī Pishāvarī *see* Shāh Ghulām Muḥammad Maʿṣūm
Herat 47, 82, 98–99, 101, 107n, 111, 114, 122n, 127, 138n, 194, 209, 215, 218–220, 222, 224–225, 228
Hindus 139, 213–214, 219, 228
Hindustan 13, 119, 120, 123–124, 126, 129, 132, 133–135, 137n, 138–139, 145, 149n, 150, 151, 156
Ḥiṣār 64, 127n
Hui *see* Dungan
Ḥusayniyya (Naqshbandī-Mujaddidī lineage) 17, 284–285, 288–289, 291, 293, 294, 296

ʿĪbādullāh Khwān Khūjam Tūra 172, 178n
Ibn ʿArabī 102n, 103–104, 107, 110
Ibn Taymiyya 240, 245, 323
Ibrāhīm b. Adham 245
Imām Rabbānī *see* Sirhindī, Aḥmad
India *see* Hindustan
infidels 19, 32, 109, 214–216, 252, 314n, 315–316, 319, 322
Ïqïlasshïlar 288
Iran 91, 102, 119n, 228
Īshān-i Pīr *see* Shahrisabzī, ʿAbd al-Karīm
Ishanism 27n, 32
Īshānlargha khiṭāb! 244, 249
Isḥāqī *khwājas* 43–44, 163
Ismatŭlla Maqsŭm 17, 286–287, 290–294, 296

Jadīds 16, 34–35, 48, 53, 54n, 61–62, 171, 238–240, 242–244, 246, 249–250, 252
Jahriyya 17–18, 61n, 286–287, 290
Jalālābād, Afghanistan 134n, 154
Jalalabat, Kyrgyzstan 262, 265, 270, 272–275, 277–280
Jāmī, ʿAbd al-Raḥmān 81–84, 87n, 94, 103–104, 107n, 114, 231
javānmardī 21, 112
Jīo Bābā *see* Niyāz Aḥmad
Jungars 32n
jurisprudence *see fiqh*
Jūybārī, Khwāja Muḥammad Islām 85, 144n
Jūybārī shaykhs/*khwājas* 42, 43n, 55, 85, 130, 139, 144, 163, 191

Kaʿba 310–311, 316n, 317, 319n, 322
Kabul 13, 121, 126–127, 130–131, 133–134, 136f, 137, 138n, 139, 145, 153–155, 196, 198, 200, 202n, 209–210, 212–213, 215–216, 218, 220, 221–222, 225, 227–228, 231, 233
kāfir see infidels
Kafiristan 140n
Kalmyks 32n
Kandahar *see* Qandahar
karāmāt see miracles
Kāsānī, Aḥmad *see* Makhdūm-i Aʿẓam
Kashghar 13, 24, 119, 154n, 163, 175–176, 183, 186
Kāshgharī, Saʿd al-Dīn 98–99, 114
Kāshifī, Kamāl al-Dīn Ḥusayn b. ʿAlī Vāʿiẓ 12–13, 98–115
Kashmir 126, 127, 145

von Kaufman, Konstantin 166–167, 169–170, 182–183, 185
Kazakhs 257n, 284, 290, 293, 295–296; *see also* Qazaqs
Kazakhstan 17–18, 26n, 266n, 274, 284–296, 317n
Kazan 13, 119, 120, 122n, 123, 131, 153, 154, 240
Khālidī-Naqshbandī 241
Khalvat-i ṣūfīhā 244, 249
khānaqāh 2, 4n, 13, 15, 19, 33, 61, 101, 122n, 123–124, 126–128, 129f, 131, 134–135, 137–138, 139n, 145, 147, 149–151, 153–154, 155f, 197, 199, 248, 291, 303, 307, 312n, 320, 327n
Khavāriq-i Naqshband dar ʿilm-i sayr 87
khirqa 47, 114, 191; *see also* Muḥammad, cloak of
Khiva 60, 145, 151, 244, 248
Khiyābānī, Jalāl al-Dīn 250–252
Khiżr 251, 310–311, 314
Khoqand 14, 60, 64, 120, 122n, 125f, 145, 151, 153, 154, 162–163, 165–167, 169, 171, 173–183, 187–188, 262, 275, 276n
Khrushchev, Nikita 272–273, 275, 281
Khudāyār Khān 166–169, 171, 181, 276n
Khujand 47, 167–169
Khurasan 2, 13, 21, 99, 112, 119, 120, 123, 124, 129, 134, 135, 138n, 139n, 141, 148n, 149n, 150, 153
Khwājagān 93
Khwājas of Eastern Turkistan 6, 7; *see also* Āfāqī *khwājas*, Isḥāqī *khwājas*
Khwāndamīr 99
Khwārazm 23, 29n, 44, 47
Khwārazmī, Ḥusayn (16th century) 42–44, 85
Khwārazmī, Kamāl al-Dīn Ḥusayn (15th century) 106–107
Khyber Pass 127, 138, 139n
Kīrgīl mausoleum 172–173, 178n
Kīsh 85
Kok Yanghaq 267, 269–270, 281
Kubrā, Najm al-Dīn 5–6, 47
Kubraviyya 2, 42, 43, 50, 56, 251
Kunta Ḥājjī 286
Kunūz al-ḥaqā'iq fī rumūz al-daqā'iq 106, 107n
Kyrgyzstan 26n, 27n, 28n, 259, 260n, 261n, 262, 265–269, 270n, 272n, 274, 281, 317n
Lahore 124, 127, 133n, 136f
Lohochi 273
Lubb al-lubāb-i maʿnavī 105–109
Lucknow 196, 211
Luqmān 104–105

Madaripov, Tursunboy 271–274
madrasa 2, 53, 101, 123–124, 130–131, 135, 137, 138n, 145, 149, 151, 176, 193, 197, 199, 201, 203, 204, 211, 249, 260, 264n, 266n, 286, 293
Maghribī, Abū ʿAbdullāh 111
Maghribī, Muḥammad Ibn al-Ḥājj al-Tilimsānī 111
Majālis al-nafā'is 98, 111
Makhdūm-i Aʿẓam 14, 42–45, 55, 85, 144n, 162–163, 174, 176, 186
Makhdūmzāda 162–163, 165, 173, 175, 176
Makhmŭdshïlar 288
Maktūbāt (Shaykh Aḥmad Sirhindī) 124, 245, 247
Malakand 122n, 135n, 154
Malla Khān 181, 308n
Mamadshukurov, Äbduluakhit Sheykh (ʿAbd al-Vāḥid-Shaykh) 284–285, 288–289, 291, 293, 294
Mamatqulov, Hazrat Ibrohim 289, 291, 293–294
Manghït 60, 140, 144, 145, 146, 148, 150, 195, 246
Maqsŭm-ŭlï, Äbdïlghappar *see* Ismatulla Maqsŭm
Marathas 126
Marghīnān 14, 162–163, 165–167, 169–176, 179–180, 182–186, 188
Marghīnānī, Mullā ʿAzīz 166
Marjānī, Shihāb al-Dīn 154, 240, 245–246, 252
Mashhad 112, 222n
Maṣnavī-yi Maʿnavī 13, 103–109, 112
Masson, Charles 138
Maʿṣūmī, Miyān Fażl Aḥmad 13, 119–131, 134–140, 142–143, 145–156
Mawarannahr 13, 24, 41n, 119–121, 123–124, 129, 132, 135, 137–140, 144, 145, 149n, 150–151, 153, 155, 156, 303, 315, 322, 327
mazār see shrine
Mazārī, Niẓām al-Dīn Balkhī 122n, 132n

Mazār-i Sharīf, Afghanistan 127, 131, 140, 195n, 202n, 220, 228, 286
Mazār-i Sharīf, Tajikistan 299n, 300, 308n, 309n, 316n, 322n, 327–328
Ming Dynasty 163
miracles 60, 63, 66n, 76, 78, 83, 90–91, 95, 110, 174, 176, 179, 248
Mīr ʿIzzatullāh 135, 149
Miyān Fażl-i Ḥaqq 122n, 127, 130n, 132n, 134–135n, 140, 153, 154
Miyān Ghulām Qādir 131, 132n, 134n, 135
Miyānkāl 64, 130n
Mohan Lal 153
Mongol era 2, 5, 6, 37–38, 257
Moorecroft, William 240
Moses 311, 313
Mughal Empire 119–120, 124, 126, 133, 175, 178, 225
Muḥammad the Prophet 19, 21–22, 47, 104, 113–114, 125, 193, 215, 232n, 247, 251, 291–292, 300, 303, 311–316, 317n, 319, 321–323, 324n, 326–327
  cloak (*khirqa*) of 14–15, 191, 194–205, 208, 210–214, 216, 218–221, 223–232, 233f
  hair of 191, 194–196, 223–224, 230–232
  traditions of *see ḥadīth*
Muḥammad b. Bashshār 19, 322; *see also* Basharā, Muḥammad
Muhammadi Bashoro 300–301, 303n, 309n, 312, 321, 323, 326–327
Muḥammadzāʾī amīrs 191, 203, 214, 219
Mujaddidiyya-Naqshbandiyya 13, 14, 18, 44–45, 48, 50, 56, 59–61, 64, 119–120, 121n, 123–127, 131–133, 136f, 137, 138n, 141, 144–151, 155, 156, 176, 178, 191, 250–251, 284–285, 288–289, 293
Mullā Isḥāq b. Ḥasan *see* Fūlād Khān
Mullā of Kotah *see* ʿUsmānzāʾī, Sayyid Amīr
Multan 131n, 136f
Murtażā ʿAlī *see* ʿAlī b. Abī Ṭālib
muruvvat 113
Musulmān-qul 167n

Nādir Shāh 133, 139n, 144, 196, 228
Namangan 169, 171, 266n, 272n, 294
Namangānī, Majẕūb 45, 273
Naqshband, Bahāʾ al-Dīn 6, 12, 30n, 75–76, 78, 81–88, 90, 92–95, 131, 139, 140n, 149n, 317n
Naqshbandiyya 2, 6, 7n, 14, 17, 26n, 27n, 35n, 38n, 42–44, 48, 50, 53, 54n, 55, 56, 60–66, 82, 83n, 85, 98, 101, 114, 123n, 125, 126n, 130, 132n, 135, 151, 162–163, 174, 178, 191, 199n, 240, 245–247, 259, 263–265, 267, 268, 275–276, 279, 280, 288, 294, 327; *see also* Ḥusayniyya, Khālidiyya, and Mujaddidiyya
Näsĭrĭdin Ishan 285, 289, 293–294
Navāʾī, ʿAlī-shīr 98–102, 111n
Nīshāpūr 111n
Nīshāpūrī, Luṭfullāh 114
Niyāz Aḥmad 124, 125f, 126, 154n
Nizhnii Novgorod 241
Nur Ata 47, 308n
Nūrbakhsh, Sayyid Muḥammad 84
Nurshĭlar 288

Occult sciences 12, 48, 98, 110–111
Oqŭshĭlar 288
Orenburg 169, 171, 244
Osh 47, 168, 260n, 265n, 274, 317n
  Throne of Solomon (*Takht-i Sulaymān*) 268n, 278–279, 317n
Osman Topbashshĭlar 288
Oxus *see* Amu Darya

Pādshāh Khān Tūra 174–178, 180–181, 184, 186
Panjikant 303, 308n, 314n
Pārsā, Abū Naṣr 195n, 199n
Pārsā, Khwāja Muḥammad 82n, 83n, 85–86, 87n
Pashtuns 121, 122n, 123, 131, 133n, 138n, 154, 219
Penjikent *see* Panjikant
Peshawar 13, 119–121, 122n, 124, 125f, 126–127, 130–140, 142–143f, 144–145, 150–151, 153–155
pilgrimage *see ḥajj, ziyārat*
Pīr ʿUmar of Chamkanni 133–134, 136f
Pishāvar *see* Peshawar
Pishāvarī, Ḥażrat Jīo Ṣāḥib *see* Maʿṣūmī, Miyān Fażl Aḥmad
Pishāvarī, ʿAbd al-Raḥīm 122n, 134n, 139n
Polish Tatars 242
Punjab 120, 129, 138n, 150–151

Qādiriyya 17–18, 28n, 56, 126, 132n, 135n, 259, 270, 285–286, 290, 292, 296

Qalandars 52, 261–262
Qandahar 14–15, 126, 130, 133, 136f, 137, 138n, 191, 194–198, 200, 202n, 203–207, 209–232
  Shrine of the Cloak *see* Muḥammad, cloak of
Qarghalï 244
Qārghālī, Muḥammad-Ḥarrāṣ Āydārōf 239, 244, 247–249
Qārī ʿAbdullāh (Qori Abdullo) 289, 293–294
Qarshi 150
Qāsim-i Anvār 111–112
Qāyinī, Jalāl al-Dīn 114n
Qāyinī, Nūr al-Dīn Aḥmad b. Muḥammad 114
Qazānī, ʿUbaydullāh b. Subḥān-qul 241
Qazānī, Qāsim Shaykh 240
Qazaqs 16, 28n, 64, 175, 242, 247, 248; *see also* Kazakhs
Qïpchāq 64–65, 167–168
Qïrghïz 166–168, 181
Qizilbāsh 228
Qïzïl-Orda 290, 293, 295
Qoqand *see* Khoqand
Quetta 207, 209, 213, 220
Qurʾān 30n, 52, 93, 98–100, 102–105, 107–108, 124, 147, 153, 278, 291, 302, 314, 319, 327
Qūrṣavī, Abū'l-Nāṣir 245
Qŭsshï-Ata, Kazakhstan 284–285

Rampur 126
Rasā, Muḥammad 125–126, 127n
Rashaḥāt-i ʿayn al-ḥayāt 114
Rasulev, Zaynullāh 54n, 240
Rawalpindi 205
Rawżat al-ansāb 174, 177, 179, 181
Rawżat al-awliyāʾ 122n, 127n, 147
Rawżat al-shuhadāʾ 99
rīmiyā (prestidigitation) 110
Risolai Khoja Muhammad Bashoro 299n, 300, 310n, 311–317, 319–323, 326–327
Rostov-na-Donu 246
Rūm 320
Rūmī, Jalāl al-Dīn 13, 103–109, 112
Russia 119, 139, 147, 154n, 239–240, 242–246, 249–250, 252–253, 289, 295
  Muslim opposition to 25, 26n, 31, 35, 162, 165–172, 183, 188
  Tsarist era conquest and rule of Central Asia 1, 14, 32n, 34, 36, 38–39, 50, 62, 156, 162, 165–172, 180, 182–185, 188, 196n, 205, 222n, 238, 252, 276n
Russian sources 7, 14, 16, 48, 123n, 167–168, 288
Russian Orthodox Church 242, 260n

Sabzavār 98–99
Ṣadr Atāʾī family 56
SADUM (*Sredneaziatskoe Dukhovnoe Upravlenie Musul'man*) 17, 259–260, 261n, 263–270, 273n, 274–276, 278, 280–281
Sadūzāʾī dynasty 203
Ṣafavid Empire 104, 110n, 111n, 119, 199, 228
Ṣafī, Fakhr al-Dīn 101
Ṣāḥibzādas 130n, 131, 135, 153–156
saint, sainthood 2, 14–15, 19, 28n, 33, 47–48, 51n, 55, 56n, 66n, 81, 84, 86, 89–95, 101, 106, 110–111, 119–120, 124, 139, 149, 151, 153, 156, 163, 169, 172–174, 176–178, 181, 186, 191, 194n, 199n, 231–232, 240, 242–243, 258–259, 269, 275, 276, 292, 295, 300, 303, 310–311, 314, 326
Salafism 19, 30n, 61, 239, 245–246, 292, 295–296, 301, 322
Salāmov, ʿĀdil-Khān-Qārī 294
samāʿ 47, 57
Samangan *see* Aybak
Samara 244
Samariyya 303, 311–312, 322–323, 327
Samarqand 19, 47, 64, 101, 127, 138n, 150–151, 195n, 303, 307, 308n, 311, 312, 314n, 315, 325
Samarqandī, Dawlatshāh 111
SAMK (Spiritual Administration of the Muslims of Kazakhstan) 287, 290, 292, 293n, 298
Sanāʾī, Ḥakīm 107
Ṣārātāghī, Sirāj al-Dīn Bukhārī 246
Sarts 168
Sayrām 47, 314
Sayyid Atāʾī family 55–56
Shāh-i Mardān 179, 279n
Shāh Mashrab 52
Shāh Murād (Manghït) 60, 128, 140, 145–150
Shahr-i Khān 168

Shahrisabzī, ʿAbd al-Karīm 250–252
Shāh Shujāʿ 135
Shamanism 27n, 30n, 33n, 51, 63
Shāh Niʿmatullāh Valī 84
sharīʿa 52, 59–60, 107–108, 113, 119n, 124, 147n, 148–149, 169, 174, 200n, 219, 233, 242–243, 247, 249, 290, 292, 314
Shaṭṭārīs 2
Shaykh Khāvand-i Ṭahūrī family 56
Shīʿism, Shīʿīs 112, 192, 209, 227–228
Shikarpur 137, 139
Shīrvānī, Aḥmad-Farīd 246
Shoh Fozil, Kyrgyzstan 272n, 279n
Shokirkhojayev, Olimkhon tora 265n, 266–269, 276
Shor Bāzār 130, 136f, 137, 145n, 155
Shrine of the Cloak (Qandahar)
    see Muḥammad, cloak of
shrines 2, 7n, 14–16, 18, 19–20, 26, 28n, 29n, 32–33, 36, 47–48, 51n, 56, 60, 62, 64, 66n, 85, 101, 112, 122n, 124, 131, 133n, 137n, 139n, 140n, 142–143f, 151, 153, 155, 163, 177n, 178, 186, 187–188f, 191–233, 240, 243, 259–261, 263, 272, 275n, 276, 278, 279n, 295, 296, 299–328
Sialkot 127
Siberia 13, 131, 154n, 239
Siḥr al-ʿuyūn 110–111
Sikhs 126, 127n, 134n, 136n, 138n, 156, 232
silsila 41, 43, 45, 47, 48, 50, 55–56, 85, 91, 120, 124, 130–132, 133n, 135, 140, 145, 151, 153–155, 244, 247, 249, 251, 258, 287–288
    bundled *silsilas* 50, 56, 132, 244, 251, 258
Sīmāwī, Abū'l-Qāsim Aḥmad al-ʿIrāqī 110
sīmiyā 110
Sīnā Ibn al-Ḥarb 314n, 315–316
Sind 136f, 137n, 155
sīra 91, 322
Sirāj al-tawārīkh 198
Sirhind 13, 120, 124, 126–127 133, 135
Sirhindī, Shaykh Aḥmad 119–120, 124–125, 126n, 132, 137, 144, 145n, 149, 155, 246–247, 288
Sorocha 244
Soviet Union, Muslim opposition to 25, 26n, 28n, 31, 35
Stalin, Joseph 17, 260, 263, 265, 272, 276, 285
Sterlitamak 239
Subkī, Tāj al-Dīn 101
Sufism
    and Sovietology 3–4, 7–8n, 10, 20, 23, 24, 51, 58–59, 63
    anthropological and ethnographical studies of 29, 36–37, 50, 65–66n
    as more than mysticism 3
    "folk" characterization 26, 30n, 33–34
    what is Sufism and where to find it 21–22, 32–33, 49–54, 63–64, 261–262
Suhaylī, Niẓām al-Dīn Shaykh Aḥmad 100
Suhravardī Sufis 56, 132n
Süleymenshĭler 288
Sulṭān-Abū Saʿīd 99
Sulṭān-Aḥmad Mīrzā 101
Sulṭān Murād Bék 167, 170, 171
Survivals paradigm 30n, 33–34, 51, 63, 66n
Swat 123, 134n, 135, 136, 138n, 154
Syr Darya 169, 171

Tajikistan 18, 28n, 51n, 115, 261n, 262–263, 265, 294, 299–302, 304f, 308, 309n, 314, 322, 323n, 326, 328
Tajiks 28n, 168, 293
Takht-i Sulaymān see Osh
Tanīqul Dādkhwāh 168
taraqqī 241–242
Taraz 285, 289n, 293
Tarĭbayev, Qĭdĭrälĭ 295
Tashkent 46–47, 53–54, 82, 131, 166, 169, 175, 182–185, 248, 264–266, 289, 293, 300n
Tashqurghan 127n
tavajjuh 136, 147, 289
Tavārīkh-i Bulghāriyya 240
Ṭāyy, Ḥāṭim 114
Thaʿlabī, Abū Isḥāq Aḥmad 104–105
Thana 122n
Throne of Solomon *see* Osh
Timurids 6, 7n, 8, 12, 38, 98–102, 107, 111–112, 114, 175, 194n, 305n
Tirmidhī, al-Ḥakīm 5, 325
Tordher, Shaykh Shuʿayb 135n, 136f
Transoxiana *see* Mawarannahr
Turkistan (Türkĭstan), Kazakhstan 274
Turkmānī, Niyāz-Qulī 145n, 246, 252
Türkmen 64
Turkmenistan 26n, 27n, 28n, 119n, 205, 265n
Tursunov, Dust-Muhammad 294

ʿUbaydullāh Khān (Ashtarkhānid) 59, 144n
Ufa 54n
ʿulamā 2, 51–53, 63–64, 83, 120–121, 128, 132, 133n, 134n, 137–138, 144–145, 146f, 147, 148n, 170, 172, 178, 180, 192, 198, 200, 210–211, 226, 239–240, 250, 264–265, 267, 270
ʿUmar Khān 175, 178
Ura Tepe 153n
Urgench 248
ʿUs̱mānzāʾī, Sayyid Amīr 136
Utïz-Imäni, ʿAbd al-Raḥīm al-Bulghārī 245–246
Uvaysī 51n, 251
Uyghurs 263
Uzbek conquest of Central Asia 39
Uzbekistan 13, 24n, 29n, 35n, 45n, 46, 115, 260, 264, 265n, 266, 268, 271, 272n, 279n, 285, 289, 292, 294, 302, 308
Uzbeks 30n, 65, 144, 148, 163, 261n, 262n, 263, 273, 293, 296
Uzgen 167

valāyat see saint
valī see saint
Valī Khān Tūra 14, 162–188
Vambery, Armenius 145n
Volga Tatars 154
Volga-Ural region 16, 25n, 54n, 238–253
Vyatka 239, 250

Wahhābīs, Wahhābism 30n, 35, 61, 136n, 138n, 192, 240–241
waqf 15, 201–202, 209, 249, 288, 309, 320
waqfiyya see waqf
Waziristan 120, 122n, 154–155

Xinjiang 13, 44n, 263, 266n, 299n, 314n, 317n

Yaʿqūb Bék 183
Yarkand 137n
Yasavī, Aḥmad (Qozha Akhmet Yasaui) 6n, 274, 284, 287, 290, 292–294, 296, 317n
Yasaviyya 2, 4, 27n, 37n, 42–44, 50, 55–56, 61, 294
Yazıcılar 288

Zād al-sālikīn 107
Zagiev, Vis Ḥājjī 286
Zakori 122n
Zakorī, Imām Muḥammad Ḥusayn 122n, 131
ẕikr 18, 33, 47, 60–62, 86, 179, 251, 289–292, 294
ziyārat 16, 19, 28n, 33, 123, 131, 133n, 135, 139, 153n, 179, 197, 220–221, 227, 231, 240–241, 243, 275–276, 278–279, 286, 295–296, 303, 304, 306, 311n, 316n, 320, 322, 326–328

Printed in the United States
By Bookmasters